The War of 1812

The War of 1812

Henry Adams

Edited by Major H. A. DeWeerd
New Introduction by Colonel John R. Elting

Cooper Square Press

New introduction copyright © 1999 by John R. Elting

First Cooper Square Press edition 1999

This Cooper Square Press paperback edition of *The War of 1812* is an unabridged republication of the edition first published in Washington, D.C. in 1944. It consists of chapters extracted from the nine-volume *History of the United States during the Administrations of Jefferson and Madison* (1889–1891) by Henry Adams, and is here supplemented with a new introduction by Colonel John R. Elting.

Published by Cooper Square Press,
An Imprint of Rowman & Littlefield Publishers, Inc.
150 Fifth Avenue, Suite 911
New York, New York 10011

Distributed by National Book Network

Library of Congress Cataloging-in-Publication Data

Adams, Henry, 1838–1918
    The War of 1812 / by Henry Adams ; edited by H. A. DeWeerd ; new introduction by John R. Elting. —1st Cooper Square Press ed.
        p.   cm.
    Originally published: Washington : The Infantry Journal, 1944.
    Includes index.
    ISBN 0-8154-1013-1 (alk. paper)
    1. United States—History—War of 1812.   I. DeWeerd, Harvey A. (Harvey Arthur), 1902–1979. II. Title.
    E354.A24   1999
    973.5'2—dc21   99–38133
                                                                              CIP

⊖™ The paper used in this publication meets the minimum requirements of American National Standard for Information Sciences—Permanence of Paper for Printed Library Materials, ANSI/NISO Z39.48-1992.
Manufactured in the United States of America.

INTRODUCTION

"A nation learns its most important military lessons from a study of its defeats and frustrations, not from a study of its successes."

—Major H. A. DeWeerd,
The Infantry Journal

The United States is a nation created, built, shaped, and preserved by wars. (My own lifetime has so far included five, plus various minor punitive expeditions, pacifications, and interventions.) Yet of all our wars, that of 1812 has until recently remained something of an unwanted orphan of tainted legitimacy. To English historians it seemed a shocking case of American ingratitude toward an England desperately waging the battle for truth, virtue, and justice against the Corsican ogre. (At least one normally balanced author concluded that Napoleon and Madison had been actively in cahoots in planning America's entry.) The war itself had been sheer frustration—a minor, distant border brawl that steadily sucked more and more of England's limited manpower into useless victories and unexpected, humiliating defeats—the black sheep of England's Napoleonic wars and so best ignored. Some Americans considered it a war of disgraceful, unprovoked aggression; others were repelled by its too-frequent displays of American incompetence, treason, and sheer cowardice. The United States Navy might cherish its record of victories in lake battles and occasional ship-to-ship engagements; a few tall tales, such as that of Andrew Jackson's hawk-eyed Kentucky sharpshooters leveling their long rifles across a breastwork of cotton bales at New Orleans, would be taken into popular history, but serious historians largely avoided the subject.

The one major exception was Henry B. Adams (1838–1918) in his literally monumental *A History of the United States during the Administrations of Jefferson and Madison* (nine volumes; published by Scribner's, New York, 1889–1891). This work, though still justly regarded as one of the true classics of American historical writing, has never become popular. Apparently its very size, exacting detail, and impartiality has daunted the average prospective reader. (Adams would wryly conclude that its limited sales proved that history was the "most aristocratic of all literary pursuits, because it obliges the historian to be rich as well as educated.")

Not until 1944 did a truly reliable account of the War of 1812 become available. At that time the editors of *The Infantry Journal*, convinced that "the war of 1812 still has many things to teach a nation prone to find easy confirmation of its policies and methods in the ultimate success of its military enterprises," secured permission from Scribner's and the Adams heirs to publish the relevant chapters of Adams' *History* as a single volume. Enough political coverage was retained to give the necessary background to the military and naval campaigns—and, incidentally, to make it painfully evident that the Armed Forces of the United States have never operated under such a combination of strategic ignorance, administrative ineptitude, and blind political folly. The editors omitted Adams' extensive documentation, two major wars having destroyed or scattered much of its sources, but retained the original maps and place names, which provide a better idea of the state of geographical knowledge when Henry Adams wrote his history than modernized versions would.

Henry Adams was uniquely qualified as a historian by birth, education, and experience. Great-grandson of John and Abigail Adams (respectively the second president of the United States and the "first fully emancipated woman in American history"), and grandson of John Quincy Adams, the sixth president, he inherited a family tradition that placed the good of the United States and personal integrity above any consideration of political expediency or success. John Adams, zealous patriot, successfully defended the British soldiers accused of murder after defending themselves during the so-called "Boston Massacre." John Quincy Adams capped a difficult presidency by almost seventeen years of highly independent service in the House of Representatives, disregarding constant opposition and threats in his condemnation of slavery. Graduating from Harvard in 1858, Henry continued his study of law in Germany for the next two years, but found the legal profession unsatisfying. His true education came as private secretary to his father, Charles Francis Adams, during the latter's seven years of indispensable service as American Minister to Great Britain from 1861 to 1868. Many leading Englishmen were Confederate sympathizers. There was considerable British interest in recognizing the Confederate States as a legal belligerent. Confederate agents sought English recognition, weapons, and ships. Charles Adams met these challenges with intelligence, adroitness, wit, understanding, and a flinty resolution. In the process, his son Henry witnessed and learned the inner workings of governments, the grim linkage of diplomacy and military power, and the myriad ways in which domestic peanut politics can hamper crucial matters of national policy.

Returning to America, Henry Adams was for two years assistant professor of history at Harvard, but gradually found historical writing the proper expression of his inquiring, perfectionist mind. His first major work was a biography (1879) of Albert Gallatin. His preparations for his *History* began with eighteen months of ransacking English, Spanish, and French archives, a task much facilitated by the Adams reputation; at home, he had free access to any official records. (For relaxation he wrote, under a pen name, the novel *Democracy*, a scathing, satirical depiction of contemporary Washington politics that caused a sensation both here and in England, and resulted in his only financially successful book.) Later works included *Mont-Saint-Michel and Chartres* (1904), an account of medieval culture; a partial autobiography, *The Education of Henry Adams* (1907); and a second pseudonymous novel, *Esther* (1884), apparently inspired by his wife and his favorite among his works.

The *History*, however, remains his chief accomplishment. Written with painstaking attention to detail, whether recounting the speeches of long-and-deservedly-forgotten congressmen or a warship's exact armament, it was almost entirely based on original documentation. His older brother Charles Francis Adams, Jr.—veteran cavalryman (first lieutenant in 1861 and brevet brigadier general by 1865), railroad expert, and minor historian in his own right—helped Adams achieve his objective of complete impartiality by peppering the first draft with "suppress the patriotic glow" and similar admonitions.

The finished *History*—and thus this book—is a model of balance and fairness, albeit tinged with a cool irony. Simply and in their own words he describes—and eviscerates—the members of the United States Congress during late 1814–early 1815, as they refused to take any measure to provide for the United States Army while yammering of States' rights, demanding that the individual states be authorized to raise their own armies, and boasting that the individual state would thus be competent to defeat any aggression. With equal clarity he dissects the famous Hartford Convention, pointing out that its demands implied the dissolution of the United States and the establishment of an independent New England Confederation, which would cheerfully sacrifice the western states and even a slice of Maine to make peace with Great Britain. Yet, the members of the convention, mostly "elderly men, who detested democracy, but disliked enthusiasm almost as much," actually attempted to keep "young hot-heads from getting into mischief by delaying any open break with the Federal government." (Typically, the aging John Adams supported the war and derided New England's defeatist attitude.)

In military matters Adams' conclusions take an even sharper edge. There can hardly be an icier verdict on the military incompetence of the Madison administration than his description of the 1814 British advance on Washington: "Thus for five days . . . [A] British army, which though small [approximately 4,000] was larger than any single body of American regulars then in the field, marched in a leisurely manner through a long-settled country, and met no show of resistance before coming within sight of the Capitol. Such an adventure resembled the stories of Cortez and De Soto; and the conduct of the United States Government offered no contradiction to the resemblance." And, recounting the British conduct after their capture of Washington: "They burned the Capitol, the White House, and the Department buildings because they thought it proper, as they would have burned a Negro kraal or a den of pirates. Apparently they assumed as a matter of course that the American government stood beyond the pale of civilization; and, in truth, a government which showed so little capacity to defend its Capitol, could hardly wonder at whatever treatment it received."

His recording of Jackson's defense of New Orleans shows a similar precision. Jackson, rough-and-tumble Indian fighter, always pugnacious, but ignorant alike of strategy and logistics, allowed himself to be caught unready, with only a portion of his available troops, by the British strike at New Orleans. "The record of American generalship offered many examples of misfortune but none so complete as this. . . . a British army, heralded long in advance, [had been allowed] to arrive within seven miles, unseen and unsuspected, and without so much as an earthwork, a man, or a gun between them and their object." But then he fairly compares Jackson's reactions with that of the unfortunate General Winder who had attempted to defend Washington: "[Jackson's] conduct thence forward offered a contrast the more striking because it proved how Washington might have been saved. Winder lost his head when he saw an enemy. Jackson needed to see his enemy in order to act; he thought rightly only at the moment when he struck." Thereafter, Adams notes Jackson's courage and decisiveness, yet shows him consistently handicapped by his ignorance of conventional warfare, and strangely incurious as to the enemy's movements. As a minor buffet to frontier legends, Adams notes that American artillery inflicted most of the British casualties at New Orleans; American riflemen played a very minor part in breaking the British attack.

Quietly, deftly, Adams rubbed his fellow Americans' noses in their manifest political and military failures. Even so, there are passages—as when Oliver Hazard Perry snatches victory out of looming defeat on Lake Erie, or when Winfield Scott's brigade swings forward like gray doom at Chippawa to meet and break an equal line of veteran British infantry—that ring with honest, heartfelt pride.

More than a century of use and further study has naturally found errors and omissions in Adams' work. None are serious, and his judgments of men and events remain impeccable. Recent years have brought a revival of interest in the War of 1812 and, with it, a number of excellent new books: George F. G. Stanley's *War of 1812: Land Operations* (Toronto: Macmillan, 1983), valuable for its detailed picture of Canada at war; as well as Donald E. Graves' meticulously researched *Red Coats and Grey Jackets* (Toronto: Dundam Press, 1994) and *Where Right and Glory Lead* (Toronto: Robin Brass, 1997) covering, respectively, the battles of Chippawa and Lundy's Lane. But all our books on this subject are merely supplements to Henry Adams' *The War of 1812*. If you read only one history of that war, it still should be Adams!

COLONEL JOHN R. ELTING, USA, RET.
Cornwall-on-Hudson, New York
March 1999

TABLE OF CONTENTS

MAPS AND SKETCHES

FOREWORD

The need for an adequate short history of the War of 1812 has long been felt by general readers and students of military affairs. This need prompted *Infantry Journal* to request permission to publish the relevant chapters of Henry Adams's nine-volume *History of the United States, 1801-1817* (Charles Scribner's Sons, New York, 1889-1891), as a single-volume history of that war. The generosity of the publisher and the heirs of the author make the appearance of this book possible.

Henry Adams's *History of the United States* is one of the classics of American history, but present-day readers are often discouraged by the mere bulk of the series. The result has been that his treatment of the unhappiest war in our history has been among the neglected treasures of American letters. It is an axiom that a nation learns its most important military lessons from a study of its defeats and frustrations, not from a study of its successes. Thus the War of 1812 still has many things to teach a nation prone to find easy confirmation of its policies and methods in the ultimate success of its military enterprises.

In making the selection of chapters to be included in this volume, we have been governed by the general policy of retaining merely enough political discussion to give a background to the military and naval campaigns. Chapters dealing with the causes of the war have been omitted because they are assumed to be fairly well known by the average reader. The naval and military campaigns are not so well known and these chapters are given *in extenso*. On the advice of archival specialists we have eliminated the documentation which the author provided in the first edition of his work. In many cases the documents and papers to which he referred are no longer located in the places cited and the body of the text clearly reveals the nature of the sources used. No attempt has been made to edit the chapters presented or to modernize the spelling of place names. The maps which accompanied the original edition have been reproduced because they convey a better impression of the state of geographical knowledge and cartographical science when Henry Adams wrote this history than a modernized version would do.

It is hoped that this handy volume on the War of 1812 will give many readers who know Henry Adams only through his famous *Education of Henry Adams* (1918) or his *Mont St. Michel and Chartres* (1913) an opportunity to become acquainted with at least a portion of his major work, the *History of the United States*.

MAJOR H. A. DeWEERD,
Associate Editor,
Infantry Journal.

Washington.
March, 1944.

CHAPTER I
INVASION OF CANADA

For civil affairs Americans were more or less trained; but they had ignored war, and had shown no capacity in their treatment of military matters. Their little army was not well organized or equipped; its civil administration was more imperfect than its military, and its military condition could hardly have been worse. The ten old regiments, with half-filled ranks, were scattered over an enormous country on garrison service, from which they could not be safely withdrawn; they had no experience, and no organization for a campaign, while thirteen new regiments not yet raised were expected to conquer Canada.

If the army in rank and file was insufficient, its commanding officers supplied none of its wants. The senior major general appointed by President Madison in February, 1812, was Henry Dearborn, who had retired in 1809 from President Jefferson's Cabinet into the Custom-House of Boston. Born in 1751, Dearborn at the time of his nomination as major general was in his sixty-second year, and had never held a higher grade in the army than that of deputy quartermaster-general in 1781, and colonel of a New Hampshire regiment after active service in the Revolutionary War had ended.

The other major general appointed at the same time was Thomas Pinckney, of South Carolina, who received command of the Southern Department. Pinckney was a year older than Dearborn; his military service was chiefly confined to the guerrilla campaigns of Marion and Sumter, and to staff duty as aide to General Gates in the Southern campaign of 1780; he had been minister in England and Envoy Extraordinary to Spain, where he negotiated the excellent treaty known by his name; he had been also a Federalist member of Congress in the stormy sessions from 1797 to 1801—but none of these services, distinguished as they were, seemed to explain his appointment as major general. Macon, whose opinions commonly reflected those of the Southern people, was astonished at the choice.

"The nomination of Thomas Pinckney for major-general," he wrote, "is cause of grief to all men who wish proper men appointed; not that he is a Federal or that he is not a gentleman, but because he is thought not to possess the talents necessary to his station. I imagine his nomination must have been produced through the means of P. Hamilton, who is about as fit for his place as the Indian Prophet would be for Emperor of Europe. I never was more at a loss to account for any proceeding than the nomination of Pinckney to be major-general."

Even the private report that Pinckney had become a Republican did not reconcile Macon, whose belief that the "fighting secretaries" would not do for real war became stronger than ever, although he admitted that some of the military appointments were supposed to be tolerably good.

Of the brigadier generals, the senior was James Wilkinson, born in 1757, and fifty-five years old in 1812. Wilkinson had recently been tried by court-martial on a variety of charges, beginning with that of having been a pensioner of Spain and engaged in treasonable conspiracy; then of being an accomplice of Aaron Burr; and finally, insubordination, neglect of duty, wastefulness, and corruption. The court acquitted him, and February 14 President Madison approved the decision, but added an irritating reprimand. Yet in spite of acquittal Wilkinson stood in the worst possible odor, and returned what he considered his wrongs by bitter and contemptuous hatred for the President and the Secretary of War.

The next brigadier was Wade Hampton of South Carolina who entered the service in 1808 and was commissioned as brigadier in 1809. Born in 1754, he was fifty-seven years old, and though understood to be a good officer, he had as yet enjoyed no opportunity of distinguishing himself. Next in order came Joseph Bloomfield of New Jersey, nominated as brigadier general of the regular army March 27, 1812; on the same day James Winchester, of Tennessee, was named fourth brigadier; and April 8 William Hull, of Massachusetts, was appointed fifth in rank. Bloomfield, a major in the Revolutionary War, had been for the last ten years Governor of New Jersey. Winchester, another old Revolutionary officer, originally from Maryland, though mild, generous, and rich, was not the best choice that might have been made from Tennessee. William Hull, civil Governor of Michigan since 1805, was a third of the same class. All were sixty years of age or thereabout, and none belonged to the regular service, or had ever commanded a regiment in face of an enemy.

Of the inferior appointments, almost as numerous as the enlistments, little could be said. Among the officers of the regiment of Light Artillery raised in 1808, after the "Chesapeake" alarm, was a young captain named Winfield Scott, born near Petersburg, Virginia, in 1786, and in the prime of his energies when at the age of twenty-six he saw the chance of distinction before him. In after life Scott described the condition of the service as he found it in 1808.

"The army of that day," he said, "including its general staff, the three old and the nine new regiments, presented no pleasing aspect. The old officers had very generally sunk into either sloth, ignorance, or habits of intemperate drinking. . . . Many of the appointments were positively bad, and a majority of the remainder indifferent. Party spirit of that day knew no bounds, and of course was blind to policy. Federalists were almost entirely excluded from selection, though great numbers were eager for the field, and in New England and some other States there were but very few educated Republicans; hence the selections from those communities consisted mostly of coarse and ignorant men. In the other States, where there was no lack of educated men in the dominant party, the appointments consisted generally of swaggerers, dependents, decayed gentlemen, and others, 'fit for nothing else,' which always turned out utterly unfit for any military purpose whatever."

This account of the army of 1808 applied equally, said Scott, to the appointments of 1812. Perhaps the country would have fared as well without a regular army, by depending wholly on volunteers, and allowing the States to choose general officers. In such a case Andrew Jackson would have taken the place of James Winchester, and William Hull would never have received an appointment from Massachusetts.

No one in the government gave much thought to the military dangers created by the war, yet these dangers seemed evident enough to warrant keen anxiety. The seashore was nowhere capable of defense; the lakes were unguarded; the Indians of the Northwestern Territory were already in arms, and known to be waiting only a word from the Canadian governor-general; while the whole country beyond the Wabash and Maumee rivers stood nearly defenseless. At Detroit one hundred and twenty soldiers garrisoned the old British fort; eighty-five men on the Maumee held Fort Wayne; some fifty men guarded the new stockade called Fort Harrison, lately built on the Wabash; and fifty-three men, beyond possibility of rescue, were stationed at Fort Dearborn, or Chicago; finally, eighty-eight men occupied the Island of Michillimackinaw in the straits between Lake Huron and Lake Michigan. These were all the military defenses of a vast territory, which once lost would need another war to regain; and these petty garrisons, with the settlers about them, were certain, in the event of an ordinary mischance, to be scalped as well as captured. The situation was little better in the south and southwest, where the Indians needed only the support of a British army at New Orleans or Mobile to expel every American garrison from the territory.

No serious preparations for war had yet been made when the war began. In January, Congress voted ten new regiments of infantry, two of artillery, and one of light dragoons; the recruiting began in March, and in June the Secretary of War reported to Congress that although no returns had been received from any of the recruiting offices, yet considering the circumstances "the success which has attended this service will be found to have equalled any reasonable expectations." Eustis was in no way responsible for the failure of the service, and had no need to volunteer an opinion as to the reasonable expectations that Congress might entertain. Everyone knew that the enlistments fell far below expectation; but not the enlistments alone showed torpor. In February, Congress authorized the President to accept fifty thousand volunteers for one year's service. In June, the number of volunteers who had offered themselves was even smaller than that of regular recruits. In April Congress authorized the President to call out one hundred thousand State militia. In June no one knew whether all the States would regard the call, and still less whether the militia would serve beyond the frontier. One week after declaring war Congress fixed the war establishment at twenty-five regiments of infantry, four of artillery, two of dragoons, and one of riflemen—making, with the engineers and artificers, an army of thirty-six thousand seven hundred men; yet the actual force under arms did not exceed ten thousand, of whom four thousand were new recruits. Toward no part of the service did the people show a sympathetic spirit before the war was declared; and even where the war was most popular, as in Kentucky and Tennessee, men showed themselves determined to fight in their own way or not at all.

However inexperienced the Government might be, it could not overlook the necessity of providing for one vital point. Detroit claimed early attention and received it. The dangers surrounding Detroit were evident to anyone who searched the map for that remote settlement, within gunshot of British territory and surrounded by hostile Indian tribes. The Governor of Michigan, William Hull, a native of Connecticut, had done good service in the Revolutionary War, but had reached the age of sixty years without a wish to resume his military career. He preferred to remain in his civil post, leaving to some officer of the army the charge of military operations; but he came to Washington in February, 1812, and urged the Government to take timely measures for holding the Indians in check. He advised the President and Cabinet to increase the naval force on Lake Erie, although he already had at Detroit an armed brig ready to launch, which he thought sufficient to control the upper lakes. The subject was discussed; but the delay necessary to create a fleet must have risked, if it did not insure, the loss of the whole Northwestern Territory, and the President necessarily decided to march first a force to Detroit strong enough to secure the frontier, and, if possible, to occupy the whole or part of the neighboring and friendly British territory in Upper Canada. This decision Hull seems to have suggested, for he wrote March 6 to Secretary Eustis:

"A part of your army now recruiting may be as well supported and disciplined at Detroit as at any other place. A force adequate to the defence of that vulnerable point would prevent a war with the savages, and probably induce the enemy to abandon the province of Upper Canada without opposition. The naval force on the Lakes would in that event fall into our possession, and we should obtain the command of the waters without the expense of building such a force."

This hazardous plan required energy in the American armies, timely cooperation from Niagara if not from Lake Champlain, and, most of all, assumed both incompetence and treason in the enemy. Assuming that Hull would capture the British vessels on the Lakes, the President made no further provision for a fleet; but, apparently to provide for simultaneous measures against Lower Canada, the Secretary of War sent to Boston for General Dearborn, who was to command operations on Lake Ontario and the St. Lawrence River. Dearborn hastened to Washington in February, where he remained until the last of April. He submitted to the Secretary of War what was called a plan of campaign, recommending that a main army should advance by way of Lake Champlain upon Montreal, while three corps, composed chiefly of militia, should enter Canada from Detroit, Niagara, and Sackett's Harbor. Neither Dearborn, Hull, Eustis, nor Madison settled the details of the plan or fixed the time of the combined movement. They could not readily decide details before Congress acted, and before the ranks of the army were filled.

While these matters were under discussion in March, the President, unable to find an army officer fitted to command the force ordered to Detroit, pressed Governor Hull to reconsider his refusal; and Hull, yielding to the President's wish, was appointed, April 8, 1812, brigadier general of the United States army, and soon afterward set out for Ohio. No further understanding had then been reached between him and Dearborn, or Secretary Eustis, in regard to the military movements of the coming campaign.

The force destined for Detroit consisted of three regiments of Ohio militia under Colonels McArthur, Findlay, and Cass, a troop of Ohio dragoons, and the Fourth Regiment of United States Infantry which fought at Tippecanoe—in all about sixteen hundred effective men, besides a few volunteers. April 1 the militia were ordered to rendezvous at Dayton, and there, May 25, Hull took command. June 1 they marched, and June 10 were joined at Urbana by the Fourth Regiment. Detroit was nearly two hundred miles away, and the army as it advanced was obliged to cut a road through the forest, to bridge streams and construct causeways; but for such work the militia were well fitted, and they made good progress.

The energy with which the march was conducted excited the surprise of the British authorities in Canada, and contrasted well with other military movements of the year; but vigorous as it was it still lagged behind events. Hull had moved only some seventy-five miles, when, June 26, he received from Secretary Eustis a dispatch, forwarded by special messenger from the Department, to warn him that war was close at hand. "Circumstances have recently occurred," wrote Secretary Eustis, "which render it necessary you should pursue your march to Detroit with all possible expedition. The highest confidence is reposed in your discretion, zeal, and perseverance."

The dispatch, dated June 18, was sent by the secretary on the morning of that day in anticipation of the vote taken in Congress a few hours later. Hull had every reason to understand its meaning for he expected to lead his army against the enemy. "In the event of hostilities," he had written June 24, "I feel a confidence that the force under my command will be superior to any which can be opposed to it. It now exceeds two thousand rank and file." On receiving the secretary's pressing orders Hull left his heavy camp-equipage behind, and hurried his troops to the Miami, or Maumee, River thirty-five miles away. There he arrived June 30, and there, to save transportation, loading a schooner with his personal baggage, his hospital stores, entrenching tools, and even a trunk containing his instructions and the muster-rolls of his army, he dispatched it, July 1, up the Lake toward Detroit. He took for granted that he should receive from his own government the first notice of war; yet he knew that the steamboat from New York to Albany and the road from Albany to Buffalo, which carried news to the British forces at Malden, was also the regular mode of conveyance for Detroit; and he had every reason to suspect that as his distance in time from Washington was greater, he might learn of war first from actual hostilities. Hull considered "there was no hazard" in sending his most valuable papers past Malden; but within twenty-four hours he received a dispatch from Secretary Eustis announcing the declaration of war, and the same day his schooner was seized by the British in passing Malden to Detroit.

This first disaster told the story of the campaign. The declaration made at Washington June 18 was published by General Bloomfield at New York June 20, and reached Montreal by express June 24; the same day it reached the British Fort George on the Niagara River and was sent forward to Malden, where it arrived June 30. The dispatch to Hull reached Buffalo two days later than the British express, for it went by ordinary mail; from Cleveland it was forwarded by express, June 28, by way of Sandusky, to Hull, whom it reached at last, July 2, at Frenchtown on the river Raisin, forty miles below Detroit.

The slowness of transportation was made conspicuous by another incident. John Jacob Astor, being engaged in extensive trade with the Northwestern Indians, for political reasons had been encouraged by the government. Anxious to save the large amount of property exposed to capture, he not only obtained the earliest intelligence of war, and warned his agents by expresses, but he also asked and received from the Treasury orders addressed to the Collectors on the Lakes, directing them to accept and hold such goods as might be brought from Astor's trading-posts. The business of the Treasury as well as that of Astor was

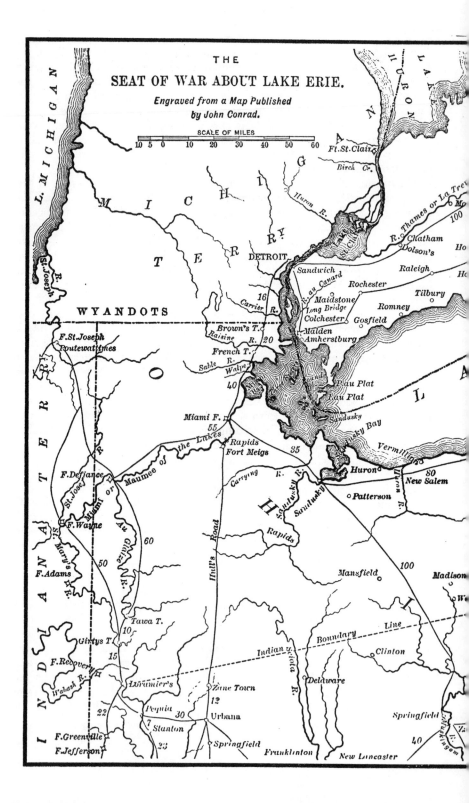

THE
SEAT OF WAR ABOUT LAKE ERIE.
*Engraved from a Map Published
by John Conrad.*

SCALE OF MILES
10 5 0   10   20   30   40   50   60

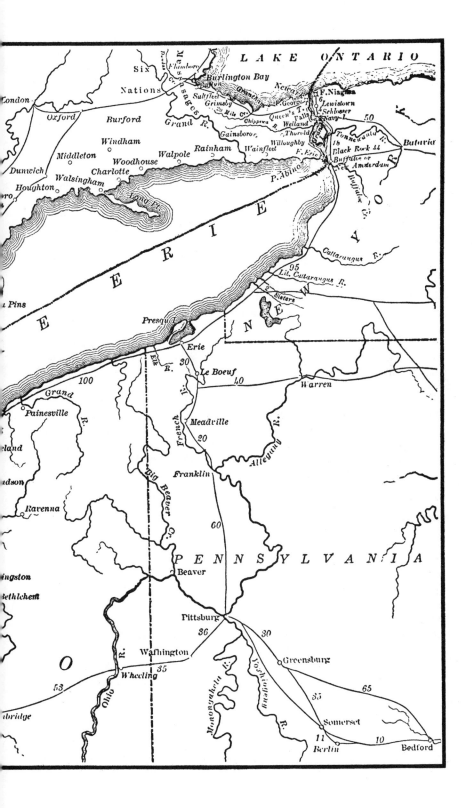

better conducted than that of the War Department. Gallatin's letters reached Detroit before Eustis's dispatch reached Hull; and this incident gave rise to a charge of misconduct and even of treason against Gallatin himself.

Hull reached Detroit July 5. At that time the town contained about eight hundred inhabitants within gunshot of the British shore. The fort was a square enclosure of about two acres, surrounded by an embankment, a dry ditch, and a double row of pickets. Although capable of standing a siege, it did not command the river; its supplies were insufficient for many weeks; it was two hundred miles distant from support, and its only road of communication ran for sixty miles along the edge of Lake Erie, where a British fleet on one side and a horde of savages on the other could always make it impassable. The widely scattered people of the territory, numbering four or five thousand, promised to become a serious burden in case of siege or investment. Hull knew in advance that in a military sense Detroit was a trap.

July 9, four days after his arrival, Hull received orders from Washington authorizing him to invade Canada:

"Should the force under your command be equal to the enterprise, consistent with the safety of your own post, you will take possession of Malden, and extend your conquests as circumstances may justify."

He replied immediately the same day:

"I am preparing boats, and shall pass the river in a few days. The British have established a post directly opposite this place. I have confidence in dislodging them, and of being in possession of the opposite bank. . . . The British command the water and the savages. I do not think the force here equal to the reduction of Amherstburg (Malden); you therefore must not be too sanguine."

Three days later, July 12, his army crossed the river. Not a gun was fired. The British militia force retired behind the Canard River, twelve miles below, while Hull and his army occupied Sandwich, and were well received by the inhabitants.

Hull had many reasons for wishing to avoid a battle. From the first he looked on the conquest of Canada as a result of his mere appearance. He began by issuing a proclamation intended to win a peaceful conquest.

"You will be emancipated," said the proclamation to the Canadians, "from tyranny and oppression, and restored to the dignified station of freemen. . . . I have a force which will break down all opposition, and that force is but the vanguard of a much greater. . . . The United States offer you peace, liberty, and security—your choice lies between these and war, slavery, or destruction. Choose then; but choose wisely." . . .

This proclamation, dated July 12, was spread throughout the province with no small effect, although it contained an apparently unauthorized threat, that "no white man found fighting by the side of an Indian will be taken prisoner; instant death will be his lot." The people of the western province were strongly American, and soon to the number of three hundred and sixty-seven, including deserters from the Malden garrison, sought protection in the American lines. July 19 Hull described the situation in very hopeful terms:

"The army is encamped directly opposite to Detroit. The camp is entrenched. I am mounting the 24-pounders and making every preparation for the siege of

Malden. The British force, which in numbers was superior to the American, including militia and Indians, is daily diminishing. Fifty or sixty (of the militia) have deserted daily since the American standard was displayed, and taken protection. They are now reduced to less than one hundred. In a day or two I expect the whole will desert. The Indian force is diminishing in the same proportion. I have now a large council of ten or twelve nations sitting at Brownstown, and I have no doubt but the result will be that they will remain neutral. The brig 'Adams' was launched on the 4th of July. I have removed her to Detroit under cover of the cannon, and shall have her finished and armed as soon as possible. We shall then have the command of the upper lakes."

To these statements Hull added a warning which carried at least equal weight:

"If you have not a force at Niagara, the whole force of the province will be directed against this army. . . . It is all important that Niagara should be invested. All our success will depend upon it."

While Hull reached this position, July 19, he had a right to presume that the Secretary of War and Major General Dearborn were straining every nerve to support him; but in order to understand Hull's situation, readers must know what Dearborn and Eustis were doing. Dearborn's movements, compared day by day with those of Hull, show that after both officers left Washington in April to take command of their forces, Hull reached Cincinnati May 10, while Dearborn reached Albany May 3, and wrote May 8, to Eustis that he had fixed on a site to be purchased for a military station. "I shall remain here until the erection of buildings is commenced. . . . The recruiting seems going on very well where it has been commenced. There are nearly three hundred recruits in this State." If Dearborn was satisfied with three hundred men as the result of six weeks' recruiting in New York State in immediate prospect of a desperate war, he was likely to take his own duties easily; and in fact, after establishing his headquarters at Albany for a campaign against Montreal, he wrote, May 21, to the Secretary announcing his departure for Boston: "As the quartermaster general arrived here this day I hope to be relieved from my duties in that line, and shall set out for Pittsfield, Springfield, and Boston; and shall return here as soon as possible after making the necessary arrangements at those places."

Dearborn reached Boston May 26, the day after Hull took command at Dayton. May 29 he wrote again to Eustis: "I have been here three days. . . . There are about three hundred recruits in and near this town. . . . Shall return to Albany within a few days." Dearborn found business accumulate on his hands. The task of arranging the coast defenses absorbed his mind. He forgot the passage of time, and while still struggling with questions of gunboats, garrisons, field pieces, and enlistments he was surprised, June 22, by receiving the declaration of war. Actual war threw still more labor and anxiety upon him. The State of Massachusetts behaved as ill as possible. "Nothing but their fears," he wrote, "will prevent their going all lengths." More used to politics than to war, Dearborn for the time took no thought of military movements.

Madison and Eustis seemed at first satisfied with this mode of conducting the campaign. June 24 Eustis ordered Hull to invade West Canada, and extend his conquests as far as practicable. Not until June 26 did he write to Dearborn:

"Having made the necessary arrangements for the defence of the sea-coast, it is the wish of the President that you should repair to Albany and prepare the force to be collected at that place for actual service. It is understood that being possessed of a full view of the intentions of Government, and being also acquainted with the disposition of the force under your command, you will take your own time and give the necessary orders to the officers on the sea coast. It is altogether uncertain at what time General Hull may deem it expedient to commence offensive operations. The preparations it is presumed will be made to move in a direction for Niagara, Kingston, and Montreal. On your arrival at Albany you will be able to form an opinion of the time required to prepare the troops for action."

Such orders as those of June 24 to Hull, and of June 26 to Dearborn, passed beyond bounds of ordinary incapacity, and approached the line of culpable neglect. Hull was to move when he liked, and Dearborn was to take his own time at Boston before beginning to organize his army. Yet the letter to Dearborn was less surprising than Dearborn's reply. The major general in charge of operations against Montreal, Kingston, and Niagara should have been able to warn his civil superior of the risks incurred in allowing Hull to make an unsupported movement from an isolated base such as he knew Detroit to be; but no thought of Hull found place in Dearborn's mind. July 1 he wrote:

"There has been nothing yet done in New England that indicates an actual state of war, but every means that can be devised by the Tories is in operation to depress the spirits of the country. Hence the necessity of every exertion on the part of the Government for carrying into effect the necessary measures for defence or offence. We ought to have gunboats in every harbor on the coast. Many places will have no other protection, and all require their aid. I shall have doubts as to the propriety of my leaving this place until I receive your particular directions after you shall have received my letter."

Dearborn complained with reason of the difficulties that surrounded him. Had Congress acted promptly, a large body of volunteers would have been already engaged, general officers would have been appointed and ready for service, whereas no general officer except himself was yet at any post north of New York City. Every day he received from every quarter complaints of want of men, clothing, and supplies; but his remaining at Boston to watch the conduct of the State government was so little likely to overcome these difficulties that at last it made an unfavorable impression on the Secretary, who wrote, July 9, a more decided order from Washington:

"The period has arrived when your services are required at Albany, and I am instructed by the President to direct, that, having made arrangements for placing the works on the sea-coast in the best state of defence your means will permit . . . you will then order all the recruits not otherwise disposed of to march immediately to Albany, or some station on Lake Champlain, to be organized for the invasion of Canada."

With this official letter Eustis sent a private letter of the same date, explaining the reason for his order:

"If . . . we divide, distribute, and render inefficient the force authorized by law, we play the game of the enemy within and without. District among the field-officers the sea-board! . . . Go to Albany or the Lake! The troops shall come to you as fast as the season will admit, and the blow must be struck. Congress must not meet without a victory to announce to them."

Dearborn at Boston replied to these orders, July 13, a few hours after Hull's army, six hundred miles away, crossed the Detroit River into Canada and challenged the whole British force on the lakes.

"For some time past I have been in a very unpleasant situation, being at a loss to determine whether or not I ought to leave the sea-coast. As soon as war was declared [June 18] I was desirous of repairing to Albany, but was prevented by your letters of May 20 and June 12, and since that time by the extraordinary management of some of the governors in this quarter. On the receipt of your letter of June 26 I concluded to set out in three or four days for Albany, but the remarks in your letter of the 1st inst. prevented me. But having waited for more explicit directions until I begin to fear that I may be censured for not moving, and having taken such measures as circumstances would permit for the defence of the sea-coast, I have concluded to leave this place for Albany before the end of the present week unless I receive orders to remain."

A general-in-chief unable to decide at the beginning of a campaign in what part of his department his services were most needed was sure to be taught the required lesson by the enemy. Even after these warnings Dearborn made no haste. Another week passed before he announced, July 21, his intended departure for Albany the next day, but without an army. "Such is the opposition in this State as to render it doubtful whether much will be done to effect in raising any kind of troops. " The two months he passed in Boston were thrown away; the enlistments were so few as to promise nothing, and the governor of Massachusetts barely condescended to acknowledge without obeying his request for militia to defend the coast.

July 26, one week after Hull had written that all his success depended on the movements at Niagara, Dearborn reached Albany and found there some twelve hundred men not yet organized or equipped. He found also a letter, dated July 20, from the Secretary of War, showing that the Government had begun to feel the danger of its position. "I have been in daily expectation of hearing from General Hull, who probably arrived in Detroit on the 8th inst." In fact, Hull arrived in Detroit July 5, and crossed into Canada July 12; but when the secretary wrote, July 20, he had not yet heard of either event. "You will make such arrangements with Governor Tompkins," continued Eustis, "as will place the militia detached by him for Niagara and other posts on the lakes under your control; and there should be a communication, and if practicable a coöperation, throughout the whole frontier."

The secretary as early as June 24 authorized Hull to invade Canada West, and his delay in waiting till July 20 before sending similar orders to the general commanding the force at Niagara was surprising; but if Eustis's letter seemed singular, Dearborn's answer passed belief. For the first time General Dearborn then asked a question in regard to his own campaign—a question so extraordinary that every critic found it an enigma: "Who is to have command of the operations in Upper Canada? I take it for granted that my command does not extend to that distant quarter."

July 26, when Hull had been already a fortnight on British soil, a week after he wrote that his success depended on coöperation from Niagara, the only force at Niagara consisted of a few New York militia, not coöperating with Hull or under the control of any United States officer, while the major general of the Department took it for granted that Niagara was not included in his command. The Government therefore expected General Hull, with a force which it knew did not at the outset exceed two thousand effectives, to march two hundred miles, constructing a road as he went; to garrison Detroit; to guard at least sixty miles of road under the enemy's guns; to face a force in the field equal to his own, and another savage force of unknown numbers in his rear; to sweep the Canadian peninsula of British troops; to capture the fortress at Malden and the British fleet on Lake Erie—and to do all this without the aid of a man or a boat between Sandusky and Quebec.

CHAPTER II

HULL'S SURRENDER

General Hull, two days after entering Canada, called a council of war which decided against storming Malden and advised delay. Their reasons were sufficiently strong. After allowing for the sick-list and garrison-duty, the four regiments could hardly supply more than three hundred men each for active service, besides the Michigan militia, on whom no one felt willing to depend. Hull afterward affirmed that he had not a thousand effectives; the highest number given in evidence two years later by Major Jesup was the vague estimate of sixteen or eighteen hundred men. Probably the utmost exertion could not have brought fifteen hundred effectives to the Canadian shore. The British force opposed to them was not to be despised. Colonel St. George commanding at Malden had with him two hundred men of the Forty-First British line, fifty men of the Royal Newfoundland regiment, and thirty men of the Royal Artillery. Besides these two hundred and eighty veteran troops with their officers, he had July 12 about six hundred Canadian militia and two hundred and thirty Indians. The militia deserted rapidly; but after allowing for the desertions, the garrison at Malden, including Indians, numbered nearly nine hundred men. The British had also the advantage of position, and of a fleet whose guns covered and supported their left. They were alarmed and cautious, but though they exaggerated Hull's force they meant to meet him in front of their fortress. Hull's troops would have shown superiority to other American forces engaged in the campaign of 1812 had they won a victory.

The Ohio militia, although their officers acquiesced in the opinion of the council of war, were very unwilling to lose their advantage. If nothing was to be gained by attack, everything was likely to be lost by delay. Detachments scoured the country, meeting at first little resistance, one detachment even crossing the Canard River, flanking and driving away the guard at the bridge; but the army was not ready to support the unforeseen success, and the bridge was abandoned. Probably this moment was the last when an assault could have been made with a chance of success. July 19 and 24 strong detachments were driven back with loss, and the outlook became suddenly threatening.

Hull tried to persuade himself that he could take Malden by siege. July 22 he wrote to Eustis that he was pressing the preparation of siege guns:

"I find that entirely new carriages must be built for the 24-pounders and mortars. It will require at least two weeks to make the necessary preparations. It is in the power of this army to take Malden by storm, but it would be attended in my opinion with too great a sacrifice under the present circumstances. . . . If Malden was in our possession, I could march this army to Niagara or York (Toronto) in a very short time."

This was Hull's last expression of confidence or hope. Thenceforward every day brought him fatal news. His army lost respect for him in consequence of his failure to attack Malden; the British strengthened the defenses of Malden, and August 8 received sixty fresh men of the Forty-first under Colonel Proctor from Niagara; but worse than mutiny or British reinforcement, news from the Northwest of the most disastrous character reached Hull at a moment when his hopes of taking Malden had already faded. August 3 the garrison of Michillimackinaw arrived at Detroit as prisoners-of-war on parole, announcing that Mackinaw had capitulated July 17 to a force of British and savages, and that Hull must prepare to receive the attack of a horde of Indians coming from the Northwest to fall upon Detroit in the rear.

Hull called another council of war August 5, which, notwithstanding this news, decided to attack Malden August 8, when the heavy artillery should be ready; but while they were debating this decision, a party of Indians under Tecumthe crossing the river routed a detachment of Findlay's Ohio regiment on their way to protect a train of supplies coming from Ohio. The army mail bags fell into British hands. Hull then realized that his line of communication between Detroit and the Maumee River was in danger, if not closed. On the heels of this disaster he received, August 7, letters from Niagara announcing the passage of British reinforcements up Lake Ontario to Lake Erie and Malden. Thus he was called to meet in his front an intrenched force nearly equal to his own, while at least a thousand Indian warriors were descending on his flank from Lake Huron, and in the rear his line of communication and supply could be restored only by detaching half his army for the purpose.

Hull decided at once to recross the river, and succeeded in effecting this movement on the night of August 8 without interference from the enemy; but his position at Detroit was only one degree better than it had been at Sandwich. He wished to abandon Detroit and retreat behind the Maumee, and August 9 proposed the measure to some of his principal officers. Colonel Cass replied that if this were done every man of the Ohio militia would refuse to obey, and would desert their general, that the army would fall to pieces if ordered to retreat. Hull considered that this report obliged him to remain where he was.

This was the situation at Detroit August 9—a date prominent in the story; but Hull's true position could be understood only after learning what had been done in Canada since the declaration of war.

The difficulties of Canada were even greater than those of the United States. Upper Canada, extending from Detroit River to the Ottawa within forty miles of Montreal, contained not more than eighty thousand persons. The political capital was York, afterward Toronto, on Lake Ontario. The civil and military command of this vast territory was in the hands of Brigadier General Isaac Brock, a native of Guernsey, forty-two years old, who had been colonel of the Forty-ninth regiment of the British line, and had served since 1802 in Canada. The appointment of Brock in October, 1811, to the chief command at the point of greatest danger was for the British a piece of good fortune, or good judgment, more rare than could have been appreciated at the time, even though Dearborn, Hull, Winchester, Wilkinson, Sir George Prevost himself, and Colonel Proctor were examples of the common standard. Brock was not only a man of unusual powers, but his powers were also in their prime. Neither physical nor mental fatigue such as followed his rivals' exertions paralyzed his plans. No scruples about bloodshed stopped him midway to victory. He stood alone in his superiority as a soldier. Yet his civil difficulties were as great as his military, for he had

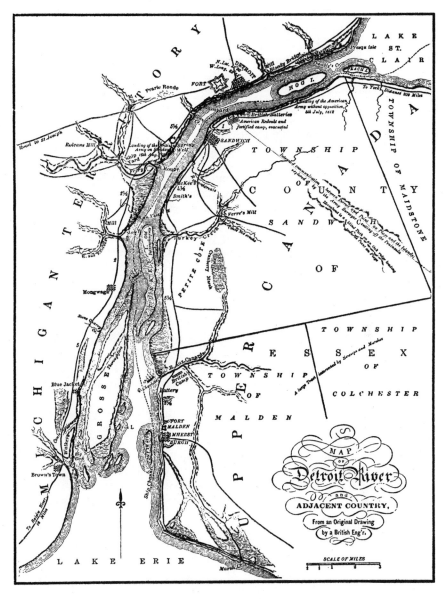

to deal with a people better disposed toward his enemies than toward himself; and he succeeded in both careers.

Under Brock's direction, during the preceding winter vessels had been armed on Lake Erie, and Malden had been strengthened by every means in his power. These precautions gave him from the outset the command of the lake, which in itself was almost equivalent to the command of Detroit. Of regular troops he had but few. The entire regular force in both Canadas at the outbreak of the war numbered six thousand three hundred and sixty rank and file, or about seven thousand men including officers. More than five thousand of these were stationed in Lower Canada. To protect the St. Lawrence, the Niagara, and the Detroit, Brock had only fourteen hundred and seventy-three rank and file, or including his own regiment—the Forty-ninth then at Montreal—two thousand one hundred and thirty-seven men at the utmost.

When the news of war reached him, not knowing where to expect the first blow, Brock waited, moving between Niagara and Toronto, until Hull's passage of the Detroit River, July 12, marked the point of danger and startled the province almost out of its dependence on England. Sir George Prevost, the governor-general, reported with much mortification the effect of Hull's movement on Upper Canada:

"Immediately upon the invasion of the province and upon the issuing of the proclamation by General Hull, which I have the honor of herewith transmitting, it was plainly perceived by General Brock that little reliance could be placed upon the militia, and as little dependence upon the active exertions of any considerable proportion of the population of the country, unless he was vested with full power to repress the disaffected spirit which was daily beginning to show itself, and to restrain and punish the disorders which threatened to dissolve the whole militia force which he had assembled. He therefore called together the provincial legislature of July 27 in the hope that they would adopt prompt and efficient measures for strengthening the hands of the Government at a period of such danger and difficulty. . . . In these reasonable expectations I am sorry to say General Brock has been miserably disappointed; and a lukewarm and temporizing spirit, evidently dictated either by the apprehension or the wish that the enemy might soon be in complete possession of the country, having prevented the Assembly from adopting any of the measures proposed to them, they were prorogued on the 5th instant."

Brock himself wrote to Lord Liverpool a similar account of his trials:

"The invasion of the western district by General Hull was productive of very unfavorable sensations among a large portion of the population, and so completely were their minds subdued that the Norfolk militia when ordered to march peremptorily refused. The state of the country required prompt and vigorous measures. The majority of the House of Assembly was likewise seized with the same apprehensions, and may be justly accused of studying more to avoid by their proceedings incurring the indignation of the enemy than the honest fulfilment of their duty. . . . I cannot hide from your Lordship that I considered my situation at that time extremely perilous. Not only among the militia was evinced a disposition to submit tamely, five hundred in the western district having deserted their ranks, but likewise the Indians of the Six Nations, who are placed in the heart of the country on the Grand River, positively refused, with the exception of a few individuals, taking up arms. They audaciously announced their intention after the return of some of their chiefs from General Hull to remain neutral, as if they wished to impose upon the Government the belief that it was possible they could sit quietly in the midst of war. This unexpected conduct of the Indians deterred many good men from leaving their families and joining the militia; they became more apprehensive of the internal than of the external enemy, and would willingly have compromised with the one to secure themselves from the other."

Brock's energy counterbalanced every American advantage. Although he had but about fifteen hundred regular troops in his province, and was expected to remain on the defensive, the moment war was declared, June 26, he sent to Amherstburg all the force he could control and ordered the commandant of the British post at the island of St. Joseph on Lake Huron to seize the American fort at Michillimackinaw. When Hull issued his proclamation of July 12, Brock replied by a proclamation of July 22. To Hull's threat that no quarter should be given to soldiers fighting by the side of Indians, Brock responded by "the certain assurance of retaliation"; and he justified the employment of his Indian allies by arguments which would have been more conclusive had he ventured to reveal his desperate situation. In truth the American complaint that the British employed Indians in war meant nothing to Brock, whose loss of his province by neglect of any resource at his command might properly have been punished by the utmost penalty his Government could inflict.

Brock's proclamation partly restored confidence. When his legislature showed backwardness in supporting him he peremptorily dismissed them, August 5, after they had been only a week in session, and the same day he left York for Burlington Bay and Lake Erie. Before quitting Lake Ontario he could not fail to inquire what was the American force at Niagara and what it was doing. Every one in the neighborhood must have told him that on the American side five or six hundred militiamen, commanded by no general officer, were engaged in patrolling thirty-six miles of river front; that they were undisciplined, ill-clothed, without tents, shoes, pay, or ammunition, and ready to retreat at any sign of attack. Secure at that point, Brock hurried toward Malden. He had ordered reinforcements to collect at Long Point on Lake Erie; and August 8, while Hull was withdrawing his army from Sandwich to Detroit, Brock passed Long Point, taking up three hundred men whom he found there, and coasted night and day to the Detroit River.

Meanwhile, at Washington, Eustis sent letter after letter to Dearborn, pressing for a movement from Niagara. July 26 he repeated the order of July 20. August 1 he wrote, enclosing Hull's dispatch of July 19: "You will make a diversion in his favor at Niagara and at Kingston as soon as may be practicable, and by such operations as may be within your control."

Dearborn awoke August 3 to the consciousness of not having done all that man could do. He began arrangements for sending a thousand militia to Niagara, and requested Major General Stephen Van Rensselaer of the New York State militia to take command there in person. In a letter of August 7 to the Secretary of War, he showed sense both of his mistakes and of their results:

"It is said that a detachment [of British troops] has been sent from Niagara by land to Detroit; if so, I should presume before they can march two hundred and fifty miles General Hull will receive notice of their approach, and in season to cut them off before they reach Fort Malden. It is reported that no ordnance or ammunition have reached Niagara this season, and that there is great deficiency of these articles. Not having considered any part of the borders of Upper Canada as within the command intended for me, I have received no reports or returns from that quarter, and did not until since my last arrival at this place give any orders to the commanding officers of the respective posts on that frontier."

The consequences of such incapacity showed themselves without an instant's delay. While Dearborn was writing from Albany, August 7, General Brock, as has been told, passed from Lake Ontario to Lake Erie; and the next morning, when Brock reached his detachment at Long Point, Hull evacuated Sandwich and retired to Detroit. Had he fallen back on the Maumee or even to Urbana or Dayton, he would have done only what Wellington had done more than once in circumstances hardly more serious, and what Napoleon was about to do three months afterward in leaving Moscow.

Desperate as Hull's position was, Dearborn succeeded within four-and-twenty hours by an extraordinary chance in almost extricating him, without being conscious that his action more than his neglect affected Hull's prospects. This chance was due to the reluctance of the British government to accept the war. Immediately after the repeal of the Orders in Council the new Ministry of Lord Liverpool ordered their minister, Foster, to conclude an armistice in case hostilities had begun, and requested their governor-general to avoid all extraordinary preparations. These orders given in good faith by the British government were exceeded by Sir George Prevost, who had every reason to wish for peace. Although he could not make an armistice without leaving General Hull in possession of his conquests in Upper Canada, which might be extensive, Prevost sent his adjutant general, Colonel Baynes, to Albany to ask a cessation of hostilities, and the same day, August 2, wrote to General Brock warning him of the proposed step. Colonel Baynes reached headquarters at Albany August 9, and obtained from Dearborn an agreement that his troops, including those at Niagara, should act only on the defensive until further orders from Washington:

"I consider the agreement as favorable at this period," wrote Dearborn to Eustis, "for we could not act offensively except at Detroit for some time, and there it will not probably have any effect on General Hull or his movements."

What effect the armistice would have on Hull might be a matter for prolonged and serious doubt, but that it should have no effect at all would have occurred to no ordinary commander. Dearborn had been urgently ordered, August 1, to support Hull by a vigorous offensive at Niagara, yet August 9 he agreed with the British general to act only on the defensive at Niagara. Detroit was not under Dearborn's command, and therefore was not included in the armistice; but Dearborn stipulated that the arrangement should include Hull if he wished it. Orders were sent to Niagara August 9, directing the commanding officers "to confine their respective operations to defensive measures," and with these orders Dearborn wrote to Hull proposing a concurrence in the armistice. Had Brock moved less quickly, or had the British government sent its instructions a week earlier, the armistice might have saved Detroit. The chance was narrow, for even an armistice unless greatly prolonged would only have weakened Hull, especially as it could not include Indians other than those actually in British service; but even the slight chance was lost by the delay until August 9 in sending advices to Niagara and Detroit, for Brock left Long Point August 8, and was already within four days of Detroit when Dearborn wrote from Albany. The last possibility of saving Hull was lost by the inefficiency of American mail service. The distance from Albany to Buffalo was about three hundred miles. A letter written at Albany August 9 should have reached Niagara by express August 13; Dearborn's letter to Hull arrived there only on the evening of August 17, and was forwarded by General Van Rensselaer the next morning. Even through the British lines it could hardly reach Detroit before August 24.

Slowness such as this in the face of an enemy like Brock, who knew the value of time, left Hull small chance of escape. Brock with his little army of three hundred men leaving Long Point August 8 coasted the shore of the lake, and sailing at night reached Malden late in the evening of August 13, fully eight days in advance of the armistice.

Meanwhile Hull was besieged at Detroit. Immediately after returning there, August 8, he sent nearly half his force—a picked body of six hundred men, including the Fourth U. S. Regiment—to restore his communications with Ohio. Toward afternoon of the next day, when this detachment reached the Indian village of Maguaga fourteen miles south of Detroit, it came upon the British force consisting of about one hundred and fifty regulars of the Forty-first Regiment, with forty or fifty militia and Tecumthe's little band of twenty-five Indians —about two hundred and fifty men all told. After a sharp engagement the British force was routed and took to its boats, with a loss of thirteen men or more, while the Indians disappeared in the woods. For some unsatisfactory reason the detachment did not then march to the river Raisin to act as convoy for the supplies, and nothing but honor was acquired by the victory. "It is a painful consideration," reported Hull, "that the blood of seventy-five gallant men could only open the communication as far as the points of their bayonets extended." On receiving a report of the battle Hull at first inclined to order the detachment to the Raisin, but the condition of the weather and the roads changed his mind, and August 10 he recalled the detachment to Detroit.

The next four days were thrown away by the Americans. August 13 the British began to establish a battery on the Canadian side of the river to bombard Detroit. Within the American lines the army was in secret mutiny. Hull's vacillations and evident alarm disorganized his force. The Ohio colonels were ready to remove him from his command, which they offered to Lieutenant Colonel Miller of the U. S. Fourth Regiment; but Colonel Miller declined this manner of promotion, and Hull retained control. August 12 the three colonels united in a letter to the governor of Ohio, warning him that the existence of the army depended on the immediate dispatch of at least two thousand men to keep open the line of communication. "Our supplies must come from our State; this country does not furnish them." A postscript added that even a capitulation was talked of by the commander-in-chief. In truth, Hull, who like most commanders-in-chief saw more of the situation than was seen by his subordinates, made no concealment of his feelings. Moody, abstracted, wavering in his decisions, and conscious of the low respect in which he was held by his troops, he shut himself up and brooded over his desperate situation.

Desperate the situation seemed to be; yet a good general would still have saved Detroit for some weeks, if not altogether. Hull knew that he must soon be starved into surrender; but though already short of supplies he might by vigorous preparations and by rigid economy have maintained himself a month, and he had always the chance of a successful battle. His effective force, by his own showing, still exceeded a thousand men to defend the fort; his supplies of ammunition were sufficient; and even if surrender were inevitable, after the mortifications he had suffered and those he foresaw, he would naturally have welcomed a chance of dying in battle. Perhaps he might have chosen this end, for he had once been a brave soldier; but the thought of his daughter and the women and children of the settlement left to the mercy of Indians overcame him. He shrank from it with evident horror, exaggerating the numbers and brooding over the "greedy violence" of the bands, "numerous beyond any former example," who were descending from the Northwest. Doubtless his fears were well-founded but a general-in-chief whose mind was paralyzed by such thoughts could not measure himself with Isaac Brock.

On the evening of August 14 Hull made one more effort. He ordered two of the Ohio colonels, McArthur and Cass, to select the best men from their regiments, and to open if possible a circuitous route of fifty miles through the woods to the river Raisin. The operation was difficult, fatiguing, and dangerous; but the supplies so long detained at the Raisin, thirty-five miles away by the direct road, must be had at any cost, and the two Ohio colonels aware of the necessity promptly undertook the service. Their regiments in May contained nominally about five hundred men each, all told. Two months of severe labor with occasional fighting and much sickness had probably reduced the number of effectives about one-half. The report of Colonel Miller of the U. S. Fourth Regiment in regard to the condition of his command showed this proportion of effectives, and the Fourth Regiment was probably in better health than the militia. The two Ohio regiments of McArthur and Cass numbered perhaps six or seven hundred effective men, and from these the two colonels selected three hundred and fifty, probably the best. By night time they were already beyond the river Rouge, and the next evening, August 15, were stopped by a swamp less than half way to the river Raisin.

After their departure on the night of August 14 Hull learned that Brock had reached Malden the night before with heavy reinforcements. According to Hull's later story, he immediately sent orders to McArthur and Cass to return to Detroit, giving the reasons for doing so; in fact, he did not send till the afternoon of the next day, and the orders reached the detachment four-and-twenty miles distant only at sunset August 15. So it happened that on the early morning of

August 16 Hull was guarding the fort and town of Detroit with about two hundred and fifty effective men of the Fourth Regiment, about seven hundred men of the Ohio militia, and such of the Michigan militia and Ohio volunteers as may have been present—all told, about a thousand effectives. Hull estimated his force as not exceeding eight hundred men; Major Jesup, the acting adjutant general, reported it as one thousand and sixty, including the Michigan militia. If the sickness and loss of strength at Detroit were in proportion to the waste that soon afterward astonished the generals at Niagara, Hull's estimate was perhaps near the truth.

Meanwhile Brock acted with rapidity and decision. After reaching Malden late at night August 13, he held a council the next day, said to have been attended by a thousand Indian warriors.

"Among the Indians whom I found at Amherstburg," he reported to Lord Liverpool, "and who had arrived from distant parts of the country, I found some extraordinary characters. He who attracted most my attention was a Shawnee chief, Tecumset, brother to the Prophet, who for the last two years has carried on contrary to our remonstrances an active warfare against the United States. A more sagacious or more gallant warrior does not, I believe, exist. He was the admiration of every one who conversed with him."

Brock consumed one day in making his arrangements with them, and decided to move his army immediately across the Detroit River and throw it against the fort.

"Some say that nothing could be more desperate than the measure," he wrote soon afterward; "but I answer that the state of the province admits only of desperate remedies. I got possession of the letters my antagonist addressed to the Secretary of War, and also the sentiments which hundreds of his army uttered to their friends. Confidence in their general was gone, and evident despondency prevailed throughout. I crossed the river contrary to the opinion of Colonel Proctor, etc. It is therefore no wonder that envy should attribute to good fortune what, in justice to my own discernment, I must say proceeded from a cool calculation of the *pours* and *contres*."

Probably Brock received then Sir George Prevost's letter of August 2 warning him of the intended armistice, for Hull repeatedly and earnestly asserted that Brock spoke to him of the armistice August 16; and although twelve days was a short time for an express to pass between Montreal and Malden, yet it might have been accomplished at the speed of about fifty miles a day. If Brock had reason to expect an armistice, the wish to secure for his province the certainty of future safety must have added a motive for hot haste.

At noon August 15 Brock sent a summons of surrender across the river to Hull. "The force at my disposal," he wrote, "authorizes me to require of you the surrender of Detroit. It is far from my inclination to join in a war of extermination, but you must be aware that the numerous body of Indians who have attached themselves to my troops will be beyond my control the moment the contest commences." The threat of massacre or Indian captivity struck Hull's most sensitive chord. After some delay he replied, refusing to surrender, and then sent orders recalling McArthur's detachment; but the more he thought of his situation the more certain he became that the last chance of escape had vanished. In a few days or weeks want of provisions would oblige him to capitulate, and the bloodshed that would intervene could serve no possible purpose. Brock's movements increased the general's weakness. As soon as Hull's reply reached the British lines, two British armed vessels—the *Queen Charlotte* of seventeen guns and the *Hunter* of ten guns—moved up the river near Sandwich, while a battery of guns and mortars opened fire from the Canadian shore and continued firing irregularly all night on the town and fort. The fire was returned, but no energetic measures were taken to prepare either for an assault or a siege.

During the night Tecumthe and six hundred Indians crossed the river some two miles below and filled the woods, cutting communication between McArthur's detachment and the fort. A little before daylight of August 16 Brock himself, with three hundred and thirty regulars and four hundred militia, crossed the river carrying with them three six-pound and two three-pound guns. He had intended to take up a strong position and force Hull to attack it; but learning from his Indians that McArthur's detachment, reported as five hundred strong, was only a few miles in his rear he resolved on an assault, and moved in close column within three-quarters of a mile of the American twenty-four-pound guns. Had Hull prayed that the British might deliver themselves into his hands, his prayers could not have been better answered. Even under trial for his life he never ventured to express a distinct belief that Brock's assault could have succeeded; and in case of failure the small British force must have retreated at least a mile and a half under the fire of the fort's heavy guns, followed by a force equal to their own, and attacked in flank and rear by McArthur's detachment, which was within hearing of the battle and marching directly toward it.

"Nothing but the boldness of the enterprise could have insured its success," said Richardson, one of Brock's volunteers. "When within a mile and a half of the rising ground commanding the approach to the town we distinctly saw two long, heavy guns, afterward proved to be 24-pounders, planted in the road, and around them the gunners with their fuses burning. At each moment we expected that they would be fired . . . and fearful in such case must have been the havoc; for moving as we were by the main road, with the river close upon our right flank and a chain of alternate houses and close fences on our left, there was not the slightest possibility of deploying. In this manner and with our eyes riveted on the guns, which became at each moment more visible, we silently advanced until within about three quarters of a mile of the formidable battery, when General Brock, having found at this point a position favorable for the formation of the columns of assault, caused the whole to be wheeled to the left through an open field and orchard leading to a house about three hundred yards off the road, which he selected as his headquarters. In this position we were covered."

All this time Hull was in extreme distress. The cannon-shot from the enemy's batteries across the river were falling in the fort. Uncertain what to do, the General sat on an old tent on the ground with his back against the rampart. "He apparently unconsciously filled his mouth with tobacco, putting in quid after quid more than he generally did; the spittle colored with tobacco-juice ran from his mouth on his neckcloth, beard, cravat, and vest." He seemed preoccupied, his voice trembled, he was greatly agitated, anxious, and fatigued. Knowing that sooner or later the fort must fall, and dreading massacre for the women and children; anxious for the safety of McArthur and Cass, and treated with undisguised contempt by the militia officers—he hesitated, took no measure to impede the enemy's advance, and at last sent a flag across the river to negotiate. A cannonball from the enemy's batteries killed four men in the fort; two companies of the Michigan militia deserted—their behavior threatening to leave the town exposed to the Indians—and from that moment Hull determined to surrender on the best terms he could get.

As Brock, after placing his troops under cover, ascended the brow of the rising ground to reconnoiter the fort, a white flag advanced from the battery before him and within an hour the British troops, to their own undisguised astonishment, found themselves in possession of the fortress. The capitulation included McArthur's detachment and the small force covering the supplies at the river Raisin. The army, already mutinous, submitted with what philosophy it could command to the necessity it could not escape.

On the same day at the same hour Fort Dearborn at Chicago was in flames. The Government provided neither for the defense nor for the safe withdrawal of the little garrison, but Hull had sent an order to evacuate the fort if practicable. In the process of evacuation, August 15, the garrison was attacked and massacred by an overwhelming body of Indians. The next morning the fort was burned, and with it the last vestige of American authority on the western lakes disappeared. Thenceforward the line of the Wabash and the Maumee became the military boundary of the United States in the Northwest, and the country felt painful doubt whether even that line could be defended.

CHAPTER III

THE NIAGARA CAMPAIGN

Although the loss of Detroit caused the greatest loss of territory that ever before or since befell the United States, the public at large understood little of the causes that made it inevitable, and saw in it only an accidental consequence of Hull's cowardice. Against this victim, who had no friend in the world, every voice was raised. He was a coward, an imbecile, but above all unquestionably a traitor, who had, probably for British gold, delivered an army and a province, without military excuse, into the enemy's hands. If any man in the United States was more responsible than Hull for the result of the campaign it was ex-President Jefferson, whose system had shut military efficiency from the scope of American government; but to Jefferson, Hull and his surrender were not the natural products of a system, but objects of hatred and examples of perfidy that had only one parallel. "The treachery of Hull, like that of Arnold, cannot be a matter of blame to our government," he wrote, on learning the story of Lewis Cass and the Ohio militia officers, who told with the usual bitterness of betrayed men what they knew of the causes that had brought their betrayal to pass. "The detestable treason of Hull," as Jefferson persisted in calling it, was the more exasperating to him because even as late as August 4 he had written with entire confidence to the same correspondent that "the acquisition of Canada this year, as far as the neighborhood of Quebec, will be a mere matter of marching, and will give us experience for the attack of Halifax the next, and the final expulsion of England from the American continent." Perhaps the same expectation explained the conduct of Hull, Madison, Eustis, and Dearborn; yet at the moment when Jefferson wrote thus, Madison was beginning to doubt. August 8, the often-mentioned day when Brock reached Long Point and Hull decided to retreat from Canada, Madison wrote to Gallatin:

"Should he [Hull] be able to descend upon Niagara and an adequate co-operation be there afforded, our prospect as to Upper Canada may be good enough. But what is to be done with respect to the expedition against Montreal? The enlistments for the regular army fall short of the most moderate calculation; the Volunteer Act is extremely unproductive; and even the militia detachments are either obstructed by the disaffected governors or chilled by the Federal spirit diffused throughout the region most convenient to the theatre. I see nothing better than to draw on this resource as far as the detachments consist of volunteers, who, it may be presumed, will cross the line without raising Constitutional or legal questions."

In contrast with these admissions and their satirical "it may be presumed," the tone of the governor-general, Sir George Prevost, at the same crisis was masterful.

"The Eighth or King's Regiment," he wrote August 17 from Montreal, "has arrived this morning from Quebec to relieve the Forty-ninth Regiment. This fine and effective regiment of the Eighth, together with a chain of troops established in the vicinity of this place consisting of a regular and militia force, the whole amounting to near four thousand five hundred men, effectually serve to keep in check the enemy in this quarter, where alone they are in any strength."

[24]

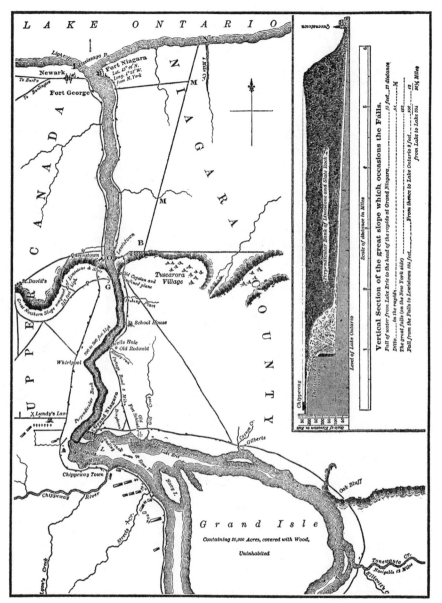

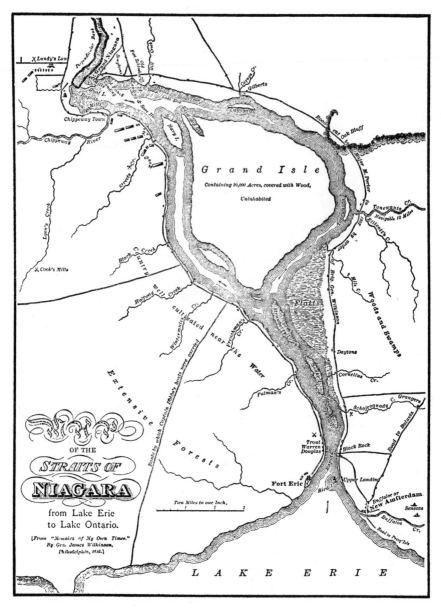

OF THE

STRAITS OF

NIAGARA

from Lake Erie
to Lake Ontario.

[From "Memoirs of My Own Times."
By Gen. James Wilkinson,
Philadelphia, 1816.]

Two Miles to one Inch.

The Canadian outnumbered the American forces at every point of danger on the frontier. A week later Sir George claimed another just credit:

"The decided superiority I have obtained on the Lakes in consequence of the precautionary measures adopted during the last winter has permitted me to move without interruption, independently of the arrangement [armistice], both troops and supplies of every description toward Amherstburg, while those for General Hull, having several hundred miles of wilderness to pass before they can reach Detroit, are exposed to be harassed and destroyed by the Indians."

Not only were the British forces equal or superior to the American at Detroit, Niagara, and Montreal, but they could be more readily concentrated and more quickly supplied.

The storm of public wrath which annihilated Hull and shook Eustis passed harmless over the head of Dearborn. No one knew that Dearborn was at fault, for he had done nothing; and a general who did nothing had that advantage over his rivals whose activity or situation caused them to act. Dearborn threw the whole responsibility on the War Department. August 15 he wrote to President Madison:

"The particular circumstances which have created the most unfortunate embarrassments were my having no orders or directions in relation to Upper Canada (which I had considered as not attached to my command) until my last arrival at this place, and my being detained so long at Boston *by direction*. If I had been directed to take measures for acting offensively on Niagara and Kingston, with authority such as I now possess, for calling out the militia, we might have been prepared to act on those points as early as General Hull commenced his operations at Detroit; but unfortunately no explicit orders had been received by me in relation to Upper Canada until it was too late even to make an effectual diversion in favor of General Hull. All that I could do was done without any delay."

For the moment such pleas might serve; but after the capture of Detroit, Dearborn's turn came, and nothing could save him from a fate as decided if not as fatal as that of Hull. His armistice indeed would have answered the purpose of protection had the Government understood its true bearing; but Dearborn's letter announcing the armistice reached Washington August 13, and the Secretary of War seeing the dangers and not the advantages of a respite replied, August 15, in language more decided than he had yet used:

"I am commanded by the President to inform you that there does not appear to him any justifiable cause to vary or desist from the arrangements which are in operation; and I am further commanded to instruct you that from and after the receipt of this letter and allowing a reasonable time in which you will inform Sir George Prevost thereof, you will proceed with the utmost vigor in your operations. How far the plan originally suggested by you of attacking Niagara, Kingston, and Montreal at the same time can be rendered practicable, you can best judge. Presuming that not more than a feint, if that should be deemed expedient, with the troops on Lake Champlain aided by volunteers and militia can be immediately effected against Montreal, and considering the urgency of a diversion in favor of General Hull under the circumstances attending his situation, the President thinks it proper that not a moment should be lost in gaining possession of the British posts at Niagara and Kingston, or at least the former, and proceeding in co-operation with General Hull in securing Upper Canada."

The same day, August 15, the eve of Hull's surrender Dearborn wrote to the Secretary of War:

"If the troops are immediately pushed on from the southward, I think we may calculate on being able to possess ourselves of Montreal and Upper Canada before the winter sets in. . . . I am pursuing measures with the view of being able to operate with effect against Niagara and Kingston, at the same time that I move toward Lower Canada. If the Governor of Pennsylvania turns out two thousand good militia from the northwesterly frontier of his State, as I have requested him to do, and the quartermaster-general furnishes the means of transportation and camp-equipage in season, I am persuaded we may act with effect on the several points in the month of October at farthest."

As yet nothing had been done. August 19 General Van Rensselaer reported from Lewiston that between Buffalo and Niagara he commanded less than a thousand militia, without ordnance heavier than six-pounders and but few of these, without artillerists to serve the few pieces he had, and the troops in a very indifferent state of discipline. In pursuance of his orders he collected the force within his reach, but August 18 received notice of Dearborn's armistice and immediately afterward of Hull's surrender. August 23 Brock, moving with his usual rapidity, reappeared at Fort George with Hull's army as captives.

Fortunately, not only were the Americans protected by the armistice, but both Prevost and Brock were under orders, and held it good policy, to avoid irritating the Americans by useless incursions. Prevost, about the equal of Madison as a military leader, showed no wish to secure the positions necessary for his safety. Had he at once seized Sackett's Harbor, as Brock seized Detroit, he would have been secure, for Sackett's Harbor was the only spot from which the Americans could contest the control of Lake Ontario. Brock saw the opportunity, and wanted to occupy the harbor, but Prevost did not encourage the idea; and Brock, prevented from making a correct movement, saw no advantage in making an incorrect one. Nothing was to be gained by an offensive movement at Niagara, and Brock at that point labored only to strengthen his defense.

Van Rensselaer, knowing the whole American line to be at Brock's mercy, felt just anxiety. August 31 he wrote to Governor Tompkins:

"Alarm pervades the country, and distrust among the troops. They are incessantly pressing for furloughs under every possible pretence. Many are without shoes; all clamorous for pay; many are sick. . . . While we are thus growing weaker our enemy is growing stronger. They hold a very commanding position on the high ground above Queenstown, and they are daily strengthening themselves in it with men and ordnance. Indeed, they are fortifying almost every prominent point from Fort Erie to Fort George. At present we rest upon the armistice, but should hostilities be recommenced I must immediately change my position. I receive no reinforcements of men, no ordnance or munitions of war."

Dearborn replied to this letter September 2, and his alarm was certainly not less than that of Van Rensselaer:

"From the number of troops which have left Montreal for Upper Canada, I am not without fear that attempts will be speedily made to reduce you and your forces to the mortifying situation of General Hull and his army. If such an attempt of the enemy should be made previous to the arrival of the principal part of the troops destined to Niagara, it will be necessary for you to be prepared for all events, and to be prepared to make good a secure retreat as the last resort."

To the Secretary of War, Dearborn wrote that he hoped there would be nothing worse than retreat. Under such circumstances the armistice became an advantage, for the offensive had already passed into the enemy's hands. Detroit and Lake Erie were lost beyond salvation, but on Lake Ontario supplies and cannon were brought to Niagara by water from Oswego; the vessels at Ogdensburg were moved to Sackett's Harbor and became the nucleus of a fleet; while all the troops, regular and militia, that could be gathered from New England, New York, and Pennsylvania were hurried to the front. September 1 Dearborn wrote to Eustis that he had at Plattsburg, on Lake Champlain, or under marching orders there, five thousand troops, more than half of them regulars, while six thousand, including three regular regiments from the southward, were destined for Niagara.

"When the regular troops you have ordered for Niagara arrive at that post," he wrote to Eustis, September 1, "with the militia and other troops there or on their march, they will be able I presume to cross over into Canada, carry all the works in Niagara, and proceed to the other posts in that province in triumph."

Yet the movement of troops was slow. September 15 Van Rensselaer had only sixteen hundred militia. Not till then did the reaction from Hull's disaster make itself felt. Commodore Chauncey came to Lake Ontario with unbounded authority to create a fleet, and Lieutenant Elliott of the navy was detached to Lake Erie for the same purpose; ordnance and supplies were hurried to Buffalo, and Dearborn sent two regiments from Albany with two companies of artillery.

"When they arrive," he wrote September 17 to Van Rensselaer, "with the regular troops and militia from the southward and such additional numbers of militia as I reckon on from this State, the aggregate force will I presume amount to upward of six thousand. It is intended to have a force sufficient to enable you to act with effect, though late."

The alarm still continued; and even a week afterward Dearborn wrote as though he expected disaster:

"A strange fatality seems to have pervaded the whole arrangements. Ample reinforcements of troops and supplies of stores are on their way, but I fear their arrival will be too late to enable you to maintain your position. . . . By putting on the best face that your situation admits, the enemy may be induced to delay an attack until you will be able to meet him and carry the war into Canada. At all events we must calculate on possessing Upper Canada before winter sets in."

In Dearborn's letters nothing was said of the precise movement intended, but through them all ran the understanding that as soon as the force at Niagara should amount to six thousand men a forward movement should be made. The conditions supposed to be needed for the advance were more than fulfilled in the early days of October, when some twenty-five hundred militia, with a regiment of Light Artillery without guns, and the Thirteenth U. S. Infantry were in the neighborhood of Lewiston; while a brigade of United States troops, sixteen hundred and fifty strong, commanded by Brigadier General Alexander Smyth, were on the march to Buffalo. October 13 Dearborn wrote to Van Rensselaer: "I am confidently sure that you will embrace the first practicable opportunity for effecting a forward movement." This opportunity had then already arrived. Smyth reached Buffalo, September 29, and reported by letter to General Van Rensselaer; but before seeing each other the two generals quarrelled. Smyth held the opinion that the army should cross into Canada above the Falls, and therefore camped his brigade at Buffalo. Van Rensselaer had made his arrangements to cross below the Falls. October 5 Van Rensselaer requested Smyth to fix a day for a council of war, but Smyth paid no attention to the request; and as he was independent of Van Rensselaer, and could not be compelled to obey the orders of a major general of New York militia, Van Rensselaer decided to act without regard to Smyth's brigade or to his opinions. He knew that the force under his immediate orders below the Falls was sufficient for his purpose.

Van Rensselaer's decision was supported by many different motives—the lateness of the season, the weather, the sickness and the discontent of the militia threatening actual disbandment, the jealousy of a militia officer toward the regular service, and the additional jealousy of a Federalist toward the Government; for Van Rensselaer was not only a Federalist, but was also a rival candidate against Tompkins for the governorship of New York, and the Republicans were eager to charge him with intentional delay. A brilliant stroke by Lieutenant Elliott at the same moment added to the restlessness of the army. On the night of October 8 Elliott and Captain Towson of the Second Artillery, with fifty sailors and fifty soldiers of Smyth's brigade, cut out two British vessels under the guns of Fort Erie. One of these vessels was the *Adams*, captured by Brock at Detroit, the other had belonged to the Northwestern Fur Company, and both were of great value to the British as a reinforcement to their fleet on Lake Erie. The larger was destroyed; the smaller, named the *Caledonia*, was saved, and served to increase the little American fleet. Brock felt keenly the loss of these two vessels, which "may reduce us to incalculable distress," he wrote to Prevost, October 11. He watched the progress of Elliott's and Chauncey's naval preparations with more anxiety than he showed in regard to Dearborn's military movements, although he spared no labor in fortifying himself against these.

General Van Rensselaer conceived a plan for a double attack by throwing one body of troops across the river to carry Queenston, while a strong force of regulars should be conveyed in boats by way of the Lake and landed on the Lake shore in the rear of Fort George to take the fort by storm—a movement afterward successfully made; but owing to Smyth's conduct the double attack was abandoned, and Van Rensselaer decided to try only the simpler movement against Queenston. Brock with less than two thousand men guarded nearly forty miles of front along the Niagara River, holding at Queenston only two companies of the Forty-ninth Regiment with a small body of militia—in all about three hundred men. Brock was himself at Fort George, some five miles below Queenston, with the greater part of the Forty-first Regiment, which he had brought back from Detroit, and a number of Indians. The rest of his force was at Chippawa and Fort Erie, opposite Buffalo, where the real attack was expected.

Van Rensselaer fixed the night of October 10 for his movement, and marched the troops to the river at the appointed time; but the crossing was prevented by some blunder in regard to boats, and the troops after passing the night exposed to a furious storm returned to camp. After this miscarriage Van Rensselaer would have waited for a council of war, but the tone of his officers and men satisfied him that any sign of hesitation would involve him in suspicion and injure the service. He postponed the movement until the night of October 12 giving the command of the attack to Colonel Solomon Van Rensselaer of the State militia, whose force was to consist of three hundred volunteers and three hundred regular troops under Lieutenant Colonel Christie of the Thirteenth Regiment.

At three o'clock on the morning of October 13 the first body of troops embarked. Thirteen boats had been provided. Three of these lost their way, or were forced by the current down stream until obliged to return. Colonel Christie was in one of the boats that failed to land. The command of his men fell to young Captain Wool of the Thirteenth Regiment. The British were on the alert and although after a volley of musketry they withdrew toward Queenston they quickly returned with reinforcements and began a sharp action, in which Colonel Van Rensselaer was severely wounded and the advance on Queenston was effectually stopped. Daylight appeared and at a quarter before seven Brock himself galloped up and mounted the hill above the river to watch the contest from an 18-pounder battery on the hilltop. At the same moment Captain Wool with a few men of his regiment climbed up the same heights from the riverside by a path which had been reported to Brock as impassable, and was left unguarded. Reaching the summit, Wool found himself about thirty yards in the rear of the battery from which Brock was watching the contest below. By a rapid flight on foot Brock escaped capture, and set himself immediately to the task of recovering the heights. He had early sent for the Forty-first Regiment under General Sheaffe from Fort George, but without waiting reinforcements he collected a few men— about ninety, it is said—of the Forty-ninth Regiment who could be spared below, and sent them to dislodge Wool. The first British attack was beaten back. The second, in stronger force with the York Volunteers, was led by Brock in person; but while he was still at the foot of the hill an American bullet struck him in the breast and killed him on the spot.

At ten o'clock in the morning, Captain Wool, though painfully wounded, held the heights with two hundred and fifty men; but the heights had no value except to cover or assist the movement below, where the main column of troops with artillery and intrenching tools should have occupied Queenston, and advanced or fortified itself. When Lieutenant Colonel Christie, at about seven o'clock, having succeeded in crossing the river, took command of the force on the river bank, he could do nothing for want of men, artillery, and intrenching tools. He could not even dislodge the enemy from a stone house whence two light pieces of artillery were greatly annoying the boats. Unable to move without support he recrossed the river, found General Van Rensselaer half a mile beyond, and described to him the situation. Van Rensselaer sent orders to General Smyth to march his brigade to Lewiston "with every possible despatch," and ordered Captain Totten of the Engineers across the river, with intrenching tools, to lay out a fortified camp.

Toward noon General Van Rensselaer himself crossed with Christie to Queenston and climbed the hill, where Lieutenant Colonel Winfield Scott had appeared as a volunteer and taken the command of Captain Wool's force. Toward three o'clock Lieutenant Colonel Christie joined the party on the hill. Brigadier General William Wadsworth of the New York militia was also on the ground, and some few men arrived, until three hundred and fifty regulars and two hundred and fifty militia are said to have been collected on the heights. From their position, at two o'clock, Van Rensselaer and Scott made out the scarlet line of the Forty-first Regiment advancing from Fort George. From Chippawa every British soldier who could be spared hurried to join the Forty-first, while a swarm of Indians swept close on the American line, covering the junction of the British forces and the turning movement of General Sheaffe round the foot of the hill. About one thousand men, chiefly regulars, were concentrating against the six hundred Americans on the heights. General Van Rensselaer, alarmed at the sight, hastened to recross the river to Lewiston for reinforcements.

"By this time," concluded Van Rensselaer in his report of the next day, "I perceived my troops were embarking very slowly. I passed immediately over to accelerate their movements; but to my utter astonishment I found that at the very moment when complete victory was in our hands the ardor of the unengaged troops had entirely subsided. I rode in all directions, urged the men by every consideration to pass over; but in vain. Lieutenant Colonel Bloom who had been wounded in the action returned, mounted his horse, and rode through the camp, as did also Judge Peck who happened to be here, exhorting the companies to proceed; but all in vain."

More unfortunate than Hull, Van Rensselaer stood on the American heights and saw his six hundred gallant soldiers opposite slowly enveloped, shot down, and at last crushed by about a thousand men who could not have kept the field a moment against the whole American force. Scott and his six hundred were pushed over the cliff down to the bank of the river. The boatmen had all fled with the boats. Nothing remained but to surrender; and under the Indian fire even surrender was difficult. Scott succeeded only by going himself to the British line through the Indians, who nearly killed him as he went.

In this day's work ninety Americans were reported as killed. The number of wounded can only be estimated. Not less than nine hundred men surrendered, including skulkers and militia-men who never reached the heights. Brigadier General William Wadsworth of the New York militia, Lieutenant Colonel Fenwick of the U. S. Light Artillery, Lieutenant Colonel Winfield Scott of the Second Artillery, and, among officers of less rank, Captain Totten of the Engineers were among the prisoners. Van Rensselaer's campaign did not, like that of Hull, cost a province, but it sacrificed nearly as many effective troops as were surrendered by Hull.

General Van Rensselaer the next day sent his report of the affair to General Dearborn, and added a request to be relieved of his command. Dearborn, who knew little of the circumstances, ordered him to transfer the command to General Smyth, and wrote to Washington a bitter complaint of Van Rensselaer's conduct, which he attributed to jealousy of the regular service.

Hitherto the military movements against Canada had been directed by Eastern men. Alexander Smyth belonged to a different class. Born in Ireland in 1765, his fortunes led him to Virginia, where he became a respectable member of the Southwestern bar and served in the State legislature. Appointed in 1808 by President Jefferson colonel of the new rifle regiment, in 1812 he became inspector general, with the rank of brigadier. By his own request he received command of the brigade ordered to Niagara, and his succession to Van Rensselaer followed of course. Dearborn, knowing little of Smyth, was glad to intrust the army to a regular officer in whom he felt confidence; yet an Irish temperament with a Virginian education promised the possibility of a campaign which if not more disastrous than that led by William Hull of Massachusetts, or by Stephen Van Rensselaer of New York, might be equally eccentric.

October 24 Smyth took command at Buffalo, and three weeks later the public read in the newspapers an address issued by him to the "Men of New York," written in a style hitherto unusual in American warfare.

"For many years," Smyth announced to the Men of New York, "you have seen your country oppressed with numerous wrongs. Your government, although above all others devoted to peace, has been forced to draw the sword, and rely for redress of injuries on the valor of the American people. That valor has been conspicuous. But the nation has been unfortunate in the selection of some of those who have directed it. One army has been disgracefully surrendered and lost. Another has been sacrificed by a precipitate attempt to pass it over at the strongest point of the enemy's lines with most incompetent means. The cause of these miscarriages is apparent. The commanders were popular men, 'destitute alike of theory and experience' in the art of war."

Unmilitary as such remarks were, the address continued in a tone more and more surprising, until at last it became burlesque.

"In a few days the troops under my command will plant the American standard in Canada. They are men accustomed to obedience, silence, and steadiness. They will conquer, or they will die.

"Will you stand with your arms folded and look on this interesting struggle? Are you not related to the men who fought at Bennington and Saratoga? Has the race degenerated? Or have you, under the baneful influence of contending factions, forgot your country? Must I turn from you and ask the men of the Six Nations to support the government of the United States? Shall I imitate the officers of the British king, and suffer our ungathered laurels to be tarnished by ruthless deeds? Shame, where is thy blush! No!"

The respectable people of the neighborhood were not wholly discouraged by this call or by a second proclamation, November 17, as little military as the first; or even by an address of Peter B. Porter offering to lead his neighbors into Canada under the command of the "able and experienced officer" who within a few days could and would "occupy all the British fortresses on the Niagara River." A certain number of volunteers offered themselves for the service, although not only the attack but also its details were announced in advance. The British responded by bombarding Black Rock and Fort Niagara; and although their cannon did little harm, they were more effective than the proclamations of the American generals.

November 25 General Smyth issued orders for the invasion, which were also unusual in their character, and prescribed even the gestures and attitudes of the attacking force: "At twenty yards distance the soldiers will be ordered to trail arms, advance with shouts, fire at five paces distance, and charge bayonets. The soldiers will be *silent* above all things." In obedience to these orders, everything was prepared, November 27, for the crossing, and once more orders were issued in an inspiring tone:

"Friends of your country! ye who have 'the will to do, the heart to dare!' the moment ye have wished for has arrived! Think on your country's honors torn! her rights trampled on! her sons enslaved! her infants perishing by the hatchet! Be strong! be brave! and let the ruffian power of the British king cease on this continent!"

Two detachments were to cross the river from Black Rock before dawn, November 28, to surprise and disable the enemy's batteries and to destroy a bridge five miles below; after this should be done the army was to cross. The British were supposed to have not more than a thousand men within twenty miles to resist the attack of three thousand men from Buffalo. Apparently Smyth's calculations were correct. His two detachments crossed the river at three o'clock on the morning of November 28 and gallantly, though with severe loss, captured and disabled the guns and tore up a part of the bridge without destroying it. At sunrise the army began to embark at the navy yard, but the embarkation continued so slowly that toward afternoon, when all the boats were occupied, only twelve hundred men, with artillery, were on board. "The troops thus embarked," reported Smyth, "moved up the stream to Black Rock without sustaining loss from the enemy's fire. It is now afternoon, and they were ordered to disembark and dine."

This was all. No more volunteers appeared, and no other regulars fit for service remained. Smyth would not cross without three thousand men, and doubtless was right in his caution; but he showed want of courage not so much in this failure to redeem his pledges, as in his subsequent attempt to throw responsibility on subordinates, and on Dearborn who had requested him to consult some of his officers occasionally, and be prepared if possible to cross into Canada with three thousand men at once. Smyth consulted his officers at the moment when consultation was fatal.

"Recollecting your instructions to cross with three thousand men *at once,* and to consult some of my principal officers in 'all important movements,' I called for the field officers of the regulars and twelve-months volunteers embarked."

The council of war decided not to risk the crossing. Winder, who was considered the best of Smyth's colonels, had opposed the scheme from the first, and reported the other officers as strongly against it. Smyth was aware of their opinions, and his appeal to them could have no object but to shift responsibility. After receiving their decision, Smyth sent a demand for the surrender of Fort Erie, "to spare the effusion of blood," and then ordered his troops to their quarters. The army obeyed with great discontent, but fifteen hundred men still mustered in boats, when two days afterward Smyth issued another order to embark. Once more Smyth called a council of war, and once more decided to abandon the invasion. With less than three thousand men in the boats at once, the General would not stir.

Upon this, General Smyth's army dissolved. "A scene of confusion ensued which it is difficult to describe," wrote Peter B. Porter soon afterward—"about four thousand men without order or restraint discharging their muskets in every direction." They showed a preference for General Smyth's tent as their target, which caused the General to shift his quarters repeatedly. A few days afterward Peter B. Porter published a letter to a Buffalo newspaper attributing the late disgrace "to the cowardice of General Smyth." The General sent a challenge to his subordinate officer, and exchanged shots with him. Smyth next requested permission to visit his family, which Dearborn hastened to grant; and three months afterward, as General Smyth did not request an inquiry into the causes of his failure, the President without express authority of law dropped his name from the army roll.

When Dearborn received the official report of Smyth's grotesque campaign, he was not so much annoyed by its absurdities as he was shocked to learn that nearly four thousand regular troops sent to Niagara in the course of the campaign could not supply a thousand for crossing the river. Further inquiry explained that sickness had swept away more than half the army. The brigade of regulars at Buffalo, which with the exception of Winder's regiment had never fired a musket, was reduced to less than half its original number, and both officers and men were unfit for active duty. Only rest and care could restore the army to efficiency.

The failures of Hull, Van Rensselaer, and Smyth created a scandal so noisy that little was thought of General Dearborn; yet Dearborn still commanded on Lake Champlain the largest force then under arms, including seven regiments of the regular army, with artillery and dragoons. He clung to the idea of an attack on Montreal simultaneous with Smyth's movement at Niagara. November 8 he wrote from Albany to Eustis that he was about to join the army under General Bloomfield at Plattsburg.

"I have been detained several days by a severe rheumatic attack, but I shall, by the aid of Dr. Mann, be able to set off this day toward Lake Champlain, where I trust General Bloomfield will be able to move toward Montreal, and with the addition of three thousand regular troops that place might be carried and held this winter; but I cannot consent to crossing the St. Lawrence with an uncertainty of being able to remain there."

Whatever were Dearborn's motives for undertaking the movement, his official report explained that on arriving at Plattsburg he found General Bloomfield ill, and was himself obliged to take command, November 19, when he marched the army about twenty miles to the Canadian line. At that point the militia declined to go further, and Dearborn as quietly as possible, November 23, marched back to Plattsburg. His campaign lasted four days, and he did not enter Canada.

Whether Dearborn, Smyth or William Hull would have improved the situ-

ation by winning a victory or by losing a battle was a question to be answered
by professional soldiers; but the situation at best was bad, and when the report
of Smyth's crowning failure reached Dearborn it seemed for a moment to overcome his sorely tried temper. "I had anticipated disappointment and misfortune
in the commencement of the war," he wrote to Eustis, "but I did by no means apprehend such a deficiency of regular troops and such a series of disasters as we
have witnessed." He intimated his readiness to accept the responsibility which
properly belonged to him, and to surrender his command. "I shall be happy to
be released by any gentleman whose talents and popularity will command the
confidence of the Government and the country." To the President he wrote at
the same time; "It will be equally agreeable to me to employ such moderate
talents as I possess in the service of my country, or to be permitted to retire to the
shades of private life, and remain a mere but interested spectator of passing
events."

CHAPTER IV

NAVAL BATTLES

Culpable as was the helplessness of the War Department in 1812, the public neither understood nor knew how to enforce responsibility for disasters which would have gone far to cost a European war minister his life, as they might have cost his nation its existence. By fortune still kinder, the Navy Department escaped penalty of any sort for faults nearly as serious as those committed by its rival. The navy consisted, besides gunboats, of three heavy frigates rated as carrying forty-four guns; three lighter frigates rated at thirty-eight guns; one of thirty-two, and one of twenty-eight; besides two ships of eighteen guns, two brigs of sixteen, and four brigs of fourteen and twelve—in all sixteen seagoing vessels, twelve of which were probably equal to any vessels afloat of the same class. The eight frigates were all built by Federalist Congresses before President Jefferson's time; the smaller craft, except one, were built under the influence of the war with Tripoli. The Administration which declared war against England did nothing to increase the force. Few of the ships were in first-rate condition. The officers complained that the practice of laying up the frigates in port hastened their decay, and declared that hardly a frigate in the service was as sound as she should be. For this negligence Congress was alone responsible; but the Department perhaps shared the blame for want of readiness when war was declared.

The only ships actually ready for sea, June 18, were the *President*, 44, commanded by Commodore Rodgers, at New York, and the *United States*, 44, which had cruised to the southward with the *Congress*, 38, and *Argus*, 16, under the command of Commodore Decatur. Secretary Hamilton, May 21, sent orders to Decatur to prepare for war, and June 5 wrote more urgently: "Have the ships under your command immediately ready for extensive active service, and proceed with them to New York where you will join Commodore Rodgers and wait further orders. Prepare for battle which I hope will add to your fame." To Rodgers he wrote on the same day in much the same words: "Be prepared in all respects for extensive service." He asked both officers for their advice how to make the navy most useful. Rodgers's reply, if he made one, was not preserved; but Decatur answered from Norfolk, June 8:

"The plan which appears to me to be the best calculated for our little navy . . . would be to send them out with as large a supply of provisions as they can carry, distant from our coast and singly, or not more than two frigates in company, without giving them any specific instructions as to place of cruising, but to rely on the enterprise of the officers."

The Department hesitated to adopt Decatur's advice, and began by an effort to concentrate all its ships at New York—an attempt in which Secretary Hamilton could not wholly succeed, for the *Constellation* and the *Chesapeake*, 38-gun frigates, and the *Adams*, 28, were not in condition for sea; the *Essex*, 32, was not quite ready, and the *Wasp*, 18, was bringing dispatches from Europe, while the *Constitution*, 44, detained at Annapolis by the difficulty of shipping a new crew, could not sail within three weeks. The secretary ordered Captain Hull, who commanded the *Constitution*, to make his way to New York with the utmost

speed, and if his crew were in proper condition, to look for the British frigate
Belvidera on the way. The only ships that could be brought to New York without delay were those of Decatur at Norfolk. To him the secretary, on the
declaration of war, sent orders to proceed with all dispatch northwards, and "to
notice the British flag if it presents itself" on the way. "The *Belvidera* is said to
be on our coast," added the secretary. Before this letter reached Norfolk, Decatur
and his squadron sailed from the Chesapeake and were already within sight of
Sandy Hook; so that the only orders from the Navy Department which immediately affected the movement of the frigates were those sent to New York for
Commodore Rodgers and the frigate *President,* but which included Decatur's
squadron when it should arrive.

"For the present," wrote the secretary to Rodgers, "it is desirable that with the
force under your command you remain in such position as to enable you most
conveniently to receive further more extensive and more particular orders, which
will be conveyed to you through New York. But as it is understood that there
are one or more British cruisers on the coast in the vicinity of Sandy Hook, you
are at your discretion free to strike them, returning immediately after into port.
You are free to capture or destroy them."

These orders reached New York June 21. Rodgers in his fine frigate the
President, with the *Hornet,* 18, was eager to sail. The hope of capturing the
Belvidera, which had long been an intolerable annoyance to New York commerce, was strong both in the Navy Department and in the navy; but the
chance of obtaining prize money from the British West India convoy, just then
passing eastward only a few days' sail from the coast, added greatly to the commodore's impatience. Decatur's squadron arrived off Sandy Hook June 19. June
21, within an hour after receiving the secretary's orders of June 18, the whole
fleet, including two forty-four and one thirty-eight-gun frigates, with the *Hornet*
and the *Argus,* stood out to sea.

The secretary might have spared himself the trouble of giving further orders,
for many a week passed before Rodgers and Decatur bethought themselves of his
injunction to return immediately into port after striking the *Belvidera.* They
struck the *Belvidera* within forty-eight hours, and lost her; partly on account of
the bursting of one of the *President's* main-deck guns, which blew up the forecastle deck, killing or wounding sixteen men, including Commodore Rodgers
himself, whose leg was broken; partly, and according to the British account
chiefly, on account of stopping to fire at all, when Rodgers should have run
alongside and in that case could not have failed to capture his enemy. Whatever
was the reason, the *Belvidera* escaped; and Rodgers and Decatur, instead of returning immediately into port as they had been ordered, turned in pursuit of the
British West India convoy, and hung doggedly to the chase without catching
sight of their game, until after three weeks' pursuit they found themselves within
a day's sail of the British Channel and the convoy safe in British waters.

This beginning of the naval war was discouraging. The American ships
should not have sailed in a squadron, and only their good luck saved them from
disaster. Rodgers and Decatur showed no regard to the wishes of the Government, although had they met with misfortune, the navy would have lost its last

hope. Yet if the two commodores had obeyed the secretary's commands their cruise would probably have been in the highest degree disastrous. The Government's true intentions have been a matter of much dispute; but beyond a doubt the President and a majority of his advisers inclined to keep the navy within reach at first—to use them for the protection of commerce, to drive away the British blockaders; and aware that the British naval force would soon be greatly increased, and that the American navy must be blockaded in port, the Government expected in the end to use the frigates as harbor defenses rather than send them to certain destruction.

With these ideas in his mind, Secretary Hamilton, in his orders of June 18, told Rodgers and Decatur that "more extensive" orders should be sent to them on their return to New York. A day or two afterward Secretary Gallatin complained to the President that these orders had not been sent.

"I believe the weekly arrivals from foreign ports," said Gallatin, "will for the coming four weeks average from one to one-and-a-half million dollars a week. To protect these and our coasting vessels, while the British have still an inferior force on our coasts, appears to me of primary importance. I think that orders to that effect, ordering them to cruise accordingly, ought to have been sent yesterday, and that at all events not one day longer ought to be lost."

June 22 the orders were sent according to Gallatin's wish.. They directed Rodgers with his part of the squadron to cruise from the Chesapeake eastwardly, and Decatur with his ships to cruise from New York southwardly, so as to cross and support each other and protect with their united force the merchantmen and coasters entering New York harbor, the Delaware, and the Chesapeake. Rodgers and Decatur were then beginning their private cruise across the ocean, and never received these orders until the commerce they were to protect either reached port in safety or fell into British hands.

Probably this miscarriage was fortunate, for not long after Rodgers and Decatur passed the Banks the British Vice Admiral Sawyer sent from Halifax a squadron to prevent the American navy from doing what Secretary Hamilton had just ordered to be done. July 5 Captain Broke, with his own frigate, the *Shannon*, 38, the *Belvidera*, 36, the *Africa*, 64, and *Æolus*, 32, put to sea from Halifax and was joined, July 9, off Nantucket by the *Guerrière*, 38. Against such a force Rodgers and Decatur, even if together, would have risked total destruction, while a success would have cost more than it was worth. The Americans had nothing to gain and everything to lose by fighting in line-of-battle.

As Broke's squadron swept along the coast it seized whatever it met, and July 16 caught one of President Jefferson's 16-gun brigs, the *Nautilus*. The next day it came on a richer prize. The American navy seemed ready to outstrip the army in the race for disaster. The *Constitution*, the best frigate in the United States service, sailed into the midst of Broke's five ships. Captain Isaac Hull, in command of the *Constitution*, had been detained at Annapolis shipping a new crew, until July 5—the day when Broke's squadron left Halifax;—then the ship got under way and stood down Chesapeake Bay on her voyage to New York. The wind was ahead and very light. Not till July 10 did the ship anchor off Cape Henry lighthouse, and not till sunrise of July 12 did she stand to the eastward and northward. Light head-winds and a strong current delayed her progress till July 17 when at two o'clock in the afternoon off Barnegat on the New Jersey coast the lookout at the masthead discovered four sails to the northward, and two hours later a fifth sail to the northeast. Hull took them for Rodgers's squadron. The wind was light and Hull being to windward determined to speak the nearest vessel, the last to come in sight. The afternoon passed without bringing the ships together, and at ten in the evening, finding that the nearest ship could not answer the night signal, Hull decided to lose no time in escaping.

Then followed one of the most exciting and sustained chases recorded in naval history. At daybreak the next morning one British frigate was astern within five or six miles, two more were to leeward, and the rest of the fleet some ten miles astern, all making chase. Hull put out his boats to tow the *Constitution*; Broke summoned the boats of his squadron to tow the *Shannon*. Hull then bent all his spare rope to the cables, dropped a small anchor half a mile ahead, in twenty-six fathom water, and warped his ship along. Broke quickly imitated the device, and slowly gained on the chase. The *Guerrière* crept so near Hull's lee-beam as to open fire, but her shot fell short. Fortunately the wind, though slight, favored Hull. All night the British and American crews toiled on, and when morning came the *Belvidera,* proving to be the best sailor, got in advance of her consorts, working two kedge-anchors, until at two o'clock in the afternoon she tried in her turn to reach the *Constitution* with her bow guns, but in vain. Hull expected capture, but the *Belvidera* could not approach nearer without bringing her boats under the *Constitution's* stern guns; and the wearied crews toiled on, towing and kedging, the ships barely out of gunshot, till another morning came. The breeze, though still light, then allowed Hull to take in his boats, the *Belvidera* being two and a half miles in his wake; the *Shannon* three and a half miles on his lee, and the three other frigates well to leeward. The wind freshened, and the *Constitution* drew ahead, until toward seven o'clock in the evening of July 19 a heavy rain-squall struck the ship, and by taking skillful advantage of it Hull left the *Belvidera* and *Shannon* far astern; yet until eight o'clock the next morning they were still in sight keeping up the chase.

Perhaps nothing during the war tested American seamanship more thoroughly than these three days of combined skill and endurance in the face of an irresistible enemy. The result showed that Hull and the *Constitution* had nothing to fear in these respects. There remained the question whether the superiority extended to his guns; and such was the contempt of British naval officers for American ships that with this experience before their eyes they still believed one of their 38-gun frigates to be more than a match for an American forty-four, although the American, besides the heavier armament, had proved his capacity to out-sail and outmaneuver the Englishman. Both parties became more eager than ever for the test. For once, even the Federalists of New England felt their blood stir; for their own President and their own votes had called these frigates into existence, and a victory won by the *Constitution*, which had been built by their hands, was in their eyes a greater victory over their political opponents than over the British. With no half-hearted spirit, the sea-going Bostonians showered well-weighed praises on Hull when his ship entered Boston harbor, July 26, after its narrow escape; and when he sailed again, New England waited with keen interest to learn his fate.

Hull could not expect to keep command of the *Constitution*. Bainbridge was much his senior, and had the right to a preference in active service. Bainbridge then held and was ordered to retain command of the *Constellation*, fitting out at the Washington Navy Yard; but Secretary Hamilton, July 28, ordered him to take command also of the *Constitution* on her arrival in port. Doubtless Hull expected this change, and probably the expectation induced him to risk a dangerous experiment; for without bringing his ship to the Charlestown Navy Yard, but remaining in the outer harbor, after obtaining such supplies as he needed, August 2, he set sail without orders, and stood to the eastward. Having reached Cape Race without meeting an enemy he turned southward, until on the night of August 18 he spoke a privateer, which told him of a British frigate near at hand. Following the privateersman's directions the *Constitution* the next day, August 19, at two o'clock in the afternoon, latitude 41° 42′, longitude 55° 48′, sighted the *Guerrière*.

The meeting was welcome on both sides. Only three days before, Captain Dacres had entered on the log of a merchantman a challenge to any American frigate to meet him off Sandy Hook. Not only had the *Guerrière* for a long time been extremely offensive to every sea-faring American, but the mistake which caused the *Little Belt* to suffer so seriously for the misfortune of being taken for the *Guerrière* had caused a corresponding feeling of anger in the officers of the British frigate. The meeting of August 19 had the character of a preconcerted duel.

The wind was blowing fresh from the northwest, with the sea running high. Dacres backed his maintop-sail and waited. Hull shortened sail and ran down before the wind. For about an hour the two ships wore and wore again, trying to get advantage of position; until at last, a few minutes before six o'clock, they came together side by side, within pistol-shot, the wind almost astern, and running before it they pounded each other with all their strength. As rapidly as the guns could be worked, the *Constitution* poured in broadside after broadside, double-shotted with round and grape—and, without exaggeration, the echo of these guns startled the world. "In less than thirty minutes from the time we got alongside of the enemy," reported Hull, "she was left without a spar standing, and the hull cut to pieces in such a manner as to make it difficult to keep her above water."

That Dacres should have been defeated was not surprising; that he should have expected to win was an example of British arrogance that explained and excused the war. The length of the *Constitution* was 173 feet; that of the *Guerrière* was 156 feet; the extreme breadth of the *Constitution* was 44 feet; that of the *Guerrière* was 40 feet, or within a few inches in both cases. The *Constitution* carried thirty-two long 24-pounders, the *Guerrière* thirty long 18-pounders and two long 12-pounders; the *Constitution* carried twenty 32-pound carronades, the *Guerrière* sixteen. In every respect, and in proportion of ten to seven, the *Constitution* was the better ship; her crew was more numerous in proportion of ten to six. Dacres knew this very nearly as well as it was known to Hull, yet he sought a duel. What he did not know was that in a still greater proportion the American officers and crew were better and more intelligent seamen than the British, and that their passionate wish to repay old scores gave them extraordinary energy. So much greater was the moral superiority than the physical, that while the *Guerrière's* force counted as seven against ten, her losses counted as though her force were only two against ten.

Dacres' error cost him dear, for among the *Guerrière's* crew of two hundred and seventy-two, seventy-nine were killed or wounded; and the ship was injured beyond saving before Dacres realized his mistake, although he needed only thirty minutes of close fighting for the purpose. He never fully understood the causes of his defeat, and never excused it by pleading, as he might have done, the great superiority of his enemy.

Hull took his prisoners on board the *Constitution,* and after blowing up the *Guerrière* sailed for Boston, where he arrived on the morning of August 30. The Sunday silence of the Puritan city broke into excitement as the news passed through the quiet streets that the *Constitution* was below, in the outer harbor with Dacres and his crew prisoners on board. No experience of history ever went to the heart of New England more directly than this victory, so peculiarly its own; but the delight was not confined to New England, and extreme though it seemed it was still not extravagant, for however small the affair might appear on the general scale of the world's battles, it raised the United States in one half hour to the rank of a first-class Power in the world.

Hull's victory was not only dramatic in itself, but was also supremely fortunate in the moment it occurred. The *Boston Patriot* of September 2, which announced the capture of the *Guerrière,* announced in the next column that Rodgers and Decatur, with their squadron, entered Boston harbor within four-and-twenty hours after Hull's arrival, returning empty-handed after more than two months of futile cruising; while in still another column the same newspaper announced "the melancholy intelligence of the surrender of General Hull and his whole army to the British General Brock." Isaac Hull was nephew to the unhappy General, and perhaps the shattered hulk of the *Guerrière,* which the nephew left at the bottom of the Atlantic Ocean, eight hundred miles east of Boston, was worth for the moment the whole province which the uncle had lost, eight hundred miles to the westward; it was at least the only equivalent the people could find, and they made the most of it. With the shock of new life, they awoke to the consciousness that after all the peace teachings of Pennsylvania and Virginia, the sneers of Federalists and foreigners; after the disgrace of the *Chesapeake* and the surrender of Detroit—Americans could still fight. The public had been taught, and had actually learned, to doubt its own physical courage; and the reaction of delight in satisfying itself that it still possessed the commonest and most brutal of human qualities was the natural result of a system that ignored the possibility of war.

Hull's famous victory taught the pleasures of war to a new generation, which had hitherto been sedulously educated to think only of its cost. The first taste of blood maddens; and hardly had the *Constitution* reached port and told her story than the public became eager for more. The old Jeffersonian jealousy of the navy vanished in the flash of Hull's first broadside. Nothing would satisfy the craving of the popular appetite but more battles, more British frigates, and more daring victories. Even the cautious Madison was dragged by the public excitement upon the element he most heartily disliked.

The whole navy, was once more, September 1, safe in port except only the *Essex*, a frigate rated at thirty-two but carrying forty-four guns, commanded by Captain David Porter. She left New York July 3 with orders dated June 24 to join Rodgers, or failing this to cruise southwardly as far as St. Augustine. July 11 she met a convoy of seven transports conveying a battalion of the First Regiment, or Royal Scots, from the West Indies to reinforce Prevost and Brock in Canada. Porter cut out one transport. With the aid of another frigate he could have captured the whole, to the great advantage of Dearborn's military movements; but the British commander managed his convoy so well that the battalion escaped, and enabled Prevost to strengthen the force at Niagara which threatened and defeated Van Rensselaer. August 13 the British 20-gun sloop-of-war *Alert* came in sight, bore down within short pistolshot, and opened fire on the *Essex*. Absurd as the idea seemed, the British captain behaved as though he hoped to capture the American frigate, and not until Porter nearly sunk him with a broadside did the Englishman strike his colors. After taking a number of other prizes, but without further fighting, September 7 Porter brought his ship back to the Delaware River.

The return of the *Essex* to port, September 7, brought all the national vessels once more under the direct control of the Department. Nearly every ship in the service was then at Boston. The three forty-fours—the *Constitution, United States,* and *President*—were all there; two of the thirty-eights—the *Congress* and *Chesapeake*—were there, and the *Constellation* was at Washington. The *Adams*, 28, was also at Washington; but the *Hornet*, 18, and *Argus*, 16, were with Rodgers and Decatur at Boston. The *Syren*, 16, the *New Orleans*; the *Essex*, 32, and the *Wasp*, 18, were in the Delaware.

Carried away by Hull's victory, the Government could no longer hesitate to give its naval officers the liberty of action they asked, and which in spite of orders they had shown the intention to take. A new arrangement was made. The vessels were to be divided into three squadrons, each consisting of one forty-four, one light frigate, and one sloop-of-war. Rodgers in the *President* was to command one squadron, Bainbridge in the *Constitution* was to command another, and Decatur in the *United States* was to take the third. Their sailing orders, dated October 2, simply directed the three commodores to proceed to sea; "You are to do your utmost to annoy the enemy, to afford protection to our commerce, pursuing that course which to your best judgment may under all circumstances appear the best calculated to enable you to accomplish these objects as far as may be in your power, returning into port as speedily as circumstances will permit consistently with the great object in view."

Before continuing the story of the frigates, the fate of the little *Wasp* needs to be told. Her career was brief. The *Wasp*, a sloop-of-war rated at eighteen guns, was one of President Jefferson's additions to the navy to supply the loss of the *Philadelphia*; she was ship-rigged, and armed with two long 12-pounders and sixteen 32-pound carronades. She carried a crew of one hundred and thirty-seven men, commanded by Captain Jacob Jones, a native of Delaware, lieutenant in the *Philadelphia* when lost in the war with Tripoli. The *Wasp* was attached to Rodgers's squadron, and received orders from the commodore to join him at sea. She sailed from the Delaware October 13, and when about six hundred miles east of Norfolk, October 17, she fell in with the British 18-gun brig *Frolic*, convoying fourteen merchantmen to England. The two vessels were equal in force, for the *Frolic's* broadside threw a weight of two hundred and seventy-four pounds, while that of the *Wasp* threw some few pounds less; the *Frolic* measured, by British report, one hundred feet in length, the *Wasp* one hundred and six; their breadth on deck was the same; and although the *Wasp's* crew exceeded that of her enemy, being one hundred and thirty-five men against one hundred and ten, the British vessel had all the men she needed, and suffered little from this inferiority. The action began at half-past eleven in the morning, the two sloops running parallel, about sixty yards apart, in a very heavy sea, which caused both to pitch and roll so that marksmanship had the most decisive share in victory. The muzzles of the guns went under water, and clouds of spray dashed over the crews, while the two vessels ran side by side for the first fifteen minutes. The British fire cut the *Wasp's* rigging, while the American guns played havoc with the *Frolic's* hull and lower masts. The vessels approached each other so closely that the rammers of the guns struck the enemy's side, and at last they fell foul—the *Wasp* almost squarely across the *Frolic's* bow. In the heavy sea boarding was difficult; but as soon as the *Wasp's* crew could clamber down the *Frolic's* bowsprit, they found on the deck the British captain and lieutenant, both severely wounded, and one brave sailor at the wheel. Not twenty of the British crew were left unhurt, and these had gone below to escape the American musketry. The *Wasp* had only ten men killed and wounded. The battle lasted forty-three minutes.

If the American people had acquired a taste for blood the battle of the *Wasp* and *Frolic* gratified it, for the British sloop was desperately defended, and the battle, won by the better marksmanship of the Americans, was unusually bloody. Captain Jones lost the full satisfaction of his victory, for a few hours afterward the *Poictiers*, a British seventy-four, came upon the two disabled combatants and carried both into Bermuda; but the American people would have been glad to part with their whole navy on such terms, and the fight between the *Wasp* and the *Frolic* roused popular enthusiasm to a point where no honors seemed to satisfy their gratitude to Captain Jones and his crew.

The *Wasp's* brilliant career closed within a week from the day she left the Delaware. A week afterward another of these ship-duels occurred, which made a still deeper impression. Rodgers and Decatur sailed from Boston October 8 with the *President*, the *United States, Congress,* and *Argus*, leaving the *Constitution, Chesapeake,* and *Hornet* in port. Rodgers in the *President*, with the *Congress,* cruised far and wide, but could find no enemy to fight, and after making prize of a few merchantmen returned to Boston, December 31. The *Argus* also made some valuable prizes, but was chased by a British squadron, and only by excellent management, escaped capture, returning January 3, 1813, to New York. Decatur in the *United States,* separating from the squadron October 12, sailed eastward to the neighborhood of the Azores, until, October 25, he sighted a sail to windward. The stranger made chase. The wind was fresh from south-southeast, with a heavy sea. Decatur stood toward his enemy, who presently came about, abreast of the *United States* but beyond gunshot, and both ships being then on the same tack approached each other until the action began at long range. The British ship was the 38-gun frigate *Macedonian* commanded by Captain Carden, and about the same force as the *Guerrière*. At first the *United States* used only her long 24-pounders, of which she carried fifteen on her broadside, while the *Macedonian* worked a broadside of fourteen long 18-pounders. So unequal a contest could not continue. Not only was the American metal heavier, but the American fire was quicker and better directed than that of the Englishman; so that Carden, after a few minutes of this experience, bore down to close. His maneuver made matters worse. The carronades of the *United States* came into play; the *Macedonian's* mizzen-mast fell, her fore and main top-mast were shot away, and her main-yard; almost all her rigging was cut to pieces, and most of the guns on her engaged side were dismounted. She dropped gradually to leeward, and Decatur, tacking and coming up under his enemy's stern hailed, and received her surrender.

The British ship had no right to expect a victory for the disparity of force was even greater than between the *Constitution* and *Guerrière*; but in this case the British court-martial subsequently censured Captain Carden for mistakes. The battle lasted longer than that with the *Guerrière*, and Decatur apologized for the extra hour because the sea was high and his enemy had the weather-gauge and kept at a distance; but the apology was not needed. Decatur proved his skill by sparing his ship and crew. His own loss was eleven men killed and wounded; the *Macedonian's* loss was nine times as great. The *United States* suffered little in her hull, and her spars and rigging suffered no greater injury than could be quickly repaired; while the *Macedonian* received a hundred shot in her hull, and aloft nothing remained standing but her fore and main masts and her fore-yard.

Decatur saved the *Macedonian*, and brought her back to New London—the only British frigate ever brought as a prize into an American port. The two ships arrived December 4, and from New London the *Macedonian* was taken to New York and received in formal triumph. Captain Jones of the *Wasp* took command of her in reward for his capture of the *Frolic*.

Before the year closed, the *Constitution* had time for another cruise. Hull at his own request received command of the Navy Yard at Charlestown, and also took charge of the naval defenses in New York harbor, but did not again serve at sea during the war. The *Constitution* was given to Captain Bainbridge, one of the oldest officers in the service. A native of New Jersey, Bainbridge commanded the *Philadelphia* when lost in the Tripolitan war, and was held for eighteen months a prisoner in Tripoli. In 1812 when he took command of the *Constitution*, though a year older than Hull and five years older than Decatur, he had not yet reached his fortieth year, while Rodgers, born in 1771, had but lately passed it. The difference in age between these four naval officers and the four chief generals—Dearborn, Wilkinson, Wade Hampton, and William Hull—was surprising; for the average age of the naval commanders amounted barely to thirty-seven years, while that of the four generals reached fifty-eight. This difference alone accounted for much of the difference in their fortune, and perhaps political influence accounted for the rest.

Bainbridge showed no inferiority to the other officers of the service, and no one grumbled at the retirement of Hull. The *Constitution* sailed from Boston, October 25, with the *Hornet*. The *Essex*, then in the Delaware, was ordered to join the squadron at certain specified ports in the south Atlantic, and sailed October 28 expecting a very long cruise. December 13 Bainbridge arrived at San Salvador, on the coast of Brazil, where he left the *Hornet* to blockade the *Bonne Citoyenne*, a British 18-gun sloop-of-war bound to England with specie. Cruising southward, within sight of the Brazilian coast, in latitude 13° 6′ south, Bainbridge sighted the British frigate *Java*, a ship of the same tonnage as the *Guerrière*, throwing a slightly heavier broadside and carrying a large crew of four hundred and twenty-six men, if the American account was correct. Bainbridge tacked and made sail off shore, to draw the stranger away from a neutral coast; the British frigate followed him, until at half-past one o'clock in the afternoon Bainbridge shortened sail, tacked again, and stood for his enemy. Soon after two o'clock the action began, the two ships being on the same tack, the *Java* to windward and the better sailer, and both fighting their long-range guns. The British frigate insisted upon keeping at a distance, obliging Bainbridge after half an hour to risk the danger of being raked; and at twenty minutes before three o'clock the *Constitution* closed within pistol-shot. At ten minutes before three the ships were foul, the *Java's* jibboom in the *Constitution's* mizzen rigging; and from that point the battle became slaughter. In fifteen minutes the *Java's* bowsprit, fore-mast, and main top-mast were cut away, and a few minutes after four o'clock she ceased firing. Her captain, Lambert, was mortally wounded; the first lieutenant was wounded; forty-eight of her officers and crew were dead or dying; one hundred and two were wounded; little more than a hulk filled with wreck and with dead or wounded men floated on the water.

The *Constitution* had but twelve men killed and twenty-two wounded, and repaired damages in an hour. Owing perhaps to the death of Captain Lambert the reports of the battle were more contradictory than usual, but no one disputed that although the *Java* was to windward and outsailed the American frigate, and although her broadside counted as nearly nine against her enemy's ten—for the *Constitution* on this cruise carried two guns less than in her fight with the *Guerrière*,—yet the *Java* inflicted no more damage than she ought to have done had she been only one fourth the size of the American frigate, although she was defended more desperately than either the *Guerrière* or the *Macedonian*.

With this battle the year ended. Bainbridge was obliged to blow up his prize, and after landing and paroling his prisoners at San Salvador sailed for Boston, where he arrived in safety, February 27, 1813. During the six months the war had lasted the little United States navy captured three British frigates, besides the 20-gun *Alert* and the 18-gun *Frolic*; privateers by scores had ravaged British commerce, while the immense British force on the ocean had succeeded only in capturing the little *Nautilus*, the 12-gun brig *Vixen*, and the *Wasp*. The commerce of America had indeed suffered almost total destruction; but the dispute was to be decided not so much by the loss which England could inflict upon America, as by that which America could inflict upon England.

CHAPTER V

THE RIVER RAISIN

The fall of Detroit and Chicago in August, 1812, threw the American frontier back to the line of the Wabash and the Maumee, and threatened to throw it still farther back to the Indian boundary itself. The Miami or Maumee River was defended by Fort Wayne; the Wabash had no other defense than the little fort or blockhouse which Harrison built during the Tippecanoe campaign, and named after himself. Fort Harrison stood near the later city of Terre Haute, close to the border of Illinois; Fort Wayne stood within twenty miles of the Ohio border. The width of Indiana lay between the two.

Had Brock been able, after the capture of Detroit, to lead his little army into Ohio, he might have cleared not only the Maumee River but the whole western end of Lake Erie from American possession. Recalled in haste to defend Niagara, Brock left only two or three companies of troops as garrison at Detroit and Malden. The Indians could do little without the aid of regular forces, but they tried to carry both Fort Wayne and Fort Harrison by stratagem. The attacks were made almost simultaneously a few days after September 1, and not without skill. In the case of Fort Harrison the Indians were nearly successful, not so much in fighting as in burning it. With great difficulty its young captain, Zachary Taylor, of the Seventh Infantry, succeeded in saving his post. Fort Wayne was held by Captain James Rhea of the First Infantry until reinforcements arrived, September 12. Except the usual massacres of scattered families, the Indians accomplished nothing.

Upon the State of Ohio, with its quarter of a million inhabitants, and of Kentucky with four hundred thousand, fell the immediate burden of defending the border between the Ohio and the Lakes. Governor William Henry Harrison of the Indiana Territory leaving Vincennes June 19, the day after the declaration of war, was at Cincinnati when threatening news began to arrive from Detroit. Harrison had military knowledge and instincts. He saw that after the capture of Mackinaw Detroit must fall, and that Hull could save himself only by evacuating it. Harrison's ambition, which had drawn him to Tippecanoe, drew him also to lead the new crusade for the relief or recovery of Detroit. He went to Kentucky at the invitation of Governor Scott, and under the patronage of Scott and Henry Clay he took the direction of military affairs. August 24 news reached Kentucky that Hull was shut in Detroit, and must surrender unless immediately relieved. The Governor of Kentucky at once summoned what was then called a *caucus*, composed of himself, his successor elect Governor Shelby, Henry Clay, Justice Todd of the United States Supreme Court, Major General Hopkins of the Kentucky militia, various Congressmen, judges, and other citizens, whose whole authority was needed to warrant giving to Harrison, who was not a citizen of Kentucky, the commission of major general and the command of the expedition to Detroit. By general acclamation, and on the warm assurances of universal popular approval, the measure was taken; and Harrison started at once for Cincinnati and Detroit to organize the campaign. The news of Hull's surrender met him as he left Frankfort.

By this combination of skill and accident, Harrison reached the object of his ambition—the conduct of war on a scale equal to his faith in his own powers; but the torrent of Western enthusiasm swept him forward faster than his secret judgment approved. Appointed by caucus the general of volunteers, he could keep his position only by keeping his popularity. Without deciding precisely where to march, or what military object to pursue, he talked and acted on the idea that he should recover Detroit by a *coup de main*. He knew that the idea was baseless as a practical plan, and futile as a military measure; but nothing less would satisfy the enthusiasm of his Kentucky volunteers, and the national government almost compelled him to pretend what he did not at heart believe possible.

The confusion thus created was troublesome. First, Harrison insisted on commanding the troops marching to relieve Fort Wayne, and obliged the good-natured General Winchester, who outranked him, to yield the point. Then after a forced march with the Kentuckians down the St. Mary's River, having relieved Fort Wayne, Harrison was obliged, September 19, to surrender the command to Winchester, who arrived with orders from the Secretary of War to take general charge of the northwestern army. Harrison then left Fort Wayne for Piqua. Meanwhile the President and Eustis, learning what had been done in Kentucky, September 17, after much debate decided to give to Harrison the commission of brigadier general, with the command of the northwestern army, to consist of ten thousand men, with unlimited means and no orders except to retake Detroit. Brigadier General Winchester, who was already at Fort Wayne, was given the option of serving under Harrison or of joining the army at Niagara.

These new orders reached Harrison September 25 at Piqua. Harrison then resumed command and two days afterward, September 27, wrote to the secretary announcing his plan for the autumn campaign. Three columns of troops, from widely distant quarters, were to move to the Maumee Rapids—the right column consisting of Virginia and Pennsylvania troops by way of the Sandusky River; the center column of twelve hundred Ohio militia by Hull's road; the left column consisting of four Kentucky regiments and the Seventeenth U. S. Infantry was to descend the Auglaize River to Fort Defiance on the Maumee, and thence to fall down that river to the point of junction with the two other columns.

Compared with Hull's resources Harrison's were immense; and that he had no serious enemy to fear was evident from his dividing the army into three columns which marched by lines far beyond supporting distance of each other. At the same time he ordered Major General Hopkins of the Kentucky militia to march with two thousand men up the Wabash into the Indian country and to destroy the Indian settlements on the Wabash and Illinois rivers. Had a British force been opposed to the Americans, its general would have had little difficulty in destroying some one of these four isolated columns and driving Harrison back to central Ohio; but only bands of Indians, not exceeding five hundred at most, were to be feared before the army should cross the Maumee, and little anxiety existed on account of enemies unless for the safety of Fort Wayne.

Harrison's anxieties bore a different character. September 23 he wrote to the Secretary of War: "If the fall should be very dry I will take Detroit before the winter sets in; but if we should have much rain it will be necessary to wait at the rapids until the Miami of the Lakes is sufficiently frozen to bear the army and its baggage." The promise was rash. However dry the season might be, the task of marching an army with siege-artillery past Malden to Detroit, and of keeping it supplied from a base two hundred miles distant, with the British commanding the Lake, was one which Harrison had too much sense to attempt. Nothing but disaster could have resulted from it, even if Detroit had been taken. In the actual condition of that territory, no army could be maintained beyond the Maumee River without controlling the Lake. Perhaps Harrison was fortunate that constant rains throughout the month of October brought the army to a halt long before it reached the Maumee. Only the left division of five Kentucky regiments succeeded in getting to the river, and camped in the neighborhood of old Fort Defiance, waiting for the other columns to reach the rapids. There the Kentuckians remained, under the command of General Winchester, without food, clothing, or sufficient shelter, in a state of increasing discontent and threatening mutiny, till the year closed.

Within a month after assuming command Harrison found himself helpless either to advance or to retreat, or to remain in any fixed position. The supplies required for ten thousand troops could not be sent forward by any means then known. October 22 the left column, consisting of the Kentucky regiments and some regulars, was at Defiance on the Maumee; the central column of a thousand Ohio troops under General Tupper was on Hull's road, a hundred miles from the Maumee, unable to march beyond Urbana, where its supplies were collecting; the right column of Pennsylvanians and Virginians was still farther from the front, slowly approaching the Sandusky River from the southeast, but far out of reach. General Hopkins's expedition up the Wabash ended in failure, his troops becoming a mere mob, and at last disbanding, leaving their general to follow them home. Harrison himself was riding indefatigably through the mud, from one end to the other of his vast concave line—now at Defiance, making speeches to pacify Winchester's Kentuckians; then at Piqua and Urbana with the Ohioans; soon a hundred miles away at the river Huron, east of Sandusky; next at Wooster, Delaware, or Franklinton, afterward Columbus, in the center of Ohio, looking for his right wing; but always searching for a passable ridge of dry land, on which his supplies could go forward to the Maumee Rapids. The result of his search was given in a letter of October 22 from Franklinton to the Secretary of War:

"I am not able to fix any period for the advance of the troops to Detroit. It is pretty evident that it cannot be done upon proper principles until the frost shall become so severe as to enable us to use the rivers and the margin of the Lake for transportation of the baggage and artillery upon the ice. To get them forward through a swampy wilderness of near two hundred miles in wagons or on packhorses which are to carry their own provisions, is absolutely impossible."

The obstacle which brought Harrison's autumn campaign to this sudden close was the vast swamp that extended from the Sandusky River on his right to the Auglaize River on his left, and for the moment barred the passage of his necessary supplies as effectually as though it had been the Andes. Hull had crossed it, cutting a road as he went, and no one had then appreciated his effort; but he had marched with a small force in May and June. Harrison tried to transport supplies, heavy guns, military stores, and all the material for an army of ten thousand men on a long campaign, as the autumn rains set in. On the extreme right, with great effort and expense, a considerable quantity of rations was accumulated on the Sandusky River to be sent to the Maumee Rapids whenever the frosts should harden the swamps. On the extreme left, desperate efforts were made to carry supplies to Winchester's army at Defiance by way of the Auglaize and St. Mary's rivers. Hull's road was impassable, and for that reason the column of Ohio troops and their supplies were stopped in the neighborhood of Urbana.

Throughout the month of October and November Harrison's army stood still, scattered over the State of Ohio, while wagons and packhorses wallowed in mud toward the Maumee Rapids. None arrived. Sometimes the wagons were abandoned in the mud; sometimes the packhorses broke down; sometimes the rivers were too low for boats; then they froze and stopped water-transport. Universal confusion, want of oversight and organization, added to physical difficulties, gave play to laziness, incapacity, and dishonesty. No bills of lading were used; no accounts were kept with the wagoners; and the teams were valued so high, on coming into service, that the owners were willing to destroy them for the price to be received. The waste of government funds was appalling, for nothing short of a million rations at the Maumee Rapids could serve Harrison's objects, and after two months of effort not a ration had been carried within fifty miles of the spot. In Winchester's camp at Defiance the men were always on half rations except when they had none at all. During the greater part of December they had no flour, but lived on poor beef and hickory roots. Typhus swept them away by scores; their numbers were reduced to about one thousand. The exact force which Harrison had in the field was matter of conjecture, for he sent no return of any description to the adjutant general's office. The Government gave him *carte blanche,* and he used it. Chaos and misconduct reigned in every department while he, floundering through the mud along his line of two hundred miles front, sought in vain for a road.

For the train of errors and disasters in the northwest Secretary Eustis was chiefly responsible, and his resignation, December 3, 1812, left the campaign in this hopeless condition. From December 3, 1812, until January 13, 1813, Monroe acted as Secretary of War; and to him Harrison next wrote from Delaware, December 12, a letter which not only disheartened the Government but was calculated to create a prejudice against the writer in the mind of any Secretary of War who was not invincibly prejudiced in his favor:

"If there were not some important political reason" said Harrison, "urging the recovery of the Michigan Territory and the capture of Malden as soon as those objects can possibly be effected, and that to accomplish them a few weeks sooner expense was to be disregarded, I should not hesitate to say that if a small proportion of the sums which will be expended in the quartermaster's department in the active prosecution of the campaign during the winter was devoted to obtaining the command of Lake Erie, the wishes of the Government, in their utmost extent, could be accomplished without difficulty in the months of April and May. Malden, Detroit, and Mackinaw would fall in rapid succession. On the contrary, all that I can certainly promise to accomplish during the winter, unless the strait should afford us a passage on the ice, is to recover Detroit. I must further observe that no military man would think of retaining Detroit, Malden being in possession of the enemy, unless his army was at least twice as strong as the disposable force of the enemy. An army advancing to Detroit along a line of operation passing so near the principal force of the enemy as to allow them access to it whenever they think proper, must be covered by another army more considerable than the disposable force of the enemy. I mention this circumstance to show that the attack ought not to be directed against Detroit, but against Malden; and that it depends upon the ice affording a safe passage across the strait, whether I shall be able to proceed in this way or not. Detroit is not tenable. Were I to take it without having it in my power to occupy the opposite shore, I should be under the necessity of hiding the army in the adjacent swamp to preserve it from the effects of the shot and shells which the enemy would throw with impunity from the opposite shore. This result is so obvious to every man who has the least military information, that it appears to me as extraordinary as any other part of General Hull's conduct that he should choose to defend Detroit rather than attack Malden."

Hull could have asked no better apology for his surrender. Harrison did not know that the insubordination and refusal of the Ohio colonels to evacuate Detroit had forced Hull to remain there; but that Detroit was not tenable came at last to the surface as a self-evident truth of the campaign—which Hull had always seen, and which Harrison himself announced almost as clearly in August as in December, but which he ignored in the interval.

"If it should be asked," he continued, "why these statements were not made sooner—I answer that although I was always sensible that there were great difficulties to be encountered in the accomplishment of the wishes of the President in relation to the recovery of Detroit and the conquest of the adjacent part of Upper Canada in the manner proposed, I did not make sufficient allowance for the imbecility and inexperience of the public agents and the villany of the contractors. I am still, however, very far from believing that the original plan is impracticable. I believe on the contrary that it can be effected."

The excuse did not satisfy the Cabinet who thought they saw that Harrison wished to throw upon Government the responsibility for a military failure fatal to himself. Perhaps a simpler motive guided Harrison, who from the first never had known precisely what to do, or had seen any clear path to success. He wrote, January 4, from Franklinton:

"When I was directed to take the command in the latter end of September, I thought it possible by great exertions to effect the objects of the campaign before the setting in of winter. . . . The experience of a few days was sufficient to convince me that the supplies of provisions could not be procured for our autumnal advance; and even if this difficulty was removed, another of equal magnitude existed in the want of artillery. There remained then no alternative but to prepare for a winter campaign."

According to this account he had seen early in October that advance was impossible, yet he wasted millions of money and many of his best troops in attempting it. Winter had come, and he was pledged to a winter campaign as impracticable as the autumn campaign had proved to be. Without the control of the Lake, any army beyond the Maumee must starve or surrender. The government had already paid a vast price in money and men in order to obtain this knowledge; yet Harrison proposed a winter campaign, with full persuasion of its uselessness.

December 20 he sent orders to Winchester to descend the Maumee River from Defiance to the rapids, there to prepare sleds for an expedition against Malden, to be made by a choice detachment when the whole army should concentrate at the rapids. Early in January, the ground being at last frozen, provisions in large quantities were hurried to the Maumee River. Artillery was sent forward. The Pennsylvania and Virginia brigades moved to the Sandusky River, making an effective force of fifteen hundred men at that point. The whole effective force on the frontier amounted to six thousand three hundred infantry. Harrison intended to move his headquarters forward from the Sandusky, and to reach the Maumee Rapids January 20, to which point he supposed General Winchester already in motion from Defiance.

This was the situation January 12; and although Harrison hinted in his reports of January 4 and 8 that his winter campaign would probably fail, he showed the intention of advancing at least as far as the strait opposite Malden, about thirty-five miles beyond the Maumee. This he might venture without much danger; and if he reached that point, supposing the straits to be frozen, the enemy to show little sign of resistance, and the weather to favor, he might attack Malden. Hull had been expected to take Malden with twelve or fourteen hundred men, with an open river behind him, a British fleet on his flank, fifty miles of road to cover, and supplies for only a few days at Detroit; but Harrison with six thousand men, the river frozen and the British fleet frozen in it, a secure base, with a million rations close in his rear, and no Isaac Brock in his front, still spoke with extreme doubt of his prospects, and said that "most of the well-informed men who knew the character of the country" expected a suspension of operations for the winter.

Aware that from a military point of view no land campaign could, except by accident, effect any result proportionate to its cost, Harrison had placed himself at the head of a popular movement so strong that he would have met the fate of Hull and Alexander Smyth, had he not made at least a demonstration against an enemy whose face he had not yet seen. Forced by his own pledges and the public discontent to enter on an unmilitary campaign, he was anxious to risk as little as possible where he could hardly expect to gain anything; and he would probably have contented himself with his first scheme of a *coup de main* against Malden or Detroit, without attempting to hold either place, had not his subordinate, General Winchester, rescued him from an awkward position by a blunder that relieved Harrison of further responsibility.

Brigadier General Winchester was a planter of Tennessee, sixty-one years old, and formerly an officer in the Revolutionary War. Though outranking Harrison, he had allowed himself to be set aside by what he thought intrigue, and consented to conduct the left wing of the force under Harrison's command. Winchester was not a favorite with his Kentucky militiamen, who had no choice in electing him to their command. Their term of service was to expire in February; they had been imprisoned since September in a wilderness at

Defiance—hungry, cold, sick, and mutinous, able to find no enemy willing to fight them, and disgusted with idleness. No sooner was the ground frozen and the general movement of concentration possible, than Winchester's command by common consent, under Harrison's orders, broke up their camp near Defiance and marched to the rapids, where Hull's road crossed the Maumee. There they arrived January 10, as Harrison expected. They fortified themselves on the north bank, and waited for the arrival of Harrison, who intended to join them January 20.

Winchester's force included three regiments of Kentucky militia, numbering nine hundred effectives, and the Seventeenth United States Infantry, numbering three hundred men, also Kentuckians. Altogether he had under his command at the rapids about thirteen hundred men—a force barely sufficient to hold the exposed position it had taken on the north bank of the river. The three Kentucky militia regiments were soon to go home. The other columns were not yet within supporting distance. If Colonel Proctor, who commanded at Malden, were capable of imitating Brock's enterprise, he would hardly throw away an opportunity which might never recur to strike a blow at the Kentuckians, and by defeating them to drive Harrison's army behind the Sandusky River. Every military motive warned Winchester not to divide, detach, or expose his troops without caution. He was himself a detachment, and he had no support nearer than the Sandusky.

While the troops were busily engaged in building a storehouse and throwing up log-works in an injudicious and untenable position, two Frenchmen came into camp, begging protection for the inhabitants of Frenchtown on the River Raisin, thirty miles in front, and within the British lines. Thirty-three families, or about one hundred and fifty persons, were resident at Frenchtown, and the place was held by a few Canadian militia, supposed to consist of two companies, with about as many Indians—in all, some three hundred men. This force might easily be destroyed, and the loss to the British would be serious. Winchester's troops became eager to dash at them. A council of war decided, January 16, without a voice in remonstrance, that the movement should be made. The most ardent supporter of the adventure was Colonel John Allen of the Kentucky Rifle regiment; but no one offered opposition, and Winchester agreed to the council's opinion.

The next morning, January 17, 1813, Colonel William Lewis, of the Fifth Kentucky militia, started for the river Raisin, with four hundred and fifty men. A few hours afterward he was followed by Colonel Allen with one hundred and ten men. No reports told what regiments were taken, or where they were at any moment stationed; but Lewis and Allen probably led twelve companies, drawn from four Kentucky regiments—the Seventeenth United States Infantry, recruited in Kentucky, commanded by Colonel Samuel Wells; the Kentucky Rifles, Colonel John Allen; the First Kentucky Infantry; and Colonel Lewis's regiment, the Fifth Kentucky Infantry—in all, six hundred and sixty men, representing the flower of Kentucky.

They marched on the ice, along the shore of Maumee Bay and Lake Erie, until nightfall, when they camped and at two o'clock the next afternoon, Janu-

ary 18, reached without meeting resistance the houses on the south bank of the
river Raisin. The north bank was occupied, according to British authority, by
fifty Canadian militia and two hundred Indians. The British force opened fire
with a three-pound howitzer. The action began at three o'clock and lasted till
dark, when the enemy after an obstinate resistance was driven about two miles
into the woods with inconsiderable loss. The action was sharp, and cost the
Americans not less than twelve killed and fifty-five wounded, reducing their
effective number to six hundred.

Colonel Lewis had orders to take possession of Frenchtown, and hold it. He
reported his success to General Winchester at the rapids, and remained at
Frenchtown waiting further orders. Winchester became then aware that the
situation was hazardous. Six hundred men were with him in a half-fortified camp
on the north bank of the Maumee; six hundred more were thirty miles in advance at the Raisin River; while fully two thousand—or, according to Harrison's
estimate, four thousand—enemies held two fortresses only eighteen miles beyond
the Raisin. The Kentuckians at the Maumee, equally aware of their comrades'
peril, insisted on going to their aid. Winchester promptly started on the evening of January 19, and arrived at Frenchtown the next morning. Colonel Wells's
Seventeenth United States Infantry, two hundred and fifty men, followed,
arriving at Frenchtown in the evening.

Winchester, before leaving the Maumee Rapids, sent a dispatch to Harrison
with a report of the battle of the 18th, which met Harrison on the road hurrying
to the Maumee Rapids. The next morning, January 20, Harrison arrived at the
camp on the Maumee, and found there about three hundred Kentucky troops,
the remainder being all with Winchester at the river Raisin. Probably Harrison,
whose own caution was great, felt the peril of Winchester's situation, but he
sent his inspector general, Captain Hart, forward with orders to Winchester "to
hold the ground we had got at any rate," while he wrote to the Secretary of War.

"Upon my way to this place [Maumee Rapids] last evening, I received the
letter from the General [Winchester] of which the enclosed is a copy, informing
me of the complete success of the enterprise in the defeat of the enemy and taking
the stores they had collected. The detachment under Colonel Lewis remain at
the river Raisin, and General Winchester very properly marched yesterday with
two hundred and fifty men to reinforce him and take the command. . . . It is
absolutely necessary to maintain the position at the river Raisin, and I am assem-
bling the troops as fast as possible for the purpose."

Harrison added that his only fear was lest Winchester should be overpowered.
He waited at the Maumee Rapids two days, until at noon, January 22, a messenger arrived with disastrous tidings from the front.

Winchester afterward told the story of his own proceedings with so much
candor that his narrative became a necessary part of any explanation of his
disaster:

"Suspecting that Proctor would make an attempt to avenge this stroke, and
knowing that our wounded men could not be removed, I hastened to reinforce
Colonel Lewis with Wells's regiment, two hundred and fifty men; and set out
myself to join him, and arrived on the morning of the 20th. The town, lying on

the north side of the river, was picketed on three sides, the longest facing the
north, and making the front. Within these pickets Colonel Lewis's corps was
found. Not thinking the position eligible, nor the pickets a sufficient defense
against artillery, I would have retreated but for the wounded, of whom there were
fifty-five; but having no sufficient means for transporting these, and being equally
destitute of those necessary for fortifying strongly, I issued an order for putting
the place in the best condition for defense that might be practicable, intending
to construct some new works as soon as the means for getting out timber might be
had. On the evening of the 20th Wells arrived, and was directed to encamp on
the right in an open field immediately without the picketing. On the 21st a patrol
as far as Brownstown [opposite Malden] was sent out, and returned without
seeing anything of an enemy. On the same day a man from Malden came in who
reported that the enemy were preparing to attack us; but knowing nothing of the
kind or extent of the preparation made or making, what he brought was thought
to be only conjecture and such as led to a belief that it would be some days before
Proctor would be ready to do anything. . . . Neither night-patrol nor night-
pickets were ordered by me, from a belief that both were matters of routine and
in constant use. . . . Not to discommode the wounded men . . . I took quarters
for myself and suite in a house on the southern bank, directly fronting the troops
and only separated from them by the river, then firmly frozen, and but between
eighty and a hundred yards wide."

The only educated officer under Harrison's command was Major E. D. Wood
of the Engineers, one of the early graduates of West Point, and an officer of
high promise. He was not with Winchester's division, but with the right wing
on the Sandusky, and arrived at the Maumee Rapids some ten days afterward,
where he built Fort Meigs, in February. During the campaign he kept a diary,
and his criticisms of Winchester, Lewis, Allen, and their command were quoted
with approval by the Kentucky historian, as well as by Harrison's biographer.

"The troops were permitted to select, each for himself, such quarters on the
west side of the river as might please him best, whilst the general . . . took his
quarters on the east side—not the least regard being paid to defence, order, regularity, or system, in the posting of the different corps. . . . With only one third
or one fourth of the force destined for that service; destitute of artillery, of engineers, of men who had ever seen or heard the least of an enemy; and with but a
very inadequate supply of ammunition—how he ever could have entertained the
most distant hope of success, or what right he had to presume to claim it, is to me
one of the strangest things in the world. . . . Winchester was destitute of every
means of supporting his corps long at the river Raisin; was in the very jaws of
the enemy, and beyond the reach of succor. He who fights with such flimsy
pretensions to victory will always be beaten, and eternally ought to be."

Defeat under such conditions was disgraceful enough; but defeat by Colonel
Proctor was one of the worst misfortunes that happened to an American general.
The Prince Regent took occasion, at the close of the war, to express his official
opinion of this officer, then Major General Proctor, in language of unusual
severity. Yet Proctor's first movements at the Raisin River showed no apparent
sign of his being "so extremely wanting in professional knowledge, and deficient

in those active, energetic qualities which must be required of every officer," as his later career, in the Prince Regent's opinion, proved him to be. He had opposed Brock's bold movement on Detroit; but he did not hesitate to make a somewhat similar movement himself. January 21 he marched with artillery across the river on the ice, to Brownstown opposite Malden, in full view of any American patrol in the neighborhood. His force consisted of six hundred whites, all told, besides either four hundred and fifty, six hundred or eight hundred Indians, under the chief Round Head, Tecumthe being absent collecting reinforcements on the Wabash. This large body of more than a thousand men, without an attempt at concealment, crossed to Brownstown and marched twelve miles, January 21, camping at night within five miles of Frenchtown. If the British historian James was correct, they numbered eleven hundred and eighty men, of whom five hundred and thirty were white, and the rest Indians; but the official return reported the whites, including every person present, at five hundred and ninety-seven men. Two hours before dawn, January 22, they again advanced, and before daybreak approached within musket-shot of the picket-fence, and half-formed their line before an alarm was given.

Had Proctor dashed at once on the defenseless Seventeenth regiment and the fence that covered the militia, he would probably have captured the whole without loss; but he preferred to depend on his three-pound guns, which gave the Kentuckians opportunity to use their rifles. In such fighting the Americans had much the advantage, especially as British regulars were opposite them. Within an hour the Forty-first regiment lost fifteen killed and ninety-eight wounded, and of the entire body of six hundred British troops not less than twenty-four were killed and one hundred and sixty-one wounded. Their three-pound guns were abandoned, so murderous were the Kentucky rifles. Had all the American troops been under cover, the battle would have been theirs; but Wells's Seventeenth regiment was a hundred yards away on open ground outside the picket-fence on the right where it was flanked by the Canadian militia and Indians and driven back toward the river until Allen's Rifle regiment went out to help it. Gradually forced toward the rear, across the river, this part of the line was at last struck with a panic and fled, carrying with it Winchester himself, Colonel Allen, and Colonel Lewis; while six hundred Indians were in hot pursuit, or already in advance of them.

In the deep snow escape was impossible. Nearly a hundred Kentuckians fell almost side by side, and were scalped. Among these was Colonel Allen. General Winchester and Colonel Lewis were so fortunate as to fall into the hands of the chief Round Head, who first stripped them and then took them to Proctor, who had for the time withdrawn his forces and ceased firing. By Proctor's advice, General Winchester sent an order to the men within the picket-fence to surrender.

By eight o'clock all resistance had ceased except from three hundred and eighty-four Kentuckians who remained within the picket-fence, under the command of Major Madison of the Rifle regiment. Surrounded by a thousand enemies, they had no chance of escape. Their ammunition was nearly exhausted; retreat was impossible; they could choose only between surrender and massacre, and they surrendered. The British officers looked at them with curiosity, as they came within the British line.

"Their appearance," said Major Richardson, "was miserable to the last degree. They had the air of men to whom cleanliness was a virtue unknown, and their squalid bodies were covered by habiliments that had evidently undergone every change of season, and were arrived at the last stage of repair. . . . It was the depth of winter; but scarcely an individual was in possession of a great coat or cloak, and few of them wore garments of wool of any description. They still retained their summer dress, consisting of cotton stuff of various colors shaped into frocks, and descending to the knee. Their trousers were of the same material. They were covered with slouched hats, worn bare by constant use, beneath which their long hair fell matted and uncombed over their cheeks; and these, together with the dirty blankets wrapped round their loins to protect them against the inclemency of the season, and fastened by broad leathern belts, into which were thrust axes and knives of an enormous length, gave them an air of wilderness and savageness which in Italy would have caused them to pass for brigands of the Apennines. The only distinction between the garb of the officer and that of the soldier was that the one, in addition to his sword, carried a short rifle instead of a long one, while a dagger, often curiously worked and of some value, supplied the place of the knife."

This description gave a lifelike idea of what Harrison justly thought the best material in the world for soldiery, had it been properly handled. Men who for four months had suffered every hardship and were still unclothed, unfed, uncared for, and sacrificed to military incompetence, but hardened to cold, fatigue, and danger, had no reason to be ashamed of their misfortunes or of their squalor. Fortunately about five hundred were saved as prisoners and thirty or forty escaped to the rapids; the rest, four hundred in number, were killed in battle or massacred afterward.

Had Proctor acted with energy, he might have advanced to the rapids and there have captured Harrison with his remaining force of nine hundred men, his artillery train and stores. Even with the utmost celerity Harrison could hardly have escaped if an active pursuit had been made by Indians through the swamp which he had with extreme difficulty crossed two days before, and in the heavy rain which followed the battle; but Proctor had no wish for fighting. So far from thinking of attack, he thought only of escaping it and hurried back to Malden at noon the same day, leaving the wounded prisoners behind without a guard. Nothing excused such conduct for Proctor knew the fate to which he was exposing his prisoners. That night the Indians, drunk with whiskey and mad with their grievances and losses, returned to Frenchtown and massacred the wounded. About thirty perished, some apparently burned. Fortunately for the United States the glamor of Proctor's victory hid his true character, and he was made a major general—the most favorable event of the war for the American armies he was to meet and one which cost Great Britain even more in pride than in power.

CHAPTER VI

PROCTOR AND PERRY

If Proctor was afraid of Harrison, with more military reason Harrison was afraid of Proctor; and while the British colonel, deserting his wounded prisoners, hurried from the field of battle and felt himself in danger until the next day he was again entrenched at Malden, at the same moment Harrison, burning the post at the Maumee Rapids and destroying such stores as were collected there, hastened back to the Portage or Carrying River some fifteen miles in the rear. Within thirty-six hours after the battle the two enemies were sixty miles apart. At the Portage River Harrison remained a week until he had collected a force of two thousand men. With these he returned to the rapids February 1 and began to construct a regularly fortified camp on the south bank of the river. Fort Meigs, as it was called, did credit to the skill of Major Wood, the engineer officer who constructed it; but such a fortress seemed rather intended for defense than for the conquest of Canada.

In fact, Harrison had succeeded only in making the most considerable failure that had thus far marked the progress of the war; but while the public was still assuming treason and cowardice in William Hull, who had been sent with fifteen hundred men to hold Detroit and conquer Canada, and had been left unsupported to face destruction—the same public admitted the excuses of Harrison who with ten thousand men, unlimited means, and active support at Niagara, after four months of effort, failed even to pass the Maumee River except with a detachment so badly managed that only thirty-three men in a thousand escaped. This was the crowning misfortune which wrung from Gallatin the complaint that a "real incapacity" for war existed in the government itself, and must inevitably exhaust its resources without good result; but although it drove Gallatin to Europe, it left Harrison on the Maumee. Harrison would not take on himself the disgrace of admitting his inability to recapture Detroit, and the President would not, without his express admission, order him to desist. As Armstrong afterward explained: "The Cabinet, not inexpert at deciphering military diplomacy, and peculiarly shy of incurring any responsibility it could avoid, determined, with perhaps less of patriotism than of prudence, to leave the question of continuing the winter campaign exclusively with the General." The General, not inclined to sink into obscurity or to admit failure, set himself to a third campaign as hopeless as either of its predecessors. Ordering all the troops in his rear to join him, making a body of four thousand men, he fixed February 11 as the day for his advance on Malden, not expecting to reduce that place, but merely to raid it. When the day arrived the roads had again become impassable, the ice was no longer safe; and Harrison, "with much reluctance and mortification," was reduced to write from the Maumee Rapids to the Secretary of War that the campaign must cease.

Thus the Western movement, likened by Henry Clay to a tenth-century crusade, ended in failure. The Government would have been in a better position had it never sent a man to the Maumee, but merely built a few sloops at Cleveland. The entire result of six months' immense effort was confined to raids into the Indian country; and even these were costly beyond proportion to their results.

When the militia of Kentucky and Ohio, which had been mustered in August for six months' service, returned to their homes in February, 1813, not only had they failed to reoccupy a foot of the ground abandoned by Hull, but they left Harrison almost alone at Fort Meigs, trembling lest the enemy should descend on his rear and destroy his supplies, or force him back to protect them. He had accumulated artillery, ammunition, and stores at the Maumee Rapids, in a fortress which itself required a garrison of two thousand men and from which he could neither fall back, as he thought the wiser course, nor remain with safety exposed to an active enemy. He called for more militia from Kentucky and Ohio, but the people no longer felt enthusiasm for war.

"I am sorry to mention," reported Harrison, March 17, "the dismay and disinclination to the service which appear to prevail in the Western country; numbers must give that confidence which ought to be produced by conscious valor and intrepidity, which never existed in any army in a superior degree than amongst the greater part of the militia who were with me through the winter. The new drafts from this State [Ohio] are entirely of another character, and are not to be depended on."

In short, Harrison, who had in 1812 commanded ten thousand militia, seemed to think double the number necessary for 1813 besides regular troops and a fleet.

President Madison and two successive Secretaries of War had allowed themselves, for fear of displeasing Kentucky, to give Harrison *carte blanche*, which Harrison had used without other limit than that of the entire resources of the West. The time at last came when such management must be stopped, and Secretary Armstrong, naturally impatient under the load of Eustis's and Monroe's failures, quickly decided to stop it. Harrison's letter of February 11, announcing his failure, reached the Department March 1. March 5 the secretary wrote to Harrison ordering him to maintain a threatening attitude, but altering the mode of warfare. Henceforward the army was to be made subordinate—the navy was to take the lead; and until the middle of May, when the fleet on Lake Erie should be constructed, Harrison was to maintain a strict defensive, and to protect the line of the Maumee with six regular regiments, only three of which had been yet partly raised.

Meanwhile, Harrison had but a few hundred regulars and some Pennsylvania and Virginia militia—perhaps five hundred men in all—to hold Fort Meigs, and mere squads of militia to guard eight other posts which had cost the government some millions of dollars. These five hundred troops, whose service was mostly near its end, he left at Fort Meigs, and in the middle of March he set out for Chillicothe and Cincinnati. Greatly annoyed at the summary manner in which Armstrong had put an end to his campaigning, he protested only against the inadequacy of his force for the defense required of it, and insisted on a temporary reinforcement of militia to garrison the fortress that had cost him so much effort to construct at the Maumee Rapids.

Then the value of General Proctor to his enemy became immense. Between January 22, when he attacked Winchester, and the end of April, when he moved on Fort Meigs, Proctor molested in no way the weak and isolated American garrisons. With hundreds of scouts and backwoodsmen at his command, he had not the energy or the knowledge to profit by his opponents' exposed and defense-less condition. He allowed Major Wood to make Fort Meigs capable of standing a siege; he let Harrison, unmolested, pass a month away from his command; he looked on while the Virginia militia marched home, leaving only a handful of sickly men, under a major of artillery, to defend the unfinished fort; he made no attempt to waylay Harrison who returned with reinforcements by way of the Auglaize River; and not until Harrison had enjoyed all the time necessary to pre-pare for attack did Proctor disturb him.

Harrison, expecting an assault, hurried back from Cincinnati to Fort Meigs with some three hundred men, leaving a brigade of Kentucky militia to follow him. April 12 he reached the fort, but not till April 28 did Proctor appear at the mouth of the Maumee, with about five hundred regulars and nearly as many militia—nine hundred and eighty-three whites, all told, and twelve hundred Indians under Tecumthe and other chiefs. Besides this large force he brought two twenty-four pound guns with other artillery from Detroit, and two gunboats supported the land battery. While the guns were placed in position on the north bank of the river, the Indians crossed and surrounded the fort on the south. May 1 the batteries opened, and during four days kept up a heavy fire. Proctor, like Harrison, moved in the wilderness as though he were conducting a campaign on the Rhine; he liked regular modes of warfare, and with a force almost wholly irregular, after allowing Fort Meigs to be built, he besieged it as though he could take it by battering its earthen ramparts. Untaught by his losses at the river Raisin, he gave once more advantage to the Kentucky rifle; and with every oppor-tunity of destroying the reinforcement which he knew to be near, he allowed him-self to be surprised by it.

The Kentucky brigade of twelve hundred men, under Brigadier General Green Clay, had descended the Auglaize River in boats, and arrived at Defiance May 3, where they learned that Fort Meigs was invested. So neglectful of his ad-vantages was Proctor that he not only failed to prevent General Clay from ad-vancing, but failed to prevent communication between the besieged fort and the relief-column, so that Harrison was able to arrange a general attack on the in-vesting lines, and came near driving the British force back to Malden with the loss of all its artillery and baggage. At about nine o'clock on the morning of May 5 Clay's brigade descended the rapids, and eight hundred and sixty-six men under Colonel William Dudley, landing on the north side of the river, surprised and took possession of the British batteries, which were entirely unsupported. Had Clay's whole force been on the ground, and had it been vigorously pushed forward, the small British division which held the north bank must have aban-doned all its positions; but Dudley's men were under no discipline, and though ready to advance were in no hurry to retreat, even when ordered. Three com-panies of the British Forty-first, and some of the Canadian militia soon gathered together; and although these could hardly have been half the number of Dudley's force, yet with Tecumthe and a body of Indians they attacked the batteries, drove the Kentuckians out, dispersed them, and either captured or massacred the whole body under the eyes of Harrison and Fort Meigs.

This affair, though little less fatal to the Americans than that of the river Raisin, was much less dearly bought by the British. Five hundred prisoners fell into Proctor's hands; two or three hundred more of the Kentucky brigade, including "the weak and obstinate but brave" Dudley himself, must have been either killed in battle or massacred after surrender; only one hundred and seventy escaped; the boats with the baggage were captured; while the whole British loss on the north side of the river hardly exceeded fifty killed and wounded. A bitter feeling against Proctor was caused by the massacre of some forty American prisoners while under a British guard, and also, as was alleged, under the eyes of General Proctor, who did not interpose, although a soldier of the Forty-first was murdered in trying to protect them. Probably all the prisoners would have been massacred had Tecumthe not ridden up at full speed, tomahawk in hand, and threatened to kill the first Indian who defied his authority.

On the south side Harrison had better fortune, and Colonel John Miller of the Nineteenth U. S. Infantry by a sortie gallantly captured a battery with some forty prisoners; but neither on the north nor on the south did the fighting of May 5 decide any immediate military result. Besides losing on the north bank half the reinforcement brought by General Green Clay, Harrison had lost in the siege and in the sorties on the south bank nearly three hundred men in killed and wounded. If the numbers loosely reported in the American accounts were correct, the siege cost Harrison one thousand men, or fully half his entire force, including his reinforcements. After the fighting of May 5 he withdrew once more into the fort; the British batteries reopened fire, and the siege went on. No further attempt was made to trouble the enemy in open field. Harrison felt himself too weak for further ventures; yet never had his chance of a great success been so fair.

Proctor's siege of Fort Meigs was already a failure. Not only had the fort proved stronger than he expected, but the weather was bad; his troops were without shelter; dysentery and loss in battle rapidly weakened them; half his militia went home and, what was fatal to further action, his Indians could not be held together. Within three days after the battle of May 5 the twelve hundred Indians collected by Tecumthe's influence and exertions in the northwest territory dispersed, leaving only Tecumthe himself and a score of other warriors in the British camp. Proctor had no choice but to retire as rapidly as possible and May 9 embarked his artillery and left his encampment without interference from Harrison, who looked on as a spectator while the movement was effected.

From that time until the middle of July Proctor remained quiet. Harrison moved his headquarters to Upper Sandusky and to Cleveland, and began to prepare for advance under cover of a naval force; but he was not allowed to rest, even though Proctor might have preferred repose. Proctor's position was difficult. Told by Sir George Prevost that he must capture what supplies he needed from the Americans, and must seek them at Erie and Cleveland, since Lower Canada could spare neither food nor transport, he was compelled to look for support to the American magazines. He was issuing ten thousand rations a day to the Indian families at Malden, and his resources were near an end. Leaving Malden with either three hundred and ninety-one regulars, or about five hundred regulars and militia, and by one British account nearly a thousand Indians, by another between three and four thousand, Proctor returned by water to the Maumee Rapids July

20 and tried to draw the garrison of Fort Meigs into an ambush. The attempt failed. General Green Clay, who was in command, had learned caution, and imposed it on his troops. Proctor then found that his Indians were leaving him and returning to Detroit and Amherstburg. To occupy them Proctor took again to his boats and coasted the Lake shore as far as the Sandusky River, while the Indians who chose to accompany him made their way by land. August 1 the expedition effected a landing at the mouth of the Sandusky, and scattered panic into the heart of Ohio.

In truth nothing could be more alarming than this movement, which threatened Harrison in all directions—from Fort Meigs on the Maumee to Erie or Presqu'isle, where Perry's fleet was building. On Sandusky River Harrison had collected his chief magazines. All the supplies for his army were lying at Upper Sandusky, some thirty miles above the British landing place, and he had only eight hundred raw recruits to defend their unfortified position. Nothing but an untenable stockade, called Fort Stephenson, on the Sandusky River, where the town of Fremont afterward grew, offered an obstacle to the enemy in ascending; and Tecumthe with two thousand Indians was said to be moving from Fort Meigs by the direct road straight for the magazines, thus flanking Fort Stephenson and every intermediate position on the Sandusky.

In just panic for the safety of his magazines, the only result of a year's campaigning, Harrison's first thought was to evacuate Fort Stephenson in order to protect Upper Sandusky. The flank-attack from two thousand Indians, who never showed themselves, impelled him to retire before Proctor, and to leave the river open. July 29, after a council of war, he sent down a hasty order to young Major Croghan who commanded Fort Stephenson, directing him immediately to burn the fort and retreat up the river or along the Lake shore, as he best could, with the utmost haste. Croghan, a Kentuckian, and an officer of the Seventeenth U. S. regiment, refused to obey. "We have determined to maintain this place, and by Heaven, we will," he wrote back. Harrison sent Colonel Wells, of the same regiment, to relieve him; but Croghan went to headquarters and by somewhat lame excuses carried his point and resumed his command the next day. Harrison gave him only conditional orders to abandon the fort—orders which Croghan clearly could not regard and which Harrison seemed to feel no confidence in his wishing to follow. In the face of British troops with cannon he was to retreat; but "you must be aware that the attempt to retreat in the face of an Indian force would be vain." Proctor's main force was believed to be Indian.

Neither evacuating nor defending Fort Stephenson, Harrison remained at Seneca, ten miles behind it, watching for Tecumthe and the flank attack, and arranging a plan of battle for his eight hundred men by which he could repel the Indians with dragoons in the open prairie. Croghan remained at Fort Stephenson with one hundred and sixty men, making every preparation to meet an attack. August 1 the woods were already filled with Indians, and retreat was impossible, when the British boats appeared on the river and Proctor sent to demand surrender of the fort. Immediately on Croghan's refusal, the British howitzers opened fire and continued until it became clear that they were too light to destroy the stockade.

If experience had been of service to Proctor, he should have learned to avoid direct attack on Americans in fortified places; but his position was difficult, and he was as much afraid of Harrison as Harrison was afraid of him. Fearing to leave Croghan's little fort in the rear, and to seek Harrison himself, ten miles above, on the road to Upper Sandusky; fearing delay, which would discontent his Indian allies; fearing to go on to Cleveland or Erie without crippling Harrison; still more afraid to retire to Malden without striking a blow—Proctor again sacrificed the Forty-first regiment which had suffered at the river Raisin and had been surprised at Fort Meigs. On the afternoon of August 2 the Forty-first regiment and the militia, in three columns of about one hundred and twenty men each with the utmost gallantry marched to the pickets of Fort Stephenson, and were shot down. After two hours' effort, and losing all its officers, the assaulting column retired, leaving twenty-six dead, forty-one wounded, and about thirty missing, or more than one fifth of their force. The same night the troops reëmbarked and returned to Malden.

Proctor's report of this affair was filled with complaints of the Indians, who could not be left idle and who would not fight. At Sandusky he said, "we could not muster more hundreds of Indians than I might reasonably have expected thousands."

"I could not, therefore, with my very small force remain more than two days, from the probability of being cut off, and of being deserted by the few Indians who had not already done so. . . . On the morning of the 2d inst. the gentlemen of the Indian department who have the direction of it, declared formally their decided opinion that unless the fort was stormed we should never be able to bring an Indian warrior into the field with us, and that they proposed and were ready to storm one face of the fort if we would attempt another. I have also to observe that in this instance my judgment had not that weight with the troops I hope I might reasonably have expected. . . . The troops, after the artillery had been used for some hours, attacked two faces, and impossibilities being attempted, failed. The fort, from which the severest fire I ever saw was maintained during the attack, was well defended. The troops displayed the greatest bravery, the much greater part of whom reached the fort and made every effort to enter; but the Indians who had proposed the assault, and, had it not been assented to, would have ever stigmatized the British character, scarcely came into fire before they ran out of its reach. A more than adequate sacrifice having been made to Indian opinion, I drew off the brave assailants."

Sir George Prevost seemed to doubt whether Proctor's excuse for the defeat lessened or increased the blame attached to it. The defeat at Sandusky ruined Proctor in the esteem of his men. On the American side Harrison's conduct roused a storm of indignation. Through the whole day, August 2, he remained at Seneca with eight hundred men, listening to the cannonade at Fort Stephenson till late at night when he received an express from Croghan to say that the enemy were embarking. The story ran that as the distant sound of Croghan's guns reached the camp at Seneca, Harrison exclaimed: "The blood be on his own head; I wash my hands of it." Whatever else might be true, his conduct betrayed an extravagant estimate of his enemy's strength. The only British eye-witness who left an account of the expedition reckoned Proctor's force, on its departure from Malden, at about four hundred troops, and "nearly a thousand Indians." The Indians dispersed until those with Proctor at Fort Stephenson probably numbered two or three hundred, the rest having returned to Detroit and Malden. Harrison reported the British force as five thousand strong, on the authority of General Green Clay.

Whether the British force was large or small, Harrison's arrangements to meet it did not please Secretary Armstrong. "It is worthy of notice," he wrote long afterward, "that of these two commanders, always the terror of each other, one [Proctor] was now actually flying from his supposed pursuer; while the other [Harrison] waited only the arrival of Croghan at Seneca to begin a camp-conflagration and flight to Upper Sandusky."

The well-won honors of the campaign fell to Major George Croghan, with whose name the whole country resounded. Whatever were the faults of the two generals, Major Croghan showed courage and intelligence, not only before and during the attack, but afterward in supporting Harrison against the outcry which for a time threatened to destroy the General's authority. Immediately after the siege of Fort Stephenson every energy of the northwest turned toward a new offensive movement by water against Malden, and in the task of organizing the force required for that purpose, complaints of past failures were stifled. Secretary Armstrong did not forget them, but the moment was not suited for making a change in so important a command. Harrison organized, under Armstrong's orders, a force of seven thousand men to cross the Lake in boats, under cover of a fleet.

The fleet, not the army, was to bear the brunt of reconquering the northwest; and in nothing did Armstrong show his ability so clearly as in the promptness with which, immediately after taking office, he stopped Harrison's campaign on the Maumee, while Perry was set to work at Erie. February 5, 1813, Armstrong entered on his duties. March 5 his arrangements for the new movements were already made. Harrison did not approve them, but he obeyed. The Navy Department had already begun operations on Lake Erie, immediately after Hull's surrender; but though something was accomplished in the winter, great difficulties had still to be overcome when February 17 Commander Perry, an energetic young officer on gunboat service at Newport, received orders from Secretary Jones to report to Commodore Chauncey on Lake Ontario. Chauncey ordered him to Presqu'isle, afterward called Erie, to take charge of the vessels under construction on Lake Erie. March 27 he reached the spot, a small village in a remote wilderness where timber and water alone existed for the supply of the fleets.

When Perry reached Presqu'isle the contractors and carpenters had on the stocks two brigs, a schooner, and three gunboats. These were to be launched in May, and to be ready for service in June. Besides these vessels building at Erie, a number of other craft, including the prize brig *Caledonia*, were at the Black Rock navy yard in the Niagara River, unable to move on account of the British fort opposite Buffalo and the British fleet on the Lake. Perry's task was to unite the two squadrons, to man them, and to fight the British fleet, without allowing his enemy to interfere at any stage of these difficult operations.

The British squadron under Commander Finnis, an experienced officer, had entire control of the Lake and its shores. No regular garrison protected the harbor of Presqu'isle; not two hundred men could be armed to defend it, nor was any military support to be had nearer than Buffalo, eighty miles away. Proctor or Prevost were likely to risk everything in trying to destroy the shipyard at Erie; for upon that point, far more than on Detroit, Fort Meigs, Sandusky, or Buffalo, their existence depended. If Perry were allowed to control the Lake, the British must not only evacuate Detroit, but also Malden, must abandon Tecumthe and the military advantages of three or four thousand Indian auxiliaries, and must fall back on a difficult defensive at the Niagara River. That they would make every effort to thwart Perry seemed certain.

Superstition survived in nothing more obstinately than in faith in luck; neither sailors nor soldiers ever doubted the value of this inscrutable quality in the conduct of war. The *Chesapeake* was an unlucky ship to the luckiest commanders, even to the British captain who captured it. The bad luck of the *Chesapeake* was hardly steadier than the good luck of Oliver Perry. Whatever he touched seemed to take the direction he wanted. He began with the advantage of having Proctor for his chief enemy; but Harrison, also a lucky man, had the same advantage and yet suffered constant disasters. Commander Finnis was a good seaman, yet Finnis failed repeatedly, and always by a narrow chance, to injure Perry. Dearborn's incompetence in 1813 was not less than it had been in 1812; but the single success which in two campaigns Dearborn gained on the Niagara obliged the British, May 27, to evacuate Fort Erie opposite Buffalo, and to release Perry's vessels at Black Rock. June 6, at leisure, Perry superintended the removal of the five small craft from the navy yard at Black Rock; several hundred soldiers, seamen, and oxen warped them up stream into the Lake. Loaded with stores, the little squadron sailed from Buffalo June 13; the wind was ahead; they were five days making eighty miles; but June 19 they arrived at Presqu'isle, and as the last vessel crossed the bar, Finnis and his squadron came in sight. Finnis alone could explain how he, a first-rate seaman, with a strong force and a fair wind, in such narrow seas, could have helped finding Perry's squadron when he knew where it must be.

From June 19 to August 1 Perry's combined fleet lay within the bar at Presqu'-isle, while Proctor, with a sufficient fleet and a military force superior to anything on the Lake, was planning expeditions from Malden against every place except the one to which military necessity and the orders of his Government bade him go. August 4 Perry took out the armaments of his two brigs and floated both over the bar into deep water. Had the British fleet been at hand, such a movement would have been impossible or fatal; but the British fleet appeared just as Perry's vessels got into deep water and when for the first time an attack could not be made with a fair hope of success.

These extraordinary advantages were not gained without labor, energy, courage, and wearing anxieties and disappointments. Of these Perry had his full share, but no more; and his opponents were no better off than himself. By great exertions alone could the British maintain themselves on Lake Ontario, and to this necessity they were forced to sacrifice Lake Erie. Sir George Prevost could spare only a new commander with a few officers and some forty men from the lower Lake to meet the large American reinforcements on the upper. When the commander, R. H.

Barclay, arrived at Malden in June, he found as many difficulties there as Perry found at Presqu'isle. Barclay was a captain in the British Royal Navy, thirty-two years old; he had lost an arm in the service, but he was fairly matched as Perry's antagonist, and showed the qualities of an excellent officer.

Perry's squadron, once on the Lake, altogether overawed the British fleet, and Barclay's only hope lay in completing a vessel called the *Detroit,* then on the stocks at Amherstburg. Rough and unfinished, she was launched, and while Perry blockaded the harbor, Barclay, early in September, got masts and rigging into her, and armed her with guns of every caliber, taken from the ramparts. Even the two American twenty-four pound guns, used by Proctor against Fort Meigs, were put on board the *Detroit.* Thus equipped, she had still to be manned; but no seamen were near the Lake. Barclay was forced to make up a crew of soldiers from the hard-worked Forty-first regiment and Canadians unused to service. September 6 the *Detroit* was ready to sail, and Barclay had then no choice but to fight at any risk. "So perfectly destitute of provisions was the port that there was not a day's flour in store, and the crews of the squadron under my command were on half allowance of many things; and when that was done there was no more."

Early on the morning of September 9 Barclay's fleet weighed and sailed for the enemy, who was then at anchor off the island of Put-in-Bay near the mouth of Sandusky River. The British squadron consisted of six vessels—the *Detroit,* a ship of four hundred and ninety tons, carrying nineteen guns, commanded by Barclay himself; the *Queen Charlotte* of seventeen guns, commanded by Finnis; the *Lady Prevost* of thirteen guns; the *Hunter* of ten; the *Little Belt* carrying three, and the *Chippeway* carrying one gun—in all, sixty-three guns, and probably about four hundred and fifty men. The American squadron consisted of nine vessels—the *Lawrence,* Perry's own brig, nearly as large as the *Detroit,* and carrying twenty guns; the *Niagara,* commander Jesse D. Elliott, of the same tonnage, with the same armament; the *Caledonia,* a three-gun brig; the schooners *Ariel, Scorpion, Somers, Porcupine,* and *Tigress,* carrying ten guns; and the sloop *Trippe,* with one gun—in all, fifty-four guns, with a nominal crew of five hundred and thirty-two men, and an effective crew probably not greatly differing from the British. In other respects Perry's superiority was decided, as it was meant to be. The Americans had thirty-nine thirty-two pound carronades; the British had not a gun of that weight, and only fifteen twenty-four pound carronades. The lightest guns on the American fleet were eight long twelve-pounders, while twenty-four of the British guns threw only nine-pound shot, or less. The American broadside threw at close range about nine hundred pounds of metal; the British threw about four hundred and sixty. At long range the Americans threw two hundred and eighty-eight pounds of metal; the British threw one hundred and ninety-five pounds. In tonnage the Americans were superior as eight to seven. In short, the Navy Department had done everything reasonably necessary to insure success; and if the American crews, like the British, were partly made up of landsmen, soldiers or volunteers, the reason was in each case the same. Both governments supplied all the seamen they had.

Between forces so matched, victory ought not to have been in doubt; and if it was so, the fault certainly lay not in Perry. When, at daylight September 10 his lookout discovered the British fleet, Perry got his own squadron under way and came down with a light wind from the southeast against Barclay's line, striking it obliquely near the head. Perry must have been anxious to fight at close range, where his superiority was as two to one, while at long range his ship could use only two long twelve-pounders against the *Detroit's* six twelves, one eighteen, and two twenty-fours—an inferiority amounting to helplessness. Both the *Lawrence* and the *Niagara* were armed for close fighting, and were intended for nothing else. At long range their combined broadside, even if all their twelve-pounders were worked on one side, threw but forty-eight pounds of metal; at short range the two brigs were able to throw six hundred and forty pounds at each broadside.

Perry could not have meant to fight at a distance, nor could Commander Elliott have thought it good seamanship. Yet Perry alone acted on this evident scheme; and though his official account showed that he had himself fought at close range, and that he ordered the other commanders to do the same, it gave no sufficient reasons to explain what prevented the whole fleet from acting together, and made the result doubtful. He did not even mention that he himself led the line in the *Lawrence*, with two gunboats, the *Ariel* and the *Scorpion*, supporting him, the *Caledonia, Niagara,* and three gunboats following. The *Lawrence* came within range of the British line just at noon, the wind being very light, the Lake calm, and Barclay, in the *Detroit*, opposite. Perry's report began at that point:

"At fifteen minutes before twelve the enemy commenced firing; at five minutes before twelve the action commenced on our part. Finding their fire very destructive, owing to their long guns, and its being mostly directed to the *Lawrence*, I made sail (at quarter-past twelve) and directed the other vessels to follow, for the purpose of closing with the enemy. Every brace and bowline being shot away, she became unmanageable, notwithstanding the great exertions of the sailing-master. In this situation she sustained the action upwards of two hours, within canister-shot distance, until every gun was rendered useless, and a greater part of the crew either killed or wounded. Finding she could no longer annoy the enemy, I left her in charge of Lieutenant Yarnall, who, I was convinced from the bravery already displayed by him, would do what would comport with the honor of the flag. At half-past two, the wind springing up, Captain Elliott was enabled to bring his vessel, the *Niagara*, gallantly into close action. I immediately went on board of her, when he anticipated my wish by volunteering to bring the schooners, which had been kept astern by the lightness of the wind, into close action. . . . At forty-five minutes past two the signal was made for 'close action.' The *Niagara* being very little injured, I determined to pass through the enemy's line; bore up, and passed ahead of their two ships and a brig, giving a raking fire to them from the starboard guns, and to a large schooner and sloop, from the larboard side, at half pistol-shot distance. The smaller vessels at this time having got within grape and canister distance, under the direction of Captain Elliott, and keeping up a well-directed fire, the two ships, a brig, and a schooner surrendered, a schooner and sloop making a vain attempt to escape."

From this reticent report any careful reader could see that for some reason, not so distinctly given as would have been the case if the wind alone were at fault, the action had been very badly fought on the American side. The British official account confirmed the impression given by Perry. Barclay's story was as well told as his action was well fought:

"At a quarter before twelve I commenced the action by a few long guns; about a quarter-past the American commodore, also supported by two schooners, . . . came to close action with the *Detroit*. The other brig [the *Niagara*] of the enemy, apparently destined to engage the *Queen Charlotte*, kept so far to windward as to render the *Queen Charlotte's* twenty-four pounder carronades useless, while she was, with the *Lady Prevost*, exposed to the heavy and destructive fire of the *Caledonia* and four other schooners, armed with heavy and long guns. . . . The action continued with great fury until half-past two, when I perceived my opponent [the *Lawrence*] drop astern, and a boat passing from him to the *Niagara*, which vessel was at this time perfectly fresh. The American commodore, seeing that as yet the day was against him . . . made a noble and, alas! too successful an effort to regain it; for he bore up, and supported by his small vessels, passed within pistol-shot and took a raking position on our bow. . . . The weather-gage gave the enemy a prodigious advantage, as it enabled them not only to choose their position, but their distance also, which they [the *Caledonia, Niagara*, and the gunboats] did in such a manner as to prevent the carronades of the *Queen Charlotte* and *Lady Prevost* from having much effect, while their long ones did great execution, particularly against the *Queen Charlotte*."

Barclay's report, agreeing with Perry's, made it clear that while Perry and the head of the American line fought at close quarters, the *Caledonia, Niagara*, and the four gunboats supporting them preferred fighting at long range—not because they wanted wind, but because the *Caledonia* and gunboats were armed with long thirty-two and twenty-four pounders, while the British vessels opposed to them had only one or two long twelve-pounders. Certainly the advantage in this respect on the side of the American brig and gunboats was enormous; but these tactics threw the *Niagara*, which had not the same excuse, out of the battle, leaving her, from twelve o'clock till half-past two, firing only two twelve-pound guns, while her heavy armament was useless, and might as well have been left ashore. Worse than this, the persistence of the *Caledonia, Niagara*, and their gunboats in keeping beyond range of their enemies' carronades nearly lost the battle by allowing the British to concentrate on the *Lawrence* all their heavy guns, and in the end compelling the *Lawrence* to strike. On all these points no reasonable doubt could exist. The two reports were the only official sources of information on which an opinion as to the merits of the action could properly be founded. No other account. contemporaneous and authoritative, threw light on the subject, except a letter by Lieutenant Yarnall, second in command to Perry on the *Lawrence*, written September 15 and published in the Ohio newspapers about September 29,—in which Yarnall said that if Elliott had brought his ship into action when the signal was given, the battle would have ended in much less time and with less loss to the *Lawrence*. This statement agreed with the tenor of the two official reports.

Furious as the battle was, a more furious dispute raged over it when in the year 1834 the friends of Perry and of Elliott wrangled over the action. With their dispute history need not concern itself. The official reports left no reasonable doubt that Perry's plan of battle was correct; that want of wind was not the reason it failed; but that the *Niagara* was badly managed by Elliott, and that the victory, even actually forfeited by this mismanagement, was saved by the personal energy of Perry, who, abandoning his own ship, brought the *Niagara* through the enemy's line, and regained the advantage of her heavy battery. The luck which attended Perry's career on the Lake saved him from injury, when every other officer on the two opposing flagships and four-fifths of his crew were killed or wounded, and enabled him to perform a feat almost without parallel in naval warfare, giving him a well-won immortality by means of the disaster unnecessarily incurred. No process of argument or ingenuity of seamanship could deprive Perry of the fame justly given him by the public, or detract from the splendor of his reputation as the hero of the war. More than any other battle of the time, the victory on Lake Erie was won by the courage and obstinacy of a single man.

Between two opponents such as Perry and Barclay, no one doubted that the ships were fought to their utmost. Of the *Lawrence* not much was left; ship, officers, and crew were shot to pieces. Such carnage was not known on the ocean for even the cockpit where the sick and wounded lay, being above water, was riddled by shot, and the wounded were wounded again on the surgeon's board. Of one hundred and three effectives on the *Lawrence*, twenty-two were killed and sixty-one wounded. The brig herself when she struck was a wreck, unmanageable, her starboard bulwarks beaten in, guns dismounted, and rigging cut to pieces. The British ships were in hardly better condition. The long guns of the gunboats had raked them with destructive effect. Barclay was desperately wounded; Finnis was killed; Barclay's first lieutenant was mortally wounded; not one commander or second in command could keep the deck; the squadron had forty-one men killed and ninety-four wounded, or nearly one man in three; the *Detroit* and *Queen Charlotte* were unmanageable and fell foul; the *Lady Prevost* was crippled, and drifted out of the fight. Perry could console himself with the thought that if his ship had struck her flag, she had at least struck to brave men.

CHAPTER VII
THE BATTLE OF THE THAMES

General Harrison, waiting at Seneca, on the Sandusky River received September 12 Perry's famous dispatch of September 10: "We have met the enemy, and they are ours." The navy having done its work, the army was next to act.

The force under Harrison's command was ample for the required purpose, although it contained fewer regular troops than Armstrong had intended. The seven regular regiments assigned to Harrison fell short in numbers of the most moderate expectations. Instead of providing seven thousand rank-and-file, the recruiting service ended in producing rather more than twenty-five hundred. Divided into two brigades under Brigadier Generals McArthur and Lewis Cass, with a light corps under Lieutenant Colonel Ball of the Light Dragoons, they formed only one wing of Harrison's army.

To supply his main force, Harrison had still to depend on Kentucky; and once more that State made a great effort. Governor Shelby took the field in person, leading three thousand volunteers, organized in eleven regiments, five brigades, and two divisions. Besides the militia, who volunteered for this special purpose, Harrison obtained the services of another Kentucky corps, which had already proved its efficiency.

One of Armstrong's happiest acts, at the beginning of his service as War Secretary, was to accept the aid of Richard M. Johnson in organizing for frontier defense a mounted regiment of a thousand men, armed with muskets or rifles, tomahawks, and knives. Johnson and his regiment took the field about June 1, and from that time anxiety on account of Indians ceased. The regiment patrolled the district from Fort Wayne to the river Raisin, and whether in marching or fighting proved to be the most efficient corps in the Western country. Harrison obtained the assistance of Johnson's regiment for the movement into Canada, and thereby increased the efficiency of his army beyond the proportion of Johnson's numbers.

While the mounted regiment moved by the road to Detroit Harrison's main force was embarked in boats September 20, and in the course of a few days some forty-five hundred infantry were safely conveyed by way of Bass Island and Put-in-Bay to Middle Sister Island, about twelve miles from the Canadian shore. Harrison and Perry then selected a landing place, and the whole force was successfully set ashore, September 27, about three miles below Malden.

Although Proctor could not hope to maintain himself at Malden or Detroit without control of the Lake, he had still the means of rendering Harrison's possession insecure. According to the British account, he commanded at Detroit and Malden a force of nine hundred and eighty-six regulars, giving about eight hundred effectives. Not less than thirty-five hundred Indian warriors had flocked to Amherstburg, and although they greatly increased the British general's difficulties by bringing their families with them, they might be formidable opponents to Harrison's advance. Every motive dictated to Proctor the necessity of resisting Harrison's approach. To Tecumthe and his Indians the evacuation of Malden and Detroit without a struggle meant not only the sacrifice of their cause, but also cowardice; and when Proctor announced to them, September 18, that he

[70]

meant to retreat, Tecumthe rose in the council and protested against the flight, likening Proctor to a fat dog that had carried its tail erect, and now that it was frightened dropped its tail between its legs and ran. He told Proctor to go if he liked, but the Indians would remain.

Proctor insisted upon retiring at least toward the Moravian town, seventy miles on the road to Lake Ontario and the Indians yielded. The troops immediately began to burn or destroy the public property at Detroit and Malden, or to load on wagons or boats what could not be carried away. September 24, three days before Harrison's army landed, the British evacuated Malden and withdrew to Sandwich, allowing Harrison to establish himself at Malden without a skirmish, and neglecting to destroy the bridge over the Canard River.

Harrison was surprised at Proctor's tame retreat.

"Nothing but infatuation," he reported, "could have governed General Proctor's conduct. The day that I landed below Malden he had at his disposal upward of three thousand Indian warriors; his regular force reinforced by the militia of the district would have made his number nearly equal to my aggregate, which on the day of landing did not exceed forty-five hundred. . . . His inferior officers say that his conduct has been a series of continued blunders."

This crowning proof of Proctor's incapacity disorganized his force. Tecumthe expressed a general sentiment of the British army in his public denunciation of Proctor's cowardice. One of the inferior British officers afterward declared that Proctor's "marked inefficiency" and "wanton sacrifice" of the troops raised more than a doubt not only of his capacity but even of his personal courage, and led to serious thoughts of taking away his authority. The British at Sandwich went through the same experience that marked the retreat of Hull and his army from the same spot, only the year before.

Harrison on his side made no extreme haste to pursue. His army marched into Malden at four o'clock on the afternoon of September 27, and he wrote to Secretary Armstrong that evening: "I will pursue the enemy tomorrow, although there is no probability of my overtaking him, as he has upwards of a thousand horses, and we have not one in the army." The pursuit was not rapid. Sandwich, opposite Detroit, was only thirteen miles above Malden, but Harrison required two days to reach it, arriving at two o'clock on the afternoon of September 29. From there, September 30, he wrote again to Secretary Armstrong that he was preparing to pursue the enemy on the following day; but he waited for R. M. Johnson's mounted regiment, which arrived at Detroit September 30, and was obliged to consume a day in crossing the river. Then the pursuit began with energy, but on the morning of October 2 Proctor had already a week's advance and should have been safe.

Proctor seemed to imagine that the Americans would not venture to pursue him. Moving, according to his own report, "by easy marches," neither obstructing the road in his rear nor leaving detachments to delay the enemy, he reached Dolson's October 1, and there halted his army, fifty miles from Sandwich, while he went to the Moravian town some twenty-six miles beyond. He then intended to make a stand at Chatham, three miles behind Dolson's.

"I had assured the Indians," said Proctor's report of October 23, "that we would not desert them, and it was my full determination to have made a stand at the Forks (Chatham), by which our vessels and stores would be protected; but after my arrival at Dover [Dolson's] three miles lower down the river, I was induced to take post there first, where ovens had been constructed, and where there was some shelter for the troops, and had accordingly directed that it should be put into the best possible state of defence that time and circumstances would admit of; indeed it had been my intention to have opposed the enemy nearer the mouth of the river, had not the troops contrary to my intention been moved, during my absence of a few hours for the purpose of acquiring some knowledge of the country in my rear."

The British army, left at Dolson's October 1, without a general or orders, saw the American army arrive in its front, October 3, and retired three miles to Chatham, where the Indians insisted upon fighting; but when, the next morning, October 4, the Americans advanced in order of battle, the Indians after a skirmish changed their minds and retreated. The British were compelled to sacrifice the supplies they had brought by water to Chatham for establishing their new base, and their retreat precipitated on the Moravian town the confusion of flight already resembling rout.

Six miles on their way they met General Proctor returning from the Moravian town, and as much dissatisfied with them as they with him. Pressed closely by the American advance, the British troops made what haste they could over excessively bad roads until eight o'clock in the evening, when they halted within six miles of the Moravian town. The next morning, October 5, the enemy was again reported to be close at hand, and the British force again retreated. About a mile and a half from the Moravian town it was halted. Proctor had then retired as far as he could, and there he must either fight, or abandon women and children, sick and wounded, baggage, stores, and wagons, desert his Indian allies, and fly to Lake Ontario. Probably flight would not have saved his troops. More than a hundred miles of unsettled country lay between them and their next base. The Americans had in their advance the mounted regiment of R. M. Johnson, and could outmarch the most lightly equipped British regulars. Already, according to Proctor's report, the rapidity of the Americans had destroyed the efficiency of the British organization:

"In the attempt to save provisions we became encumbered with boats not suited to the state of navigation. The Indians and the troops retreated on different sides of the river, and the boats to which sufficient attention had not been given became particularly exposed to the fire of the enemy who were advancing on the side the Indians were retiring, and most unfortunately fell into possession of the enemy, and with them several of the men, provisions, and all the ammunition that had not been issued to the troops and Indians. The disastrous circumstance afforded the enemy the means of crossing and advancing on both sides of the river. Finding the enemy were advancing too near I resolved to meet him, being strong in cavalry, in a wood below the Moravian town, which last was not cleared of Indian women and children, or of those of the troops, nor of the sick."

The whole British force was then on the north bank of the river Thames, retreating eastward by a road near the river bank. Proctor could hardly claim to have exercised choice in the selection of a battleground, unless he preferred placing his little force under every disadvantage. "The troops were formed with their left to the river," his report continued, "with a reserve and a six-pounder on the road, near the river; the Indians on the right." According to the report of officers of the Forty-first regiment, two lines of troops were formed in a thick forest, two hundred yards apart. The first line began where the six-pound field-piece stood, with a range of some fifty yards along the road. A few Canadian Light Dragoons were stationed near the gun. To the left of the road was the river; to the right a forest, free from underbrush that could stop horsemen, but offering cover to an approaching enemy within twenty paces of the British line. In the wood about two hundred men of the British Forty-first took position as well as they could behind trees, and there as a first line they waited some two hours for their enemy to appear.

The second line, somewhat less numerous, two hundred yards behind the first, and not within sight, was also formed in the wood; and on the road, in rear of the second line, Proctor and his staff stationed themselves. The Indians were collected behind a swamp on the right, touching and covering effectually the British right flank, while the river covered the left.

Such a formation was best fitted for Harrison's purposes, but the mere arrangement gave little idea of Proctor's weakness. The six-pound field-piece, which as he afterward reported "certainly should have produced the best effect if properly managed," had not a round of ammunition, and could not be fired. The Forty-first regiment was almost mutinous, but had it been in the best condition it could not have held against serious attack. The whole strength of the Forty-first was only three hundred and fifty-six rank-and-file, or four hundred and eight men all told. The numbers of the regiment actually in the field were reported as three hundred and fifteen rank-and-file, or three hundred and sixty-seven men all told. The dragoons were supposed not to exceed twenty. This petty force was unable to see either the advancing enemy or its own members. The only efficient corps in the field was the Indians, who were estimated by the British sometimes at five hundred, at eight hundred, and twelve hundred in number, and who were in some degree covered by the swamp.

Harrison came upon the British line soon after two o'clock in the afternoon, and at once formed his army in regular order of battle. As the order was disregarded and the battle was fought, as he reported, in a manner "not sanctioned by anything that I had seen or heard of," the intended arrangement mattered little. In truth, the battle was planned as well as fought by Richard M. Johnson, whose energy impressed on the army a new character from the moment he joined it. While Harrison drew up his infantry in order of battle, Johnson, whose mounted regiment was close to the British line, asked leave to charge, and Harrison gave him the order, although he knew no rule of war that sanctioned it.

Johnson's tactics were hazardous, though effective. Giving to his brother, James Johnson, half the regiment to lead up the road against the six-pound gun and the British Forty-first regiment, R. M. Johnson with the other half of his regiment wheeled to the left, at an angle with the road, and crossed the swamp to attack twice his number of Indians posted in a thick wood.

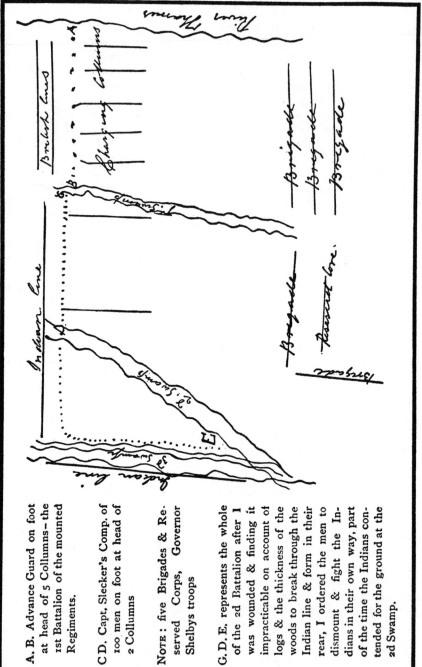

A. B. Advance Guard on foot at head of 5 Collumns – the 1st Battalion of the mounted Regiments.

C.D. Capt. Slecker's Comp. of 100 men on foot at head of 2 Collumns

NOTE: five Brigades & Reserved Corps, Governor Shelbys troops

G.D.E. represents the whole of the 2d Battalion after 1 was wounded & finding it impracticable on account of logs & the thickness of the woods to break through the Indian line & form in their rear, I ordered the men to dismount & fight the Indians in their own way, part of the time the Indians contended for the ground at the 2d Swamp.

James Johnson, with his five hundred men, galloped directly through the British first line, receiving a confused fire, and passing immediately to the rear of the British second line, so rapidly as almost to capture Proctor himself, who fled at full speed. As the British soldiers straggled in bands or singly toward the rear, they found themselves among the American mounted riflemen, and had no choice but to surrender. About fifty men, with a single lieutenant, contrived to escape through the woods; all the rest became prisoners.

R. M. Johnson was less fortunate. Crossing the swamp to his left he was received by the Indians in underbrush which the horses could not penetrate. Under a sharp fire his men were obliged to dismount and fight at close quarters. At an early moment of the battle, Johnson was wounded by the rifle of an Indian warrior who sprang forward to dispatch him, but was killed by a ball from Johnson's pistol. The fighting at that point was severe, but Johnson's men broke or turned the Indian line, which was uncovered after the British defeat, and driving the Indians toward the American left, brought them under fire of Shelby's infantry when they fled.

In this contest Johnson maintained that his regiment was alone engaged. In a letter to Secretary Armstrong, dated six weeks after the battle, he said:

"I send you an imperfect sketch of the late battle on the river Thames, fought solely by the mounted regiment; at least, so much so that not fifty men from any other corps assisted. . . . Fought the Indians, twelve hundred or fifteen hundred men, one hour and twenty minutes, driving them from the extreme right to the extreme left of my line, at which last point we came near Governor Shelby, who ordered Colonel Simrall to reinforce me; but the battle was over, and although the Indians were pursued half a mile, there was no fighting."

Harrison's official report gave another idea of the relative share taken by the Kentucky infantry in the action; but the difference in dispute was trifling. The entire American loss was supposed to be only about fifteen killed and thirty wounded. The battle lasted, with sharpness, not more than twenty minutes; and none but the men under Johnson's command enjoyed opportunity to share in the first and most perilous assault.

The British loss was only twelve men killed and thirty-six wounded. The total number of British prisoners taken on the field and in the Moravian town, or elsewhere on the day of battle, was four hundred and seventy-seven; in the whole campaign, six hundred. All Proctor's baggage, artillery, small arms, stores, and hospital were captured in the Moravian town. The Indians left thirty-three dead on the field, among them one reported to be Tecumthe. After the battle several officers of the British Forty-first, well acquainted with the Shawnee warrior, visited the spot and identified his body. The Kentuckians had first recognized it, and had cut long strips of skin from the thighs, to keep, as was said, for razor-straps, in memory of the river Raisin.

After Perry's victory on Lake Erie Tecumthe's life was of no value to himself or his people and his death was no subject for regret; but the manner chosen for producing this result was an expensive mode of acquiring territory for the United States. The Shawnee warrior compelled the government to pay for once something like the value of the lands it took. The precise cost of the Indian war could not be estimated, being combined in many ways with that of the war with England; but the British counted for little, within the northwestern territory, except so far as Tecumthe used them for his purposes. Not more than seven or eight hundred British soldiers ever crossed the Detroit River; but the United States raised fully twenty thousand men, and spent at least five million dollars and many lives in expelling them. The Indians alone made this outlay necessary. The campaign of Tippecanoe, the surrender of Detroit and Mackinaw, the massacres at Fort Dearborn, the river Raisin, and Fort Meigs, the murders along the frontier, and the campaign of 1813 were the price paid for the Indian lands in the Wabash Valley.

No part of the war more injured British credit on the American continent than the result of the Indian alliance. Except the capture of Detroit and Mackinaw at the outset, without fighting, and the qualified success at the river Raisin, the British suffered only mortifications, ending with the total loss of their fleet, the abandonment of their fortress, the flight of their army, and the shameful scene before the Moravian town, where four hundred British regulars allowed themselves to be ridden over and captured by five hundred Kentucky horsemen, with hardly the loss of a man to the assailants. After such a disgrace the British ceased to be formidable in the northwest. The Indians recognized the hopelessness of their course, and from that moment abandoned their dependence on England.

The battle of the Thames annihilated the right division of the British army in Upper Canada. When the remnants of Proctor's force were mustered, October 17, at Ancaster, a hundred miles from the battlefield, about two hundred rank-and-file were assembled. Proctor made a report of the battle blaming his troops, and Prevost issued a severe reprimand to the unfortunate Forty-first regiment on the strength of Proctor's representations. In the end the Prince Regent disgraced both officers, recognizing by these public acts the loss of credit the government had suffered; but its recovery was impossible.

So little anxiety did General Harrison thenceforward feel about the Eighth Military District which he commanded, that he returned to Detroit October 7; his army followed him, and arrived at Sandwich, October 10, without seeing an enemy. Promptly discharged, the Kentucky Volunteers marched homeward October 14; the mounted regiment and its wounded colonel followed a few days later, and within a fortnight only two brigades of the regular army remained north of the Maumee.

At Detroit the war was closed, and except for two or three distant expeditions was not again a subject of interest. The Indians were for the most part obliged to remain within the United States jurisdiction. The great number of Indian families that had been collected about Detroit and Malden were rather a cause for confidence than fear, since they were in effect hostages, and any violence committed by the warriors would have caused them, their women and children, to be deprived of food and to perish of starvation. Detroit was full of savages dependent on army supplies, and living on the refuse and offal of the slaughter-yard; but their military strength was gone. Some hundreds of the best warriors followed Proctor to Lake Ontario, but Tecumthe's northwestern confederacy was broken up, and most of the tribes made submission.

CHAPTER VIII

DEARBORN'S CAMPAIGN

The new Secretaries of War and Navy who took office in January, 1813, were able in the following October to show Detroit recovered. Nine months solved the problem of Lake Erie. The problem of Lake Ontario remained insoluble.

In theory nothing was simpler than the conquest of Upper Canada. Six months before war was declared, January 2, 1812, John Armstrong, then a private citizen, wrote to Secretary Eustis a letter containing the remark—

"In invading a neighboring and independent territory like Canada, having a frontier of immense extent; destitute of means strictly its own for the purpose of defense; separated from the rest of the empire by an ocean, and having to this but one outlet—this outlet forms your true object or point of attack."

The river St. Lawrence was the true object of attack, and the Canadians hardly dared hope to defend it.

"From St. Regis to opposite Kingston," said the Quebec *Gazette* in 1814, "the southern bank of the river belongs to the United States. It is well known that this river is the only communication between Upper and Lower Canada. It is rapid and narrow in many places. A few cannon judiciously posted, or even musketry, could render the communication impracticable without powerful escorts, wasting and parcelling the force applicable to the defence of the provinces. It is needless to say that no British force can remain in safety or maintain itself in Upper Canada without a ready communication with the lower province."

Closure of the river anywhere must compel the submission of the whole country above, which could not provide its supplies. The American, who saw his own difficulties of transport between New York and the Lakes, thought well of his energy in surmounting them; but as the war took larger proportions, and great fleets were built on Lake Ontario, the difficulties of Canadian transport became insuperable. Toward the close of the war, Sir George Prevost wrote to Lord Bathurst that six thirty-two-pound guns for the fleet, hauled in winter four hundred miles from Quebec to Kingston, would cost at least £2000 for transport. Forty twenty-four-pounders hauled on the snow had cost £4,800; a cable of the largest size hauled from Sorel to Kingston, two hundred and fifty-five miles, cost £1000 for transport. In summer when the river was open the difficulties were hardly less. The commissary-general reported that the impediments of navigation were incalculable, and the scarcity of workmen, laborers, and voyagers not to be described.

If these reasons for attacking and closing the river St. Lawrence had not been decisive with the United States government, other reasons were sufficient. The political motive was as strong as the military. Americans, especially in New England, denied that treasonable intercourse existed with Canada; but intercourse needed not to be technically treasonable in order to have the effects of treason. Sir George Prevost wrote to Lord Bathurst, August 27, 1814, when the war had lasted two years:

"Two thirds of the army in Canada are at this moment eating beef provided by American contractors, drawn principally from the States of Vermont and New York. This circumstance, as well as that of the introduction of large sums of specie into this province, being notorious in the United States, it is to be ex-

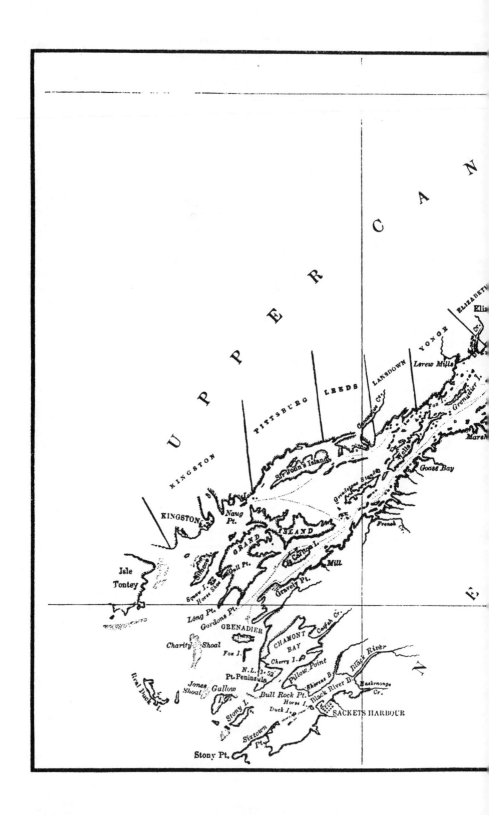

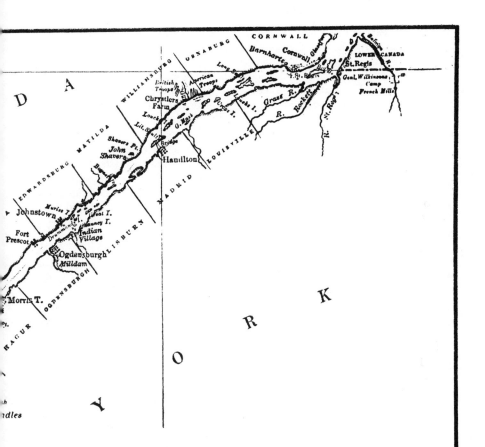

EAST END OF

LAKE ONTARIO

AND

RIVER ST. LAWRENCE

FROM

Kingston to French Mills

REDUCED FROM AN

ORIGINAL DRAWING IN THE
NAVAL DEPARTMENT

BY JOHN MELISH.

SCALE

1 2 3 4 5   10   15   20 Miles

pected Congress will take steps to deprive us of those resources, and under that apprehension large droves are daily crossing the lines coming into Lower Canada."

This state of things had then lasted during three campaigns, from the beginning of the war. The Indians at Malden, the British army at Niagara, the naval station at Kingston were largely fed by the United States. If these supplies could be stopped, Upper Canada must probably fall; and they could be easily stopped by interrupting the British line of transport anywhere on the St. Lawrence.

The task was not difficult. Indeed, early in the war an enterprising officer of irregulars, Major Benjamin Forsyth, carried on a troublesome system of annoyance from Ogdensburg, which Sir George Prevost treated with extreme timidity. The British commandant at Prescott, Major Macdonnell, was not so cautious as the governor general, but crossed the river on the ice with about five hundred men, drove Forsyth from the town, destroyed the public property, and retired in safety with a loss of eight killed and fifty-two wounded. This affair, February 23, 1813, closed hostilities in that region, and Major Forsyth was soon ordered to Sackett's Harbor. His experience, and that of Major Macdonnell, proved how easy the closure of such a river must be, exposed as it was for two hundred miles to the fire of cannon and musketry.

The St. Lawrence was therefore the proper point of approach and attack against Upper Canada. Armstrong came to the Department of War with that idea fixed in his mind. The next subject for his consideration was the means at his disposal.

During Monroe's control of the War Department for two months, between December 3, 1812, and February 5, 1813, much effort had been made to increase the army. Monroe wrote to the chairman of the Military Committee December 22, 1812, a sketch of his ideas. He proposed to provide for the general defense by dividing the United States into military districts, and apportioning ninety-three hundred and fifty men among them as garrisons. For offensive operations he required a force competent to overpower the British defense, and in estimating his wants, he assumed that Canada contained about twelve thousand British regulars, besides militia, and three thousand men at Halifax.

"To demolish the British force from Niagara to Quebec," said Monroe, "would require, to make the thing secure, an efficient regular army of twenty thousand men, with an army of reserve of ten thousand. . . . If the government could raise and keep in the field thirty-five thousand regular troops . . . the deficiency to be supplied even to authorize an expedition against Halifax would be inconsiderable. Ten thousand men would be amply sufficient; but there is danger of not being able to raise that force, and to keep it at that standard. . . . My idea is that provision ought to be made for raising twenty thousand men in addition to the present establishment."

Congress voted about fifty-eight thousand men, and after deducting ten thousand for garrisons, counted on forty-eight thousand for service in Canada. When Armstrong took control February 5, 1813, he began at once to devise a plan of operation for the army which by law numbered fifty-eight thousand men, and in fact numbered, including the staff and regimental officers, eighteen thousand nine hundred and forty-five men, according to the returns in the adjutant general's office February 16, 1813. Before he had been a week in the War Department he wrote, February 10, to Major General Dearborn announcing that four thousand men were to be immediately collected at Sackett's Harbor, and three thousand at Buffalo. April 1, or as soon as navigation opened, the four thousand troops at Sackett's Harbor were to be embarked and transported in boats under convoy of the fleet across the Lake at the entry of the St. Lawrence, thirty-five miles, to Kingston. After capturing Kingston, with its magazines, navy yards, and ships, the expedition was to proceed up the Lake to York (Toronto) and capture two vessels building there. Thence it was to join the corps of three thousand men at Buffalo, and attack the British on the Niagara River.

In explaining his plan to the Cabinet, Armstrong pointed out that the attack from Lake Champlain on Montreal could not begin before May 1; that Kingston, between April 1 and May 15, was shut from support by ice; that not more than two thousand men could be gathered to defend it; and that by beginning the campaign against Kingston rather than against Montreal, six weeks' time would be gained before reinforcements could arrive from England.

Whatever defects the plan might have, Kingston, and Kingston alone, possessed so much military importance as warranted the movement. Evidently Armstrong had in mind no result short of the capture of Kingston.

Dearborn received these instructions at Albany, and replied, February 18, that nothing should be omitted on his part in endeavoring to carry into effect the expedition proposed. Orders were given for concentrating the intended force at Sackett's Harbor. During the month of March the preparations were stimulated by a panic due to the appearance of Sir George Prevost at Prescott and Kingston. Dearborn hurried to Sackett's Harbor in person, under the belief that the governor general was about to attack it.

Armstrong estimated the British force at Kingston as nine hundred regulars, or two thousand men all told; and his estimate was probably correct. The usual garrison at Kingston and Prescott was about eight hundred rank-and-file. In both the British and American services the returns of rank-and-file were the ordinary gauge of numerical force. Rank-and-file included corporals, but not sergeants or commissioned officers; and an allowance of at least ten sergeants and officers was always to be made for every hundred rank-and-file, in order to estimate the true numerical strength of an army or garrison. Unless otherwise mentioned, the return excluded also the sick and disabled. The relative force of every army was given in effectives, or rank-and-file actually present for duty.

In the distribution of British forces in Canada for 1812-1813, the garrison at Prescott was allowed three hundred and seventy-six rank-and-file, with fifty-two officers including sergeants. To Kingston three hundred and eighty-four rank-and-file were allotted, with sixty officers including sergeants. To Montreal and the positions between Prescott and the St. John's River about five thousand rank-and-file were allotted. At Prescott and Kingston, besides the regular troops, the men employed in shipbuilding or other labor, the sailors, and the local militia were to be reckoned as part of the garrison, and Armstrong included them all in his estimate of two thousand men.

The British force should have been known to Dearborn nearly as well as his own. No considerable movement of troops between Lower and Upper Canada could occur without his knowledge. Yet Dearborn wrote to Armstrong, March 9, 1813, from Sackett's Harbor:

"I have not yet had the honor of a visit from Sir George Prevost. His whole force is concentrated at Kingston, probably amounting to six or seven thousand—about three thousand of them regular troops. The ice is good, and we expect him every day. . . . As soon as the fall [fate?] of this place [Sackett's Harbor] shall be decided, we shall be able to determine on other measures. If we hold this place, we will command the Lake, and be able to act in concert with the troops at Niagara."

A few days later March 14 Dearborn wrote again.

"Sir George," he said, had "concluded that it is too late to attack this place. . . . We are probably just strong enough on each side to defend, but not in sufficient force to hazard an offensive movement. The difference of attacking and being attacked, as it regards the contiguous posts of Kingston and Sackett's Harbor, cannot be estimated at less than three or four thousand men, arising from the circumstance of militia acting merely on the defensive."

Clearly Dearborn did not approve Armstrong's plan and wished to change it. In this idea he was supported, or instigated, by the naval commander on the Lake, Isaac Chauncey, a native of Connecticut, forty years of age, who entered the service in 1798 and became captain in 1806. Chauncey and Dearborn consulted together, and devised a new scheme, which Dearborn explained to Armstrong about March 20:

"To take or destroy the armed vessels at York will give us the complete command of the Lake. Commodore Chauncey can take with him ten or twelve hundred troops to be commanded by Pike; take York; from thence proceed to Niagara and attack Fort George by land and water, while the troops at Buffalo cross over and carry Forts Erie and Chippewa, and join those at Fort George; and then collect our whole force for an attack on Kingston. After the most mature deliberation the above was considered by Commodore Chauncey and myself as the most certain of ultimate success."

Thus Dearborn and Chauncey inverted Armstrong's plan. Instead of attacking on the St. Lawrence, they proposed to attack on the Niagara. Armstrong acquiesced. "Taking for granted," as he did on Dearborn's assertion, "that General Prevost . . . has assembled at Kingston a force of six or eight thousand men, as stated by you," he could not require that his own plan should be pursued. "The alteration in the plan of campaign so as to make Kingston the last object instead of making it the first, would appear to be necessary or at least proper," he wrote to Dearborn, March 29.

The scheme proposed by Dearborn and Chauncey was carried into effect by them. The contractors furnished new vessels, which gave to Chauncey for a time the control of the Lake. April 22 the troops, numbering sixteen hundred men, embarked. Armstrong insisted on only one change in the expedition, which betrayed perhaps a shade of malice, for he required Dearborn himself to command it, and Dearborn was suspected of shunning service in the field.

From the moment Dearborn turned away from the St. Lawrence and carried the war westward, the naval and military movements on Lake Ontario became valuable chiefly as a record of failure. The fleet and army arrived at York early in the morning of April 27. York, a village numbering in 1806, according to British account, more than three thousand inhabitants, was the capital of Upper Canada, and contained the residence of the lieutenant governor and the two brick buildings where the Legislature met. For military purposes the place was valueless, but it had been used for the construction of a few war-vessels, and Chauncey represented, through Dearborn, that "to take or destroy the armed vessels at York will give us the complete command of the Lake." The military force at York, according to British account, did not exceed six hundred men, regulars and militia; and of these, one hundred and eighty men, or two companies of the Eighth or King's regiment, happened to be there only in passing.

Under the fire of the fleet and riflemen, Pike's brigade was set ashore; the British garrison, after a sharp resistance, was driven away, and the town capitulated. The ship on the stocks was burned; the ten-gun brig *Gloucester* was made prize; the stores were destroyed or shipped; some three hundred prisoners were taken; and the public buildings, including the houses of Assembly, were burned. The destruction of the Assembly houses, afterward alleged as ground for retaliation against the capital at Washington, was probably the unauthorized act of private soldiers. Dearborn protested that it was done without his knowledge and against his orders.

The success cost far more than it was worth. The explosion of a powder magazine, near which the American advance halted, injured a large number of men on both sides. Not less than three hundred and twenty Americans were killed or wounded in the battle or explosion, or about one-fifth of the entire force. General Pike, the best brigadier then in the service, was killed. Only two or three battles in the entire war were equally bloody. "Unfortunately the enemy's armed ship the *Prince Regent*," reported Dearborn, "left this place for Kingston four days before we arrived."

Chauncey and Dearborn crossed to Niagara, while the troops remained some ten days at York, and were then disembarked at Niagara, May 8, according to Dearborn's report, "in a very sickly and depressed state; a large proportion of the officers and men were sickly and debilitated." Nothing was ready for the movement which was to drive the British from Fort George, and before active operations could begin, Dearborn fell ill. The details of command fell to his chief-of-staff, Colonel Winfield Scott.

The military organization at Niagara was at best unfortunate. One of Secretary Armstrong's earliest measures was to issue the military order previously arranged by Monroe, dividing the Union into military districts. Vermont and the State of New York north of the highlands formed the Ninth Military District under Major General Dearborn. In the Ninth District were three points of activity —Plattsburg on Lake Champlain, Sackett's Harbor on Lake Ontario, and the Niagara River. Each point required a large force and a commander of the highest ability; but in May, 1813, Plattsburg and Sackett's Harbor were denuded of troops and officers, who were all drawn to Niagara, where they formed three brigades, commanded by Brigadier Generals John P. Boyd, who succeeded Pike, John Chandler, and W. H. Winder. Niagara and the troops in its neighborhood were under the command of Major General Morgan Lewis, a man of ability, but possessing neither the youth nor the energy to lead an army in the field, while Boyd, Chandler, and Winder were competent only to command regiments.

Winfield Scott in effect assumed control of the army and undertook to carry out Van Rensselaer's plan of the year before for attacking Fort George in the rear from the Lake. The task was not very difficult. Chauncey controlled the Lake, and his fleet was at hand to transfer the troops. Dearborn's force numbered certainly not less than four thousand rank-and-file present for duty. The entire British regular force on the Niagara River did not exceed eighteen hundred rank-and-file, and about five hundred militia. At Fort George about one thousand regulars and three hundred militia were stationed, and the military object to be gained by the Americans was not so much the capture of Fort George, which was then not defensible, as that of its garrison.

Early on the morning of May 27, when the mist cleared away, the British General Vincent saw Chauncey's fleet, "in an extended line of more than two miles," standing toward the shore. When the ships took position, "the fire from the shipping so completely enfiladed and scoured the plains, that it became impossible to approach the beach," and Vincent could only concentrate his force between the Fort and the enemy, waiting attack. Winfield Scott at the head of an advance division first landed, followed by the brigades of Boyd, Winder, and Chandler, and after a sharp skirmish drove the British back along the Lake shore, advancing under cover of the fleet. Vincent's report continued:

"After awaiting the approach of the enemy for about half an hour I received authentic information that his force, consisting of from four to five thousand men, had reformed his columns and was making an effort to turn my right flank. Having given orders for the fort to be evacuated, the guns to be spiked, and the ammunition destroyed, the troops under my command were put in motion, and marched across the country in a line parallel to the Niagara River, toward the position near the Beaver Dam beyond Queenston mountain. . . . Having assembled my whole force the following morning, which did not exceed sixteen hundred men, I continued my march toward the head of the Lake."

Vincent lost severely in proportion to his numbers, for fifty-one men were killed, and three hundred and five were wounded or missing, chiefly in the Eighth or King's regiment. Several hundred militia were captured in his retreat. The American loss was about forty killed and one hundred and twenty wounded. According to General Morgan Lewis, Colonel Winfield Scott "fought nine-tenths of the battle." Dearborn watched the movements from the fleet.

For a time this success made a deep impression on the military administration of Canada, and the abandonment of the whole country west of Kingston was thought inevitable. The opportunity for achieving a decided advantage was the best that occurred for the Americans during the entire war; but whatever might be said in public, the battle of Fort George was a disappointment to the War Department as well as to the officers in command of the American army, who had hoped to destroy the British force. The chief advantage gained was the liberation of Perry's vessels to complete his fleet on Lake Erie.

On Lake Ontario, May 31, Chauncey insisted, not without cause, on returning to Sackett's Harbor. Dearborn, instead of moving with his whole force, ordered Brigadier General Winder, June 1, to pursue Vincent. Winder, with eight hundred or a thousand men, marched twenty miles and then sent for reinforcements. He was joined, June 5, by General Chandler with another brigade. Chandler then took command, and advanced with a force supposed to number in the aggregate two thousand men to Stony Creek, within ten miles of Vincent's position at Hamilton, where sixteen hundred British regulars were encamped. There Chandler and Winder posted themselves for the night, much as Winchester and his Kentuckians had camped at the river Raisin four months earlier.

Vincent was not to be treated with such freedom. Taking only seven hundred rank-and-file, he led them himself against Chandler's camp. The attack began, in intense darkness, at two o'clock in the morning of June 6. The British quickly broke the American center and carried the guns. The lines became mixed, and extreme confusion lasted till dawn. In the darkness both American generals, Chandler and Winder, walked into the British force in the center, and were captured. With difficulty the two armies succeeded in recovering their order, and then retired in opposite directions. The British suffered severely, reporting twenty-three killed, one hundred and thirty-four wounded, and fifty-five missing, or two hundred and twelve men in all; but they safely regained Burlington Heights at dawn. The American loss was less in casualties, for it amounted only to fifty-five killed and wounded, and one hundred missing; but in results the battle at Stony Creek was equally disgraceful and decisive. The whole American force, leaving the dead unburied, fell back ten miles, where Major General Lewis took command in the afternoon of June 7. An hour later the British fleet under Sir James Yeo made its appearance, threatening to cut off Lewis's retreat. Indians hovered about. Boats and baggage were lost. Dearborn sent pressing orders to Lewis directing him to return, and on the morning of June 8 the division reached Fort George.

These mortifications prostrated Dearborn, whose strength had been steadily failing. June 8 he wrote to Armstrong: "My ill state of health renders it extremely painful to attend to the current duties; and unless my health improves soon, I fear I shall be compelled to retire to some place where my mind may be more at ease for a short time." June 10, his adjutant general, Winfield Scott, issued orders devolving on Major General Morgan Lewis the temporary command not only of the Niagara army but also of the Ninth Military district. "In addition to the debility and fever he has been afflicted with," wrote Dearborn's aid, S. S. Connor, to Secretary Armstrong, June 12, "he has, within the last twenty-four hours, experienced a violent spasmodic attack on his breast, which has obliged him to relinquish business altogether." "I have doubts whether he will ever again be fit for service," wrote Morgan Lewis to Armstrong, June 14; "he has been repeatedly in a state of convalescence, but relapses on the least agitation of mind." June 20 Dearborn himself wrote in a very despondent spirit both in regard to his health and to the military situation: "I have been so reduced in strength as to be incapable of any command. Brigadier General Boyd is the only general officer present."

The sudden departure of Morgan Lewis, ordered to Sackett's Harbor, left General Boyd for a few days to act as the general in command at Niagara. Boyd, though well known for his success at Tippecanoe, was not a favorite in the army. "A compound of ignorance, vanity, and petulance," wrote his late superior, Morgan Lewis, "with nothing to recommend him but that species of bravery in the field which is vaporing, boisterous, stifling reflection, blinding observation, and better adapted to the bully than the sailor."

Galled by complaints of the imbecility of the army, Boyd, with Dearborn's approval, June 23, detached Colonel Boerstler of the Fourteenth Infantry with some four hundred men and two field-pieces, to batter a stone house at Beaver Dam, some seventeen miles from Fort George. Early in the morning of June 24 Boerstler marched to Beaver Dam. There he found himself surrounded in the woods by hostile Indians, numbering according to British authority about two hundred. The Indians, annoying both front and rear, caused Boerstler to attempt retreat, but his retreat was stopped by a few militiamen, said to number fifteen. A small detachment of one hundred and fifty men came to reinforce Boerstler, and Lieutenant Fitzgibbon of the British Forty-ninth regiment, with forty-seven men, reinforced the Indians. Unable to extricate himself, and dreading dispersion and massacre, Boerstler decided to surrender; and his five hundred and forty men accordingly capitulated to a British lieutenant with two hundred and sixty Indians, militia, and regulars.

Dearborn reported the disaster as "an unfortunate and unaccountable event"; but of such events the list seemed endless. A worse disaster, equally due to Dearborn and Chauncey, occurred at the other end of the Lake. Had they attacked Kingston, as Armstrong intended, their movement would have covered Sackett's Harbor; but when they placed themselves a hundred and fifty miles to the westward of Sackett's Harbor, they could do nothing to protect it. Sackett's Harbor was an easy morning's sail from Kingston, and the capture of the American naval station was an object of infinite desire on the part of Sir George Prevost, since it would probably decide the result of the war.

Prevost, though not remarkable for audacity, could not throw away such an opportunity without ruining his reputation. He came to Kingston, and while Dearborn was preparing to capture Fort George in the night of May 26-27, Prevost embarked his whole regular force, eight hundred men all told, on Yeo's fleet at Kingston, set sail in the night, and at dawn of May 27 was in sight of Sackett's Harbor.

Had Yeo and Prevost acted with energy, they must have captured the Harbor without serious resistance. According to Sir George's official report, "light and adverse winds" prevented the ships from nearing the Fort until evening. Probably constitutional vacillation on the part of Sir James Yeo caused delay, for Prevost left the control wholly to him and Colonel Baynes.

At Sackett's Harbor about four hundred men of different regular regiments, and about two hundred and fifty Albany volunteers were in garrison; and a general alarm, given on appearance of the British fleet in the distance, brought some

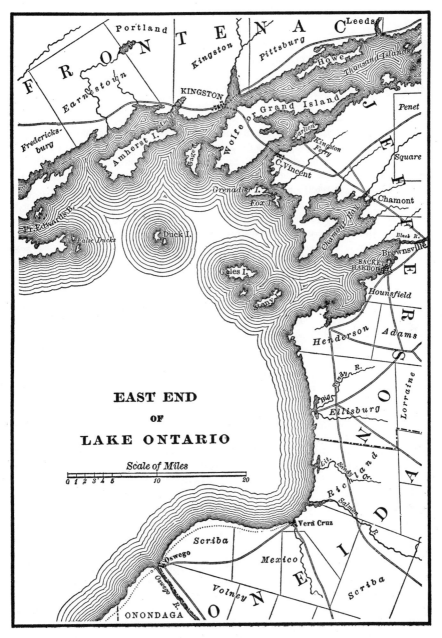

EAST END

OF

LAKE ONTARIO

Scale of Miles

0 1 2 3 4 5   10   20

hundreds of militia into the place; but the most important reinforcement was Jacob Brown, a brigadier general of State militia who lived in the neighborhood, and had been requested by Dearborn to take command in case of an emergency. Brown arrived at the Harbor in time to post the men in order of battle. Five hundred militia were placed at the point where the British were expected to land; the regulars were arranged in a second line; the forts were in the rear.

At dawn of May 28, under command of Colonel Baynes, the British grenadiers of the One Hundredth regiment landed gallantly under "so heavy and galling a fire from a numerous but almost invisible foe, as to render it impossible to halt for the artillery to come up." Pressing rapidly forward, without stopping to fire, the British regulars routed the militia and forced the second line back until they reached a block-house at the edge of the village, where a thirty-two pound gun was in position, flanked by log barracks and fallen timber. While Brown with difficulty held his own at the military barracks, the naval lieutenant in charge of the shipyard, being told that the battle was lost, set fire to the naval barracks, shipping, and storehouses. Brown's indignation of this act was intense.

"The burning of the marine barracks was as infamous a transaction as ever occurred among military men," he wrote to Dearborn. "The fire was set as our regulars met the enemy upon the main line; and if anything could have appalled these gallant men it would have been the flames in their rear. We have all, I presume, suffered in the public estimation in consequence of this disgraceful burning. The fact is, however, that the army is entitled to much higher praise than though it had not occurred. The navy are alone responsible for what happened on Navy Point, and it is fortunate for them that they have reputations sufficient to sustain the shock."

Brown's second line stood firm at the barracks, and the British attack found advance impossible. Sir George Prevost's report admitted his inability to go farther:

"A heavier fire than that of musketry having become necessary in order to force their last position, I had the mortification to learn that the continuation of light and adverse winds had prevented the co-operation of the ships, and that the gunboats were unequal to silence the enemy's elevated batteries, or to produce any effect on their block houses. Considering it therefore impracticable without such assistance to carry the strong works by which the post was defended, I reluctantly ordered the troops to leave a beaten enemy whom they had driven before them for upwards of three hours, and who did not venture to offer the slightest opposition to the re-embarkation, which was effected with proper deliberation and in perfect order."

If Sir George was correct in regarding the Americans as "a beaten enemy," his order of retreat to his own troops seemed improper; but his language showed that he used the words in a sense of his own, and Colonel Baynes's report gave no warrant for the British claim of a victory.

"At this point," said Baynes, "the further energies of the troops became unavailing. Their [American] blockhouses and stockaded battery could not be carried by assault, nor reduced by field-pieces had we been provided with them. . . . Seeing no object within our reach to attain that could compensate for the loss we were momentarily sustaining from the heavy fire of the enemy's cannon, I directed the troops to take up the position we had charged from. From this position we were ordered to re-embark, which was performed at our leisure and in perfect order, the enemy not presuming to show a single soldier without the limits of his fortress."

Another and confidential report was written by E. B. Brenton of Prevost's staff to the governor's military secretary, Noah Freer. After describing the progress of the battle until the British advance was stopped, Brenton said that Colonel Baynes came to Sir George to tell him that the men could not approach nearer the works with any prospect of success:

"It was however determined to collect all the troops at a point, to form the line, and to make an attack immediately upon the battery and barracks in front. For this purpose the men in advance were called in, the line formed a little without the reach of the enemy's musketry, and though evidently much fagged, was, after being supplied with fresh ammunition, again led in line. At this time I do not think the whole force collected in the lines exceeded five hundred men."

The attack was made, and part of the Hundred-and-Fourth regiment succeeded in getting shelter behind one of the American barracks, preparing for a farther advance. Sir George Prevost, under a fire which his aid described as tremendous —"I do not exaggerate when I tell you that the shot, both of musketry and grape, was falling about us like hail"—watched the American position through a glass, when, "at this time those who were left of the troops behind the barracks made a dash out to charge the enemy; but the fire was so destructive that they were instantly turned by it, and the retreat was sounded. Sir George, fearless of danger and disdaining to run or to suffer his men to run, repeatedly called out to them to retire in order; many, however, made off as fast as they could."

These reports agreed that the British attack was totally defeated, with severe loss, before the retreat was sounded. Such authorities should have silenced dispute; but Prevost had many enemies in Canada, and at that period of the war the British troops were unused to defeat. Both Canadians and English attacked the governor-general privately and publicly, freely charging him with having disgraced the service, and offering evidence of his want of courage in the action. Americans, though not interested in the defense of Prevost, could not fail to remark that the British and Canadian authorities who condemned him, assumed a condition of affairs altogether different from that accepted by American authorities. The official American reports not only supported the views taken by Prevost and Baynes of the hoplessness of the British attack, but added particulars which made Prevost's retreat necessary. General Brown's opinion was emphatic: "Had not General Prevost retired *most rapidly* under the guns of his vessels, he would never have returned to Kingston." These words were a part of Brown's official report. Writing to Dearborn he spoke with the same confidence:

"The militia were all rallied before the enemy gave way, and were marching perfectly in his view towards the rear of his right flank; and I am confident that even then, if Sir George had not retired with the utmost precipitation to his boats, he would have been cut off."

Unlike the Canadians, Brown thought Prevost's conduct correct and necessary, but was by no means equally complimentary to Sir James Yeo, whom he blamed greatly for failing to join in the battle. The want of wind which Yeo alleged in excuse, Brown flatly denied. From that time Brown entertained and freely expressed contempt for Yeo, as he seemed also to feel little respect for Chauncey. His experience with naval administration on both sides led him to expect nothing but inefficiency from either.

Whatever were the true causes of Prevost's failure, Americans could not admit that an expedition which cost the United States so much, and which so nearly succeeded, was discreditable to the British governor-general or was abandoned without sufficient reason. The British return of killed and wounded proved the correctness of Prevost, Baynes, and Brown in their opinion of the necessity of retreat. According to the report of Prevost's severest critics, he carried less than seven hundred and fifty rank-and-file to Sackett's Harbor. The returns showed forty-four rank-and-file killed; one hundred and seventy-two wounded, and thirteen missing—in all, two hundred and twenty-nine men, or nearly one man in three. The loss in officers was relatively even more severe; and the total loss in an aggregate which could hardly have numbered much more than eight hundred and fifty men all told, amounted to two hundred and fifty-nine killed, wounded, and missing, leaving Prevost less than six hundred men to escape, in the face of twice their numbers and under the fire of heavy guns.

The British attack was repulsed, and Jacob Brown received much credit as well as a commission of brigadier general in the United States Army for his success; but the injury inflicted by the premature destruction at the navy yard was very great, and was sensibly felt. Such a succession of ill news could not but affect the Government. The repeated failures to destroy the British force at Niagara; the disasters of Chandler, Winder, and Boerstler; the narrow and partial escape of Sackett's Harbor; the total incapacity of Dearborn caused by fever and mortification—all these evils were not the only or the greatest subjects for complaint. The two commanders, Dearborn and Chauncey, had set aside the secretary's plan of campaign, and had substituted one of their own, on the express ground of their superior information. While affirming that the garrison at Kingston had been reinforced to a strength three or four times as great as was humanly possible, they had asserted that the capture of York would answer their purpose as well as the capture of Kingston, to "give us the complete command of the Lake." They captured York, April 27, but the British fleet appeared June 6, and took from them the command of the Lake. These miscalculations or misstatements, and the disasters resulting from them, warranted the removal of Chauncey as well as Dearborn from command; but the brunt of dissatisfaction fell on Dearborn alone. Both Cabinet and Congress agreed in insisting on Dearborn's retirement, and the President was obliged to consent. July 6 Secretary Armstrong wrote:

"I have the President's orders to express to you the decision that you retire from the command of District No. 9, and of the troops within the same, until your health be re-established and until further orders."

CHAPTER IX
WILKINSON'S CAMPAIGN

Armstrong's embarrassment was great in getting rid of the generals whom Madison and Eustis left on his hands. Dearborn was one example of what he was obliged to endure, but Wilkinson was a worse. According to Armstrong's account, New Orleans was not believed to be safe in Wilkinson's keeping. The senators from Louisiana, Tennessee, and Kentucky remonstrated to the President, and the President ordered his removal. Armstrong and Wilkinson had been companions in arms, and had served with Gates at Saratoga. For many reasons Armstrong wished not unnecessarily to mortify Wilkinson, and in conveying to him, March 10, the abrupt order to proceed with the least possible delay to the headquarters of Major General Dearborn at Sackett's Harbor, the Secretary of War added, March 12, a friendly letter of advice:

"Why should you remain in your land of cypress when patriotism and ambition equally invite to one where grows the laurel? Again, the men of the North and East want you; those of the South and West are less sensible of your merits and less anxious to have you among them. I speak to you with a frankness due to you and to myself, and again advise, Come to the North, and come quickly! If our cards be well played, we may renew the scene of Saratoga."

The phrase was curious. Saratoga suggested defeated invasion rather than conquest; the surrender of a British army in the heart of New York rather than the capture of Montreal. The request for Wilkinson's aid was disheartening. No one knew better than Armstrong the feebleness of Wilkinson's true character. "The selection of this unprincipled imbecile was not the blunder of Secretary Armstrong," said Winfield Scott long afterward; but the idea that Wilkinson could be chief-of-staff to Dearborn—that one weak man could give strength to another—was almost as surprising as the selection of Wilkinson to chief command would have been. Armstrong did not intend that Wilkinson should command more than a division under Dearborn; but he must have foreseen that in the event of Dearborn's illness or incapacity, Wilkinson would become by seniority general-in-chief.

Wilkinson at New Orleans received Armstrong's letter of March 10 only May 19, and started, June 10, for Washington, where he arrived July 31, having consumed the greater part of the summer in the journey. On arriving at Washington he found that Dearborn had been removed and that he was himself by seniority in command of the Ninth Military District. This result of Dearborn's removal was incalculably mischievous, for if its effect on Wilkinson's vanity was unfortunate, its influence on the army was fatal. Almost every respectable officer of the old service regarded Wilkinson with antipathy or contempt.

Armstrong's ill-fortune obliged him also to place in the position of next importance Wilkinson's pronounced enemy, Wade Hampton. A major general was required to take command on Lake Champlain, and but one officer of that rank claimed employment or could be employed; and Wade Hampton was accordingly ordered to Plattsburg. Of all the major generals Hampton was probably the best; but his faults were serious. Proud and sensitive even for a South Carolinian; irritable, often harsh, sometimes unjust, but the soul of honor,

[91]

Hampton was rendered wholly intractable wherever Wilkinson was concerned, by the long-standing feud which had made the two generals for years the heads of hostile sections in the army. Hampton loathed Wilkinson. At the time of his appointment to command on Lake Champlain he had no reason to expect that Wilkinson would be his superior; but though willing and even wishing to serve under Dearborn, he accepted only on the express understanding that his was a distinct and separate command, and that his orders were to come directly from the War Department. Only in case of a combined movement uniting different armies was he to yield to the rule of seniority. With that agreement he left Washington, June 15, and assumed command, July 3, on Lake Champlain.

Nearly a month afterward Wilkinson arrived in Washington, and reported at the War Department. By that time Armstrong had lost whatever chance he previously possessed of drawing the army at Niagara back to a position on the enemy's line of supply. Three insuperable difficulties stood in his way—the season was too late; the army was too weak; and the generals were incompetent. Armstrong found his generals the chief immediate obstacle, and struggled perseveringly and good-humoredly to overcome it. Wilkinson began, on arriving at Washington, by showing a fancy for continuing the campaign at Niagara. Armstrong was obliged to give an emphatic order, dated August 8, that Kingston should be the primary object of the campaign, but he left Wilkinson at liberty to go there by almost any route, even by way of Montreal. Disappointed at the outset by finding Wilkinson slow to accept responsibility or decided views, he was not better pleased when the new general began his duties in Military District No. 9.

Wilkinson left Washington August 11 and no sooner did he reach Albany than he hastened to write, August 16, two letters to General Hampton, assuming that every movement of that general was directly dependent on Wilkinson's orders. Considering the relations between the two men, these letters warranted the inference that Wilkinson intended to drive Hampton out of his Military District and if possible from the service. Hampton instantly leaped to that conclusion, and wrote to Armstrong, August 23, offering his resignation in case Wilkinson's course was authorized by government. Wilkinson also wrote to the secretary August 30, substantially avowing his object to be what Hampton supposed:

"You have copies of my letters to Major-General Hampton, which I know he has received, yet I have no answer. The reflection which naturally occurs is that if I am authorized to command he is bound to obey; and if he will not respect the obligation, he should be turned out of the service."

Armstrong pacified Hampton by promising once more that all his orders and reports should pass through the Department. Hampton promised to serve cordially and vigorously through the campaign, but he believed himself intended for a sacrifice, and declared his intention of resigning as soon as the campaign was ended. Wilkinson, after having at Albany provoked this outburst, started for Sackett's Harbor, where he arrived August 20.

At Sackett's Harbor Wilkinson found several general officers. Morgan Lewis was there in command, Commodore Chauncey was there with his fleet. Jacob

Brown was also present by virtue of his recent appointment as brigadier general. The quartermaster general, Robert Swartwout, a brother of Burr's friend who went to New Orleans, was posted there. Wilkinson summoned these officers to a council of war August 26, which deliberated on the different plans of campaign proposed to it, and unanimously decided in favor of one called by Armstrong "No. 3 of the plans proposed by the government." As defined in Wilkinson's language, the scheme was:

"To rendezvous the whole of the troops on the Lake in this vicinity, and in co-operation with our squadron to make a bold feint upon Kingston, slip down the St. Lawrence, lock up the enemy in our rear to starve or surrender, or oblige him to follow us without artillery, baggage, or provisions, or eventually to lay down his arms; to sweep the St. Lawrence of armed craft, and in concert with the division under Major General Hampton to take Montreal."

Orders were given, August 25, for providing river transport for seven thousand men, forty field pieces, and twenty heavy guns, to be in readiness by September 15.

The proposed expedition closely imitated General Amherst's expedition against Montreal in 1760, with serious differences of relative situation. After Wolfe had captured Quebec and hardly twenty-five hundred French troops remained to defend Montreal, in the month of July Amherst descended the river from Lake Ontario with more than ten thousand men, chiefly British veterans, capturing every fortified position as he went. Wilkinson's council of war proposed to descend the river in October or November with seven thousand men, leaving a hostile fleet and fortresses in their rear, and running past every fortified position to arrive in the heart of a comparatively well populated country, held by a force greater than their own, with Quebec to support it, while Wilkinson would have no certain base of supplies, reinforcements, or path of escape. Knowledge of Wilkinson's favorite Quintus Curtius or of Armstrong's familiar Jomini was not required to satisfy any intelligent private, however newly recruited, that under such circumstances the army would be fortunate to escape destruction.

Wilkinson next went to Niagara, where he arrived September 4, and where he found the army in a bad condition, with Boyd still in command, but restrained by the President's orders within a strict defensive. Wilkinson remained nearly a month at Fort George making the necessary preparations for a movement. He fell ill of fever, but returned October 2 to Sackett's Harbor, taking with him all the regular troops at Niagara. At that time Chauncey again controlled the Lake.

Secretary Armstrong also came to Sackett's Harbor, September 5, and established the War Department at that remote point for nearly two months. When Wilkinson arrived, October 2, Armstrong's difficulties began. Wilkinson, then fifty-six years old, was broken by the Lake fever. "He was so much indisposed in mind and body," according to Brigadier General Boyd, "that in any other service he would have perhaps been superseded in his command." According to Wilkinson's story, he told Secretary Armstrong that he was incapable of commanding the army and offered to retire from it; but the secretary said there was no one to take his place and he could not be spared. In private Armstrong was believed to express himself more bluntly, and Wilkinson was told that the secre-

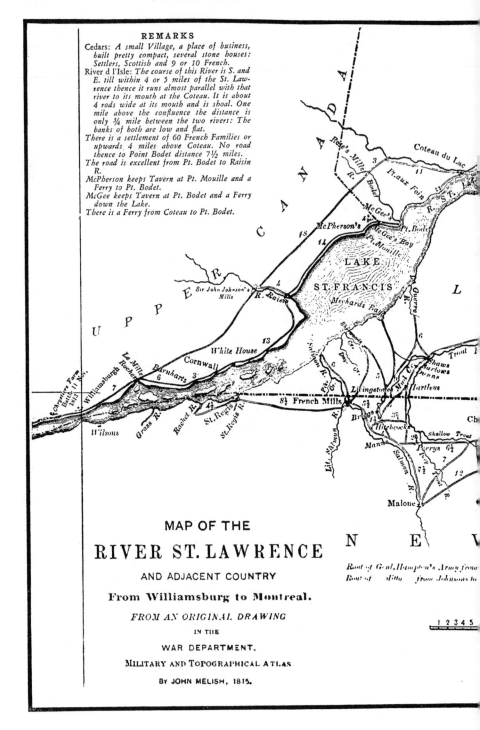

REMARKS

Cedars: *A small Village, a place of business, built pretty compact, several stone houses: Settlers, Scottish and 9 or 10 French.*

River d l'Isle: *The course of this River is S. and E. till within 4 or 5 miles of the St. Lawrence thence it runs almost parallel with that river to its mouth at the Coteau. It is about 4 rods wide at its mouth and is shoal. One mile above the confluence the distance is only 3/4 mile between the two rivers: The banks of both are low and flat.*

There is a settlement of 60 French Families or upwards 4 miles above Coteau. No road thence to Point Bodet distance 7 1/2 miles.

The road is excellent from Pt. Bodet to Raisin R.

McPherson keeps Tavern at Pt. Mouille and a Ferry to Pt. Bodet.

McGee keeps Tavern at Pt. Bodet and a Ferry down the Lake.

There is a Ferry from Coteau to Pt. Bodet.

MAP OF THE

RIVER ST. LAWRENCE

AND ADJACENT COUNTRY

From Williamsburg to Montreal.

FROM AN ORIGINAL DRAWING

IN THE

WAR DEPARTMENT.

MILITARY AND TOPOGRAPHICAL ATLAS

BY JOHN MELISH, 1815.

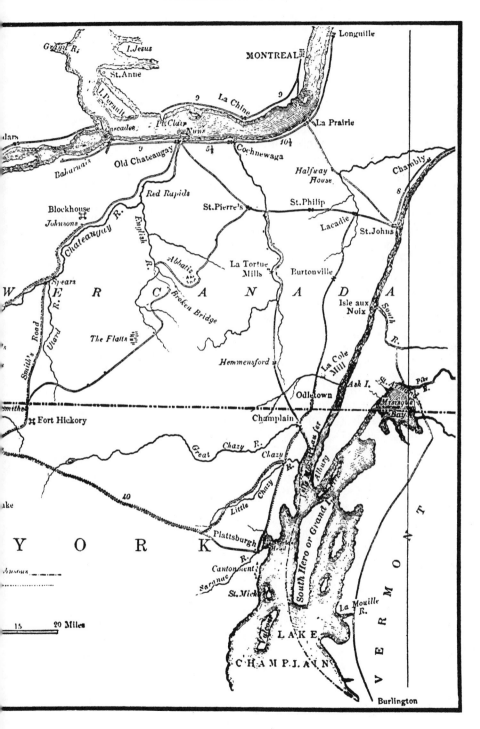

tary said: "I would feed the old man with pap sooner than leave him behind."
Wilkinson's debility did not prevent him from giving orders, or from becoming
jealous and suspicious of everyone, but chiefly of Armstrong. Whatever was
suggested by Armstrong was opposed by Wilkinson. Before returning to Sackett's
Harbor, October 4, Wilkinson favored an attack on Kingston. On reaching
Sackett's Harbor, finding that Armstrong also favored attacking Kingston, Wilkinson argued "against my own judgment" in favor of passing Kingston and
descending upon Montreal. Ten days afterward Armstrong changed his mind.
Yeo had succeeded in returning to Kingston bringing reinforcements.

"He will bring with him about fifteen hundred effectives," wrote Armstrong;
"and thanks to the storm and our snail-like movements down the Lake, they will
be there before we can reach it. The manoeuvre intended is lost, so far as regards
Kingston. What we now do against that place must be done by hard blows, at
some risk."

Accordingly, October 19, Armstrong wrote to Wilkinson a letter advising
abandonment of the attack on Kingston, and an effort at "grasping the safer and
the greater object below."

"I call it the safer and greater object, because at Montreal you find the
weaker place and the smaller force to encounter; at Montreal you meet a fresh,
unexhausted, efficient reinforcement of four thousand men; at Montreal you
approach your own resources, and establish between you and them an easy and
an expeditious intercourse; at Montreal you occupy a point which must be gained
in carrying your attacks home to the purposes of the war, and which, if seized
now, will save one campaign; at Montreal you hold a position which completely
severs the enemy's line of operations, which shuts up the Ottawa as well as the
St. Lawrence against him, and which while it restrains all below, withers and
perishes all above itself."

As Armstrong veered toward Montreal Wilkinson turned decidedly toward
Kingston, and wrote the same day to the secretary a letter of remonstrance,
closing by a significant remark:

"Personal considerations would make me prefer a visit to Montreal to the
attack of Kingston; but before I abandon this attack, which by my instructions
I am ordered to make, it is necessary to my justification that you should by the
authority of the President direct the operations of the army under my command
particularly against Montreal."

The hint was strong that Wilkinson believed Armstrong to be trying to evade
responsibility, as Armstrong believed Wilkinson to be trying to shirk it. Both
insinuations were probably well-founded; neither Armstrong nor Wilkinson
expected to capture Kingston, and still less Montreal. Wilkinson plainly said
as much at the time. "I speak conjecturally," he wrote; "but should we surmount
every obstacle in descending the river we shall advance upon Montreal ignorant
of the force arrayed against us, and in case of misfortune, having no retreat,
the army must surrender at discretion." Armstrong's conduct was more extraordinary than Wilkinson's, and could not be believed except on his own evidence. He not only looked for no capture of Montreal, but before writing his
letter of October 19 to Wilkinson, he had given orders for preparing winter

quarters for the army sixty or eighty miles above Montreal, and did this without informing Wilkinson. In later years he wrote:

"Suspecting early in October, from the lateness of the season, the inclemency of the weather, and the continued indisposition of the commanding general, that the campaign then in progress would terminate as it did—'with the disgrace of doing nothing, but without any material diminution of physical power'—the Secretary of War, then at Sackett's Harbor, hastened to direct Major General Hampton to employ a brigade of militia attached to his command, in constructing as many huts as would be sufficient to cover an army of ten thousand men during the winter."

The order dated October 16 and addressed to the quartermaster general prescribed the cantonment of ten thousand men within the limits of Canada, and plainly indicated the secretary's expectation that the army could not reach Montreal. In other ways Armstrong showed the same belief more openly.

All the available troops on or near Lake Ontario were concentrated at Sackett's Harbor about the middle of October, and did not exceed seven thousand effectives, or eight thousand men. "I calculate on six thousand combatants," wrote Wilkinson after starting, "exclusive of Scott and Randolph, neither of whom will, I fear, be up in season." The army was divided into four brigades under Generals Boyd, Swartwout, Jacob Brown, and Covington—the latter a Maryland man, forty-five years old, who entered the service in 1809 as lieutenant colonel of dragoons. The brigades of Boyd and Covington formed a division commanded by Major General Morgan Lewis. The second division was intended for Major General Hampton; a reserve under Colonel Macomb, and a park of artillery under Brigadier General Moses Porter completed the organization.

The men were embarked in bateaux, October 17, at Henderson's Bay, to the westward of Sackett's Harbor. The weather had been excessively stormy, and continued so. The first resting-point to be reached was Grenadier Island at the entrance of the St. Lawrence, only sixteen or eighteen miles from the starting-point; but the bateaux were dispersed by heavy gales of wind, October 18, 19 and 20, and the last detachments did not reach Grenadier Island until November 3. "All our hopes have been nearly blasted," wrote Wilkinson October 24; but at length, November 5, the expedition, numbering nearly three hundred boats, having safely entered the river, began the descent from French Creek. That day they moved forty miles and halted about midnight six miles above Ogdensburg. The next day was consumed in running the flotilla past Ogdensburg under the fire of the British guns at Prescott. The boats floated down by night and the troops marched by land. November 7 the army halted at the White House about twenty miles below Ogdensburg. There Wilkinson called a council of war, November 8, to consider whether the expedition should proceed. Lewis, Boyd, Brown, and Swartwout voted simply in favor of attacking Montreal. Covington and Porter were of the opinion "that we proceed from this place under great danger . . . but . . . we know of no other alternative."

More than any other cause, Armstrong's conduct warranted Wilkinson in considering the campaign at an end. If the attack on Montreal was seriously intended, every motive required Armstrong to join Hampton at once in advance of Wilkinson's expedition. No one knew so well as he the necessity of some authority to interpose between the tempers and pretensions of these two men in case a joint campaign were to be attempted, or to enforce coöperation on either side. Good faith toward Hampton, even more than toward Wilkinson, required that the secretary who had led them into such a situation should not desert them. Yet Armstrong, after waiting till Wilkinson was fairly at Grenadier Island, began to prepare for return to Washington. From the village of Antwerp, half way between Sackett's Harbor and Ogdensburg, the secretary wrote to Wilkinson, October 27, "Should my fever continue I shall not be able to approach you as I intended." Three days later he wrote again from Denmark on the road to Albany:

"I rejoice that your difficulties are so far surmounted as to enable you to say with assurance when you will pass Prescott. I should have met you there; but bad roads, worse weather, and a considerable degree of illness admonished me against receding farther from a point where my engagements call me about the 1st proximo. The resolution of treading back my steps was taken at Antwerp."

From Albany Armstrong wrote, November 12, for the last time, "in the fulness of my faith that you are in Montreal," that he had sent orders to Hampton to effect a junction with the river expedition. Such letters and orders, whatever Armstrong meant by them, were certain to impress both Wilkinson and Hampton with a conviction that the secretary intended to throw upon them the whole responsibility for the failure of an expedition which he as well as they knew to be hopeless.

Doubtless a vigorous general might still have found means if not to take Montreal, at least to compel the British to evacuate Upper Canada; but Wilkinson was naturally a weak man, and during the descent of the river he was excessively ill, never able to make a great exertion. Every day his difficulties increased. Hardly had his flotilla begun its descent when a number of British gunboats commanded by Captain Mulcaster, the most energetic officer in the British naval service on the Lake, slipping through Chauncey's blockade, appeared in Wilkinson's rear, and caused him much annoyance. Eight hundred British rank-and-file from Kingston and Prescott were with Mulcaster, and at every narrow pass of the river, musketry and artillery began to open on Wilkinson from the British bank. Progress became slow. November 7, Macomb was landed on the north bank with twelve hundred men to clear away these obstructions. The day and night of November 8 were consumed at the White House in passing troops across the river. Brown's brigade was landed on the north shore to reinforce Macomb. The boats were delayed to keep pace with Brown's march on shore, and made but eleven miles November 9, and the next day, November 10, fell down only to the Long Saut, a continuous rapid eight miles in length. The enemy pressed close, and while Brown marched in advance to clear the bank along the rapid, Boyd was ordered to take all the other troops and protect the rear.

The flotilla stopped on the night of November 10 near a farm called Chrystler's on the British bank; and the next morning, November 11, at half-past ten o'clock Brown having announced that all was clear below, Wilkinson was about to order the flotilla to run the rapids when General Boyd sent word that the enemy in the rear were advancing in column. Wilkinson was on his boat, unable to leave his bed; Morgan Lewis was in no better condition; and Boyd was left to fight a battle as he best could. Boyd never had the confidence of the army; Brown was said to have threatened to resign rather than serve under him, and Winfield Scott, who was that day with Macomb and Brown in the advance, described Boyd as amiable and respectable in a subordinate position, but "vacillating and imbecile beyond all endurance as a chief under high responsibilities."

The opportunity to capture or destroy Mulcaster and his eight hundred men was brilliant, and warranted Wilkinson in turning back his whole force to accomplish it. Boyd actually employed three brigades, and made an obstinate but not united or well-supported attempt to crush the enemy. Colonel Ripley with the Twenty-first regiment drove in the British skirmishers, and at half-past two o'clock the battle became general. At half-past four, after a stubborn engagement, General Covington was killed; his brigade gave way, and the whole American line fell back, beaten and almost routed.

This defeat was the least creditable of the disasters suffered by American arms during the war. No excuse or palliation was ever offered for it. The American army consisted wholly of regulars, and all the generals belonged to the regular service. Wilkinson could hardly have had less than three thousand men with him, after allowing for his detachments, and was alone to blame if he had not more. Boyd, according to his own account, had more than twelve hundred men and two field-pieces under his immediate command on shore. The reserve, under Colonel Upham of the Eleventh regiment, contained six hundred rank-and-file, with four field-pieces. Wilkinson's official report admitted that eighteen hundred rank-and-file were engaged; Colonel Walbach, his adjutant general, admitted two thousand, while Swartwout thought that twenty-one hundred were in action. The American force was certainly not less than two thousand with six field-pieces.

The British force officially reported by Lieutenant Colonel Morrison of the Eighty-ninth regiment, who was in command, consisted of eight hundred rank-and-file, and thirty Indians. The rank-and-file consisted of three hundred and forty-two men of the Forty-ninth regiment, about as many more of the Eighty-ninth, and some Canadian troops. They had three six-pound field-pieces, and were supported on their right flank by gunboats.

On the American side the battle was ill fought both by the generals and by the men. Wilkinson and Morgan Lewis, the two major generals, who were ill on their boats, never gave an order. Boyd, who commanded, brought his troops into action by detachments, and the men, on meeting unexpected resistance, broke and fled. The defeat was bloody as well as mortifying. Wilkinson reported one hundred and two killed, and two hundred and thirty-seven wounded, but strangely reported no missing, although the British occupied the field of battle and claimed upward of one hundred prisoners. Morrison reported twenty-two killed, one hundred and forty-eight wounded, and twelve missing. The American loss was twice that of the British, and Wilkinson's reports were so little to be trusted that the loss might well have been greater than he represented it. The story had no redeeming incident.

If three brigades, numbering two thousand men, were beaten at Chrystler's farm by eight hundred British and Canadians, the chance that Wilkinson could capture Montreal, even with ten thousand men, was small. The conduct of the army showed its want of self-confidence. Late as it was, in the dusk of the evening Boyd hastened to escape across the river. "The troops being much exhausted," reported Wilkinson, "it was considered most convenient that they should embark, and that the dragoons with the artillery should proceed by land. The embarkation took place without the smallest molestation from the enemy, and the flotilla made a harbor near the head of the Saut on the opposite shore." In truth, neither Wilkinson nor his adjutant gave the order of embarkation, nor was Boyd willing to admit it as his. Apparently the army by common consent embarked without orders.

Early the next morning, November 12, the Flotilla ran the rapids and rejoined Brown and Macomb near Cornwall, where Wilkinson learned that General Hampton had taken the responsibility of putting an end to an undertaking which had not yet entered upon its serious difficulties.

Four months had passed since Hampton took command on Lake Champlain. When he first reached Burlington, July 3, neither men nor material were ready, nor was even a naval force present to cover his weakness. While he was camped at Burlington, a British fleet, with about a thousand regulars, entered the Lake from the Isle aux Noix and the Richelieu River, and plundered the American magazines at Plattsburg, July 31, sweeping the Lake clear of American shipping. Neither Hampton's army nor McDonough's small fleet ventured to offer resistance. Six weeks afterward, in the middle of September, Hampton had but about four thousand men, in bad condition and poor discipline.

Wilkinson, though unable to begin his own movement, was earnest that Hampton should advance on Montreal. Apparently in order to assist Wilkinson's plans, Hampton moved his force, September 19, to the Canada line. Finding that a drought had caused want of water on the direct road to Montreal, Hampton decided to march his army westward to the Chateaugay River, forty or fifty miles, and establish himself there, September 26, in a position equally threatening to Montreal and to the British line of communication up the St. Lawrence. Armstrong approved the movement, and Hampton remained three weeks at Chateaugay, building roads and opening lines of communication while waiting for Wilkinson to move.

October 16 Armstrong ordered Hampton, in view of Wilkinson's probable descent of the river, to "approach the mouth of the Chateaugay, or other point which shall better favor our junction, and hold the enemy in check." Hampton instantly obeyed, and moved down the Chateaugay to a point about fifteen miles from its mouth. There he established his army, October 22, and employed the next two days in completing his road, and getting up his artillery and stores.

Hampton's movements annoyed the British authorities at Montreal. Even while he was still within American territory, before he advanced from Chateaugay Four Corners, Sir George Prevost reported, October 8, to his government:

"The position of Major-General Hampton at the Four Corners on the Chateaugay River, and which he continued to occupy, either with the whole or a part of his force, from the latest information I have been able to obtain from thence, is highly judicious—as at the same time that he threatens Montreal and obliges me to concentrate a considerable body of troops in this vicinity to protect it, he has it in his power to molest the communication with the Upper Province, and impede the progress of the supplies required there for the Navy and Army."

If this was the case, October 8, when Hampton was still at Chateaugay, fifty miles from its mouth, the annoyance must have been much greater when he advanced, October 21, to Spear's, within ten miles of the St. Lawrence on his left, and fifteen from the mouth of the Chateaugay. Hampton accomplished more than was expected. He held a position equally well adapted to threaten Montreal, to disturb British communication with Upper Canada, and to succor Wilkinson.

That Hampton, with only four thousand men, should do more than this, could not fairly be required. The defenses of Montreal were such as required ten times his force to overcome. The regular troops defending Montreal were not stationed in the town itself, which was sufficiently protected by a broad river and rapids. They were chiefly at Chambly, St. John's, Isle aux Noix, or other points on the Richelieu River, guarding the most dangerous line of approach from Lake Champlain; or they were at Coteau du Lac on the St. Lawrence about twenty miles northwest of Hampton's position. According to the general weekly return of British forces serving in the Montreal District under command of Major General Sir R. H. Sheaffe, September 15, 1813, the aggregate rank-and-file present for duty was five thousand seven hundred and fifty-two. At Montreal were none but sick, with the general staff. At Chambly were nearly thirteen hundred effectives; at St. John's nearly eight hundred; at Isle aux Noix about nine hundred. Excluding the garrison at Prescott, and including the force at Coteau du Lac, Major General Sheaffe commanded just five thousand effectives.

Besides the enrolled troops, Prevost could muster a considerable number of sailors and marines for the defense of Montreal; and his resources in artillery, boats, fortifications, and supplies of all sorts were ample. In addition to the embodied troops, Prevost could count upon the militia, a force almost as good as regulars for the defense of a forest-clad country where axes were as effective as musketry in stopping an invading army. In Prevost's letter to Bathurst of October 8 announcing Hampton's invasion, the governor general said:

"Measures had been in the mean time taken by Major-General Sir Roger Sheaffe commanding in his district, to resist the advance of the enemy by moving the whole of the troops under his command nearer to the frontier line, and by calling out about three thousand of the sedentary militia. I thought it necessary to increase this latter force to nearly eight thousand by embodying the whole of the sedentary militia upon the frontier, this being in addition to the six battalions of incorporated militia amounting to five thousand men; and it is with peculiar satisfaction I have to report to your Lordship that his Majesty's Canadian subjects have a second time answered the call to arms in defence of their country with a zeal and alacrity beyond all praise."

Thus the most moderate estimate of the British force about Montreal gave at least fifteen thousand rank-and-file under arms. Besides this large array of men, Prevost was amply protected by natural defenses. If Hampton had reached the St. Lawrence at Caughnawaga, he would still have been obliged to cross the St. Lawrence, more than two miles wide, under the fire of British batteries and gunboats. Hampton had no transports. Prevost had bateaux and vessels of every description, armed and unarmed, above and below the rapids, besides two river vessels constantly plying to Quebec.

Hampton's command consisted of four thousand infantry new to service, two hundred dragoons, and artillery. With such a force, his chance of suffering a fatal reverse was much greater than that of his reaching the St. Lawrence. His position at the Chateaugay was not less perilous than that of Harrison on the Maumee, and far more so than that which cost Dearborn so many disasters at Niagara.

The British force in Hampton's immediate front consisted at first of only three hundred militia, who could make no resistance, and retired as Hampton advanced. When Hampton made his movement to Spear's, Lieutenant Colonel de Salaberry in his front commanded about eight hundred men, and immediately entrenched himself and obstructed the road with abattis. Hampton felt the necessity of dislodging Salaberry, who might at any moment be reinforced; and accordingly in the night of October 25, sent a strong force to flank Salaberry's position, while he should himself attack it in front.

The flanking party failed to find its way, and the attack in front was not pressed. The American loss did not exceed fifty men. The British loss was reported as twenty-five. Sir George Prevost and his officers were greatly pleased by their success; but Prevost did not attempt to molest Hampton, who fell back by slow marches to Chateaugay, where he waited to hear from the Government. The British generals at Montreal showed little energy in thus allowing Hampton to escape; and the timidity of their attitude before Hampton's little army was the best proof of the incompetence alleged against Prevost by many of his contemporaries.

Hampton's retreat was due more to the conduct of Armstrong than to the check at Spear's or to the movements of Prevost. At the moment when he moved against Salaberry, October 25, a messenger arrived from Sackett's Harbor, bringing instructions from the quartermaster general, for building huts for ten thousand men for winter quarters. These orders naturally roused Hampton's suspicions that no serious movement against Montreal was intended.

"The papers sunk my hopes," he wrote to Armstrong, November 1, "and raised serious doubts of receiving that efficacious support that had been anticipated. I would have recalled the column, but it was in motion, and the darkness of the night rendered it impracticable."

In a separate letter of the same date which Hampton sent to Armstrong by Colonel King, assuming that the campaign was at an end, he carried out his declared purpose of resigning. "Events," he said, "have had no tendency to change my opinion of the destiny intended for me, nor my determination to retire from a service where I can neither feel security nor expect honor. The campaign I consider substantially at an end." The implication that Armstrong meant to sacrifice him was certainly disrespectful, and deserved punishment; but when Colonel King, bearing these letters, arrived in the neighborhood of Ogdensburg, he found that Armstrong had already done what Hampton reproached him for intending to do. He had retired to Albany, "suspecting . . . that the campaign . . . would terminate as it did."

A week afterward, November 8, Hampton received a letter from Wilkinson, written from Ogdensburg, asking him to forward supplies and march his troops to some point of junction on the river below St. Regis. Hampton replied from Chateaugay that he had no supplies to forward; and as, under such circumstances, his army could not throw itself on Wilkinson's scanty means, he should fall back on Plattsburg, and attempt to act against the enemy on some other road to be indicated. Wilkinson received the letter on his arrival at Cornwall, November 12, the day after his defeat at Chrystler's farm; and with extraordinary energy moved the whole expedition the next day to French Mills, six or seven miles up the Salmon River, within the United States lines, where it went into winter quarters.

Armstrong and Wilkinson made common cause in throwing upon Hampton the blame of failure. Wilkinson at first ordered Hampton under arrest, but after reflection decided to throw the responsibility upon Armstrong. The Secretary declined to accept it, but consented after some delay to accept Hampton's resignation when renewed in March, 1814. Wilkinson declared that Hampton's conduct had blasted his dawning hopes and the honor of the army. Armstrong sneered at Wilkinson for seizing the pretext for abandoning his campaign. Both the generals believed that Armstrong had deliberately led them into an impossible undertaking, and deserted them in order to shift the blame of failure from himself. Hampton behaved with dignity, and allowed his opinion to be seen only in his contemptuous silence; nor did Armstrong publicly blame Hampton's conduct until Hampton was dead. The only happy result of the campaign was to remove all the older generals—Wilkinson, Hampton and Morgan Lewis—from active service.

The bloodless failure of an enterprise which might have ended in extreme disaster was not the whole cost of Armstrong's and Wilkinson's friendship and quarrels. In November nearly all the regular forces, both British and American, had been drawn toward the St. Lawrence. Even Harrison and his troops, who reached Buffalo October 24, were sent to Sackett's Harbor, November 16, to protect the navy. Not a regiment of the United States army was to be seen between Sackett's Harbor and Detroit. The village of Niagara and Fort George on the British side were held by a few hundred volunteers commanded by Brigadier General McClure of the New York militia. As long as Wilkinson and Hampton threatened Montreal, Niagara was safe, and needed no further attention.

After November 13, when Wilkinson and Hampton withdrew from Canada, while the American army forgot its enemy in the bitterness of its own personal feuds, the British generals naturally thought of recovering their lost posts on the Niagara River. McClure, who occupied Fort George and the small town of Newark under its guns, saw his garrison constantly diminishing. Volunteers refused to serve longer on any conditions. The War Department ordered no reinforcements, although ten or twelve thousand soldiers were lying idle at French Mills and Plattsburg. December 10 McClure had about sixty men of the Twenty-fourth infantry, and some forty volunteers, at Fort George, while the number of United States troops present for duty at Fort George, Fort Niagara, Niagara village, Black Rock, and Buffalo, to protect the people and the magazines, amounted to four companies, or three hundred and twenty-four men.

As early as October 4 Armstrong authorized McClure to warn the inhabitants of Newark that their town might suffer destruction in case the defense of Fort George should render such a measure proper. No other orders were given, but Wilkinson repeatedly advised that Fort George should be evacuated, and Armstrong did nothing to protect it, further than to issue a requisition from Albany, November 25, upon the Governor of New York for one thousand militia.

The British, though not rapid in their movements, were not so slow as the Americans. Early in December Lieutenant General Gordon Drummond came from Kingston to York, and from York to the head of the Lake where the British had maintained themselves since losing the Niagara posts in May. Meanwhile General Vincent had sent Colonel Murray with five hundred men to retake Fort George. McClure at Fort George, December 10, hearing that Murray had approached within ten miles, evacuated the post and crossed the river to Fort Niagara; but before doing so he burned the town of Newark and as much as he could of Queenston, turning the inhabitants, in extreme cold, into the open air. He alleged as his motive to wish to deprive the enemy of winter quarters; yet he did not destroy the tents or military barracks, and he acted without authority, for Armstrong had authorized him to burn Newark only in case he meant to defend Fort George.

"The enemy is much exasperated, and will make a descent on this frontier if possible," wrote McClure from the village of Niagara, December 13; "but I shall watch them close with my handful of men until a reinforcement of militia and volunteers arrives. . . . I am not a little apprehensive that the enemy will take advantage of the exposed condition of Buffalo and our shipping there. My whole effective force on this extensive frontier does not exceed two hundred and fifty men."

Five days passed and still no reinforcements arrived, and no regular troops were even ordered to start for Niagara. "I apprehended an attack," wrote McClure; and he retired thirty miles to Buffalo, "with a view of providing for the defence." On the night of December 18 Colonel Murray, with five hundred and fifty regular rank-and-file, crossed the river from Fort George unperceived; surprised the sentinels on the glacis and at the gates of Fort Niagara; rushed through the main gate; and, with a loss of eight men killed and wounded, captured the fortress with some three hundred and fifty prisoners.

Nothing could be said on the American side in defense or excuse of this disgrace. From Armstrong at the War Department to Captain Leonard who commanded the fort, every one concerned in the transaction deserved whatever punishment the law or army regulations could inflict. The unfortunate people of Niagara and Buffalo were victims to official misconduct. The British, thinking themselves released from ordinary rules of war by the burning of Newark and Queenston, showed unusual ferocity. In the assault on Fort Niagara they killed sixty-seven Americans, all by the bayonet, while they wounded only eleven. Immediately afterward they "let loose" their auxiliary Indians on Lewiston and the country around. On the night of December 29 Lieutenant General Drummond sent a force of fifteen hundred men including Indians across the river above the falls and driving away the militia burned Black Rock and Buffalo with all their public stores and three small war-schooners.

These acts of retaliation were justified by Sir George Prevost in a long proclamation dated January 12, 1814, which promised that he would not "pursue further a system of warfare so revolting to his own feelings and so little congenial to the British character unless the future measures of the enemy should compel him again to resort to it." The Americans themselves bore Drummond's excessive severity with less complaint than usual. They partly suspected that the destruction effected on the Thames, at York and at Newark, by American troops, though unauthorized by orders, had warranted some retaliation; but they felt more strongly that their anger should properly be vented on their own government and themselves, who had allowed a handful of British troops to capture a strong fortress and to ravage thirty miles of frontier, after repeated warning, without losing two hundred men on either side, while thousands of regular troops were idle elsewhere, and the neighborhood ought without an effort to have supplied five thousand militia.

Fort Niagara, which thus fell into British hands, remained, like Mackinaw, in the enemy's possession until the peace.

CHAPTER X

MOBILE AND FORT MIMS

Military movements in the Southern department attracted little notice, but were not the less important. The Southern people entered into the war in the hope of obtaining the Floridas. President Madison, like President Jefferson, gave all the support in his power to the scheme. Throughout the year 1812 United States troops still occupied Amelia Island and the St. Mary's River, notwithstanding the refusal of Congress to authorize the occupation. The President expected Congress at the session of 1812-1813 to approve the seizure of both Floridas, and took measures in advance for that purpose.

October 12, 1812, Secretary Eustis wrote to the Governor of Tennessee calling out fifteen hundred militia for the defense of the "lower country." The force was not intended for defense but for conquest; it was to support the seizure of Mobile, Pensacola, and St. Augustine by the regular troops. For that object every man in Tennessee was ready to serve; and of all Tennesseeans, Andrew Jackson was the most ardent. Governor Blount immediately authorized Jackson, as major general of the State militia, to call out two thousand volunteers. The call was issued November 14; the volunteers collected at Nashville December 10; and January 7, 1813, the infantry embarked in boats to descend the river, while the mounted men rode through the Indian country to Natchez.

"I have the pleasure to inform you," wrote Jackson to Eustis in departing, "that I am now at the head of two thousand and seventy volunteers, the choicest of our citizens, who go at the call of their country to execute the will of the Government; who have no Constitutional scruples, and if the Government orders, will rejoice at the opportunity of placing the American eagle on the ramparts of Mobile, Pensacola and Fort St. Augustine."

The Tennessee army reached Natchez, February 15, and went into camp to wait orders from Washington, which were expected to direct an advance on Mobile and Pensacola.

While Jackson descended the Mississippi, Monroe, then acting Secretary of War, wrote, January 13, to Major General Pinckney, whose military department included Georgia: "It is intended to place under your command an adequate force for the reduction of St. Augustine should it be decided on by Congress before whom the subject will be in a few days." A fortnight later, January 30, Monroe wrote also to Wilkinson, then commanding at New Orleans: "The subject of taking possession of West Florida is now before Congress and will probably pass. You will be prepared to carry into effect this measure should it be decided on."

Neither Madison nor Monroe raised objection to the seizure of territory belonging to a friendly power; but Congress showed no such readiness to act. Senator Anderson of Tennessee, as early as December 10, 1812, moved, in secret session of the Senate, that a committee be appointed to consider the expediency of authorizing the President "to occupy and hold the whole or any part of East Florida, including Amelia Island, and also those parts of West Florida which are not now in the possession and under the jurisdiction of the United States." After much debate the Senate, December 22, adopted the resolution by eighteen votes to twelve, and the committee, consisting of Anderson, Samuel Smith, Tait of Georgia, Varnum of Massachusetts, and Goodrich of Connecticut, reported a bill, January 19, authorizing the President to occupy both Floridas, and to exercise government there, "provided . . . that the section of country herein designated that is situated to the eastward of the river Perdido may be the subject of future negotiation."

The bill met opposition from the President's personal enemies, Giles, Leib, and Samuel Smith, as well as from the Federalists and some of the Northern Democrats. January 26 Samuel Smith moved to strike out the second section, which authorized the seizure of Florida east of the Perdido; and the Senate, February 2, by a vote of nineteen to sixteen, adopted Smith's motion. The vote was sectional. North and South Carolina, Georgia, Tennessee, and Louisiana, supported the bill; Maryland, Delaware, Pennsylvania, New York, Connecticut, and Rhode Island opposed it; Virginia, Kentucky, Ohio, Massachusetts, New Hampshire, and Vermont were divided; New Jersey threw one vote in its favor, the second senator being absent. Had Leib not changed sides the next day the whole bill would have been indefinitely postponed; but the majority rallied, February 5, and by a vote of twenty-one to eleven authorized the President to seize Florida west of the Perdido, or, in other words, to occupy Mobile. The House passed the bill in secret session February 9, and the President signed it February 12.

In refusing to seize East Florida, the Senate greatly disarranged Madison's plans. Three days afterward, February 5, Armstrong took charge of the War Department, and his first orders were sent to Andrew Jackson directing him to dismiss his force, "the causes of embodying and marching to New Orleans the corps under your command having ceased to exist." Jackson, ignorant that the Administration was not to blame, and indignant at his curt dismissal, marched his men back to Tennessee, making himself responsible for their pay and rations. On learning of these circumstances, Armstrong wrote, March 22, a friendly letter thanking him for the important services his corps would have rendered "had the Executive policy of occupying the two Floridas been adopted by the national legislature."

After the Senate had so persistently refused to support Madison's occupation of East Florida, he could hardly maintain longer the illegal possession he had held during the past year of Amelia Island. February 15 Armstrong wrote to Major General Pinckney, "The late private proceedings of Congress have resulted in a decision not to invade East Florida at present;" but not until March 7 did the Secretary order Pinckney to withdraw the troops from Amelia Island and Spanish territory.

The troops were accordingly withdrawn from Amelia Island, May 16; but nothing could restore East Florida to its former repose, and the anarchy which had been introduced from the United States could never be mastered except by the power that created it. Perhaps Madison would have retained possession, as the least of evils, in spite of the Senate's vote of February 3, had not another cause, independent of legislative will, overcome his repugnance to the evacuation. The Russian offer of mediation arrived while the President was still in doubt.

The occupation of Florida, being an act of war against Spain, could not fail to excite the anger of England, and in that feeling of displeasure the Czar must inevitably share. From the moment their cause against Napoleon was common, Russia, England and Spain were more than likely to act together in resistance to any territorial aggression upon any member of their alliance. The evacuation of East Florida by the United States evaded a serious diplomatic difficulty; and probably not by mere coincidence, Armstrong's order to evacuate Amelia Island was dated March 7, while Daschkoff's letter offering the Czar's mediation was dated March 8.

The Cabinet was so little united in support of the Executive policy that Madison and Monroe ordered the seizure of Mobile without consulting Gallatin, whose persistent hostility to the Florida intrigues was notorious. When Monroe in April gave to Gallatin and Bayard the President's instructions for the peace negotiations, among the rest he directed them to assert "a right to West Florida by cession from France, and a claim to East Florida as an indemnity for spoliations." On receiving these instructions, Gallatin wrote to Monroe, May 2, asking:

"Where is the importance of taking possession of Mobile this summer? We may do this whenever we please, and is it not better to delay every operation of minor importance which may have a tendency to impede our negotiations with Great Britain and Russia? You know that to take by force any place in possession of another nation, whatever our claim to that place may be, is war; and you must be aware that both Russia and Great Britain will feel disposed, if not to support the pretensions of Spain against us, at least to take part against the aggressor."

Monroe quickly replied: "With respect to West Florida, possession will be taken of it before you get far on your voyage. That is a question settled." In fact, possession had been taken of it three weeks before he wrote, in pursuance of orders sent in February, apparently without Gallatin's knowledge. Monroe added views of his own, singularly opposed to Gallatin's convictions.

"On the subject of East Florida," wrote Monroe to Gallatin, May 6, "I think I intimated to you in my last that Colonel Lear was under the most perfect conviction, on the authority of information from respectable sources at Cadiz, that the Spanish regency had sold that and the other province to the British government, and that it had done so under a belief that we had, or should soon get, possession of it. My firm belief is that if we were possessed of both, it would facilitate your negotiations in favor of impressment and every other object, especially if it was distinctly seen by the British ministers or minister that, instead of yielding them or any part of either, we would push our fortunes in that direction, and in Canada, if they did not hasten to accommodate."

Gallatin, on the eve of sailing for Russia, replied with good temper, expressing opinions contrary to those of the President and Secretary of State.

"On the subject of Florida," Gallatin said, "I have always differed in opinion with you, and am rejoiced to have it in our power to announce the evacuation of the province. Let it alone until you shall, by the introduction of British troops, have a proof of the supposed cession. In this I do not believe. It can be nothing more than a permission to occupy it in order to defend it for Spain. By withdrawing our troops, we withdraw the pretence; but the impolitic occupancy of Mobile will, I fear, renew our difficulties. The object is at present of very minor importance, swelled into consequence by the representations from that quarter, and which I would not at this moment have attempted, among other reasons, because it was a Southern one, and will, should it involve us in a war with Spain, disgust every man north of Washington. You will pardon the freedom with which, on the eve of parting with you, I speak on this subject. It is intended as a general caution, which I think important, because I know and see every day the extent of geographical feeling, and the necessity of prudence if we mean to preserve and invigorate the Union."

No sooner did the Act of February 12 become law than Armstrong wrote, February 16, to Wilkinson at New Orleans, enclosing a copy of the Act, and ordering him immediately to take possession of Mobile and the country as far as the Perdido. Wilkinson, who had for years looked forward to that step, hastened to obey the instruction. When Gallatin remonstrated, the measure had been already taken and could not be recalled.

Since July 9, 1812, Wilkinson had again commanded at New Orleans. No immediate attack was to be feared, nor could a competent British force be collected there without warning; but in case such an attack should be made, Wilkinson had reason to fear the result, for his regular force consisted of only sixteen hundred effectives, ill equipped and without defenses. The War Department ordered him to depend on movable ordnance and temporary works rather than on permanent fortifications; but with his usual disregard of orders he began the construction or the completion of extensive works at various points on the river and coast, at a cost which the government could ill afford.

While engaged in this task Wilkinson received, March 14, Armstrong's order of February 16 for the invasion of West Florida. When the government's orders were agreeable to Wilkinson they reached him promptly and were executed with rapidity. Within three weeks he collected at Pass Christian a force of about six hundred men, supported by gunboats, and entered the Bay of Mobile on the night of April 10, while at the same time the garrison at Fort Stoddert descended the Tensaw River, and cut the communication by land between Mobile and Pensacola. At that time Mobile Point was undefended. The only Spanish fortress was Fort Charlotte at Mobile, garrisoned by one hundred and fifty combatants. Wilkinson summoned the fort to surrender, and the commandant had no choice but to obey, for the place was untenable and without supplies. The surrender took place April 15. Wilkinson then took possession of the country as far as the Perdido, and began the construction of a fort, to be called Fort Bowyer, on Mobile Point at the entrance of the Bay, some sixty miles below the town.

This conquest, the only permanent gain of territory made during the war, being effected without bloodshed, attracted less attention than it deserved. Wilkinson committed no errors, and won the President's warm approval. Wilkinson was greatly pleased by his own success, and wished to remain at New Orleans to carry out his projected defenses; but Armstrong had written as early as March 10, ordering him to the Lakes. As so often happened with orders that displeased the general, Armstrong's letter, though dated March 10, and doubtless arriving in New Orleans before April 10, was received by Wilkinson only on his return, May 19. After another delay of three weeks, he started northward, and traveled by way of Mobile through the Creek country to Washington.

Wilkinson's departure June 10 and the evacuation of Amelia Island by General Pinckney May 16 closed the first chapter of the war in the South. Armstrong wrote to Wilkinson, May 27: "The mission to Petersburg and the instructions to our envoys will put a barrier between you and Pensacola for some time to come at least, and permanently in case of peace." The sudden stop thus put by the Senate and the Russian mediation to the campaign against Pensacola and St. Augustine deranged the plans of Georgia and Tennessee, arrested the career of Andrew Jackson, and caused the transfer of Wilkinson from New Orleans to the Lakes. The government expected no other difficulties in the Southern country, and had no reason to fear them. If new perils suddenly arose, they were due less to England, Spain, or the United States than to the chance that gave energy and influence to Tecumthe.

The Southern Indians were more docile and less warlike than the Indians of the Lakes. The Chickasaws and Choctaws, who occupied the whole extent of the country on the east bank of the Mississippi River from the Ohio to the Gulf, gave little trouble or anxiety; and even the great confederacy of Muskogees, or Creeks, who occupied the territory afterward called the State of Alabama and part of Georgia, fell in some degree into a mode of life which seemed likely to make them tillers of the soil. In 1800 the Creeks held, or claimed, about three hundred miles square from the Tennessee River to the Gulf, and from the middle of Georgia nearly to the line which afterward marked the State of Mississippi. The Seminoles, or wild men, of Florida were a branch of the Muskogees, and the Creek warriors themselves were in the habit of visiting Pensacola and Mobile, where they expected to receive presents from the Spanish governor.

Two-thirds of the Creek towns were on the Coosa and Tallapoosa rivers in the heart of Alabama. Their inhabitants were called Upper Creeks. The Lower Creeks lived in towns on the Chattahooche River, the modern boundary between Alabama and Georgia. The United States government, following a different policy in 1799 from that of Jefferson toward the Northwestern Indians, induced the Creeks to adopt a national organization for police purposes; it also helped them to introduce ploughs, to learn cotton-spinning, and to raise crops. The success of these experiments was not at first great, for the larger number of Indians saw no advantage in becoming laborers, and preferred sitting in the squares of the towns, or hunting; but here and there chiefs or half-breeds had farms, slaves, stock, orchards, and spinning-wheels.

Large as the Creek county was, and wild as it had ever been, it did not abound in game. A good hunter, passing in any direction through the three hundred miles of Alabama and Georgia, found difficulty in obtaining game enough for his support. For that reason the Seminoles left their old towns and became wild people, as their name implied, making irregular settlements in Florida, where game and food were more plenty. The mass of the Creek nation, fixed in the villages in the interior, clung to their habits of hunting even when obliged to cultivate the soil, and their semi-civilization rendered them a more perplexing obstacle to the whites than though they had obstinately resisted white influence.

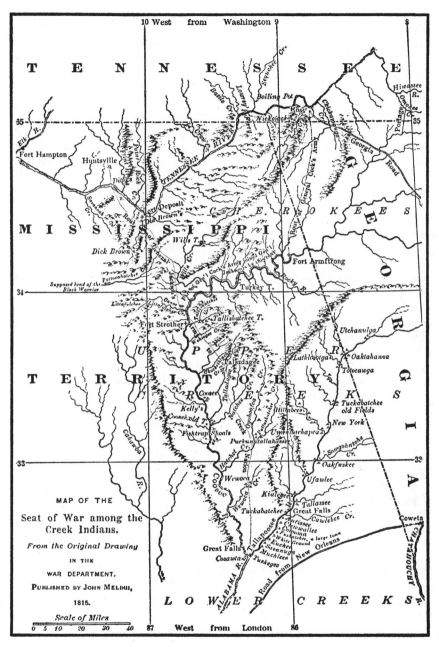

MAP OF THE

Seat of War among the
Creek Indians.

From the Original Drawing

IN THE

WAR DEPARTMENT.

PUBLISHED BY JOHN MELISH,

1815.

Scale of Miles

Had the Indian problem been left to the people of Georgia and Tennessee, the Indians would soon have disappeared; but the national government established under President Washington in 1789 put a sharp curb on Georgia, and interposed decisively between the Georgians and the Creeks. President Washington in 1796 appointed Benjamin Hawkins of North Carolina as Indian agent among the Creeks, and Hawkins protected and governed them with devotion; but the result of his friendliness was the same as that of others' greed. The Indians slowly lost ground.

The Creeks complained of grievances similar to those of the Northwestern Indians, and their position was even more helpless. They had no other outlet than Pensacola and Mobile. Except from the Spaniards they could expect no aid in case of trouble, and the Spanish governors of Florida, after the abdication of Carlos IV in 1807 could scarcely maintain their own position, much less supply the Creeks with arms or gunpowder. While the Northwestern Indians could buy at Malden all the weapons and ammunition they wanted, the Creeks possessed few firearms, and these in bad condition; nor were they skillful in using guns.

The United States government prevented the Georgians from compelling the Indians to sell their lands, but nothing could prevent them from trespass; and the Indian woods along the frontier were filled with cattle, horses, and hogs belonging to the whites, while white men destroyed the game, hunting the deer by firelight, and scaring the Indian hunters from their hunting grounds. "Every cane-swamp where they go to look for a bear—which is part of their support—is near eat out by the stocks put over by the citizens of Georgia." This complaint was made in 1796, and as time went on the Indian hunting grounds were more rapidly narrowed. Not only from Georgia but also from Fort Stoddert, along the course of the Tombigbee River, above Mobile, intruders pressed into the Creek country. The Indians had no choice but to sell their lands for annuities, and under this pressure the Creeks, in 1802 and 1803, were induced to part with the district between the Oconee and Ocmulgee in the center of Georgia. They retained their towns on the Chattahoochee, where Hawkins's agency was established in the town of Coweta, on the edge of the Creek country.

Hawkins was satisfied with their behavior, and believed the chiefs to be well disposed. They showed none of the restlessness which characterized the Northwestern Indians, until Tecumthe conceived the idea of bringing them into his general league to check the encroachments of the whites. After Tecumthe's interview with Governor Harrison at Vincennes, in July, 1811, he made a long journey through the Chickasaw and Choctaw country, and arrived among the Creeks in October, bringing with him a score of Indian warriors. The annual council of the Creeks was held in that month at the village of Tuckaubatchee—an ancient town of the Upper Creeks on the Tallapoosa. The rumor that Tecumthe would be present brought great numbers of Indians, even Cherokees and Choctaws, to the place, while Hawkins attended the council in his character as agent.

Tecumthe and his warriors marched into the center of the square and took their places in silence. That night "they danced the dance of the Indians of the

Lakes," which became thenceforward a political symbol of their party among the Creeks. Some nights afterward Tecumthe addressed the council. Versions more or less untrustworthy have been given of the speech; but the only official allusion to it by a person entitled to credit seemed to show that it was in substance the address made by Tecumthe at Vincennes. Hawkins, recalling to the Creek chiefs in 1814 the course of events which had caused their troubles, reminded them how "Tecumseh, in the square of Tuckaubatchee . . . told the Creeks not to do any injury to the Americans; to be in peace and friendship with them; not to steal even a bell from any one of any color. Let the white people on this continent manage their affairs their own way. Let the red people manage their affairs their own way." Hawkins and the old chiefs would have certainly interfered had Tecumthe incited the Creeks to war or violence; but according to Hawkins the speech was a pacific "talk," delivered by Tecumthe in the name of the British. Indian tradition preserved another form of Tecumthe's rhetoric, which seemed to complete the identity with the Vincennes address. Unable to express himself in the Muskogee language, Tecumthe used pantomime familiar to Indians. Holding his war-club with outstretched arm, he opened first the little finger, then the next and the next, till the club fell from his hand.

Indian union was unquestionably the chief theme of all Tecumthe's public addresses. Whether in private he taught other doctrines must be matter of surmise; but he certainly brought into the Creek nation a religious fanaticism of a peculiar and dangerous kind. Prophets soon appeared, chiefly among the Alabamas, a remnant of an ancient race, not of Creek blood, but members of the Creek confederacy. The prophets, with the usual phenomena of hysteria, claimed powers of magic, and promised to bring earthquakes to destroy an invading army. They preached the total destruction of everything, animate and inanimate, that pertained to civilization. As the nation generally was badly armed, and relied chiefly on their bows, arrows, and war-clubs for battle, the moral support of magic was needed to give them confidence.

So secret was the influence of Tecumthe's friends that no suspicion of the excitement reached Hawkins even when the war with England began; and the old chiefs of the nation—known to be devoted to peace and to the white alliance—were kept in ignorance of all that was done among the young warriors. The Alabamas, or Coosadas, lived below the junction of the Coosa and Tallapoosa, on the west bank of the Alabama River, about eight miles above the modern town of Montgomery; they were considered by Hawkins the most industrious and best behaved of all the Creeks, whose fields were the granaries of the upper towns and furnished supplies even to Mobile. Their town was the last place in which Hawkins expected to see conspiracy, violence, or fanaticism. The young men "sang the song of the Indians of the Lakes, and danced the dance" in secret for eighteen months after Tecumthe's visit, without public alarm, and probably would have continued to do so except for an outbreak committed by some of their nation three hundred miles away.

In 1812 a band of six Indians led by the Little Warrior of Wewocau, a Creek town on the Coosa, was sent by the nation on a public mission to the Chickasaws. Instead of delivering their "talks" and returning, they continued their journey to the northern Lakes and joined Tecumthe at Malden. They took part in the massacre at the river Raisin, January 22, 1813, and soon afterward began their return, bringing talks from the Shawanese and British and also a letter from some British officer at Malden to the Spanish officials at Pensacola, from whom they hoped to obtain weapons and powder. According to common report, Tecumthe told the Little Warrior that he was about to aid the British in capturing Fort Meigs, and as soon as the fort was taken he would come to join the Creeks. Until then his friends were to increase their party by the secret means and magic that had proved so successful, but were not to begin open war.

The Little Warrior and his party, including a warrior from Tuskegee, a Creek town at the fork of the Coosa and Tallapoosa, after crossing Indiana in the month of February reached the north bank of the Ohio River about seven miles above its mouth, where were two cabins occupied by white families. Unable to resist the temptation to spill blood, the band murdered the two families with the usual Indian horrors. This outrage was committed February 9; and the band, crossing the Ohio, passed southward through the Chickasaw country, avowing the deed and its motive.

The Little Warrior arrived at home about the middle of March, and reported that he brought talks from the Shawanese and British. The old chiefs of the Upper Creeks immediately held a council March 25, and after listening to the talks, reprimanded the Little Warrior and ordered him to leave the Council House. On the same day Hawkins wrote to them from Coweta, demanding delivery of the Little Warrior and his six companions to answer for the murders they had committed. On hearing this demand, the old chiefs at Tuckaubatchee under the lead of the Big Warrior held another council, while the Little Warrior, the Tuskegee Warrior, and the murderers took to the woods. The old chiefs in council decided to execute the murderers, and sent out parties to do it. The Little Warrior was found in the swamp, well armed, but was decoyed out and killed by treachery; "the first and second man's gun snapped at him, but the third man's gun fired and killed; . . . four men that had on pouches kept them shaking following after him, so that he could not hear the gun snap; if he had found out that, he would have wounded a good many with his arrows."

The Tuskegee Warrior and four others were found in a house on the Hickory Ground at the fork of the rivers. As long as they had ammunition, they held the attack at a distance, but at last the house was fired. The Tuskegee Warrior being wounded, was burned in the house, while his two young brothers were taken out and tomahawked. One warrior broke away but was caught and killed; two more were killed elsewhere. One escaped, and "set out the morning after to kill white people." Warriors were sent after him.

"He made battle, firing at the warriors, and was near killing one; the bullet passed near his ear. He then drew his knife and tomahawk, defended himself, and the warriors shot three balls through him. He fell, retained the power of speech till next day, and died. He said he had been to the Shawanese helping of them, and had got fat eating white people's flesh. Every one to the very last called on the Shawanese general, Tecumseh."

Such political executions, in the stifled excitement of the moment, could not but rouse violent emotion throughout the Creek nation. The old chiefs, having given life for life, felt the stronger for their assertion of authority; but they knew nothing of the true situation. For several weeks no open outbreak occurred, but the prophets were more active than ever. About June 4 the old chiefs at Tuckaubatchee, hearing that the prophets "kept as usual their fooleries," sent a runner to the Alabamas with a message:

"You are but a few Alabama people. You say that the Great Spirit visits you frequently; that he comes in the sun and speaks to you; that the sun comes down just above your heads. Now we want to see and hear what you say you have seen and heard. Let us have the same proof you have had, and we will believe what we see and hear. You have nothing to fear; the people who committed murders have suffered for their crimes, and there is an end of it."

The runner who carried this message was one of the warriors who had aided in killing the seven murderers. The Alabamas instantly put him to death, and sent his scalp to their friends at the forks of the river. Then began a general uprising, and every warrior who had aided in killing the murderers was himself killed or hunted from the Upper Creek country. The chiefs of Tuckaubatchee with difficulty escaped to the agency at Coweta, where they were under the protection of Georgia.

The Lower Creek towns did not join the outbreak; but of the Upper Creek towns twenty-nine declared for war, and only five for peace. At least two thousand warriors were believed to have taken the warclub by August 1, and got the name of Red Clubs, or Red Sticks, for that reason. Everywhere they destroyed farms, stock, and all objects of white civilization, and killed or drove away their opponents.

With all this the Spaniards had nothing to do. The outbreak was caused by the Indian War in the Northwest, and immediately by the incompetence of General Winchester and by the massacre at the river Raisin. The Creeks were totally unprepared for war, except so far as they trusted to magic; they had neither guns, powder, nor balls. For that reason they turned to the Spaniards, who could alone supply them. When the Little Warrior was put to death, the British letter which he carried from Malden for the Spanish officials at Pensacola came into the charge of another Creek warrior, Peter McQueen, a half-breed. In July, McQueen, with a large party of warriors started for Pensacola, with the letter and four hundred dollars, to get powder. On arriving there they saw the Spanish governor, who treated them civilly, and in fear of violence gave them, according to McQueen's account, "a small bag of powder each for ten towns, and five bullets to each man." With this supply, which the governor represented as a friendly present for hunting purposes, they were obliged to content themselves, and started on their return journey.

News that McQueen's party was at Pensacola instantly reached the American settlements above Mobile, where the inhabitants were already taking refuge in stockades. A large number of Americans, without military organization, under several leaders, one of whom was a half-breed named Dixon Bailey, started July 26 to intercept McQueen, and succeeded in surprising the Indians July 27 at a place called Burnt Corn, about eighty miles north of Pensacola. The whites at first routed the Indians, and captured the pack-mules with the ammunition; but the Indians quickly rallied, and in their turn routed the whites, with a loss of two killed and fifteen wounded—although they failed to recover the greater part of the pack-animals. With the small amount of powder left to him, McQueen then returned to his people.

Angry at the attack and eager to revenge the death of his warriors, McQueen summoned the warriors of thirteen towns, some eight hundred in number, and about August 20 started in search of his enemies. The Creek war differed from that on the Lakes in being partly a war of half-breeds. McQueen's strongest ally was William Weatherford, a half-breed, well-known throughout the country as a man of property and ability, as nearly civilized as Indian blood permitted, and equally at home among Indians and whites. McQueen and Weatherford were bitterly hostile to the half-breeds Bailey and Beasley, who were engaged in the affair of Burnt Corn. Both Beasley and Bailey were at a stockade called Fort Mims, some thirty-five miles above Mobile, on the eastern side of the Alabama River, where about five hundred and fifty persons were collected—a motley crowd of whites, half-breeds, Indians, and negroes, old and young, women and children, protected only by a picket wall, pierced by five hundred loop-holes three and a half feet from the ground, and two rude gates. Beasley commanded, and wrote, August 30, that he could "maintain the post against any number of Indians." To Fort Mims the Creek warriors turned, for the reason that Beasley and Bailey were there, and they arrived in the neighborhood, August 29, without giving alarm. Twice, negroes tending cattle outside rushed back to the fort reporting that painted warriors were hovering about; but the horsemen when sent out discovered no sign of an enemy, and Beasley tied up and flogged the second negro for giving a false alarm.

At noon, August 30, when the drum beat for dinner no patrols were out, the gates were open, and sand had drifted against that on the eastern side so that it could not quickly be closed. Suddenly a swarm of Indians raising the warwhoop rushed toward the fort. Beasley had time to reach the gate, but could not close it, and was tomahawked on the spot. The Indians got possession of the loop-holes outside, and of one inclosure. The whites, under Dixon Bailey, held the inner inclosure and fought with desperation; but at last the Indians succeeded in setting fire to the house in the center, and the fire spread to the whole stockade. The Indians then effected an entrance, and massacred most of the inmates. Fifteen persons escaped, and among these was Dixon Bailey mortally wounded. Most of the negroes were spared to be slaves. Two hundred and fifty scalps became trophies of the Creek warriors—a number such as had been seldom taken by Indians from the white people on a single day.

CHAPTER XI
CAMPAIGNS AMONG THE CREEKS

The Battle at Burnt Corn was regarded by the Indians as a declaration of war by the whites. Till then they seemed to consider themselves engaged in a domestic quarrel, or civil war; but after the massacre at Fort Mims they could not retreat, and yet knew that they must perish except for supernatural aid. Their destiny was controlled by that of Tecumthe. Ten days after the massacre at Fort Mims, Perry won his victory on Lake Erie, which settled the result of the Indian wars both in the North and in the South. Tecumthe had expected to capture Fort Meigs, and with it Fort Wayne and the line of the Maumee and Wabash. On the impulse of this success he probably hoped to raise the war-spirit among the Chickasaws and Choctaws, and then in person to call the Creeks into the field. Proctor's successive defeats blasted Indian hopes, and the Creeks had hardly struck their first blow in his support when Tecumthe himself fell, and the Indians of the Lakes submitted or fled to Canada.

At best the Creek outbreak would have been hopeless. Although the number of hostile Creek warriors was matter of conjecture, nothing showed that they could exceed four thousand. At Pensacola, Peter McQueen was said to have claimed forty-eight hundred "gun-men" on his side. At such a moment he probably exaggerated his numbers. The Big Warrior, who led the peace party, estimated the hostile Creeks, early in August, as numbering at least twenty-five hundred warriors. If the number of gun-men was four thousand, the number of guns in their possession could scarcely be more than one thousand. Not only had the Creeks few guns, and those in poor condition, but they had little powder or lead, and no means of repairing their weapons. Their guns commonly missed fire, and even after discharging them, the Creeks seldom reloaded, but resorted to the bow-and-arrows which they always carried. As warriors they felt their inferiority to the Shawanese and Indians of the Lakes, while their position was more desperate, for the Choctaws and Cherokees behind them refused to join in their war.

Four thousand warriors who had never seen a serious war even with their Indian neighbors, and armed for the most part with clubs, or bows-and-arrows, were not able to resist long the impact of three or four armies, each nearly equal to their whole force, coming from every quarter of the compass. On the other hand, the military difficulties of conquering the Creeks were not trifling. The same obstacles that stopped Harrison in Ohio, stopped Pinckney in Georgia. Pinckney, like Harrison, could set in motion three columns of troops on three converging lines, but he could not feed them or make roads for them. The focus of Indian fanaticism was the Hickory Ground at the fork of the Coosa and Tallapoosa, about one hundred and fifty miles distant from the nearest point that would furnish supplies for an American army coming from Georgia, Tennessee, or Mobile. Pinckney's natural line of attack was through Georgia to the Lower Creek towns and the American forts on the Chattahoochee, whence he could move along a good road about eighty miles to the Upper Creek towns, near the Hickory Ground. The next convenient line was from Mobile up the Alabama River about one hundred and fifty miles to the same point. The least convenient was the pathless, mountainous, and barren region of Upper Alabama and Georgia, through which an army from Tennessee must toil for at least a hundred miles in order to reach an enemy.

The State of Georgia was most interested in the Creek war, and was chiefly to profit by it. Georgia in 1813 had a white population of about one hundred and twenty-five thousand, and a militia probably numbering thirty thousand. Military District No. 6, embracing the two Carolinas and Georgia, was supposed to contain two thousand regular troops, and was commanded by Major General Pinckney. Under Pinckney's command, a thousand regulars and three thousand militia, advancing from Georgia by a good road eighty miles into the Indian country, should have been able to end the Creek war within six months from the massacre at Fort Mims; but for some reason the attempts on that side were not so successful as they should have been, and were neither rapid nor vigorous. Tennessee took the lead.

In respect of white population, the State of Tennessee was more than double the size of Georgia; but it possessed a greater advantage in Andrew Jackson, whose extreme energy was equivalent to the addition of an army. When news of the Mims massacre reached Nashville about the middle of September, Jackson was confined to his bed by a pistol-shot, which had broken his arm and nearly cost his life ten days before in a street brawl with Thomas H. Benton. From his bed he issued an order calling back into service his two thousand volunteers of 1812; and as early as October 12, a little more than a month after the affair at Fort Mims, he and his army of twenty-five hundred men were already camped on the Tennessee River south of Huntsville in Alabama. There was his necessary base of operations, but one hundred and sixty miles of wilderness lay between him and the Hickory Ground.

On the Tennessee River Jackson's position bore some resemblance to that of Harrison on the Maumee a year before. Energy could not save him from failure. Indeed, the greater his energy the more serious were his difficulties. He depended on supplies from east Tennessee descending the river; but the river was low and the supplies could not be moved. He had taken no measures to procure supplies from Nashville. Without food and forage he could not safely advance, or even remain where he was. Under such conditions, twenty-five hundred men with half as many horses could not be kept together. Harrison under the same difficulties held back his main force near its magazines till it disbanded, without approaching within a hundred miles of its object. Jackson suffered nearly the same fate. He sent away his mounted men under General Coffee to forage on the banks of the Black Warrior River, fifty miles to the southwest, where no Creeks were to be feared. He forced his infantry forward through rough country some twenty miles, to a point where the river made its most southern bend, and there, in the mountainous defile, he established, October 23, a camp which he called Deposit, where his supplies were to be brought when the river should permit.

Coffee's mounted men returned October 24. Then, October 25, in the hope of finding food as he went, Jackson plunged into the mountains beyond the river, intending to make a raid, as far as he could, into the Creek country. Except fatigue and famine, he had nothing to fear. The larger Creek towns were a hundred miles to the southward, and were busy with threatened attacks nearer home. After a week's march Jackson reached the upper waters of the Coosa. Within a short distance were two or three small Creek villages. Against one of these Jackson sent his mounted force, numbering nine hundred men, under General Coffee. Early in the morning of November 3 Coffee surrounded and destroyed Talishatchee His report represented that the Indians made an obstinate resistance. "Not one of the warriors escaped to tell the news—a circumstance unknown heretofore." According to Coffee's estimate, Talishatchee contained two hundred and eighty-four Indians of both sexes and all ages. If one in three could be reckoned as capable of bearing arms, the number of warriors was less than one hundred. Coffee's men after the battle counted one hundred and eighty-six dead Indians, and estimated the total loss at two hundred. In every attack on an Indian village a certain number of women and children were necessarily victims, but the proportion at Talishatchee seemed large.

"I lost five men killed, and forty-one wounded," reported Coffee,—"none mortally, the greater part slightly, a number with arrows. Two of the men killed was with arrows; this appears to form a very principal part of the enemy's arms for warfare, every man having a bow with a bundle of arrows, which is used after the first fire with the gun until a leisure time for loading offers."

Meanwhile Jackson fortified a point on the Coosa, about thirty-five miles from his base on the Tennessee, and named it Fort Strother. There he expected to be joined by a division of east Tennessee militia under General Cocke, approaching from Chattanooga, as he hoped, with supplies; but while waiting, he received, November 7, a message from Talladega, a Creek village thirty miles to the southward, reporting that the town, which had refused to join the warparty, was besieged and in danger of capture by a large body of hostile warriors. Jackson instantly started to save Talladega, and marched twenty-four miles November 8 surrounding and attacking the besieging Creeks the next morning.

"The victory was very decisive," reported Jackson to Governor Blount, November 11; "two hundred and ninety of the enemy were left dead, and there can be no doubt but many more were killed who were not found. . . . In the engagement we lost fifteen killed, and eighty-five wounded."

Coffee estimated the number of Indians, on their own report, at about one thousand. Jackson mentioned no wounded Indians, nor the number of hostile Creeks engaged. Male Indians, except infants, were invariably killed, and probably not more than five or six hundred were in the battle, for Coffee thought very few escaped unhurt.

At Talladega Jackson was sixty miles from the Hickory Ground, and still nearer to several large Indian towns, but he had already passed the limit of his powers. News arrived that the army of eastern Tennessee had turned eastward toward the Tallapoosa, and that his expected supplies were as remote as ever. Returning to Fort Strother, November 10, Jackson waited there in forced inactivity, as Harrison had waited at Fort Meigs, anxious only to avoid the disgrace of retreat. For two weeks the army had lived on the Indians. A month more passed in idle starvation, until after great efforts a supply train was organized, and difficulties on that account ceased; but at the same moment the army claimed discharge.

The claim was reasonable. Enlisted December 10, 1812, for one year, the men were entitled to their discharge December 10, 1813. Had Jackson been provided with fresh levies he would doubtless have dismissed the old; but in his actual situation their departure would have left him at Fort Strother to pass the winter alone. To prevent this, he insisted that the men had no right to count as service, within the twelve months for which they had enlisted, the months between May and October when they were dismissed to their homes. The men, unanimous in their own view of the contract, started to march home December 10; and Jackson, in a paroxysm of anger, planted two small pieces of artillery in their path and threatened to fire on them. The men, with good temper, yielded for the moment; and Jackson, quickly recognizing his helplessness, gave way, and allowed them to depart December 12 with a vehement appeal for volunteers who made no response.

Fort Strother was then held for a short time by east Tennessee militia, about fourteen hundred in number, whose term of service was a few weeks longer than that of the west Tennesseeans. Jackson could do nothing with them, and remained idle. The Governor of Tennessee advised him to withdraw to the State frontier; but Jackson, while admitting that his campaign had failed, declared that he would perish before withdrawing from the ground he considered himself to have gained. Fortunately he stood in no danger. The Creeks did not molest him and he saw no enemy within fifty miles.

While Jackson was thus brought to a stand-still, Major General Cocke of east Tennessee, under greater disadvantages, accomplished only results annoying to Jackson. Cocke with twenty-five hundred three-months militia took the field at Knoxville October 12, and moving by way of Chattanooga reached the Coosa sixty or seventy miles from Camp Strother. The nearest Creek Indians were the Hillabees, on a branch of the Tallapoosa about sixty miles from Cocke's position, and the same distance from Jackson. The Hillabees, a group of four small villages, numbered in 1800 one hundred and seventy warriors. Unaware that the Hillabees were making their submission to Jackson, and were to receive his promise of protection, Cocke sent a large detachment, which started November 12 into the Indian country, and surprised one of the Hillabee villages November 18, massacring sixty-one warriors, and capturing the other inmates, two hundred and fifty in number, without losing a drop of blood or meeting any resistance.

Jackson was already displeased with General Cocke's conduct, and the Hillabee massacre increased his anger. Cocke had intentionally kept himself and his army at a distance in order to maintain an independent command. Not until Jackson's troops disbanded and marched home, December 12, did Cocke come to Fort Strother. There his troops remained a month, guarding Jackson's camp, until January 12, 1814, when their three months' term expired.

While five thousand men under Jackson and Cocke wandered about northern Alabama, able to reach only small and remote villages, none of which was actively concerned in the outbreak, the Georgians organized a force to enter the heart of the Creek country. Brigadier General John Floyd commanded the Georgia army, and neither Major General Pinckney nor any United States troops belonged to it. Jackson's battle of Talladega was fought November 9; Cocke's expedition against the Hillabees started November 12, and surprised the Hillabee village November 18. Floyd entered the hostile country November 24. The Georgians though nearest were last to move, and moved with the weakest force. Floyd had but nine hundred and forty militia, and three or four hundred friendly warriors of the Lower Creek villages.

Floyd had heard that large numbers of hostile Indians were assembled at Autossee—a town on the Tallapoosa River near Tuckaubatchee, in the center of the Upper Creek country. He crossed the Chattahoochee November 24 with five days' rations, and marched directly against Autossee, arriving within nine or ten miles without meeting resistance. At half-past six on the morning of November 29 he formed his troops for action in front of the town.

The difference between the Northwestern Indians and the Creeks was shown in the battle of Autossee compared with Tippecanoe. Floyd was weaker than Harrison, having only militia and Indians, while Harrison had a regular regiment composing one-third of his rank-and-file. The Creeks were probably more numerous than the Tippecanoe Indians, although in both cases the numbers were quite unknown. Probably the Creeks were less well armed, but they occupied a strong position and stood on the defensive. Floyd reported that by nine o'clock he drove the Indians from their towns and burned their houses—supposed to be four hundred in number. He estimated their loss at two hundred killed. His own loss was eleven killed and fifty-four wounded. That of Harrison at Tippecanoe was sixty-one killed or mortally wounded, and one hundred and twenty-seven not fatally injured. The Creeks hardly inflicted one fourth the loss caused by the followers of the Shawnee Prophet.

General Floyd—himself among the severely wounded—immediately after the battle ordered the troops to begin their return march to the Chattahoochee. The Georgia raid into the Indian country was bolder, less costly, and more effective than the Tennessee campaign; but at best it was only a raid, like the Indian assault on Fort Mims, and offered no immediate prospect of regular military occupation. Another attempt, from a third quarter, had the same unsatisfactory result.

The successor of General Wilkinson at New Orleans and Mobile, and in Military District No. 7, was Brigadier General Thomas Flournoy. Under his direction an expedition was organized from Fort Stoddert, commanded by Brigadier General Claiborne of the Mississippi volunteers. Claiborne was given the Third United States Infantry, with a number of militia, volunteers, and Choctaw Indians—in all about a thousand men. He first marched to a point on the Alabama River, about eighty-five miles above Fort Stoddert, where he constructed a military post, called Fort Claiborne. Having established his base there, he marched, December 13, up the river till he reached, December 23, the Holy Ground, where the half-breed Weatherford lived. There Claiborne approached within about fifty miles of the point which Floyd reached a month before, but for want of coöperation he could not maintain his advantage. He attacked and captured Weatherford's town, killing thirty Indians, with a loss of one man; but after destroying the place he retreated, arriving unharmed at Fort Claiborne, on the last day of the year.

Thus the year 1813 ended without closing the Creek war. More than seven thousand men had entered the Indian country from four directions; and with a loss of thirty or forty lives had killed, according to their reports, about eight hundred Indians, or one-fifth of the hostile Creek warriors; but this carnage had fallen chiefly on towns and villages not responsible for the revolt. The true fanatics were little harmed, and could offer nearly as much resistance as ever. The failure and excessive expense of the campaign were the more annoying, because they seemed beyond proportion to the military strength of the fanatics. Major General Pinckney wrote to the War Department at the close of the year:

"The force of the hostile Creeks was estimated by the best judges to have consisted of three thousand five hundred warriors; of these it is apprehended that about one thousand have been put *hors de combat.*"

To Andrew Jackson, Pinckney wrote, January 19, 1814:

"Your letter, dated December 26, did not reach me until the last evening. Your preceding dispatches of December 14 had led me to conclude what would probably soon be the diminished state of your force. I therefore immediately ordered to your support Colonel Williams's regiment of twelve-months men, and wrote to the Governor of Tennessee urging him to complete the requisition of fifteen hundred for the time authorized by law. I learn from the person who brought your letter that Colonel Williams's regiment is marching to join you; if the fifteen hundred of the quota should also be furnished by Governor Blount, you will in my opinion have force sufficient for the object to be attained. The largest computation that I have heard of the hostile Creek warriors, made by any competent judge, is four thousand. At least one thousand of them have been killed or disabled; they are badly armed and supplied with ammunition; little doubt can exist that two thousand of our men would be infinitely superior to any number they can collect."

Jackson at Fort Strother on the departure of the east Tennesseeans, January 14, received a reinforcement of sixty-day militia, barely nine hundred in number. Determined to use them to the utmost, Jackson started three days afterward to coöperate with General Floyd in an attack on the Tallapoosa villages, aiming at a town called Emuckfaw, some forty miles north of Tuckaubatchee. The movement was much more dangerous than any he had yet attempted. His own force was fresh, motley, and weak, numbering only nine hundred and thirty militia, including "a company of volunteer officers headed by General Coffee, who had been abandoned by his men," and assisted by two or three hundred friendly Creeks and Cherokees. The sixty-day militia were insubordinate and unsteady, the march was long, and the Creek towns at which he aimed were relatively large. Emuckfaw was one of seven villages belonging to Ocfuskee, the largest town in the Creek nation—in 1800 supposed to contain four hundred and fifty warriors.

As far as Enotachopco Creek, twelve miles from Emuckfaw, Jackson had no great danger to fear; but beyond that point he marched with caution. At daylight, January 22, the Indians, who were strongly encamped at about three miles distance, made an attack on Jackson's camp, which was repulsed after half an hour's fighting. Jackson then sent Coffee with four hundred men to burn the Indian camp, but Coffee returned without attempting it. "On viewing the encampment and its strength the General thought it most prudent to return to my encampment," reported Jackson. Immediately after Coffee's return the Indians again attacked, and Coffee sallied out to turn their flank, followed by not more than fifty-four men. The Indians were again repulsed with a loss of forty-five killed, but Coffee was severely wounded, and Jackson "determined to commence a return march to Fort Strother the following day."

At that moment Jackson's situation was not unlike that of Harrison after the battle of Tippecanoe, and he escaped less happily. Fortifying his camp, he remained during the night of January 22 undisturbed. At half-past ten, January 23, he began his return march, "and was fortunate enough to reach Enotachopco before night, having passed without interruption a dangerous defile occasioned by a hurricane." Enotachopco Creek was twelve or fifteen miles from Emuckfaw Creek, and the Hillabee towns were about the same distance beyond.

At Enotachopco Jackson again fortified his camp. His position was such as required the utmost caution in remaining or moving. So hazardous was the passage of the deep creek and the defile beyond, through which the army had marched in its advance, that Jackson did not venture to return by the same path, but on the morning of January 24 began cautiously crossing the creek at a safer point:

"The front guard had crossed with part of the flank columns, the wounded were over, and the artillery in the act of entering the creek, when an alarm-gun was heard in the woods. . . . To my astonishment and mortification when the word was given by Colonel Carrol to halt and form, and a few guns had been fired, I beheld the right and left columns of the rear guard precipitately give way. This shameful retreat was disastrous in the extreme; it drew along with it the greater part of the centre column, leaving not more than twenty-five men, who being formed by Colonel Carrol maintained their ground as long as it was possible to maintain it, and it brought consternation and confusion into the centre of the army,—a consternation which was not easily removed, and a confusion which could not soon be restored to order."

The Indians were either weak or ignorant of warfare, for they failed to take advantage of the panic, and allowed themselves to be driven away by a handful of men. Jackson's troops escaped unharmed, or but little injured, their loss in the engagements of January 22 and 24 being twenty-four men killed and seventy-one wounded. Probably the Creek force consisted of the Ocfuskee warriors, and numbered about half that of Jackson. Coffee supposed them to be eight hundred or a thousand in number, but the exaggeration in estimating Indian forces was always greater than in estimating white enemies in battle. An allowance of one-third was commonly needed for exaggeration in reported numbers of European combatants; an allowance of one-half was not unreasonable in estimates of Indian forces.

In letting Jackson escape from Emuckfaw the Creeks lost their single opportunity. Jackson never repeated the experiment. He arrived at Fort Strother in safety January 29 and did not again leave his intrenchment until the middle of March, under much better conditions.

General Floyd was no more successful. Jackson started from Fort Strother for Emuckfaw January 17; Floyd left Fort Mitchell, on the Chattahoochee, January 18, for Tuckaubatchee, only forty miles south of Emuckfaw. Floyd's army, like Jackson's, was partly composed of militia and partly of Lower Creek warriors, in all about seventeen hundred men, including four hundred friendly Creeks. From the best information to be obtained at the time, the effective strength of the hostile Indians did not then exceed two thousand warriors, scattered along the Coosa and Tallapoosa rivers; while experience proved the difficulty of concentrating large bodies of Indians, even when supplies were furnished them. The British commissariat in Canada constantly issued from five to ten thousand rations for Indians and their families, but Proctor never brought more than fifteen hundred warriors into battle. The Creeks, as far as was known, never numbered a thousand warriors in any battle during the war. Floyd, with seventeen hundred men well armed, was able to face the whole Creek nation, and meant to move forward, fortifying military posts at each day's march, until he should establish himself on the Tallapoosa in the center of the Creek towns, and wait for a junction with Jackson.

When Jackson was repulsed at Emuckfaw January 22, Floyd was about forty miles to the southward, expecting to draw the chief attack of the Indians. Having advanced forty-eight miles from the Chattahoochee he arrived at a point about seven or eight miles south of Tuckaubatchee, where he fortified, on Calibee Creek, a camp called Defiance. There, before daybreak on the morning of January 27, he was sharply attacked, as Harrison was attacked at Tippecanoe, and with the same result. The attack was repulsed, but Floyd lost twenty-two killed and one hundred and forty-seven wounded—the largest number of casualties that had yet occurred in the Indian war. The Indians "left thirty-seven dead on the field; from the effusion of blood and the number of head-dresses and war-clubs found in various directions, their loss must have been considerable independent of their wounded."

The battle of Calibee Creek, January 27, was in substance a defeat to Floyd. So decided were his militia in their determination to go home that he abandoned all his fortified posts and fell back to the Chattahoochee, where he arrived February 1, four days after the battle.

Six months had then elapsed since the outbreak of hostilities at Burnt Corn; a year since the Little Warrior murders on the Ohio River, yet not a post had been permanently occupied within eighty miles of the fanatical center at the fork of the Coosa and Tallapoosa.

Pinckney was obliged to apply to the governors of North and South Carolina to furnish him with men and equipments. The Governor of Georgia also exerted himself to supply the deficiencies of the national magazines. By their aid Pinckney was able to collect an army with which to make another and a decisive movement into the Creek country; but before he could act, Jackson succeeded in striking a final blow.

Jackson's success in overcoming the obstacles in his path was due to his obstinacy in insisting on maintaining himself at Fort Strother, which obliged Governor Blount to order out four thousand more militia in January for six months. Perhaps this force alone would have been no more effectual in 1814 than in 1813, but another reinforcement was decisive. The Thirty-ninth regiment of the regular army, authorized by the Act of January 29, 1813, had been officered and recruited in Tennessee, and was still in the State. Major General Pinckney sent orders December 23, 1813, to its colonel, John Williams, to join Jackson. The arrival of the Thirty-ninth regiment February 6, 1814, gave Jackson the means of coping with his militia. February 21 he wrote to his quartermaster, Major Lewis, that he meant to use his regulars first to discipline his own army. "I am truly happy in having the Colonel [Williams] with me. His regiment will give strength to my arm, and quell mutiny." His patience with militiamen had been long exhausted, and he meant to make a warning of the next mutineer.

The first victim was no less a person than Major General Cocke of the east Tennessee militia. Cocke's division of two thousand men, mustered for six months, began January 17 its march from Knoxville to Fort Strother. Learning on the march that the west Tennessee division, mustered at the same time for the same service, had been accepted to serve only three months, Cocke's men mutinied, and Cocke tried to pacify them by a friendly speech. Jackson, learning what had passed, dispatched a sharp order to one of Cocke's brigadiers to arrest and send under guard to Fort Strother every officer of whatever rank who should be found exciting the men to mutiny. Cocke was put under arrest when almost in sight of the enemy's country; his sword was taken from him and he was sent to Nashville for trial. His division came to Fort Strother, and said no more about its term of service.

Having dealt thus with the officers, Jackson selected at leisure a test of strength with the men. The conduct of the Fayetteville company of the Twenty-eighth regiment of west Tennessee light infantry gave him ground for displeasure. Not only had they refused to obey the call for six months' service and insisted on serving for three months or not at all, but they had halted on their march, and had sent their commanding officer to bargain with Jackson for his express adhesion to their terms. Learning that Jackson made difficulties, they marched home without waiting for an official reply. Jackson ordered the whole body to be arrested as deserters, accompanying his order by an offer of pardon to such as returned to duty on their own understanding of the term of service. The company was again mustered, and arrived at Fort Strother not long after the arrival of the Thirty-ninth United States Infantry.

A few weeks later an unfortunate private of the same company, named Woods, refused to obey the officer of the day, and threatened to shoot any man who arrested him. Jackson instantly called a court-martial, tried and sentenced Woods, and March 14 caused him to be shot. The execution was a harsh measure; but Jackson gave to it a peculiar character by issuing a general order in which he misstated facts that made Wood's case exceptional, in order to let the company understand that their comrade was suffering the penalty which they all deserved.

Without giving his army time to brood over the severity, Jackson ordered a general movement, and within forty-eight hours after Woods's execution, all were well on their way toward the enemy. Jackson had with him about five thousand men, four-fifths of whom expected their discharge in a month. He left them not a day's repose.

Two lines of advance were open to him in approaching the fork of the Coosa and Tallapoosa, which was always the objective point. He might descend the Coosa, or cross to the Tallapoosa by the way he had taken in January. He descended the Coosa thirty miles, and then struck a sudden blow at the Tallapoosa towns.

The Ocfuskee Indians, elated by their success in January, collected their whole force, with that of some neighboring towns, in a bend of the Tallapoosa, where they built a sort of fortress by constructing across the neck of the Horse-shoe a breastwork composed of five large logs, one above the other, with two ranges of portholes. The interior was covered with trees and fallen timber along the river side, and caves were dug in the bank. Seven or eight hundred Indian warriors together with many women and children were within the enclosure of eighty or a hundred acres.

Jackson, after leaving a garrison at a new fort which he constructed on the Coosa, about half way to the Horse-shoe, had somewhat less than three thousand effectives. With these he camped, on the evening of March 28, about six miles northwest of the bend, and the next morning advanced to attack it. "Determined to exterminate them," he reported, he detached Coffee with the mounted force of seven hundred men and six hundred friendly Indians to surround the bend, along the river bank, while Jackson himself with all his infantry took position before the breastwork. At half-past ten o'clock he planted his cannon about two hundred yards from the center of the work and began a rapid fire of artillery and musketry, which continued for two hours without producing apparent effect. Meanwhile the Cherokee allies swam the river in the rear of the Creek warriors, who were all at the breastwork, and seizing canoes, brought some two hundred Indians and whites into the Horse-shoe, where they climbed the high ground in the rear of the breastwork and fired on the Creeks, who were occupied in defending their front.

Jackson then ordered an assault on the breastwork, which was carried with considerable loss by the Thirty-ninth regiment in the center. The Creeks sought shelter in the thickets and under the bluffs, where they were hunted or burned out, and killed. "The slaughter was greater than all we had done before," wrote Coffee; it was continued all day and the next morning. When the Horse-shoe had been thoroughly cleared, five hundred and fifty-seven dead bodies were counted within the bend; many were killed in the river, and about twenty were supposed to have escaped. According to Coffee, "we killed not less than eight hundred and fifty or nine hundred of them, and took about five hundred squaws and children prisoners." The proportion of squaws and children to the whole number of Indians showed the probable proportion of warriors among the dead. "I lament that two or three women and children were killed by accident," reported Jackson.

Jackson's loss was chiefly confined to the Thirty-ninth regiment and the friendly Indians, who were most actively engaged in the storm. The Thirty-ninth lost twenty killed and fifty-two wounded. Among the severely wounded was

Ensign Samuel Houston, struck by an arrow in the thigh. The major and two lieutenants were killed. The Cherokees lost eighteen killed and thirty-five wounded. The friendly Creeks lost five killed and eleven wounded. The Tennessee militia, comprising two-thirds of the army, lost only eight killed and fifty-two wounded. The total loss was fifty-one killed and one hundred and forty-eight wounded.

Jackson's policy of extermination shocked many humane Americans, and would perhaps have seemed less repulsive had the Creeks shown more capacity for resistance. The proportion between two hundred casualties on one side and seven or eight hundred killed on the other would have been striking in any case, but was especially so where the advantages of position were on the side of the defense. A more serious criticism was that the towns thus exterminated were not the towns chiefly responsible for the outbreak. The Alabamas and the main body of fanatical Creeks escaped.

Jackson was obliged to return to his new fort on the Coosa, a march of five days; and was delayed five days more by preparations to descend the river. When at length he moved southward, scouring the country as he went, he could find no more enemies. He effected his junction with the Georgia troops April 15, and the united armies reached the fork of the Coosa and Tallapoosa April 18, where Major General Pinckney joined them, April 20, and took command; but the Red Sticks had then fled southward. A few of the hostile leaders, including Weatherford, made submission, but McQueen and the chief prophets escaped to continue the war from Florida. The friendly Creeks did not consider the war to be finished; they reported to Hawkins:

"They did not believe the hostile Indians were ready for peace, although a part of them had suffered so severely in battle against our armies. They were proud, haughty, brave, and mad by fanaticism. Those of the towns of Tallapoosa below Tuckaubatchee and Alabama had suffered the least, although they were the most culpable; and it was probable they would mistake our object in offering terms of peace to them."

The number of refugees was never precisely known, but Hawkins reported that eight of the Tallapoosa towns had migrated in a body to Spanish territory, and probably a larger proportion of the Coosa and Alabama towns accompanied them. The Indians themselves gave out that a few more than a thousand Red Stick warriors survived, who meant to die fighting. In May the British admiral Cochrane sent Captain Pigot of the *Orpheus* to the Appalachicola to communicate with the refugee Creek Indians and supply them with arms. Pigot received ten of the principal chiefs on board his vessel May 20, and reported on their authority that "the number of the warriors ready to take up arms was about twenty-eight hundred, exclusive of one thousand unarmed warriors who had been driven by the Americans from their towns into the marshes near Pensacola, and who were expected to rejoin the main body." The Creek warriors friendly to the Americans were estimated at about twelve hundred, and the fugitive Red Sticks at one thousand. Whatever their number, they included the most fanatical followers of Tecumthe and their obstinate outlawry caused long and costly difficulties to the United States government.

Meanwhile the whites were conquerors and could take as much of the Creek lands as suited them; but an irregularity of form could not be avoided. Secretary Armstrong first authorized General Pinckney to conclude a treaty of peace with the hostile Creeks, containing a cession of land and other provisions. A few days later Armstrong saw reason to prefer that the proposed treaty with the Creeks should take a form altogether military, and be in the nature of a capitulation. His idea required a treaty with the hostile Creek chiefs; but the hostile Creeks were not a separate organization capable of making a treaty or granting lands of the Creek nation; and besides that difficulty the hostile chiefs had fled, and refused either to submit or negotiate. No chiefs remained except among the friendly Creeks, who could not capitulate because they had never been at war. They had fought in the United States service and were entitled to reward as allies, not to punishment as enemies.

The solution of this legal problem was entrusted to Andrew Jackson, whose services in the war earned for him the appointment of major general in the regular army, and the command of Military District No. 7, with headquarters at Mobile. Jackson met the Creek chiefs in July. The Indians, parties to the negotiation, were friendly chiefs, deputies, and warriors, representing perhaps one-third of the entire Creek nation. To these allies and friends Jackson presented a paper, originally intended for the hostile Indians, entitled "Articles of Agreement and Capitulation," requiring as indemnity for war expenses a surrender of two-thirds of their territory. They were required to withdraw from the southern and western half of Alabama, within the Chattahoochee on the east and the Coosa on the west. The military object of this policy was to isolate them from the Seminoles and Spaniards on one side, and from the Choctaws and Chickasaws on the other. The political object was to surround them with a white population.

Unanimously the Creeks refused to accept the sacrifice. Jackson told them in reply that their refusal would show them to be enemies of the United States; that they might retain their own part of the country, but that the part which belonged to the hostile Indians would be taken by the government; and that the chiefs who would not consent to sign the paper might join the Red Sticks at Pensacola—although, added Jackson, he should probably overtake and destroy them before they could get there. Such arguments could not be answered. A number of the Creeks at last, after long resistance, signed the capitulation or agreement, although they continued to protest against it, and refused their aid to carry it out.

Jackson's capitulation of August 9, 1814, which, without closing the Creek war, appropriated to the government the larger part of the Creek lands, was nearly simultaneous with a treaty signed July 22 by William Henry Harrison and Lewis Cass, at Greenville in Ohio, with chiefs of the Wyandots, Delawares, Shawanese, Senecas, and Miamis. This treaty contained no land-cession, but established peace between the parties and obliged the Indian signers to declare war on the British. Neither Harrison's nor Jackson's treaty embraced the chief body of hostile Indians; but Harrison's treaty served another purpose of no small value in appearing to remove an obstacle to negotiation with England.

CHAPTER XII

"THE BLOCKADE"

Badly as the United States fared in the campaign of 1813, their situation would have been easy had they not suffered under the annoyances of a blockade continually becoming more stringent. The doctrine that coasts could be blockaded was enforced against America with an energy that fell little short of demonstration. The summer was well advanced before the whole naval force to be used for the purpose could be posted at the proper stations. Not until May 26 did Admiral Warren issue at Bermuda his proclamation of "a strict and rigorous blockade of the ports and harbors of New York, Charleston, Port Royal, Savannah, and of the river Mississippi," which completed the blockade of the coast, leaving only the ports of New England open to neutrals. From that time nothing entered or left the blockaded coast except swift privateers, or occasional fast-sailing vessels which risked capture in the attempt. Toward the close of the year Admiral Warren extended his blockade eastward. Notice of the extension was given at Halifax November 16, and by the blockading squadron off New London December 2, thus closing Long Island Sound to all vessels of every description.

The pressure of the blockade was immediately felt. In August superfine flour sold at Boston for $11.87 a barrel, at Baltimore for $6.00, and at Richmond for $4.50. Upland cotton sold at Boston for twenty cents a pound; at Charleston for nine cents. Rice sold at Philadelphia for $12.00 a hundred weight; in Charleston and Savannah for $3.00. Sugar sold in Boston for $18.75 a hundred weight; in Baltimore for $26.50. Already the American staples were unsalable at the places of their production. No rate of profit could cause cotton, rice, or wheat to be brought by sea from Charleston or Norfolk to Boston. Soon speculation began. The price of imported articles rose to extravagant points. At the end of the year coffee sold for thirty-eight cents a pound, after selling for twenty-one cents in August. Tea which could be bought for $1.70 per pound in August, sold for three and four dollars in December. Sugar which was quoted at nine dollars a hundred weight in New Orleans, and in August sold for twenty-one or twenty-two dollars in New York and Philadelphia, stood at forty dollars in December.

More sweeping in its effects on exports than on imports, the blockade rapidly reduced the means of the people. After the summer of 1813, Georgia alone, owing to its contiguity with Florida, succeeded in continuing to send out cotton. The exports of New York, which exceeded $12,250,000 in 1811, fell to $209,-000 for the year ending in 1814. The domestic exports of Virginia diminished in four years from $4,800,000 to $3,000,000 for 1812, $1,819,000 for 1813, and $17,581 for the year ending September 30, 1814. At the close of 1813 exports, except from Georgia and New England, ceased.

On the revenue the blockade acted with equal effect. Owing to the increase of duties and to open ports, the New England States rather increased than diminished their customs receipts. Until the summer of 1813, when the blockade began in earnest, New York showed the same result; but after that time the receipts fell, until they averaged less than $50,000 a month instead of $500,000, which would have been a normal average if peace had been preserved. Philadelphia suffered sooner. In 1810 the State of Pennsylvania contributed more than $200,000 a month to the Treasury; in 1813 it contributed about $25,000 a month. Maryland, where was collected in 1812 no less than $1,780,000 of net revenue, paid only $182,000 in 1813, and showed an actual excess of expenditures in 1814. After the summer, the total net revenue collected in every port of the United States outside of New England did not exceed $150,000 a month or at the rate of $1,800,000 a year.

No ordinary operations of war could affect the United States so severely as this inexorable blockade. Every citizen felt it in every action of his life. The farmer grew crops which he could not sell, while he paid tenfold prices for every necessity. While the country was bursting with wealth, it was ruined. The blockade was but a part of the evil. The whole coast was systematically swept of the means of industry. Especially the Virginians and Marylanders felt the heavy hand of England as it was felt nowhere else except on the Niagara River. A large British squadron occupied Chesapeake Bay, and converted it into a British naval station. After the month of February, 1813, the coasts of Virginia and Maryland enjoyed not a moment's repose. Considering the immense naval power wielded by England, the Americans were fortunate that their chief losses were confined to the farm-yards and poultry of a few islands in Chesapeake Bay, but the constant annoyance and terror were not the less painful to the people who apprehended attack.

Fortunately the British naval officers showed little disposition to distinguish themselves, and their huge line-of-battle ships were not adapted to river service. The squadron under the general command of Admiral Sir John Borlase Warren seemed contented for the most part to close the bay to commerce. The only officer in the fleet who proved the energy and capacity to use a part of the great force lying idle at Lynnhaven Bay was Rear Admiral Sir George Cockburn, whose efficiency was attested by the execration in which his name was held for fifty years in the United States. His duties were not of a nature to make him popular, and he was an admiral of the old school, whose boisterous energy seemed to take needless pleasure in the work.

Early in April, 1813, Admiral Warren sent Cockburn with a light flotilla to the head of Chesapeake Bay to destroy everything that could serve a warlike purpose, and to interrupt, as far as possible, communication along the shore. The squadron consisted of only one light frigate, the *Maidstone,* thirty-six guns; two brigs, the *Fantome* and *Mohawk;* and three or four prize schooners, with four or five hundred seamen, marines, and soldiers. With this petty force Cockburn stationed himself at the mouth of the Susquehanna River and soon threw Maryland into paroxysms of alarm and anger. Taking possession of the islands in his neighborhood, he obtained supplies of fresh food for the whole British force in Chesapeake Bay. He then scoured every creek and inlet above his anchorage. He first moved into the Elk River and sent his boats, April 28, with one hundred and fifty marines to Frenchtown—a village of a dozen buildings which had acquired a certain importance for the traffic between Baltimore and Philadelphia since the stoppage of transit by sea. Without losing a man the expedition drove away the few Americans who made a show of resistance, and burned whatever property was found "consisting of much flour, a large quantity of army clothing, of saddles, bridles, and other equipments for cavalry, etc., together with various articles of merchandise," besides five vessels lying near the place.

Cockburn next sent the same force to destroy a battery lately erected at Havre de Grace. The attack was made on the morning of May 3, and like the attack on Frenchtown, met with only resistance enough to offer an excuse for pillage. The militia took refuge in the woods; Cockburn's troops destroyed or carried away the arms and cannon, and set fire to the town of some sixty houses "to cause the proprietors (who had deserted them and formed part of the militia who had fled to the woods) to understand and feel what they were liable to bring upon themselves by building batteries and acting toward us with so much useless rancor." While engaged in this work Cockburn was told that an extensive cannon-foundry existed about four miles up the Susquehanna River; and he immediately started for it in his boats. He met no resistance and destroyed the foundry with several small vessels. His handful of men passed the day undisturbed on the banks of the Susquehanna, capturing fifty-one cannon, mostly heavy pieces, with one hundred and thirty stand of small arms. The party then returned to their ships "where we arrived at ten o'clock after being twenty-two hours in constant exertion, without nourishment of any kind; and I have much pleasure in being able to add that, excepting Lieutenant Westphall's wound, we have not suffered any casualty whatever."

These expeditions cleared every inlet in the Upper Chesapeake except the Sassafras River on the Eastern Shore. During the night of May 5 Cockburn sent his boats into the Sassafras. Militia in considerable numbers assembled on both banks and opened a fire which Cockburn described as "most heavy," aided by one long gun. Cockburn landed, dispersed the militia, and destroyed Fredericktown and Georgetown with the vessels and stores he found there. This expedition cost him five men wounded, one severely. The next day, May 6, he reported to Admiral Warren:

"I had a deputation from Charleston in the Northeast River to assure me that that place is considered by them at your mercy, and that neither guns nor militiamen shall be suffered there; and as I am assured that all the places in the upper part of Chesapeake Bay have adopted similar resolutions, and as there is now neither public property, vessels, nor warlike stores remaining in this neighborhood, I propose returning to you with the light squadron tomorrow morning."

Thus in the course of a week and without loss of life on either side, Cockburn with a few boats and one hundred and fifty men terrorized the shores of the Upper Chesapeake, and by his loud talk and random threats threw even Baltimore into a panic, causing every one to suspend other pursuits in order to garrison the city against an imaginary attack. The people, harassed by this warfare, remembered with extreme bitterness the marauding of Cockburn and his sailors; but where he met no resistance he paid in part for what private property he took, and as far as was recorded, his predatory excursions cost the Marylanders not a wound.

For six weeks after Cockburn's return to Warren's station at Lynnhaven Bay, the British fleet remained inactive. Apparently the British government aimed at no greater object than that of clearing from Chesapeake Bay every vessel not engaged in British interests under British protection. The small craft and privateers were quickly taken or destroyed; but the three chief depots of commerce and armaments—Norfolk, Baltimore, and Washington—required a greater effort. Of these three places Norfolk seemed most open to approach, and Admiral Warren determined to attack it.

The British navy wished nothing more ardently than to capture or destroy the American frigates. One of these, the *Constellation*, lay at Norfolk, where it remained blockaded throughout the war. Admiral Warren could earn no distinction so great as the credit of capturing this frigate, which not only threatened to annoy British commerce should she escape to sea, but even when blockaded in port required a considerable squadron to watch her, and neutralized several times her force.

Another annoyance drew Warren's attention to Norfolk. June 20 fifteen gunboats issued from the harbor before daylight and under cover of darkness approached within easy range of a becalmed British frigate, the *Junon* of forty-six guns. For half an hour, from four o'clock till half-past four, the gunboats maintained, according to the official report of Commodore Cassin who commanded them, "a heavy, galling fire at about three quarters of a mile distance." Their armament was not mentioned, but probably they, like the gunboats on the Lakes, carried in part long thirty-two and twenty-four-pound guns. The attack was intended to test the offensive value of gunboats, and the result was not satisfactory. The fire of fifteen heavy guns for half an hour on a defenseless frigate within easy range should have caused great injury, but did not. When a breeze rose and enabled the *Junon* and a neighboring frigate, the *Barrosa,* to get under weigh, the gunboats were obliged to retire with the loss of one man killed and two wounded. The *Junon* also had one man killed but received only one or two shots in her hull.

The *Constellation* lay, under the guns of two forts and with every possible precaution, five miles up the Elizabeth River, at the Portsmouth navy yard. The utmost pains had been taken to provide against approach by water. Whatever incompetence or neglect was shown elsewhere, Norfolk was under the command of able officers in both services, who neglected no means of defense. General Wade Hampton had fortified the interior line immediately below the town, where two strong forts were constructed under the direction of Captain Walker Keith Armistead of the Engineers, the first graduate of the West Point Academy in 1803. Five miles below these forts, where the river widened into Hampton Roads, Brigadier General Robert Taylor of the Virginia militia and Captain John Cassin commanding at the navy yard established a second line of defense resting on Craney Island on the left, supported by fifteen or twenty gunboats moored across the channel. A battery of seven guns was established on the island covering the approach to the gunboats so that the capture of the island was necessary to the approach by water. The force on the island consisted of about seven hundred men, of whom less than a hundred were State troops. The rest were infantry of the line, riflemen, seamen, and marines. The town and forts

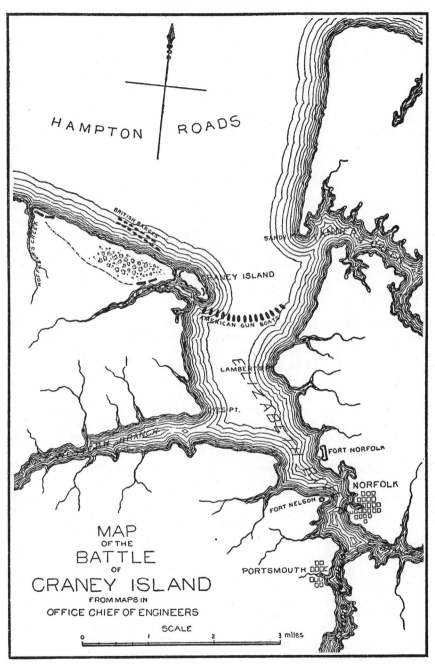

MAP
OF THE
BATTLE
OF
CRANEY ISLAND
FROM MAPS IN
OFFICE CHIEF OF ENGINEERS
SCALE

were strongly garrisoned, and a large body of State militia was constantly on service.

To deal with the defenses of Norfolk, Admiral Warren brought from Bermuda, according to newspaper account, a detachment of battalion marines eighteen hundred strong; three hundred men of the One Hundred and Second regiment of the line, commanded by Lieutenant Colonel Charles James Napier, afterward a very distinguished officer; two hundred and fifty chasseurs, or French prisoners of war who had entered the British service; and three hundred men of the royal marine artillery—in all, two thousand six hundred and fifty rank-and-file, or about three thousand men all told, besides the sailors of the fleet. At that time no less than thirteen sail of British ships, including three ships-of-the-line and five frigates, lay at anchor within thirteen miles of Craney Island.

The attack was planned for June 22. The land forces were commanded by Sir Sydney Beckwith, but the general movement was directed by Admiral Warren. The main attack, led by Major General Beckwith in person, was to land and approach Craney Island from the rear, or mainland; the second division, under command of Captain Pechell of the flagship San Domingo, 74, was to approach the island in boats directly under fire of the American guns on the island, but not exposed to those in the gunboats.

The plan should have succeeded. The island was held by less than seven hundred men in an open earthwork easily assaulted from the rear. The water was so shallow as to offer little protection against energetic attack. The British force was more than twice the American, and the plan of attack took from the gunboats the chance of assisting the land-battery.

At daylight on the morning of June 22 Beckwith, with about eight hundred men, landed on the main shore outside of Craney Island, and pushed forward to take the island in the rear. Soon afterward Captain Pechell, with about seven hundred men in fifteen boats, approached the island from the northwest along the shore, far out of the reach of the gunboats. Toward eleven o'clock the British boats came within range of the American battery on the island. Contrary to the opinions of several officers, Captain Pechell insisted on making the attack independently of Beckwith's approach, and pushed on. Two or three hundred yards from land the leading boats grounded in shoal water. Apparently the men might have waded ashore; but "one of the seamen, having plunged his boat-hook over the side found three or four feet of slimy mud at the bottom;" the leading officer's boat being aground was soon struck by a six-pound shot, the boat sunk, and himself and his crew, with those of two other launches, were left in the water. The other boats took a part of them in, and then quickly retired.

The affair was not improved by the fortunes of Sir Sydney Beckwith, who advanced to the rear of Craney Island, where he was stopped by creeks which he reported too deep to ford, and accordingly re-embarked his troops without further effort; but the true causes of the failure seemed not to be understood. Napier thought it due to the division of command between three heads, Warren, Cockburn, and Beckwith; but incompetence was as obvious as the division of command. Admiral Warren's official report seemed to admit that he was also overmatched:

"Upon approaching the island from the extreme shoalness of the water on the seaside and the difficulty of getting across from the land, as well as the island itself being fortified with a number of guns and men from the frigate [Constellation] and the militia, and flanked by fifteen gunboats, I considered, in consequence of the representation of the officer commanding the troops of the difficulty of their passing over from the land, that the persevering in the attempt would cost more men than the number with us would permit, as the other forts must have been stormed before the frigate and dockyard could be destroyed. I therefore directed the troops to be re-embarked."

On neither side were the losses serious. The American battery inflicted less injury than was to be expected. Fifteen British boats containing at least eight hundred men, all told, remained some two hours under the fire of two twenty-four-pound and four six-pound guns, at a range differently estimated from one hundred to three hundred yards, but certainly beyond musketry fire, for the American troops had to wade out before firing. Three boats were sunk; three men were killed and sixteen were wounded. Sixty-two men were reported missing, twenty-two of whom came ashore from the boats, while forty deserted from Beckwith's land force. The Americans suffered no loss.

To compensate his men for their check at Craney Island, Admiral Warren immediately afterward devised another movement which proved, what the Craney Island affair suggested, that the large British force in the Chesapeake was either ill constructed or ill led. Opposite Craney Island, ten miles away on the north shore of James River, stood the village of Hampton, a place of no importance either military or commercial. Four or five hundred Virginia militia were camped there, covering a heavy battery on the water's edge. The battery and its defenders invited attack, but Admiral Warren could have no military object to gain by attacking them. His official report said "that the enemy having a post at Hampton defended by a considerable corps commanding the communication between the upper part of the country and Norfolk, I considered it advisable, and with a view to cut off their resources, to direct it to be attacked." Hampton could not fairly be said to "command" communication with Norfolk, a place which lay beyond ten miles of water wholly commanded by the British fleet; but Warren was not obliged to excuse himself for attacking wherever he pleased, and Hampton served his object best.

At dawn of June 25 Beckwith's troops were set ashore about two miles above the village, and moved forward to the road, taking Hampton in the rear, while Cockburn's launches made a feint from the front. The militia, after resistance costing Beckwith a total loss of nearly fifty men, escaped, and the British troops entered the town where they were allowed to do what they pleased with property and persons. Lieutenant Colonel Napier of the One Hundred and Second regiment who commanded Beckwith's advance wrote in his diary that Sir Sydney Beckwith "ought to have hanged several villains at Little Hampton; had he so done, the Americans would not have complained; but every horror was perpetrated with impunity—rape, murder, pillage—and not a man was punished." The British officers in general shared Napier's disgust, but alleged that the English troops took no part in the outrages which were wholly the work of the French chasseurs.

Warren made no attempt to hold the town; the troops returned two days afterward to their ships, and the Virginia militia resumed their station; but when the details of the Hampton affair became known, the story roused natural exasperation throughout the country, and gave in its turn incitement to more violence in Canada. Admiral Warren and Sir Sydney Beckwith did not deny the wrong; they dismissed their Frenchmen from the service, and the United States had no further reason to complain of that corps; but the double mortification seemed to lower the British officers even in their own eyes to the level of marauders.

After the failure to destroy the *Constellation,* Admiral Warren could still indulge a hope of destroying the twenty-eight-gun frigate *Adams,* and the navy yard at Washington; for the defense of the Potomac had been totally neglected, and only one indifferent fort, about twelve miles below the Federal city, needed to be captured. July 1 the British squadron entered the Potomac; but beyond rousing a panic at Washington it accomplished nothing except to gain some knowledge of the shoals and windings that impeded the ascent of the river. Leaving the Potomac, Warren turned up Chesapeake Bay toward Annapolis and Baltimore, but made no atttempt on either place. During the rest of the year he cruised about the bay, meeting little resistance, and keeping the States of Virginia and Maryland in constant alarm.

Cockburn was more active. In the month of July he was detached with a squadron carrying Napier's One Hundred and Second regiment and arrived July 12 off Ocracoke Inlet where he captured two fine privateers—the *Atlas* and *Anaconda.* Thence he sailed southward and established himself for the winter on Cumberland Island near the Florida boundary where he vexed the Georgians. Besides the property consumed or wasted he gave refuge to many fugitive slaves whom he assisted to the West Indies or Florida. "Strong is my dislike" wrote Napier, "to what is perhaps a necessary part of our job; namely, plundering and ruining the peasantry. We drive all their cattle and of course ruin them. *My* hands are clean; but it is hateful to see the poor Yankees robbed and to be the robber."

Compared with the widespread destruction which war brought on these regions half a century afterward, the injury inflicted by the British navy in 1813 was trifling; but it served to annoy the Southern people who could offer no resistance and were harassed by incessant militia-calls. To some extent the same system of vexation was pursued on the Northern coast. The Delaware River was blockaded and its shores much annoyed. New York was also blockaded, and Nantucket with the adjacent Sounds became a British naval station. There Sir Thomas Hardy, Nelson's favorite officer, commanded, in his flag ship the *Ramillies.* Hardy did not encourage marauding such as Cockburn practiced but his blockade was still stringent, and its efficiency was proved by the failure of Decatur's efforts to evade it.

Decatur commanded a squadron composed of the *United States,* its prize frigate the *Macedonian,* and the sloop-of-war *Hornet,* which lay in the harbor of New York, waiting for a chance to slip out. Impatient at the steady watch kept by the British fleet off Sandy Hook, Decatur brought his three ships through the

East River into Long Island Sound. He reached Montauk Point, May 29, only to find Hardy's squadron waiting for him. June 1 he made an attempt to run out, but was chased back and took refuge in the harbor of New London. A large British squadron immediately closed upon the harbor, and Decatur not only lost hope of getting to sea but became anxious for the safety of his ships. He withdrew them as far as he could into the river, five miles above the town, and took every precaution to repel attack. The British officers were said to have declared that they would get the *Macedonian* back "even if they followed her into a cornfield." They did not make the attempt, but their vigilance never relaxed, and Decatur was obliged to remain all summer idle in port. He clung to the hope that when winter approached he might still escape; but in the month of December the country was scandalized by the publication of an official letter from Decatur to the Secretary of the Navy, charging the people of New London with the responsibility for his failure.

"Some few nights since," he wrote, December 20, 1813, "the weather promised an opportunity for this squadron to get to sea, and it was said on shore that we intended to make the attempt. In the course of the evening two blue lights were burned on both the points at the harbor's mouth as signals to the enemy; and there is not a doubt but that they have, by signals and otherwise, instantaneous information of our movements. Great but unsuccessful exertions have been made to detect those who communicated with the enemy by signal. . . . Notwithstanding these signals have been repeated, and have been seen by twenty persons at least in this squadron, there are men in New London who have the hardihood to affect to disbelieve it and the effrontery to avow their disbelief."

Decatur's charge roused much ill feeling, and remained a subject of extreme delicacy with the people of New London. Perhaps Decatur would have done better not to make such an assertion until he could prove its truth. That blue lights, as well as other lights, were often seen, no one denied; but whether they came from British or from American hands, or were burned on sea or on shore, were points much disputed. The town of New London was three miles from the river's mouth, and Decatur's squadron then lay at the town. At that distance the precise position of a light in line with the British fleet might be mistaken. Decatur's report, if it proved anything, proved that the signals were concerted, and were burnt from "both the points at the river's mouth." If the British admiral wanted information, he could have found little difficulty in obtaining it; but he would hardly have arranged a system of signals as visible to Decatur as to himself. Even had he done so, he might have employed men in his own service as well as Americans for the purpose. Decatur's letter admitted that he had made great exertions to detect the culprits, but without success.

The rigor of the British blockade extended no farther north than the Vineyard and Nantucket. Captain Broke in the *Shannon*, with a companion frigate, cruised off Boston harbor rather to watch for ships-of-war than to interfere with neutral commerce. Along the coast of Maine an illicit trade with the British provinces was so actively pursued that one of the few American sloops of war, the *Enterprise*, cruised there, holding smugglers, privateers, and petty marauders in check. On no other portion of the coast would an armed national vessel have been allowed to show itself, but the *Enterprise*, protected by the bays and inlets of Maine, and favored by the absence of a blockade, performed a useful service as a revenue cutter. She was not a first-rate vessel. Originally a schooner, carrying twelve guns and sixty men, she had taken part in the war with Tripoli. She was afterward altered into a brig, and crowded with sixteen guns and a hundred men. In 1813 she was commanded by Lieutenant William Burrows, a Pennsylvanian, who entered the navy in 1799, and, like all the naval heroes, was young—not yet twenty-eight years old.

On the morning of September 5 as the *Enterprise* was cruising eastward, Burrows discovered in a bay near Portland a strange brig, and gave chase. The stranger hoisted three English ensigns, fired several guns, and stood for the *Enterprise*. Perhaps escape would have been impossible; but the British captain might, without disgrace, have declined to fight for he was no match for the American. The *Enterprise* measured about ninety-seven feet in length; the *Boxer* as the British brig was named measured about eighty-four. The *Enterprise* was nearly twenty-four feet in extreme width; the *Boxer* slightly exceeded twenty-two feet. The *Enterprise* carried fourteen eighteen-pound carronades and two long nines; the *Boxer* carried twelve eighteen pound carronades and two long sixes. The *Enterprise* had a crew of one hundred and two men; the *Boxer* had only sixty-six men on board. With such odds against him the British captain might have entertained some desperate hope of success, but could not have expected it.

The behavior of Captain Blyth of the *Boxer* showed consciousness of his position for he nailed his colors to the mast and told his men that they were not to be struck while he lived. The day was calm and the two brigs maneuvered for a time before coming together; but at quarter-past three in the afternoon they exchanged their first broadside within a stone's throw of one another. The effect on both vessels was destructive. Captain Blyth fell dead, struck full in the body by an eighteen-pound shot. Lieutenant Burrows fell, mortally wounded, struck by a canister shot. After another broadside, at half-past three the *Enterprise* ranged ahead, crossed the *Boxer's* bow, and fired one or two more broadsides, until the *Boxer* hailed and surrendered, her colors still nailed to the mast.

Considering the disparity of force, the two brigs suffered nearly in equal proportion. The *Boxer* lost seven men killed or mortally wounded; the *Enterprise* lost four. The *Boxer* had thirteen wounded, not fatally; the *Enterprise* had eight. The *Boxer's* injuries were not so severe as to prevent her captors from bringing her as a prize to Portland; and no incident in this quasi-civil war touched the sensibilities of the people more deeply than the common funeral of the two commanders—both well known and favorites in the service, buried, with the same honors and mourners, in the graveyard at Portland overlooking the scene of their battle.

Neither the battle between the *Enterprise* and *Boxer* nor any measures that could be taken by sea or land prevented a constant traffic between Halifax and the New England ports not blockaded. The United States government seemed afraid to interfere with it. The newspapers asserted that hundreds of Americans were actually in Halifax carrying on a direct trade, and that thousands of barrels of flour were constantly arriving there from the United States in vessels carrying the Swedish or other neutral flag. In truth the government could do little to enforce its non-intercourse, and even that little might prove mischievous. Nothing could be worse than the spirit of the people on the frontier. Engaged in a profitable illicit commerce, they could only be controlled by force and any force not overwhelming merely provoked violence or treason. The Navy Department had no vessels to send there, and could not have prevented their capture if vessels in any number had been sent. The Secretary of War had abandoned to the State governments the defense of the coast. When Armstrong allotted garrisons to the various military districts, he stationed one regiment, numbering three hundred and fifty-two effectives, besides two hundred and sixty-three artillerists, in Military District No. 1, which included the whole coast north of Cape Cod, with the towns of Boston, Marblehead, Salem, Gloucester, Portsmouth, Portland, and Eastport. Such a provision was hardly sufficient for garrisoning the fort at Boston. The government doubtless could spare no more of its small army, but for any military or revenue purpose might almost as well have maintained in New England no force whatever.

CHAPTER XIII

CHESAPEAKE AND ARGUS

During the month of April, 1813, four American frigates lay in Boston Harbor fitting for sea. The *President* and *Congress* returned to that port December 31, 1812. The *Constitution*, after her battle with the *Java*, arrived at Boston February 27, 1813. The *Chesapeake* entered in safety April 9 after an unprofitable cruise of four months. The presence of these four frigates at Boston offered a chance for great distinction to the British officer stationed off the port, and one of the best captains in the service was there to seize it. In order to tempt the American frigates to come out boldly, only two British frigates, the *Shannon* and *Tenedos*, remained off the harbor. They were commanded by Captain P. B. V. Broke of the *Shannon*. Broke expected Rodgers with his ships, the *President* and *Congress* to seize the opportunity for a battle with two ships of no greater force than the *Shannon* and *Tenedos* but either Rodgers did not understand the challenge or did not trust it, or took a different view of his duties, for he went to sea on the night of April 30 leaving Broke greatly chagrined and inclined to be somewhat indignant with him for escaping.

After May 1 Broke on the watch outside as he ran in toward Nahant, could see the masts of only the *Constitution* and *Chesapeake* at the Charlestown navy yard and his anxiety became the greater as he noticed that the *Chesapeake* was apparently ready for sea. May 25 Broke sent away his consort the *Tenedos* to cruise from Cape Sable southward, ostensibly because the two frigates cruising separately would have a better chance of intercepting the *Chesapeake* than if they kept together. His stronger reason was to leave a fair field for the *Chesapeake* and *Shannon*, as he had before kept all force at a distance except the *Shannon* and *Tenedos* in order to tempt Rodgers to fight. That there might be no second misunderstanding he sent several messages to Captain Lawrence commanding the *Chesapeake*, inviting a combat.

Nothing showed so clearly that at least one object of the war had been gained by the Americans as the habit adopted by both navies in 1813 of challenging ship duels. War took an unusual character when officers like Hardy and Broke countenanced such a practice, discussing and arranging duels between matched ships, on terms which implied that England admitted half-a-dozen American frigates to be equal in value to the whole British navy. The loss of a British frigate mattered little to a government which had more than a hundred such frigates actually at sea, not to speak of heavier ships; but the loss of the *Chesapeake* was equivalent to destroying nearly one-fourth of the disposable American navy. Already the *Constellation* was imprisoned at Norfolk; the *United States* and *Macedonian* were blockaded for the war; the *Congress* though at sea was unseaworthy and never cruised again; the *Adams* was shut in the Potomac; the *Essex* was in the Pacific. The United States Navy consisted, for active service on the Atlantic, of only the *President*, 44, at sea; the *Constitution* 44, replacing her masts at the Charlestown navy yard; the *Chesapeake*, 38, ready for sea; and a few sloops of war. Under such circumstances British officers who like Broke considered every American frigate bound to offer them equal terms in a duel, seemed to admit that the American service had acquired the credit it claimed.

The first duty of a British officer was to take risks; the first duty of an American officer was to avoid them, and to fight only at his own time, on his own terms. Rodgers properly declined to seek a battle with Broke's ships. Captain James Lawrence of the *Chesapeake* was less cautious, for his experience in the war led him to think worse of the British navy than it deserved. Lawrence commanded the *Hornet* in Bainbridge's squadron at the time of the *Java's* capture. Bainbridge and Lawrence blockaded the *Bonne Citoyenne,* a twenty-gun sloop of war at San Salvador in Brazil. Lawrence sent a message to the captain of the *Bonne Citoyenne* inviting him to come out and meet the *Hornet.* The British captain declined, doubtless for proper reasons; but the reason he gave seemed to Lawrence insufficient, for it was merely that Commodore Bainbridge, in spite of his pledged word, might interfere. Bainbridge sailed about Christmas, and was absent till January 3, capturing the *Java* in the interval. January 6 he sailed for Boston, leaving Lawrence in the *Hornet* still blockading the *Bonne Citoyenne,* which showed no more disposition to fight the *Hornet* in Bainbridge's absence than before, although the British captain's letter had said that "nothing could give me greater satisfaction than complying with the wishes of Captain Lawrence" if the single alleged objection were removed.

The conduct of the *Bonne Citoyenne*—a vessel at least the equal of the *Hornet*—gave Lawrence a low opinion of the British service, and his respect was not increased by his next experience. A British seventy-four arrived at San Salvador, January 24, and obliged the *Hornet* to abandon the *Bonne Citoyenne.* During the next month the little vessel cruised northward along the Brazil coast, making a few prizes, until February 24 off the mouth of Demerara River, at half-past three o'clock in the afternoon, Captain Lawrence discovered a sail approaching him. Within the bar at the mouth of the river, seven or eight miles distant, he saw another vessel at anchor. Both were British sloops of war. The one at anchor was the *Espiègle,* carrying eighteen thirty-two-pound carronades. The other, approaching on the *Hornet's* weather-quarter was the *Peacock* carrying eighteen twenty-four-pound carronades, two long-sixes, and one or two lighter pieces.

The *Peacock,* according to British report, had long been "the admiration of her numerous visitors," and was remarkable for the elegance of her fittings; but in size she was inferior to the *Hornet.* Lawrence reported his ship to be four feet the longer, but the British believed the *Hornet* to measure one hundred and twelve feet in length while the *Peacock* measured one hundred. Their breadth was the same. The *Hornet* carried eighteen thirty-two-pounders, while the British captain, thinking his sloop too light for thirty-twos, had exchanged them for twenty-fours, and carried only sixteen. The American crew numbered one hundred and thirty-five men fit for duty; the British numbered one hundred and twenty-two men and boys.

At ten minutes past five, Lawrence tacked and stood for the brig. Fifteen minutes afterward the two vessels, sailing in opposite directions, passed each other and exchanged broadsides within a stone's throw. The British fire, even at point-blank range of forty or fifty feet, did no harm, while the *Hornet's* broadside must have decided the battle; for although both vessels instantly wore, and Lawrence at thirty-five minutes past five ran his enemy close aboard, the *Peacock* almost immediately struck at thirty-nine minutes past five in a sinking condition, and actually went down immediately afterward, carrying with her nine of the *Peacock's* wounded and three of the *Hornet's* crew.

The ease of this victory was beyond proportion to the odds. The British captain and four men were killed outright, thirty-three officers and men were wounded, and the brig was sunk in an action of less than fifteen minutes; while the *Hornet* lost one man killed and two wounded, all aloft, and not a shot penetrated her hull. If the facility of this triumph satisfied Lawrence of his easy superiority in battle, the conduct of the *Espiègle* convinced him that the British service was worse than incompetent. Lawrence, expecting every moment to see the *Espiègle* get under weigh, made great exertions to put his ship in readiness for a new battle, but to his astonishment the British brig took no notice of the action. Subsequent investigation showed that the *Espiègle* knew nothing of the battle until the next day; but Lawrence, assuming that the British captain must have seen or heard, or at least ought to have suspected what was happening, conceived that cowardice was a trait of the British navy.

When Lawrence reached New York he became famous for his victory, and received at once promotion. The *Hornet* given to Captain Biddle was attached to Decatur's squadron and blockaded at New London, while Lawrence received command of the *Chesapeake*. Lawrence was then thirty-two years old; he was born in New Jersey in 1781, entered the navy in 1798, and served in the war with Tripoli. He was first lieutenant on the *Constitution* and passed to the grade of commander in 1810, commanding successively the *Vixen*, the *Wasp*, the *Argus*, and the *Hornet*. His appointment to the *Chesapeake* was an accident owing to the ill health of Captain Evans, who commanded her on her recent cruise. The *Chesapeake's* reputation for ill luck clung to her so persistently that neither officers nor men cared greatly to sail in her, and Lawrence would have preferred to remain in the *Hornet*; but his instructions were positive, and he took command of the *Chesapeake* about the middle of May. Most of the officers and crew were new. The old crew on reaching port, April 9, had been discharged, and left the ship, dissatisfied with their share of prize money, and preferring to try the privateer service. The new crew was unequal in quality and required training; they neither knew their officers nor each other.

Lawrence's opponent, Captain Broke of the *Shannon*, was an officer whose courage could as little be questioned as his energy or skill. Among all the commanders in the British service Broke had profited most by the lessons of the war. More than seven years' experience of his ship and crew gave him every advantage of discipline and system. Nearly every day the officers at the Charlestown navy yard could see the *Shannon* outside, practicing her guns at floating targets as she sailed about the bay. Broke's most anxious wish was to fight the *Chesapeake*, which he considered to be of the same size with the *Shannon*. The two frigates were the same length within a few inches—between one hundred and fifty, and one hundred and fifty-one feet. Their breadth was forty feet within a few inches. The *Chesapeake* carried eighteen thirty-two pound carronades on the spar-deck; the *Shannon* carried sixteen. Each carried twenty-eight long eighteen-pounders on the gun deck. The *Chesapeake* carried also two long twelve-pounders and a long eighteen-pounder, besides a twelve-pound carronade. The *Shannon* carried four long nine-pounders, a long six-pounder, and three twelve-pound carronades. The *Chesapeake's* only decided advantage was in the number of her crew, which consisted of three hundred and seventy-nine men, while the *Shannon* carried three hundred and thirty all told.

Broke sent the *Tenedos* away May 25, but Lawrence was not aware of it and wrote, May 27, to Captain Biddle of the *Hornet* a letter showing that till the last moment he hoped not to sail in the *Chesapeake:*

"In hopes of being relieved by Captain Stewart, I neglected writing to you according to promise; but as I have given over all hopes of seeing him, and the *Chesapeake* is almost ready, I shall sail on Sunday, provided I have a chance of getting out clear of the *Shannon* and *Tenedos,* who are on the look-out."

Sunday, May 30, the ship was ready, though the crew was not as good or as well disciplined as it should have been, and showed some discontent owing to difficulties about prize money. On the morning of June 1 the frigate was lying in President's Roads, when between eight and nine o'clock the second lieutenant, George Budd, reported a sail in sight. Captain Lawrence went up the main rigging, and having made out the sail to be a large frigate, ordered the crew to be mustered, and told them he meant to fight. At midday he stood down the harbor and out to sea. The *Shannon,* outside, stood off under easy sail, and led the way until five o'clock, when she luffed and waited till the *Chesapeake,* came up. As the wind was westerly, Lawrence had the choice of position, but he made no attempt to profit by his advantage, although it might have been decisive. Bringing the *Chesapeake* with a fresh breeze directly down on the *Shannon's* quarter, at half-past five he luffed, at about fifty yards distance, and ranged up abeam on the *Shannon's* starboard side.

The *Shannon* opened fire as her guns began to bear, but discharged only her two sternmost guns when the *Chesapeake* replied. The two ships ran on about seven minutes, or about the length of time necessary for two discharges of the first guns fired, when, some of the *Shannon's* shot having cut away the *Chesapeake's* foretopsail tie and jib-sheet, the ship came up into the wind and was taken aback. Lying with her larboard quarter toward the *Shannon's* side, at some forty or fifty yards distance, she began to drift toward her enemy. None of the *Chesapeake's* guns then bore on the *Shannon,* and the American frigate wholly ceased firing.

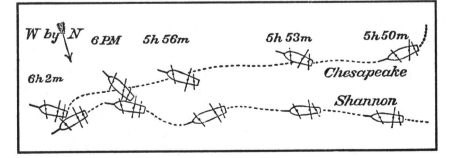

From the moment the *Chesapeake* was taken aback she was a beaten ship, and the crew felt it. She could be saved only by giving her headway, or by boarding the *Shannon;* but neither expedient was possible. The effort to make sail forward was tried, and proved futile. The idea of boarding was also in Lawrence's mind, but the situation made it impracticable. As the *Chesapeake* drifted sternforemost toward the *Shannon,* every gun in the British broadside swept the American deck diagonally from stern to stem, clearing the quarter-deck and beating in the stern-ports, while the musketry from the *Shannon's* tops killed the men at the *Chesapeake's* wheel, and picked off every officer, sailor, or marine in the afterpart of the ship. Boarders could not be rallied under a fire which obliged them to seek cover. The men on the spar-deck left their stations, crowding forward or going below.

Nevertheless, Lawrence ordered up his boarders—he could do nothing else; but the affair hurried with such rapidity to its close that almost at the same instant the *Chesapeake's* quarter touched the *Shannon* amidships. From the moment when the *Chesapeake* was taken aback until the moment when she fell foul, only four minutes were given for Lawrence to act. Before these four minutes were at an end, he was struck and mortally wounded by a musket-ball from the *Shannon.* His first lieutenant, Ludlow, had already been carried below wounded. His second lieutenant, Budd, was stationed below. His third lieutenant, Cox, improperly assisted Lawrence to reach the gun-deck. Not an officer remained on the spar-deck, and neither an officer nor a living man was on the quarter-deck when the *Chesapeake's* quarter came against the *Shannon's* gangway, as though inviting the British captain to take possession.

As the ships fouled, Broke ran forward and called for boarders. With about twenty men he stepped on the *Chesapeake's* quarter-deck and was followed by thirty more before the ships parted. The error should have cost him his life and the lives of all who were with him, for the Americans might easily have killed every man of the boarding-party in spite of the fire from the *Shannon.* For several moments Broke was in the utmost peril, not only from the American crew but from his own. His first lieutenant, Watt, hastening to haul down the American ensign, was killed by the discharge of a cannon from the *Shannon;* and when Broke, leaving the *Chesapeake's* quarter-deck, went forward to clear the forecastle, enough of the American crew were there to make a sharp resistance. Broke himself was obliged to take part in the scuffle. According to his report he "received a severe saber-wound at the first onset, whilst charging a part of the enemy who had rallied on their forecastle." According to another British account he was first knocked down with the butt-end of a musket, and then was cut by a broadsword. Of his fifty boarders, not less than thirty-seven were killed or wounded.

Had the American crew been in a proper state of discipline, the struggle would have taken an extraordinary character, and the two ships might have renewed the combat, without officers, and in a more or less unmanageable condition. Fortunately for Broke his fifty men outnumbered the Americans on the spar-deck, while the men below, for the most part, would not come up. About a score of sailors and marines were on the forecastle, and about a dozen more rushed up from below, led by the second lieutenant, George Budd, as soon as he, at his station on the main-deck, learned what was happening above; but so rapidly did the whole affair pass, that in two minutes the scuffle was over, the Americans were killed or thrown down the hatchway, and the ship was helpless with its spar-deck in the hands of Broke's boarders. The guns ceased firing, and the crew below surrendered after some musket-shots up and down the hatchways.

The disgrace to the Americans did not consist so much in the loss of a ship to one of equal force, as in the shame of suffering capture by a boarding party of fifty men. As Lawrence lay wounded in the cockpit he saw the rush of his men from the spar-deck down the after-ladders, and cried out repeatedly and loudly, "Don't give up the ship! blow her up!" He was said to have added afterward: "I could have stood the wreck if it had not been for the boarding."

Doubtless the *Shannon* was the better ship, and deserved to win. Her crew could under no circumstances have behaved like the crew of the *Chesapeake*. In discipline she was admittedly superior; but the question of superiority in other respects was not decided. The accident that cut the *Chesapeake's* jib-sheet and brought her into the wind was the only decisive part of the battle, and was mere ill luck, such as pursued the *Chesapeake* from the beginning. As far as could be seen, in the favorite American work of gunnery the *Shannon* showed no superiority.

On that point the reports agreed. The action began at half-past five o'clock in the afternoon at close range. In seven minutes the *Chesapeake* forged ahead, came into the wind and ceased firing, as none of her guns could be made to bear. Seven minutes allowed time at the utmost for two discharges of some of her guns. No more guns were fired from the *Chesapeake* till she drifted close to the *Shannon*. Then her two sternmost guns, the thirteenth and fourteenth on the main deck, again bore on the enemy, and were depressed and fired by Lieutenant Cox while the boarders were fighting on the spar-deck. Thus the number of discharges from the *Chesapeake's* guns could be known within reasonable certainty. She carried in her broadside nine thirty-two pounders and fourteen or fifteen eighteen pounders, besides one twelve pounder—twenty-five guns. Assuming them to have been all discharged twice, although the forward guns could scarcely have been discharged more than once, the *Chesapeake* could have fired only fifty-two shots, including the two eighteen pounders fired by Lieutenant Cox at the close.

According to the official report nearly every shot must have taken effect. The *Shannon* was struck by thirteen thirty-two pound shot; the *Chesapeake* fired only eighteen, if she discharged every gun twice. The *Shannon* was struck by twelve eighteen-pound shot, fourteen bar shot, and one hundred and nineteen grape shot; the *Chesapeake's* fifteen eighteen pounders could hardly have done more in the space of seven minutes. In truth, every shot that was fired probably took effect.

The casualties showed equal efficiency of fire, and when compared with other battles were severe. When the *Guerrière* struck to the *Constitution* in the previous year, she had lost in half an hour of close action twenty-three killed or mortally wounded and fifty-six more or less injured. The *Shannon* seems to have lost in eleven minutes before boarding twenty-seven men killed or mortally wounded and nineteen more or less injured.

The relative efficiency of the *Shannon's* gunnery was not so clear because the *Shannon's* battery continued to fire after the *Chesapeake* ceased. As the *Chesapeake* drifted down on the *Shannon* she was exposed to the broadside of the British frigate, while herself unable to fire a gun.

"The shot from the *Shannon's* aftermost guns now had a fair range along the *Chesapeake's* decks," said the British account, "beating in the stern-ports and sweeping the men from their quarters. The shots from the foremost guns at the same time entering the ports from the mainmast aft did considerable execution."

Broke's biographer said that the *Chesapeake* fired but one broadside, and then coming into the wind drifted down, "exposed while making this crippled and helpless movement to the *Shannon's* second and most deliberate broadside." The *Chesapeake* was very near, almost touching the British frigate during the four or five minutes of this fire, and every shot must have taken effect. Broke ordered the firing to cease when he boarded, but one gun was afterward discharged, and killed the British first lieutenant as he was lowering the American flag on the *Chesapeake's* quarter-deck.

The *Shannon's* fire lasted eleven or twelve minutes. She carried twenty-five guns in broadside. Eight of these were thirty-two pound carronades, and the official report showed that the *Chesapeake* was struck by twenty-five thirty-two pound shot, showing that three full broadsides were fired from the *Shannon*, and at least one gun was discharged four times. The *Shannon's* broadside also carried fourteen eighteen-pounders, which threw twenty-nine shot into the *Chesapeake*, besides much canister and grape. Considering that at least half the *Shannon's* shot were fired at so close a range that they could not fail to take effect, nothing proved that her guns were better served than those of the *Chesapeake*. The *Shannon*, according to the British account, fired twice as many shot under twice as favorable conditions, but the injury she inflicted was not twice the injury inflicted in return. Setting aside the grape-shot, the *Chesapeake* struck the *Shannon* thirty-nine times; the *Shannon* struck the *Chesapeake* fifty-seven times. Including the grape-shot, which Broke used freely the *Shannon* probably did better, but even with a liberal allowance for grape and canister, nothing proved her superiority at the guns.

The loss in men corresponded with the injury to the ships. The *Shannon* lost eighty-three killed and wounded; the *Chesapeake* lost one hundred and forty-six. Thirty-three of the *Shannon's* men were killed or died of their wounds; sixty-one of the *Chesapeake's* number were killed or mortally wounded.

The injuries suffered by the *Chesapeake* told the same story, for they were chiefly in the stern, and were inflicted by the *Shannon's* second and third broadsides, after the *Chesapeake* ceased firing. The *Chesapeake's* bowsprit received no injury, and not a spar of any kind was shot away. The *Shannon* carried her prize into Halifax with all its masts standing and without anxiety for its safety.

The news of Broke's victory was received in England and by the British navy with an outburst of pleasure that proved the smart of the wounds inflicted by Hull, Decatur, and Bainbridge. The two official expressions of Broke's naval and civil superiors probably reflected the unexaggerated emotion of the service.

"At this critical moment," wrote Admiral Warrren by a curious coincidence the day before his own somewhat less creditable defeat at Craney Island, "you could not have restored to the British naval service the preëminence it has always preserved, or contradicted in a more forcible manner the foul aspersions and calumnies of a conceited, boasting enemy, than by the brilliant act you have performed."

A few days later he wrote again:

"The relation of such an event restores the history of ancient times, and will do more good to the service than it is possible to conceive."

In Parliament, July 8, John Wilson Croker said:

"The action which he [Broke] fought with the *Chesapeake* was in every respect unexampled. It was not—and he knew it was a bold assertion which he made—to be surpassed by any engagement which graced the naval annals of Great Britain."

The Government made Broke a baronet, but gave him few other rewards, and his wound was too serious to permit future hard service. Lawrence died June 5 before the ships reached Halifax. His first lieutenant Ludlow also died. Their bodies were brought to New York and buried September 16 with formal services at Trinity Church.

By the Americans the defeat was received at first with incredulity and boundless anxiety, followed by extreme discouragement. The news came at a dark moment when every hope had been disappointed and the outlook was gloomy beyond all that had been thought possible.

"I remember," wrote Richard Rush in later life—"what American does not—the first rumor of it. I remember the startling sensation. I remember at first the universal incredulity. I remember how the post offices were thronged for successive days by anxious thousands; how collections of citizens rode out for miles on the highway accosting the mail to catch something by anticipation. At last when the certainty was known I remember the public gloom; funeral orations and badges of mourning bespoke it. 'Don't give up the ship!'—the dying words of Lawrence—were on every tongue."

Six weeks afterward another American naval captain lost another American vessel-of-war by reason of the same over-confidence which caused Lawrence's mistakes, and in a manner equally discreditable to the crew. The *Argus* was a small brig, built in 1803 rating sixteen guns. In the summer of 1813 she was commanded by Captain W. H. Allen of Rhode Island who had been third officer to Barron when he was attacked in the *Chesapeake* by the *Leopard*. Allen was the officer who snatched a coal from the galley and discharged the only gun that was fired that day. On leaving the *Chesapeake*, Allen was promoted to be first officer in the *United States*. To his exertions in training the men to the guns, Decatur attributed his superiority in gunnery over the *Macedonian*. To him fell one of the most distinguished honors that ever came to the share of an American naval officer—that of successfully bringing the *Macedonian* to port. Promoted to the rank of captain, he was put in command of the *Argus,* and ordered to take William Henry Crawford to his post as Minister to France.

On that errand the *Argus* sailed, June 18, and after safely landing Crawford

July 11 at Lorient in Brittany, Captain Allen put to sea again, three days afterward, and in pursuance of his instructions cruised off the mouth of the British Channel. During an entire month he remained between the coast of Brittany and the coast of Ireland, destroying a score of vessels and creating a panic among the ship-owners and underwriters of London. Allen performed his task with as much forbearance as the duty permitted, making no attempt to save his prizes for the sake of prize-money, and permitting all passengers to take what they claimed as their own without inspection or restraint. The English whose property he destroyed spoke of him without personal ill-feeling.

The anxiety and labor of such a service falling on a brig of three hundred tons and a crew of a hundred men, and the impunity with which he defied danger, seemed to make Allen reckless. On the night of August 13 he captured a brig laden with wine from Oporto. Within sight of the Welsh coast and within easy reach of Milford Haven, he burned his prize, not before part of his crew got drunk on the wine. The British brig *Pelican*, then cruising in search of the *Argus*, guided by the light of the burning prize, at five o'clock on the morning of August 14 came down on the American brig; and Captain Allen, who had often declared that he would run from no two-masted vessel, waited for his enemy.

According to British measurements, the *Argus* was ninety-five and one-half feet long; the *Pelican*, one hundred. The *Argus* was twenty-seven feet, seven and five-eighths inches in extreme breadth; the *Pelican* was thirty feet, nine inches. The *Argus* carried eighteen twenty-four pound carronades and two long twelve-pounders; the *Pelican* carried sixteen thirty-two pound carronades, four long six-pounders and a twelve-pound carronade. The number of the *Argus's* crew was disputed. According to British authority, it was one hundred and twenty-seven, while the *Pelican* carried one hundred and sixteen men and boys.

At six o'clock in the morning, according to American reckoning—at half-past five according to the British report—the *Argus* wore, and fired a broadside within grape-distance which was returned with cannon and musketry. Within five minutes Captain Allen was struck by a shot which carried away his left leg, mortally wounding him; and five minutes afterward the first lieutenant was wounded on the head by a grape-shot. Although the second lieutenant fought the brig well, the guns were surprisingly inefficient. During the first fifteen minutes the *Argus* had the advantage of position, and at eighteen minutes after six raked the *Pelican* at close range, but inflicted no great injury on the enemy's hull or rigging, and killed at the utmost but one man, wounding only five. According to an English account "the *Argus* fought well while the cannonading continued, but her guns were not levelled with precision, and many shots passed through the *Pelican's* royals." The *Pelican*, at the end of twenty-five minutes, succeeded in cutting up her opponent's rigging so that the *Argus* lay helpless under her guns. The *Pelican* then took a position on her enemy's starboard quarter and raked her with eight thirty-two pound carronades for nearly twenty minutes at close range without receiving a shot in return except from musketry. According to the report of the British captain, the action "was kept up with great spirit on both sides forty-three minutes, when we lay her alongside and were in the act of boarding when she struck her colors."

The *Argus* repeated the story of the *Chesapeake*, except that the action lasted three-quarters of an hour instead of fifteen minutes. During that time the *Pelican* should have fired all her broadside eight or ten times into the *Argus* at a range so close that no shot should have missed. Sixty thirty-two pound shot fired into a small brig less than one hundred feet long should have shivered it to atoms. Nine thirty-two pound shot from the *Hornet* seemed to reduce the *Peacock* to a sinking condition in fifteen minutes; yet the *Argus* was neither sunk nor dismasted. The British account of her condition after the battle showed no more injury than was suffered by the *Peacock*, even in killed and wounded, by one or at the utmost two broadsides of the *Hornet*.

"The *Argus* was tolerably cut up in her hull. Both her lower masts were wounded, although not badly, and her fore-shrouds on one side nearly all destroyed; but like the *Chesapeake* the *Argus* had no spar shot away. Of her carronades several were disabled. She lost in the action six seamen killed; her commander, two midshipmen, the carpenter, and three seamen mortally, her first lieutenant and five seamen severely, and eight others slightly wounded—total twenty-four; chiefly, if not wholly by the cannon-shot of the *Pelican*."

The *Pelican* lost seven men killed or wounded, chiefly by musketry. On both sides the battle showed little skill with the guns; but perhaps the *Pelican* considering her undisputed superiority during half the combat, showed even less than the *Argus*. As in the *Chesapeake's* battle, the discredit of the defeated ship lay in surrender to boarders.

Two such defeats were calculated to shake confidence in the American navy. That Allen should have been beaten in gunnery was the more strange, because his training with the guns gave him his chief credit with Decatur. Watson, the second lieutenant of the *Argus*, attributed the defeat to the fatigue of his crew. Whatever was the immediate cause, no one could doubt that both the *Chesapeake* and *Argus* were sacrificed to the over-confidence of their commanders.

CHAPTER XIV

PRIVATEERING

The people of the Atlantic coast felt the loss of the *Chesapeake* keenly. Other nations had a history to support them in moments of mortification or had learned by centuries of experience to accept turns of fortune as the fate of war. The American of the seacoast was not only sensitive and anxious, but he also saw with singular clearness the bearing of every disaster, and did not see with equal distinctness the general drift of success. The loss of the *Chesapeake* was a terrible disaster, not merely because it announced the quick recovery of England's pride and power from a momentary shock, but also because it threatened to take away the single object of American enthusiasm which redeemed shortcomings elsewhere. After the loss of the *Chesapeake,* no American frigate was allowed the opportunity to fight with an equal enemy. The British frigates, ordered to cruise in company, gave the Americans no chance to renew their triumphs of 1812.

Indeed, the experience of 1813 tended to show that the frigate was no longer the class of vessel best suited to American wants. Excessively expensive compared with their efficiency, the *Constitution, President,* and *United States* could only with difficulty obtain crews; and when after much delay they were ready for sea, they could not easily evade a blockading squadron. The original cost of a frigate varied from two hundred thousand dollars to three hundred thousand; that of a sloop-of-war, like the *Hornet, Wasp,* or *Argus,* varied between forty and fifty thousand dollars. The frigate required a crew of about four hundred men; the sloop carried about one hundred and fifty. The annual expense of a frigate in active service was about one hundred and thirty-four thousand dollars; that of the brig was sixty thousand. The frigate required much time and heavy timber in her construction; the sloop could be built quickly and of ordinary material. The loss of a frigate was a severe national disaster; the loss of a sloop was not a serious event.

For defensive purposes neither the frigate nor the brig counted heavily against a nation which employed ships-of-the-line by dozens; but even for offensive objects the frigate was hardly so useful as the sloop-of-war. The record of the frigates for 1813 showed no results equivalent to their cost. Their cruises were soon told. The *President,* leaving Boston April 30 ran across to the Azores, thence to the North Sea, and during June and July haunted the shores of Norway, Scotland, and Ireland, returning to Newport September 27 having taken thirteen prizes. The *Congress,* which left Boston with the *President,* cruised nearly eight months in the Atlantic, and returned to Boston December 14, having captured but four merchantmen. The *Chesapeake,* which sailed from Boston, December 13, 1812, cruised four months in the track of British commerce, past Madeira and Cape de Verde, across the equator, and round through the West Indies, returning to Boston April 9, having taken six prizes; at the beginning of her next cruise, June 1, the *Chesapeake* was herself captured. The adventures of the *Essex* in the Pacific were such as might have been equally well performed by a sloop-of-war, and belonged rather to the comparative freedom with which the frigates moved in 1812 than to the difficult situation that followed. No other frigates succeeded in getting to sea till December 4 when the *President* sailed again. The injury inflicted by the frigates on the Atlantic was therefore the capture of twenty-three merchantmen in a year. At the close of 1813 the *President* and the *Essex* were the only frigates at sea; the *Constitution* sailed from Boston only January 1, 1814; the *United States* and *Macedonian* were blockaded at New London; the *Constellation* was still at Norfolk; the *Adams* was at Washington, and the *Congress* at Boston.

When this record was compared with that of the sloops-of-war the frigates were seen to be luxuries. The sloop-of-war was a single-decked vessel, rigged sometimes as a ship, sometimes as a brig, but never as a sloop, measuring about one hundred and ten feet in length by thirty in breadth, and carrying usually eighteen thirty-two-pound carronades and two long twelve-pounders. Of this class the American Navy possessed in 1812 only four examples—the *Hornet*, the *Wasp*, the *Argus*, and the *Syren*. The *Wasp* was lost October 18, 1812, after capturing the *Frolic*. The *Syren* remained at New Orleans during the first year of the war, and then came to Boston, but saw no ocean service of importance during 1813. The *Hornet* made three prizes, including the sloop-of-war *Peacock*, and was then blockaded with the *United States* and *Macedonian*; but the smaller vessel could do what the frigates could not, and in November the *Hornet* slipped out of New London and made her way to New York, where she waited an opportunity to escape to sea. The story will show her success. Finally the *Argus* cruised for a month in the British Channel, and made twenty-one prizes before she was captured by the *Pelican*.

The three frigates, *President*, *Congress*, and *Chesapeake*, captured twenty-three prizes in the course of the year, and lost the *Chesapeake*. The two sloops, the *Hornet* and *Argus*, captured twenty-four prizes, including the sloop-of-war *Peacock*, and lost the *Argus*.

The government at the beginning of the war owned four smaller vessels—the *Nautilus* and *Vixen* of fourteen guns, and the *Enterprise* and *Viper* of twelve. Another brig, the *Rattlesnake*, sixteen, was bought. Experience seemed to prove that these were of little use. The *Nautilus* fell into the hands of Broke's squadron July 16, 1812, within a month after the declaration of war. The *Vixen* was captured November 22, 1812, by Sir James Yeo. The *Viper*, January 17, 1813, became prize to Captain Lumley in the British frigate *Narcissus*. The *Enterprise* distinguished itself by capturing the *Boxer*, and was regarded as a lucky vessel, but was never a good or fast one. The *Rattlesnake* though fast was at last caught on a lee shore by the frigate *Leander*, July 11, 1814, and carried into Halifax.

In the enthusiasm over the frigates in 1812 Congress voted that six forty-fours should be built, besides four ships-of-the-line. The Act was approved January 2, 1813. Not until March 3 did Congress pass an Act for building six new sloops-of-war. The loss of two months was not the only misfortune in this legislation. Had the sloops been begun in January they might have gone to sea by the close of the year. The six sloops were all launched within eleven months from the passage of the bill, and the first of them, the *Frolic*, got to sea within that time, while none of the frigates or line-of-battle ships could get to sea within two years of the passage of the law. A more remarkable oversight was the building of only six sloops, when an equal number of forty-fours and four seventy-fours were ordered. Had Congress voted twenty-four sloops, the proportion would not have been improper; but perhaps the best policy would have been to build fifty such sloops, and to prohibit privateering. The reasons for such a course were best seen in the experiences of the privateers.

The history of the privateers was never satisfactorily written. Neither their number, their measurements, their force, their captures, nor their losses were accurately known. Little ground could be given for an opinion in regard to their economy. Only with grave doubt could any judgment be reached even in regard to their relative efficiency compared with government vessels of the same class. Yet their experience was valuable, and their services were very great.

In the summer of 1812 any craft that could keep the sea in fine weather set out as a privateer to intercept vessels approaching the coast. The typical privateer of the first few months was the pilot-boat, armed with one or two long-nine or twelve-pound guns. Of twenty-six privateers sent from New York in the first four months of war, fifteen carried crews of eighty men or less. These small vessels especially infested the West Indies, where fine weather and light breezes suited their qualities. After the seas had been cleared of such prey as these petty marauders could manage, they were found to be unprofitable—too small to fight and too light to escape. The typical privateer of 1813 was a larger vessel—a brig or schooner of two or three hundred tons, armed with one long pivot-gun and six or eight lighter guns in broadside; carrying crews which varied in number from one hundred and twenty to one hundred and sixty men; swift enough to escape under most circumstances even a frigate, and strong enough to capture any armed merchantman.

After the war was fairly begun, the British mercantile shipping always sailed either under convoy or as armed "running ships" that did not wait for the slow and comparatively rare opportunities of convoy, but trusted to their guns for defense. The new American privateer was adapted to meet both chances. Two or three such craft hanging about a convoy could commonly cut off some merchantman, no matter how careful the convoying man-of-war might be. By night they could run directly into the fleet and cut out vessels without even giving an alarm, and by day they could pick up any craft that lagged behind or happened to stray too far away. Yet the "running ships" were the chief objects of their search, for these were the richest prizes; and the capture of a single such vessel, if it reached an American port in safety, insured success to the cruise. The loss of these vessels caused peculiar annoyance to the British, for they sometimes carried considerable amounts of specie, and usually were charged with a mail which was always sunk and lost in case of capture.

As the war continued, experience taught the owners of privateers the same lesson that was taught to the government. The most efficient vessel of war corresponded in size with the *Hornet* or the new sloops-of-war building in 1813. Tonnage was so arbitrary a mode of measurement that little could be learned from the dimensions of five hundred tons commonly given for these vessels; but in a general way they might be regarded as about one hundred and fifteen or one hundred and twenty feet long on the spar-deck and thirty-one feet in ex-

treme breadth. Unless such vessels were swift sailers, particularly handy in working to windward, they were worse than useless; and for that reason the utmost
effort was made both by the public and private constructors to obtain speed. At
the close of the war the most efficient vessel afloat was probably the American
sloop-of-war, or privateer, of four or five hundred tons, rigged as a ship or brig,
and carrying one hundred and fifty or sixty men, with a battery varying according to the ideas of the captain and owners, but in the case of privateers almost
invariably including one "long Tom" or pivot-gun.

Yet for privateering purposes the smaller craft competed closely with the
larger. For ordinary service no vessel could do more effective work in a more
economical way than was done by Joshua Barney's *Rossie* of Baltimore, or
Boyle's *Comet* of the same port, or Champlin's *General Armstrong* of New
York—schooners or brigs of two or three hundred tons, uncomfortable to their
officers and crews, but most dangerous enemies to merchantmen. Vessels of this
class came into favor long before the war because of their speed, quickness in
handling, and economy during the experience of twenty years in blockade-run-
ning and evasion of cruisers. Such schooners could be built in any Northern sea
port in six weeks or two months at half the cost of a government cruiser.

The government sloop-of-war was not built for privateering purposes. Every
government vessel was intended chiefly to fight, and required strength in every
part and solidity throughout. The frame needed to be heavy to support the heavier
structure; the quarters needed to be thick to protect the men at the guns from
grape and musketry; the armament was as weighty as the frame would bear. So
strong were the sides of American frigates that even thirty-two pound shot fired
at forty or fifty feet distance sometimes failed to penetrate and the British complained as a grievance that the sides of an American forty-four were thicker than
those of a British seventy-four. The American ship-builders spared no pains to
make all their vessels in every respect—in size, strength, and speed—superior to
the vessels with which they were to compete; but the government ship-carpenter
had a harder task than the private ship-builder for he was obliged to obtain
greater speed at the same time that he used heavier material than the British
constructors. As far as the navy carpenters succeeded in their double object, they
did so by improving the model and increasing the proportions of the spars.

The privateer was built for no such object. The last purpose of a privateer was
to fight at close range, and owners much preferred that their vessels, being built
to make money, should not fight at all unless much money could be made. The
private armed vessel was built rather to fly than to fight, and its value depended
far more on its ability to escape than on its capacity to attack. If the privateer
could sail close to the wind, and wear or tack in the twinkling of an eye; if she
could spread an immense amount of canvas and run off as fast as a frigate before
the wind; if she had sweeps to use in a calm, and one long-range gun pivoted
amidships, with plenty of men in case boarding became necessary—she was perfect. To obtain these results the builders and sailors ran excessive risks. Too
lightly built and too heavily sparred, the privateer was never a comfortable or a
safe vessel. Beautiful beyond anything then known in naval construction, such
vessels roused boundless admiration, but defied imitators. British constructors

could not build them, even when they had the models; British captains could not sail them; and when British admirals, fascinated by their beauty and tempted by the marvellous qualities of their model, ordered such a prize to be taken into the service, the first act of the carpenters in the British navy yards was to reduce to their own standard the long masts, and to strengthen the hull and sides till the vessel should be safe in a battle or a gale. Perhaps an American navy carpenter must have done the same; but though not a line in the model might be altered, she never sailed again as she sailed before. She could not bear conventional restraints.

Americans were proud of their privateers, as they well might be; for this was the first time when in competition with the world, on an element open to all, they proved their capacity to excel and produced a creation as beautiful as it was practical. The British navy took a new tone in regard to these vessels. Deeply as the American frigates and sloops-of-war had wounded the pride of the British navy, they never had reduced that fine service to admitted inferiority. Under one pretext or another, every defeat was excused. Even the superiority of American gunnery was met by the proud explanation that the British navy, since Trafalgar, had enjoyed no opportunity to use their guns. Nothing could convince a British admiral that Americans were better fighters than Englishmen; but when he looked at the American schooner he frankly said that England could show no such models, and could not sail them if she had them. In truth, the schooner was a wonderful invention. Not her battles, but her escapes won for her the open-mouthed admiration of the British captains, who saw their prize double like a hare and slip through their fingers at the moment when capture was sure. Under any ordinary condition of wind and weather, with an open sea, the schooner, if only she could get to windward, laughed at a frigate.

As the sailing rather than the fighting qualities of the privateer were the chief object of her construction, those were the points best worth recording; but the newspapers of the time were so much absorbed in proving that Americans could fight, as to cause almost total neglect of the more important question whether Americans could sail better than their rivals. All great nations had fought, and at one time or another every great nation in Europe had been victorious over every other; but no people, in the course of a thousand years of rivalry on the ocean, had invented or had known how to sail a Yankee schooner. Whether ship, brig, schooner, or sloop, the American vessel was believed to outsail any other craft on the ocean, and the proof of this superiority was incumbent on the Americans to furnish. They neglected to do so. No clear evidence was ever recorded of the precise capacities of their favorite vessels. Neither the lines of the hull, the dimensions of the spars, the rates of sailing by the log in different weather, the points of sailing—nothing precise was ever set down.

Of the superiority no doubts could be entertained. The best proof of the American claim was the British admission. Hardly an English writer on marine affairs—whether in newspapers, histories, or novels—failed to make some allusion to the beauty and speed of American vessels. The naval literature of Great Britain from 1812 to 1860 was full of such material. The praise of the invention was still commonly accompanied by some expression of dislike for the inventor, but even in that respect a marked change followed the experiences of 1812-1814. Among the English living on the island of Jamaica, and familiar with the course of events in the West Indies from 1806 to 1817, was one Michael Scott, born in Glasgow in 1789, and in the prime of his youth at the time of the American war. In the year 1829 at the age of forty he began the publication in *Blackwood's Magazine* of a series of sketches which rapidly became popular as *Tom Cringle's Log*. Scott was the best narrator and probably the best informed man who wrote on the West Indies at that period; and his frequent allusions to the United States and the war threw more light on the social side of history than could be obtained from all official sources ever printed.

"I don't like Americans," Scott said; "I never did and never shall like them. I have seldom met an American gentleman in the large and complete sense of the term. I have no wish to eat with them, drink with them, deal with or consort with them in any way; but let me tell the whole truth—*nor fight* with them, were it not for the laurels to be acquired by overcoming an enemy so brave, determined, and alert, and every way so worthy of one's steel as they have always proved."

The Americans did not fight the War of 1812 in order to make themselves loved. According to Scott's testimony they gained the object for which they did fight. "In gunnery and small-arm practice we were as thoroughly weathered on by the Americans during the war as we overtopped them in the bull-dog courage with which our boarders handled those genuine English weapons—the cutlass and the pike." Superiority in the intellectual branches of warfare was conceded to the Americans; but even in regard to physical qualities the British were not inclined to boast.

"In the field," said Scott, "or grappling in mortal combat on the blood-slippery quarter-deck of an enemy's vessel, a British soldier or sailor is the bravest of the brave. No soldier or sailor of any other country, saving and excepting those damned Yankees, can stand against them."

Had English society known so much of Americans in 1807 war would have been unnecessary.

Yet neither equality in physical courage nor superiority in the higher branches of gunnery and small-arms was the chief success of Americans in the war. Beyond question the schooner was the most conclusive triumph. Readers of Michael Scott could not forget the best of his sketches—the escape of the little American schooner *Wave* from two British cruisers by running to windward under the broadside of a man-of-war. With keen appreciation Scott detailed every motion of the vessels, and dwelt with peculiar emphasis on the apparent desperation of the attempt. Again and again the thirty-two-pound shot, as he described the scene, tore through the slight vessel as the two crafts raced through the heavy seas within musket-shot of one another until at last the firing from the corvette ceased. "The breeze had taken off and the *Wave* resuming her superiority in light winds, had escaped." Yet this was not the most significant part of *Tom Cringle's* experience. The *Wave*, being afterward captured at anchor, was taken into the royal service and fitted as a ship-of-war. Cringle was ordered by the vice-admiral to command her, and as she came to report he took a look at her:

"When I had last seen her she was a most beautiful little craft, both in hull and rigging, as ever delighted the eye of a sailor; but the dock-yard riggers and carpenters had fairly bedevilled her, at least so far as appearances went. First they had replaced the light rail on her gunwale by heavy solid bulwarks four feet high, surmounted by hammock nettings at least another foot; so that the symmetrical little vessel that formerly floated on the foam light as a sea-gull now looked like a clumsy, dish-shaped Dutch dogger. Her long, slender wands of masts which used to swing about as if there were neither shrouds nor stays to support them were now as taut and stiff as church-steeples, with four heavy shrouds of a side, and stays and back-stays, and the Devil knows what all."

"If them heave-'em-taughts at the yard have not taken the speed out of the little beauty I am a Dutchman" was the natural comment—as obvious as it was sound.

The reports of privateer captains to their owners were rarely published, and the logs were never printed or deposited in any public office. Occasionally, in the case of a battle or the loss of guns or spars or cargo in a close pursuit, the privateer captain described the causes of his loss in a letter which found its way into print; and from such letters some idea could be drawn of the qualities held in highest regard, both in their vessels and in themselves. The first and commonest remark was that privateers of any merit never seemed to feel anxious for their own safety so long as they could get to windward a couple of gunshots from their enemy. They would risk a broadside in the process without very great anxiety. They chiefly feared lest they might be obliged to run before the wind in heavy weather. The little craft which could turn on itself like a flash and dart away under a frigate's guns into the wind's eye long before the heavy ship could come about had little to fear on that point of sailing; but when she was obliged to run to leeward, the chances were more nearly equal. Sometimes, especially in light breezes or in a stronger wind, by throwing guns and weighty articles overboard privateers could escape; but in heavy weather the ship-of-war could commonly outcarry them and more often could drive them on a coast or into the clutches of some other man-of-war.

Of being forced to fly to leeward almost every privateer could tell interesting stories. A fair example of such tales was an adventure of Captain George Coggeshall, who afterward compiled, chiefly from newspapers, an account of the privateers, among which he preserved a few stories that would otherwise have been lost. Coggeshall commanded a two-hundred-ton schooner, the *David Porter*, in which he made the run to France with a cargo and a letter-of-marque. The schooner was at Bordeaux in March, 1814, when Wellington's army approached. Afraid of seizure by the British if he remained at Bordeaux, Coggeshall sailed from Bordeaux for La Rochelle with a light wind from the eastward, when at daylight March 15, 1814, he found a large ship about two miles to windward. Coggeshall tried to draw his enemy down to leeward, but only lost ground until the ship was not more than two gunshots away. The schooner could then not run to windward without taking the enemy's fire within pistol-shot and dared not return to Bordeaux. Nothing remained but to run before the wind. Coggeshall got out his square-sail and studding-sails ready to set, and when everything was prepared he changed his course and bore off suddenly, gaining a mile in the six or eight minutes lost by the ship in spreading her studding-sails. He then started his water-casks, threw out ballast, and drew away from his pursuer, till in a few hours the ship became a speck on the horizon.

Apparently a similar but narrower escape was made by Captain Champlin of the *Warrior*, a famous privateer-brig of four hundred and thirty tons, mounting twenty-one guns and carrying one hundred and fifty men. Standing for the harbor of Fayal, December 15, 1814, he was seen by a British man-of-war lying there at anchor. The enemy slipped her cables and made sail in chase. The weather was very fresh and squally and at eight o'clock in the evening the ship was only three miles distant. After a run of about sixty miles, the man-of-war came within grape-shot distance and opened fire from her two bow-guns. Champlin luffed a little, got his long pivot-gun to bear, and ran out his starboard guns as though to fight, which caused the ship to shorten sail for battle. Then Champlin at two o'clock in the morning threw overboard eleven guns and escaped. The British ship was in sight the next morning but did not pursue farther.

Often the privateers were obliged to throw everything overboard at the risk of capsizing, or escaped capture only by means of their sweeps. In 1813 Champlin commanded the *General Armstrong*, a brig of two hundred and forty-six tons and one hundred and forty men. Off Surinam, March 11, 1813, he fell in with the British sloop-of-war *Coquette*, which he mistook for a letter-of-marque, and approached with the intention of boarding. Having come within pistol-shot and fired his broadsides, he discovered his error. The wind was light, the two vessels had no headway, and for three-quarters of an hour, if Champlin's account could be believed, he lay within pistol-shot of the man-of-war. He was struck by a musket-ball in the left shoulder; six of his crew were killed and fourteen wounded; his rigging was cut to pieces; his foremast and bowsprit injured, and several shots entered the brig between wind and water, causing her to leak; but at last he succeeded in making sail forward, and with the aid of his sweeps crept out of range. The sloop-of-war was unable to cripple or follow him.

Sometimes the very perfection of the privateer led to dangers as great as though perfection were a fault. Captain Shaler of the *Governor Tompkins*, a schooner, companion to the *General Armstrong*, chased three sails December 25, 1812, and on near approach found them to be two ships and a brig. The larger ship had the appearance of a government transport; she had boarding-nettings almost up to her tops, but her ports appeared to be painted, and she seemed prepared for running away as she fought. Shaler drew nearer, and came to the conclusion that the ship was too heavy for him; but while his first officer went forward with the glass to take another look, a sudden squall struck the schooner without reaching the ship, and in a moment, before the light sails could be taken in, "and almost before I could turn round, I was under the guns, not of a transport, but of a large frigate, and not more than a quarter of a mile from her." With impudence that warranted punishment, Shaler fired his little broadside of nine or twelve pounders into the enemy, who replied with a broadside of twenty-four-pounders, killing three men, wounding five, and causing an explosion on deck that threw confusion into the crew; but the broadside did no serious injury to the rigging.

The schooner was then just abaft the ship's beam, a quarter of a mile away, holding the same course and to windward. She could not tack without exposing her stern to a raking fire, and any failure to come about would have been certain destruction. Shaler stood on, taking the ship's fire, on the chance of outsailing his enemy before a shot could disable the schooner. Side by side the two vessels raced for half an hour, while twenty-four pound shot fell in foam about the schooner, but never struck her, and at last she drew ahead beyond range. Even then her dangers were not at an end. A calm followed; the ship put out boats; and only by throwing deck-lumber and shot overboard, and putting all hands at the sweeps, did Shaler "get clear of one of the most quarrelsome companions that I ever met with."

The capacities of the American privateer could to some extent be inferred from its mishaps. Notwithstanding speed, skill, and caution, the privateer was frequently and perhaps usually captured in the end. The modes of capture were numerous. April 3, 1813, Admiral Warren's squadron in the Chesapeake captured by boats, after a sharp action, the privateer *Dolphin* of Baltimore, which had taken refuge in the Rappahannock River. April 27 the *Tom* of Baltimore, a schooner of nearly three hundred tons, carrying fourteen guns, was captured by his Majesty's ships *Surveillante* and *Lyra* after a smart chase. Captain Collier of the *Surveillante* reported: "She is a remarkably fine vessel of her class, and from her superior sailing has already escaped from eighteen of his Majesty's cruisers." May 11 the *Holkar* of New York was driven ashore off Rhode Island and destroyed by the frigate *Orpheus.* May 19 Captain Gordon of the British man-of-war *Ratler,* in company with the schooner *Bream* drove ashore and captured the *Alexander* of Salem, off Kennebunk "considered the fastest sailing privateer out of the United States" according to Captain Gordon's report. May 21 Captain Hyde Parker of the frigate *Tenedos,* in company with the brig *Curlew,* captured the *Enterprise* of Salem, pierced for eighteen guns. May 23 the *Paul Jones* of sixteen guns and one hundred and twenty men fell in with a frigate in a thick fog off the coast of Ireland and being crippled by her fire surrendered. July 13 Admiral Cockburn captured by boats at Ocracoke Inlet the fine privateer-brig *Anaconda* of New York with a smaller letter-of-marque. July 17 at sea three British men-of-war after a chase of four hours captured the *Yorktown* of twenty guns and one hundred and forty men. The schooner *Orders in Council* of New York, carrying sixteen guns and one hundred and twenty men, was captured during the summer after a long chase of five days, by three British cutters that drove her under the guns of a frigate. The *Matilda*, privateer of eleven guns and one hundred and four men, was captured off San Salvador by attempting to board the Brittish letter-of-marque *Lyon* under the impression that she was the weaker ship.

In these ten instances of large privateers captured or destroyed in 1813, the mode of capture happened to be recorded; and in none of them was the privateer declared to have been outsailed and caught by any single British vessel on the open seas. Modes of disaster were many, and doubtless among the rest a privateer might occasionally be fairly beaten in speed, but few such cases were recorded, although British naval officers were quick to mention these unusual victories. Unless the weather gave to the heavier British vessel-of-war the advantage of carrying more sail in a rough sea, the privateer was rarely outsailed.

The number of privateers at sea in 1813 was not recorded. The list of all private armed vessels during the entire war included somewhat more than five hundred names. Most of these were small craft, withdrawn after a single cruise. Not two hundred were so large as to carry crews of fifty men. Nearly two hundred and fifty, or nearly half the whole number of privateers, fell into British hands. Probably at no single moment were more than fifty sea-going vessels on the ocean as privateers, and the number was usually very much less; while the large privateer-brigs or ships that rivalled sloops-of-war in size were hardly more numerous than the sloops themselves.

The total number of prizes captured from the British in 1813 exceeded four hundred, four-fifths of which were probably captured by privateers, national cruisers taking only seventy-nine. If the privateers succeeded in taking three hundred and fifty prizes, the whole number of privateers could scarcely have exceeded one hundred. The government cruisers *President, Congress, Chesapeake, Hornet,* and *Argus* averaged nearly ten prizes apiece. Privateers averaged much less; but they were ten times as numerous as the government cruisers, and inflicted four times as much injury.

Such an addition to the naval force of the United States was very important. Doubtless the privateers contributed more than the regular navy to bring about a disposition for peace in the British classes most responsible for the war. The colonial and shipping interests, whose influence produced the Orders in Council, suffered the chief penalty. The West India colonies were kept in constant discomfort and starvation by swarms of semi-piratical craft darting in and out of every channel among their islands; but the people of England could have borne with patience the punishment of the West Indies had not the American cruisers inflicted equally severe retribution nearer home.

Great Britain was blockaded. No one could deny that manifest danger existed to any merchant-vessel that entered or left British waters. During the summer the blockade was continuous. Toward the close of 1812 an American named Preble living in Paris bought a small vessel, said to have belonged in turn to the British and French navy, which he fitted as a privateer-brig, carrying sixteen guns and one hundred and sixty men. The *True-Blooded Yankee* commanded by Captain Hailey, sailed from Brest March 1, 1813, and cruised thirty-seven days on the coasts of Ireland and Scotland, capturing twenty-seven valuable vessels; sinking coasters in the very bay of Dublin; landing and taking possession of an island off the coast of Ireland, and of a town in Scotland, where she burned seven vessels in the harbor. She returned safely to Brest, and soon made another cruise. At the same time the schooner *Fox* of Portsmouth burned or sunk vessel after vessel in the Irish Sea, as they plied between Liverpool and Cork. In May the schooner *Paul Jones* of New York, carrying sixteen guns and one hundred and twenty men, took or destroyed a dozen vessels off the Irish coast, until she was herself caught in a fog by the frigate *Leonidas,* and captured May 23 after a chase in which five of her crew were wounded.

While these vessels were thus engaged, the brig *Rattlesnake* of Philadelphia, carrying sixteen guns and one hundred and twenty men, and the brig *Scourge* of New York, carrying nine guns and one hundred and ten men, crossed the ocean and cruised all the year in the northern seas off the coasts of Scotland and Norway, capturing some forty British vessels, and costing the British merchants and shipowners losses to the amount of at least two million dollars. In July the *Scourge* fell in with Commodore Rodgers in the *President,* and the two vessels remained several days in company off the North Cape, while the British admiralty sent three or four squadrons in search of them without success. July 19 after Rodgers had been nearly a month in British waters, one of these squadrons drove him away, and he then made a circuit round Ireland before he turned homeward. At the same time, from July 14 to August 14 the *Argus* was destroying vessels in the British Channel at the rate of nearly one a day. After the capture of the *Argus,* August 14, the *Grand Turk* of Salem, a brig carrying sixteen guns and one hundred and five men, cruised for twenty days in the mouth of the British Channel without being disturbed. Besides these vessels, others dashed into British waters from time to time as they sailed forward and back across the ocean in the track of British commerce.

No one disputed that the privateers were a very important branch of the American navy; but they suffered under serious drawbacks which left doubtful the balance of merits and defects. Perhaps their chief advantage compared with government vessels was their lightness—a quality which no government would have carried to the same extent. The long-range pivot-gun was another invention of the privateer, peculiarly successful and easily adapted for government vessels. In other respects the same number or even half the number of sloops-of-war would have probably inflicted greater injury at less cost. The *Argus* showed how this result could have been attained. The privateer's first object was to save prizes; and in the effort to send captured vessels into port the privateer lost a large proportion by recapture. Down to the moment when Admiral Warren established his blockade of the American coast from New York southward, most of the prizes got to port. After that time the New England ports alone offered reasonable chance of safety, and privateering received a check. During the war about twenty-five hundred vessels all told were captured from the British. Many were destroyed; many released as cartels; and of the remainder not less than seven hundred and fifty, probably one-half the number sent to port, were recaptured by the British navy. Most of these were the prizes of privateers, and would have been destroyed had they been taken by government vessels. They were usually the most valuable prizes, so that the injury that might have been inflicted on British commerce was diminished nearly one-half by the system which encouraged private war as a money-making speculation.

Another objection was equally serious. Like all gambling ventures, privateering was not profitable. In the list of five hundred privateers furnished by the Navy Department, three hundred were recorded as having never made a prize. Of the remainder, few made their expenses. One of the most successful cruises of the war was that of Joshua Barney on the Baltimore schooner *Rossie* at the outbreak of hostilities, when every prize reached port. Barney sent in prizes supposed to be worth fifteen hundred thousand dollars; but after paying charges and duties and selling the goods, he found that the profits were not sufficient to counterbalance the discomforts, and he refused to repeat the experiment. His experience was common. As early as November, 1812, the owners of twenty-four New York privateers sent to Congress a memorial declaring that the profits of private naval war were by no means equal to the hazards, and that the spirit of privateering stood in danger of extinction unless the government would consent in some manner to grant a bounty for the capture or destruction of the enemy's property.

If private enterprise was to fail at the critical moment, and if the government must supply the deficiency, the government would have done better to undertake the whole task. In effect, the government in the end did so. The merchants asked chiefly for a reduction of duties on prize-goods. Gallatin pointed out the serious objections to such legislation, and the little probability that the measure would increase the profits of privateering or the number of privateers. The actual privateers, he said, were more than enough for the food offered by the enemy's trade, and privateering, like every other form of gambling, would always continue to attract more adventurers than it could support.

Congress for the time followed Gallatin's advice, and did nothing; but in the summer session of 1813, after Gallatin's departure for Europe, the privateer owners renewed their appeal, and the acting Secretary of the Treasury, Jones, wrote to the chairman of the Naval Committee July 21, 1813:

"The fact is that . . . privateering is nearly at an end; and from the best observation I have been enabled to make, it is more from the deficiency of remuneration in the net proceeds of their prizes than from the vigilance and success of the enemy in recapturing."

In deference to Jones's opinion, Congress passed an Act, approved August 2, 1813, reducing one-third the duties on prize-goods. Another Act, approved August 3, granted a bounty of twenty-five dollars for every prisoner captured and delivered to a United States agent by a private armed vessel. A third Act, approved August 2, authorized the Secretary of the Navy to place on the pension list any privateersman who should be wounded or disabled in the line of his duty.

These complaints and palliations tended to show that the privateer cost the public more than the equivalent government vessel would have cost. If instead of five hundred privateers of all sizes and efficiency, the government had kept twenty sloops-of-war constantly at sea destroying the enemy's commerce, the result would have been about the same as far as concerned injury to the enemy, while in another respect the government would have escaped one of its chief difficulties. Nothing injured the navy so much as privateering. Seamen commonly preferred the harder but more profitable and shorter cruise in a privateer, where fighting was not expected or wished, to the strict discipline and murderous battles of government ships, where wages were low and prize-money scarce. Of all towns in the United States, Marblehead was probably the most devoted to the sea; but of nine hundred men from Marblehead who took part in the war, fifty-seven served as soldiers, one hundred and twenty entered the navy, while seven hundred and twenty-six went as privateersmen. Only after much delay and difficulty could the frigates obtain crews. The *Constitution* was nearly lost by this cause at the beginning of the war; and the loss of the *Chesapeake* was supposed to be chiefly due to the determination of the old crew to quit the government service for that of the privateers.

Such drawbacks raised reasonable doubts as to the balance of advantages and disadvantages offered by the privateer system. Perhaps more careful inquiry might show that, valuable as the privateers were, the government would have done better to retain all military and naval functions in its own hands, and to cover the seas with small cruisers capable of pursuing a system of thorough destruction against the shipping and colonial interests of England.

CHAPTER XV

MONROE AND ARMSTRONG

John Armstrong was an unusual character. The local influences which shaped Americans were illustrated by the leaders whom New York produced and by none better than by Armstrong. Virginians could not understand, and could still less trust, such a combination of keenness and will, with absence of conventional morals as the Secretary of War displayed. The Virginians were simple in everything; even their casuistry was old-fashioned. Armstrong's mind belonged to modern New York. The Virginians were a knot of country gentlemen, inspired by faith in rural virtues, and sustained by dislike for the city tendencies of Northern society. Among themselves they were genial, reluctant to offend, and eager to remove causes of offense. The domestic history of the government at Washington repeated the Virginian traits. Jefferson and his friends passed much time in making quarrels, and more in making peace. Unlike Pennsylvania, New York, and New England, Virginia stood stoutly by her own leaders; and however harsh Virginians might be in their judgment of others they carried delicacy to an extreme in their treatment of each other. Even John Randolph and W. B. Giles, who seemed to put themselves beyond the social pale, were treated with tenderness and regarded with admiration.

The appearance of a rough and harshly speaking friend in such a society was no slight shock, and for that reason William Henry Crawford was socially one of themselves, while Armstrong belonged to a different type and class. The faculty of doing a harsh act in a harsh way, and of expressing rough opinions in a caustic tone, was not what the Virginians most disliked in Armstrong. His chief fault in their eyes, and one which they could not be blamed for resenting, was his avowed want of admiration for the Virginians themselves. Armstrong's opinion on that subject, which was but the universal opinion of New York politicians, became notorious long before he entered the Cabinet, and even then annoyed Madison. The newspapers gossiped about the mean estimate which Armstrong expressed for the capacities of the Virginia statesmen. So old and fixed was the feud, that from the first the Virginians lost no opportunity to express their opinion of Armstrong, especially in the Senate, whenever he was nominated for office. Madison unwillingly selected him for the post of secretary after Crawford refused it, but neither of the Virginia senators voted on the question of confirmation. In appointing Armstrong, Madison bestowed on him neither respect nor confidence. He afterward declared the reasons that caused him to invite a person whom he distrusted into a position of the highest importance.

"Should it be asked," wrote Madison ten years after the war, "why the individual in question was placed, and after such developments of his career continued, at the head of the War Department, the answer will readily occur to those best acquainted with the circumstances of the period. Others may be referred for an explanation to the difficulty, which had been felt in its fullest pressure, of obtaining services which would have been preferred, several eminent citizens to whom the station had been offered having successively declined it. It was not unknown at the time that objections existed to the person finally appointed, as appeared when his nomination went to the Senate, where it received the reluctant sanction of a scanty majority [eighteen to fifteen]. Nor was the President unaware or unwarned of the temper and turn of mind ascribed to him, which might be uncongenial with the official relations in which he was to stand. But these considerations were sacrificed to recommendations from esteemed friends; a belief that he possessed, with known talents, a degree of military information which might be useful; and a hope that a proper mixture of conciliating confidence and interposing control would render objectionable peculiarities less in practice than in prospect."

Possibly Armstrong took a different view of Madison's conduct, and regarded his own acceptance of the War Department in January, 1813, as proof both of courage and disinterestedness. He knew that he could expect no confidence from Virginians; but apparently he cared little for Virginian enmity, and was chiefly fretted by what he thought Virginian incompetence. No one could fail to see that he came into the Government rather as a master than a servant. According to General Wilkinson he was quite as much feared as hated. "I am indeed shocked," wrote Wilkinson in his Memoirs "when I take a retrospect of the evidence of the terror in which the minister kept more than one great man at Washington." Wilkinson, who hated Madison even more than he hated Armstrong, evidently believed that the President was afraid of his secretary. Madison himself explained that he thought it better to bear with Armstrong's faults than to risk another change in the Department of War.

In that decision Madison was doubtless right. Whatever were Armstrong's faults, he was the strongest Secretary of War the government had yet seen. Hampered by an inheritance of mistakes not easily corrected, and by a chief whose methods were unmilitary in the extreme, Armstrong still introduced into the army an energy wholly new. Before he had been a year in office he swept away the old generals with whom Madison and Eustis had encumbered the service, and in their place substituted new men. While Major Generals Dearborn, Pinckney and Morgan Lewis were set over military districts where active service was unnecessary, and while Major General Wilkinson was summoned to the last of his many courts of inquiry, the President sent to the Senate, January 21 and February 21 the names of two new major generals and six brigadiers of a totally different character from the earlier appointments.

The first major general was George Izard of South Carolina, born at Paris in 1777, his father Ralph Izard being then American commissioner with Franklin and Deane. Returning to America only for a few years after the peace, George Izard at the age of fifteen was sent abroad to receive a military education in England, Germany, and France in the great school of the French Revolution. As far as education could make generals, Izard was the most promising officer in the United States service. Appointed in March, 1812, colonel of the Second Artillery, promoted to brigadier in March, 1813, he served with credit under Hampton at Chateaugay, and received his promotion over the heads of Chandler, Boyd, and one or two other brigadiers his seniors. He was intended to succeed Hampton on Lake Champlain.

The second new major general was Jacob Brown, who after receiving the appointment of brigadier, July 19, 1813, was suddenly promoted to major general at the same time with Izard. The selection was the more remarkable because Brown had no military education, and was taken directly from the militia. Born in Pennsylvania in 1775 of Quaker parentage, Brown began life as a school-master. At the instance of the Society of Friends, he taught their public school in New York city for several years with credit. He then bought a large tract of land near Sackett's Harbor, and in 1799 undertook to found a town of Brownville. He soon became a leading citizen in that part of New York, and in 1809 was appointed to the command of a militia regiment. In 1811 he was made a briga-dier of militia and at the beginning of the war distinguished himself by activity and success at Ogdensburg. His defense of Sackett's Harbor in 1813 won him a brigade in the regular service, and his share in Wilkinson's descent of the St. Lawrence led to his further promotion.

Wilkinson, who regarded Brown as one of his enemies, declared that he knew not enough of military duty to post the guards of his camp, and that he compelled his battery to form in a hollow for the advantage of elevating the pieces to fire at the opposite heights. Winfield Scott, who was one of Brown's warmest friends, described him as full of zeal and vigor, but not a technical soldier, and but little acquainted with organization, tactics, police, and camp duties in gen-eral. The promotion of an officer so inexperienced to the most important com-mand on the frontier gave a measure of Armstrong's boldness and judgment.

The six new brigadiers were also well chosen. They were Alexander Macomb, T. A. Smith, Daniel Bissell, Edmund P. Gaines, Winfield Scott, and Eleazer W. Ripley, all colonels of the regular army selected for their merits. Armstrong sup-plied Brown's defects of education by giving him the aid of Winfield Scott and Ripley, who were sent to organize brigades at Niagara.

The energy thus infused by Armstrong into the regular army lasted for half a century; but perhaps his abrupt methods were better shown in another in-stance, which brought upon him the displeasure of the President. Against Har-rison, Armstrong from the first entertained a prejudice. Believing him to be weak and pretentious, the Secretary of War showed the opinion by leaving him in nominal command in the northwest, but sending all his troops in different di-rections, without consulting him even in regard to movements within his own military department. Harrison, taking just offense, sent his resignation as major general May 11, 1814 but at the same time wrote to Governor Shelby of Ken-tucky a letter which caused the governor to address to the President a remon-strance against accepting the resignation.

At that moment Armstrong and Madison were discussing the means of pro-moting Andrew Jackson in the regular service for his success in the Creek cam-paigns. No commission higher than that of brigadier was then at their disposal, and a commission as brigadier was accordingly prepared for Jackson May 22 with a brevet of major general. Harrison's resignation had been received by Armstrong two days before issuing Jackson's brevet, and had been notified to the President who was then at Montpelier. The President replied May 25 sug-gesting that in view of Harrison's resignation, the better way would be to send a commission as major general directly to Jackson: "I suspend a final decision, however, till I see you, which will be in two or three days after the arrival of this." No sooner did Armstrong receive the letter, than without waiting for the President's return he wrote to Jackson, May 28: "Since the date of my letter of the 24th Major General Harrison has resigned his commission in the army and thus is created a vacancy in that grade, which I hasten to fill with your name."

Armstrong's course was irregular, and his account to Jackson of the circumstances was incorrect; for Harrison's resignation had been received before, not after, Armstrong's letter of the 24th. Madison believed that Armstrong wished to appear as the source of favor to the army. Armstrong attributed Madison's hesitation to the wish of Madison and Monroe that Harrison, rather than Jackson, should take command of Mobile and New Orleans. Both suspicions might be wrong or right; but Armstrong's conduct, while betraying the first motive, suggested the fear that the President might change his mind; and Harrison believed that the President would have done so, had not Armstrong's abrupt action made it impossible. "The President expressed his great regret," said Harrison's biographer, "that the letter of Governor Shelby had not been received earlier, as in that case the valuable services of General Harrison would have been preserved to the nation in the ensuing campaign."

Little as the President liked his Secretary of War, his antipathy was mild when compared with that of Monroe. The failure of the Canada campaign gave a serious blow to Armstrong; but he had still recovered Detroit, and was about to finish the Creek war. His hold upon the army was becoming strong. His enemies charged him with ambition; they said he was systematically engaged in strengthening his influence by seducing the young officers of talent into his personal support, teaching them to look for appreciation not to the President but to himself, and appointing to office only his own tools, or the sons of influential men. He was believed to favor a conscription and to aim at the position of lieutenant general. These stories were constantly brought to Monroe, and drove him to a condition of mind only to be described as rabid. He took the unusual step of communicating them to the President, with confidential comments that, if known to Armstrong, could hardly have failed to break up the Cabinet.

"It is painful to me to make this communication to you," wrote the Secretary of State December 27, 1813; "nor should I do it if I did not most conscientiously believe that this man if continued in office will ruin not you and the Administration only, but the whole Republican party and cause. He has already gone far to do it, and it is my opinion, if he is not promptly removed, he will soon accomplish it. Without repeating other objections to him, if the above facts are true . . . he wants a head fit for his station. Indolent except to improper purposes, he is incapable of that combination and activity which the times require. My advice to you, therefore, is to remove him at once. The near prospect of a conscription, adopted and acted on without your approbation or knowledge, is a sufficient reason. The burning of Newark, if done by his orders, is another. The failure to place troops at Fort George is another. In short there are abundant reasons for it. His removal for either of the three would revive the hopes of our party now desponding, and give a stimulus to measures. I do not however wish you to act on my advice—consult any in whom you have confidence. Mr. A. has, as you may see, few friends, and some of them cling to him rather as I suspect from improper motives, or on a presumption that you support him."

Armstrong's faults were beyond dispute, but his abilities were very considerable; and the President justly thought that nothing would be gained by dismissing him, even to restore Monroe to the War Department. Armstrong, struggling with the load of incapable officers and insufficient means, for which Madison and Congress were responsible, required the firm support of his chief and his colleagues, as well as of the army and of Congress, to carry the burden of the war; but he had not a friend to depend upon. Secretary Jones was as hostile as Monroe. Pennsylvania and Virginia equally distrusted him, and the fate of any public man distrusted by Pennsylvania and Virginia was commonly fixed in advance. Armstrong was allowed to continue his preparations for the next campaign, but Monroe remained actively hostile. In a private letter to Crawford, written probably about the month of May, 1814, and preserved with a memorandum that it was not sent, Monroe said:

"There is now no officer free to command to whom the public looks with any sort of confidence or even hope. Izard stands next, but he is as you see otherwise engaged on a court of inquiry on Wilkinson. Thus the door is left open for some new pretender, and Mr. Armstrong is that pretender. This has been his object from the beginning. . . . The whole affair is beyond my control."

Thus the elements of confusion surrounding Armstrong were many. A suspicious and hesitating President; a powerful and jealous Secretary of State; a South Carolinian major general educated in the French engineers commanding on Lake Champlain; a Pennsylvania schoolmaster, of Quaker parentage, without military knowledge, commanding at Sackett's Harbor and Niagara; a few young brigadiers eager to distinguish themselves, and an army of some thirty thousand men—these were the elements with which Armstrong was to face the whole military power of England; for Paris capitulated March 31 and the war in Europe was ended.

In one respect, Armstrong's conduct seemed inconsistent with the idea of selfishness or intrigue. The duty of organizing a court-martial for the trial of William Hull fell necessarily upon him. Hull's defense must inevitably impeach Hull's superiors; his acquittal was possible only on the ground that the Government had been criminally negligent in supporting him. As far as Armstrong was interested in the result, he was concerned in proving the incapacity of his predecessor Eustis, and of the President, in their management of the war. He could have had no personal object to gain in procuring the conviction of Hull, but he might defend his own course by proving the imbecility of Dearborn.

The President ordered a court-martial on Hull before Armstrong entered the War Department. A. J. Dallas drew up the specifications, and inserted, contrary to his own judgment, a charge of treason made by the Department. The other charges were cowardice, neglect of duty, and unofficer-like conduct. Monroe, while temporarily at the head of the Department, organized the first court to meet at Philadelphia February 25, 1813. Major General Wade Hampton was to preside.

Before the trial could be held, Armstrong came into office and was obliged to order the members of the court to active service. Hampton was sent to Lake Champlain, and when his campaign ended in November, 1813 he returned under charges resembling those against Hull. Finding that neither Wilkinson nor Armstrong cared to press them, and satisfied that no inquiry could be impartial, Hampton determined to settle the question by once more sending in his resignation, which he did in March, 1814, when it was accepted. Armstrong in effect acquitted Hampton by accepting his resignation, and never publicly affirmed any charge against him until after Hampton's death, when he attributed to the major general "much professional error and great moral depravity." Hampton's opinion of Armstrong could be gathered only from his conduct and his letters to the Secretary of War, but was not materially different from Armstrong's opinion of Hampton.

Meanwhile Hull waited for trial. During the summer of 1813 he saw nearly all his possible judges disgraced and demanding courts-martial like himself. Hampton was one; Wilkinson another; Dearborn a third. Dearborn had been removed from command of his army in face of the enemy, and loudly called for a court of inquiry. Instead of granting the request the President again assigned him to duty in command of Military District No. 3 comprising the city of New York, and also made him President of the court-martial upon General Hull.

The impropriety of such a selection could not be denied. Of all men in the United States, Dearborn was most deeply interested in the result of Hull's trial, and the President, next to Dearborn, would be most deeply injured by Hull's acquittal. The judgment of Dearborn, or of any court over which Dearborn presided, in a matter which affected both court and government so closely could not command respect. That Armstrong lent himself to such a measure was a new trait of character never explained; but that Madison either ordered or permitted it showed that he must have been unconscious either of Dearborn's responsibility for Hull's disaster, or of his own.

Hull offered no objection to his court, and the trial began at Albany, January 3, 1814, Dearborn presiding, and Martin Van Buren acting as special judge advocate. March 26 the court sentenced Hull to be shot to death for cowardice, neglect of duty, and unofficer-like conduct. April 25 President Madison approved the sentence, but remitted the execution, and Hull's name was ordered to be struck from the army roll.

That some one should be punished for the loss of Detroit was evident, and few persons were likely to complain because Hull was a selected victim; but many thought that if Hull deserved to be shot, other men, much higher than he in office and responsibility, merited punishment; and the character of the court-martial added no credit to the Government, which in effect it acquitted of blame.

CHAPTER XVI
CHIPPAWA AND LUNDY'S LANE

After the close of the campaign on the St. Lawrence, in November, 1813, General Wilkinson's army, numbering about eight thousand men, sick and well, went into winter quarters at French Mills, on the Canada line, about eight miles south of the St. Lawrence. Wilkinson was unfit for service, and asked leave to remove to Albany, leaving Izard in command; but Armstrong was not yet ready to make the new arrangements, and Wilkinson remained with the army during the winter. His force seemed to stand in a good position for annoying the enemy and interrupting communications between Upper and Lower Canada; but it lay idle between November 13 and February 1, when, under orders from Armstrong, it was broken up. Brigadier-General Brown, with two thousand men, was sent to Sackett's Harbor. The rest of the army was ordered to fall back to Plattsburg—a point believed most likely to attract the enemy's notice in the spring.

Wilkinson obeyed, and found himself, in March, at Plattsburg with about four thousand effectives. He was at enmity with superiors and subordinates alike; but the chief object of his antipathy was the Secretary of War. From Plattsburg, March 27, he wrote a private letter to Major-General Dearborn whose hostility to the secretary was also pronounced: "I know of his (Armstrong's) secret underworkings, and have therefore, to take the bull by the horns, demanded an arrest and a court-martial. . . . Good God! I am astonished at the man's audacity, when he must be sensible of the power I have over him." Pending the reply to his request for a court-martial, Wilkinson determined to make a military effort. "My advanced post is at Champlain on this side. I move today; and the day after tomorrow, if the ice, snow, and frost should not disappear, we shall visit the Lacolle, and take possession of that place. This is imperiously enjoined to check the reinforcements he (Prevost) continues to send to the Upper Province."

The Lacolle was a small river, or creek, emptying into the Sorel four or five miles beyond the boundary. According to the monthly return of the troops commanded by Major-General de Rottenburg, the British forces stationed about Montreal numbered, January 22, 1814, eight thousand rank-and-file present for duty. Of these, eight hundred and eighty-five were at St. John's; six hundred and ninety were at Isle aux Noix, with outposts at Lacadie and Lacolle of three hundred and thirty-two men.

Wilkinson knew that the British outpost at the crossing of Lacolle Creek, numbering two hundred men all told, was without support nearer than Isle aux Noix ten miles away; but it was stationed in a stone mill, with thick walls and a solid front. He took two twelve-pound field-guns to batter the mill, and crossing the boundary, March 30, with his four thousand men, advanced four or five miles to Lacolle Creek. The roads were obstructed and impassable, but his troops made their way in deep snow through the woods until they came within sight of the mill. The guns were then placed in position and opened fire; but Wilkinson was disconcerted to find that after two hours the mill was unharmed. He ventured neither to storm it nor flank it; and after losing more than two hundred men by the fire of the garrison, he ordered a retreat, and marched his army back to Champlain.

With this last example of his military capacity Wilkinson disappeared from the scene of active life, where he had performed so long and extraordinary a part. Orders arrived, dated March 24, relieving him from duty under the form of granting his request for a court of inquiry. Once more he passed the ordeal of a severe investigation, and received the verdict of acquittal; but he never was again permitted to resume his command in the army.

The force Wilkinson had brought from Lake Ontario, though united with that which Wade Hampton had organized, was reduced by sickness, expiration of enlistments, and other modes of depletion to a mere handful when Major-General Izard arrived at Plattsburg on the first day of May. Izard's experience formed a separate narrative, and made a part of the autumn campaign. During the early summer, the war took a different and unexpected direction, following the steps of the new Major-General Brown; for wherever Brown went, fighting followed.

General Brown marched from French Mills, February 13, with two thousand men. February 28, Secretary Armstrong wrote him a letter suggesting an attack on Kingston, to be covered by a feint on Niagara. Brown, on arriving at Sackett's Harbor, consulted Chauncey, and allowed himself to be dissuaded from attacking Kingston. "By some extraordinary mental process," Armstrong thought, Brown and Chauncey "arrived at the same conclusion,—that the main action, an attack on Kingston, being impracticable, the *ruse*, intended merely to mask it, might do as well." Brown immediately marched with two thousand men for Niagara.

When the secretary learned of this movement, although it was contrary to his ideas of strategy; he wrote an encouraging letter to Brown, March 20:

"You have mistaken my meaning. . . . If you hazard anything by this mistake, correct it promptly by returning to your post. If on the other hand you left the Harbor with a competent force for its defence, go on and prosper. Good consequences are sometimes the result of mistakes."

The correspondence showed chiefly that neither the secretary nor the general had a distinct idea, and that Brown's campaign, like Dearborn's the year before, received its direction from Chauncey, whose repugnance to attacking Kingston was invincible.

Brown was shown his mistake by Gaines, before reaching Buffalo March 24, and leaving his troops he hurried back to Sackett's Harbor, "the most unhappy man alive." He resumed charge of such troops as remained at the Harbor, while Winfield Scott formed a camp of instruction at Buffalo, and, waiting for recruits who never came, personally drilled the officers of all grades. Scott's energy threw into the little army a spirit and an organization strange to the service. Three months of instruction converted the raw troops into soldiers.

Meanwhile Brown could do nothing at Sackett's Harbor. The British held control of the Lake, while Commodore Chauncey and the contractor Eckford were engaged in building a new ship which was to be ready in July. The British nearly succeeded in preventing Chauncey from appearing on the Lake during the entire season, for no sooner did Sir James Yeo sail from Kingston in the spring than he attempted to destroy the American magazines. Owing to the remote situation of Sackett's Harbor in the extreme northern corner of the State, all supplies and war material were brought first from the Hudson River to Oswego by way of the Mohawk River and Oneida Lake. About twelve miles above Oswego the American magazines were established, and there the stores were kept until they could be shipped on schooners, and forwarded fifty miles along the Lake-shore to Sackett's Harbor—always a hazardous operation in the face of an enemy's fleet. The destruction of the magazines would have been fatal to Chauncey, and even the capture or destruction of the schooners with stores was no trifling addition to his difficulties.

Sir James Yeo left Kingston May 4, and appeared off Oswego the next day, bringing a large body of troops, numbering more than a thousand rank-and-file. They found only about three hundred men to oppose them, and having landed May 6, they gained possession of the fort which protected the harbor of Oswego. The Americans made a resistance which caused a loss of seventy-two men killed and wounded to the British, among the rest Captain Mulcaster of the Royal Navy, an active officer, who was dangerously wounded. The result was hardly worth the loss. Four schooners were captured or destroyed, and some twenty-four hundred barrels of flour, pork, and salt, but nothing of serious importance. Yeo made no attempt to ascend the river, and retired to Kingston after destroying whatever property he could not take away.

Although the chief American depot escaped destruction, the disgrace and discouragement remained, that after two years of war the Americans, though enjoying every advantage, were weaker than ever on Lake Ontario, and could not defend even so important a point as Oswego from the attack of barely a thousand men. Their coastwise supply of stores to Sackett's Harbor became a difficult and dangerous undertaking, to be performed mostly by night. Chauncey remained practically blockaded in Sackett's Harbor; and without his fleet in control of the Lake the army could do nothing effectual against Kingston.

In this helplessness, Armstrong was obliged to seek some other line on which the army could be employed against Upper Canada; and the idea occurred to him that although he had no fleet on Lake Ontario he had one on Lake Erie, which by a little ingenuity might enable the army to approach the heart of Upper Canada at the extreme western end of Lake Ontario. "Eight or even six thousand men," Armstrong wrote to the President, April 30, "landed in the bay between Point Abino and Fort Erie, and operating either on the line of the Niagara, or more directly if a more direct route is found, against the British post at the head of Burlington Bay, cannot be resisted with effect without compelling the enemy so to weaken his more eastern posts as to bring them within reach of our means at Sackett's Harbor and Plattsburg."

Armstrong's suggestion was made to the President April 30. Already time was short. The allies had entered Paris March 31; the citadel of Bayonne capitulated to Wellington April 28. In a confidential despatch dated June 3, Lord Bathurst notified the governor-general of Canada that ten thousand men had been ordered to be shipped immediately for Quebec. July 5, Major-General Torrens at the Horse-guards informed Prevost that four brigades—Brisbane's, Kempt's, Power's, and Robinson's; fourteen regiments of Wellington's best troops—had sailed from Bordeaux for Canada. Prevost could afford in July to send westward every regular soldier in Lower Canada, sure of replacing them at Montreal by the month of August.

"A discrepancy in the opinions of the Cabinet," according to Armstrong, delayed adoption of a plan till June, when a compromise scheme was accepted, but not carried out.

"Two causes prevented its being acted upon *in extenso,*" Armstrong afterward explained—"the one, a total failure in getting together by militia calls and volunteer overtures a force deemed competent to a campaign of demonstration and manoeuvre on the peninsula; the other, an apprehension that the fleet, which had been long inactive, would not yet be found in condition to sustain projects requiring from it a vigorous coöperation with the army."

Brown might have been greatly strengthened at Niagara by drawing from Detroit the men that could be spared there; but the Cabinet obliged Armstrong to send the Detroit force—about nine hundred in number—against Mackinaw. Early in July the Mackinaw expedition, commanded by Lieutenant-Colonel Croghan, started from Detroit, and August 4 it was defeated and returned. Croghan's expedition did not even arrive in time to prevent a British expedition from Mackinaw crossing Wisconsin and capturing, July 19, the distant American post at Prairie du Chien.

Armstrong did not favor Croghan's expedition, wishing to bring him and his two batteries to reinforce Brown, but yielded to the Secretary of the Navy, who wished to capture Mackinaw, and to the promises of Commodore Chauncey that on or before July 1 he would sail from Sackett's Harbor, and command the Lake. In reliance on Chauncey, the Cabinet, except Monroe, decided that Major-General Brown should cross to the Canadian side, above the Fall of Niagara, and march, with Chauncey's support, to Burlington Heights and to York.

This decision was made June 7, and Armstrong wrote to Brown, June 10, describing the movement intended. The Secretary of the Navy, he said, thought Chauncey could not be ready before July 15:

"To give, however, immediate occupation to your troops, and to prevent their blood from stagnating, why not take Fort Erie and its garrison, stated at three or four hundred men? Land between Point Abino and Erie in the night; assail the fort by land and water; push forward a corps to seize the bridge at Chippawa; and be governed by circumstances in either stopping there or going farther. Boats may follow and feed you. If the enemy concentrates his whole force on this line, as I think he will, it will not exceed two thousand men."

Brown had left Sackett's Harbor, and was at Buffalo when these orders reached him. He took immediate measures to carry them out. Besides his regular force, he called for volunteers to be commanded by Peter B. Porter; and he wrote to Chauncey, June 21, an irritating letter, complaining of having received not a line from him, and giving a sort of challenge to the navy to meet the army before Fort George, by July 10. The letter showed that opinion in the army ran against the navy and particularly against Chauncey, whom Brown evidently regarded as a sort of naval Wilkinson. In truth, Brown could depend neither upon Chauncey nor upon volunteers. The whole force he could collect was hardly enough to cross the river, and little exceeded the three thousand men on whose presence at once in the boats Alexander Smyth had insisted eighteen months before, in order to capture Fort Erie.

So famous did Brown's little army become, that the details of its force and organization retained an interest equalled only by that which attached to the frigates and sloops-of-war. Although the existence of the regiments ceased with the peace, and their achievements were limited to a single campaign of three or four months, their fame would have insured them in any other service extraordinary honors and sedulous preservation of their identity. Two small brigades of regular troops, and one still smaller brigade of Pennsylvania volunteers, with a corps of artillery, composed the entire force. The first brigade was commanded by Brigadier-General Winfield Scott, and its monthly return of June 30, 1814, reported its organization and force as follows:

STRENGTH OF THE FIRST, OR SCOTT'S, BRIGADE

	Non-com Officers, Rank-and file	Officers	Aggregate Present and absent
Ninth Regiment	332	16	642
Eleventh Regiment	416	17	577
Twenty-second Regiment	217	12	287
Twenty-fifth Regiment	354	16	619
General Staff		4	4
Total	1,319	65	2,129

The Ninth regiment came from Massachusetts, and in this campaign was usually commanded by its lieutenant-colonel, Thomas Aspinwall, or by Major Henry Leavenworth. The Eleventh was raised in Vermont, and was led by Major John McNeil. The Twenty-second was a Pennsylvania regiment, commanded by its colonel, Hugh Brady. The Twenty-fifth was enlisted in Connecticut, and identified by the name of T. S. Jesup, one of its majors. The whole brigade, officers and privates, numbered thirteen hundred and eighty-four men present for duty on the first day of July, 1814.

The Second, or Ripley's, brigade was still smaller, and became even more famous. Eleazar Wheelock Ripley was born in New Hampshire, in the year 1782. He became a resident of Portland in Maine, and was sent as a representative to the State legislature at Boston, where he was chosen speaker of the Massachusetts House of Representatives, January 17, 1812, on the retirement of Joseph Story to become a Justice of the Supreme Court of the United States. A few weeks afterward, March 12, 1812, Ripley took the commission of lieutenant-colonel of the Twenty-first regiment, to be enlisted in Massachusetts. A year afterward he became colonel of the same regiment, and took part in the battle of Chrystler's Field. Secretary Armstrong made him a brigadier-general April 15, 1814, his commission bearing date about a month after that of Winfield Scott. Both the new brigadiers were sent to Niagara, where Scott formed a brigade from regiments trained by himself; and Ripley was given a brigade composed of his old regiment, the Twenty-first, with detachments from the Seventeenth and Nineteenth and Twenty-third. The strength of the brigade, July 1, 1814, was reported in the monthly return as follows:

Strength of the Second, or Ripley's, Brigade

	Present for Duty Non-com. Officers, Rank-and-file	Officers	Aggregate Present and absent
Twenty-first Regiment	651	25	917
Twenty-third Regiment	341	8	496
General Staff		2	2
Total	992	35	1,415

Ripley's old regiment, the Twenty-first, was given to Colonel James Miller, who had served in the Tippecanoe campaign as major in the Fourth Infantry, and had shared the misfortune of that regiment at Detroit. The other regiment composing the brigade—the Twenty-third—was raised in New York, and was usually commanded by one or another of its majors, McFarland or Brooke. Ripley's brigade numbered one thousand and twenty-seven men present for duty, on the first day of July.

The artillery, under the command of Major Hindman, was composed of four companies.

Strength of Hindman's Battalion of Artillery

	Present for Duty	Aggregate
Towson's Company	89	101
Biddle's Company	80	104
Ritchie's Company	96	133
Williams's Company	62	73
Total	327	411

The militia brigade was commanded by Peter B. Porter, and consisted of six hundred Pennsylvania volunteer militia, with about the same number of Indians, comprising nearly the whole military strength of the Six Nations.

Strength of Major-General Brown's Army, Buffalo, July 1, 1814

	Present for Duty Non-com. Officers, Rank-and-file	Officers	Aggregate Present and absent
Artillery	330	15	413
Scott's Brigade	1,312	65	2,122
Ripley's Brigade	992	36	1,415
Porter's Brigade	710	43	830
Total...................	3,344	159	4,780

Thus the whole of Brown's army consisted of half-a-dozen skeleton regiments, and including every officer, as well as all Porter's volunteers, numbered barely thirty-five hundred men present for duty. The aggregate, including sick and absent, did not reach five thousand.

The number of effectives varied slightly from week to week, as men joined or left their regiments; but the entire force never exceeded thirty-five hundred men, exclusive of Indians.

According to the weekly return of June 22, 1814, Major-General Riall, who commanded the right division of the British Army, had a force of four thousand rank-and-file present for duty; but of this number the larger part were in garrison at York, Burlington Heights, and Fort Niagara. His headquarters were at Fort George, where he had nine hundred and twenty-seven rank-and-file present for duty. Opposite Fort George, in Fort Niagara on the American side, five hundred and seventy-eight rank-and-file were present for duty. At Queenston were two hundred and fifty-eight; at Chippawa, four hundred and twenty-eight; at Fort Erie, one hundred and forty-six. In all, on the Niagara River Riall commanded two thousand three hundred and thirty-seven rank-and-file present for duty. The officers, musicians, etc., numbered three hundred and thirty-two. At that time only about one hundred and seventy men were on the sick list. All told, sick and well, the regular force numbered two thousand eight hundred and forty men. They belonged chiefly to the First, or Royal Scots; the Eighth, or King's; the Hundredth, the Hundred-and-third regiments, and the Artillery, with a few dragoons.

As soon as Porter's volunteers were ready, the whole American army was thrown across the river. The operation was effected early in the morning of July 3; and although the transport was altogether insufficient, the movement was accomplished without accident or delay. Scott's brigade with the artillery landed below Fort Erie; Ripley landed above; the Indians gained the rear; and the Fort, which was an open work, capitulated at five o'clock in the afternoon. One hundred and seventy prisoners, including officers of all ranks, being two companies of the Eighth and Hundredth British regiments were surrendered by the major in command.

The next British position was at Chippawa, about sixteen miles below. To Chippawa Major-General Riall hastened from Fort George, on hearing that the American army had crossed the river above; and there, within a few hours, he collected about fifteen hundred regulars and six hundred militia and Indians, behind the Chippawa River, in a position not to be assailed in front. The American army also hastened toward Chippawa. On the morning of July 4 Scott's brigade led the way, and after an exhausting march of twelve hours, the enemy tearing up the bridges in retiring, Scott reached Chippawa plain toward sunset, and found Riall's force in position beyond the Chippawa River. Scott could only retire a mile or two, behind the nearest water,—a creek, or broad ditch, called Street's Creek,—where he went into camp. Brown and Ripley, with the second brigade and artillery, came up two or three hours later, at eleven o'clock in the night. Porter followed the next morning.

Brown, knowing his numbers to be about twice those of Riall, was anxious to attack before Riall could be reinforced; and on the morning of July 5, leaving Ripley and Porter's brigades encamped in the rear, he reconnoitered the line of the Chippawa River, and gave orders for constructing a bridge above Riall's position. The bridge was likely to be an affair of several days, and Riall showed a disposition to interfere with it. His scouts and Indians crossed and occupied the woods on the American left, driving in the pickets and annoying the reconnoitring party, and even the camp. To dislodge them, Porter's volunteers and Indians were ordered forward to clear the woods; and at about half-past four o'clock in the afternoon, Porter's advance began to drive the enemy's Indians back, pressing forward nearly to the Chippawa River. There the advancing volunteers and Indians suddenly became aware that the whole British army was in the act of crossing the Chippawa Bridge on their flank. The surprise was complete, and Porter's brigade naturally broke and fell back in confusion.

No one could have been more surprised than Brown, or more incredulous than Scott, at Riall's extraordinary movement. The idea that a British force of two thousand men at most should venture to attack more than three thousand, with artillery, covered by a deep, miry creek, had not entered their minds. Riall drew up his little army in three columns on the Chippawa plain,—the King's regiment four hundred and eighty strong in advance, supported by the Royal Scots five hundred strong, and the Hundredth four hundred and fifty strong, with a troop of dragoons and artillerists; in all about fifteen hundred regular troops, with two twenty-four-pound field-pieces and a five-and-a-half inch howitzer. Six hundred militia and Indians occupied the woods. The whole force advanced in order of battle toward Street's Creek.

Brown was at the front when this movement was made. Porter was routed. Ripley with the second brigade was in the rear. Scott, having rested his brigade in the morning and given them a dinner to celebrate the Fourth of July, had ordered a grand parade "to keep his men in breath," as he said; and while Riall's regular force, fifteen hundred strong, formed on the Chippawa plain a mile away, Scott's brigade—which a week before had been reported as containing thirteen hundred men present for duty, and if all its details had been called in could hardly have exceeded thirteen hundred men in the ranks on the afternoon of July 5—was forming, before crossing the little bridge over Street's Creek to parade on the plain already occupied by the British. Owing to the brushwood that lined the creek Scott could not see the plain, and received no notice of danger until he approached the bridge at the head of his brigade. At that moment General Brown in full gallop from the front rode by, calling out in passing, "You will have a battle!" Scott remarked that he did not believe he should find three hundred British to fight, and crossed the bridge.

If Riall was unwise to attack, Scott tempted destruction by leaving his secure position behind the creek; but at that moment he was in his happiest temper. He meant to show what he and his brigade could do. As his thin column crossed the bridge, the British twenty-four-pound guns opened upon it; but the American line moved on, steady as veterans, and formed in order of battle beyond. Towson's three twelve-pounders were placed in position near the river on the

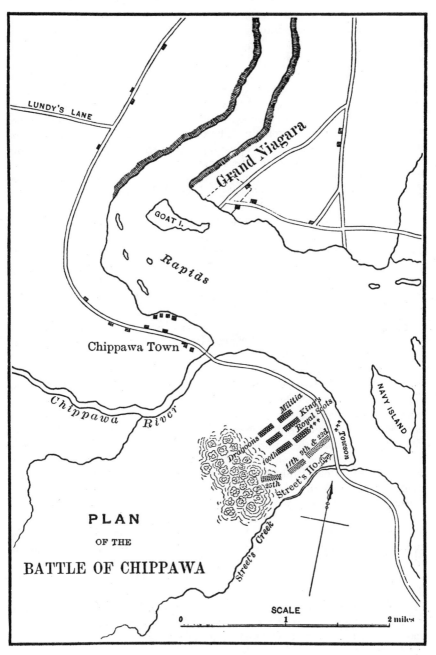

LUNDY'S LANE

Grand Niagara

GOAT I.

Rapids

Chippawa Town

Chippawa River

NAVY ISLAND

Militia
King's
Royal Scots
Dragoons
100th
11th, 9th & 22d
Towson
25th
Street's Ho.

PLAN

OF THE

BATTLE OF CHIPPAWA

Street's Creek

SCALE

0   1   2 miles

extreme right, and opened fire on the heavier British battery opposite. The infantry deployed in three battalions,—the right, under Major Leavenworth of the Ninth; the centre, under Major McNeil of the Eleventh; the left, under Major Jesup of the Twenty-fifth. Throwing the flanks obliquely forward, and extending Jesup's battalion into the woods on the left to prevent outflanking, Scott ordered an advance; and at the same time Riall directed the Royal Scots and the Hundredth to charge. The two lines advanced, stopping alternately to fire and move forward, while Towson's guns, having blown up a British caisson, were turned on the British column. The converging American fire made havoc in the British ranks, and when the two lines came within some sixty or seventy paces of each other in the centre, the flanks were actually in contact. Then the whole British line broke and crumbled away. Ripley's brigade, arriving soon afterward, found no enemy on the plain. The battle had lasted less than an hour.

Riall's report made no concealment of his defeat.

"I placed two light twenty-four-pounders and a five-and-a-half inch howitzer," he said, "against the right of the enemy's position, and formed the Royal Scots and Hundredth regiment with the intention of making a movement upon his left, which deployed with the greatest regularity and opened a very heavy fire. I immediately moved up the King's regiment to the right, while the Royal Scots and Hundredth regiments were directed to charge the enemy in front, for which they advanced with the greatest gallantry under a most destructive fire. I am sorry to say, however, in this attempt they suffered so severely that I was obliged to withdraw them, finding their further efforts against the superior numbers of the enemy would be unavailing."

For completeness, Scott's victory at Chippawa could be compared with that of Isaac Hull over the *Guerrière*; but in one respect Scott surpassed Hull. The *Constitution* was a much heavier ship than its enemy; but Scott's brigade was weaker, both in men and guns, than Riall's force. Even in regulars, man against man, Scott was certainly outnumbered. His brigade could not have contained, with artillerists, more than thirteen hundred men present on the field, while Riall officially reported his regulars at fifteen hundred, and his irregular corps at six hundred. Scott's flank was exposed and turned by the rout of Porter. He fought with a creek in his rear, where retreat was destruction. He had three twelve-pound field-pieces, one of which was soon dismounted, against two twenty-four-pounders, and a five-and-a-half inch howitzer. He crossed the bridge and deployed under the enemy's fire. Yet the relative losses showed that he was the superior of his enemy in every respect, and in none more than in the efficiency of his guns.

Riall reported a total loss in killed, wounded, and missing of five hundred and fifteen men, not including Indians. Scott and Porter reported a total loss of two hundred and ninety-seven, not including Indians. Riall's regular regiments and artillery lost one hundred and thirty-seven killed, and three hundred and five wounded. Scott's brigade reported forty-eight killed and two hundred and twenty-seven wounded. The number of Riall's killed was nearly three times the number of Scott's killed, and proved that the battle was decided by the superior accuracy or rapidity of the musketry and artillery fire, other military qualities being assumed to be equal.

The battle of Chippawa was the only occasion during the war when equal bodies of regular troops met face to face, in extended lines on an open plain in broad daylight, without advantage of position; and never again after that combat was an army of American regulars beaten by British troops. Small as the affair was, and unimportant in military results, it gave to the United States army a character and pride it had never before possessed.

Riall regained the protection of his lines without further loss; but two days afterward Brown turned his position, and Riall abandoned it with the whole peninsula except Fort George. Leaving garrisons in Fort George and Fort Niagara, he fell back toward Burlington Bay to await reinforcements. Brown followed as far as Queenston, where he camped July 10, doubtful what next to do. Fretting under the enforced delay, he wrote to Commodore Chauncey, July 13, a letter that led to much comment:—

"I have looked for your fleet with the greatest anxiety since the 10th. I do not doubt my ability to meet the enemy in the field, and to march in any direction over his country, your fleet carrying for me the necessary supplies. . . . There is not a doubt resting in my mind but that we have between us the command of sufficient means to conquer Upper Canada within two months, if there is a prompt and zealous co-operation and a vigorous application of these means."

Brown, like Andrew Jackson, with the virtues of a militia general, possessed some of the faults. His letter to Chauncey expressed his honest belief; but he was mistaken, and the letter tended to create a popular impression that Chauncey was wholly to blame. Brown could not, even with Chauncey's help, conquer Upper Canada. He was in danger of being himself destroyed; and even at Queenston he was not safe. Riall had already received, July 9, a reinforcement of seven hundred regulars; at his camp, only thirteen miles from Brown, he had twenty-two hundred men; in garrison at Fort George and Niagara he left more than a thousand men; Lieutenant-General Drummond was on his way from Kingston with the Eighty-ninth regiment four hundred strong, under Colonel Morrison, who had won the battle of Chrystler's Field, while still another regiment, DeWatteville's, was on the march. Four thousand men were concentrating on Fort George, and Chauncey, although he might have delayed, could not have prevented their attacking Brown, or stopping his advance.

Brown was so well aware of his own weakness that he neither tried to assault Fort George nor to drive Riall farther away, although Ripley and the two engineer officers McRee and Wood advised the attempt. After a fortnight passed below Queenston, he suddenly withdrew to Chippawa July 24, and camped on the battle-field. Riall instantly left his camp at eleven o'clock in the night of July 24, and followed Brown's retreat with about a thousand men, as far as Lundy's Lane, only a mile below the Falls of Niagara. There he camped at seven o'clock on the morning of July 25, waiting for the remainder of his force, about thirteen hundred men, who marched at noon, and were to arrive at sunset.

The battle of Chippawa and three weeks of active campaigning had told on the Americans. According to the army returns of the last week in July, Brown's army at Chippawa, July 25, numbered twenty-six hundred effectives.

STRENGTH OF MAJOR-GENERAL BROWN'S ARMY, CHIPPAWA, JULY 25, 1814

	Present for Duty Non-com. Officers and Privates	Aggregate Present and absent
Scott's Brigade	1,072	1,422
Ripley's Brigade	895	1,198
Porter's Brigade	441	538
Artillery	236	260
Total	2,644	3,418

Thus Brown at Chippawa Bridge, on the morning of July 25, with twenty-six hundred men present for duty, had Riall within easy reach three miles away at Lundy's Lane, with only a thousand men; but Brown expected no such sudden movement from the enemy, and took no measures to obtain certain information. He was with reason anxious for his rear. His position was insecure and unsatisfactory except for attack. From the moment it became defensive, it was unsafe and needed to be abandoned.

The British generals were able to move on either bank of the river. While Riall at seven o'clock in the morning went into camp within a mile of Niagara Falls, Lieutenant-General Gordon Drummond with the Eighty-ninth regiment disembarked at Fort George, intending to carry out a long-prepared movement on the American side.

Gordon Drummond, who succeeded Major-General de Rottenburg in the command of Upper Canada in December, 1813, and immediately distinguished himself by the brilliant capture of Fort Niagara and the destruction of Buffalo, was regarded as the ablest military officer in Canada. Isaac Brock's immediate successors in the civil and military government of Upper Canada were Major-Generals Sheaffe and de Rottenburg. Neither had won distinction; but Gordon Drummond was an officer of a different character. Born in 1772, he entered the army in 1789 as an ensign in the First regiment, or Royal Scots, and rose in 1794 to be lieutenant-colonel of the Eighth, or King's regiment. He served in the Netherlands, the West Indies, and in Egypt, before being ordered to Canada in 1808. In 1811 he became lieutenant-general. He was at Kingston when his subordinate officer, Major-General Riall, lost the battle of Chippawa and retired toward Burlington Heights. Having sent forward all the reinforcements he could spare, Drummond followed as rapidly as possible to take command in person.

No sooner did Drummond reach Fort George than, in pursuance of orders previously given, he sent a detachment of about six hundred men across the river to Lewiston. Its appearance there was at once made known to Brown at Chippawa, only six or seven miles above, and greatly alarmed him for the safety of his base at Fort Schlosser, Black Rock, and Buffalo. Had Drummond advanced up the American side with fifteen hundred men, as he might have done, he would have obliged Brown to recross the river, and might perhaps have destroyed or paralyzed him; but Drummond decided to join Riall, and accordingly, recalling the detachment from Lewiston at four o'clock in the afternoon, he began his march up the Canadian side with eight hundred and fifteen rank-and-file to Lundy's Lane.

At five o'clock, July 25, the British army was nearly concentrated. The advance under Riall at Lundy's Lane numbered nine hundred and fifty rank-and-file, with the three field-pieces which had been in the battle of Chippawa, and either two or three six-pounders. Drummond was three miles below with eight hundred and fifteen rank-and-file, marching up the river; and Colonel Scott of the One Hundred-and-third regiment, with twelve hundred and thirty rank-and-file and two more six-pound field-pieces, was a few miles behind Drummond. By nine o'clock in the evening the three corps, numbering three thousand rank-and-file, with eight field-pieces, were to unite at Lundy's Lane.

At a loss to decide on which bank the British generals meant to move, Brown waited until afternoon, and then, in great anxiety for the American side of the river, ordered Winfield Scott to march his brigade down the road toward Queenston on the Canadian side, in the hope of recalling the enemy from the American side by alarming him for the safety of his rear. Scott, always glad to be in motion, crossed Chippawa bridge, with his brigade and Towson's battery, soon after five o'clock, and to his great surprise, in passing a house near the Falls, learned that a large body of British troops was in sight below. With his usual audacity he marched directly upon them, and reaching Lundy's Lane, deployed to the left in line of battle. Jesup, Brady, Leavenworth, and McNeil placed their little battalions, numbering at the utmost a thousand rank-and-file, in position, and Towson opened with his three guns. The field suited their ambition. The sun was setting at the end of a long, hot, midsummer day. About a mile to their right the Niagara River flowed through its chasm, and the spray of the cataract rose in the distance behind them.

At the first report that the American army was approaching, Riall ordered a retreat, and his advance was already in march from the field when Drummond arrived with the Eighty-ninth regiment, and countermanded the order. Drummond then formed his line, numbering according to his report sixteen hundred men, but in reality seventeen hundred and seventy rank-and-file,—the left resting on the high road, his two twenty-four-pound brass field-pieces, two six-pounders, and a five-and-a-half-inch howitzer a little advanced in front of his centre on the summit of the low hill, and his right stretching forward so as to overlap Scott's position in attacking. Lundy's Lane, at right angles with the river, ran close behind the British position. Hardly had he completed his formation, when, in his own words, "the whole front was warmly and closely engaged."

With all the energy Scott could throw into his blow, he attacked the British left and centre. Drummond's left stopped slightly beyond the road, and was assailed by Jesup's battalion, the Twenty-fifth regiment, while Scott's other battalions attacked in front. So vigorous was Jesup's assault that he forced back the Royal Scots and Eighty-ninth, and got into the British rear, where he captured

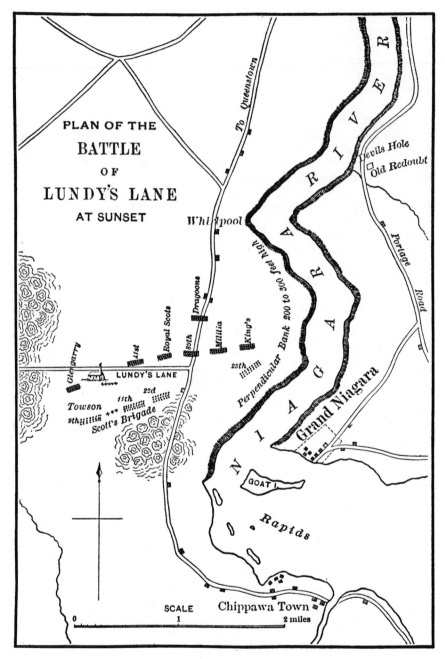

PLAN OF THE
BATTLE
OF
LUNDY'S LANE
AT SUNSET

Major-General Riall himself, as he left the field seriously wounded. "After repeated attacks," said Drummond's report, "the troops on the left were partially forced back, and the enemy gained a momentary possession of the road." In the centre also Scott attacked with obstinacy; but the British artillery was altogether too strong and posted too high for Towson's three guns, which at last ceased firing. There the Americans made no impression, while they were overlapped and outnumbered by the British right.

From seven till nine o'clock Scott's brigade hung on the British left and centre, charging repeatedly close on the enemy's guns; and when at last with the darkness their firing ceased from sheer exhaustion, they were not yet beaten. Brady's battalion, the Ninth and Twenty-second, and McNeil's, the Eleventh, were broken up; their ammunition was exhausted, and most of their officers were killed or wounded. The Eleventh and Twenty-second regiments lost two hundred and thirty men killed, wounded, and missing, or more than half their number; many of the men left the field, and only with difficulty could a battalion be organized from the debris. McNeil and Brady were wounded, and Major Leavenworth took command of the remnant. With a small and exhausted force which could not have numbered more than six hundred men, and which Drummond by a vigorous movement might have wholly destroyed, Scott clung to the enemy's flank until in the darkness Ripley's brigade came down on the run. The American line was also reinforced by Porter's brigade; by the First regiment, one hundred and fifty strong, which crossed from the American side of the river; and by Ritchie's and Biddle's batteries.

At about the same time the rest of Riall's force, twelve hundred and thirty rank-and-file, with two more six-pound guns, appeared on the field, and were placed in a second line or used to prolong the British right. If Scott had lost four hundred men from the ranks Drummond had certainly lost no more, for his men were less exposed. Brown was obliged to leave details of men for camp duty; Drummond brought three thousand rank-and-file on the field. At nine o'clock Drummond could scarcely have had fewer than twenty-six hundred men in Lundy's Lane, with seven field-pieces, two of which were twenty-four-pounders. Brown could scarcely have had nineteen hundred, even allowing Porter to have brought five hundred of his volunteers into battle. He had also Towson's, Ritchie's, and Biddle's batteries,—seven twelve-pound field-pieces in all.

As long as the British battery maintained its fire in the centre, victory was impossible and escape difficult. Ripley's brigade alone could undertake the task of capturing the British guns, and to it the order was given. Colonel Miller was to advance with the Twenty-first regiment against the British battery in front. Ripley himself took command of the Twenty-third regiment on the right, to lead it by the road to attack the enemy's left flank in Lundy's Lane. According to the story that for the next fifty years was told to every American schoolboy as a model of modest courage, General Brown gave to Miller the order to carry the enemy's artillery, and Miller answered, "I'll try!"

The two regiments thus thrown on the enemy's centre and left numbered probably about seven hundred men in the ranks, according to Ripley's belief. The Twenty-first regiment was the stronger, and may have contained four hundred and fifty men, including officers; the Twenty-third could scarcely have brought three hundred into the field. In a few minutes both battalions were in motion. The Twenty-third, advancing along the road on the right, instantly attracted the enemy's fire at about one hundred and fifty yards from the hill, and was thrown back. Ripley reformed the column, and in five minutes it advanced again. While the Twenty-third was thus engaged on the right, the Twenty-first silently advanced in front, covered by shrubbery and the darkness, within a few rods of the British battery undiscovered, and with a sudden rush carried the guns, bayoneting the artillery-men where they stood.

So superb a feat of arms might well startle the British general, who could not see that less than five hundred men were engaged in it; but according to the British account the guns stood immediately in front of a British line numbering at least twenty-six hundred men in ranks along Lundy's Lane. Drummond himself must have been near the spot, for the whole line of battle was but five minutes' walk; apparently he had but to order an advance, to drive Miller's regiment back without trouble. Yet Miller maintained his ground until Ripley came up on his right. According to the evidence of Captain McDonald of Ripley's staff, the battle was violent during fifteen or twenty minutes:—

"Having passed the position where the artillery had been planted, Colonel Miller again formed his line facing the enemy, and engaged them within twenty paces distance. There appeared a perfect sheet of fire between the two lines. While the Twenty-first was in this situation, the Twenty-third attacked the enemy's flank, and advanced within twenty paces of it before the first volley was discharged,—a measure adopted by command of General Ripley, that the fire might be effectual and more completely destructive. The movement compelled the enemy's flank to fall back immediately by descending the hill out of sight, upon which the firing ceased."

Perhaps this feat was more remarkable than the surprise of the battery. Ripley's Twenty-third regiment, about three hundred men, broke the British line, not in the centre but on its left, where the Eighty-ninth, the Royal Scots, King's, and the Forty-first were stationed, and caused them to retire half a mile from the battle-field before they halted to reform.

When the firing ceased, Ripley's brigade held the hill-top, with the British guns, and the whole length of Lundy's Lane to the high-road. Porter then brought up his brigade on the left; Hindman brought up his guns, and placed Towson's battery on Ripley's right, Ritchie's on his left, while Biddle's two guns were put in position on the road near the corner of Lundy's Lane. Jesup with the Twenty-fifth regiment was put in line on the right of Towson's battery; Leavenworth with the remnants of the Ninth, Eleventh, and Twenty-second formed a second line in the rear of the captured artillery; and thus reversing the former British order of battle, the little army stood ranked along the edge of Lundy's Lane, with the British guns in their rear.

The British force was then in much confusion, a part of it marching into the American line by mistake, and suffering a destructive fire; a part of it firing into the regiment on its own right, and keeping up the fire persistently. In order to recover their artillery they must assault, without guns, a steep hill held by an

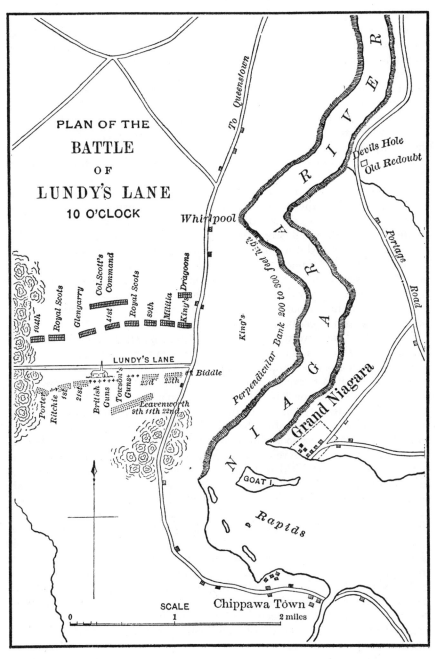

PLAN OF THE
BATTLE
OF
LUNDY'S LANE
10 O'CLOCK

enemy with several field-pieces. Had Brown been able to put a reserve of only a few hundred men into the field, his victory was assured; but the battle and exhaustion were rapidly reducing his force. He had at ten o'clock not more than fifteen hundred men in the ranks, and almost every officer was wounded.

After a long interval the British line was reformed, and brought to the attack. General Drummond's report said nothing of this movement, but according to the American account the two lines were closely engaged their whole length at a distance of ten or twelve yards. In the darkness the troops could aim only at the flash of the muskets. "We having much the advantage of the ground, the enemy generally fired over our heads," said Captain McDonald of Ripley's staff; "but the continual blaze of light was such as to enable us distinctly to see their buttons." After a sharp combat of some twenty minutes the enemy retreated. Three times, at intervals of half an hour or more, the British line moved up the hill, and after the exchange of a hot fire retired; between the attacks, for half an hour at a time, all was darkness and silence, hardly interrupted by a breath of air. Brown and Scott were with Porter on the extreme left. In the centre, by the captured cannon, Ripley sat on his horse, ten or twelve paces in rear of his line. Two bullets passed through his hat, but he was unhurt. Captain Ritchie was killed at his battery on the left; Jesup was wounded on the right. Each attack sorely diminished the number of men in the ranks, until at the close of the third about seven hundred rank-and-file, with few officers, were believed to remain in position.

Scott, with Leavenworth's consolidated battalion, after ranging somewhat wildly the entire length of the line in the attempt to turn the enemy's flank, and receiving the fire of both armies, joined Jesup's Twenty-fifth regiment on the right, and was at last severely wounded. At about the same time Brown was wounded on the extreme left, where Porter's volunteers held the line. Major Leavenworth, with the remnants of the first brigade, moving from the left to reinforce Jesup on the right after the third repulse of the enemy, met Scott retiring from the field, and soon afterward was hailed by General Brown, who was also returning to camp severely wounded. The time was then about eleven o'clock, and every one felt that the army must soon retreat. Farther in the rear General Brown met Major Hindman of the artillery, who was bringing up his spare ammunition wagons. Brown ordered Hindman to collect his artillery as well as he could, and retire immediately; "we shall all march to camp." He said that they had done as much as they could do; that nearly all their officers were killed or wounded; that he was himself wounded, and he thought it best to retire to camp. Hindman on arriving at the hill, firing having wholly ceased, immediately began to withdraw the guns. Ripley first learned the order to withdraw by discovering the artillery to be already gone. Next came a peremptory order to collect the wounded and retire. The order was literally obeyed. The enemy in no way molested the movement; and at about midnight the wearied troops marched for camp, in as good order and with as much regularity as they had marched to the battle-field.

Hindman withdrew his own guns, and having with some difficulty procured horses to haul off the British pieces, on returning to the hill after Ripley's withdrawal found the enemy again in possession, and some men and wagons captured. He left the field at once, with the British in possession of their guns, and followed the retreating column.

Lieutenant-General Drummond's report of the battle, though silent as to the repeated British repulses, declared that the Americans fought with uncommon gallantry: —

"In so determined a manner were the attacks directed against our guns that our artillery-men were bayoneted by the enemy in the act of loading, and the muzzles of the enemy's guns were advanced within a few yards of ours. The darkness of the night during this extraordinary conflict occasioned several uncommon incidents; our troops having for a moment been pushed back, some of our guns remained for a few minutes in the enemy's hands."

Drummond's "few minutes" were three hours. According to the British account, the One-Hundred-and-third regiment, with its two field-pieces, arrived on the field just at nine, and "passed by mistake into the centre of the American army now posted upon the hill." The regiment "fell back in confusion" and lost its two field-pieces, which were captured by Miller, with Riall's five pieces. By British report, Miller was at nine o'clock "in possession of the crest of the hill and of seven pieces of captured artillery." Drummond admitted that in retiring "about midnight" the Americans carried away one of his light pieces, having limbered it up by mistake and leaving one of their own. During the entire action after nine o'clock Drummond did not fire a cannon, although, according to Canadian authority, the fighting was desperate: —

"The officers of the army from Spain who have been engaged in Upper Canada have acknowledged that they never saw such determined charges as were made by the Americans in the late actions. . . . In the action on the 25th July the Americans charged to the very muzzles of our cannon, and actually bayoneted the artillery-men who were at their guns. Their charges were not once or twice only, but repeated and long, and the steadiness of British soldiers alone could have withstood them."

CHAPTER XVII

FORT ERIE

The battle of Lundy's Lane lasted five hours, and Drummond believed the American force to be five thousand men. In truth, at no moment were two thousand American rank-and-file on the field. "The loss sustained by the enemy in this severe action," reported Drummond, "cannot be estimated at less than fifteen hundred men, including several hundred prisoners left in our hands." Drummond's estimate of American losses, as of American numbers, was double the reality. Brown reported a total loss, certainly severe enough, of eight hundred and fifty-three men—one hundred and seventy-one killed, five hundred and fifty-nine wounded, one hundred and ninety-three missing, and forty-two prisoners. On both sides the battle was murderous. Brown and Scott were both badly wounded, the latter so severely that he could not resume his command during the war. Drummond and Riall were also wounded. On both sides, but especially on the Americans, the loss in officers was very great.

The effect of the British artillery on Scott's brigade, while daylight lasted, had been excessive, while at that period of the battle the British could have suffered comparatively little. Among Scott's battalions the severest loss was that of Brady's Twenty-second regiment, from Pennsylvania—at the opening of the campaign two hundred and twenty-eight strong, officers and men. After Lundy's Lane the Twenty-second reported thirty-six killed, ninety wounded, and seventeen missing. The Ninth, Leavenworth's Massachusetts regiment, which was returned as numbering three hundred and forty-eight officers and men June 31, reported sixteen killed, ninety wounded, and fifteen missing at Lundy's Lane. The Eleventh, McNeil's Vermont battalion, which numbered three hundred and four officers and men June 31, returned twenty-eight killed, one hundred and two wounded, and three missing. The Twenty-fifth, Jesup's Connecticut corps. numbering three hundred and seventy officers and men at the outset, reported twenty-eight killed, sixty-six wounded, and fifteen missing. These four regiments composing Scott's brigade, numbered thirteen hundred and eighty-eight officers and men June 31, and lost in killed, wounded, and missing at Lundy's Lane five hundred and six men, after losing two hundred and fifty-seven at Chippawa.

Ripley's brigade suffered less; but although, after the British guns were captured, the Americans were exposed only to musketry fire, the brigades of Ripley and Porter reported a loss of two hundred and fifty-eight men, killed, wounded, and missing. The three artillery companies suffered a loss of forty-five men, including Captain Ritchie. The total loss of eight hundred and fifty-three men was as nearly as possible one third of the entire army, including the unengaged pickets and other details.

When Ripley, following the artillery, arrived in camp toward one o'clock in the morning, Brown sent for him, and gave him an order to return at day-break to the battle-field with all the force he could collect, "and there to meet and beat the enemy if he again appeared." The order was impossible to execute. The whole force capable of fighting another battle did not exceed fifteen or sixteen hundred effectives, almost without officers, and exhausted by the night battle. The order was given at one o'clock in the morning; the army must employ the remainder of the night to reorganize its battalions and replace its officers, and was expected to march at four o'clock to regain a battle-field which Brown had felt himself unable to maintain at midnight, although he then occupied it, and held all the enemy's artillery. The order was futile. Major Leavenworth of the Ninth regiment, who though wounded commanded the first brigade after the disability of Scott, Brady, Jesup, and McNeil, thought it "the most consummate folly to attempt to regain possession of the field of battle," and declared that every officer he met thought like himself.

Yet Ripley at dawn began to collect the troops, and after the inevitable delay caused by the disorganization, marched at nine o'clock with about fifteen hundred men, to reconnoitre the enemy. At about the same time Drummond advanced a mile, and took position in order of battle near the Falls, his artillery in the road, supported by a column of infantry. A month earlier Drummond, like Riall, would have attacked, and with a force greater by one half could hardly have failed to destroy Ripley's shattered regiments; but Chippawa and Lundy's Lane had already produced an effect on the British army. Drummond believed that the Americans numbered five thousand, and his own force in the ranks was about twenty-two hundred men. He allowed Ripley to retire unmolested, and remained at the Falls the whole day.

Ripley returned to camp at noon and made his report to Brown. The question requiring immediate decision was whether to maintain or abandon the line of the Chippawa River. Much could be said on both sides, and only officers on the spot could decide with certainty how the enemy could be placed under most disadvantage, and how the army could be saved from needless dangers. Ripley, cautious by nature, recommended a retreat to Fort Erie. With the assent, as he supposed, of Brown and Porter, Ripley immediately broke up the camp at Chippawa, and began the march to Fort Erie, sixteen miles in the rear. Although complaint was made of the retreat as confused, hasty, and unnecessary, it was conducted with no more loss or confusion than usual in such movements, and its military propriety was to be judged by its effects on the campaigns.

The same evening, July 26, the army arrived at Fort Erie and camped. Brown was taken from Chippawa across the river to recover from his wound. Scott was also removed to safe quarters. Ripley was left with the remains of the army camped on a plain, outside the unfinished bastions of Fort Erie, where the destruction of his entire force was inevitable in case of a reverse. Ripley favored a withdrawal of the army to the American side; but Brown, from his sick bed at Buffalo, rejected the idea of a retreat, and fortunately Drummond's reinforcements arrived slowly. The worst result of the difference in opinion was to make Brown harsh toward Ripley, who—although his record was singular in showing only patient, excellent, and uniformly successful service—leaned toward caution, while Brown and Scott thought chiefly of fighting. The combination produced admirable results; but either officer alone might have failed.

Distrusting Ripley, and angry at losing the British cannon at Lundy's Lane as well as at the retreat from Chippawa, Brown wrote, August 7, to the Secretary of War a report containing an improper implication, which he afterward with-

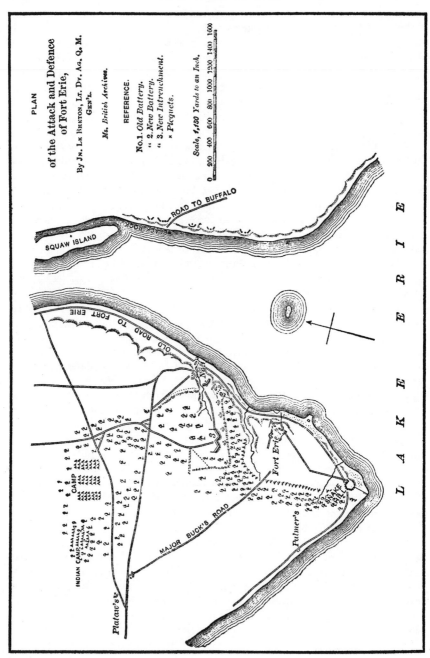

PLAN
of the Attack and Defence
of Fort Erie,
By Jn. Le Breton, Lr. Dy. Ag. Q. M.
Gen'l.

Ms. British Archives.

REFERENCE.

No.1. *Old Battery.*
"   2. *New Battery.*
"   3. *New Intrenchment.*
×   *Picquets.*

Scale, 1,150 Yards to an Inch.

0 200 400 600 800 1000 1200 1400 1600

drew, that Ripley was wanting either in courage or capacity. He also summoned Brigadier-General Gaines from Sackett's Harbor to command the army. Gaines arrived, and as senior brigadier assumed command at Fort Erie, August 4, while Ripley resumed command of his brigade. During the week that elapsed before Gaines's arrival, the army, under Ripley's orders, worked energetically to intrench itself in lines behind Fort Erie; and after Gaines took command the same work was continued without interruption or change of plan, under the direction of Major McRee, Major Wood, and Lieutenant Douglass of the Engineers.

The result was chiefly decided by Drummond's errors. Had he followed Ripley closely, and had he attacked instantly on overtaking the retreating army at Fort Erie or elsewhere, he would have had the chances in his favor. Had he crossed the river and moved against Buffalo, he would have obliged Brown to order the instant evacuation of Fort Erie, and would have recovered all the British positions without the loss of a man. Drummond took neither course. He waited two days at Chippawa before he moved up the river within two miles of Fort Erie. About August 1 his reinforcements arrived—DeWatteville's regiment from Kingston, and the Forty-first from Fort George—replacing his losses, and giving him three thousand one hundred and fifty rank-and-file; but he seemed still undecided what course to adopt. The battles of Chippawa and Lundy's Lane had given the British army respect for American troops, and Drummond hesitated to assault the unfinished works at Fort Erie, although he was fully one half stronger in men than Gaines and Ripley, who had barely two thousand rank-and-file after obtaining such reinforcements as were at hand.

STRENGTH OF SCOTT'S BRIGADE, FORT ERIE, JULY 31, 1814

	Present for Duty Non-com. Officers, Rank-and-file	Officers	Aggregate Present and absent
Ninth Regiment	139	8	569
Eleventh Regiment	293	11	624
Twenty-second Regiment	218	10	408
Twenty-fifth Regiment	255	7	676
General Staff		4	4
Total	905	40	2,281

STRENGTH OF RIPLEY'S BRIGADE

First Regiment	141	6	220
Twenty-first Regiment	441	20	849
Twenty-third Regiment	292	12	713
General Staff		4	4
Total	874	42	1,786

MONTHLY RETURN OF TROOPS UNDER MAJOR-GENERAL BROWN,

FORT ERIE, JULY 31, 1814

Bombardiers, etc.	58	2	69
Light Dragoons	47	1	64
Artillery Corps	241	12	364
First Brigade	905	40	2,281
Second Brigade	874	42	1,786
Total	2,125	97	4,564

Drummond began operations by ordering a detachment of six hundred men to cross the river and destroy the magazines at Black Rock and Buffalo. During the night of August 3 Colonel Tucker of the Forty-first, with four hundred and sixty rank-and-file of his own and other regiments, landed two or three miles below Black Rock, and advanced against it. They were met at the crossing of a creek by two hundred and forty men of Morgan's Rifles, then garrisoning Black Rock, with some volunteers. The effect of the rifles was so deadly that the British troops refused to face them, and Tucker returned after losing twenty-five men. This repulse, as creditable in its way to the American army as the battles at Chippawa and Lundy's Lane, caused much annoyance to Drummond, who issued an order, August 5, expressing "the indignation excited by discovering that the failure of an expedition, the success of which . . . would have compelled the enemy's forces to surrender or . . . encounter certain defeat, was attributable to the misbehavior of the troops employed." The only success achieved by the British detachments was the cutting out of two American schooners which covered the approach to Fort Erie, near the shore.

Drummond having decided not to assault the lines of Fort Erie until he had made an impression on the works, next sent for guns of heavy calibre. Ten days were passed in opening trenches and constructing batteries. Gaines and Ripley employed the time in completing their defences. Of these, the so-called Fort Erie was the smallest part, and made only the salient angle toward Drummond's approaches. As the British had constructed the fort, it was a small, unfinished work, about one hundred and fifty yards from the Lake-shore, open in the rear, and mounting three guns. The American engineers completed its rear bastions, and constructed an earthwork seven feet high with a ditch, to the shore, where a small stone-work completed the defence on that side, and brought the lines to the water's edge. The stone-work was called the Douglass battery, after the lieutenant of engineers who built it. Fort Erie, Battery Douglass, and their connecting breastwork secured the camp on the right. A similar breastwork, nearly at right angles with the first, was extended three hundred and fifty yards farther till it neared the Lake-shore, where it was finished on Snake Hill by a projecting battery called Towson's. Traverses were constructed, and a strongly intrenched camp, about seven hundred yards by two hundred and fifty, was thus formed, open on its rear to the Lake.

Hindman had general charge of the artillery. Battery Douglass mounted one gun; another was mounted on the neighboring line; Fort Erie contained six, under Captain Williams; Biddle's and Fanning's (Ritchie's) four guns were placed on the long line in the front; and Towson had six field-pieces at the extreme left. Scott's brigade, commanded by Lieutenant-Colonel Aspinwall, was posted on the right; Porter's volunteers and the First Rifles occupied the centre; and Ripley with the Twenty-first and Twenty-third regiments defended the left.

Drummond opened with six guns, August 13, and prepared for assault the following day. His arrangements were somewhat complicated. He divided the attacking force into three columns, retaining another division in reserve. The strongest column, commanded by Lieutenant-Colonel Fischer of DeWatteville's regiment, was composed of portions of four regular regiments, and numbered about thirteen hundred men; these were to assault Towson and Ripley on Snake Hill. The centre column, commanded by Lieutenant-Colonel Drummond of the One-Hundred-and-fourth, numbered only one hundred and ninety rank-and-file, including a party of seamen and marines; these were to attack Fort Erie. The third column, under Colonel Scott of the One-Hundred-and-third regiment, numbered six hundred and fifty rank-and-file; these were to assault the breastworks between Fort Erie and Battery Douglass. According to these numbers, Drummond meant to assault with twenty-one hundred and forty rank-and-file, or about twenty-four hundred men all told. His reserve numbered one thousand men. Some further number must have been detailed in camp duty.

Drummond's instructions, dated August 14, to Colonel Fischer were minute. Fischer's column was to march immediately, in order to pass through the woods before dark, and halt for the night opposite the point of attack, with every precaution against discovery: —

"You are to advance to the attack precisely at two o'clock. You are to enter the enemy's position betwixt Snake Hill and the Lake, which is represented to be sufficiently open; but this is not to prevent your making your arrangements for assaulting any other part of the position by means of the short ladders and hay-bags with which you will be furnished. In order to *insure success*, the Lieutenant-General most strongly recommends that the flints be taken out of the fire-locks, with the exception of a reserve of select and steady men who may be permitted to retain their flints, if you think it necessary or advisable, not exceeding one third of your force. This reserve, with the detachment of artillery, should take post on Snake Hill."

A demonstration was to be made a few minutes before two o'clock against the American pickets opposite the centre of the line.

Drummond's general orders concluded by encouraging his men to consider their task easy: —

"The Lieutenant-General most strongly recommends a free use of the bayonet. The enemy's force does not exceed fifteen hundred fit for duty, and those are represented as much dispirited."

The British general underestimated Gaines's force, which probably contained at least two thousand rank-and-file fit for duty August 14, who though possibly overworked and inclined to grumble, were ready to fight. Neither Gaines nor

Ripley, nor any of the excellent officers of engineers and artillery who defended the lines of Fort Erie, were likely to allow themselves to be surprised or even approached by a force no greater than their own without ample resistance. They kept strong pickets far in advance of their lines, and were alive to every sign of attack. Soon after midnight of August 14 the fire of the British siege-guns slackened and ceased. At the same moment Gaines left his quarters and Ripley ordered his brigade to turn out. Both officers looked for an assault, and were not mistaken. At two o'clock the pickets fired and fell back, and at half-past two o'clock Colonel Fischer's advancing column moved against Snake Hill.

There at the breastworks were Towson's guns and the Twenty-first regiment commanded by Major Wood of the Engineers, only two hundred and fifty strong, but as steady as at Lundy's Lane. A part of Fischer's brigade marched gallantly up to the abattis, bayonets charged and guns without flints, and approached within ten feet of the breastwork, but failed to reach it. The other column, DeWatteville's regiment at its head, "marching too near the Lake," according to Colonel Fischer's report, "found themselves entangled between the rocks and the water, and by the retreat of the flank companies were thrown in such confusion as to render it impossible to give them any kind of formation during the darkness of the night, at which time they were exposed to a most galling fire of the enemy's battery." A part of DeWatteville's regiment waded through the water round the American line, and came into the camp on the flank, but found there two companies posted to meet such an attempt, and were all captured, so that Colonel Fischer, writing his report the next day, seemed ignorant what had become of them.

The attack and repulse of Colonel Fischer on the extreme American left were soon over, and the story was easy to understand; but the attack on Fort Erie and the extreme right was neither quickly ended nor easily understood. There a column of more than seven hundred men, all told, under Colonel Scott of the One-Hundred-and-third, was to attack the Douglass battery. Another column, numbering somewhat more than two hundred men, all told, under Lieutenant-Colonel Drummond of the One-Hundred-and-fourth, was to assault Fort Erie. The American line between Battery Douglass and Fort Erie was held by the Ninth regiment and the volunteers, and was covered by the battery. Fort Erie was defended by about one hundred and eighteen men of the Nineteenth regiment under Major Trimble, and about sixty artillerists under Captain Williams.

The most intelligible account of the battle at the eastern end of the lines was given neither in Gaines's nor Drummond's reports, but in some charges afterward brought against Gaines by Major Trimble, who was angry at the language of Gaines's report. Trimble's charges were judged to be frivolous, but his story of the battle was more precise than any other.

According to Major Trimble, Lieutenant-Colonel Drummond's column was directed against the north curtain of the fort, and was repulsed, but continued the assault. Colonel Scott's column at the same time advanced within about sixty yards of the Douglass battery, but deterred by the fire of the guns served under the direction of Major McRee and Lieutenant Douglass of the Engineers, and by the loss of its commanding officer Colonel Scott, who fell before the

American line, the column moved quickly to the right, gained the ditch of the northeast bastion of Fort Erie, and under cover of the smoke and darkness entered the bastion. There they were joined by Drummond's men. They surprised the artillerists, and in the scuffle Captain Williams and his lieutenants—McDonough, Fontaine, and Watmough—were killed or disabled.

Without support the British columns could do no more, and Lieutenant-General Drummond did not come to their support. None of the reports mentioned the time at which the bastion was captured; but the small British force, which could not have exceeded six or seven hundred men, remained for more than two hours in or about the bastion, exposed to the American fire, to which they could not reply with effect, and waiting for Drummond and the reserve, which the Americans also expected and trained their guns to enfilade. The British in the bastion repeatedly attempted to advance from the bastion to gain possession of the Fort, and twice tried to force the door of the stone mess-house from which the men of the Nineteenth regiment kept up a destructive fire. They repulsed the attacks made by reinforcements ordered by Gaines into the Fort to recover the bastion; yet their destruction was inevitable as soon as the dawn should arrive, for they could neither advance nor escape, nor remain where they were, under the guns of the garrison.

After maintaining themselves till five o'clock in this difficult position, the British soldiers and sailors in the bastion were panic-struck by the explosion of an ammunition-chest under the platform. According to General Drummond's official report, "Some ammunition, which had been placed under the platform, caught fire from the firing of guns in the rear, and a most tremendous explosion followed, by which almost all the troops which had entered the place were dreadfully mangled. Panic was instantly communicated to the troops, who could not be persuaded that the explosion was accidental; and the enemy at the same time pressing forward and commencing a heavy fire of musketry, the Fort was abandoned, and our troops retreated toward the battery."

The explosion merely hastened the rout. Probably the attacking columns would have fared still worse, had they remained. Even their panic-stricken flight saved only a remnant. Of Drummond's column, said to number one hundred and ninety rank-and-file, one hundred and eighty-eight officers and men were reported as missing, wounded, or killed. Of Scott's column, said to number six hundred and fifty rank-and-file—the Royal Scots and the One-Hundred-and-third regiments—four hundred and ninety-six officers and men were returned as killed, wounded, or missing. Of the whole rank-and-file engaged under Fischer, Scott, and Drummond, numbering two thousand one hundred and fifty men, if the British report was correct, seven hundred and eighty were officially reported among the casualties. The loss in officers was equally severe. Colonel Scott was killed before the lines. Lieutenant-Colonel Drummond was killed in the bastion. One major, ten captains, and fifteen lieutenants were killed, wounded, or missing. The total British loss was nine hundred and five among some twenty-four hundred engaged. The total American loss was eighty-four men.

General Drummond was excessively mortified by his failure, in truth the severest blow that British arms could suffer at that moment. For the fourth time in six weeks a large body of British troops met a bloody and unparalleled check, if not rout, from an inferior force. In a private letter to Prevost, dated August 16, Drummond attributed the disaster to the misconduct of DeWatteville's regiment, a foreign corps, which was struck by panic:—

"It appears that part of the forlorn hope and about half of Watteville's Light Company, by wading through the water, though the footing was excessively rough and rocky along the Lake-shore, turned the left flank of an abattis which extended from the enemy's battery on Snake Hill, the left of their position, to the Lake, and part penetrated through the abattis itself, and thereby gained the rear of the enemy's works. The fire of the enemy at this time being extremely heavy both from artillery and musketry, it would seem as if a simultaneous shock of panic pervaded the greater part of those not in immediate advance; and the forlorn hope, not finding itself sufficiently supported, was reluctantly under the necessity of relinquishing the advantages they had gained, and of retiring again through the water under a most galling fire. They lost many men, and DeWatteville's Light Company nearly half their number. The Light Company of the Eighty-ninth, notwithstanding they were almost overwhelmed by the grenadiers of DeWatteville in the precipitancy of their retreat, was the only body that preserved its order and remained firm upon its ground. By this act of steadiness they fortunately lost scarcely a man. The main body of DeWatteville's regiment retreated in such confusion that they carried the King's regiment before them like a torrent. Thus by the misconduct of this foreign corps has the opportunity been totally lost."

The mortification of Drummond was acute in having to charge both his attacking columns with being panic-stricken: "The agony of mind I suffer from the present disgraceful and unfortunate conduct of the troops committed to my superintendence, wounds me to the soul!" Yet he offered no evidence to show that his troops fled before they were beaten, nor did he explain why he had thought it useless to order the reserve to their support after they had captured the bastion. In reality the battle of Fort Erie was more creditable to the British than the battles of Chippawa or Lundy's Lane, and the Americans could not admit that in either of the three the conduct of Drummond's troops was "disgraceful."

The defeat so much weakened Drummond that he could no longer keep the field without support, and immediately sent for two more regiments,—the Sixth and the Eighty-second from Burlington and York,—numbering about one thousand and forty rank-and-file, and making good his losses.

At that time Chauncey was in control of Lake Ontario. The anxieties and delays in fitting out his new ship had ended in a fever, under which he was still suffering when he received General Brown's challenge of July 13 to meet him opposite Fort George. Chauncey did not immediately reply except by message through General Gaines. July 31, everything being at last ready, he was carried on board his ship, and the next day he sailed, arriving August 5 off Fort George. Brown's army was then besieged in Fort Erie, and could not approach the fleet. This situation gave to Chauncey the opportunity of writing a letter to Brown, repaying the harshness that Brown had shown to him.

"Was it friendly or just or honorable," asked Chauncey, "not only to furnish an opening for the public, but thus to assist them to infer that I had pledged myself to meet you on a particular day at the head of the Lake, for the purpose of co-operation, and in case of disaster to your army, thus to turn their resentment from you, who are alone responsible, upon me, who could not by any possibility have prevented, or retarded even, your discomfiture? You well know, sir, that the fleet could not have rendered you the least service during your late incursion upon Upper Canada. You have not been able to approach Lake Ontario on any point nearer than Queenston."

Brown's quarrel with Chauncey made much noise in its day, and, like the less defensible quarrel with Ripley, proved that Brown was unnecessarily aggressive; but in the situation of the United States, aggressiveness was the most valuable quality in the service. That Brown might have become a great general was possible, had his experience been larger; but whatever was his merit as a general, his qualities as a fighter were more remarkable than those of any other general officer in the war. Except immediately after receiving his wound at Lundy's Lane, when his army was exhausted by four hours of extreme effort, he never seemed satiated with fighting. Among all the American major-generals, he alone made raw troops as steady as grenadiers, and caused militia to storm entrenched lines held by British regulars.

Brown might have been well satisfied to let Drummond exhaust his strength in attacking Fort Erie. From a military point of view, Fort Erie was worthless for any other purpose than to draw the enemy to the extreme end of their line, where they could with difficulty obtain supplies, and could take no part in the serious campaigning intended on Lake Champlain. For that object, no more pitched battles were needed. Drummond's force was wasting away by sickness and exposure.

After the battle of August 15, the British continued to bombard Fort Erie. No great damage was done; but a shell exploded in Gaines's quarters August 29, injuring him severely and obliging him to relinquish command. Brown was still unfit for service, but was bent upon more fighting, and knew that Ripley preferred to abandon Fort Erie altogether. Accordingly he resumed command at Buffalo, September 2, and set himself to study the situation.

The situation was uncomfortable, but in no way perilous. The lines of Fort Erie were stronger than ever, and beyond danger of capture from any British force that could be brought to assault them, until Drummond should discover some new means of supplying troops with subsistence. The army return of August 31 gave the precise strength of the garrison.

Strength of the Army at Fort Erie, Aug. 31, 1814

	Present for Duty		Aggregate
	Non-com. Officers rank-and-file	Officers	Present and absent
Dragoons	27	1	48
Bombardiers, etc.	34		51
Artillery Corps	206	10	369
First Brigade	725	39	2,311
Second Brigade	698	42	1,646
Porter's Brigade	220	16	599
First and Fourth Rifles	217	11	504
Total	2,127	119	5,528

The regular force in Fort Erie numbered two thousand and thirty-three effectives September 4, and though annoyed by the enemy's fire and worn by hard work, they were in both these respects better situated than the besiegers. Sooner or later the British would be obliged to retreat; and Brown was informed by deserters that Drummond was then contemplating withdrawal. Brown estimated the British force very loosely at three or four thousand; and it was in fact about the smaller number.

Drummond's situation was told in his reports to Sir George Prevost. September 8 he wrote that he should not fail to seize any favorable opportunity to attack; "but should no such opportunity present itself, I feel it incumbent on me to prepare your Excellency for the possibility of my being compelled by sickness or suffering of the troops, exposed as they will be to the effects of the wet and unhealthy season which is fast approaching, to withdraw them from their present position to one which may afford them the means of cover. Sickness has, I am sorry to say, already made its appearance in several of the Corps." Three days afterward, September 11, Drummond was warned by several signs that his lines were to be attacked by Brown, although "whether the account which is *invariably* given by deserters of his intention to act offensively . . . be correct, I have not yet been able accurately to ascertain." Drummond's batteries had been almost silent for several days for want of ammunition, and he could do nothing till the arrival of reinforcements,—the Ninety-seventh regiment,—unaccountably delayed. Rain had begun, and he dreaded its effect on the troops. In his next despatch, dated September 14, he said that the rain had been incessant, and "as the whole of the troops are without tents, and the huts in which they are placed are wholly incapable of affording shelter against such severe weather, their situation is most distressing." The roads were impassable; the nearest depot of supplies was Fort George, and Drummond had not cattle enough to move a third of his heavy ordnance if a sudden movement should be necessary. The enemy seemed about to cross the river in his rear, and the Ninety-seventh regiment had not yet arrived:

"In the meantime I have strong grounds for thinking that the enemy will risk an attack,—an event which though from the necessity of defending my batteries in the first instance with the pickets alone I shall have to meet under every possible disadvantage, yet I am very much disposed to hope may be the most fortunate circumstance which can happen, as it will bring us in contact with the enemy at a far cheaper rate than if we were to be the assailants."

While Drummond struggled between the necessity of retreat and the difficulty of retreating, Brown was bent on attacking his lines. The plan was open to grave objections, and a council of war, September 9, discouraged the idea. Brown was much disappointed and irritated at the result of the council, especially with Ripley; but while giving the impression that he acquiesced, he brought over all the volunteers he could obtain. The number was never precisely given, but according to the official reports of General Peter B. Porter who commanded them, and of General Brown himself, they did not exceed one thousand. With these, and an equal number of regular troops, Brown undertook to assault Drummond's entrenchments.

The nearest British line was about six hundred yards from old Fort Erie. From the first British battery on the Lake-shore, to Battery No. 3 in the woods, the line extended nearly half a mile, covered by abattis, but defended only by the brigade of troops on actual duty. If carried, the first line could not be held without capturing the second line, about fifty yards distant, and a third line, farther in the rear; while the main British force was encamped, for reasons of health and comfort, a mile behind, and was supposed to number at least three thousand six hundred men, or quite sufficient to recover their works. Brown professed no intention of fighting the British army. He proposed only "to storm the batteries, destroy the cannon, and roughly handle the brigade upon duty, before those in reserve could be brought into action."

Although Drummond expected and wished to be attacked, he kept no proper pickets or scouts in the woods, and all day of September 16 American fatigue parties were at work opening a path through the forest the distance of a mile, from Snake Hill on the extreme left to the extremity of the British line in the woods. So little precaution had Drummond's engineers taken that they left the dense forest standing within pistol-shot of the flank and rear of their Battery No. 3 on their extreme right, and the American parties opened a path within one hundred and fifty yards of the flank of the British line without being discovered.

At noon, September 17, General Porter led a column of sixteen hundred men —of whom one thousand were militia volunteers, and a part were the Twenty-third regiment—along the path through the woods, in three divisions, commanded by Colonel Gibson of the Fourth rifles, Colonel E. D. Wood of the Engineers, and Brigadier-General Davis of the New York militia. At three o'clock, under cover of heavy rain, the whole force fell suddenly on the block-house which covered the flank and rear of the British battery No. 3, and succeeded in capturing the blockhouse and mastering the battery held by DeWatteville's regiment. While detachments spiked the guns and blew up the magazine, the main column advanced on Battery No. 2, while at the same time General Miller, promoted to the command of Scott's old brigade, moved with "the remains of the Ninth and Eleventh Infantry and a detachment of the Nineteenth" from a ravine in front of Battery No. 3 to pierce the centre of the British line between Battery No. 3 and Battery No. 2.

Within half an hour after the first gun was fired, Porter and Miller had effected their junction within the British lines, had captured Battery No. 2, and moved on Battery No. 1, by the Lake-shore. There the success ended. Battery No. 1 could not be carried. By that time the Royal Scots, the Eighty-ninth, the Sixth, and the Eighty-second British regiments had arrived—probably about one thousand men. A sharp engagement followed before Brown, after ordering his reserve under Ripley to the assistance of Porter and Miller, could disengage his troops. The three commanders of Porter's division—Gibson, Wood, and Davis—were killed or mortally wounded—Gibson at the second battery, Davis and Wood in assaulting the shore battery. Ripley was desperately wounded at the same time. General Porter, Lieutenant-Colonel Aspinwall, of the Ninth, and Major Trimble of the Nineteenth, as well as a number of other officers, were severely wounded. That the last action was sharp was proved by the losses suffered by the British reinforcements. According to the British official return, the four regiments which came last into the field—the Royal Scots, Sixth, Eighty-second and Eighty-ninth—lost thirty-six killed, one hundred and nine wounded, and fifty-four missing—a total of two hundred men, in a short action of half an hour at the utmost, without artillery.

The American forces were recalled by Brown and Miller as soon as their progress was stopped, and they retired without serious pursuit beyond the British lines. Their losses were very severe, numbering five hundred and eleven killed, wounded, and missing, or about one fourth of their number. Among them were several of the best officers in the United States service, including Ripley, Wood, and Gibson. Drummond's loss was still more severe, numbering six hundred and nine, probably almost one man in three of the number engaged. The British killed numbered one hundred and fifteen. The Americans reported seventy-nine killed—sixty regulars, and nineteen militia.

The next day Drummond issued a general order claiming a victory over an American force of "not less than five thousand men, including militia;" but his situation, untenable before the sortie, became impossible after it. Three out of six battering cannon were disabled; he had lost six hundred men in battle, and his losses by sickness were becoming enormous. "My effective numbers are reduced to considerably less than two thousand firelocks," he reported, September 21. Immediately after the sorties, although reinforced by the Ninety-seventh regiment, he made his arrangements to retreat.

"Within the last few days," he wrote to Prevost, September 21, "the sickness of the troops has increased to such an alarming degree, and their situation has really become one of such extreme wretchedness from the torrents of rain which have continued to fall for the last thirteen days, and from the circumstance of the Division being entirely destitute of camp-equipage, that I feel it my duty no longer to persevere in a vain attempt to maintain the blockade of so vastly superior and increasing a force of the enemy under such circumstances. I have therefore given orders for the troops to fall back toward the Chippawa, and shall commence my movement at eight o'clock this evening."

CHAPTER XVIII

PLATTSBURG

Weak as was the army at Niagara, it was relatively stronger than the defence at any other threatened point. Sackett's Harbor contained only seven hundred effectives. On Lake Champlain, Major-General Izard tried to cover Plattsburg and Burlington with about five thousand regular troops. Already Armstrong knew that large British reinforcements from Wellington's army were on their way to Canada; and within a few weeks after the battle of Lundy's Lane eleven thousand of the best troops England ever put in the field were camped on or near the Sorel River, about to march against Izard's five thousand raw recruits.

They could march nowhere else. Not only was the line of Lake Champlain the natural and necessary path of an invading army, but the impossibility of supplying any large number of troops in Upper Canada made Lake Champlain the only region in which a large British force could exist. Sir George Prevost had reached the limit of his powers in defending Upper Canada. His commissary-general, W. H. Robinson, wrote to him, August 27, expressing "the greatest alarm" on account of deficient supplies at Burlington Heights and Niagara, where instead of nine thousand rations daily as he expected, he was required to furnish fourteen thousand, half of them to Indians. Much as Prevost wanted to attack Sackett's Harbor, and weak as he knew that post to be, he could not attempt it, although he had thirteen or fourteen thousand rank-and-file idle at Montreal. In October he went to Kingston expressly to arrange such an attack, and found it impossible.

"An investigation of the state of the stores at this post," he wrote to Lord Bathurst October 18, "proved that the articles for the armament and equipment for a ship of the class of the *St. Lawrence,* carrying upward of one hundred guns, had absorbed almost the whole of the summer transport-service from Montreal, leaving the materials for an undertaking of the magnitude of the destruction of Sackett's Harbor still at the extremity of the line of communication; and now, by giving precedence to that supply of provisions and stores without which an army is no longer to be maintained in Upper Canada, its removal is inevitably postponed until the winter roads are established."

Not only were military operations on a large scale impossible in Upper Canada, but for the opposite reason occupation of Lake Champlain by a British force was necessary. Northern New York and Vermont furnished two thirds of the fresh beef consumed by the British armies. General Izard reported to Armstrong, July 31:

"From the St. Lawrence to the ocean, an open disregard prevails for the laws prohibiting intercourse with the enemy. The road to St. Regis is covered with droves of cattle, and the river with rafts, destined for the enemy. The revenue officers see these things, but acknowledge their inability to put a stop to such outrageous proceedings. On the eastern side of Lake Champlain the high roads are found insufficient for the supplies of cattle which are pouring into Canada. Like herds of buffaloes they press through the forest, making paths for themselves. . . . Nothing but a cordon of troops from the French Mills to Lake Memphramagog could effectually check the evil. Were it not for these supplies, the British forces in Canada would soon be suffering from famine, or their government be subjected to enormous expense for their maintenance."

After Chauncey, August 1, regained possession of Lake Ontario, any British campaign against Sackett's Harbor or Detroit became doubly impossible, and the occupation of Lake Champlain became doubly necessary. Prevost wrote to Bathurst, August 27:

"In fact, my Lord, two thirds of the army in Canada are at this moment eating beef provided by American contractors, drawn principally from the States of Vermont and New York. This circumstance, as well as that of the introduction of large sums in specie into the province, being notorious in the United States, it is to be expected that Congress will take steps to deprive us of those resources; and under that apprehension large droves are daily crossing the lines coming into Lower Canada."

The fear that Izard might at any moment take efficient measures to cut off the British supplies gave double force to the reasons for occupying Lake Champlain, and forcing the military frontier back beyond Plattsburg and Burlington.

The political reasons were not less strong or less notorious than the military. England made no secret of her intention to rectify the Canadian frontier by lopping away such territory as she could conquer. July 5, the day of the battle of Chippawa, Lieutenant-Colonel Pilkington sailed from Halifax, and under the naval protection of Sir Thomas Hardy in the *Ramillies,* landed at Eastport, July 11, with the One-Hundred-and-second regiment, some engineers and artillery,—a detachment of six hundred men,—and took possession of Moose Island. Fort Sullivan, with six officers and eighty men, capitulated, and Great Britain took permanent possession of the place.

Moose Island was disputed territory, and its occupation was not necessarily conquest; but the next step showed wider views. August 26, Lieutenant-General Sir J. C. Sherbrooke, the British governor of Nova Scotia, set sail from Halifax with a powerful fleet, carrying near two thousand troops, and arrived September 1 at the Penobscot. At his approach, the American garrison of the small battery at Castine blew up their fort and dispersed. In all Massachusetts, only about six hundred regular troops were to be found, and beyond the Penobscot, in September, 1814, hardly a full company could have been collected. The able-bodied, voting, male population of the counties of Kennebeck and Hancock, on either side of the Penobscot River, capable of bearing arms, was at that time about twelve thousand, on an estimate of one in five of the total population, but they offered no resistance to the British troops.

One misfortune led to another. A few days before Sherbrooke's arrival at Castine the United States ship *Adams,* a heavy corvette carrying twenty-eight guns, having escaped from Chesapeake Bay and cruised some months at sea struck on a reef on the Isle of Haut, and was brought into the Penobscot in a sinking condition. Captain Morris, who commanded her, took the ship up the river about twenty-five miles, as far as Hampden near Bangor, and removed her guns in order to repair her. Sherbrooke, on occupying Castine, sent a detachment of some six hundred men in boats up the river to destroy the ship, while he occupied Belfast with another regiment. Captain Morris hastily put his guns in battery, and prepared to defend the ship with his crew, numbering probably more than two hundred men, relying on the militia to cover his flanks. On the morning of September 3, in a thick fog, the enemy's boats approached and landed their infantry, which attacked and routed the militia, and obliged Captain Morris to set fire to the *Adams,* abandon his guns, and disperse his men. The British force then marched to Bangor, which they occupied without opposition. Their entire loss was one man killed and eight wounded. At Bangor they remained nearly a week, destroying vessels and cargoes; but Sir John Sherbrooke had no orders to occupy the country west of the Penobscot, and his troops returned September 9 to Castine.

At Castine the British remained, while another detachment occupied Machias. All the province of Maine east of the Penobscot was then in Sherbrooke's hands. The people formally submitted. One hundred miles of Massachusetts sea-coast passed quietly under the dominion of the King of England. The male citizens were required to take the oath of allegiance to King George, and showed no unwillingness to remain permanently British subjects. After September 1 the United States government had every reason to expect that Great Britain would require, as one condition of peace, a cession of the eastern and northern portions of Maine.

For this purpose the British needed also to occupy Lake Champlain, in order to make their conquests respectable. The British general might move on Platts-burg or on Burlington; but in order to maintain his position he must gain naval possession of the Lake. In such a case the difficulties of the American govern-ment would be vastly increased, and the British position would be impregnable. Armstrong knew these circumstances almost as well as they were known to Sir George Prevost.

In May the British flotilla entered Lake Champlain from the Sorel River, and cruised, May 9, as far southward as Otter Creek, terrifying Vermont for the safety of the American flotilla under Lieutenant Thomas Macdonough at Ver-gennes. Irritated and alarmed by this demonstration, Armstrong ordered Izard to seize and fortify Rouse's Point, or the mouth of Lacolle River, or Ash Island, and so close the entrance to the Lake. Apparently Armstrong gave the order in ignorance that Lacolle River and Ash Island were strongly fortified British positions, and that a battery established at Rouse's Point, in the relative situation of forces, must have fallen into British hands. On this point the opinion of Izard was more valuable than that of Armstrong; and Izard, after much study and inquiry, decided to erect his fortifications at Plattsburg. He preferred the task of taking a position which he could certainly hold, although it would not prevent the enemy from passing if they chose to leave it behind them. At Plattsburg, therefore, he collected his troops, amounting to five or six thousand men, and constructed strong forts, while Macdonough's fleet took position in the bay.

While thus occupied, Izard cast anxious glances westward, doubting whether, in case of a reverse at Niagara or Sackett's Harbor, he ought not to move on the St. Lawrence and threaten the British communications between Montreal and Kingston. The same idea occurred to Armstrong, who in a letter dated

July 27 recommended Izard to carry it out. The letter reached Izard August 10, when he had advanced with his army to Chazy, and had learned enough of the concentration of British troops in his front to be assured that they meant to direct their serious attack against Lake Champlain. He wrote Armstrong a letter, August 11, which failed only in saying too little, rather than too much, of the dangers risked in obeying Armstrong's order:

"I will make the movement you direct, if possible; but I shall do it with the apprehension of risking the force under my command, and with the certainty that everything in this vicinity but the lately erected works at Plattsburg and Cumberland Head will in less than three days after my departure be in the possession of the enemy. He is in force superior to mine in my front; he daily threatens an attack on my position at Champlain; we are in hourly expectation of a serious conflict. That he has not attacked us before this time is attributable to caution on his part, from exaggerated reports of our numbers, and from his expectation of reinforcements. . . . It has always been my conviction that the numerical force of the enemy has been under-rated. I believe this to be the strong point of our frontier for either attack or defence, and I know that a British force has been kept in check in Lower Canada for many weeks past, greatly superior to that which I could oppose to it."

Izard was right. Every week new British forces poured into Quebec and were forwarded to Montreal. The arrival of the first division at Quebec was announced in the American newspapers early in August. Within a few weeks three brigades arrived and were sent to the front. When Izard wrote, he was probably faced by ten thousand veteran British troops within twenty or thirty miles of his position, and more were known to be on their way. At such a moment the danger of attempting a diversion was great; but Armstrong refused to believe it. Irritated by Izard's remonstrance, the secretary not only persisted in his own opinion, but, abandoning the idea of a movement against the British communications along the St. Lawrence, ordered Izard to march his army to Sackett's Harbor, and from there to operate either directly in force against Kingston, or to go on to Niagara and assist Brown, then hard pressed at Fort Erie. "It is very distinctly my opinion," wrote the secretary August 12, "that it has become good policy on our part to carry the war as far to the westward as possible, particularly while we have an ascendency on the Lakes."

Izard obeyed. His troops, numbering four thousand men, began their march August 29 for Sackett's Harbor, and for several weeks at the crisis of the campaign ceased to exist for military purposes. Within the fortifications at Plattsburg Izard left a miscellaneous body of three thousand, three hundred men, without an organized battalion except four companies of the Sixth regiment. Brigadier-General Alexander Macomb, who as senior officer was left in command, reported his force as not exceeding fifteen hundred effectives.

Armstrong's policy of meeting the enemy's main attack by annihilating the main defence never received explanation or excuse. At times Armstrong seemed to suggest that he meant to rely on the Navy—and indeed nothing else, except Izard's forts, was left to rely upon; but in truth he rather invited the invasion of a British army into New York to "renew the scene of Saratoga." As Izard predicted, the enemy crossed the frontier at once after his departure, occupying Chazy September 3, and approaching, September 5, within eight miles of Plattsburg.

Great Britain had never sent to America so formidable an armament. Neither Wolfe nor Amherst, neither Burgoyne nor Cornwallis, had led so large or so fine an army as was under the command of Sir George Prevost. According to his proposed arrangement, the light brigade, under Major-General Robinson, contained four battalions of the Twenty-seventh, Thirty-ninth, Seventy-sixth, and Eighty-eighth foot, with artillery, and numbered two thousand eight hundred and eighty-four rank-and-file. The second brigade, under Major-General Brisbane, contained battalions of the Eighth, Thirteenth, and Forty-ninth, De Meuron's regiment and Canadian voltigeurs and chasseurs, numbering four thousand and forty-eight rank-and-file. The third brigade, under Major-General Power, contained battalions of the Third, Fifth, Twenty-seventh, and Fifty-eighth, and numbered three thousand eight hundred and one rank-and-file. The reserve, under Major-General Kempt, contained battalions of the Ninth, Thirty-seventh, Fifty-seventh, and Eighty-first, numbering three thousand five hundred and forty-nine rank-and-file. Finally, fourteen hundred and eighty-eight men of the Sixteenth and Seventieth regiments, under command of Major-General DeWatteville, were stationed between Coteau du Lac and Gananoque on the St. Lawrence.

Thus the left division of the British army in Canada numbered fifteen thousand seven hundred and seventy effectives, or, including officers, probably eighteen thousand men, without reckoning the Canadian militia, either incorporated or sedentary. Two lieutenant-generals and five major-generals were in command. Amply provided with artillery and horses, every brigade well equipped, they came fresh from a long service in which the troops had learned to regard themselves as invincible. As they were at last organized, four brigades crossed the border, numbering not less than "eleven thousand men with a proportionate and most excellent train of artillery, commanded in chief by Sir George Prevost, and under him by officers of the first distinction in the service." A reserve of about five thousand men remained behind.

The fleet was almost as formidable as the army. As the force of the flotilla was reported to Prevost, it consisted of a thirty-six-gun ship, the *Confiance;* an eighteen-gun brig, the *Linnet;* two ten-gun sloops and twelve gunboats, carrying sixteen guns—all commanded by Captain Downie, of the Royal Navy, detached by Sir James Yeo for the purpose.

Such an expedition was regarded with unhesitating confidence, as able to go where it pleased within the region of Lake Champlain. About every other undertaking in America the British entertained doubts, but in regard to this affair they entertained none. Every movement of the British generals showed conviction of their irresistible strength. Had Prevost doubted the result of attacking Plattsburg, he could have advanced by St. Albans on Burlington, which would have obliged Macomb and Macdonough to leave their positions. So little did his army apprehend difficulty, that in advancing to Plattsburg in face of Macomb's skirmishers they did not once form in line, or pay attention to the troops and militia who obstructed the road. "The British troops did not deign to fire on them except by their flankers and advanced patrols," reported Macomb. "So undaunted was the enemy that he never deployed in his whole march, always pressing on in column."

The fleet felt the same certainty. According to the best Canadian authority, "the strongest confidence prevailed in the superiority of the British vessels, their weight of metal, and in the capacity and experience of their officers and crews." Captain Downie informed Sir George Prevost's staff-officer that he considered himself with the *Confiance* alone a match for the whole American squadron. Taking the British account of the *Confiance* as correct, she was one hundred and forty-six feet long on the gundeck, and thirty-six feet broad; she carried a crew of three hundred officers and men; her armament was thirty-seven guns—twenty-seven long twenty-four-pounders, six thirty-two-pound carronades, and four twenty-four-pound carronades—throwing in all nine hundred and thirty-six pounds. The American account, which was more trustworthy because the *Confiance* became better known in the American than in the British service, gave her thirty-one long twenty-four-pounders and six carronades.

Macdonough's best ship was the *Saratoga*. Her dimensions were not recorded. Her regular complement of men was two hundred and ten, but she fought with two hundred and forty; she carried eight twenty-four-pounders, twelve thirty-two and six forty-two-pound carronades—or twenty-six guns, throwing eight hundred and twenty-eight pounds. Her inferiority to the *Confiance* at long range was immense, and within carronade range it was at least sufficient to satisfy Captain Downie. He believed that a few broadsides would dispose of the *Saratoga*, and that the other American vessels must then surrender.

Assuming Sir George Prevost's report to have been correct, the two fleets compared as follows:

FORCE OF BRITISH FLEET

Vessels	Guns	Long	Short	Long metal	Short metal	Weight of metal
Confiance	37	31	6	744	192	936
Linnet	16	16		192		192
Chubb	11	1	10	6	180	186
Finch	10	4	6	24	108	132
Twelve gunboats	16	8	8	162	256	418
Total	90	60	30	1,128	736	1,864

FORCE OF AMERICAN FLEET

Vessels	Guns	Long	Short	Long metal	Short metal	Weight of metal
Saratoga	26	8	18	192	636	828
Eagle	20	8	12	144	384	528
Ticonderoga	17	12	5	168	146	314
Preble	7	7		63		63
Ten gunboats	16	10	6	192	108	300
Total	86	45	41	759	1,274	2,033

In this calculation the possible error consists only in one disputed eighteen-pound columbiad on the *Finch,* and three disputed guns—one long and two short —on the British gunboats. In one case the British would have thrown about nineteen hundred pounds of metal—in the other, about eighteen hundred. A glance at the two tables shows that in one respect Downie held a decisive superiority in his guns. He had no less than sixty long-range pieces, while Macdonough had but forty-five. Downie's long-range guns threw at least eleven hundred pounds of metal; Macdonough's threw but seven hundred and sixty. If Downie chose his own distance beyond range of the thirty-two-pound carronades, and fought only his long guns, nothing could save Macdonough except extreme good fortune, for he had but fourteen twenty-four-pound guns against Downie's thirty-four. Firing by broadsides, Downie could throw from his single ship, the *Confiance,* sixteen twenty-four-pound shot, to which Macdonough could reply only with eight, even if he used all his long guns on the same side.

The Americans had a decided advantage only in their commander. Thomas Macdonough, born in Delaware in 1783, was thirty years old when this responsibility fell upon him. He had been educated, like most of the naval heroes, in the hard service of the Tripolitan war, and had been sent to construct and command the naval force on Lake Champlain in the spring of 1813. Macdonough's superiority over ordinary commanders consisted in the intelligent forethought with which he provided for the chances of battle. His arrangement showed that he foresaw and as far as possible overcame in advance, every conceivable attack. He compelled the enemy to fight only as pleased himself.

Macdonough anchored his four large vessels across Plattsburg Bay, where it was a mile and a half wide, and placed his gunboats in their rear to fill the gaps. Cumberland Head on his left and front, and Crab Island on his right obliged the enemy to enter in a line so narrow that Downie would find no room to anchor on his broadside out of carronade range, but must sail into the harbor under the raking fire of the American long guns, and take a position within range of the American carronades. As the battle was to be fought at anchor, both squadrons would as a matter of course be anchored with springs on their cables; but Macdonough took the additional precaution of laying a kedge off each buoy of the *Saratoga,* bringing their hawsers in on the two quarters, and letting them hang in bights under water. This arrangement enabled him to wind his ship at any time without fear of having his cables cut by the enemy's shot, and to use his larboard broadside, if his starboard guns should be disabled. In effect, it doubled his fighting capacity.

Sir George Prevost and the army were ready to move before Downie's fleet could be prepared. Marching directly forward with the utmost confidence, Sir George turned the advanced American position at Dead Creek Bridge and drove away the gunboats that covered it. He reached the Saranac River September 6, and saw beyond it a ridge "crowned with three strong redoubts and other field-works, and blockhouses armed with heavy ordnance, with their flotilla at anchor out of gunshot from the shore." The description was not exaggerated. Izard was himself a trained engineer, and the works built by him, under the direction of Major Totten of the Engineer Corps, were believed capable of resisting for three

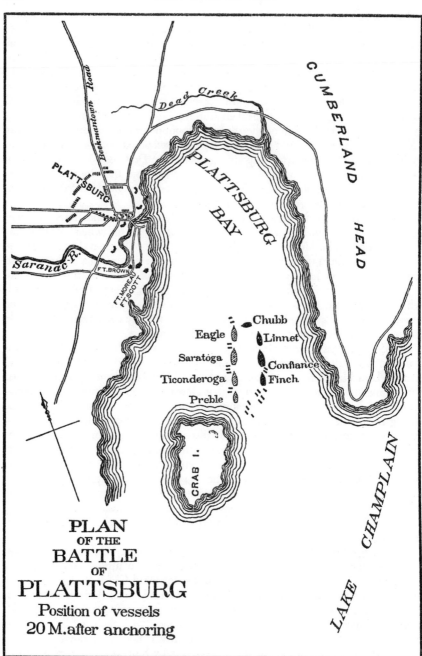

PLAN
OF THE
BATTLE
OF
PLATTSBURG
Position of vessels
20 M. after anchoring

weeks a combined attack by land and water, even if the British fleet were victorious. Three good companies of artillery manned the guns. Excellent officers of every arm were in command.

Prevost properly halted, and declined to assault without the coöperation of the fleet. He waited five days impatiently for Downie to appear. Not till seven o'clock on the morning of September 11 did the British flotilla sail round Cumberland Head. At the same time Prevost ordered his troops to cross the Saranac and storm the American works.

Downie intended, without regarding his superiority in long-range guns, to sail in and to lay the *Confiance* alongside of the *Saratoga,* but the wind was light and baffling, and his approach was so slow that he could not long bear the raking fire of the American guns. As he came within carronade range the wind baffling, he was obliged to anchor at two cables' lengths, or three hundred yards, and begin action. With the same discipline that marked the movements of the troops on shore, Downie came to, anchored, made everything secure, and then poured a full broadside into Macdonough's ship. The *Saratoga* shivered under the shock of sixteen twenty-four-pound shot and canister charges striking her hull; almost one-fifth of her crew were disabled; but she stood stoutly to her work, and the whole line was soon hotly engaged.

Americans usually had a decided advantage in their better gunnery, but three hundred yards was a long range for thirty-two-pound carronades, which at point-blank carried less than two hundred and fifty yards, and lost accuracy in proportion to elevation. Macdonough was slow to prove superiority. Early in the battle the British suffered a severe, and perhaps in the experience of this war a decisive, loss in their commander, Captain Downie, instantly killed by one of his own guns thrown off its carriage against him by a solid shot. Yet at the end of two hours' combat the British squadron was on the whole victorious, and the American on the point of capture. Of the three smaller American vessels, the *Preble* on the extreme right was driven out of the engagement, and the British gunboats, turning the American flank, attacked the *Ticonderoga,* which maintained a doubtful battle. The American left was also turned, the *Eagle* having been driven to take refuge between the *Saratoga* and *Ticonderoga,* in the centre. Macdonough's ship was then exposed to the concentrated fire of the *Confiance* and *Linnet,* and his battery was soon silenced. The *Saratoga* could not longer use a gun on the engaged side, and the battle was nearly lost.

Then Macdonough's forethought changed the impending defeat into victory. His fire had nearly silenced the *Confiance,* and disregarding the *Linnet,* he ceased attention to the battle in order to direct the operation of winding ship. Little by little hauling the ship about, he opened on the *Confiance* with one gun after another of the fresh broadside, as they bore; and the *Confiance,* after trying in vain to effect the same operation, struck her colors. Then the British fleet was in the situation which Downie had anticipated for the Americans in the event of silencing the *Saratoga.* The three smaller vessels were obliged to surrender, and the gunboats alone escaped. The battle had lasted from quarter past eight till quarter before eleven.

By land, the British attack was much less effective than by water. The troops

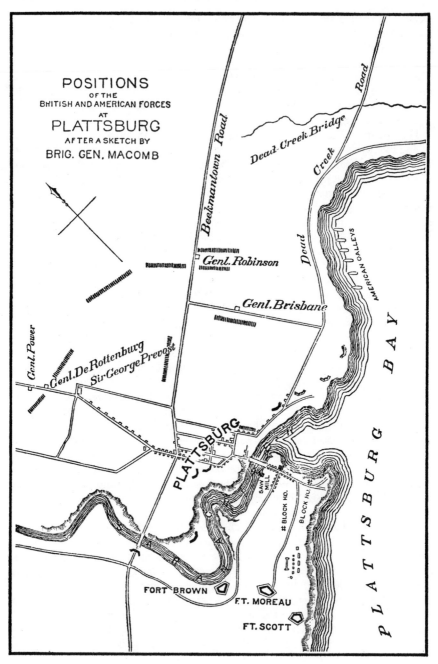

POSITIONS
OF THE
BRITISH AND AMERICAN FORCES
AT
PLATTSBURG
AFTER A SKETCH BY
BRIG. GEN. MACOMB

were slow in reaching their positions, and had time to make no decisive movement. A column under Major-General Robinson was ordered to move round by the right flank to a ford previously reconnoitered, some distance up the Saranac, in order to gain a position whence they could reverse the American works and carry them by assault; but Robinson's column missed its way, and before reaching the ford heard the cheers of the American troops, and halted to ascertain its cause. The remainder of the army waited for Robinson's column to assault. The casualties showed that nothing like a serious engagement took place. The entire loss of the British army from September 6 to September 14 was officially reported as only thirty-seven killed and one hundred and fifty wounded, and of this loss a large part occurred previous to the battle of September 11. The entire American loss was thirty-seven killed and sixty-two wounded.

In the naval battle, Macdonough reported fifty-two killed and fifty-eight wounded, among about eight hundred and eighty men. The British reported fifty-seven killed and seventy-two wounded, in crews whose number was never precisely known, but was probably fully eight hundred. In neither case was the loss, though severe, as great relatively to the numbers as the severity of the action seemed to employ. The *Saratoga* lost twenty-eight killed in a crew of two hundred and forty. In Perry's battle on Lake Erie, the *Lawrence* lost twenty-two men killed in a crew of one hundred and thirty-one. About one man in eight was killed on Macdonough's ship; about one man in six on Perry's.

With needless precipitation, Prevost instantly retreated the next day to Champlain, sacrificing stores to a very great amount, and losing many men by desertion. The army was cruelly mortified, and Prevost lost whatever military reputation he still preserved in Canada. In England the impression of disgrace was equally strong. "It is scarcely possible to conceive the degree of mortification and disappointment," said the *Annual Register,* "which the intelligence of this defeat created in Great Britain." Yeo brought official charges of misconduct against Prevost, and Prevost defended himself by unusual arguments.

"With whatever sorrow I may think of the unfortunate occurrences to which I allude," he wrote to Bathurst, three weeks later, "I consider them as light and trivial when compared to the disastrous results which I am solemnly persuaded, would have ensued had any considerations of personal glory, or any unreflecting disregard of the safety of the province, or of the honor of the army committed to my charge, induced me to pursue those offensive operations by land, independent of the fleet, which it would appear by your Lordship's despatch were expected of me. Such operations, my Lord, have been attempted before, and on the same ground. The history of our country records their failure; and had they been undertaken again with double the force placed under my command, they would have issued in the discomfiture of his Majesty's arms, and in a defeat not more disastrous than inevitable."

The Duke of Wellington was not so severe as other critics, and hesitated to say that Prevost was wrong; "though of this I am certain, he must equally have returned . . . after the fleet was beaten; and I am inclined to think he was right. I have told the ministers repeatedly that a naval superiority on the Lakes is a *sine qua non* of success in war on the frontier of Canada, even if our object should be wholly defensive." Yet the Duke in conversation seemed to think that his army in Canada was also at fault. "He had sent them some of his best troops from Bordeaux," he said five-and-twenty years afterward, "but they did not turn out quite right; they wanted this iron fist to command them."

Meanwhile Major-General Izard, by Armstrong's order, marched his four thousand men as far as possible from the points of attack. Starting from Champlain, August 29, the army reached Sackett's Harbor September 17, having marched about two hundred and eighty miles in twenty days. At Sackett's Harbor Izard found no orders from the government, for the government at that time had ceased to perform its functions; but he received an earnest appeal from General Brown to succor Fort Erie. "I will not conceal from you," wrote Brown, September 10, "that I consider the fate of this army very doubtful unless speedy relief is afforded." Izard, who had no means of testing the correctness of this opinion, decided to follow Brown's wishes, and made, September 17, the necessary preparations. Violent storms prevented Chauncey from embarking the troops until September 21; but September 27 the troops reached Batavia, and Izard met Brown by appointment. The army had then been a month in movement. The distance was more than four hundred miles, and no energy could have shortened the time so much as to have affected the result of the campaign. At one end of the line Sir George Prevost retreated from Plattsburg September 12; at the other end, Lieutenant-General Drummond retreated from Fort Erie September 21; and Izard's force, constituting the largest body of regular troops in the field, had been placed where it could possibly affect neither result.

Izard was a friend of Monroe, and was therefore an object of Armstrong's merciless criticism. Brown was a favorite of Armstrong and shared his prejudices. The position of Izard at Buffalo was calculated to excite jealousy. He had implicitly obeyed the wishes of Armstrong and Brown; in doing so, he had sacrificed himself—yielding to Macomb the credit of repulsing Prevost, and to Brown, who did not wait for his arrival, the credit of repulsing Drummond. As far as could be seen, Izard had acted with loyalty toward both Armstrong and Brown; yet both distrusted him. Brown commonly inclined toward severity, and was the more sensitive because Izard, as the senior officer, necessarily took command.

Until that moment Izard had enjoyed no chance of showing his abilities in the field, but at Niagara he saw before him a great opportunity. Drummond lay at Chippawa, with an army reduced by battle and sickness to about twenty-five hundred men. Izard commanded fifty-five hundred regular troops and eight hundred militia. He had time to capture or destroy Drummond's entire force before the winter should set in, and to gather the results of Brown's desperate fighting. Brown was eager for the attack, and Izard assented. October 13 the army moved on Chippawa, and stopped. October 16, Izard wrote to the War Department,

"I have just learned by express from Sackett's Harbor that Commodore Chauncey with the whole of his fleet has retired into port, and is throwing up batteries for its protection. This defeats all the objects of the operations by land in this quarter. I may turn Chippawa, and should General Drummond not retire, may succeed in giving him a good deal of trouble; but if he falls back on Fort George or Burlington Heights, every step I take in pursuit exposes me to be cut off by the large reinforcements it is in the power of the enemy to throw in twenty-four hours upon my flank or rear."

In this state of mind, notwithstanding a successful skirmish, October 19, between Bissell's brigade and a strong detachment of the enemy, Izard made a decision which ruined his military reputation and destroyed his usefulness to the service. He reported to the Department, October 23.

"On the 21st, finding that he (Drummond) still continued within his works, which he had been assiduously engaged in strengthening from the moment of our first appearance, the weather beginning to be severe, and a great quantity of our officers and men suffering from their continued fatigues and exposure, at twelve at noon I broke up my encampment, and marched to this ground (opposite Black Rock) in order to prepare winter quarters for the troops."

Nothing remained but to break up the army. Brown was sent at his own request to Sackett's Harbor, where the next fighting was expected. A division of the army went with him. The remainder were placed in winter quarters near Buffalo. Fort Erie was abandoned and blown up, November 5, and the frontier at Niagara relapsed into repose.

Izard felt the mortification of his failure. His feelings were those of a generous character, and his tone toward Brown contrasted to his advantage both in candor and in temper with Brown's language toward him; but great energy generally implied great faults, and Brown's faults were better suited than Izard's virtues for the work of an American general at Niagara. Greatly to Izard's credit, he not only saw his own inferiority, but advised the government of it. He wrote to the Secretary of War, November 20,

"The success of the next campaign on this frontier will in a great measure depend on concert and good understanding among the superior officers . . . General Brown is certainly a brave, intelligent, and active officer. Where a portion of the forces is composed of irregular troops, I have no hesitation in acknowledging my conviction of his being better qualified than I to make them useful in the public service."

So sensitive was Izard to the public feeling and his loss of standing that he sent his resignation to the secretary, December 18, in terms which betrayed and even asserted his consciousness of shrinking under the weight of responsibility:

"I am fully aware that attempts have been made to lessen the confidence of government as well as of the public in my ability to execute the important duties intrusted to me—duties which were imposed unexpectedly and much against my inclination. It is therefore not improbable that my voluntary retirement will relieve the Department of War from some embarrassment, and that my individual satisfaction will accord with the public advantage—especially as my view of the connection between military command and responsibility differs materially from that entertained by persons in high authority."

A man who showed so little confidence in himself could not claim the confidence of others, and in contact with stronger characters like Armstrong, Brown, Scott, or Andrew Jackson could play no part but that of a victim. His resignation was not accepted, but his career was at an end. When he relieved the pressure

kept by Brown constantly applied to the extremity of the British line, the movement of war necessarily turned back to its true object, which was Sackett's
Harbor. Drummond no sooner saw Fort Erie evacuated and his lines re-established, November 5, than he hurried on board ship with a part of his troops, and
reached Kingston, November 10, where Sir George Prevost had already prepared for an attack on Sackett's Harbor as soon as supplies could be brought from
Quebec to Kingston over the winter roads. Soon afterward Sir George Prevost
was recalled to England, and a new commander-in-chief, Sir George Murray,
supposed to be a man of higher capacity, was sent to take direction of the next
campaign. Reinforcements continued to arrive. About twenty-seven thousand
regular troops, including officers, were in Canada; a seventy-four-gun ship and
a new frigate were launched at Kingston; and no one doubted that with the
spring, Sackett's Harbor would be formally besieged. Izard remained at Buffalo,
doing nothing, and his only influence on the coming as on the past campaign
was to leave the initiative to the enemy.

CHAPTER XIX

BLADENSBURG

Armstrong's management of the Northern campaign caused severe criticism; but his neglect of the city of Washington exhausted the public patience. For two years Washington stood unprotected; not a battery or a breastwork was to be found on the river bank except the old and untenable Fort Washington, or Warburton. A thousand determined men might reach the town in thirty-six hours, and destroy it before any general alarm could be given. Yet no city was more easily protected than Washington, at that day, from attack on its eastern side; any good engineer could have thrown up works in a week that would have made approach by a small force impossible. Armstrong neglected to fortify. After experience had proved his error, he still argued in writing to a committee of Congress that fortifications would have exhausted the Treasury; "that bayonets are known to form the most efficient barriers; and that there was no reason in this case to doubt beforehand the willingness of the country to defend itself"—as though he believed that militia were most efficient when most exposed! He did not even provide the bayonets.

In truth, Armstrong looking at the matter as a military critic decided that the British having no strategic object in capturing Washington, would not make the attempt. Being an indolent man, negligent of detail, he never took unnecessary trouble; and having no proper staff at Washington, he was without military advisers whose opinion he respected. The President and Monroe fretted at his indifference, the people of the District were impatient under it, and every one except Armstrong was in constant terror of attack; but according to their account the secretary only replied: "No, no! Baltimore is the place, sir; that is of so much more consequence." Probably he was right, and the British would have gone first to Baltimore had his negligence not invited them to Washington.

In May the President began to press Armstrong for precautionary measures. In June letters arrived from Gallatin and Bayard in London which caused the President to call a Cabinet meeting. June 23 and 24 the Cabinet met and considered the diplomatic situation. The President proposed then for the first time to abandon impressment as a *sine qua non* of negotiation, and to approve a treaty that should be silent on the subject. Armstrong and Jones alone supported the idea at that time, but three days afterward, June 27, Monroe and Campbell acceded to it. The Cabinet then took the defences of Washington in hand, and July 1 decided to organize a corps of defence from the militia of the District and the neighboring States. July 2, the first step toward efficient defence was taken by creating a new military district on the Potomac, with a military head of its own. Armstrong wished to transfer Brigadier-General Moses Porter from Norfolk, to command the new Potomac District; but the President selected Brigadier-General Winder, because his relationship to the Federalist governor of Maryland was likely to make coöperation more effective.

Political appointments were not necessarily bad; but in appointing Winder to please the governor of Maryland Madison assumed the responsibility, in Armstrong's eyes, for the defence of Washington. The Secretary of War seemed to think that Madison and Monroe were acting together to take the defence of

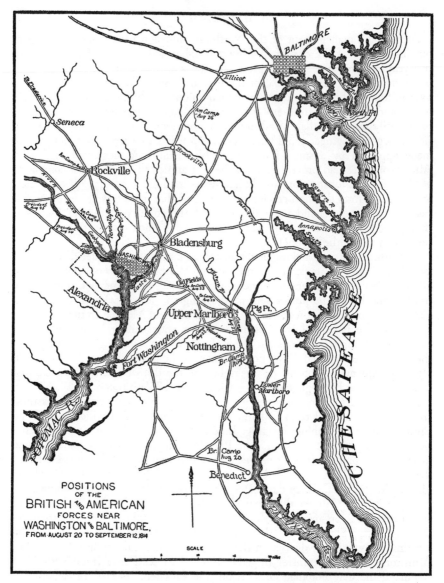

POSITIONS
OF THE
BRITISH AND AMERICAN
FORCES NEAR
WASHINGTON AND BALTIMORE,
FROM AUGUST 20 TO SEPTEMBER 12, 1814

Washington out of his hands, and to put it in hands in which they felt confidence. Armstrong placed Winder instantly in command and promptly issued orders arranged in Cabinet; but he left further measures to Winder, Monroe, and Madison. His conduct irritated the President; but no one charged that the secretary refused to carry out the orders, or to satisfy the requisitions of the President or of General Winder. He was merely passive.

Winder received his appointment July 5, and went to Washington for instructions. He passed the next month riding between Washington, Baltimore, and points on the lower Potomac and Patuxent, obtaining with great fatigue a personal knowledge of the country. August 1 he established his permanent headquarters in Washington, and the entire result of his labors till that time was the presence of one company of Maryland militia at Bladensburg. No line of defence was selected, no obstructions to the roads were prepared, and not so much as a ditch or a breastwork was marked out or suggested between Annapolis and Washington. Another fortnight passed, and still Winder got no further advanced. He had no more men, arms, fortifications, and no more ideas, on the 18th of August than on the 5th of July. "The call for three thousand militia under the requisition of July 4 had produced only two hundred and fifty men at the moment the enemy landed at Benedict." Winder had then been six weeks in command of the Washington defences.

Meanwhile a British expedition under command of Major-General Robert Ross, a distinguished officer of the Peninsula army, sailed from the Gironde, June 27, to Bermuda. Ross was instructed "to effect a diversion on the coasts of the United States of America in favor of the army employed in the defence of Upper and Lower Canada." The point of attack was to be decided by Vice-Admiral Cochrane, subject to the general's approval; but the force was not intended for "any extended operation at a distance from the coast," nor was Ross to hold permanent possession of any captured district.

"When the object of the descent which you may make on the coast is to take possession of any naval or military stores, you will not delay the destruction of them in preference to the taking them away, if there is reasonable ground of apprehension that the enemy is advancing with superior force to effect their recovery. If in any descent you shall be enabled to take such a position as to threaten the inhabitants with the destruction of their property, you are hereby authorized to levy upon them contributions in return for your forbearance; but you will not by this understand that the magazines belonging to the government, or their harbors, or their shipping, are to be included in such an arrangement. These, together with their contents, are in all cases to be taken away or destroyed."

Negroes were not to be encouraged to rise upon their masters, and no slaves were to be taken away as slaves; but any negro who should expose himself to vengeance by joining the expedition or lending it assistance, might be enlisted in the black corps, or carried away by the fleet.

Nothing in these orders warranted the destruction of private or public property, except such as might be capable of military uses. Ross was not authorized, and did not intend, to enter on a mere marauding expedition; but Cochrane was independent of Ross, and at about the time when Ross reached Bermuda Cochrane received a letter from Sir George Prevost which gave an unexpected character to the Chesapeake expedition. A small body of American troops had crossed Lake Erie to Long Point, May 15, and destroyed the flour-mills, distilleries, and some private houses there. The raid was not authorized by the United States government, and the officer commanding it was afterward court-martialed and censured; but Sir George Prevost, without waiting for explanations, wrote to

Vice-Admiral Cochrane, June 2, suggesting that he should "assist in inflicting that measure of retaliation which shall deter the enemy from a repetition of similar outrages."

When Cochrane received this letter, he issued at Bermuda, July 18, orders to the ships under his command, from the St. Croix River to the St. Mary's, directing general retaliation. The orders were interesting as an illustration of the temper the war had taken.

"You are hereby required and directed," wrote the Vice-Admiral to the British blockading squadrons, "to destroy and lay waste such towns and districts upon the coast as you may find assailable. You will hold strictly in view the conduct of the American army toward his Majesty's unoffending Canadian subjects, and you will spare merely the lives of the unarmed inhabitants of the United States. For only by carrying this retributory justice into the country of our enemy can we hope to make him sensible of the impropriety as well as of the inhumanity of the system he has adopted. You will take every opportunity of explaining to the people how much I lament the necessity of following the rigorous example of the commander of the American forces. And as these commanders must obviously have acted under instructions from the Executive government of the United States, whose intimate and unnatural connection with the late government of France has led them to adopt the same system of plunder and devastation, it is therefore to their own government the unfortunate sufferers must look for indemnification for their loss of property."

This ill-advised order was to remain in force until Sir George Prevost should send information "that the United States government have come under an obligation to make full remuneration to the injured and unoffending inhabitants of the Canadas for all the outrages their troops have committed." Cochrane further wrote to Prevost that "as soon as these orders have been acted upon," a copy would be sent to Washington for the information of the Executive government.

Cochrane's relatiatory order was dated July 18, and Ross's transports arrived at Bermuda July 24. As soon as the troops were collected and stores put on board, Cochrane and Ross sailed, August 3, for Chesapeake Bay. They arrived a few days in advance of the transports, and passing up the bay to the mouth of the Potomac, landed, August 15, with Rear Admiral Cockburn, to decide on a plan for using to best effect the forces under their command.

Three objects were within reach. The first and immediate aim was a flotilla of gunboats, commanded by Captain Joshua Barney, which had taken refuge in the Patuxent River, and was there blockaded. The next natural object of desire was Baltimore, on account of its shipping and prize-money. The third was Washington and Alexandria, on account of the navy-yard and the vessels in the Potomac. Baltimore was the natural point of attack after destroying Barney's flotilla; but Cockburn, with a sailor's recklessness, urged a dash at Washington. Ross hesitated, and postponed a decision till Barney's flotilla should be disposed of.

Two days afterward, August 17, the troops arrived, and the squadron, commanded by Vice-Admiral Cochrane, moved twenty miles up the bay to the mouth of the Patuxent—a point about fifty miles distant from Annapolis on the north, and from Washington on the northwest. Having arrived there August 18,

Cochrane wrote, or afterward ante-dated, an official letter to Secretary Monroe:

"Having been called on by the Governor-General of the Canadas to aid him in carrying into effect measures of retaliation against the inhabitants of the United States for the wanton destruction committed by their Army in Upper Canada, it has become imperiously my duty, conformably with the nature of the Governor-General's application, to issue to the naval force under my command an order to destroy and lay waste such towns and districts upon the coast as may be found assailable."

The notice was the more remarkable because Cochrane's order was issued only to the naval force. The army paid no attention to it. Ross's troops were landed at Benedict the next day, August 19; but neither there nor elsewhere did they destroy or lay waste towns or districts. They rather showed unusual respect for private property.

At Benedict, August 19, the British forces were organized in three brigades, numbering, according to different British accounts, four thousand five hundred, or four thousand rank-and-file. Cockburn with the boats of the fleet the next day, August 20, started up the river in search of Barney's flotilla; while the land force began its march at four o'clock in the afternoon abreast of the boats, and camped four miles above Benedict without seeing an enemy, or suffering from a worse annoyance than one of the evening thunder-storms common in hot weather.

The next day at dawn the British army started again, and marched that day, Sunday, August 21, twelve miles to the village of Nottingham, where it camped. The weather was hot, and the march resembled a midsummer picnic. Through a thickly wooded region, where a hundred militia-men with axes and spades could have delayed their progress for days, the British army moved in a solitude apparently untenanted by human beings, till they reached Nottingham on the Patuxent—a deserted town, rich in growing crops and full barns.

At Nottingham the army passed a quiet night, and the next morning, Monday, August 22, lingered till eight o'clock, when it again advanced. Among the officers in the Eighty-fifth regiment was a lieutenant named Gleig, who wrote afterward a charming narrative of the campaign under the title, "A Subaltern in America." He described the road as remarkably good, running for the most part through the heart of thick forests, which sheltered it from the rays of the sun. During the march the army was startled by the distant sound of several heavy explosions. Barney had blown up his gunboats to prevent their capture. The British naval force had thus performed its part in the enterprise, and the army was next to take the lead. Ross halted at Marlboro after a march of only seven miles, and there too he camped, undisturbed by sight or sound of an armed enemy, although the city of Washington was but sixteen miles on his left, and Baltimore thirty miles in his front. Ross had then marched twenty or twenty-one miles into Maryland without seeing an enemy, although an American army had been close on his left flank, watching him all day.

At Marlboro Ross was obliged to decide what he should next do. He was slow in forming a conclusion. Instead of marching at daybreak of August 23, and moving rapidly on Baltimore or Washington, the army passed nearly the whole day at Marlboro in idleness, as though it were willing to let the Americans do their utmost for defence. "Having advanced within sixteen miles of Washington," Ross officially reported, "and ascertained the force of the enemy to be such as might authorize an attempt to carry his capital, I determined to make it, and accordingly put the troops in movement on the evening of the 23d." More exactly, the troops moved at two o'clock in the afternoon, and marched about six miles on the road to Washington, when they struck American outposts at about five o'clock, and saw a force posted on high ground about a mile in their front. As the British formed to attack, the American force disappeared, and the British army camped about nine miles from Washington by way of the navy-yard bridge over the Eastern Branch.

Thus for five days, from August 18 to August 23, a British army, which though small was larger than any single body of American regulars then in the field, marched in a leisurely manner through a long-settled country, and met no show of resistance before coming within sight of the Capitol. Such an adventure resembled the stories of Cortez and DeSoto; and the conduct of the United States Government offered no contradiction to the resemblance.

News of the great fleet that appeared in the Patuxent August 17 reached Washington on the morning of Thursday, August 18, and set the town in commotion. In haste the President sent fresh militia requisitions to the neighboring States, and ordered out the militia and all the regular troops in Washington and its neighborhood. Monroe started again as a scout, arriving in the neighborhood of Benedict at ten o'clock on the morning of August 20, and remaining there all day and night without learning more than he knew before starting. Winder was excessively busy, but did, according to his own account, nothing. "The innumerably multiplied orders, letters, consultations, and demands which crowded upon me at the moment of such an alarm can more easily be conceived than described, and occupied me nearly day and night, from Thursday the 18th of August till Sunday the 21st, and had nearly broken down myself and assistants in preparing, dispensing, and attending to them." Armstrong, at last alive to the situation, made excellent suggestions, but could furnish neither troops, means, nor military intelligence to carry them out; and the President could only call for help. The single step taken for defence was taken by the citizens, who held a meeting Saturday evening, and offered at their own expense to erect works at Bladensburg. Winder accepted their offer. Armstrong detailed Colonel Wadsworth, the only engineer officer near the Department, to lay out the lines, and the citizens did such work as was possible in the time that remained.

After three days of confusion, a force was at last evolved. Probably by Winder's order, although no such order was preserved, a corps of observation was marched across the navy-yard bridge toward the Patuxent, or drawn from Bladensburg, to a place called the Woodyard, twelve miles beyond the Eastern Branch. The force was not to be despised. Three hundred infantry regulars of different regiments, with one hundred and twenty light dragoons, formed the nucleus; two hundred and fifty Maryland militia, and about twelve hundred District volunteers or militia, with twelve six-pound field-pieces, composed a body of near two thousand men, from whom General Brown or Andrew Jackson would have got good service. Winder came out and took command Sunday evening, and Monroe, much exhausted, joined them that night.

There the men stood Monday, August 22, while the British army marched by them, within sight of their outposts, from Nottingham to Marlboro. Winder rode forward with his cavalry and watched all day the enemy's leisurely movements close in his front, but the idea of attack did not appear to enter his mind. "A doubt at that time," he said, "was not entertained by anybody of the intention of the enemy to proceed direct to Washington." At nine o'clock that evening Monroe sent a note to the President, saying that the enemy was in full march for Washington; that Winder proposed to retire till he could collect his troops; that preparations should be made to destroy the bridges, and that the papers in the government offices should be removed. At the same time Monroe notified Serurier, the only foreign minister then in Washington, that the single hope of saving the capital depended on the very doubtful result of an engagement, which would probably take place the next day or the day after, at Bladensburg.

At Bladensburg, of necessity, the engagement must take place, unless Winder made an attack or waited for attack on the road. One of two courses was to be taken,—Washington must be either defended or evacuated. Perhaps Winder would have done better to evacuate it, and let the British take the undefended village; but no suggestion of the sort was made, nor did Winder retreat to Bladensburg as was necessary if he meant to unite his troops and make preparations for a battle. Instead of retreating to Bladensburg as soon as he was satisfied—at noon of Monday, August 22—that the British were going there, he ordered his troops to fall back, and took position at the Old Fields, about five miles in the rear of the Woodyard, and about seven miles by road from the navy-yard. Another road led from the Old Fields to Bladensburg about eight miles away. The American force might have been united at Bladensburg Monday evening, but Winder camped at the Old Fields and passed the night.

That evening the President and the members of the Cabinet rode out to the camp, and the next morning the President reviewed the army, which had been reinforced by Commodore Barney with four hundred sailors, the crews of the burned gunboats. Winder then had twenty-five hundred men, of whom near a thousand were regulars, or sailors even better fighting troops than ordinary regulars. Such a force vigorously led was sufficient to give Ross's army a sharp check, and at that moment Ross was still hesitating whether to attack Washington. The loss of a few hundred men might have turned the scale at any moment during Tuesday, August 23; but Winder neither fought nor retreated, but once more passed the day on scout. At noon he rode with a troop of cavalry toward Marlboro. Satisfied that the enemy was not in motion and would not move that day, he started at one o'clock for Bladensburg, leaving his army to itself. He wished to bring up a brigade of militia from Bladensburg.

Winder had ridden about five miles, when the British at two o'clock suddenly broke up their camp and marched directly on the Old Fields. The American army hastily formed in line, and sent off its baggage to Washington. Winder was summoned back in haste, and arrived on the field at five o'clock as the British appeared. He ordered a retreat. Every military reason required a retreat to Bladensburg. Winder directed a retreat on Washington by the navy-yard bridge.

The reasons which actuated him to prefer the navy-yard to Bladensburg, as explained by him, consisted in anxiety for the safety of that "direct and important pass," which could not without hazard be left unguarded. In order to guard a bridge a quarter of a mile long over an impassable river covered by the guns of war-vessels and the navy-yard, he left unguarded the open high-road which led through Bladensburg directly to the Capitol and the White House. After a very rapid retreat that "literally became a run of eight miles," Winder encamped in Washington near the bridge-head at the navy-yard at eight o'clock that night, and then rode three miles to the White House to report to the President. On returning to camp, he passed the night until three or four o'clock in the morning making in person arrangement to destroy the bridge "when necessary," assuring his officers that he expected the enemy to attempt a passage there that night. Toward dawn he lay down, exhausted by performing a subaltern's duty all day, and snatched an hour or two of sleep.

The British in their camp that evening were about eight miles from Bladensburg battle-field. Winder was about five miles distant from the same point. By a quick march at dawn he might still have arrived there, with six hours to spare for arranging his defence. He preferred to wait till he should know with certainty that the British were on their way there. On the morning of Wednesday, August 24, he wrote to Armstrong:—"I have found it necessary to establish my headquarters here, the most advanced position convenient to the troops, and nearest information. I shall remain stationary as much as possible, that I may be the more readily found, to issue orders, and collect together the various detachments of militia, and give them as rapid a consolidation and organization as possible. . . . The news up the river is very threatening. Barney's or some other force should occupy the batteries at Greenleaf's Point and the navy-yard. I should be glad of the assistance of counsel from yourself and the Government. If more convenient, I should make an exertion to go to you the first opportunity."

This singular note was carried first to the President, who, having opened and read it, immediately rode to headquarters. Monroe, Jones, and Rush followed. Armstrong and Campbell arrived last. Before Armstrong appeared, a scout arrived at ten o'clock with information that the British army had broken up its camp at daylight, and was probably more than half way to Bladensburg.

Winder's persistence in remaining at the navy-yard was explained as due to the idea that the enemy might move toward the Potomac, seize Fort Washington or Warburton, secure the passage of his ships, and approach the city by the river. The general never explained how his presence at the navy-yard was to prevent such a movement if it was made.

The whole eastern side of Washington was covered by a broad estuary called the Eastern Branch of the Potomac, bridged only at two points, and impassable, even by pontoons, without ample warning. From the Potomac River to Bladensburg, a distance of about seven miles, the city was effectually protected. Bladensburg made the point of a right angle. There the Baltimore road entered the city as by a pass; for beyond, to the west, no general would venture to enter, leaving

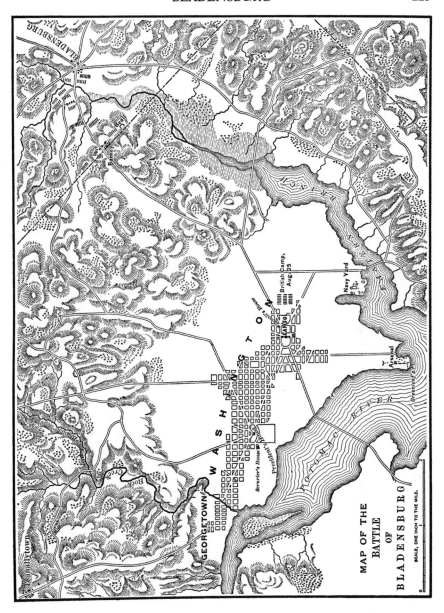

MAP OF THE
BATTLE
OF
BLADENSBURG

SCALE, ONE INCH TO THE MILE.

an enemy at Bladensburg in his rear. Roads were wanting, and the country was difficult. Through Bladensburg the attacking army must come; to Bladensburg Winder must go, unless he meant to retreat to Georgetown, or to re-cross the Eastern Branch in the enemy's rear. Monroe notified Serurier Monday evening that the battle would be fought at Bladensburg. Secretary Jones wrote to Commodore Rodgers, Tuesday morning, that the British would probably "advance to-day toward Bladensburg." Every one looked instinctively to that spot, yet Winder to the last instant persisted in watching the navy-yard bridge, using the hours of Wednesday morning to post Barney's sailors with twenty-four-pound guns to cover an approach where no enemy could cross.

No sooner did Winder receive intelligence at ten o'clock Wednesday morning that the British were in march to Bladensburg, than in the utmost haste he started for the same point, preceded by Monroe and followed by the President and the rest of the Cabinet and the troops. Barney's sailors and their guns would have been left behind to guard the navy-yard bridge had Secretary Jones not yielded to Barney's vigorous though disrespectful remonstrances, and allowed him to follow.

In a long line the various corps, with their military and civil commanders, streamed toward Bladensburg, racing with the British, ten miles away, to arrive first on the field of battle. Monroe was earliest on the ground. Between eleven and twelve o'clock he reached the spot where hills slope gently toward the Eastern Branch a mile or more in broad incline, the little straggling town of Bladensburg opposite, beyond a shallow stream, and hills and woods in the distance. Several militia corps were already camped on the ground, which had been from the first designated as the point of concentration. A Baltimore brigade, more than two thousand strong, had arrived there thirty-six hours before. Some Maryland regiments arrived at the same time with Monroe. About three thousand men were then on the field, and their officers were endeavoring to form them in line of battle. General Stansbury of the Baltimore brigade made such an arrangement as he thought best. Monroe, who had no military rank, altered it without Stansbury's knowledge. General Winder arrived at noon, and rode about the field. At the same time the British light brigade made its appearance, and wound down the opposite road, a mile away, a long column of red-coats, six abreast, moving with the quick regularity of old soldiers, and striking directly at the American centre. They reached the village on one side of the stream as Winder's troops poured down the hill on the other; and the President with two or three of his Cabinet officers, considerably in advance of all their own troops, nearly rode across the bridge into the British line, when a volunteer scout warned them of their danger.

Much the larger portion of the American force arrived on the ground when the enemy was in sight, and were hastily drawn up in line wherever they could be placed. They had no cover. Colonel Wadsworth's intrenchments were not used, except in the case of one field-work which enfiladed the bridge at close range, where field-pieces were placed. Although some seven thousand men were present, nothing deserving the name of an army existed. "A few companies only," said the Subaltern, "perhaps two or at the most three battalions, wearing the blue jacket

which the Americans have borrowed from the French, presented some appearance
of regular troops. The rest seemed country-people, who would have been much
more appropriately employed in attending to their agricultural occupations than
in standing with muskets in their hands on the brow of a bare, green hill."
Heterogeneous as the force was, it would have been sufficient had it enjoyed the
advantage of a commander.

The British light brigade, some twelve or fifteen hundred men, under Colonel
Thornton of the Eighty-fifth regiment, without waiting for the rear division,
dashed across the bridge, and were met by a discharge of artillery and musketry
directly in their face. Checked for an instant, they pressed on, crossed the bridge
or waded the stream, and spread to the right and left, while their rockets flew
into the American lines. Almost instantly a portion of the American line gave
way; but the rest stood firm, and drove the British skirmishers back under a
heavy fire to the cover of the bank with its trees and shrubs. Not until a fresh
British regiment, moving well to the right, forded the stream and threatened to
turn the American left, did the rout begin. Even then several strong corps stood
steady, and in good order retired by the road that led to the Capitol; but the mass,
struck by panic, streamed westward toward Georgetown and Rockville.

Meanwhile Barney's sailors, though on the run, could not reach the field in
time for the attack, and halted on the hillside, about a mile from Bladensburg, at
a spot just outside the District line. The rout had then begun, but Barney put
his five pieces in position and waited for the enemy. The American infantry and
cavalry that had not fled westward moved confusedly past the field where the
sailors stood at their guns. Winder sent Barney no orders, and Barney, who was
not acting under Winder, but was commander-in-chief of his own forces under
authority of the Navy Department, had no idea of running away. Four hundred
men against four thousand were odds too great even for sailors, but a battle was
not wholly disgraceful that produced such a commander and such men. Barney's
account of the combat was as excellent as his courage:—

"At length the enemy made his appearance on the main road in force and in
front of my battery, and on seeing us made a halt. I reserved our fire. In a few
minutes the enemy again advanced, when I ordered an eighteen-pounder to be
fired, which completely cleared the road; shortly after, a second and a third attempt
was made by the enemy to come forward, but all were destroyed. They then
crossed over into an open field, and attempted to flank our right. He was met
there by three twelve-pounders, the marines under Captain Miller, and my men
acting as infantry, and again was totally cut up. By this time not a vestige of the
American army remained, except a body of five or six hundred posted on a height
on my right, from which I expected much support from their fine situation."

Such a battle could not long continue. The British turned Barney's right;
the corps on the height broke and fled, and the British, getting into the rear,
fired down upon the sailors. The British themselves were most outspoken in
praise of Barney's men. "Not only did they serve their guns with a quickness and
precision that astonished their assailants," said the Subaltern, "but they stood
till some of them were actually bayoneted with fuses in their hands; nor was it
till their leader was wounded and taken, and they saw themselves deserted on all

sides by the soldiers, that they left the field." Barney held his position nearly half an hour, and then, being severely wounded, ordered his officers to leave him where he lay. There he was taken by the British advance, and carried to their hospital at Bladensburg. The British officers, admiring his gallantry, treated him, he said, "with the most marked attention, respect, and politeness as if I was a brother,"—as though to show their opinion that Barney instead of Winder should have led the American army.

After the sailors retired, at about four o'clock, the British stopped two hours to rest. Their victory, easy as it seemed, was not cheaply bought. General Ross officially reported sixty-four killed and one hundred and eighty-five wounded. A loss of two hundred and fifty men among fifteen hundred said to be engaged was not small; but Gleig, an officer of the light brigade, himself wounded, made twice, at long intervals, an assertion which he must have intended as a contradiction of the official report. "The loss on the part of the English was severe," he said, "since out of two thirds of the army which were engaged upward of five hundred men were killed and wounded." According to this assertion, Ross lost five hundred men among three thousand engaged, or one in six. Had Winder inflicted that loss while the British were still on the Patuxent, Ross would have thought long before risking more, especially as Colonel Thornton was among the severely injured. The Americans reported only twenty-six killed and fifty-one wounded.

At six o'clock, after a rest of two hours, the British troops resumed their march; but night fell before they reached the first houses of the town. As Ross and Cockburn, with a few officers, advanced before the troops, some men, supposed to have been Barney's sailors, fired on the party from the house formerly occupied by Gallatin, at the northeast corner of Capitol Square. Ross's horse was killed, and the general ordered the house to be burned, which was done. The army did not enter the town, but camped at eight o'clock a quarter of a mile east of the Capitol. Troops were then detailed to burn the Capitol, and as the great building burst into flames, Ross and Cockburn, with about two hundred men, marched silently in the darkness to the White House, and set fire to it. At the same time Commodore Tingey, by order of Secretary Jones, set fire to the navy-yard and the vessels in the Eastern Branch. Before midnight the flames of three great conflagrations made the whole country light, and from the distant hills of Maryland and Virginia the flying President and Cabinet caught glimpses of the ruin their incompetence had caused.

Serurier lived then in the house built by John Tayloe in 1800, called the Octagon, a few hundred yards from the War and Navy Departments and the White House. He was almost the only civil official left in Washington, and hastened to report the event to Talleyrand:—

"I never saw a scene at once more terrible and more magnificent. Your Highness, knowing the picturesque nature and the grandeur of the surroundings, can form an idea of it. A profound darkness reigned in the part of the city that I occupy, and we were left to conjectures and to the lying reports of negroes as to what was passing in the quarter illuminated by these frightful flames. At eleven o'clock a colonel, preceded by torches, was seen to take the direction of the

White House, which is situated quite near mine; the negroes reported that it was to be burned, as well as all those pertaining to government offices. I thought best, on the moment, to send one of my people to the general with a letter, in which I begged him to send a guard to the house of the Ambassador of France to protect it. . . . My messenger found General Ross in the White House, where he was collecting in the drawing-room all the furniture to be found, and was preparing to set fire to it. The general made answer that the King's Hotel should be respected as much as though his Majesty were there in person; that he would give orders to that effect; and that if he was still in Washington the next day, he would have the pleasure to call on me."

Ross and Cockburn alone among military officers, during more than twenty years of war, considered their duty to involve personal incendiarism. At the time and subsequently various motives were attributed to them,—such as the duty of retaliation,—none of which was alleged by either of them as their warranty. They burned the Capitol, the White House, and the Department buildings because they thought it proper, as they would have burned a negro kraal or a den of pirates. Apparently they assumed as a matter of course that the American government stood beyond the pale of civilization; and in truth a government which showed so little capacity to defend its capitol, could hardly wonder at whatever treatment it received.

A violent thunder-storm checked the flames; but the next morning, Thursday, August 24, fresh detachments of troops were sent to complete the destruction of public property. Without orders from his Government, Ross converted his campaign, which till then had been creditable to himself and flattering to British pride, into a marauding raid of which no sensible Englishman spoke without mortification. Cockburn amused himself by revenging his personal grievances on the press which had abused him. Mounted on a brood mare, white, un-curried, with a black foal trotting by her side, the Admiral attacked the office of the *National Intelligencer,* and superintended the destruction of the types. "Be sure that all the C's are destroyed," he ordered, "so that the rascals cannot any longer abuse my name." Ross was anxious to complete the destruction of the public buildings with the least possible delay, that the army might retire without loss of time; and the work was pressed with extreme haste. A few private buildings were burned, but as a rule private property was respected, and no troops except small detachments were allowed to leave the camp.

Soon after noon, while the work was still incomplete, a tornado burst on the city and put an end to the effort. An accidental explosion at the navy-yard helped to check destruction. Ross could do no more, and was in haste to get away. With precautions wholly unnecessary, leaving its camp-fires burning, the British column in extreme silence, after nine o'clock at night, began its march. Passing Bladensburg, where the dead were still unburied, Ross left his wounded in the hospital to American care, and marched all night till seven o'clock Friday morning, when the troops, exhausted with fatigue, were allowed a rest. At noon they were again in motion, and at night-fall, after marching twenty-five miles within twenty-four hours, they arrived at Marlboro.

CHAPTER XX

BALTIMORE

While Ross and Cockburn were hastily burning the White House and the Department buildings, anxious only to escape, and never sending more than two hundred soldiers beyond Capitol Square, the President, his Cabinet, his generals, and his army were performing movements at which even the American people, though outraged and exasperated beyond endurance, could not but laugh. The President, after riding over the battle-field until the action began, remarked to Monroe and Armstrong that "it would be now proper for us to retire in the rear, leaving the military movement to military men," which they did. A moment afterward the left of the line gave way, and the panic-stricken militia poured along the road leading westward toward the point which in later times became known as the Soldier's Home. The President retired with them, "continuing to move slowly toward the city," according to Monroe, in company with Attorney-General Rush. The slowness of movement, on which Monroe seemed to lay stress, was compensated by steadiness. The President left Bladensburg battle-field toward two o'clock. He had already ridden in the early morning from the White House to the navy-yard, and thence to Bladensburg,—a distance of eight miles at the least. He had six miles to ride, on a very hot August day, over a road encumbered by fugitives. He was sixty-three years old, and had that day already been in the saddle since eight o'clock in the morning, probably without food. Soon after three o'clock he reached the White House, where all was confusion and flight. He had agreed with his Cabinet, in case of disaster, to meet them at Frederick in Maryland, fifty miles away, but he did not go toward Frederick. Before six o'clock he crossed the Potomac in a boat from the White House grounds, and started by carriage westward, apparently intending to join his wife and accompany her to his residence at Montpelier in Loudoun County, adjoining Frederick County, on the south side of the Potomac. Secretary Jones, Attorney-General Rush, and one or two other gentlemen accompanied him. In the midst of a troop of fugitives they travelled till dark, and went about ten miles, passing the night at a house "a few miles above the lower falls."

The next morning, August 25, the President travelled about six miles and joined his wife at an inn on the same road, where he remained during the tornado, subjected to no little discomfort and some insult from fugitives who thought themselves betrayed. Although far beyond reach of the British troops and some twenty miles from their camp, the panic was still so great as to cause an alarm on the following night, which drove Madison from his bed for refuge in the Virginia woods, at the time when Ross's army, more than twenty miles distant, was marching at the utmost speed in the opposite direction.

Of all the rulers, monarchical or republican, whose capitals were occupied by hostile armies in the Napoleonic wars, Madison was personally the most roughly treated. Monroe's adventures were not less mortifying. As a scout the Secretary of State's services were hardly so valuable as those of a common trooper, for he was obliged to be more cautious; as a general, his interference with the order of battle at Bladensburg led to sharp criticisms from General Stansbury, whose arrangements he altered, and to the epithet of "busy and blundering tactician" from Armstrong. After the battle he was not less busy, and opinions greatly differed whether he was less blundering. He did not return to the White House with Madison, but joined Winder and rode with him to the Capitol, where he assented to an evacuation, and retired after the flying troops through Georgetown, passing the night on the Maryland side of the Potomac. The next morning, August 24, he crossed the river and overtook the President. After an interview with him, Monroe recrossed the river to Winder's headquarters at Montgomery Court House, where he resumed military functions.

The Secretary of the Treasury, G. W. Campbell, on the morning of the battle went to the Cabinet meeting at the navy-yard, but his health, which had become much affected, obliged him to return to his lodgings instead of riding to Bladensburg. In parting from Madison, Campbell lent him a pair of pistols, which the President put in his holsters. Federalists were curious to know whether the pistols were the same with which he shot Barent Gardenier, but learned only that they were fine duelling pistols, and that they were stolen from the President's holsters during his short stay at the White House after the battle. The secretary's duelling pistols became the best known of all the weapons unused that day; but the secretary himself made no further appearance on the scene. He went to Frederick. The Secretary of the Navy and the Attorney-General accompanied the President, and shared his fortunes.

Although ridicule without end was showered on the President and the other civilians, their conduct was on the whole creditable to their courage and character; but of the commanding general no kind word could be said. Neither William Hull, Alexander Smyth, Dearborn, Wilkinson, nor Winchester showed such incapacity as Winder either to organize, fortify, fight or escape. When he might have prepared defences, he acted as scout; when he might have fought, he still scouted; when he retreated, he retreated in the wrong direction; when he fought, he thought only of retreat; and whether scouting, retreating, or fighting, he never betrayed an idea. In the brief moment of his preparations on the field at Bladensburg he found time to give the characteristic order to his artillery: "When you retreat, take notice that you must retreat by the Georgetown road." When he left the field of Bladensburg he rode past Barney's sailors, at their guns, and sent his aide to Colonel Beall, on the hill covering Barney's right, with an order to retreat. "After accompanying the retreating army within two miles of the Capitol, I rode forward for the purpose of selecting a position." He reached the Capitol first, and was presently joined there by Monroe and Armstrong. Having decided not to fight at the Capitol, or at any point between the Capitol and Georgetown, he rode to Georgetown. Behind Rock Creek his army would have been safe, and he could certainly have rallied more than a thousand men to stop the panic; but he thought a farther retreat necessary, and went on to the heights. On the heights nothing could reach him without hours of warning, but he rode three miles farther to Tenallytown. At Tenallytown his exhausted men stopped a moment from inability to run farther, yet he seemed angry at their fatigue. Struck by a fresh panic at the glare of the burning city, he pressed his men on at midnight. "After waiting in this position [Tenallytown] until I supposed I collected all the force that could be gathered, I proceeded about five miles farther on the river road, which leads a little wide to the left of Montgomery Court House, and in the morning gave orders for the whole to assemble at Montgomery Court House." The river road was the road that led farthest from the enemy westward, when every motive required retreat toward Baltimore if anywhere. The next morning Winder returned to the Rockville road, till he reached Rockville, or Montgomery Court House, sixteen miles from Washington, where at last he paused.

From the beginning to the end of the campaign Winder showed no military quality. In other respects his conduct tallied with his behavior in the field. He lost no opportunity of throwing responsibility on the President and on his troops, and he so far succeeded as to save himself from public anger by encouraging the idea that the President and the Cabinet had directed the campaign. Universal as that belief was, and continued to be, it was without foundation. While Winder courted advice from every quarter, and threw on the President at every instant the responsibility for every movement, neither the President nor the Cabinet showed a disposition to interfere with his authority in any way except to give the support he asked. Under the strongest temptation they abstained even from criticism.

More than all the rest, Armstrong refrained from interference with the movements of Winder. Of all the unfortunate or incapable generals of the war, Winder was the one whom Armstrong treated with least bitterness, although he was not Armstrong's choice, and was the direct cause of the secretary's ruin. So careful was Armstrong not to interfere, that his non-interference became the chief charge against him. At one moment the President told the secretary that he interfered too much, at another moment that he should interfere more; but in truth Armstrong was the only man connected with the defence of Washington whom no one charged with being ridiculous. After August 20 his conduct was not open to reproach. He was cool when others were excited; he tried to check the panic; his suggestions were sensible; he gave all possible aid to both Winder and to the citizens; he attended the President in his expeditions, used wisely such power as he had, and indulged in few words. At the President's request he went to Bladensburg to support and assist Winder; at the President's order he retired after the battle began. He returned, after Winder, to the Capitol, hoping to convert that strong building into a fortress,—a measure not unreasonable, if the regulars and sailors were rallied to make a stand there. When Winder decided to retire to Georgetown, the secretary acquiesced without a word. Then, in pursuance of a Cabinet decision made a few hours before, he set out in company with Secretary Campbell for Frederick, and arrived there in the course of the next day.

Armstrong and Campbell were at Frederick when the British army began its retreat Thursday night; the President was in Virginia, sixteen miles up the river; Winder and Monroe, with the remaining troops, were at Montgomery Court House, sixteen miles from Washington. There they learned, Friday morning, that the British had marched toward Bladensburg, probably going to Baltimore; and at about ten o'clock in the morning Winder marched from Montgomery Court House toward Brookville and Baltimore with all his force. Passing through

Brookville, they camped, Friday night, "about half way between Montgomery Court House and Ellicott's upper mills," and Winder there left them, starting late that evening alone for Baltimore, and leaving Monroe and Stansbury in command, with directions to follow.

Meanwhile the President had crossed the Potomac that morning, expecting to find Winder and Monroe at Montgomery Court House; but on arriving there at six o'clock in the evening, and learning that the army had marched toward Baltimore, he followed as far as Brookville, about ten miles, where he passed the night. Attorney-General Rush was with him. Saturday morning, August 27, the President sent notes to all his Cabinet requesting them to unite in Washington. The same afternoon he returned with Monroe and Rush to the city, which they reached at about six o'clock, after three days' absence.

Armstrong and Campbell, ignorant of the change in plan, waited at Frederick for the President's arrival, while the President and Monroe, Sunday, August 28, began the task of restoring the functions of government. The task was difficult, not so much on account of the British ravages, which had been confined to public property, as on account of the general irritation and the continued panic. Hardly had Ross's army disappeared when a squadron of British war-vessels, under Captain Gordon of the frigate Seahorse, worked its way up the river, approaching Fort Washington or Warburton August 27. The commander of that post, misunderstanding his orders, abandoned it and crossed the river with his men. Gordon's squadron reached Alexandria the next day, and the town capitulated, since it could not resist. Until August 31 the frigates remained at Alexandria, loading such vessels as were there with the tobacco and other produce which the warehouses contained.

The citizens of Washington and Georgetown, expecting to be visited in their turn, and conscious of their inability to resist, talked of a capitulation. Public feeling ran strong against the President. Armstrong was absent. Winder was at Baltimore. Monroe alone was in a position to act, and upon Monroe the President was obliged to depend.

"Under these circumstances," said Monroe in the only authentic account of the event which remains, "the President requested Mr. Monroe to take charge of the Department of War and command of the District *ad interim*, with which he immediately complied. On the 28th, in the morning, the President with Mr. Monroe and the Attorney-General visited the navy-yard, the arsenal at Greenleaf's Point, and passing along the shore of the Potomac up toward Georgetown. Mr. Monroe, as Secretary of War and military commander, adopted measures under sanction of the President for the defence of the city and of Georgetown."

Colonel W[adsworth?] who was placing some guns on the opposite shore refused to obey an order of Monroe to change their position. Monroe rode across the bridge and gave the order in person. The colonel replied that he did not know Mr. Monroe as Secretary of War or commanding general. Monroe ordered him to obey or leave the field, and the colonel left the field.

Monroe's act, whether such was his intention or not, was a *coup d'état*. The citizens, unable to punish the President, were rabid against Armstrong. No one could deny that they had reason for their anger, although the blame for their misfortunes was so evenly distributed between every officer and every branch of government that a single victim could not justly be selected for punishment. Monroe, instead of giving to Armstrong in his absence such support as might have sustained him, took a position and exercised an authority that led necessarily to his overthrow. The influence of such acts on the citizens was obvious. That evening the first brigade of militia held a meeting, and passed a formal and unanimous resolution that they would no longer serve under the orders or military administration of General Armstrong, whom they denounced as the willing cause of the fate of Washington. This mutinous resolution, adopted in the immediate presence of the enemy, was taken to the President by two officers of the brigade, one of whom at least was a strong friend of Monroe.

The resolution of the first brigade was communicated to the President the next morning, Monday, August 29. All the President's recorded acts and conversation for months after the capture of Washington implied that he was greatly shaken by that disaster. He showed his prostration by helplessness. He allowed Monroe for the first time to control him; but he did not dismiss Armstrong. At one o'clock on the afternoon of the same day the Secretary of War arrived in Washington. The President that evening rode to his lodgings. Madison preserved a memorandum of their conversation, and Armstrong also immediately afterward recorded what passed. The President described to the secretary the violent prejudices which existed in the city against the Administration, and especially against himself and the Secretary of War. "Before his arrival there was less difficulty, as Mr. Monroe, who was very acceptable to them, had, as on preceding occasions of his absence, though very reluctantly on this, been the medium for the functions of Secretary of War"; but since Armstrong had returned, something must be done.

Armstrong replied that he was aware of the excitement, and knew its sources; that evidently he could not remain if his functions were exercised by any one else; that he would resign, or retire from Washington at once, as the President preferred.

Madison deprecated resignation, and recommended "a temporary retirement, as he suggested"; and after some further conversation, in which the President complained of the secretary's mistakes, they parted with the understanding that Armstrong should leave Washington the next morning. Armstrong behaved with dignity and with his usual pride; but he understood, if Madison did not, the necessary consequences of his retirement, and on reaching Baltimore sent his resignation to the President. At the same time he announced it to the public in a letter, dated September 3, containing comments on the weakness of Madison's conduct calculated to close their relations.

Between conscious intrigue and unconscious instinct no clear line of division was ever drawn. Monroe, by the one method or the other, gained his point and drove Armstrong from the Cabinet; but the suspicion that he had intrigued for that object troubled his mind to the day of his death. Even after Armstrong's departure, the dangers and disadvantages of appointing Monroe his successor were so great that for three weeks the post remained unfilled, until, after many doubts and hesitations, Monroe wrote to Madison a letter claiming the appointment of Secretary of War.

"I have thought much of the state of the Departments at this time," he informed the President, September 25, "and of the persons whom it may be proper to place in them, and have concluded that whatever may be the arrangement with respect to other Departments, the Department of War ought to be immediately filled. I think also that I ought to take charge of it. . . . By taking charge of the Department twice, and withdrawing from it a second time, it may be inferred that I shrink from the responsibility from a fear of injuring my reputation; and this may countenance the idea that the removal of the others was an affair of intrigue in which I partook, especially in the latter instance, from selfish and improper motives, and did not proceed from his incompetency or misconduct. It seems due, therefore, to my own reputation to go through with the undertaking by accepting permanently a trust which I have not sought, never wished, and is attended with great responsibility and hazard. By taking the place, all clamor will be silenced. It is known, here at least, that I was put into it when the other could no longer hold it. Those who wished it in the first instance will be satisfied, and I shall go on with your support and a favorable expectation of the public that I shall discharge to advantage its duties."

While Monroe in private communications with Madison thus treated Armstrong's retirement as a "removal," due to his "incompetency or misconduct," and Madison apparently acquiesced in that view, in public Madison seemed inclined to convey the idea that Armstrong was not removed or meant to be removed from office, but rather deserted it. Whichever view was correct, Madison certainly dreaded the political effect of appearing to remove Armstrong; and while he gave to Monroe the appointment of Secretary of War, he wrote, September 29, to Governor Tompkins of New York, offering him the State Department.

Governor Tompkins declined the offer. Apart from the great need of his services as governor, the experience of Northern men in Virginia Cabinets was not calculated to encourage any aspirant to the Presidency in seeking the position. Monroe remained Secretary of State as well as Secretary of War. As Secretary of State he had little or nothing to do, which was partly the cause of his activity in military matters; but as Secretary of War he was obliged to undertake a task beyond the powers of any man.

During an entire month after the appearance of the British in the Patuxent, the United States government performed few or none of its functions. The war on the frontiers was conducted without orders from Washington. Every energy of the government was concentrated on its own immediate dangers, as though Washington were a beleaguered fortress. Slowly the tide of war ebbed from the Potomac and Chesapeake, and not until it had wholly subsided could men cease to dread its possible return.

Captain Gordon's squadron began its descent of the river September 1, greatly annoyed by batteries erected on the banks by Commodore Rodgers, Perry, and Porter, who were sent from Baltimore, by order of Secretary Jones, for the purpose. Not until September 6 did Captain Gordon escape from his perilous position and rejoin the fleet. Meanwhile the shores of Chesapeake Bay continued to be ravaged with all the severity threatened by Cochrane. Frederick Chamier, afterward the author of several popular sea-stories, was then a lieutenant on the *Menelaus* in Cochrane's squadron, and his recollections in *The Life of a Sailor* gave a lively picture of the marauding in which he took part. Like Napier, Chamier was too tender-hearted for his work. "I am willing to make oath," he wrote, in reply to Captain Scott's contradictions, "that on the day that the *Menelaus* entered the Potomac, three houses were burning at the same time on the left-hand bank of the river. We burnt more than five ourselves." War was commonly accompanied by destruction, but the war in the Chesapeake was remarkable for the personal share taken by the highest officers, especially Cockburn and Ross, in directing the actual operation of setting fire to private and public property.

At last the practice caused a disaster that cost the British navy a life more valuable than all the property it could destroy or carry away. The *Menelaus,* commanded by Sir Peter Parker, was sent up Chesapeake Bay to divert attention from the general movement of troops and ships on the Potomac. The *Menelaus* took position off the Sassafras River, which Cockburn had cleared of vessels the year before. Nothing in the river could injure the navy, but the *Menelaus* was ordered to make a diversion; and Sir Peter Parker learned from negroes that two hundred militia, encamped behind a wood half a mile from the beach, intended to cross the bay for the protection of Baltimore. One hundred and twenty-four men were landed at eleven o'clock on the night of August 30, and went in search of the militia. Instead of half a mile, they were led by their guides three or four miles, and at last found the militia drawn up, ready to receive them. Sir Peter Parker ordered an attack, and while cheering it on in the moonlight was struck by a buckshot, which severed the femoral artery. The sailors carried him back to the ship, but he died long before reaching it. His party escaped with a loss of thirteen killed and twenty-seven wounded besides their captain.

The Americans regretted only that the punishment had fallen on the wrong person, for Cochrane and Cockburn rather than Parker were the true marauders; but the lesson was effectual, and the British became more cautious after Parker's death. Indeed, their activity in the Chesapeake centered thence-forward in an effort to capture Baltimore, which required all their strength.

Baltimore should have been first attacked, but Cockburn's influence by diverting Ross to Washington gave the larger city time to prepare its defence. The citizens themselves, headed by the mayor, took charge of the preparations; and their first act, contrary to the course pursued by Armstrong and Winder at Washington, was to construct intrenchments round the city, and to erect semi-circular batteries at a number of points, mounted with cannon and connected by a line of works. After the capture of Washington the citizens toiled still more earnestly at their task, until a formidable line of redoubts protected the town, and, though not wholly finished, gave cover to the militia. The batteries were manned by sailors, commanded by officers of the navy. The harbor was protected by Fort McHenry, small but capable of defence, and occupied by a strong force of regular troops, sailors, and volunteer artillerists numbering about one thousand, under the command of Lieutenant-Colonel Armistead of the Artillery.

These precautions made the capture of Baltimore impossible by such a force as had taken Washington, even though aided by the fleet. The precise number of troops present in the city, according to the official return for September 10, was twelve thousand nine hundred and ninety-one men present for duty, with eight hundred and ninety-seven officers. The aggregate of present and absent was sixteen thousand eight hundred and five men. The force was ample to man the works, but the fortifications chiefly decided the result. No army on either side during the war succeeded in storming works in face, except by surprise; and to turn the works of Baltimore a larger army was required than Ross had at his command.

The militia major-general commanding at Baltimore was no other than Samuel Smith, senator of the United States. He had lately passed his sixty-second year. The brigadier-general in the United States service who commanded the military district was W. H. Winder, whose defence of Washington ended abruptly August 24, and who left that neighborhood on the evening of August 26 to take command of the defences of Baltimore. Winder was a Baltimore lawyer, only three years Smith's junior, when Eustis and Madison gave him a regiment in March, 1812. Smith was not disposed to accept the idea of subordination to a man of inferior rank, military and civil, who knew no more of war than Smith knew, and whose career had been twice marked by unusual ridicule. Winder on arriving in Baltimore notified Smith that he should take command, and was astonished when the senator declined to surrender his authority. Winder appealed to the President and to the governor of Maryland, his cousin Levin Winder; but nothing could be done to assist him, and in the end he submitted. Samuel Smith remained in command.

The British leaders having succeeded in turning their demonstration up the Patuxent into an attack on Washington, next decided to make "a demonstration upon the city of Baltimore, which might be converted into a real attack should circumstances appear to justify it," and sailed from the Potomac September 6 for the Patapsco River. They anchored September 11 off its mouth. From that point Ross's army when landed had only fourteen miles to march, and no water in their way, while Cochrane's fleet had but twelve miles to sail. Compared with the approaches to Washington, the approach to Baltimore was easy.

Ross's troops were all landed at daylight on the northern point, and were in motion by eight o'clock September 12, without firing a shot. Their numbers were differently given by British authorities,—one reporting them at three thousand two hundred and seventy rank-and-file; the other reckoning them at upward of five thousand. Ross made on the Patapsco no such leisurely movements as on the Patuxent, but began his march at once, and proceeded about five miles without meeting resistance. The light brigade with the Eighty-fifth regiment was in advance; the second brigade, under Colonel Brooke of the Forty-fourth, followed; and the third brigade, under Colonel Patterson of the Twenty-first, formed the rear. At the same time the fleet moved up the channel toward Fort McHenry.

The city was naturally excited at the news that the British had arrived. General Smith, on receiving the intelligence September 11, detached a brigade of Baltimore militia, under General Stricker, to check the enemy if possible, and Stricker advanced that evening about seven miles toward North Point. His

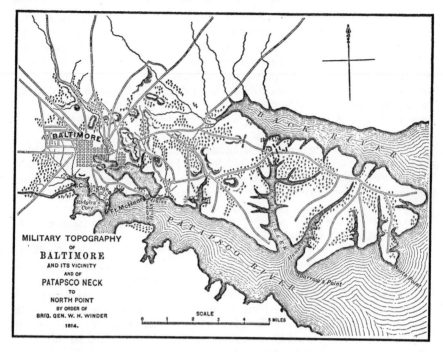

MILITARY TOPOGRAPHY
OF
BALTIMORE
AND ITS VICINITY
AND OF
PATAPSCO NECK
TO
NORTH POINT
BY ORDER OF
BRIG. GEN. W. H. WINDER
1814.

SCALE

force numbered about three thousand two hundred men; and with that body of raw militia, a part of whom had been routed at Bladensburg only a fortnight before, General Stricker attempted to fight a battle with five thousand old soldiers. On the morning of September 12 he formed his troops in three lines three hundred yards apart, apparently in close order, without cover or protection of any kind, standing in fields more or less open, and with an exposed flank. Of all his arrangements, the only one which showed ordinary caution was to send a detachment of cavalry and riflemen a mile or two in his front. As the British advance approached, the American outposts fell back, and General Stricker sent forward some four hundred men, partly rifles, as skirmishers. The British advanced guard coming up, the skirmishing party fired, but was soon driven back. Ross and Cockburn were walking together with the advance, and after the firing ceased, Ross turned back alone to order up the light companies in anticipation of more serious resistance. On his way he was shot through the breast from the wood, and fell in the road, where he lay till he was found by the light companies hurrying forward to the scene of the firing. He barely spoke afterward.

The loss of their commanding general was the second heavy penalty paid by the British for their contempt of militia. Colonel Brooke immediately took command, and the advance was not checked; but the loss was not the less serious. When Brooke saw Stricker's line stretching across the field, he did not dash at them at once with the light brigade as Thornton had attacked the larger force and stronger position at Bladensburg, but deployed the whole army and formed a regular order of battle. Although his force easily overlapped and outflanked the American, the engagement that followed was sharp, and the Americans were not routed without considerable loss to the British, who reported forty-six killed and two hundred and seventy-three wounded,—or more than they reported at Bladensburg. The Americans, though routed, suffered less, losing only twenty-four killed, one hundred and thirty-nine wounded, and fifty prisoners, with two field-pieces.

This spirited little battle detained the British so long that they bivouacked on the field, and passed the night in a drenching rain, resuming their march the next morning, September 13, when they found the roads obstructed, and were obliged to move so slowly that evening arrived before they came in sight of Baltimore. When at last they saw on the distant heights the long line of intrenchments that surrounded Baltimore on the side of their approach, they stopped short. Colonel Brooke had gone forward with the advance, and was engaged all day, at about a mile and a half distance, in studying the American lines. He made arrangements for a night attack, hoping to avoid the effects of the American artillery, and then waited for the fleet to support him.

The fleet all day bombarded the forts and batteries that covered the entrance to the harbor, and continued the bombardment till past midnight. Unlike most naval engagements during the war, this battle was harmless to either party. The heavier British ships feared to approach within range, owing to a barrier of sunken vessels, covered by the guns on shore and by gunboats. Without the heavy ships, the lighter vessels could not maintain a position. The fort sustained no great injury, and only four men were killed and twenty-four wounded. The fleet as far as was reported sustained no injury whatever. The firing ceased toward midnight, and Admiral Cochrane sent word to Colonel Brooke that he could do no more.

"Under these circumstances," reported Colonel Brooke, "and keeping in view your Lordship's instructions, it was agreed between the Vice-admiral and myself that the capture of the town would not have been a sufficient equivalent to the loss which might probably be sustained in storming the heights."

Sir George Prevost at Plattsburg only two days before with three times the number of troops and a much smaller number of opponents, came to the same conclusion. That both officers were probably wise was shown by the experience of Lieutenant-General Drummond, a month earlier, in attempting to storm the lines of Fort Erie. Brooke and Prevost followed the same course in another respect, for Brooke withdrew his army so rapidly that at noon of September 14 it had already passed the battle-field of two days before, and in another day the whole force was re-embarked.

As soon as the wind allowed, the fleet returned to the lower Chesapeake; and September 19 Admiral Cochrane sailed for Halifax to prepare for a new expedition. The troops remained till October 14 in their transports in the bay, and then set sail for Jamaica, leaving Virginia and Maryland to a long repose, which the vexed shores sorely needed.

CHAPTER XXI
SLOOPS-OF-WAR AND PRIVATEERS

After balancing gains and losses, the result of the campaign favored Great Britain by the amount of plunder which the navy obtained in Alexandria, and by the posts which Governor Sherbrooke occupied between the Penobscot and the Passamaquoddy in Maine. Considering the effort made and the waste of money, the result was a total disappointment to the British people; but even these advantages on land could not be regarded as secure until the British navy and mercantile marine had summed up their profits and losses on the ocean.

At the beginning of the year 1814 the American navy had almost disappeared. Porter in the *Essex* still annoyed British interests in the Pacific; but of the five large frigates only the *President* was at sea. January 1 the *Constitution*, Captain Charles Stewart, left Boston and cruised southward, making a few prizes and destroying a British fourteen-gun schooner, but fighting no battle and effecting no object equivalent to her cost. In returning to Boston, April 3, she narrowly escaped capture by the two British frigates blockading the port, and with difficulty got into Marblehead harbor. The *Constitution* did not again go to sea until December 17. During her cruise of three months, from January 1 to April 3, she made four prizes.

The *President* regained New York February 18, and was blockaded during the rest of the year. The *United States* and *Macedonian* remained blockaded at New London. The *Constellation* remained blockaded at Norfolk. The corvette *Adams*, twenty-eight guns, ran the blockade of Chesapeake Bay January 18, and cruised until August 17, making nine prizes and several narrow escapes before striking on the Isle of Haut and taking refuge in the Penobscot as the British forces occupied Castine. The story of her destruction has been told. Her fate was the same she would have met had she remained in Washington, where a week earlier the new forty-four-gun frigate *Columbia* and the new twenty-two-gun sloop-of-war *Argus* were burned to prevent them from falling prize to the British army.

This short abstract accounted for all the frigates except the *Essex*, whose fortune was no happier than that of the larger ships. October 27, 1812, the *Essex*, Captain David Porter, left the Delaware, intending to meet Bainbridge and form part of a squadron under his command. Failing to meet Bainbridge, though constantly near him, Porter at last decided to sail southward; and when Bainbridge in the *Constitution* reached Boston February 27, 1813, the *Essex* had already passed Cape Horn, and was running up the western coast of South America to Valparaiso.

At Valparaiso Porter arrived March 14, 1813, to the consternation of commerce. Chili had recently asserted independence of Spain, and as yet no English war-vessels were stationed in the Pacific. The chief British interest was the whale fishery which centred in the Galapagos Islands—a group lying under the equator, about a thousand miles from Panama. Although the influence of England was supreme, on account of her naval power, her commerce, and her political alliance with the Spanish people, and although Porter had neither a harbor of his own, nor the support of a diplomatic officer on the Pacific, he had nothing to fear. He was well received at Valparaiso, where since 1811 J. R. Poinsett had held the post of United States Consul-General for Buenos Ayres, Chili, and Peru; but the *Essex* tarried only for supplies, and soon sailed for the Galapagos Islands. There she arrived in April, 1813, and in the course of the summer captured all the British whalers known to be in those seas. These were twelve in number, and after sending some of them away, Porter still had a fleet of five armed ships besides his own, and nothing more to do.

The *Essex* had then been a year at sea, and needed repairs. Porter determined to take his entire fleet of six vessels about three thousand miles to the Marquesas Islands,—as though to make a voyage of discovery, or to emulate the mutineers of the *Bounty*. The squadron sailed three weeks over the southern seas, until, October 23, the Marquesas Islands were sighted. There Porter remained seven weeks, amusing himself and his crew by intervention in native Marquesan politics, ending in his conquest of the principal tribes, and taking possession of the chief island in the name of his Government. That he should have brought away his whole crew after such relaxation, without desertion, was surprising. The men were for a time in a state of mutiny on being ordered to sea; but they did not desert, and the squadron sailed, Dec. 12, 1813, for Valparaiso.

Porter would have done better to sail for the China seas or the Indian Ocean. He knew that British war-vessels were searching for him, and that Valparaiso was the spot where he would be directly in their way. He arrived February 3, and five days afterward two British vessels of war sailed into the harbor, making directly for the *Essex* with the appearance of intending to attack and board her. The crew of the *Essex* stood at quarters ready to fire as the larger ship ran close alongside, until her yards crossed those of the *Essex*, and Porter probably regretted to the end of his life that he did not seize the opportunity his enemy gave him; but the British captain, from his quarter-deck only a few feet away, protested that the closeness of his approach was an accident, and that he intended no attack. The moment quickly passed, and then Porter found himself overmatched.

The British frigate *Phoebe*, thirty-six guns, had sailed from England in March, 1813, under secret orders to break up the United States fur-establishment on the Columbia River. At Rio Janeiro the *Phoebe* was joined by the *Cherub*, a sloop-of-war rated at eighteen guns, and both sailed in search of the *Essex*. The *Phoebe* was one hundred and forty-three and three quarters feet in length, by thirty-eight and a quarter in breadth; the *Essex* was one hundred and thirty-eight and a half feet in length, and thirty-seven and a quarter in breadth. The *Phoebe* carried a crew of three hundred men and boys; the *Essex* carried two hundred and fifty-five. The *Essex* was the better sailer, and the result of an action depended on her ability to use this advantage. The broadside of the *Essex* consisted of seventeen thirty-two-pound carronades and six long twelve-pounders; the *Phoebe* showed only eight carronades, but had thirteen long eighteen-pounders, one long twelve-pounder, and one long nine-pounder. At close range, Porter's battery would overpower the *Phoebe's* long guns, but the *Phoebe's* thirteen long-range eighteen-pounders could destroy her enemy without receiving a shot in return. Porter knew all this, and knew also that he could not depend on Chilian protection. No British captain in such a situation could afford to be delicate in regard to the neutrality of Chili, which was not even a recognized nation. At most Porter could hope for immunity only in the port of Valparaiso.

Captain Hillyar of the *Phoebe* made no mistakes. During an entire month he blockaded the *Essex* with his two vessels, acting with extreme caution. At last Porter determined to run out, trusting to a chase to separate the blockading cruisers; and March 28, 1814, with a strong southerly wind, he got under way. As he rounded the outermost point a violent squall carried away his maintopmast. The loss threw on Porter a sudden emergency and a difficult, instantaneous decision. He decided to return to harbor. A young midshipman, David Farragut, who made his first cruise in the *Essex*, gave his high authority in after years to the opinion that Porter's decision was wrong. "Being greatly superior in sailing powers," said Farragut, "we should have borne up, and run before the wind." The chance of outsailing the *Phoebe*, or separating her from her consort, was better than that of regaining the anchorage.

The wind did not allow of a return to port, and the *Essex* was run into a small bay three miles from Valparaiso, and anchored within pistol-shot of the shore. There Hillyar had her wholly at his mercy. At first he attacked somewhat timidly. Although Porter could bring only three long twelve-pounders to bear, he damaged the *Phoebe's* rigging until Hillyar, in half an hour, hauled off to repair the injury—or, according to Hillyar's account, the *Phoebe* was prevented by the freshness of the wind from holding a position. Finally the *Phoebe* anchored, and began firing her broadsides of long eighteen-pounders into the *Essex's* quarter. The *Cherub* kept under way, using only her bow guns. Reply was impossible. The crew of the *Essex* fired what guns would bear, and got the ship under way; but the *Phoebe* kept her distance, throwing thirteen eighteen-pound shot into the *Essex* every five or ten minutes, until the *Essex* was cut to pieces and her decks were shambles.

The last attack continued, according to Captain Hillyar, from 5:35 till 6:20 P.M., when the *Essex* struck. The entire battle lasted from four o'clock until the surrender. The carnage was frightful and useless. Porter declared that fifty-eight of his crew were killed. Hillyar claimed one hundred and nineteen unwounded prisoners, while Porter declared the number of unwounded prisoners to be seventy-five. The British ships, with five hundred men, lost only fifteen killed and wounded.

The loss of the *Essex*, like the loss of the *Chesapeake* and *Argus*, was unnecessary. Porter need not have gone to Valparaiso, or might have tried to run out at night, or might have fought, even after the loss of his maintopmast, under less disadvantage. The disaster completed the unfortunate record of the frigates for the year. They made some sixteen prizes and busied many British cruisers, but won no victories and suffered one bloody defeat.

The sloops told a different story. Early in 1814 three of the new sloops-of-war were ready for sea—the *Frolic*, the *Peacock*, and the *Wasp*. They were heavy vessels of their class, about one hundred and twenty feet long on the main-deck, and thirty-two feet in extreme breadth; carrying crews of about one hundred and sixty men, with an armament of twenty thirty-two-pound carronades and two long eighteen-pounders. Although only one third the tonnage of the forty-four-gun frigates, and carrying only one third the crew, the new sloops-of-war threw nearly half the weight of metal—for the broadside of the *Constitution* commonly exceeded but little the weight of seven hundred pounds, while the sloops threw three hundred and thirty-eight. The difference was due not to the weight, but to the range. The frigates carried thirty long twenty-four-pounders; the sloops carried only two long eighteen-pounders. The sloops were rigged as ships, and built with the usual solidity of war-vessels, costing about seventy-five thousand dollars each.

The first to sail was the *Frolic*, from Boston, in February. She captured only two prizes before she was herself taken, April 20, off Matanzas, after a chase by the thirty-six gun British frigate *Orpheus*, assisted by a twelve-gun schooner.

The second sloop-of-war, the *Peacock*, commanded by Lewis Warrington, sailed from New York in March. Warrington was a Virginian, thirty-two years old and fourteen years in the service, with the rank of master-commandant in 1813. Cruising down the coast, the *Peacock* first ran in to St. Mary's on the Florida frontier; and then continuing southward, on the morning of April 29, off the Indian River Inlet, she discovered a small convoy on its way from Havana to Bermuda, under charge of the British eighteen-gun brig *Epervier*. The British brig was no match for the American ship. She was smaller, and carried only sixteen thirty-two and two eighteen-pound carronades, with a crew of one hundred and three men and fifteen boys. The inferiority was something like four to three; but Captain Wales of the *Epervier* gallantly brought his vessel into action at the usual close-range of these murderous combats.

Captain Wales told the result in an official report, dated May 8, to Vice-Admiral Cochrane. The report was not published, the British Admiralty having become sensitive to the popular outcry against their naval management.

"At eight A.M.," reported Captain Wales, "the wind being about east-south-east, I saw a strange sail in the south-west apparently in chase of us; at nine, perceiving her to near very fast and to be a square-rigged vessel-of-war, I shortened sail and hauled to the wind on the larboard tack to be between her and the convoy, being rather ahead of them. The wind at this time veering round to the southward enabled the stranger to lay up for us. . . . At 9:50 A.M. we weathered her and exchanged broadsides; having passed her beam, we tacked, shortened sail, and continued in close action until eleven A.M., when—five of our larboard guns being disabled by the breeching-bolts giving way, and three others by shot, and unable to manoeuvre so as to get the starboard guns to bear in consequence of the rigging and sails being cut to pieces in the early part of the action by star-shot, the main boom shot away, the foremast wounded in several places, and several shot between wind and water, with four-and-a-half feet of water in the hold, and the enemy seemingly in a state to continue the action—I deemed it prudent to surrender."

The giving way of the breeching-bolts did not wholly disable the guns, for Captain Wales specially commended "Mr. Lawrence Kennedy the Purser, who rendered much service in his exertions at the after-guns by getting them in a fighting state again when unshipped by the fighting-bolts coming out of their places."

At the close of the battle the *Peacock's* hull had not been touched; aloft, her foreyard was disabled and a few upper stays were cut away; of her crew, two men were slightly wounded—but this was all the injury sustained in running for three quarters of an hour under the close fire of nine heavy guns. The *Epervier* was reported by Captain Warrington as showing forty-five shot-holes in her hull; masts and rigging much cut up, and twenty-three men killed or wounded in a crew of one hundred and twenty-eight. The difference between the force of the two vessels amply accounted for the capture; but the Admiralty might well show unwillingness to admit the bad condition of the vessels-of-war to which it intrusted the duty of convoying British mercantile shipping. So complete was the *Epervier's* disaster that no excuse was offered for it, except the plea that she was in almost every respect inferior to the standard that British vessels of her class were supposed to maintain.

Captain Warrington saved the *Epervier* and brought her into Savannah in spite of two British frigates encountered on the way. He sailed again early in June, and passed the months of July and August in British waters or in the track of British commerce from the Faroe Islands to the Canaries. He burned or sunk twelve prizes, besides making cartels of two more, and brought his ship through the blockade into New York harbor, October 30, without injury, with only one man lost and the crew in fine health.

The third new sloop was named the *Wasp* after the famous victory over the *Hornet*. The new *Wasp* sailed from Portsmouth, New Hampshire, May 1, under command of Johnston Blakeley. Born in Ireland in 1781, Blakeley was from infancy a North Carolinian. He became in 1800 an officer in the navy. Blakeley and the *Wasp* of 1814, like Jones and the *Wasp* of 1813, ran a career in which tragedy gave a deeper tinge than usual to the bloody colors they won; but their success was on the whole greater than that of any other national cruiser from the beginning to the end of the war. Merely as a story of adventure Blakeley's career was exciting, but romance was its smallest interest. For several reasons the sloop battles and cruises afforded one of the best relative tests of American character and skill among all that were furnished in the early period of the national history; and among the sloops, Blakeley's *Wasp* was the most distinguished.

Blakeley ran directly across the ocean into soundings at the mouth of the British Channel. There he remained during the month of June, searching every vessel that passed. The number of neutrals constantly diverting his attention kept him actively employed, and led him farther into the Channel than was intended; but although three British frigates and fourteen sloops were at sea for the protection of British waters, the *Wasp* continued to burn and sink such British merchantmen as she met—the first, June 2, and subsequently June 13, 18, 23, and 26—until on the morning of June 28 a man-of-war brig appeared to windward, and bore down on the American ship.

The day was warm and overcast. During the whole morning the two vessels approached each other so slowly that each had more than time to study his opponent. Once more the foresight of the American ship-builders secured a decisive advantage. The British brig, the *Reindeer*, was altogether unequal to the contest. In tonnage she resembled the *Epervier*, and her armament was even lighter. Captain Manners, her commander, had substituted twenty-four-pound carronades for the usual thirty-two-pounders, and his broadside of ten guns threw only two hundred and ten pounds of metal, while the *Wasp's* eleven guns threw three hundred and thirty-eight pounds. The American crew numbered one hundred and seventy-three men; the British numbered one hundred and eighteen. Contest under such conditions was a forlorn hope, but the *Reindeer's* crew were the pride of Portsmouth, and Manners was the idol of his men. They might cripple the *Wasp* if they could not capture her; and probably the fate of the *Argus,* a year before, encouraged the hope that the *Reindeer* could do at least as well as the *Pelican.*

Each captain manoeuvred for the weather-gauge, but the Englishman gained it, and coming up on the *Wasp's* weatherquarter, repeatedly fired his light twelve-pound bow-carronade, filled with round and grape shot, into the American ship. Blakeley, "finding the enemy did not get sufficiently on the beam to enable us to bring our guns to bear, put the helm a-lee," and fired as his guns bore. The firing began at 3:26 P.M. and lasted until 3:40, fourteen minutes, at close range. In that space of time each gun in the broadside could be fired at the utmost three times. Apparently Manners felt that he had no chance with his guns, for he brought his vessel's bow against the *Wasp's* quarter and repeatedly attempted boarding. Early in the action the calves of his legs were shot away; then a shot passed through both his thighs; yet he still climbed into the rigging to lead his boarders, when two balls at the same moment struck him in the head. His fall ended the battle; and such had been the losses of his company that the highest officer remaining unhurt on the British brig to surrender the vessel was said to be the captain's clerk. At 3:45 the *Reindeer's* flag was struck—the whole action, from the *Wasp's* first gun, having lasted nineteen minutes.

Had every British vessel fought like the *Reindeer,* Englishmen would have been less sensitive to defeat. In this desperate action the *Wasp* suffered severely. Her foremast was shot through; her rigging and spars were much injured; her hull was struck by six round shot and much grape; eleven men were killed and fifteen wounded, or nearly one man in six, "chiefly in repelling boarders," reported Blakeley. The *Reindeer* was a wreck, and was blown up as soon as the wounded could be removed. Of her crew, numbering one hundred and eighteen, thirty-three lost their lives; thirty-four were wounded—in all, sixty-seven, or more than half the brig's complement.

Ten days afterward Blakeley ran into Lorient, where his ship was well received by the French, whose British antipathies were increased rather than lessened by their enforced submission. After refitting, the *Wasp* sailed again August 27, and four days later cut out a valuable ship from a convoy under the eyes of a seventy-four. The same evening, September 1, at half-past six, Blakeley sighted four vessels, two on either bow, and hauled up for the one most to windward. At 9:26 at night the chase, a brig, was directly under the *Wasp's* lee-bow, and Blakeley began firing a twelve-pound bow-cannonade, which he must have taken from the *Reindeer,* for no such gun made part of his regular armament.

The battle in the dark which followed has been always deeply interesting to students of naval history, the more because the British Admiralty suppressed the official reports, and left an air of mystery over the defeat which rather magnified than diminished its proportions. The British brig was the sloop-of-war *Avon,* commanded by Captain James Arbuthnot, and carrying the usual armament of sixteen thirty-two-pound carronades with two long six-pounders. Her crew was reported as numbering one hundred and four men and thirteen boys. Captain Arbuthnot's official report said that the *Avon* had been cruising in company with the sloop-of-war *Castilian*, when at daylight, September 1, he "discovered an enemy's schooner in the rear of the Kangaroo convoy," and gave chase. The *Castilian* also gave chase, and at seven o'clock the twenty-gun ship *Tartarus* was signalled, also in chase. All day the *Castilian's* superiority in sailing free left the *Avon* out of sight, nine miles astern. The position of the *Tartarus* was not mentioned in the reports, but she could hardly have been ahead of the *Castilian*. The three British sloops were then within ten miles of each other, under full sail, with a ten-knot wind. The weather was hazy, and neither the *Castilian* nor the *Tartarus* could see that the *Avon* was signalling the *Castilian* a recall. The *Avon* saw at four o'clock a large sail on her weather-beam standing directly for her, and knowing that the *Wasp* was cruising in these waters, Captain Arbuthnot felt natural anxiety to rejoin his consort.

Captain Arbuthnot's report continued:—

"The stranger closing with us fast, I kept away and set the weather studding-sails in hopes of nearing the *Castilian* or *Tartarus*, the latter of which I had only lost sight of at 3 P.M. At 7:30 P.M. the stranger had approached within hail, and being unable to get a satisfactory answer I had not a doubt of her being an enemy's corvette. At 8:30 he fired a shot over us which was instantly returned with a broadside. He then bore up and endeavored to rake us, but was prevented. The action then became general within half pistol-shot, and continued without intermission until 10:30 P.M., when—having seven feet of water in the hold, the magazine drowned; tiller, foreyard, main-boom, and every shroud shot away, and the other standing and the running rigging cut to pieces; the brig quite unmanageable, and the leak gaining fast on the pumps; with forty killed and wounded, and five of the starboard guns dismounted; and conceiving further resistance only would cause a useless sacrifice of lives—I was under the painful necessity of ordering the colors to be struck to the American corvette *Wasp*, the mainmast, almost immediately after, going over the side."

Lieutenant George Lloyd, commanding the *Castilian*, reported September 2 the circumstances attending the loss of the *Avon*, as far as they concerned his share in the matter. At nine o'clock the *Castilian* heard a very heavy firing in the north-northeast, and immediately wore and made all possible sail in that direction, burning blue lights. At quarter past ten the firing ceased, "and on coming up I had the mortification to observe the *Avon* a totally dismantled and ungovernable wreck, with her mainmast gone—the enemy, apparently a large ship corvette, lying to, to leeward of her, who on my closing made all sail, and evinced every wish to avoid a contest with us."

"I immediately used means to enable me to bring her to close action; and from our superior sailing I had in a few minutes the gratification to be within half a cable's length on her weather quarter. But I lament to state at this anxious crisis the *Avon's* situation became most alarming; she had commenced firing minute guns, and making every other signal of distress and of being in want of immediate assistance. I must here (as my pen can but inadequately describe) leave you, sir, to judge the feelings of myself, officers, and crew, as, from the confusion which evidently prevailed on board the enemy, the damage she had sustained, and her bad steerage, together with the cool and steady conduct of the officers and men I have the honor to command, I had no doubt of her falling an easy prey could we have persisted in attacking her, but which was not to be done without sacrificing the lives of the surviving gallant crew of our consort. Thus situated . . . I was obliged . . . to leave the flying enemy to escape; but I feel somewhat gratified the situation of the *Castilian* enabled me to give him a raking, and I doubt not from the closeness of the vessels a most destructive broadside, which he did not return even with a single gun—a circumstance that, I trust, cannot fail to prove how destructive the *Avon's* fire must have been."

Lieutenant Lloyd did not explain how his enemy was to bring guns to bear under the circumstances, the *Castilian* tacking under the *Wasp's* stern at half a cable's length distance, and immediately standing in the opposite direction, nor did he say what had become of the *Tartarus*. Doubtless the *Wasp* steered badly, her rigging being much damaged; and Blakeley was chiefly intent on keeping off till he could reeve new braces. The *Castilian's* broadside cut the *Wasp's* rigging and sails, and shot away a lower main cross-tree, but did no other serious damage.

The *Avon* lost ten men killed and thirty-two wounded, besides being reduced to a sinking condition in an hour of night action in a ten-knot wind, with two more ships-of-war in sight and hearing. The *Wasp* lost two men killed and one wounded, four round shot in the hull, and "rigging and sails suffered a great deal."

Blakeley had done enough, and could hardly do more. Besides two eighteen-gun brigs, he made in his cruise fourteen prizes, which he destroyed, several of great value. In that year all the frigates in the United States service had not done as much. With a single-decked ship of five hundred tons, armed with carronades, Blakeley blockaded the British Channel for two months, capturing vessels in sight of ships-of-the-line, and destroying two sloops-of-war in rapid succession, without serious injury to himself, and to the consternation of the British marine.

After sinking the *Avon*, September 1, Blakeley held on his course toward Madeira, and there, September 21, captured the brig *Atlanta*, which he sent to Savannah. Still later, October 9, near the Cape de Verde Islands, he spoke a Swedish brig, which reported him. After that day no word was ever received from the *Wasp*. Somewhere under the waters of the Atlantic, ship and crew found an unknown grave.

Besides the large sloops-of-war, three smaller vessels—the *Syren, Enterprise,* and *Rattlesnake*—went to sea in 1814. The *Syren* was captured after a chase of eleven hours, nearly on a wind, by the *Medway*, seventy-four; her sixteen guns, and everything else that could be spared, were thrown overboard during the chase. The *Rattlesnake* and *Enterprise* cruised in company toward the West Indies, and made some prizes. The *Rattlesnake* was fast, the *Enterprise* a very dull sailer; but after repeated hairbreadth escapes, the *Rattlesnake* was caught, July 11, by the frigate *Leander*, with Cape Sable to windward, and was obliged to surrender. The *Enterprise*, with her usual good fortune, was never taken, but became a guardship.

After November 1 the United States government had not a ship at sea. In port, three seventy-fours were building, and five forty-fours were building or blockaded. Three thirty-six-gun frigates were laid up or blockaded. Four sloops-of-war were also in port, the *Peacock* having just returned from her long cruise. Such a result could not be called satisfactory. The few war-vessels that existed proved rather what the government might have done than what the British had to fear from any actual or probable American navy. The result of private enterprise showed also how much more might easily have been done by government.

The year 1814 was marked by only one great and perhaps decisive success on either side, except Macdonough's victory. This single success was privateering. Owners, captains, and crews had then learned to build and sail their vessels, and to hunt their prey with extraordinary skill. A few rich prizes stimulated the building of new vessels as the old were captured, and the ship-yards turned them out as rapidly as they were wanted. In the neighborhood of Boston, in the summer of 1814, three companion ships were built—the *Reindeer, Avon* and *Blakeley*; and of these the *Reindeer* was said to have been finished in thirty-five working days, and all three vessels were at sea in the following winter. No blockade short of actual siege could prevent such craft from running out and in. Scores of them were constantly on the ocean.

On the Atlantic privateers swarmed. British merchantmen were captured, recaptured, and captured again, until they despaired of ever reaching port. One British master who was three times taken and as often retaken, reported that he had seen ten American privateers crossing his course. A letter from Halifax printed in the London *Times* of December 19 said: "There are privateers off this harbor which plunder every vessel coming in or going out, notwithstanding we have three line-of-battle ships, six frigates, and four sloops here." The West Indies and the Canaries were haunted by privateers. The *Rambler, Hyder Ali,* and *Jacob Jones* of Boston penetrated even the Chinese seas, and carried prize-goods into Macao and Canton. Had these pests confined their ravages to the colonies or the ocean, the London clubs and the lobbies of Parliament would have thought little about them; but the privateer had discovered the weakness of Great Britain, and frequented by preference the narrow seas which England regarded as her own. The quasi-blockade of the British coasts which American cruisers maintained in 1813 became a real and serious blockade in 1814. Few days passed without bringing news of some inroad into British waters, until the Thames itself seemed hardly safe.

The list of privateers that hung about Great Britain and Ireland might be made long if the number were necessary to the story, but the character of the blockade was proved by other evidence than that of numbers. A few details were enough to satisfy even the English. The *Siren,* a schooner of less than two hundred tons, with seven guns and seventy-five men, had an engagement with her Majesty's cutter *Landrail* of four guns, as the cutter was crossing the British Channel with despatches. The *Landrail* was captured after a somewhat sharp action, and sent to America, but was recaptured on the way. The victory was not remarkable, but the place of capture was very significant; and it happened July 12, only a fortnight after Blakeley captured the *Reindeer* farther westward.

The *Siren* was but one of many privateers in those waters. The *Governor Tompkins* burned fourteen vessels successively in the British Channel. The *Young Wasp* of Philadelphia cruised nearly six months about the coasts of England and Spain and in the course of West India commerce. The *Harpy* of Baltimore, another large vessel of some three hundred and fifty tons and fourteen guns, cruised nearly three months off the coast of Ireland, in the British Channel and in the Bay of Biscay, and returned safely to Boston filled with plunder, including, as was said, upward of £100,000 in British Treasury notes and bills of exchange. The *Leo*, a Boston schooner of about two hundred tons, was famous for its exploits in these waters, but was captured at last by the frigate *Tiber* after a chase of eleven hours. The *Mammoth*, a Baltimore schooner of nearly four hundred tons, was seventeen days off Cape Clear, the southernmost point of Ireland. The most mischievous of all was the *Prince of Neufchatel* of New York, which chose the Irish Channel as its favorite haunt, where during the summer it made ordinary coasting traffic impossible. The most impudent was probably the *Chausseur*, commanded by Captain Boyle, who cruised three months, and amused himself, when off the British coast, by sending to be posted at Lloyd's a "Proclamation of Blockade" of "all the ports, harbors, bays, creeks, rivers, inlets, outlets, islands, and sea-coast of the United Kingdom." The jest at that moment was too sardonic to amuse the British public.

As the announcement of these annoyances, recurring day after day, became a practice of the press, the public began to grumble in louder and louder tones. "That the whole coast of Ireland, from Wexford round by Cape Clear to Carrickfergus," said the *Morning Chronicle* of August 31, "should have been for above a month under the unresisted dominion of a few petty 'fly-by-nights' from the blockaded ports of the United States, is a grievance equally intolerable and disgraceful." The Administration mouthpiece, the *Courier*, admitted, August 22, that five brigs had been taken in two days between the Smalls and the Tuskar, and that insurance on vessels trading between Ireland and England had practically ceased. The *Annual Register* for 1814 recorded as a "most mortifying reflection," that with a navy of nearly a thousand ships of various sizes, and while at peace with all Europe, "it was not safe for a vessel to sail without convoy from one part of the English or Irish Channel to another." Such insecurity had not been known in the recent wars.

As early as August 12, the London Assurance Corporations urged the government to provide a naval force competent to cope with the privateers. In September the merchants of Glasgow, Liverpool, and Bristol held meetings, and addressed warm remonstrances to government on the want of protection given to British commerce. The situation was serious, and the British merchants did not yet know all. Till that time the East India and China trade had suffered little, but at last the American privateers had penetrated even the Chinese seas; and while they were driving the British flag into port there, they attacked the East India Company's ships, which were really men-of-war, on their regular voyages. In August the *Countess of Harcourt* of more than five hundred tons, carrying six heavy guns and ninety men, was captured in the British Channel by the privateer *Sabine* of Baltimore, and sent safely to America. The number and value of the prizes stimulated new energy in seeking them, and British commerce must soon yield to that of neutral nations if the war continued.

The merchants showed that a great change had come over their minds since they incited or permitted the Tories to issue the Impressment Proclamation and the Orders in Council seven years before. More than any other class of persons, the ship-owners and West India merchants were responsible for the temper which caused the war, and they were first to admit their punishment. At the Liverpool meeting, where Mr. Gladstone, who took the chair, began by declaring that some ports, particularly Milford, were under actual blockade, a strong address was voted; and at a very numerous meeting of merchants, manufacturers, ship-owners, and underwriters at Glasgow, September 7, the Lord Provost presiding, resolutions were unanimously passed—

"That the number of American privateers with which our channels have been infested, the audacity with which they have approached our coasts, and the success with which their enterprise has been attended, have proved injurious to our commerce, humbling to our pride, and discreditable to the directors of the naval power of the British nation, whose flag till of late waved over every sea and triumphed over every rival.

"That there is reason to believe, in the short space of twenty-four months, above eight hundred vessels have been captured by the power whose maritime strength we have hitherto impolitically held in contempt."

The war was nearly at an end, and had effected every possible purpose for the United States, when such language was adopted by the chief commercial interests of Great Britain. Yet the Glasgow meeting expressed only a part of the common feeling. The rates of insurance told the whole story. The press averred that in August and September underwriters at Lloyd's could scarcely be induced to insure at any rate of premium, and that for the first time in history a rate of thirteen per cent had been paid on risks to cross the Irish Channel. Lloyd's list then showed eight hundred and twenty-five prizes lost to the Americans, and their value seemed to increase rather than diminish.

Weary as the merchants and ship-owners were of the war, their disgust was not so intense as that of the navy. John Wilson Croker, Secretary of the Admiralty Board, whose feelings toward America were at best unkind, showed a temper that passed the limits of his duties. When the London underwriters made their remonstrance of August 12, Croker assured them, in a letter dated August 19, that at the time referred to "there was a force adequate to the purpose of protecting the trade both in St. George's Channel and the Northern Sea." The news that arrived during the next two weeks threw ridicule on this assertion; and Croker was obliged to reply to a memorial from Bristol, September 16, in a different tone. He admitted that the navy had not protected trade, and could not protect it; but he charged that the merchants were to blame for losing their own ships. His letter was a valuable evidence of the change in British sentiment:—

"Their Lordships take this opportunity of stating to you, for the information of the memorialists, that from the accounts which their Lordships have received of the description of vessels which had formed the largest proportion of the captures in the Irish and Bristol channels, it appears that if their masters had availed themselves of the convoys appointed for their protection from foreign ports, or had not in other instances deserted from the convoys under whose protection they had sailed, before the final conclusion of the voyage, many of the captures would not have been made. It is their Lordships' determination, as far as they may be enabled, to bring the parties to punishment who may have been guilty of such illegal acts, and which attended with such injurious consequences to the trade of the country."

Little by little the Americans had repaid every item of the debt of insult they owed, and after Croker's letter the account could be considered settled. Even the *Times* was not likely to repeat its sneer of 1807, that the Americans could hardly cross to Staten Island without British permission. Croker's official avowal that no vessel could safely enter or leave one port in the British Islands for another except under guard of a man-of-war, was published on the same page with the memorialists' assertion that the rate of insurance had gradually risen till it exceeded twofold the usual rates prevailing during the wars on the Continent.

The spirit of exasperation shown by Croker extended through the navy. The conduct of Cochrane and Cockburn has been already told. That of Captain Hillyar at Valparaiso was equally significant. Under the annoyance of their mortifications the British commanders broke through ordinary rules. Captain Lloyd of the *Plantagenet*, seventy-four, on arriving in the harbor of Fayal, September 26, saw a large brig in the roads, which he must have known to be an American privateer. He was so informed by his pilot. It was the *General Armstrong*, Captain Samuel C. Reid, a brig which for two years had fretted and escaped the British navy. The *Plantagenet*, with two other ships-of-war, appeared at sunset. Reid dared not run out to sea, and the want of wind would in any case have prevented success. A little after dusk, Reid, seeing the suspicious movements of the enemy, began to warp his vessel close under the guns of the castle. While doing so, at about eight o'clock four boats filled with men left the ships and approached him. As they came near he repeatedly hailed and warned them off, and at last fired. His fire was returned, but the boats withdrew with the loss of a number of men.

Captain Lloyd, in a somewhat elaborate report to explain the propriety of his conduct, enclosed affidavits to prove that the Americans had violated the neutrality of the port. The affidavits proved that, knowing the character of the vessel, he sent two boats from his own ship to assist the boats of the *Carnation* to "watch" the privateer. His report told the story as he wished it to be understood:

"On the evening of the 26th instant I put into this port for refreshments, previous to my return to Jamaica. In shore was discovered a suspicious vessel at anchor. I ordered Captain Bentham of the *Carnation* to watch her movements, and sent the pinnace and cutter of this ship to assist him on that service; but on his perceiving her under way, he sent Lieut. Robert Faussett in the pinnace, about eight o'clock, to observe her proceedings. On his approaching the schooner, he was ordered to keep off or they would fire into him, upon which the boat was immediately backed off; but to his astonishment he received a broadside or round, grape, and musketry, which did considerable damage. He then repeatedly requested them to leave off firing, as he was not come to molest them; but the enemy still continued his destructive fire until they had killed two men and wounded seven, without a musket being returned by the boat."

Lieutenant Faussett's affidavit threw more light on this curious story of British naval management. He deposed—

"That on Monday, the 26th instant, about eight o'clock in the evening, he was ordered to go in the pinnace as guard-boat unarmed on board her Majesty's brig *Carnation,* to know what armed vessel was at anchor in the bay, when Captain Bentham of said brig ordered him to go and inquire of said vessel (which by information was said to be a privateer). When said boat came near the privateer, they hailed (to say, the Americans), and desired the English boat to keep off or they would fire into her; upon which said Mr. Faussett ordered his men to back astern, and with a boat-hook was in the act of so doing, when the Americans in the most wanton manner fired into said English boat, killed two men and wounded seven, some of them mortally—and this notwithstanding said Faussett frequently called out not to murder them, that they struck and called for quarter. Said Faussett solemnly declares that no resistance of any kind was made, nor could they do it, not having any arms, nor of course sent to attack said vessel."

Lieutenant Faussett's affidavit proved that the *General Armstrong* had good reason for firing into the British boats. The *Carnation* had anchored within pistol-shot of the privateer; four boats of the *Plantagenet* and *Carnation,* filled with men, were on the water watching her in the moonlight; every act of the British squadron pointed to an attack, when Captain Bentham ordered the pinnace "to go and inquire" of the vessel, known to be an American privateer, what armed vessel it was. If Captain Bentham did not intend to provoke a shot from the privateer, his order was wanting in intelligence. Lieutenant Faussett accordingly approached in the pinnace, the other boats being not far behind. That his men were unarmed was highly improbable to the privateer, which affirmed that their fire killed one of the American crew and wounded the first lieutenant; but their armament had little to do with the matter. They approached as enemies, in the night, with a large armed force immediately behind them. The privateer repeatedly warned them off. Instead of obeying the order, Lieutenant Faussett came alongside. When he was fired on, he was so near that by his own account he shoved off with the boat-hook. Considering who and where he was, he had reason to be thankful that any of his boat's-crew escaped.

Captain Lloyd's report continued:

"This conduct, in violating the neutrality, of this port, I conceive left me no alternative but that of destroying her. I therefore repeatedly ordered Captain Bentham to tow in the brig and take that step immediately. All the boats of this ship and the *Rota* were sent under his orders to tow him alongside or assist him in the attack, as circumstances might require; but from continued light baffling winds and a lee tide he was not able, as he informed me, with his utmost exertions to put my orders in execution."

Meanwhile Captain Reid of the *General Armstrong* warped his vessel close to the beach, under the fort, and made all his preparations for the attack which he knew must come. The people of the town, with the governor among them, lined the shore, and witnessed the affair. Captain Lloyd's report told the result:

"Finding the privateer was warping under the fort very fast, Captain Bentham judged it prudent to lose no time, and about twelve o'clock ordered the boats to make the attack. A more gallant, determined one never was made, led on by Lieutenants Matterface of the *Rota* and Bowerbank of this ship; and every officer and man displayed the greatest courage in the face of a heavy discharge of great guns and musketry. But from her side being on the rocks (which was not known at the time), and every American in Fayal, exclusive of part of the crew, being armed and concealed in these rocks, which were immediately over the privateer, it unfortunately happened when these brave men gained the deck they were under the painful necessity of returning to their boats, from the very destructive fire kept up by those above them from the shore, who were in complete security— and I am grieved to add, not before many lives were lost exclusive of the wounded."

As far as the accounts agree, the boats were twelve in number, with about two hundred men. The privateersmen numbered ninety. As the boats approached, the guns opened on them; and when they came alongside the privateer they found the boarding-nettings up, with a desperate crew behind. So vigorously did the British seamen attack, that they gained the forecastle for a time. All three American lieutenants were killed or disabled, and Captain Reid fought his brig alone; but the deck was at last cleared, and the surviving assailants dropped into their boats or into the water.

Proverbially, an unsuccessful boat-attack was the most fatal of all services. The British loss was excessive. According to their report at the time, "Lieutenants Bowerbank, Coswell, and Rogers of the *Rota* were killed, as well as thirty-eight seamen, and eighty-three wounded; the first, fourth, and fifth lieutenants of the *Plantagenet* were wounded, and twenty-two seamen killed, and twenty-four wounded."

According to the official report, thirty-four were killed and eighty-six were wounded. The *Guerrière* in her battle with the *Constitution* lost only seventy-eight men altogether. The *Macedonian* lost only one hundred and four. The attack on the *General Armstrong* was one of the bloodiest defeats suffered by the British navy in the war. Not only was the privateer untaken, but she lost few of her crew—nine in all, killed and wounded.

Captain Lloyd then declared that he would destroy the privateer if he had to destroy Fayal in doing it, and ordered Captain Bentham of the *Carnation* to attack her with his guns. Reid abandoned and scuttled the *General Armstrong*, taking his men on shore. The *Carnation's* shot inflicted some injury on the town, before the privateer was set on fire by the *Carnation's* boats.

If the British navy cared to pay such a price for the shell of an old privateer brig, which had already cost British commerce, as Captain Lloyd believed, a million dollars, the privateers were willing to gratify the wish, as was shown a few days afterward when the *Endymion* tried to carry the *Prince of Neufchatel* by boarding. This privateer had made itself peculiarly obnoxious to the British navy by the boldness of its ravages in British waters. It was coming to America filled with plunder, and with a prize in company, when off Gay Head the *Endymion* was sighted, October 11, and gave chase.

Captain Hope of the *Endymion* made an official report, explaining with much detail that he chased the privateer till evening, when the wind failed, and he then sent out his boats:

"I sent all the boats under command of Lieutenants Hawkins, Ormond, and Fanshaw. In approaching the ship an alarm was fired. The boats had been previously rowing up under a shoal, and had not felt the effects of a rapid tide which they almost instantaneously became exposed to. The second barge in taking the station assigned by Lieutenant Hawkins on the schooner's starboard bow, having her larboard oars shot away, unfortunately was swept by the stream athwart the first barge; thereby all the boats became entangled; and it is with extreme concern I acquaint you that the attack was in consequence at this moment only partially made. Notwithstanding this disadvantage at the first onset, every exertion that human skill could devise was resorted to to renew the contest; and they succeeded in again getting alongside, but not in the position intended. Their failure, therefore, is to be ascribed in the first instance to the velocity of the tide, the height of the vessel's side, not having channel plates to assist the men in getting on her deck, and her very superior force (a schooner of the largest dimensions, the *Prince of Neufchatel,* three hundred and twenty tons, eighteen guns, long-nine and twelve-pounders, with a complement of one hundred and forty men of all nations, commanded by Mons. Jean Ordronaux). The boats' painters being now shot away, they again fell astern without ever being able to repeat the attack, and with great difficulty regained the ship, with the exception of the second barge."

Captain Ordronaux of the privateer had a crew of less than forty men then at quarters, and they suffered severely, only nine men escaping injury. The boarders gained the deck, but were killed as fast as they mounted; and at last more than half the British party were killed or captured. According to the British account, twenty-eight men, including the first lieutenant of the *Endymion,* were killed; and thirty-seven men, including the second lieutenant, were wounded. This report did not quite agree with that of the privateer, which claimed also twenty-eight prisoners, including the second lieutenant, who was unhurt. In any case, more than seventy men of the *Endymion's* crew, besides her first and second lieutenant, were killed, wounded, or captured; and the *Prince of Neufchatel* arrived in safety in Boston.

In the want of adjacent rocks lined with armed Americans, such as Captain Lloyd alleged at Fayal, Captain Hope was reduced to plead the tides as the cause of his defeat. These reports, better than any other evidence, showed the feelings of the British naval service in admitting discomfiture in the last resort to its pride. Successively obliged to plead inferiority at the guns, inferiority in sailing qualities, inferiority in equipment, the British service saw itself compelled by these repeated and bloody repulses to admit that its supposed pre-eminence in hand-to-hand fighting was a delusion. Within a single fortnight two petty privateers, with crews whose united force did not amount to one hundred and fifty men, succeeded in repulsing attacks made by twice their number of the best British seamen, inflicting a loss, in killed and wounded, officially reported at one hundred and eighty-five.

Such mortifying and bloody experiences made even the British navy weary of the war. Valuable prizes were few, and the service, especially in winter, was severe. Undoubtedly the British cruisers caught privateers by dozens, and were as successful in the performance of their duties as ever they had been in any war in Europe. Their blockade of American ports was real and ruinous, and nothing pretended to resist them. Yet after catching scores of swift cruisers, they saw scores of faster and better vessels issue from the blockaded ports and harry British commerce in every sea. Scolded by the press, worried by the Admiralty, and mortified by their own want of success, the British navy was obliged to hear language altogether strange to its experience.

"The American cruisers daily enter in among our convoys," said the *Times* of February 11, 1815, "to seize prizes in sight of those that should afford protection, and if pursued 'put on their sea-wings' and laugh at the clumsy English pursuers. To what is this owing? Cannot we build ships? . . . It must indeed be encouraging to Mr. Madison to read the logs of his cruisers. If they fight, they are sure to conquer; if they fly, they are sure to escape."

CHAPTER XXII
EXHAUSTION

In the tempest of war that raged over land and ocean during the months of August and September, 1814, bystanders could not trust their own judgment of the future; yet shrewd observers, little affected either by emotion or by interest, inclined to the belief that the United States government was near exhaustion. The immediate military danger on Lake Champlain was escaped, and Baltimore was saved; but the symptoms of approaching failure in government were not to be mistaken, and the capture of Washington, which was intended to hurry the collapse, produced its intended effect.

From the first day of the war the two instruments necessary for military success were wanting to Madison—money and men. After three campaigns, the time came when both these wants must be supplied, or the national government must devolve its duties on the States. When the President, preparing his Annual Message, asked his Cabinet officers what were the prospects of supplying money and men for another campaign, he received answers discouraging in the extreme.

First, in regard to money. In July, Secretary Campbell advertised a second loan, of only six million dollars. He obtained but two and a half millions at eighty. His acceptance of this trifling sum obliged him to give the same terms to the contractors who had taken the nine millions subscribed in the spring of eighty-eight. Barker found difficulty in making his payments, and from both loans the Treasury could expect to obtain only $10,400,000, owing to the contractors' failures. The authorized loan was twenty-five millions. The secretary could suggest no expedient, except Treasury notes, for filling the deficit.

Bad as this failure was—though it showed Secretary Campbell's incapacity so clearly as to compel his retirement, and obliged the President to call a special session of Congress—the Treasury might regard it as the least of its embarrassments. Commonly governments had begun their most desperate efforts only after ordinary resources failed; but the United States government in 1814 had so inextricably involved its finances that without dictatorial powers of seizing property its functions could not much longer continue. The general bankruptcy, long foreseen, at length occurred.

The panic caused by the capture of Washington, August 24, obliged the tottering banks of Philadelphia and Baltimore to suspend specie payments. The banks of Philadelphia formally announced their suspension, August 31, by a circular explaining the causes and necessity of their decision. The banks of New York immediately followed, September 1; and thence-forward no bank between New Orleans and Albany paid its obligations except in notes. Only the banks of New England maintained specie payments, with the exception of those in least credit which took the opportunity to pay or not pay as they pleased. The suspension was admitted to be permanent. Until the blockade should be raised and domestic produce could find a foreign market, the course of exchange was fixed, and specie payments could not be resumed. The British navy and the Boston Federalists held the country firmly bound, and peace alone could bring relief.

Suspension mattered little, and had the National Bank been in existence the failure might have been an advantage to the government; but without a central

[254]

authority the currency instantly fell into confusion. No medium of exchange existed outside of New England. Boston gave the specie standard, and soon the exchanges showed wide differences. New York money stood at twenty per cent discount, Philadelphia at twenty-four per cent, Baltimore at thirty per cent. Treasury notes were sold in Boston at twenty-five per cent discount, and United States six-per-cents stood at sixty in coin. The Treasury had no means of transferring its bank deposits from one part of the country to another. Unless it paid its debts in Treasury notes, it was unable to pay them at all. No other money than the notes of suspended banks came into the Treasury. Even in New England, taxes, customs-duties, and loans were paid in Treasury notes, and rarely in local currency. Thus, while the government collected in the Middle and Southern States millions in bank-notes, it was obliged to leave them in deposit at the local banks where the collection was made, while its debts in Boston and New York remained unpaid. The source of revenue was destroyed. The whole South and West, and the Middle States as far north as New York, could contribute in no considerable degree to the support of government.

The situation was unusual. The government might possess immense resources in one State and be totally bankrupt in another; it might levy taxes to the amount of the whole circulating medium, and yet have only its own notes available for payment of debt; it might borrow hundreds of millions and be none the better for the loan. All the private banknotes of Pennsylvania and the Southern country were useless in New York and New England where they must chiefly be used. An attempt to transfer such deposits in any quantity would have made them quite worthless. The Treasury already admitted bankruptcy. The interest on the national obligations could not be paid.

The President's second inquiry regarded men. The new Secretary of War, Monroe, gave him such information as the Department possessed on the numbers of the army. A comparative account showed that in June, 1813, the regular troops numbered 27,609; in December, 34,325. In January, 1814, the number was nominally 33,822; in July the aggregate was 31,503, the effectives being 27,010. Since July the recruits had declined in numbers. The three months of March, April, and May produced 6,996 recruits; the three months of July, August, and September were reported as furnishing 4,477. The general return of September 30 reported the strength of the army at 34,029 men. The government was not able to provide the money necessary to pay bounties due for the last three months' recruiting. The Secretary of War admitted the failure of the recruiting service, and attributed it to the high bounties given for substitutes in the militia detached for United States service.

The smallness of the armies in the field showed worse results than were indicated by the returns. Macomb at Plattsburg claimed to have only fifteen hundred effectives. Izard carried with him to Buffalo only four thousand men. Brown's effectives at Fort Erie numbered two thousand. Apparently these three corps included the entire force in the field on the Canada frontier, and their combined effective strength did not exceed eight thousand men. The year before, Wilkinson and Hampton commanded fully eleven thousand effectives in their movements against Montreal. Nothing showed that the victories at Niagara and

Plattsburg had stimulated enlistments, or that the army could be raised above thirty thousand effectives even if the finances were in a condition to meet the expense.

Much was said of the zeal shown by the State militia in hastening to the defence of their soil, and the New England Federalists were as loud as the Kentucky and Tennessee Democrats in praise of the energy with which the militia rose to resist invasion; but in reality this symptom was the most alarming of the time. Both in the military and in the political point of view, the persistence on depending on militia threatened to ruin the national government.

The military experience of 1814 satisfied the stanchest war Democrats that the militia must not be their dependence. In Maine the militia allowed themselves with hardly a show of resistance to be made subjects of Great Britain. At Plattsburg volunteers collected in considerable numbers, but the victory was won by the sailors and the engineers. At Niagara, Brown never could induce more than a thousand volunteers to support him in his utmost straits. Porter's efforts failed to create a brigade respectable in numbers, and at Chippawa his Indians outnumbered his whites. Four days after the repulse of Drummond's assault on Fort Erie, at the most anxious moment of the Niagara campaign, Major-General Brown wrote to Secretary Armstrong—

"I very much doubt if a parallel can be found for the state of things existing on this frontier. A gallant little army struggling with the enemies of their country, and devoting their lives for its honor and its safety, left by that country to struggle alone, and that within sight and within hearing."

A month afterward Brown succeeded in obtaining a thousand volunteers, and by some quality of his own made them assault and carry works that old soldiers feared to touch. The feat was the most extraordinary that was performed on either side in the remarkably varied experience of the war; but it proved Brown's personal energy rather than the merits of a militia system. At Washington the militia were thoroughly tested; their rout proved chiefly the incompetence of their general, but the system was shown, before the battle, to be more defective than the army it produced. At Baltimore the militia were again routed, and the town was saved chiefly by the engineers and sailors. In Virginia, where more than forty thousand militia were in the field, they protected nothing, and their service was more fatal to themselves than though they had fought severe battles. Nearly all the Virginia militia summoned for the defence of Norfolk suffered from sickness, and the mortality when compared with that of the regular service was enormous; five militia-men sickened and died where one regular soldier suffered. In Tennessee and Georgia the experience was equally unfortunate; the Georgia militia could do nothing with the Creeks, and Andrew Jackson himself was helpless until he obtained one small regiment of regulars.

Besides its military disadvantages the militia service was tainted with fraud. Habitually and notoriously in New England and New York, the militia-men when called out attended muster, served a few days in order to get their names on the pay-roll, and then went home. The United States government wasted millions of dollars in pay and pensions for such men. Another source of waste was in the time required to place them in the field. The government struggled to avoid a call to militia, even though risking great disasters by the neglect.

The worst of all evils lay still further in the background. The militia began by rendering a proper army impossible, and ended by making government a form. The object of Massachusetts in praising the conduct of militia, and in maintaining its own at a high state of efficiency, was notorious. The Federalists knew that the national government must sooner or later abandon the attempt to support an army. When that time should come, the only resource of the government would lie in State armies, and Massachusetts was the best equipped State for that object. Her militia, seventy thousand strong, well-armed, well-drilled, and as yet untouched by war, could dictate to the Union. Whenever Massachusetts should say the word, the war must stop; and Massachusetts meant to say the word when the government fairly ceased to possess either money or arms.

That moment, in the belief of the Massachusetts Federalists, had come. Their course in the summer and autumn of 1814 left no doubt of their intentions. No act of open rebellion could be more significant than their conduct when Sherbrooke's expedition occupied Castine. Then at last Governor Strong consented to call out the militia, which he refused to do two years before, because, he asserted, Castine and the other coast towns were sufficiently defended; but the governor was careful to avoid the suspicion that these troops were in the national service. He acted independently of the national government in the terms of his general order of September, 1814, placing his militia under the command of a major-general of their own, and making only a bare inquiry of the Secretary of War whether their expenses would be reimbursed—an inquiry which Monroe at once answered in the negative. The force was a State army, and could not fail to cause the President more anxiety than it was likely ever to cause the Prince Regent.

At the same time the governor of Connecticut withdrew from the command of Brigadier-General Cushing the brigade of State militia then in the national service, and placed it under a major-general of State militia, with injunctions to obey no orders except such as were issued by State authority. The evil of these measures was greatly aggravated by coinciding with the crisis which stopped the course of national government. Connecticut withdrew her militia, August 24; Washington was captured the same day; the Philadelphia banks suspended payment August 29; Castine was taken August 31; and Governor Strong called out the Massachusetts militia September 6. The government was prostrate, and New England was practically independent when Sir George Prevost crossed the frontier, September 3. So complete was the paralysis that Governor Chittenden of Vermont, on receiving official notice that the British army and navy were advancing on Lake Champlain, refused to call out the militia, because neither the Constitution nor the laws gave him authority to order the militia out of the State. He could only recommend that individuals should volunteer to assist in the defence of Plattsburg. Chittenden's conduct was the more suggestive because of his undoubted honesty and the absence of factious motive for his refusal.

The full meaning of Governor Strong's course was avowed a few days afterward. Having called a special meeting of the State legislature for October 5, he addressed to it a message narrating the steps he had taken, and the refusal of the President to assume the expenses of the militia called into service for the defence of the State.

"The situation of this State is peculiarly dangerous and perplexing," said Governor Strong; "we have been led by the terms of the Constitution to rely on the government of the Union to provide for our defence. We have resigned to that Government the revenues of the State with the expectation that this object would not be neglected. . . . Let us then, relying on the support and direction of Providence, unite in such measures for our safety as the times demand and the principles of justice and the law of self-preservation will justify."

The sense which this invitation was intended to bear could be best understood by appreciating the temper of the body thus addressed and the time when the appeal was made. The national government had for practical purposes ceased. The Boston *Centinel*, a newspaper of large circulation, said to reach six thousand copies, announced September 10, 1814, that the Union was already practically dissolved, and that the people must rise in their majesty, protect themselves, and compel their unworthy servants to obey their will. Governor Strong knew that the legislature was controlled by extreme partisans of the Pickering type, who wished, to use his phrase, to "let the ship run aground." Even Josiah Quincy, one of the most vehement Federalists, was aware that the members of the General Court stood in danger of doing too much rather than too little.

Strong's message of October 5 was echoed by Pickering from Washington, October 12, in a letter which closed with the exhortation to seize the national revenues:

"As, abandoned by the general government except for taxing us, we must defend ourselves, so we ought to secure and hold fast the revenues indispensable to maintain the force necessary for our protection against the foreign enemy and the still greater evil in prospect—domestic tyranny."

The Massachusetts legislature could not fail to understand Governor Strong's message as an invitation to resume the powers with which the State had parted in adopting the Constitution.

The legislature referred the message to a committee, which reported only three days afterward through its chairman, Harrison Gray Otis:

"The state of the national Treasury as exhibited by the proper officer requires an augmentation of existing taxes; and if in addition to these the people of Massachusetts, deprived of their commerce and harassed by a formidable enemy, are compelled to provide for the indispensable duty of self-defense, it must soon become impossible for them to sustain this burden. There remains to them therefore no alternative but submission to the enemy, or the control of their own resources to repel his aggressions. It is impossible to hesitate in making the election. This people are not ready for conquest or submission; but being ready and determined to defend themselves, they have the greatest need of those resources derivable from themselves which the national government has hitherto thought proper to employ elsewhere."

The report further showed that the United States Constitution had failed to secure to New England the rights and benefits expected from it, and required immediate change. The prescribed mode of amendment was insufficient:

"When this deficiency becomes apparent, no reason can preclude the right of the whole people who were parties to it to adopt another. . . . But as a proposition for such a convention from a single State would probably be unsuccessful, and our danger admits not of delay, it is recommended by the committee that in the first instance a conference should be invited between those States the affinity of whose interests is closest."

Thus, after ten years' delay, the project of a New England Convention was brought forward by State authority, through the process of war with England, which George Cabot from the first declared to be the only means of producing it. As Otis's committee presented the subject, the conference was in the first place to devise some mode of common defence; and, in the second, "to lay the foundation for a radical reform in the national compact by inviting to a future convention a deputation from all the States in the Union." The report closed by offering seven Resolutions, recommending the enlistment of a State army of ten thousand men, a loan of a million dollars at six per cent, and the appointment of delegates "to meet and confer with delegates from the States of New England or any of them" on the defence of those States and the redress of their grievances.

The Senate committee also made a strenuous argument against the President's decision that State militia were in State service unless called for by a United States officer and placed under his direction, and recommended that the subject should be referred to the next session. To the proposition for a conference of the New England States, and to Otis's other Resolutions, the Senate and House assented, October 13, by large majorities, varying in numbers, but amounting to two hundred and sixty against ninety in the case of the proposed convention. The minority in both Houses presented protests, charging the majority with intending more than was avowed. "The reasoning of the report," said the Protest signed by seventy-six members of the House, "is supported by the alarming assumption that the Constitution has failed in its objects, and the people of Massachusetts are absolved from their allegiance, and at liberty to adopt another. In debate it has been reiterated that the Constitution is no longer to be respected, and that revolution is not to be deprecated." The House refused to receive the Protest, as disrespectful. The minority withdrew from further share in these proceedings; and the majority then, October 19, chose twelve delegates "to meet and confer on the 15th December next with such as may be chosen by any or all the other New England States upon our public grievances and concerns." The choice was marked by a conservative spirit not altogether pleasing to Timothy Pickering. George Cabot and Harrison Gray Otis stood at the head of the delegation.

The remonstrances and threats of the minority made the majority cautious, but did not check them. The legislature of Connecticut immediately appointed seven delegates to meet those of Massachusetts at Hartford, December 15, for the purpose of recommending "such measures for the safety and welfare of these States as may consist with our obligations as members of the national Union." In this clause the legislature intended to draw a distinction between obligations to the Union and obligations to the Constitution. To the former the people avowed no hostility; to the latter they thought the war had put an end. On that point the committee's report was clear.

Besides Massachusetts and Connecticut the legislature of Rhode Island, by a vote of thirty-nine to twenty-three, appointed November 5, four delegates to confer at Hartford upon the measures which might be in their power to adopt to restore their rights under the Constitution, "consistently with their obligations." These three States alone chose delegates. The governor and legislature of New Hampshire would probably have joined them had not the Republican council stood in the way. The legislature of Vermont, including its Federalist minority, unanimously declined the invitation.

Immediately after these steps were taken, the autumn elections occurred. Members of Congress were to be chosen, and the people were obliged to vote for or against the Hartford Convention as the issue expressly avowed. President Madison might safely assume that no man voted for Federalist Congressmen in November, 1814, unless he favored the project of a New England Convention. The result was emphatic. Massachusetts chose eighteen Federalists and two Republicans; Vermont, New Hampshire, Rhode Island, and Connecticut chose only Federalists. In all, New England chose thirty-nine Federalist Congressmen and two Republicans for the Fourteenth Congress. In the Thirteenth Congress, chosen in 1812, when the feeling against the war was supposed to be strongest, the Federalist members from New England numbered thirty, the Republicans eleven.

Beyond New England the autumn elections were less significant, but were still unsatisfactory to the Administration. New Jersey returned to her true sympathies, and as far as her Congressmen expressed her opinions gave unanimous support to the war; but Pennsylvania, owing to local quarrels, elected five Federalist members; and Maryland elected five Federalists and four Republicans. In spite of the great loss in Federalist members which had occurred in the spring elections in New York, the Federalists numbered sixty-five in the Fourteenth Congress; in the Thirteenth they numbered sixty-eight. The administration had hoped, and freely asserted, that a strong reaction in favor of the war had followed the burning of Washington and the avowal of England's designs against Maine and the Northwestern territory. The elections showed no such reaction. The war was no more popular than before.

The public apathy was the more alarming because, whatever was the true object of the Hartford Convention, all Republicans believed it to be intended as a step to dissolve the Union, and they supported the Administration chiefly because Madison represented the Union. Federalists might deceive themselves. Probably the men who voted for the Hartford Convention saw its necessary consequences less clearly than they were seen by the men who voted against it. The Republican vote represented the strength of Union sentiment more closely than the disunion sentiment was represented by the Federalist vote. Yet the States from Maryland to Maine chose a majority of Congressmen who were not Republicans. The New England States, New York, New Jersey, Pennsylvania, Delaware, and Maryland returned much more than half the members of Congress—one hundred and eight in one hundred and eighty-two; and of these fifty-seven were Federalists, while only fifty-one were Republicans. The unpopularity of the Administration was not easily overestimated when Madison could win no more support than this, at a time when the public believed a vote for Federalism to be a vote for disunion.

"I give you the most serious assurance," wrote Randolph in an open letter to James Lloyd, of Massachusetts, remonstrating against the Convention, "that nothing less than the shameful conduct of the enemy and the complection of certain occurrences to the eastward could have sustained Mr. Madison after the disgraceful affair at Washington. The public indignation would have overwhelmed in one common ruin himself and his hireling newspapers."

Randolph's political judgments were commonly mistaken, but in this instance he proved himself to be at least partially right; for at the next election, six months later, when the current had turned decidedly in Madison's favor, Randolph after a sharp contest defeated Eppes and recovered control of his district. Virginia could hardly have chosen a representative less calculated to please Madison.

The President himself betrayed unusual signs of distress. Nothing in Madison's character was more remarkable than the placidity with which he commonly met anxieties that would have crushed a sensitive man; but the shock of defeat at Bladensburg, the flight from Washington, and the anxieties that followed broke him down. William Wirt visited Washington October 14, before the action of the Massachusetts legislature was yet completed. After viewing the ruins of the White House, a "mournful monument of American imbecility and improvidence," he called upon the President at Colonel Tayloe's Octagon House, which Serurier had occupied, but which Madison took for his residence after his return.

"P— and I called on the President," wrote Wirt in a private letter. "He looks miserably shattered and woe-begone. In short, he looked heart-broken. His mind is full of the New England sedition. He introduced the subject and continued to press it, painful as it obviously was to him. I denied the probability, even the possibility, that the yeomanry of the North could be induced to place themselves under the power and protection of England, and diverted the conversation to another topic; but he took the first opportunity to return to it, and convinced me that his heart and mind were painfully full of the subject."

No misconduct of New England alone would have so unmanned a Virginia President. Madison's worst troubles lay nearer home; Massachusetts made only the last straw in his burden. Jefferson, with his usual kindliness, tried to console and encourage him; but Jefferson's consolations proved only the difficulty of finding words or arguments to warrant satisfaction with the past or hope for the future.

"In the late events at Washington," wrote Jefferson, September 24, "I have felt so much for you that I cannot withhold the expression of my sympathies. For although every reasonable man must be sensible that all you can do is to order—that execution must depend on others, and failures be imputed to them alone—yet I know that when such failures happen they affect even those who have done everything they could to prevent them. Had General Washington himself been now at the head of our affairs, the same event would probably have happened."

Jefferson's estimate of Washington's abilities was lower than that commonly accepted; and his rule that a President's responsibility ceased after giving an order, besides ignoring the President's responsibility for the selection of agents, seemed to destroy the foundation of the public service. "I never doubted that the plans of the President were wise and sufficient," wrote Jefferson to Monroe. "Their failure we all impute, (1) to the insubordinate temper of Armstrong, and (2) to the indecision of Winder." The rule that an administrator might select any agent, however incompetent, without incurring responsibility for the agent's acts, was one which in private affairs Jefferson would hardly have accepted.

Yet Jefferson's opinions probably expressed Republican sentiment in Virginia, and showed better than any other evidence the course of thought among Madison's friends. In that respect his expressions retained permanent value. The Virginians were willing to throw off responsibility for public disaster; and they naturally threw it on New England, since New England challenged it. Writing to his friend William Short, Jefferson spoke of the threatening attitude of Massachusetts:

"Some apprehend danger from the defection of Massachusetts. It is a disagreeable circumstance, but not a dangerous one. If they become neutral, we are sufficient for one enemy without them, and in fact we get no aid from them now."

Probably most Virginians shared this belief, at least as far as concerned the aid rendered by Massachusetts to the war. In truth, Massachusetts gave little aid, and made a profession of her wish to give none at all; but the difficulty did not end there. Massachusetts and Virginia were States of the first class. The census of 1810 allotted to Massachusetts, including Maine, a population of about seven hundred thousand; to Virginia, a white population of five hundred and fifty-one thousand, and a colored population of four hundred and twenty-three thousand, —nine hundred and seventy-four thousand in all. In the ratio of representation Massachusetts counted for twenty, Virginia for twenty-three. The quota of Massachusetts in the direct tax was $316,000; that of Virginia was $369,000. On the scale furnished by these data, Virginia should have contributed in support of the war about one eighth or one seventh more men and money than were required from Massachusetts. The actual result was different.

The amount of money contributed by Massachusetts could not be compared with that contributed by Virginia, partly because of the severe blockade which closed the Virginian ports. The net revenue from customs derived from Virginia in 1814 was $4,000; that from Massachusetts was $1,600,000. Unlike the customs revenue, the receipts from internal revenue were supposed to be reasonably equalized, so that each state should contribute in due proportion. According to the official return dated Nov. 24, 1815, the total internal duties which had then been paid to the collectors for the year 1814 in Massachusetts was $198,400; in Virginia it was $193,500. The total amount then paid to the Treasury was $178,-400 in Massachusetts, and $157,300 in Virginia. The direct tax was fixed by Congress and was assumed by the State in Virginia, but regularly assessed in Massachusetts. One paid $316,000; the other, $369,000. The total revenue derived from Massachusetts was therefore $2,114,400 in the year 1814; that from

Virginia, $566,500. Of the loans effected in the same year, Massachusetts took a small part considering her means—hardly a million dollars. Virginia took still less—only two hundred thousand.

In money, Massachusetts contributed four times as much as Virginia to support the war, and her contributions were paid in Treasury notes or paper equivalent to coin—not in the notes of banks worthless beyond the State. In men, the estimate was affected by the inquiry whether the militia were to be considered as protecting the national government or the State. Owing to the presence of the British in the Chesapeake, Virginia kept a large force of militia on foot, some of which were in garrison at Norfolk, and a few were on the field of Bladensburg. Massachusetts also was obliged to call out a considerable force of Militia to protect or garrison national posts.

The relative numbers of regular troops were also somewhat doubtful; but the paymaster of the army reported Oct. 26, 1814, that he had distributed in bounties during the year $237,400 for Massachusetts, and $160,962 for Virginia. During the year, six regular regiments—the Ninth, Twenty-first, Thirty-third, Thirty-fourth, Fortieth, and Forty-fifth—recruited in Massachusetts. Three—the Twelfth, Twentieth, and Thirty-fifth—recruited in Virginia. Perhaps the military aid furnished by the different sections of the seaboard could be better understood by following the familiar division. New England furnished thirteen regiments. New York, New Jersey, and Pennsylvania furnished fifteen. The Southern States, from Delaware to South Carolina inclusive, furnished ten. Of all the States in the Union New York alone supplied more regular soldiers than Massachusetts, and Massachusetts supplied as many as were furnished by Virginia and the two Carolinas together.

Judged by these standards, either Massachusetts had done more than her share, or Virginia had done less than hers. The tests were material, and took no moral element in account; but in moral support the relative failure of Massachusetts was not beyond dispute. Public opinion in New England was almost equally divided, and the pronounced opposition to the war was much greater in the Eastern States than in the Southern; but in the serious work of fighting, New England claimed a share of credit. In the little army at Niagara New York supplied the Major-General, Virginia and Massachusetts the two brigadiers; but Winfield Scott's brigade was chiefly composed of New England men; and when, nearly half a century afterward, Scott in his old age was obliged to choose between his allegiance to his State and allegiance to the Union, the memory of the New England troops who had won for him his first renown had its influence in raising his mind above the local sympathies which controlled other Virginia officers. Without reflecting on Virginia courage or patriotism, the New England Republicans were warranted in claiming that not the Virginia regiments, but the Massachusetts Twenty-first and the Connecticut Twenty-fifth routed the Royal Scots at Chippawa, and bayoneted the British artillerymen at Lundy's Lane, and stormed Drummond's intrenchments at Fort Erie. They could add that without their sailors the war might have been less successful than it was; and they would have been justified had they asked Jefferson to glance at his latest newspaper as he wrote that Massachusetts gave no aid to the war, and read the despatch of Johnston Blakeley reporting that the New England crew of the *Wasp* had sunk the *Avon* in the middle of a British fleet. Virginians did not take kindly to the ocean; and on land, owing to the accidents of war, no Virginia regiment was offered a chance to win distinction.

These comparisons were of little weight to prove that New England was either better or worse than other parts of the Union, but they showed that the difficulties that depressed Madison's mind were not merely local. He might have disregarded the conduct of the State governments of Massachusetts and Connecticut had he enjoyed the full support of his own great Republican States, Pennsylvania, Virginia, and North Carolina. Except New York, Kentucky, Tennessee, and perhaps Ohio, no State gave to the war the full and earnest cooperation it needed. Again and again, from the beginning of the troubles with England, Madison had acted on the conviction that at last the people were aroused; but in every instance he had been disappointed. After the burning of Washington, he was more than ever convinced that the moment had come when the entire people would rally in their self-respect but he was met by the Hartford Convention and the November elections. If the people would not come to the aid of their government at such a moment, Madison felt that nothing could move them. Peace was his last hope.

CHAPTER XXIII
CONGRESS AND THE ARMY

While Dallas struggled with Congress to obtain the means of establishing a currency in order to pay the army, Monroe carried on a similar struggle in order to obtain an army to pay. On this point, as on the financial issue, Virginian ideas did not accord with the wishes of Government. The prejudice against a regular army was stimulated by the evident impossibility of raising or supporting it. Once more Jefferson expressed the common feeling of his Virginia neighbors. "We must prepare for interminable war," he wrote to Monroe, October 16. "To this end we should put our house in order by providing men and money to an indefinite extent. The former may be done by classing our militia, and assigning each class to the description of duties for which it is fit. It is nonsense to talk of regulars. They are not to be had among a people so easy and happy at home as ours. We might as well rely on calling down an army of angels from heaven."

As Jefferson lost the habits of power and became once more a Virginia planter, he reverted to the opinions and prejudices of his earlier life and of the society in which he lived. As Monroe grew accustomed to the exercise and the necessities of power, he threw aside Virginian ideas and accepted the responsibilities of government. On the same day when Jefferson wrote to Monroe that it was nonsense to talk of regulars, Monroe wrote to Congress that it was nonsense to talk of militia. The divergence between Monroe and Jefferson was even greater than between Dallas and Eppes.

"It may be stated with confidence," wrote Monroe to Congress, "that at least three times the force in militia has been employed at our principal cities, along the coast and on the frontier, in marching to and returning thence, that would have been necessary in regular troops; and that the expense, attending it has been more than proportionately augmented from the difficulty if not the impossibility of preserving the same degree of system in the militia as in the regular service."

In Monroe's opinion a regular force was an object "of the highest importance." He told the Senate committee that the army, which was only thirty-four thousand strong on the first of October, should be raised to its legal limit of sixty-two thousand, and that another permanent army of forty thousand men should be raised for strictly defensive service. In the face of Jefferson's warning that he might as well call down an army of angels from heaven, Monroe called for one hundred thousand regular troops, when no exertions had hitherto availed to keep thirty thousand effectives on the rolls.

The mere expression of such a demand carried with it the train of consequences which the people chiefly dreaded. One hundred thousand troops could be raised only by draft. Monroe affirmed the power as well as the need of drafting. "Congress have a right, by the Constitution," he said, "to raise regular armies, and no restraint is imposed on the exercise of it. . . . It would be absurd to suppose that Congress could not carry this power into effect otherwise than by accepting the voluntary service of individuals." Absurd as it was, such had been the general impression, and Monroe was believed to have been one of the most emphatic in maintaining it. "Ask him," suggested Randolph, "what he would have done, while governor of Virginia and preparing to resist Federal usurpation, had such an attempt been made by Mr. Adams and his ministers, especially in 1800. He *can* give the answer." Doubtless the silence of the Constitution in respect to conscription was conclusive to some minds in favor of the power; but the people preferred the contrary view, the more because militia service seemed to give more pay for less risk.

The chance of carrying such a measure through Congress was not great, yet Monroe recommended it as his first plan for raising men. He proposed to enroll the free male population between eighteen and forty-five years of age into classes of one hundred, each to furnish four men and to keep their places supplied. The second plan varied from the first only in the classification, not in the absence of compulsion. The militia were to be divided into three sections according to age, with the obligation to serve, when required, for a term of two years. A third plan suggested the exemption from militia service of every five militia-men who could provide one man for the war. If none of these schemes should be approved by Congress, additional bounties must be given under the actual system. Of the four plans, the secretary preferred the first.

The Senate committee immediately summoned Monroe to an interview. They wished an explanation of the failure in the recruiting service, and were told by Monroe that the failure was chiefly due to the competition of the detached militia for substitutes. The military committee of the House then joined with the military committee of the Senate in sounding the members of both bodies in order to ascertain the most rigorous measure that could be passed. According to the report of Troup of Georgia, chairman of the House committee, they "found that no efficacious measure, calculated certainly and promptly to fill the regular army, could be effectually resorted to. Measures were matured and proposed by the (House) committee, but were not pressed on the House, from the solemn conviction that there was no disposition in the Legislature to act finally on the subject."

Yet the issue was made at a moment of extreme anxiety and almost despair. In October, 1814, the result of the war was believed to depend on the establishment of an efficient draft. The price of United States six-per-cents showed better than any other evidence the opinion of the public; but the military situation, known to all the world, warranted deep depression. Sir George Prevost, about to be succeeded by an efficient commander—Sir George Murray, was then at Kingston organizing a campaign against Sackett's Harbor, with an army of twenty thousand regular troops and a fleet that controlled the Lake. Another great force, military and naval, was known to be on its way to New Orleans; and the defences of New Orleans were no stronger than those of Washington. One half the province of Maine, from Eastport to Castine, was already in British possession.

To leave no doubt of England's intentions, despatches from Ghent, communicating the conditions on which the British government offered peace, arrived from the American commissioners and were sent, October 10, to Congress. These conditions assumed rights of conquest. The British negotiators demanded four territorial or proprietary concessions, and all were vital to the integrity of the Union. First, the whole Indian Territory of the Northwest, including about one third of the State of Ohio, two thirds of Indiana, and nearly the entire region from which the States of Illinois, Wisconsin, and Michigan were afterward created, was to be set aside forever as Indian country under British guaranty. Second, the United States were to be excluded from military or naval contact with the Lakes. Third, they had forfeited their rights in the fisheries. Fourth, they were to cede a portion of Maine to strengthen Canada.

These demands, following the unparalleled insult of burning Washington, foreshadowed a war carried to extremities, and military preparations such as the Union had no means ready to repel. Monroe's recommendations rested on the conviction that the nation must resort to extreme measures. Dallas's financial plan could not have been suggested except as a desperate resource. Congress understood as well as the Executive the impending peril, and stood in even more fear of it.

Under these circumstances, when Troup's committee refused to act, Giles reported, on behalf of the Senate committee, two military measures. The first, for filling the regular army, proposed to extend the age of enlistment from twenty-one to eighteen years; and to double the land-bounty; and to exempt from militia duty every militia-man who should furnish a recruit for the regular service.

The second measure, reported the same day, November 5, purported to authorize the raising an army of eighty thousand militia-men by draft, to serve for two years within the limits of their own or an adjoining State. The provisions of this measure were ill-conceived, ill-digested, and unlikely to answer their purpose. The moment the debate began, the bill was attacked so vigorously as to destroy whatever credit it might have otherwise possessed.

Of all the supporters of the war, Senator Varnum of Massachusetts was one of the steadiest. He was also the highest authority in the Senate on matters pertaining to the militia. When Giles's bill came under discussion November 16, Varnum began the debate by a speech vehemently hostile to the proposed legislation. He first objected that although the bill purported to call for an army of eighty thousand men, "yet in some of the subsequent sections of it we find that instead of realizing the pleasing prospect of seeing an ample force in the field, the force is to be reduced to an indefinite amount—which contradiction in terms, inconsistency in principle, and uncertainty in effect, cannot fail to produce mortification and chagrin in every breast." Varnum objected to drafting men from the militia for two years' service because the principle of nine months' service was already established by the common law. If the nation wanted a regular force, why not make it a part of the regular army without a system of drafting militia "unnecessary, unequal, and unjust?" The machinery of classification and draft was "wholly impracticable." The limit of service to adjoining States abandoned the objects for which the Union existed. The proffered bounties which ruin the recruiting service for the regular army; the proffered exemptions and reductions in term of duty left no permanency to the service. The bill inflicted no penalties and charged no officers with the duty of making the draft. "I consider the whole system as resolving into a recommendation upon the patriotism of the States and Territories and upon the patriotism of the classes."

The justice of Varnum's criticism could not fairly be questioned. The bill authorized the President "to issue his orders to such officers of the militia as he may think proper," and left the classification and draft in the hands of these militia officers. Every drafted man who had performed any tour of duty in the militia since the beginning of the war was entitled to deduct a corresponding term from his two years of service; and obviously the demand created for substitutes would stop recruiting for the regular army.

Hardly had Varnum sat down when Senator Daggett of Connecticut spoke.

"The bill," said the Connecticut senator, "is incapable of being executed, as well as unconstitutional and unjust. It proceeds entirely upon the idea that the State governments will lend their aid to carry it into effect. If they refuse, it becomes inoperative. Now, sir, will the Executives, who believe it a violation of the Constitution, assist in its execution? I tell you they will not."

Every member of the Senate who heard these words knew that they meant to express the will of the convention which was to meet at Hartford within a month. The sentiment thus avowed was supported by another New England senator, whose State was not a party to the convention. Jeremiah Mason of New Hampshire was second to no one in legal ability or in personal authority, and when he followed Daggett in the debate, he spoke with full knowledge of the effect his words would have on the action of the Hartford Convention and of the State executives.

"In my opinion," he said, "this system of military conscription thus recommended by the Secretary of War is not only inconsistent with the provisions and spirit of the Constitution, but also with all the principles of civil liberty. In atrocity it exceeds that adopted by the late Emperor of France for the subjugation of Europe. . . . Such a measure cannot, it ought not to be submitted to. If it could in no other way be averted, I not only believe, but I hope, it would be resisted."

Mason pointed to the alternative—which Massachusetts was then adopting, as the necessary consequence of refusing power to the government—that the States must resume the powers of sovereignty:

"Should the national defence be abandoned by the general government, I trust the people, if still retaining a good portion of their resources, may rally under their State governments against foreign invasion, and rely with confidence on their own courage and virtue."

At that time the State of Massachusetts was occupied for one hundred miles of its sea-coast by a British force, avowedly for purposes of permanent conquest; and the State legislature, October 18, refused to make an inquiry, or to consider any measure for regaining possession of its territory, or to coöperate with the national government for the purpose, but voted to raise an army of ten thousand men. The object of this State army was suggested by Christopher Gore, the Federalist senator from Massachusetts who followed Mason in the debate. In personal and political influence Gore stood hardly second to Mason, and his opinions were likely to carry the utmost weight with the convention at Hartford. With this idea necessarily in his mind, Gore told the Senate,

"This (bill) is the first step on the odious ground of conscription—a plan, sir, which never will and never ought to be submitted to by this country while it retains one idea of civil freedom; a plan, sir, which if attempted will be resisted by many States, and at every hazard. In my judgment, sir, it should be resisted by all who have any regard to public liberty or the rights of the several States."

These denunciations were not confined to New England. Senator Goldsborough of Maryland, also a Federalist, affirmed that the sentiment of abhorrence for military duty was almost universal:

"Sir, you dare not—at least I hope you dare not—attempt a conscription to fill the ranks of your regular army. When the plan of the Secretary of War made its appearance, it was gratifying to find that it met with the abhorrence of almost every man in the nation; and the merit of the bill before you, if such a measure can be supposed to have merit at all, is that it is little else, as regards the militia, than a servile imitation of the secretary's plan."

Nevertheless, when Goldsborough took his seat the Senate passed the Militia Bill by a vote of nineteen to twelve—Anderson of Tennessee and Varnum of Massachusetts joining the Federalists in opposition. The regular Army Bill, which was in effect a bill to sacrifice the regular army, passed November 11, without a division. Both measures then went to the House and were committed, November 12, to the Committee of the Whole.

Ordinarily such a measure would have been referred to the Military Committee, but in this instance the Military Committee would have nothing to do with the Senate bill. Troup, the chairman, began the debate by denouncing it. The measure, he said, was inadequate to its object. "It is proposed to give you a militia force when you wanted, not a militia, but a regular force. . . . You have a deficiency of twenty-odd thousand to supply. How will you supply it? Assuredly the (Regular Army) bill from the Senate will not supply it. No, sir, the recruiting system has failed." On the nature of the force necessary for the next campaign Troup expressed his own opinion and that of his committee, as well as that of the Executive, in language as strong as he could use at such a time and place. "If, after what has happened, I could for a moment believe there could be any doubt or hesitation on this point, I would consider everything as lost; then indeed there would be an end of hope and of confidence." Yet on precisely this point Congress showed most doubt. Nothing could induce it to accept Troup's view of the necessity for providing a regular army. "The bill from the Senate," remonstrated Troup, "instead of proposing this, proposes to authorize the President to call upon the States for eighty thousand raw militia; and this is to be our reliance for the successful prosecution of the war! Take my word for it, sir, that if you do rely upon it (the military power of the enemy remaining undivided) defeat, disaster, and disgrace, must follow."

The House refused to support Troup or the President. Calhoun was first to yield to the general unwillingness, and declared himself disposed to accept the Senate bill as a matter of policy. Richard M. Johnson, though sympathizing with Troup, still preferred to accept the bill as the only alternative to nothing: "If it was rejected, they would have no dependence for defence but on six months' militia." On the other hand, Thomas K. Harris of Tennessee protested that if the British government had it in their power to control the deliberations of Congress, they could not devise the adoption of a measure of a military character better calculated to serve their purposes. The people he said, were in his part of the country prepared to make every sacrifice, and expected Congress, after the news from Ghent, to do its share; but Congress was about to adopt a measure of all others the best calculated to prolong the war.

While the friends of the government spoke in terms of open discouragement and almost despair of the strongest military measure which Congress would consent to consider, the Federalists made no concealment of their wishes and intentions. Daniel Webster used similar arguments to those of his friend Jeremiah Mason in the Senate, affirming that the same principle which authorized the enlistment of apprentices would equally authorize the freeing of slaves, and echoing pathetic threats of disunion. Other Federalists made no professions of sadness over the approaching dissolution of government. Artemas Ward of Massachusetts spoke December 14, the day before the Hartford Convention was to meet, and announced the course which events were to take:

"That the Treasury is empty I admit; that the ranks of the regular army are thin I believe to be true; and that our country must be defended in all events, I not only admit but affirm. But, sir, if all the parts of the United States are defended, of course the whole will be defended. If every State in the Union, with such aid as she can obtain from her neighbors, defends herself, our whole country will be defended. In my mind the resources of the States will be applied with more economy and with greater effect in defence of the country under the State governments than under the government of the United States."

Such avowals of the intent to throw aside Constitutional duties were not limited to members from New England. Morris S. Miller of New York made a vehement speech on the failure of national defence, and declared the inevitable result to be "that the States must and will take care of themselves; and they will preserve the resources of the States for the defence of the States." He also declared that conscription would be resisted, and echoed the well-remembered declamation of Edward Livingston against the Alien Bill in 1798, when the Republican orator prayed to God that the States would never acquiesce in obedience to the law.

"This house," replied Duval of Kentucky, "has heard discord and rebellion encouraged and avowed from more than one quarter." Indeed, from fully one fourth of its members the House heard little else. Under the shadow of the Hartford Convention the Federalist members talked with entire frankness. "This great fabric seems nodding and tottering to its fall," said Z. R. Shipherd of New York, December 9; "and Heaven only knows how long before the mighty ruin will take place." J. O. Moseley of Connecticut "meant no improper menace" by predicting to the House, "if they were determined to prosecute the war by a recourse to such measures as are provided in the present bill, that they would have no occasion for future committees of investigation into the causes of the failure of their arms." The latest committee of investigation had recently made a long report on the capture of Washington, carefully abstaining from expressing opinions of its own, or imputing blame to any one, and Moseley's remark involved a double sneer. None of these utterances was resented. Richard Stockton of New Jersey was allowed unanswered to denounce in measured terms the mild Militia Bill then under debate, from which the committee had already struck the term of two years' service by substituting one year; and Stockton concluded his fine-drawn arguments by equally studied menace:

"This bill also attacks the right and sovereignty of the State governments. Congress is about to usurp their undoubted rights—to take from them their militia. By this bill we proclaim that we will have their men, as many as we please, when and where and for as long a time as we see fit, and for any service we see proper. Do gentlemen of the majority seriously believe that the people and the State governments will submit to this claim? Do they believe that all the States of this Union will submit to this usurpation? Have you attended to the solemn and almost unanimous declaration of the legislature of Connecticut? Have you examined the cloud arising in the East? Do you perceive that it is black, alarming, portentous?"

The Resolution of the Connecticut legislature to which Stockton referred was adopted in October, and authorized the governor in case of the passage of the Militia Bill to convoke the General Assembly forthwith, to consider measures "to secure and preserve the rights and liberties of the people of this State, and the freedom, sovereignty, and independence of the same." Stockton's speech was made December 10, and "the cloud arising in the East," as he figured the Hartford Convention, was to take form December 15. The ·Republican speakers almost as earnestly used the full influence of these national fears to rouse the energies of the House. They neither denied nor disguised the helplessness of government. All admitted dread of approaching disaster. Perhaps C. J. Ingersoll was the only member who declared that the war had been successful, and that Americans need no longer blush to be Americans; but Ingersoll disliked the Militia Bill as cordially as it was disliked by Troup or Varnum, and voted for it only because "something must be done."

"When our army," said Samuel Hopkins of Kentucky, in closing the debate, "is composed of a mere handful of men, and our treasury empty so that it cannot provide for this gallant handful; when an enemy, powerful and active, is beating against our shores like the strong wave of the ocean; when everything is at stake— surely such is not the moment for parsimonious feelings in raising taxes, or for forced constructions to defeat the means for raising men."

Notwithstanding every effort of the war-leaders, the opposition steadily won control over the House. Daniel Webster during his entire lifetime remembered with satisfaction that he shared with Eppes the credit of overthrowing what he called Monroe's conscription. December 10, at Eppes's motion, the House voted by a majority of sixty-two to fifty-seven to reduce the term of service from two years to one. A motion made by Daniel Webster to reduce the term to six months was lost by only one voice, the vote standing seventy-eight to seventy-nine. The bill passed at last, December 14, by a vote of eighty-four to seventy-two, in a House where the true war majority was forty-six. When the Senate insisted on its provision of two years' service, Troup, in conference committee, compromised on eighteen months. Then the House, December 27, by a vote of seventy-three to sixty-four, rejected the report of its conference committee. The next day, December 28, in the Senate, Rufus King made an unpremeditated motion for indefinite postponement. Some members were absent; no debate occurred. The question was immediately put, and carried by a vote of fourteen to thirteen. The effect of this action was to destroy the bill.

With this failure the attempt to supply an army was abandoned, and Congress left the government to conduct the war in 1815, as in 1814, with thirty thousand regular troops and six months' militia. Monroe's effort to fill the ranks of the army ended in doubling the land-bounty; in authorizing the enlistment of minors, who had till then been enlisted without authorization; and in exempting from militia duty such persons as should furnish a recruit for the regular army. The prospect was remote that such inducements could do more than repair the waste of the actual force; but the government was unable to pay a larger number even if the force could be raised, and Monroe was obliged to prepare for the next campaign with such slight means of defence as remained to him. The last effort to induce the House to consider a serious method of raising troops was made February 6, and was referred to the Committee of the Whole, with tacit understanding that ordinary process of recruiting was not to be disturbed. According to the returns in the adjutant-general's office, the whole number of men—non-commissioned officers, privates, musicians, and artificers, present or absent, sick or well—in the regular army February 16, 1815, was thirty-two thousand three hundred and sixty men. Nothing showed a possibility of greatly increasing the force by the means prescribed by Congress.

The navy requiring little new legislation, readily obtained the little it asked. Almost the first Act of the session, approved Nov. 15, 1814, authorized the purchasing or building of twenty sixteen-guns sloops-of-war. Another Act of Feb. 7, 1815, created a Board of Commissioners for the navy to discharge all the ministerial duties of the secretary, under his superintendence.

This legislation, with the various tax-bills, comprised all that was accomplished by Congress between the months of September and February toward a vigorous prosecution of the war. For the navy the prospect of success in the coming year was sufficiently fair, and privateering promised to be more active than ever; but the army was threatened with many perils. The most serious of all dangers to the military service of the Union was supposed by Federalists to be the establishment of armies by the separate States. The attempt to establish such an army by Massachusetts in time of peace had been one of the causes which led to the Constitution of 1789; and at the close of 1814, when Massachusetts voted to raise an army of ten thousand men, the significance of the step was more clearly evident than in the time of the Confederation.

The State of Massachusetts might be supposed to act in a spirit of hostility to the Constitution; but no such motive actuated States outside of New England. If they followed the same course, they did so because the national government was believed to be incompetent to the general defence. Of all the States Massachusetts alone possessed considerable resources, and could command both credit and specie; yet the creation of a State army of ten thousand men overburdened her finances, and obliged her to claim her share of the national revenues. No other State could expect to support an army without immediate financial trouble. Yet Governor Tompkins of New York recommended to the legislature in September the establishment of a State army of twenty thousand men, and the legislature passed Acts for the purpose. The legislature of Pennsylvania took a similar measure into consideration. The legislature of Maryland passed an Act for raising five thousand State troops. Virginia decided also to create a State army, with two major-generals. South Carolina passed a law for raising a brigade of State troops, and appointed the officers. Kentucky took measures for raising a State army of ten thousand men.

The national government, unable to create an efficient army of its own, yielded to necessity, and looked already to the State armies as levies to be taken into the national service in case of need. The States, on their side, unable to bear the expense of separate armies, expected to be relieved of the burden by the national government. Yet for the moment the States, however deficient their means might be, seemed better able than the general government not only to raise men but to support them. In January, 1815, the financial resources of the government were exhausted, so that the Treasury could not meet the drafts drawn by Major-General Jackson and the pressing demands of the paymaster at New Orleans. The Secretary of War was obliged to go from bank to bank of Washington and Georgetown asking, as a personal favor, loans of their bank-notes already depreciated about fifty per cent. So desperate, according to Monroe's account, was the situation that his success depended on adding his own guaranty to that of the government. At no time of his life were Monroe's means sufficient to supply his private needs, and nothing could express so strongly his sense of national bankruptcy as the assertion that his credit was required to support that of the United States.

The State armies were the natural result of such a situation. Congress could not resist the movement, and passed an Act, approved Jan. 27, 1815, authorizing the President to receive into the national service a certain proportion of the State troops, not exceeding forty thousand men in the aggregate. Little was said in debate on the bearings of the Act, which seemed to concede the demand of Massachusetts that the States should be allowed to raise troops at the expense of the United States. The Hartford Convention had then met, deliberated, and adjourned. Its report had been published, and among its demands was one that "these States might be allowed to assume their own defence." The Federalists considered the Act of Jan. 27, 1815, as a "full and ample" concession of the demand. Senator Gore wrote to Governor Strong, January 22, while the measure was before the President, commenting on the financial and military expedients of Dallas and Monroe:

"These appear to me the spasms of a dying government. . . . The bill authorizing the raising of State troops by the States, according to the plan sent you some time since, has passed both Houses. Thus one part of the recommendations of the Hartford Convention seems to be adopted. The other—that to authorize the States to receive the taxes—will probably be more difficult to be attained. The accession to this seems not to accord with Mr. Monroe's intimation in your letter, or rather in his letter to you. Indeed, if they have fears of the State governments, one can hardly account for this government's authorizing the States to raise and keep in pay, at the expense of the United States, troops which may be used for purposes hostile to, or not conformable with, the views of the paymaster."

The accession to the principle of State armies which surprised Gore could be explained only by the government's consciousness of helplessness. Gore was somewhat careful to express no opinion of the probable consequences, but other Federalists spoke with entire candor. Timothy Pickering expected a division of the Union. Less extreme partisans looked only to a dissolution of government. A year afterward, in the calmer light of peace and union, Joseph Hopkinson, a very distinguished Federalist of Philadelphia, not deluded like the New Englanders by local pride or prejudice, declared publicly in Congress the common conviction of his party on the probable consequences of another year of war:

"The federal government was at the last gasp of existence. But six months longer and it was no more. . . . The general government would have dissolved into its original elements; its powers would have returned to the States from which they were derived; and they doubtless would have been fully competent to their defence against any enemy. Does not everybody remember that all the great States, and I believe the small ones too, were preparing for this state of things, and organizing their own means for their own defence?"

Calhoun contradicted Hopkinson and denied his assertions; but on that subject Hopkinson was at least an equal authority. Calhoun knew well his own State, but he knew little of New England; and he had yet to learn, perhaps, to his own surprise, how easily a section of the Union could be wrought to treason.

CHAPTER XXIV
THE HARTFORD CONVENTION

The Massachusetts legislature issued, October 17, its invitation to the New England States for a conference, and on the same day the newspapers published the despatches from Ghent, to August 20, containing British conditions of peace—which required, among greater sacrifices, a cession of Massachusetts territory, and an abandonment of fisheries and fishing rights conceded with American independence. Two counties of the State beyond the Penobscot were then in British military possession, and a third, Nantucket, was a British naval station. Yet even under these circumstances the British demands did not shock the Federalist leaders. Governor Strong, after reading the Ghent documents October 17, wrote to Pickering at Washington,

"If Great Britain had discovered a haughty or grasping spirit, it might naturally have excited irritation; but I am persuaded that in the present case there is not a member of Congress who, if he was a member of Parliament, would have thought that more moderate terms ought in the first instance to have been offered."

The argument seemed to prove only that members of Congress could also be haughty and grasping; but Governor Strong thought the British demands reasonable, and began at once to sound his friends in regard to the proposed concessions. The following day he wrote that the Essex people expected to lose the fisheries, but were ready to give up a portion of Maine to retain them.

Pickering wrote in reply, acquiescing in the proposed barter of territory for fisheries, and also in the more extravagant British demands for the Indians and the Lakes. "I was gratified," said Pickering, "to find my own sentiments corresponding with yours." The leading Federalists united with Pickering and Strong in blaming the American negotiators and the government for rejecting the British offers. The same view was taken by the chief Federalist newspaper of the State, the Boston *Centinel*.

Thus, in the November election, a few weeks later, two issues were impressed on the people of New England. In regard to neither issue did the Federalist leaders attempt concealment. The people were invited, as far as the press of both parties could decide the points of dispute, to express their opinion—first, whether the British conditions of peace should have been taken into consideration; second, whether the States should be represented at the Hartford Convention. The popular response was emphatic. Everywhere in New England the Republican candidates were defeated; and the Federalists encouraged by the result—believing the Hartford Convention to be the most popular action taken by Massachusetts since the State adopted the Federal Constitution—prepared to support measures, looking to the restoration of peace and to the establishment of a new Federal compact comprising either the whole or a portion of the actual Union.

However varied the wishes of the majority might be, they agreed in requiring a radical change in the organic law. This intention was their chief claim to popularity. The Boston *Centinel*, announcing November 9 the adhesion of Connecticut and Rhode Island to the Hartford Convention, placed over the announcement the head-line, "Second and third Pillars of a new Federal Edifice reared." During November and December, almost every day, the newspapers discussed the question what the convention should do; and the chief divergence of opinion seemed to regard rather the immediate than the ultimate resort to forcible means of stopping the war. The extremists, represented in the press by John Lowell, asked for immediate action.

"Throwing off all connection with this wasteful war"—wrote "A New England Man" in the *Centinel* of December 17—"making peace with our enemy and opening once more our commerce with the world," would be a wise and manly course. The occasion demands it of us, and the people at large are ready to meet it."

Apparently Lowell was right. The people showed no sign of unwillingness to meet any decision that might be recommended by the convention. As the moment approached, the country waited with increasing anxiety for the result. The Republican press—the *National Intelligencer* as well as the Boston *Patriot*—at first ridiculed the convention, then grew irritable, and at last betrayed signs of despair. On both sides threats were openly made and openly defied; but in Massachusetts the United States government had not five hundred effective troops, and if the convention chose to recommend that the State should declare itself neutral and open its ports, no one pretended that any national power existed in Massachusetts capable of preventing the legislature from carrying the recommendation into effect if it pleased.

From immediate extravagance Massachusetts was saved by the leaders who, knowing the popular excitement, feared lest the convention should be carried too fast into disorder, and for that reason selected representatives who could be trusted to resist emotion. When George Cabot was chosen as the head of the State delegation, the character of the body was fixed. The selection of Cabot did not please the advocates of action. Pickering wrote to Lowell suggesting doubts whether Cabot was the fittest choice. Lowell replied that he shared these doubts, and that in consequence he had been led to oppose the convention altogether, because it would not withdraw the State resources from the general government. Cabot, he said, was "most reluctantly dragged in like a conscript to the duty of a delegate;" he had always been despondent as to the course of public affairs, and felt no confidence in the possibility of awakening the people to their true disease—which was not the war or the Union, but democracy. Lowell did not know "a single bold and ardent man" among the Massachusetts or Connecticut delegates. In the *Centinel* of December 7 he described Cabot's tendencies in language evidently intended as a warning to Cabot himself:

"There are men who know that our troubles are not the offspring of this war alone, and will not die with it. But they despair of relief, and think resistance unavailing. They consider the people in their very nature democratic, and that nothing but the severity of their sufferings has driven them from those men and that system out of which have grown all our evils; that should they be restored to that state of prosperity which they once enjoyed, the same passions and opinions would diffuse themselves through the country, and the same course of conduct be again followed out."

Cabot shocked Pickering by expressing all his favorite political views in one brief question: "Why can't you and I let the world ruin itself its own way?"

Such a turn of mind was commonly the mark of a sceptical spirit, which doubted whether the world at best was worth the trouble of saving; and against this inert and indifferent view of human affairs New England offered a constant protest. Yet the Massachusetts delegation to Hartford was in sympathy with Cabot, while the Massachusetts legislature seemed to sympathize with Pickering. William Prescott, another member of the delegation, was chiefly remarkable for prudence and caution; Nathan Dane bore the same stamp; Harrison Gray Otis took character and color from his surroundings. The Connecticut delegation— James Hillhouse, Chauncey Goodrich, Roger M. Sherman, and others—were little likely to recommend "effectual measures." The convention consisted of men supposed to be inclined to resist popular pressure, and Cabot was probably serious in replying to a young friend who asked him what he was to do at Hartford: "We are going to keep you young hot-heads from getting into mischief."

In the Council Chamber of the State House at Hartford the delegates assembled, December 15, and gave instant evidence of their intention to discourage appeals to popular emotion. Their earliest steps decided their whole course. They chose George Cabot as their President, and they made their sessions secret. Under no circumstances could the convention have regarded itself as a popular body, for the delegates numbered only twenty-three persons, mostly cautious and elderly men, who detested democracy, but disliked enthusiasm almost as much. Two new members, appointed by popular meetings in New Hampshire, were next admitted; and toward the close of the sessions another member, representing the county of Windham in Vermont, was given a seat. Thus enlarged, the convention over which George Cabot presided numbered twenty-six members besides the secretary, Theodore Dwight.

Excess of caution helped to give the convention an air of conspiracy, which warned future conspirators to prefer acting, or appearing to act, in public. The secrecy of the Hartford conference was chiefly intended to secure freedom for the exchange of opinion, and also in some degree to prevent premature excitement and intrusion of popular feeling; but the secrecy created a belief that the debates would not bear publicity. Possibly much was said which verged on treasonable conspiracy; but the members were not men of a class likely to act beyond their instructions, and they adhered strictly to the practical task imposed on them. Some years afterward, Harrison Gray Otis, laboring to clear his political reputation from the stigma of membership, caused the official journal of the convention to be published; and the record, though revealing nothing of what was said, proved that nothing was formally done or proposed which contradicted the grave and restrained attitude maintained in its public expression.

On the first day of its meeting the convention appointed a committee to consider and report upon the business to be done. Chauncey Goodrich, Otis, and three other members formed this committee, which reported the next day the points in dispute between the States and the national government,—the militia power, conscription power, duty and means of defence, and matters of a like nature. After two days of discussion, the convention appointed another committee to frame a general project of measures, and again placed a Connecticut man— Nathaniel Smith—at its head, with Otis second. Still another committee was appointed, December 21, to prepare a report showing the reasons which guided the convention to its results; and of that committee Otis was chairman.

Clearly, Otis took the chief burden of business; and the result could scarcely fail to reflect in some degree the character of the man as well as of the body for which he was acting. Though ambitious of leading, Otis never led. John Lowell described his character, as it was understood in Boston, perhaps somewhat harshly, for Otis was no favorite with any class of men who held fixed opinions:

"Mr. Otis is naturally timid and frequently wavering—to-day bold, and to-morrow like a hare trembling at every breeze. It would seem by his language that he is prepared for the very boldest measures, but he receives anonymous letters every day or two threatening him with bodily harm. It seems the other party suspect his firmness. He is sincere in wishing thorough measures, but a thousand fears restrain him."

Otis was the probable author of the report, adopted December 24, recommending a course to the convention; and he was chairman of the larger committee to which that report was referred, and within which the final report—after a discussion lasting from December 24 to December 30—was framed. The discussions, both in committee and in convention, took much time and caused some difficulties; but nothing was ever known of the speeches made, or of the motions proposed, or of the amendments offered. All the reports were finally adopted by the convention; and all proposed business then having been finished, January 5 the convention adjourned *sine die*, authorizing Cabot to call another meeting at Boston if he should at any time see occasion for it.

The report, therefore, contained all the information which the convention intended to make public, and only from that document could the ultimate object of the members be inferred. It was immediately published in Connecticut, and at the meeting of the legislatures of Massachusetts and Connecticut in January it was laid before them for approval.

Considering the conservative temper of the delegates and their dislike for extreme measures, the report bore striking evidence of the popular passion which urged them forward. A few paragraphs in its first pages showed the spirit of its recommendations, and a few more showed the effect expected from them.

"It is a truth not to be concealed that a sentiment prevails to no inconsiderable extent . . . that the time for a change is at hand. . . . This opinion may ultimately prove to be correct; but as the evidence on which it rests is not yet conclusive, . . . some general considerations are submitted in the hope of reconciling all to a course of moderation and firmness which may . . . probably avert the evil, or at least insure consolation and success in the last resort. . . . A severance of the Union by one or more States against the will of the rest, and especially in time of war, can be justified only by absolute necessity."

Having thus discouraged precipitation, and argued in favor of firm and moderate measures as a probable means of preserving the Union, the report sketched the limits of the Union that was to be preserved. In a paragraph closely following the precedent of the Virginia Resolutions of 1798, the report asserted the right and duty of a State to "interpose its authority" for the protection of its citizens from infractions of the Constitution by the general government.

In the immediate crisis, this interposition should take the form of State laws to protect the militia or citizens from conscriptions and drafts; of an arrangement with the general government authorizing the States to assume their own defence, and to retain "a reasonable portion of the taxes collected within the said States" for the purpose; and of State armies to be held in readiness to serve for the defence of the New England States upon the request of the governor of the State invaded.

Such measures involved the establishment of a New England Confederation. The proposed union of the New England States for their own defence ignored any share to be taken by the general government in the defence of the national territory, and reduced that government to helplessness. What could be done by New England might be done by all; and the Federalists assumed that all would be obliged to do it.

If the general government should reject the request for the proposed arrangement, the ultimate emergency must arise; but with the measures to be then taken the convention would not interfere.

"It would be inexpedient for this convention to diminish the hope of a successful issue to such an application by recommending, upon supposition of a contrary event, ulterior proceedings. Nor is it indeed within their province. In a state of things so solemn and trying as may then arise, the legislatures of the States, or conventions of the whole people or delegates appointed by them for the express purpose in another convention, must act as such urgent circumstances may then require."

Besides the measures of urgency which must be immediately accepted by the national government, the convention recommended seven amendments to the Constitution; but on these no immediate action was required. The single issue forced on the government by the convention was that of surrendering to Massachusetts, Connecticut, and Rhode Island "a reasonable portion of the taxes collected within said States," and consenting to some arrangement "whereby the said States may, separately or in concert, be empowered to assume upon themselves the defence of their territory against the enemy." If the United States government should decline such an arrangement, the State legislatures were to send delegates to another convention to meet at Boston, June 15, "with such powers and instructions as the exigency of a crisis so momentous may require."

While the convention was preparing its report, from December 15 to January 5, the public waited with the utmost curiosity for the result. Major Jesup, famous at Chippawa and Lundy's Lane, was then recruiting for the Twenty-fifth United States Infantry at Hartford, and reported constantly to the President and War Department; but he could tell nothing of the convention that was not notorious. His letters were mere surmises or unmilitary comments on the treasonable intentions of the meeting. The Federalists knew no more than was known to the Republicans; but while they waited, they expressed fear only lest the convention should fall short of their wishes.

"I care nothing more for your actings and doings," wrote Gouverneur Morris to Pickering in Congress. "Your decree of conscriptions and your levy of contributions are alike indifferent to one whose eyes are fixed on a star in the East, which he believes to be the day-spring of freedom and glory. The traitors and madmen assembled at Hartford will, I believe, if not too tame and timid, be hailed hereafter as the patriots and sages of their day and generation."

As far as newspapers reflected public opinion, the people of New England held the same views as those expressed by Gouverneur Morris. The Boston *Centinel* contained, December 28, an address to the Hartford Convention announcing that the once venerable Constitution had expired: "At your hands, therefore, we demand deliverance. New England is unanimous. And we announce our irrevocable decree that the tyrannical oppression of those who at present usurp the powers of the Constitution is beyond endurance. And we will resist it." A meeting at Reading in Massachusetts, January 5, pledged itself to make no more returns for taxation and to pay no more national taxes until the State should have made its decision known.

A newspaper paragraph copied by the Federalist press advised the President to provide himself with a swifter horse than he had at Bladensburg if he meant to attempt to subjugate the Eastern States. "He must be able to escape at a greater rate than forty miles a day, or the swift vengeance of New England will overtake the wretched miscreant in his flight." Such expressions of the press on either side were of little authority, and deserved no great attention; but the language of responsible and representative bodies could not be denied weight. Opposition to the convention seemed cowed. Apparently the State was ready for immediate action; and the convention, in recommending a delay of six months, risked general disapproval.

While the public was in this temper, the convention adjourned and its report was given to the press. No one doubted that moderate men would approve it. The only persons whose approval was in question were "bold and ardent" partisans, like Gouverneur Morris, Pickering, and John Lowell, who wanted instant action. Chiefly for the sake of unanimity, these men gave in their adhesion. John Lowell hastened to publish his acquiescence in the convention's report. Pickering also approved it, although Pickering's approval was partly founded on the belief that the Union was already dissolved, and no further effort in that direction need be made.

"If the British succeed in their expedition against New Orleans," Pickering wrote to Lowell,—"and if they have tolerable leaders I see no reason to doubt of their success,—I shall consider the Union as severed. This consequence I deem inevitable. I do not expect to see a single representative in the next Congress from the Western States."

Governor Strong and Senator Gore also approved the convention's report. On receiving it at Washington, January 14, Gore wrote to Strong: "The result of the Hartford Convention is here, and affords satisfaction to most if not to all,— to some because they see not the point nor consequence of the recommendation as relates to taxes." The point and consequence of that recommendation were clear to Gore, and he approved of both.

If any leading Federalist disapproved the convention's report, he left no record of the disapproval. In such a case, at such a moment, silence was acquiescence. As far as could be inferred from any speeches made or letters written at the time, the Federalist party was unanimous in acquiescing in the recommendations of the Hartford Convention.

In Massachusetts and Connecticut the acquiescence was express. The legislature, convened at Boston, January 18, hastened to refer the convention's report to a joint committee, which reported, January 24, Resolutions that the legislature "do highly approve" the proceedings of the convention, and that State commissioners should immediately proceed to Washington to effect the arrangement proposed. By a very large majority of three to one, the legislature adopted the Resolutions, making the acts of the convention their own. Three commissioners were quickly appointed,—Harrison Gray Otis at their head,—and in the early days of February started for Washington.

Massachusetts was then more than ever convinced that it must peremptorily insist on taking its share of the national revenue into its own hands. Already the first step toward providing a State army had plunged the State treasury into financial difficulties, and measures for defence were stopped until new resources could be obtained. To the surprise of Governor Strong, the Massachusetts banks, restrained by their charters, applied to the State government the same rigorous refusal of credit which they had applied to the national government, and Strong found himself unable to obtain even the loan of one million dollars authorized by the legislature at its autumn session. The miscarriage cast a shade of ridicule on the character of the State which criticised so severely the failure of the national government to defend it, and found itself unable to take the first step toward defence without the aid of the national government, bankrupt and impotent though it was. Governor Strong sent to the legislature on the first day of its winter session a message that might have been sent by Madison to Congress. He reminded the legislature that it had, by a Resolution of Oct. 11, 1814, authorized a loan of a million dollars from the banks.

"At that time," continued Strong's message, "it was supposed that there would be no difficulty in procuring the requisite sums from that source, and the treasurer soon obtained loans to a considerable amount; but the directors of some of the banks declared themselves unable to lend, and others have expressed such reluctance as forbids an expectation that the whole amount can be obtained in that way during the continuance of the present cautious operations of the banks."

The treasurer had obtained $631,000, and with the expenditure of that sum the work of defence and the organization of the State army ceased. "The efforts of defensive preparation which were made in this State the last year," Governor Strong declared, "will, if continued at the expense of the Commonwealth, be fatal to our finances." The necessary consequence followed, that the State must take the national revenues. Accordingly the committee of both Houses, to which the subject was referred, reported an approval of suspending the organization of State troops "until in virtue of some arrangement to be made with the national government sufficient funds can be provided for their pay and support, without recourse to additional taxes." Under such circumstances the national government was little likely to surrender its resources, and every symptom showed that the State then meant to seize them.

The same committee formally approved the governor's course in declining to co-operate with the national government in expelling the enemy from Maine. The public excuse for the refusal was founded on the condition of the Treasury. In Federalist society the weightier motive was supposed to be the wish to leave on the national government the odium of failure to defend the State.

While Massachusetts sustained the Hartford Convention, and pressed to an issue the quarrel with the national government, Connecticut acted with equal zeal in the same sense. The governor, John Cotton Smith, was an old man, and neither his opinions nor his passions were extreme; but as far as concerned the Hartford Convention, his views differed little from those of Pickering and Lowell. He called a special session of the legislature for January 25, to act on the delegates' report; and his speech at the opening of the session would have been taken for irony, had his moderation of character not been known. "The temperate and magnanimous course proposed for our adoption cannot fail to allay the apprehensions which many have professed to entertain, and to enliven the hopes of all who cherish our national Union, and are disposed to place it on a solid and durable basis." The legislature without delay approved the measures recommended by the convention, and appointed delegates to accompany those sent from Massachusetts to effect the proposed arrangement with the government at Washington.

In later times the Hartford Convention was often and vigorously defended by writers whose works were friendly to the national government, and whose influence was popular. The wisdom, loyalty, and patriotism of George Cabot and his associates became the theme of authors whose authority was above dispute. Nearly always the defence rested on the argument that popular opinion went beyond the convention's report, and that the convention risked its credit by refusing to advise instant withdrawal from the Union. This view was apparently correct. The efforts of the moderate Federalists to praise the moderation of the report, and the labored protests of the extremists against the possible suspicion that they objected to its moderation, showed that the convention was then believed to have offered resistance to what Governor Smith stigmatized as "rash councils or precipitate measures." The tone of the press and the elections bore out the belief that a popular majority would have supported an abrupt and violent course.

The tone of the minority at the time showed a similar belief that Massachusetts favored disunion. During all the proceedings of the State legislatures and the convention, the loyal press and citizens never ceased to point out the dangerous, treasonable, and absurd results to be expected from the course pursued. In the Massachusetts Senate John Holmes of Maine attacked the convention and its doings in a speech that gave him wide reputation. Threats of civil war were freely uttered and defied. Among the least violent of Federalists was James Lloyd, recently United States senator from Massachusetts; and to him as a man of known patriotism John Randolph addressed a letter, Dec. 15, 1814, remonstrating against the Hartford Convention that day to meet. Lloyd replied in a letter also published, advising Randolph and the Virginians to coerce Madison into retirement, and to place Rufus King in the Presidency as the alternative to a fatal issue. The assertion of such an alternative showed how desperate the situation was believed by the moderate Federalists to be.

A long letter of a similar kind was written, Nov. 26, 1814, by Jonathan Mason to Wilson Cary Nicholas. The opinion of the men among whom Mason lived was expressly declared by Mason to the effect that "Great Britain will not treat with Mr. Madison. He must retire, or the country and the Union are at an end. . . . This is plain language, but in my soul I believe it true. We shall not be destroyed to-day or to-morrow, but it will come; and the end of these measures (of the Administration) will be disunion and disgrace."

In the Republican party the belief was universal that the Hartford Convention could lead only to a New England Confederation; and the belief was not confined to partisans. An anecdote that George Ticknor delighted in telling, illustrated the emotion that then agitated men far beyond the passing and fitful excitements of party politics. Ticknor, a young Federalist twenty-three years old, wished for letters of introduction to Virginia, and asked them from John Adams, then a man of eighty, whose support of the war made him an object of antipathy to the party he had led.

"When I visited him in Quincy to receive these letters," related Ticknor, "I had a remarkable interview with him, which at the time disturbed me not a little. . . . Soon after I was seated in Mr. Adams's parlor,—where was no one but himself and Mrs. Adams, who was knitting,—he began to talk of the condition of the country with great earnestness. I said not a word; Mrs. Adams was equally silent; but Mr. Adams, who was a man of strong and prompt passions, went on more and more vehemently. He was dressed in a single-breasted dark-green coat, buttoned tightly by very large white metal buttons over his somewhat rotund person. As he grew more and more excited in his discourse, he impatiently endeavored to thrust his hand into the breast of his coat. The buttons did not yield readily; at last he *forced* his hand in, saying, as he did so, in a very loud voice and most excited manner: 'Thank God! thank God! George Cabot's close-buttoned ambition has broke out at last: he wants to be President of New England, sir!' "

Whether George Cabot wanted it or not, he was in danger of becoming what John Adams predicted. He was far from being the first man who had unwillingly allowed himself to be drawn into a position from which escape was impossible. After going so far, neither leaders nor people could retreat. The next and easy step of sequestrating the direct and indirect taxes was one to which the State stood pledged in the event of a refusal by President Madison and Congress to surrender them. After such an act, the establishment of a New England Confederation could hardly be matter of choice.

If so considerable a mass of concurrent testimony did not prove the gravity of the occasion, as it was understood by the most intelligent and best-informed men of the time, ample evidence could be drawn from other sources. William Wirt described the painful anxiety of Madison as early as the month of October. Throughout Virginia the depression was akin to despair. John Randolph and Wilson Cary Nicholas gave expression to it in letters to prominent New Englanders; but Jefferson in private was still more pronounced in his fears. "The war, had it proceeded, would have upset our government," he wrote to Gallatin a year later, "and a new one, whenever tried, will do it." George Ticknor, after obtaining at Quincy his letter of introduction from John Adams to Jefferson, delivered it at Monticello at a time when the anxiety for the safety of New Orleans was acute. He found Jefferson convinced that the city must fall, and Jefferson expressed the expectation that the British would hold it indefinitely. Pickering felt the same conviction, and regarded the event as a dissolution of the Union.

The *Federal Republican* of Baltimore published, January 5, the day when the Hartford Convention adjourned, a letter from Washington announcing "an explosion at hand; that the President would be called on to resign; and there must be peace by that or a future Administration." The fall of New Orleans was to be the signal for a general demand that Madison should resign, and the Federalist press already prepared the ground by insisting that "Mr. Madison has scarcely raised his little finger to preserve New Orleans," and would finally determine to abandon the State of Louisiana. That Madison's authority could survive two such blows as the capture of Washington and the loss of Louisiana seemed improbable; but that he should resign was impossible, though the alternative was a collapse of government.

When the month of February arrived, government and people were waiting with keen apprehension for some new disaster, and the least probable solution was that England knowing the situation would consent to any tolerable peace. The *Federal Republican* of January 28, commenting on the expected bank veto, summed up the consequences, not unfairly from its point of view, in few words:

"It is impossible, as Mr. Giles said in his luminous and eloquent argument upon the measure (of a national bank), that the government can stand these reiterated shocks. . . . The interest upon the public debt remains unpaid, and there exists not the means, without making the most ruinous sacrifices to pay it. The government is in arrears to the army upward of nine million dollars; to the navy, about four millions. . . . The condition of our finances is known to the enemy; and is it possible he will be such a fool as to give us peace, after the mortal blow we aimed at him, when he knows we cannot pay the interest on the public debt, that we cannot pay our army or our navy, and when he finds us unable to defend any part of the country at which he strikes?"

CHAPTER XXV
NEW ORLEANS IN DANGER

A despatch from Lord Bathurst, marked "most secret," and dated July 30, 1814, informed Major-General Ross that, after finishing his operations in Chesapeake Bay, he was to sail with his whole force to Jamaica, where he would join an expedition then preparing in England to rendezvous at Cape Negril on the west coast of Jamaica about November 20. Lieutenant-General Lord Hill was to command the combined land-forces. These orders were given before the arrival of a long report from Vice-Admiral Cochrane concerning the military condition of the American territories on the Gulf of Mexico, which Cochrane considered such "that he had no doubt in his mind that three thousand British troops landed at Mobile, where they would be joined by all the Indians, with the disaffected French and Spaniards, would drive the Americans entirely out of Louisiana and the Floridas."

Circumstances induced the British government to defer sending Lord Hill, with a large force, to the Gulf; and Cochrane was informed by a despatch, dated August 10, that Major-General Ross was directed to carry out the Vice-Admiral's plans, which required fewer men. Orders were sent to Ross, of the same date, informing him that reinforcements amounting to more than twenty-one hundred rank-and-file were preparing to sail from England, which with the Fifth West India regiment and two hundred black pioneers from Jamaica would enable Ross to carry more than five thousand effective rank-and-file to the theatre of his operations.

Ross's detailed instructions were dated September 6. They began by recounting the force which was intended to act against New Orleans. The brigade from the Gironde which Ross took to the Chesapeake was estimated at about twenty-three hundred effectives, and a battalion which he had taken from Bermuda was supposed to have raised his rank-and-file to thirty-four hundred men. In addition to this force, a brigade under Major-General Keane, numbering twenty-one hundred and fifty men, was under orders for Jamaica, which with the black troops would enable Ross to proceed to his destination "with near six thousand men, exclusive of the marines and seamen. . . . About the same time you will be joined by the First West India regiment from Guadeloupe."

The objects which rendered the success of the expedition "extremely important" were two: first, the command of the mouth of the Mississippi, so as to deprive the back settlements of America of their communication with the sea; second, "to occupy some important and valuable possession by the restoration of which we may improve the conditions of peace, or which may entitle us to exact its cession as the price of peace."

The point of attack was left to the discretion of Cochrane and Ross. They might proceed directly against New Orleans, or move in the first instance into the back parts of Georgia and the country of the friendly Indians. In either case, the second object in view could not be attained against the will of the inhabitants. "With their favor and co-operation, on the other hand, we may expect to rescue the whole province of Louisiana from the United States."

"If therefore you shall find in the inhabitants a general and decided disposi-

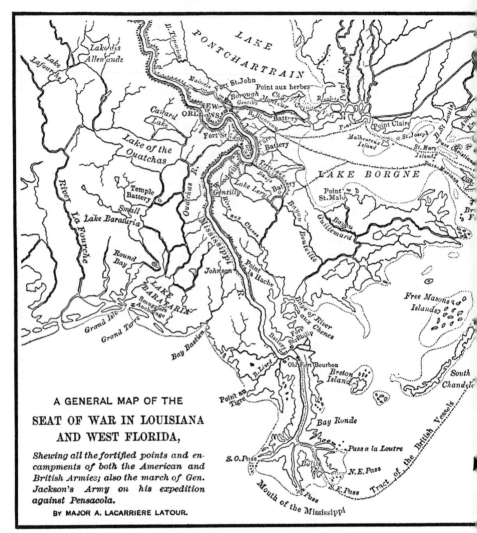

A GENERAL MAP OF THE

SEAT OF WAR IN LOUISIANA
AND WEST FLORIDA,

*Shewing all the fortified points and en-
campments of both the American and
British Armies; also the march of Gen.
Jackson's Army on his expedition
against Pensacola.*

BY MAJOR A. LACARRIERE LATOUR.

tion to withdraw from their recent connection with the United States, either
with the view of establishing themselves as an independent people or of returning under the dominion of the Spanish Crown, you will give them every
support in your power; you will furnish them with arms and clothing, and
assist in forming and disciplining the several levies, provided you are fully
satisfied of the loyalty of their intentions, which will be best evinced by their
committing themselves in some act of decided hostility against the United
States. . . . You will discountenance any proposition of the inhabitants to
place themselves under the dominion of Great Britain; and you will direct their
disposition toward returning under the protection of the Spanish Crown rather
than to the attempting to maintain what it will be much more difficult to secure

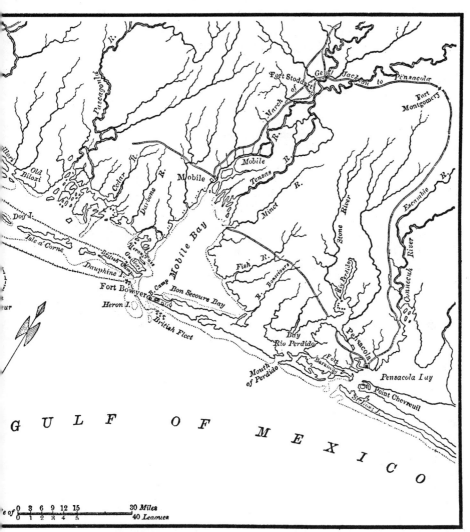

substantially,—their independence as a separate State; and you must give them clearly to understand that Great Britain cannot pledge herself to make the independence of Louisiana, or its restoration to the Spanish Crown, a *sine qua non* of peace with the United States."

After occupying New Orleans, Ross and Cochrane were to decide whether any further military operations could be carried on; and if nothing of material importance could be attempted, they were to send the disposable part of their force to Bermuda.

Ross's report of the capture of Washington reached Lord Bathurst September 27, and caused so much satisfaction that the British government decided to show its approval by placing another major-general, Lambert, with a brigade numbering twenty-two hundred rank-and-file, under Ross's command, to be used without restriction, either in the Middle or the Southern States. The Prince Regent highly applauded the ability with which Ross had conducted the capture of Washington, "an enterprise so creditable to his Majesty's arms, and so well calculated to humble the presumption of the American government, which contrary to the real interests, and as it is believed involved that country in an unnecessary and unjust war against his Majesty." Only in one respect did Bathurst hint a criticism on the course pursued by Ross. While informing him, September 29, that reinforcements were on their way which would place upward of ten thousand men under his command, to be used very much at his discretion, Bathurst added:

"You and your troops have gained great credit in the discipline you observed at Washington. It is no disparagement of your merit to say that it was prudent as well as merciful to show such forbearance. If, however, you should attack Baltimore, and could, consistent with that discipline *which it is essential for you not to relax,* make its inhabitants *feel* a little more the effects of your visit than what has been experienced at Washington, you would make that portion of the American people experience the consequences of the war who have most contributed to its existence."

When this despatch was written, Ross had made his attack on Baltimore, and had failed. The report of his failure and death was received by the War Department in London October 17, and Bathurst as soon as possible selected a new commander for the expedition to New Orleans. Orders, dated October 24, were sent to Major-Generals Sir Edward Pakenham and Gibbs to join Vice-Admiral Cochrane forthwith, detailing the force at their command. Pakenham was to follow the instructions already given to Ross, and was especially enjoined to conciliate the people of Louisiana:

"You will for that purpose cause the force under your command to observe the strictest discipline; to respect the lives and the property of all those who are inclined to a peaceable deportment, and by no means to excite the black population to rise against their masters."

The *Statira* received orders, October 28, to convey Major-Generals Pakenham and Gibbs to the rendezvous at Negril Bay in Jamaica, whither the large force intended for New Orleans was already moving from several distant quarters. The day for beginning the movement on New Orleans was already fixed for November 20, and Pakenham could at that season hardly expect to reach Jamaica in time to sail with his troops. Meanwhile the English press talked openly of the expedition and its object.

Military District No. 7, in which New Orleans and Mobile were situated, had not been neglected by the United States government. The regular force assigned by Secretary Armstrong for its defence consisted of five regiments of United States Infantry,—the Second, Third, Seventh, Thirty-ninth, and Forty-fourth, with three hundred and fifty artillerists,—an aggregate of two thousand three hundred and seventy-eight men. The provision was relatively liberal. District No. 5, on Chesapeake Bay, contained an aggregate of two thousand two hundred and eight regular troops; District No. 6, including North and

South Carolina and Georgia, was allotted two thousand two hundred and forty-four men. One half the regular army was employed in such garrison duty, and a greater number could not have been allotted consistently with retaining an army in the field. Indeed, the only means by which Armstrong could provide so strong a defence, aggregating nearly eight thousand men, for the Southern States, was by stripping Massachusetts. District No. 1, including Massachusetts and Maine, contained only six hundred and fifty-five regular troops; and District No. 2, including Rhode Island and Connecticut, contained only seven hundred and fourteen. Besides the regular troops, New Orleans enjoyed the protection of gunboats and one or two larger armed vessels. The city needed only an efficient commander to defy any ordinary attack.

Armstrong supplied a commander who might, as he believed, be safely considered efficient. In the month of May Andrew Jackson was appointed to the command of Military District No. 7, with headquarters at Mobile. At that moment Jackson, having finished the Creek war, was about to make the necessary arrangements for the future control of the Creek nation, and he did not take immediate command of his district. No occasion for haste existed. During the summer of 1814 no British force of consequence approached the Gulf of Mexico, or was likely to approach it until the frosts began. Jackson was detained in the centre of Alabama, undisturbed by fears for New Orleans, until the so-called Treaty of Capitulation of August 9 with the Creeks released him from further duties in that region. He left the Creek country August 11, with his regular troops, going by water down the Alabama River, and arriving at Mobile about August 15.

At the same moment government was brought to a stand-still at Washington by the appearance of General Ross's army in the Patuxent, and the raids on Washington and Baltimore. Between August 20 and September 25 the War Department could do little more than attend to its own pressing dangers. Jackson was left independent, substantially dictator over the Southwest. If New England carried out its intentions, and the government sank, as seemed probable, into helplessness, his dictatorship was likely to be permanent.

When Jackson arrived at Mobile, August 15, the defence of New Orleans was not in his mind. The people of Tennessee and Georgia had long been bent on the seizure of the Floridas, and Jackson had been one of the most ardent in favoring the step. The Creek war and the escape of the hostile Creeks to East Florida strengthened his conviction that the Spaniards must be expelled. He had begun the war with the idea of pushing his army directly through the Creek country to Pensacola, which he meant to hold. The instant he succeeded in destroying the military power of the Creeks, he began preparations for invading Florida. As early as July he wrote to the War Department suggesting an attack on Pensacola:

"Will you only say to me, Raise a few hundred militia (which can be quickly done), and with such a regular force as can be conveniently collected, make a descent upon Pensacola and reduce it?"

At the same time Jackson entered, July 12, into an angry correspondence with the Spanish governor of Pensacola, and requested him to deliver up the

Creek warriors who had taken refuge in East Florida,—a demand with which he knew that the Spaniard had no means of complying. August 10 he wrote to Armstrong announcing that he had given orders for the reoccupation of Mobile Point. "The United States in possession of Pensacola and Mobile, well defended, our whole coast and country in this quarter would be secure." A direct attack by the British on New Orleans had not occurred to his mind.

Although Jackson received no answer from Washington to his suggestion, he came to Mobile, August 15, determined to pursue his object; and his decision was confirmed by the eccentric conduct of Major Nicholls, an Irish officer, who was sent to Pensacola, July 23, with the sloops-of-war *Hermes* and *Carron*, with four officers, eleven non-commissioned officers, and ninety-seven privates of the Royal Marines, taking two howitzers, a field-piece, a thousand stand of arms, and three hundred suits of clothing for the Creek warriors. Nicholls landed his marines, seized Fort Barrancas, disembarked arms, and began to collect the fugitive Creeks, commonly known as Red Sticks, with a view to invading Louisiana, while he spread extravagant stories of his plans.

Had the British government sent Nicholls to Pensacola expressly to divert Jackson's attention from New Orleans, he could not have used his means more successfully for his purpose. Jackson at Mobile, some sixty miles away, learned within forty-eight hours what Nicholls was doing at Pensacola, and wrote instantly, August 27, to Governor Blount of Tennessee, calling out the whole quota of Tennessee militia, twenty-five hundred men, who were to march instantly to Mobile. "It is currently reported in Pensacola," he added, "that the Emperor of Russia has offered his Britannic Majesty fifty thousand of his best troops for the conquest of Louisiana, and that this territory will fall a prey to the enemy before the expiration of one month."

During the next three months Nicholls with a mere handful of men distracted Jackson's whole attention. From Pensacola, August 29, Nicholls issued a proclamation calling on the natives of Louisiana to assist him "in liberating from a faithless, imbecile government" their paternal soil. A few days afterward, September 3, a British sloop-of-war, the *Sophie*, appeared at Barataria, forty miles south of New Orleans. There for several years smugglers and pirates had established a station, to the scandal of society and with its connivance. Three Frenchmen, the brothers Laffite,—Jean, Pierre, and Dominique,—ruled over this community, and plundered impartially the commerce of England and Spain, while defying the laws of the United States and the power of the national government. The British sloop-of-war brought to Jean Laffite a letter from Major Nicholls asking him and his men, with their vessels, to enter into British service, under penalty of destruction of their establishment. Laffite, preferring to make terms with the United States, and knowing that the authorities at New Orleans were about to break up his establishments in any case, sent to Governor Claiborne the letters he received from Captain Lockyer of the *Sophie*, and offered his services to defend Barataria.

Nothing in these demonstrations suggested a direct attack on New Orleans. Nicholls constantly gave out that he meant to attack Mobile, and from there "push for New Orleans"; but his force was wholly inadequate, and his rank was much too low, to warrant the belief that he intended a serious campaign. Yet such noisy and insulting conduct was adapted to irritate a man of Jackson's temper, and to keep his attention fixed on Mobile and Pensacola. Nicholls even undertook to annoy Jackson in his headquarters.

On a bare sand-point at the entrance of Mobile Bay, General Wilkinson, on taking possession of Mobile in April, 1813, established a battery which he armed with Spanish cannon. The redoubt, which was called Fort Bowyer, could not hold against a land attack properly supported, and offered a temptation to the enemy; but in the absence of a land force competent to besiege it,

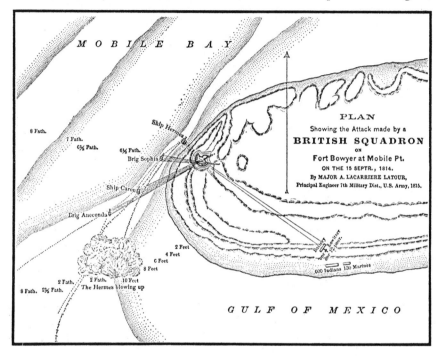

the fortification was useful to close the entrance of Mobile Bay against marauders. In Fort Bowyer Jackson placed one hundred and sixty men of the Second United States Infantry, commanded by Major William Lawrence. Twenty guns were mounted on the platforms, but according to the American account only two twenty-four pounders and six twelve-pounders were likely to prove serviceable.

The British force at Pensacola consisted chiefly of four sloops, commanded by Captain W. H. Percy,—the *Hermes,* twenty-two guns, the *Carron,* twenty, and the *Sophie* and *Childers* of eighteen guns each. The usual armament of such vessels consisted of thirty-two-pound carronades, with two long-nines or sixes. Apparently the British squadron threw thirty-four thirty-two-pound shot, and four nine or six pound balls at a broadside. Whether the armament was greater or smaller mattered little, for Captain Percy was unable to use with effect the batteries of either the *Carron* or the *Childers*. With much difficulty, owing to the shoals, he brought his squadron within range of Fort Bowyer, and with more gallantry than discretion prepared for the attack.

According to the British account, the land force at Percy's command consisted of sixty marines and one hundred and twenty Indians, with one five-and-a-half-inch howitzer. Such a force was insufficient to do more than intercept the garrison if it should be driven out of the fort. The brunt of the action fell on the ships, and experience did not warrant Percy in believing that his sloops, with their carronades, could silence a work like Fort Bowyer.

Nevertheless Percy gallantly made the attempt. At half-past four of the afternoon of September 15, he brought the *Hermes* close in, and opened fire within musket-shot of the fort. The *Sophie* came to anchor some distance astern, but within range. The *Carron* and the *Childers* anchored so far out that their carronades were useless, and apparently even the American twenty-four-pounders did not touch them. The *Hermes* and the *Sophie* alone sustained injury, but their experience was decisive. After an hour's action, the cable of the *Hermes* being cut, she became unmanageable, and at last grounded and was abandoned. Captain Percy set her on fire, and carried his crew, including the wounded, with much difficulty to his other vessels. The *Sophie* withdrew from fire, and the squadron returned at once to Pensacola.

Assuming that Captain Percy could use with effect only the twenty guns of the broadsides of the *Hermes* and *Sophie* against the twenty guns of the fort, the American gunnery was evidently superior to the British. The *Hermes* lost twenty-five men killed and twenty-four wounded,—a very severe loss in a crew which could not much have exceeded one hundred and fifty men. A better test of marksmanship was offered by the *Sophie*, which received comparatively little attention from the fort, but lost six killed and sixteen wounded. The whole American loss was reported as four killed and five wounded, under the combined fire of both ships at close range, the fort having no casemates, and parapets only on the front and flanks. Three guns were dismounted.

Greatly pleased by this success, Jackson issued a counter-proclamation to the people of Louisiana, somewhat in the style of that which Nicholls had issued three weeks before.

"The base, the perfidious British," it began, "have attempted to invade your country. They had the temerity to attack Fort Bowyer with their incongruous horde of Indians and negro assassins. . . . The proud, vain-glorious boaster Colonel Nicholls, when he addressed you, Louisianians and Kentuckians, had forgotten that you were the votaries of freedom. . . . I ask you, Louisianians, can we place any confidence in the honor of men who have courted an alliance with pirates and robbers? Have not these noble Britons, these honorable men, Colonel Nicholls and the honorable Captain W. H. Percy, the true representatives of their royal master, done this? Have they not made offers to the pirates of Barataria to join them and their holy cause? And have they not dared to insult you by calling on you to associate as brethren with them and this hellish banditti?"

With the exception of this proclamation and another of the same date to the free negroes of Louisiana, Jackson paid no attention to the defence of New Orleans, but left it entirely to Governor Claiborne. He disregarded a memorial from the citizens, dated September 18, urging his personal attention and presence. "My whole force would not satisfy the demands they make," he wrote to the War Department, October 10. "As soon as security is given to this section of my district, which is first indispensably necessary, I shall hasten to New Orleans," he wrote from Mobile, October 14. He entertained no doubt that at Mobile he stood between the British and their object. "Unless Pensacola were reduced," said his confidential biographer ten years afterward, "it was vain to think of defending the country. . . . The attack on Mobile Point was a confirmation of his previous conjectures as to the views of the enemy."

The Government at Washington became alarmed. While Jackson waited at Mobile for the arrival of General Coffee with his Tennesseeans to attack Pensacola, Monroe at Washington received warnings from Europe, Halifax, and Bermuda that the British force which had just laid Washington in ashes was but a division of a larger army on its way to attack New Orleans. He wrote to Jackson, September 25,—

"There is great cause to believe that the enemy have set on foot an expedition against Louisiana, through the Mobile, in the expectation that while so strong a pressure was made from Canada and in this quarter, whereby the force of the country and attention of the government would be much engaged, a favorable opportunity would be afforded them to take possession of the lower part of that State, and of all the country along the Mobile."

The President, he continued, had ordered five thousand additional troops from Tennessee to march to Jackson's aid, and had directed the governor of Georgia to hold twenty-five hundred more subject to Jackson's orders. He had also sent one hundred thousand dollars in Treasury notes to Governor Blount of Tennessee, to be applied to the necessary expenses of the campaign, and Jackson could draw on him for the necessary funds. The orders to the governor of Tennessee were sent the same day, September 25. A week later, October 3, Monroe wrote to Governor Shelby of Kentucky, requesting him to send twenty-five hundred men to Jackson. Again, October 10, Monroe wrote to Jackson, informing him that not less than twelve thousand five hundred men were already subject to his orders, from Kentucky, Tennessee, and Georgia:

"There is strong reason to presume, from intelligence just received from our ministers at Ghent, that a British force consisting of twelve or fifteen thousand men sailed from Ireland early in September for New Orleans and the Mobile, with intention to take possession of that city and of the country through which the great rivers of which the whole of the United States westward of the Alleghany Mountains so essentially depends."

When Monroe received a letter from Jackson, dated September 9, indicating his intention of attacking Pensacola, the secretary replied October 21, forbidding the step. "I hasten to communicate to you the directions of the President that you should at present take no measures which would involve this government in a contest with Spain." He reiterated the warning that British forces would probably be directed against Louisiana; but he did not order Jackson to New Orleans, nor did he notify him that arms would be sent there. Not until November 2 were orders given that four thousand stands of arms should be sent from Pittsburgh, and only November 11 and 15 were the arms shipped, not by steamer but by the ordinary flatboat. Even then the arms were in advance of the men. The governor of Tennessee could not appoint an earlier day than November 13 for mustering the new levies, and on that day three thousand men assembled at Nashville, while two thousand collected at Knoxville. Not till November 20 did the Nashville division start down the river, to arrive a month later at New Orleans.

Jackson quietly waited at Mobile for the twenty-five hundred men he had summoned from Tennessee by his letter of August 27. Two months were consumed in this manner. The Tennessee brigade, under command of General Coffee, marched promptly, and passing through the Indian country arrived October 25 at Mobile. Coffee brought with him somewhat more than the number of men required by the call. His force was about twenty-eight hundred. Jackson held at Mobile the Second, Third, Thirty-ninth, and Forty-fourth United States Infantry, besides some Mississippi troops and Choctaw Indians. With the Tennesseeans he could dispose of more than four thousand troops.

Notwithstanding Monroe's warning letter of September 25, Jackson still paid no immediate attention to New Orleans. October 28 he wrote to Monroe, acknowledging a letter from him of September 27, and announcing that he was then organizing an attack of Pensacola. Having no authority for the act, and aware that the government was anxious about New Orleans, he added: "I hope in a few weeks to place this quarter in perfect security, and to be able to move to New Orleans with General Coffee's mounted men." October 31, Jackson wrote, apparently for the first time, that he needed arms, and that half the arms of the militia were not fit for use.

Taking four thousand one hundred men, without trains, Jackson marched November 3 against Pensacola, which he occupied, November 7, with little resistance, although "Spanish treachery," he said, "kept us out of possession of the fort until nearly twelve o'clock at night." The next morning the British blew up Fort Barrancas, six miles below, where they had established themselves, and Colonel Nicholls sailed away no farther than the Appalachicola River, leaving Jackson to do what he pleased with Pensacola, a position of no value to either party.

Even Armstrong, who favored Jackson against what he thought the ill-will of Madison and Monroe, afterward condemned the movement against Pensacola. "The general's attack and capture of the town on the 7th of November, 1814, was to say the least of it decidedly ill-judged, involving at once an offense to a neutral power, and a probable misapplication of both time and force as regarded the defence of New Orleans." Jackson remained only two days at the place, and then returned to Mobile, where he arrived November 11 and remained until November 22, as though still in doubt. He detached Major Blue of the Thirty-ninth United States Infantry, with a thousand mounted men, to the Appalachicola to break up the depot established there for supplying assistance to the Red Stick Indians. Nothing indicated that he felt anxiety for the safety of New

Orleans, although the British expedition, comprising some fifty vessels, was then at Jamaica, and November 26 actually sailed for the Mississippi.

Jackson's conduct greatly alarmed the President and the Secretary of War. When the despatches arrived at Washington announcing what was taking place at Mobile and Pensacola, Monroe hastened to order General Gaines to Mobile. He wrote to Jackson, December 7—

"General Gaines is ordered to join you and act under you in the defence of New Orleans and of the district under your command. Full confidence is entertained that this appointment of an officer of his merit will afford to you a very acceptable aid in the discharge of your highly important duties. . . . Much anxiety is felt lest you should remain too long on the Mobile. The city (New Orleans), it is presumed, is the principal object of the enemy, and it cannot be defended on either of the passes by which it may be approached—one by the river Mississippi itself, another by the Fourche, the third by Lake Pontchartrain—without occupying the ground bearing on these passes."

Three days afterward, December 10, Monroe wrote again in stronger terms:

"It is hoped that you will have long since taken a suitable position on the river to afford complete protection to that city. Mobile is a comparatively trifling object with the British government. Your presence at such a point on the river with the main body of your troops will be of vital importance."

Jackson left Mobile November 22, four days before the British expedition under Sir Edward Pakenham sailed from Jamaica. Both Jackson and Pakenham were moving to New Orleans at the same time. Pakenham brought with him an immense fleet and a large army. Jackson, instead of taking, as Monroe hoped, "the main body" of his troops, left at Mobile the main body, consisting of the Second, Third, and Thirty-ninth regiments, about a thousand or twelve hundred men.

According to his friend's biography, probably founded on his own information, Jackson's "principal fears at present were that Mobile might fall, the left bank of the Mississippi be gained, all communication with the Western States cut off, and New Orleans be thus unavoidably reduced." That the British should advance against the Mississippi by way of Mobile was improbable, as Monroe pointed out; but they could have taken no course which better suited the resources of Jackson. A march of near two hundred miles, through a barren and wooded country, with Jackson's whole force concentrated in their front, was an undertaking that promised little success.

Leaving at Mobile three regular regiments, Jackson ordered the Forty-fourth regiment to New Orleans, and directed Coffee with two thousand of his mounted brigade to march to Baton Rouge. He was himself ill and suffering, and made no excessive haste. "I leave this (sic) for New Orleans on the 22nd instant," he wrote to Monroe November 20, "and if my health permits, shall reach there in twelve days. I travel by land, to have a view of the points at which the enemy might effect a landing." Starting from Mobile November 22, he arrived at New Orleans, about one hundred and twenty-five miles, only December 2. His troops were then much scattered. The main body was at Mobile. The Forty-fourth regiment was in march from Mobile to New Orleans, where the Seventh regiment was already stationed. A thousand volunteer horsemen, part of Coffee's brigade, under Major Blue of the Thirty-ninth Infantry, were scouring the Escambia, Yellow Water, and other remote Florida recesses. The remainder of Coffee's brigade was at Baton Rouge December 4, greatly reduced by various causes, and numbering only twelve hundred men. A few Mississippi dragoons were near them. A division of Tennessee militia, twenty-five hundred strong, under General Carroll, had started from Nashville November 20, and might be expected at New Orleans about December 20. A division of Kentucky militia, also twenty-five hundred strong, was on its way, and might arrive about the new year. Meanwhile the British expedition was sailing, with much deliberation, past the shores of Cuba, toward Florida.

At New Orleans nothing had yet been done for defence; but inaction was not the worst. Jackson found the people despondent and distrustful. The legislature showed incompetence and, as Jackson believed, indifference. The whole population of Louisiana was but small, containing certainly not more than twenty thousand persons including slaves. The State government supplied one thousand militia under the general requisition of the President. The city raised a battalion of volunteers nearly three hundred strong, a rifle company numbering sixty-two men when in the field, and a battalion of free mulattoes, chiefly refugees from St. Domingo, which produced two hundred and ten men—in all, between five and six hundred troops. Jackson immediately reviewed the companies, December 2, and could expect no further aid from these sources. No arms were in store, even if men could be found, and none of the necessary supplies of an army had been provided.

Jackson's first act after arriving at New Orleans showed no consciousness of danger. Armstrong, criticising his measures, afterward said: "Had the general been better acquainted with military history, he would not have suffered a single day of the twenty he had for preparation to have passed without forming one or more intrenched camps for the protection of the city." Instead of doing this, Jackson did what had been done by Armstrong and Winder at Washington in August. Having arrived in the city December 2, he started two days afterward to inspect Fort St. Philip on the river sixty miles below. He returned to New Orleans December 11, believing that the British would approach by the river, and prepared works to arrest their advance. He then rode out to Chef Menteur and Lake Pontchartrain on the north, which he thought the next probable point of attack. He was still absent, December 15, examining the situation of different works northward of the city, when the British expedition struck its first blow.

Six American gunboats, the whole force on the lakes, watched the entrance of Lake Borgne through which the British must pass if they attacked New Orleans by way of the lakes. They were stationed for observation rather than for resistance—although for observation a few fishermen's boats would have been more useful. The British expedition, upward of fifty sail, made land December 10, and was seen by the gunboats, which retired within the lake. The British land-forces were transferred from the heavy ships into the lighter vessels, and under convoy of sloops-of-war entered Lake Borgne December 13.

The boats of the squadron, carrying about a thousand seamen and marines, left the ships during the night of December 12 in search of the American gunboats, which tried to escape, but were becalmed and obliged by the tide to anchor. After a tedious row of thirty-six hours the British boats overtook the gunboat flotilla December 14, and after a sharp struggle succeeded in capturing the whole, with a loss of seventeen men killed and seventy-seven wounded. The American crews numbered one hundred and eighty-two men, and lost six killed and thirty-five wounded.

News of the capture of the gunboats, which occurred at noon December 14 about forty miles to the eastward of New Orleans, arrived on the evening of December 15, and produced the utmost consternation. Jackson hurried back to the city, where his presence was no longer a matter of choice but necessity. Instantly on hearing the news he sent expresses to Coffee at Baton Rouge, and to Carroll and Thomas, wherever they might be found on the river, urging them to hasten with all possible speed to New Orleans. He issued a proclamation to the people of the city, in which he threatened them with punishment if they were not unanimous, and at the same time he recommended the legislature to suspend the writ of habeas corpus. Finding the legislature hesitant, Jackson declared martial law by proclamation the same day, December 16, and assumed dictatorial powers.

Feverish activity followed. General Coffee above Baton Rouge received Jackson's summons on the evening of December 17, and marched the next morning with twelve hundred and fifty men. In two days he made one hundred and twenty miles, camping on the night of December 19 within fifteen miles of New Orleans, with eight hundred men. Carroll, with the Tennessee brigade which left Nashville November 27, arrived at New Orleans December 21, and a squadron of mounted Mississippi volunteers hurried down. The British also lost no time. Their advance disembarked on the Isle aux Poix in Lake Borgne on the night of December 14, and during the following week all the boats and seamen of the fleet were occupied in transporting seven thousand men, with their equipment, thirty miles from the fleet to the island. During the night of December 18 two British officers reconnoitred the head of Lake Borgne. At the mouth of Bayou Bienvenu, not fifteen miles from New Orleans, was a fishermen's village. The fishermen were Spaniards, with no love for the United States, and ready to accept British pay. They received the two British officers, and conveyed them in a canoe up the bayou to the Villeré plantation on the bank of the Mississippi only six miles from New Orleans. There, at their leisure, Lieutenant Peddie of the quartermaster's department and Captain Spencer of the *Carron* selected the line of advance for the British army, and returned, unmolested and unseen, through the bayou to the lake and the Isle aux Poix.

Only December 21, two days after the British reconnaissance, was an American picket of eight men and a sergeant placed at the fishermen's village, where they remained thirty-six hours without learning that British officers had been on the spot, or that the fishermen were all away, acting as pilots for the approaching British boats. Meanwhile the troops at Isle aux Poix were ready

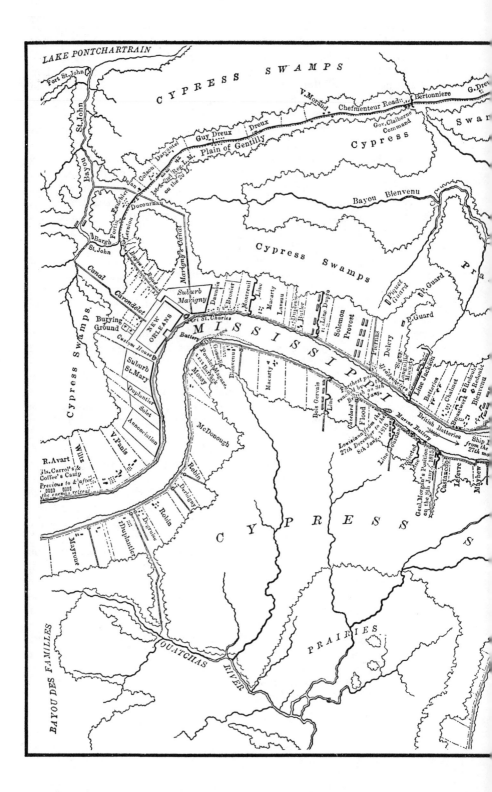

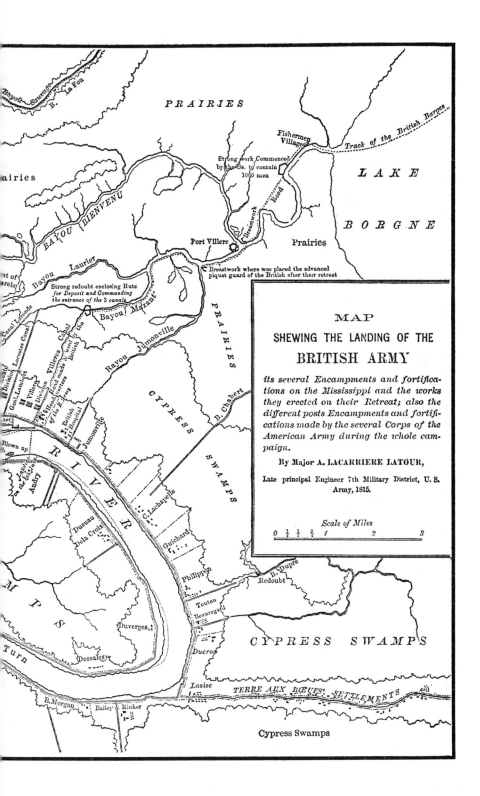

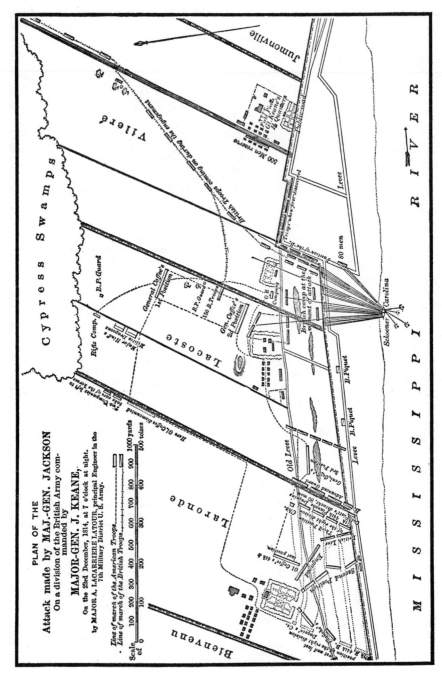

PLAN OF THE
Attack made by MAJ.-GEN. JACKSON
On a division of the British Army commanded by
MAJOR-GEN. J. KEANE,
On the 23rd December, 1814, at 7 o'clock at night.
by MAJOR A. LACARRIERE LATOUR, principal Engineer in the
7th Military District U. S. Army.

Line of march of the American Troops.
Line of march of the British Troops.

Scale of 0 100 200 300 400 500 600 700 800 900 1000 yards
                100   200   300   400 500 toises

to move almost as soon as Lieutenant Peddie could return to show them the way. At ten o'clock on the morning of December 22 the light brigade—sixteen hundred and eighty-eight rank-and-file, under Colonel Thornton, who had led the advance at Bladensburg—embarked in boats, and after a day on the lake arrived the next morning, December 23, at daylight, without giving alarm, at the fishermen's village, where they surprised and captured the picket, and then passing up the bayou five miles, landed at a point about three miles from the Mississippi River. No attempt at concealment was made. The troops were formed in column, and found no obstacles to their march except the soft ground and the ditches. Through reeds and cypress swamp they made their way about three miles, when their advance suddenly entered open fields skirted by an orange-grove, with the broad Mississippi beyond. They were on the Villeré plantation; and they surprised and captured Major Villeré and his militia company, in his own house at noon-day, after a march of three miles with sixteen hundred men, from a point which had been recognized by Jackson as one of two or three necessary avenues of approach.

The record of American generalship offered many examples of misfortune, but none so complete as this. Neither Hull nor Harrison, neither Winder nor Samuel Smith, had allowed a large British army, heralded long in advance, to arrive within seven miles unseen and unsuspected, and without so much as an earthwork, a man, or a gun between them and their object. The disaster was unprecedented, and could be repaired only by desperate measures.

CHAPTER XXVI

THE ARTILLERY BATTLE

The defence of New Orleans resembled the defence of Washington until the moment when in each case the British expedition came within sight. Jackson was even slower than Winder to see the point of danger or to concentrate his forces. At Washington, Winder took command July 1, and the British expedition arrived August 16; at Mobile, Jackson took command August 16, and the British expedition arrived December 14. In neither case was the interval seriously employed for defence. So much was Jackson misled that he collected no troops, and made no inquiry as to the military means at his disposal at New Orleans. Had he gone there September 1, he would have been able to supply them. During the summer, while yet among the Creeks, he was said to have made requisition for a quantity of war material to be sent to New Orleans; but he certainly showed no interest in its shipment or the causes for its delay in arrival. The arms should have reached New Orleans in October, when he would have had ample time to correct any failure or want of supply. He could have used in case of necessity, the steamboat *Enterprise,* which was then regularly plying on the Mississippi, and was not the only steamboat on those waters. If New Orleans was deficient in many articles of military necessity, the fault was not wholly in the War Department.

A similar criticism applied to the political situation at New Orleans. Governor Claiborne wanted authority to control the factions in his legislature, and the legislature wanted an impulse sufficiently energetic to overcome its inertia. Probably Jackson's presence would at any time have given authority to Claiborne and energy to the entire State government. From the moment of his actual arrival, difficulties of this kind seemed to cease. "It is hardly possible," said the military historian of the campaign, "to form an idea of the change which his arrival produced on the minds of the people."

When the British expedition was once known to have appeared at the entrance of Lake Borgne, Jackson's task was perhaps simpler than Winder's, for Winder might doubt whether the British meant to attack Washington, and in fact General Ross took the decision only at the last moment; but no one could doubt that New Orleans was the object of Pakenham's expedition. Jackson had only to choose his positions and collect his resources. These were small; but on the other hand the British were opposed by natural difficulties much greater at New Orleans than at Washington. Even their greater numbers were a disadvantage when they were obliged to move in widely separated detachments, in open boats, from a point far distant from their column's head, and toward a point easily fortified.

If until the moment of the enemy's appearance Jackson showed no more military capacity than was shown by Winder, his conduct thenceforward offered a contrast the more striking because it proved how Washington might have been saved. Winder lost his head when he saw an enemy. Jackson needed to see his enemy in order to act; he thought rightly only at the moment when he struck. At noon, December 23, New Orleans was in greater danger than Washington on the afternoon of August 23, when the British advanced from the

Patuxent. Had Colonel Thornton followed his impulses and marched directly on the city, he must have reached it before a gun could have been fired by the Americans; his own muskets would have given the first news of his arrival. Major-General Keane, his commanding officer, preferred caution, and his delay gave a few hours' time for Jackson to show his qualities.

News that a British column had reached Villeré plantation was brought to Jackson at headquarters in New Orleans, at about half-past one o'clock, much as the news was brought to Winder, August 24, that the British were marching on Bladensburg. The distances were about the same. Winder and Jackson both allowed the enemy to approach within seven miles before anything had been done for defence. In one respect Jackson was more unfortunate than Winder, for his troops were not ready to march; they were not even collected. Jackson sent orders to the different corps, but several hours passed before the men could be brought down and posted between the city and the British.

Fortunately Major Latour, chief-engineer in Military District No. 7, had been sent that morning to examine the approaches from Lake Borgne, and as he rode down the road at noon he met persons flying toward town with news that the British had penetrated through the canal to Villeré's house. Latour was a trained French engineer, whose services were extremely valuable, not only during the campaign but afterward; for he subsequently wrote a "History of the War in West Florida and Louisiana," which was far the best military work published in the United States till long after that time, and furnished the only accurate maps and documents of the campaign at New Orleans. On the morning of December 23 Latour approached within rifle-shot of the British force, and judged their number accurately as sixteen or eighteen hundred men. Such exact information, which could not have been gained from any ordinary scout, was invaluable. Latour hastened to headquarters, and reported at two o'clock to Jackson the position and numbers of the enemy. The general, on that information, decided to attack.

For such a purpose Jackson's resources were ample. Four miles above the city his Tennessee militia were camped—Carroll's brigade numbering probably about two thousand effectives, and the remnants of Coffee's mounted brigade numbering some seven hundred men, besides three regiments of city militia. The Seventh United States Infantry produced four hundred and sixty-five men in the ranks; the Forty-fourth counted three hundred and thirty-one; while a detachment of artillerists, twenty-two in number, with two six-pound field-pieces, added greatly to the numerical strength of the Infantry. Against Thornton's force, numbering one thousand six hundred and eighty-eight rank-and-file, or about nineteen hundred men all told, Jackson could oppose about five thousand Infantry with two field-pieces.

Besides these land forces Jackson was provided with another resource. In the river at New Orleans lay a war-schooner, the *Carolina*, rated at fourteen guns, armed with one long twelve-pounder and six twelve-pound carronades on a broadside. A sixteen-gun sloop-of-war, the *Louisiana,* was also at New Orleans, but not ready for immediate use. The *Carolina* could be brought instantly into action, and her broadside of seven twelve-pounders, added to the field-battery of two six-pounders, gave Jackson immense advantage over the British, who had no artillery except two three-pounders and rockets, and whose lines must be enfiladed by the *Carolina's* fire.

Jackson, aware of his superiority, expected with reason to destroy the British detachment. He did not even think more than half his force necessary for the purpose, but detached the whole of Carroll's brigade and the three regiments of city militia—fully twenty-five hundred men—to guard the town against an apprehended attack from the north. Without giving the reasons which led him to believe that the British could approach on that side without ample warning, his report said—

"Apprehending a double attack by the way of Chef Menteur, I left General Carroll's force and the militia of the city posted on the Gentilly road, and at five o'clock P. M. marched to meet the enemy, whom I was resolved to attack in his first position, with Major Hind's dragoons, General Coffee's brigade, parts of the Seventh and Forty-fourth regiments, the uniformed companies of militia under the command of Major Plauché, two hundred men of color chiefly from St. Domingo, raised by Colonel Savary and acting under the command of Major Daquin, and a detachment of artillery under the direction of Lieutenant Spots—not exceeding in all fifteen hundred."

More exact returns showed that Jackson carried with him eight hundred and eighty-four regular troops and two field-pieces, five hundred and sixty-three mounted riflemen of Coffee's brigade, five hundred and fifty-nine Louisiana militia, one hundred and seven Mississippians, and eighteen Choctaw Indians— in all, twenty-one hundred and thirty-one men and two guns, besides the *Carolina*, which dropped down the river at four o'clock.

Jackson did not, like Winder, pass the hours in looking at his enemy, nor did he, like General Smith at Baltimore, send out militia under militia officers, to stand in close order on an open field and wait attack. His chief difficulty was due to the ground, which obliged him to make his main assault in a narrow column along the road. To gain the advantage of his numbers, he detached Coffee with seven hundred and thirty-two men, mostly armed with rifles, to make a detour toward the left and fall on the British flank and rear, while Jackson himself, with fourteen hundred men and two guns, should strike the British advance where it was posted on the levee.

The signal for battle was to be given by the *Carolina's* guns. Commodore Patterson in the *Carolina* received his orders at half-past six, and getting out sweeps, brought his vessel in a few minutes abreast of the British camp, where he anchored close in shore and began a heavy fire, soon after seven o'clock. Ten minutes later, Jackson, waiting about two miles above, ordered his men to advance, and moving down the road with his regulars and New Orleans companies struck the British outposts about a mile below his point of departure, at a few minutes before eight o'clock. At the same time Coffee, as he marched along the edge of the swamp, hearing the signal, wheeled to the right, and moved toward the British flank.

Night had then fallen. The weary British troops had lain down, when their sentries on the levee gave the alarm, and immediately afterward the roar of seven cannon close beside them threw their camp into confusion. About half an hour afterward, while the *Carolina* still swept the camp with its shot, the British sentries on the levee a mile above gave another alarm, and in a few moments the outposts were sharply attacked.

The accounts of the battle fought along the levee, under the command of Jackson in person, were both confused and contradictory. Thornton's brigade was composed of the Eighty-fifth and Ninety-fifth regiments, a company of rocketeers, one hundred sappers and miners, and the Fourth regiment as a support—in all, sixteen hundred and eighty-eight rank-and-file. At the point where the fighting began the British had merely an outpost, which was forced back by Jackson's attack, with some difficulty, about one hundred and fifty yards. Colonel Thornton ordered two of his regiments—the Eighty-fifth and Ninety-fifth, eight hundred rank-and-file—to support the outpost, and their arrival checked Jackson's advance. Indeed, the American line was driven back and lost ground, until the two field-pieces were in danger, and were hastily withdrawn. Each party claimed that the other first withdrew from fire; but the American report admitted that the battle which began on the levee at eight ceased before nine, while Jackson seemed not to regard his attack as successful. His first brief report, written December 26, said—

"The heavy smoke occasioned by an excessive fire rendered it necessary that I should draw off my troops, after a severe conflict of upward of an hour."

Jackson's official report of December 27, said—

"There can be but little doubt that we should have succeeded on that occasion with our inferior force in destroying, or capturing the enemy, had not a thick fog which arose about eight o'clock occasioned some confusion among the different corps. Fearing the consequences, under this circumstance, of the further prosecution of a night attack with troops then acting together for the first time, I contented myself with lying on the field that night."

Although the battle was severest where Jackson commanded, it was most successful where Coffee attacked. On hearing the *Carolina* open fire, Coffee turning to the right advanced on the British flank, striking it nearly opposite to the *Carolina's* position. The British, thus surrounded, were placed in a situation which none but the steadiest troops could have maintained. So great was the confusion that no organized corps opposed Coffee's men. Squads of twenty or thirty soldiers, collecting about any officer in their neighborhood, made head as they best could against Coffee's riflemen, and the whole British position seemed encircled by the American fire. Forced back toward the river, the British rallied behind an old levee which happened at that point to run parallel with the new levee, at a distance of about three hundred yards. Knots of men, mixed in great disorder, here advancing, there retreating, carried on a desultory battle over the field, often fighting with clubbed weapons, knives, and fists. At last the British centre, finding a strong protection in the old levee which answered for an earthwork, held firm against Coffee's further advance, and were also sheltered by the new levee in their rear from the fire of the *Carolina's* guns. At about the same time several companies of the Twenty-first and Ninety-third regiments arrived from Lake Borgne, and raised the

British force to two thousand and fifty rank-and-file. Coffee then despaired of further success, and withdrew his men from the field.

"My brigade," wrote Coffee immediately afterward, "met the enemy's line near four hundred yards from the river. The fire on both sides was kept up remarkably brisk until we drove them to the river-bank, where they gave a long, heavy fire, and finally the enemy fell behind the levee or river-bank that is thrown up. The battle had now lasted near two and a half hours. The regulars had ceased firing near one hour before I drew my men back."

The *Carolina* began firing soon after seven o'clock, and ceased at nine. Jackson's attack with the regulars began at eight o'clock, and his force ceased firing before nine. Coffee withdrew his men at about half-past nine. The hope of destroying the British force was disappointed; and brilliant as the affair was, its moral effect was greater than the material injury it inflicted. Major-General Keane officially reported his loss as forty-six killed, one hundred and sixty-seven wounded, and sixty-four missing—two hundred and sixty-seven in all. Jackson reported twenty-four killed, one hundred and fifteen wounded, and seventy-four missing—two hundred and thirteen in all. The two regular regiments suffered most, losing fifteen killed and fifty-four wounded. Coffee's Tennesseeans lost nine killed and forty-three wounded. The New Orleans volunteer corps and the colored volunteers lost seventeen wounded.

Compared with the night battle at Lundy's Lane, the night battle of December 23 was not severe. Brown's army, probably not more numerous than Jackson's, lost one hundred and seventy-one men killed, while Jackson lost twenty-four. Brown lost five hundred and seventy-one wounded, while Jackson lost one hundred and fifteen. Drummond at Lundy's Lane reported a British loss of eighty-four killed, while Keane reported forty-six. Drummond reported five hundred and fifty-nine wounded, while Keane reported one hundred and sixty-seven. The total British loss at Lundy's Lane was eight hundred and seventy-eight men; that of December 23 was two hundred and sixty-seven. Jackson's battle was comparatively short, lasting an hour and a half, while the fighting at Lundy's Lane continued some five hours. Lundy's Lane checked the enemy only for a day or two, and the battle of December 23 could hardly be expected to do more.

Conscious that the British army would advance as soon as its main body arrived, Jackson, like Brown, hastened to place his men under cover of works. Falling back the next morning about two miles, he took position behind an old canal or ditch which crossed the strip of cultivated ground where it was narrowest. The canal offered no serious obstacle to an enemy, for although ten feet wide it was shallow and dry, and fully three quarters of a mile long. Had the British been able to advance in force at any time the next day, December 24, directing their attack toward the skirts of the swamp to avoid the *Carolina's* fire, they might have forced Jackson back upon New Orleans; but they were in no disposition to do on the 24th what they had not ventured to do on the 23d, when they possessed every advantage. Keane believed that Jackson's force in the night battle amounted to five thousand men. Keane's troops, weary, cold, without food, and exposed to the *Carolina's* fire, which imprisoned them all day between the two levees, were glad to escape further attack, and entertained no idea of advance. The day and night of December 24 were occupied by the British in hurrying the main body of their troops from the Isle aux Poix across Lake Borgne to the Bayou Bienvenu.

By very great efforts the boats of the fleet transported the whole remaining force across the lake, until, on the morning of December 25, all were concentrated at the Villeré plantation. With them arrived Major-General Sir Edward Pakenham, and took command. Hitherto the frequent British disasters at Plattsburg, Sackett's Harbor, Fort Erie, and the Moravian towns had been attributed to their generals. Sir George Prevost, Major-Generals Drummond and Riall, and Major-General Proctor were not officers of Wellington's army. The British government, in appointing Sir Edward Pakenham to command at New Orleans, meant to send the ablest officer at their disposal. Pakenham was not only one of Wellington's best generals, but stood in the close relation of his brother-in-law, Pakenham's sister being Wellington's wife. In every military respect Sir Edward Pakenham might consider himself the superior of Andrew Jackson. He was in the prime of life and strength, thirty-eight years of age, while Jackson, nearly ten years older, was broken in health and weak in strength. Pakenham had learned the art of war from Wellington, in the best school in Europe. He was supported by an efficient staff and a military system as perfect as experience and expenditure could make it, and he commanded as fine an army as England could produce, consisting largely of Peninsula veterans.

Their precise number, according to British authority, was five thousand and forty rank-and-file, on Christmas Day, when Pakenham took command. Afterward many more arrived, until January 6, when ten regiments were in camp at Villeré's plantation—Royal Artillery; Fourteenth Light Dragoons; Fourth, Seventh, Twenty-first, Forty-third, Forty-fourth, Eighty-fifth, Ninety-third, and Ninety-fifth Infantry—numbering, with sappers and miners and staff-corps, five thousand nine hundred and thirteen rank-and-file; or with a moderate allowance of officers, an aggregate of at least sixty-five hundred Europeans. Two West India regiments of black troops accompanied the expedition, numbering ten hundred and forty-three rank-and-file. The navy provided about twelve hundred marines and seamen, perhaps the most efficient corps in the whole body. Deducting eight hundred men for camp-duty, Pakenham, according to British official reports, could put in the field a force of eight thousand disciplined troops, well-officered, well-equipped, and confident both in themselves and in their commander. More were on their way.

The Duke of Wellington believed such a force fully competent to capture New Orleans, or to rout any American army he ever heard of; and his confidence would have been, if possible still stronger, had he known his opponent's resources, which were no greater and not very much better than those so easily overcome by Ross at Bladensburg. The principal difference was that Jackson commanded.

Jackson's difficulties were very great, and were overcome only by the desperate energy which he infused even into the volatile creoles and sluggish negroes. When he retired from the field of the night battle, he withdrew, as

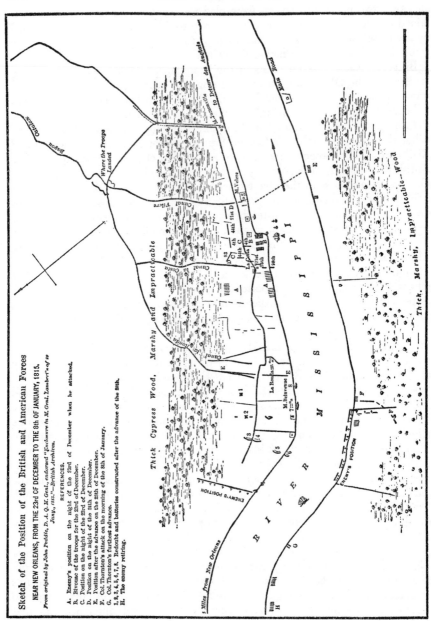

Sketch of the Position of the British and American Forces

NEAR NEW ORLEANS, FROM THE 23rd OF DECEMBER TO THE 8th OF JANUARY, 1815.

From original by John Peddie, D. A. Q. M. Genl., endorsed "Enclosure in M. Genl. Lambert's of 10 Jany, 1815."—British Archives.

REFERENCES.

A. Enemy's position on the night of the 23rd of December when he attacked.
B. Bivouac of the troops for the 23rd of December.
C. Position on the night of the 23rd of December.
D. Position on the night of the 24th of December.
E. Position after the advance on the 28th of December.
F. Col. Thornton's attack on the morning of the 8th of January.
G. Col. Thornton's furthest advance.
1, 2, 3, 4, 5, 6, 7, 8. Redoubts and batteries constructed after the advance of the 28th.
H. The enemy retiring.

has been told, only two miles. About five miles below New Orleans he halted his troops. Between the river and the swamp, the strip of open and cultivated land was there somewhat narrower than elsewhere. A space of a thousand yards, or about three fifths of a mile, alone required strong defence. A shallow, dry canal, or ditch, ten feet wide, crossed the plain and opened into the river on one side and the swamp on the other. All day the troops, with the negroes of the neighborhood, worked, deepening the canal, and throwing up a parapet behind it. The two six-pound field-pieces commanded the road on the river-bank, and the *Louisiana* descended the river to a point about two miles below Jackson's line. A mile below the *Louisiana* the *Carolina* remained in her old position, opposite the British camp. By nightfall the new lines were already formidable, and afforded complete protection from musketry. For further security the parapet was continued five hundred yards, and turned well on the flank in the swamp; but this task was not undertaken until December 28.

The first act of Sir Edward Pakenham gave the Americans at least three days for preparation. Even veteran soldiers, who were accustomed to storming mountain fortresses held by French armies, were annoyed at exposing their flank to the fire of fifteen or twenty heavy guns, which hampered not only every military movement but also every motion beyond cover of the bank. Pakenham sent instantly to the fleet for cannon to drive the ships away. In reality he could not so relieve himself, for the American commodore soon placed one twenty-four-pound gun and two twelve-pounders in battery on the opposite bank of the river, where they answered every purpose of annoyance, while the ships after December 28 took little part in action. Pakenham gained nothing by waiting; but he would not advance without artillery, and the sailors, with much labor, brought up a number of light guns—nine field-pieces, it was said, two howitzers, and a mortar. Pakenham passed two days, December 25 and 26, organizing his force and preparing the battery. At daylight, December 27, the guns were ready. Five pieces suddenly opened with hot shot and shell on the *Carolina*, and in half an hour obliged the crew to abandon her. The *Louisiana*, by extreme exertion, was hauled beyond range while the British battery was occupied in destroying the *Carolina*.

Nothing then prevented Pakenham's advance, and the next morning, December 28, the whole army moved forward.

"On we went," said the Subaltern, "for about three miles, without any halt or hindrance, either from man or inanimate nature coming in our way. But all at once a spectacle was presented to us, such indeed as we ought to have looked for, but such as manifestly took our leaders by surprise. The enemy's army became visible. It was posted about forty yards in rear of a canal, and covered, though most imperfectly, by an unfinished breastwork."

The British left, coming under the fire of the *Louisiana*, was immediately halted and placed as far as possible under cover. The skirmishers in the swamp were recalled. In the evening the whole army was ordered to retire beyond cannon-shot and hut themselves. They obeyed; but "there was not a man among us who failed to experience both shame and indignation."

Beyond doubt, such caution was not expected from Sir Edward Pakenham.

Sir George Prevost at Sackett's Harbor and Plattsburg, and Colonel Brooke at Baltimore had retired before American works; but those works had been finished forts, strongly held and situated on elevated points. Even with such excuses, and after suffering severe losses, Prevost was discredited for his retreats. Pakenham did not live to make a report, and his reasons remained unavowed; but Admiral Cochrane reported that it was "thought necessary to bring heavy artillery against this work, and also against the ship which had cannonaded the army when advancing." The decision implied that Pakenham considered the chances unfavorable for storming the American line.

In effect, Pakenham's withdrawal December 28 was equivalent to admitting weakness in his infantry, and to calling on the artillery as his strongest arm. The experiment showed little self-confidence. Not only must he sacrifice two or three days in establishing batteries, but he must challenge a contest with cannon—weapons which the Americans were famous for using, both afloat and ashore, with especial skill. Jackson could also mount heavy guns and allow Pakenham to batter indefinite lines. Sooner or later Pakenham must storm, unless he could turn the American position.

The seamen were once more set to work, and "with incredible labor" rowed their boats, laden with heavy guns, from the fleet to the bayou, and dragged the guns through three miles of bog to the British headquarters. The Americans also prepared batteries. From the lines one thirty-two-pounder, three twenty-four-pounders, and one eighteen-pounder commanded the plain in their front. Besides these heavy guns, three twelve-pounders, three six-pounders, a six-inch howitzer or mortar, and a brass carronade, useless from its bad condition—in all, twelve or thirteen guns, capable of replying to the British batteries, were mounted along the American lines. On the west bank of the river, three quarters of a mile away, Commodore Patterson established, December 30 and 31, a battery of one twenty-four-pounder and two long twelve-pounders, which took the British batteries in flank. Thus the Americans possessed fifteen effective guns, six of which were heavy pieces of long range. They were worked partly by regular artillerists, partly by sailors, partly by New Orleans militia, and partly by the "hellish banditti" of Barataria, who to the number of twenty or thirty were received by General Jackson into the service and given the care of two twenty-four-pounders.

The number and position of the British guns were given in Lieutenant Peddie's sketch of the field. Before the reconnaissance of December 28, field-pieces had been placed in battery on the river-side to destroy the Carolina and Louisiana. Canon Gleig said that "nine field-pieces, two howitzers, and one mortar" were placed in battery on the river-side during the night of December 25. Captain Henley of the Carolina reported that five guns opened upon him on the morning of December 26. Captain Peddie's sketch marked seven pieces mounted in battery on the river-side, bearing on Commodore Patterson's battery opposite, besides four pieces in two batteries below. Their range was sufficient to destroy the Carolina and pierce the breastwork across the river, and therefore they were probably twelve and nine pounders.

Besides these lighter long-range guns, the British constructed three batteries in the night of December 31.

"Four eighteen-pounders," reported Major Forrest, British assistant-quartermaster-general, "were placed in a battery formed of hogsheads of sugar, on the main road, to fire upon the ship if she dropped down. Preparations were also made to establish batteries—one of six eighteen-pounders, and one of four twenty-four-pound carronades; also batteries for the field-pieces and howitzers, the latter to keep the fire of the enemy under, while the troops were to be moved forward in readiness to storm the works as soon as a practicable breach was effected."

According to Peddie's sketch the Battery No. 6, on the road or new levée, contained not four but two guns. Battery No. 5, some fifty yards from No. 6, contained six guns, as Major Forrest reported. Battery No. 4, to the left of the old levee, contained four guns, probably the carronades. Battery No. 3, to the right of the old levee, contained five guns, probably the field-pieces and howitzers. In all, seventeen guns bore on the American lines—besides seven, in Batteries No. 7 and No. 8, bearing on Commodore Patterson's three-gun battery across the river. According to Gleig, the British had thirty guns; but in any case they used not less than twenty-four guns, throwing a heavier weight of metal than was thrown by the fifteen pieces used by the Americans. The British artillery was served by regular artillerists.

These details were particularly interesting, because the artillery battle of Jan. 1, 1815, offered the best test furnished during the war of relative skill in the use of that arm. The attack had every advantage over the defence. The British could concentrate their fire to effect a breach for their troops to enter; the Americans were obliged to disperse their fire on eight points. The American platforms being elevated, offered a better target than was afforded by the low British batteries, and certainly were no better protected. Three of the American guns were in battery across the river, three quarters of a mile from the main British battery of six eighteen-pounders, while the Louisiana's carronades were beyond range, and the Louisiana herself was not brought into action. On the American side the battle was fought entirely by the guns in Jackson's lines and in Patterson's battery across the river—one thirty-two-pounder, four twenty-four-pounders, one eighteen-pounder, five twelve-pounders, three six-pounders, and a howitzer—fifteen American guns in all, matched against ten British eighteen-pounders, four twenty-four-pound carronades, and ten field-pieces and howitzers—twenty-four guns in all. If the British field-pieces were twelves and nines, the weight of metal was at least three hundred and fifty pounds on the British side against two hundred and twenty-four pounds on the American side, besides two howitzers against one.

The main British batteries were about seven hundred yards distant from Jackson's line. Opposite to the battery of six eighteen-pounders were the American thirty-two and three twenty-four-pounders. Behind the British batteries the British army waited for the order to assault. Toward eight o'clock on the morning of Jan. 1, 1815, the British opened a hot fire accompanied by a shower of rockets. The American guns answered, and the firing continued

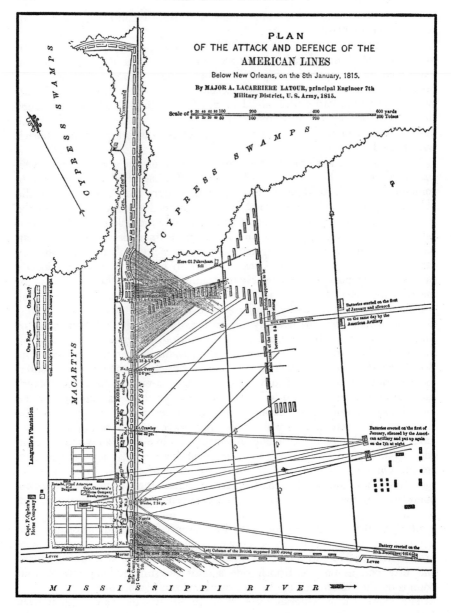

PLAN
OF THE ATTACK AND DEFENCE OF THE
AMERICAN LINES
Below New Orleans, on the 8th January, 1815.

By MAJOR A. LACARRIERE LATOUR, principal Engineer 7th
Military District, U. S. Army, 1815.

without intermission until toward noon, when the British fire slackened, and at one o'clock the British artillerists abandoned their batteries, leaving the guns deserted.

During the entire war, no other battle was fought in which the defeated party had not some excuse to offer for inferiority. Usually the excuse ascribed greater force to the victor than to the vanquished, or dwelt upon some accident or oversight which affected the result. For the defeat of the British artillery, Jan. 1, 1815, no excuse was ever suggested. The British army and navy frankly admitted that the misfortune was due to American superiority in the use of artillery. British evidence on that point was ample, for their surprise and mortification were extreme; while the Americans seemed never fully to appreciate the extraordinary character of the feat they performed. The most detailed British account was also the most outspoken.

"Never was any failure more remarkable or unlooked-for than this," said Gleig. . . . "The sun, as if ashamed to shine upon our disgrace, was slow of making its appearance; a heavy mist obscured him, and the morning was far advanced before it cleared away. At last, however, the American lines were visible, and then began a fire from our batteries, so brisk and so steadily kept up that we who were behind made not the smallest doubt of its effect. It was answered for a while faintly, and with seeming difficulty. By and by, however, the enemy's salutation became more spirited, till it gradually surpassed our own, both in rapidity and precision. We were a good deal alarmed at this, and the more that a rumor got abroad that our batteries were not proof against the amazing force of the American shot. We had, it may be stated, imprudently rolled into the parapets barrels filled with sugar, under the impression that sugar would prove as effectual as sand in checking the progress of cannon-balls. But the event showed that we had been completely mistaken. The enemy's shot penetrated these sugar-hogsheads as if they had been so many empty casks, dismounting our guns and killing our artillery-men in the very centre of their works. There could be small doubt, as soon as these facts were established, how the cannonading would end. Our fire slackened every moment; that of the Americans became every moment more terrible, till at length, after not more than two hours and a half of firing, our batteries were all silenced. The American works, on the other hand, remained as little injured as ever, and we were completely foiled."

Admiral Codrington, writing from the British headquarters three days after the battle, expressed equal astonishment and annoyance: —

"On the 1st we had our batteries, by severe labor, ready in situations from which the artillery people were, as a matter of course, to destroy and silence the opposing batteries, and give opportunity for a well-arranged storm. But instead of so doing, not a gun of the enemy appeared to suffer, and our firing too high was not made out until we had expended too much of our hardly-collected ammunition to push the matter further. Such a failure in this boasted arm was not to be expected, and I think it a blot in the artillery escutcheon."

Codrington somewhat under-estimated the effect of the British fire. Three of the American guns, including the thirty-two-pounder, were more or less damaged, and the cotton-bales which formed the cheeks of the embrasures proved to be as little serviceable as the hogsheads of sugar in the British river battery. Two artillery caissons were exploded by the British rockets. Thirty-four men were killed or wounded; while the British reported a loss of seventy-six killed and wounded between Jan. 1 and 5, 1815, most of whom fell in the artillery battle.

The British official reports said less, but their silence was equally significant.

"Our batteries made little impression upon the enemy's parapet," wrote Major Forrest. "The order for the assault was therefore not carried into effect. The troops remained in this advanced position, and orders were given to retire the guns in the night. The evening changed to wet, and the ground became in consequence so deep that it required the exertions of the whole army as a working-party, aided by the seamen, to retire the guns a short distance before daylight. The army then fell back to the position it occupied on the 31st."

Admiral Cochrane's official report was still more brief, and best understood by the comments already quoted from his friend Admiral Codrington:—

"On the 1st instant batteries were opened; but our fire not having the desired effect, the attack was deferred until the arrival of the troops under Major-General Lambert, which was daily expected."

If the Subaltern was right, the British defeat resulted in the loss of several guns.

"The enemy having made no attempt to carry off our heavy guns, which we abandoned to their fate," continued Gleig, "it was judged advisable to bring them into the camp as soon as circumstances would allow; and for this purpose working parties were again sent out as soon as the darkness screened them. It was my fortune to accompany them. The labor of dragging a number of huge ship's guns out of the soft soil into which they had sunk, crippled too as most of them were in their carriages, was more extreme by far than any one expected to find it. Indeed, it was not till four o'clock in the morning that our task came to the conclusion, and even then it had been very imperfectly performed. Five guns were eventually left behind. These were rendered useless, it is true, by breaking their trunnions; but it cannot be said that in the course of the late operations the British army came off without the loss of some of its artillery."

CHAPTER XXVII

THE BATTLE OF NEW ORLEANS

Effectually stopped by these repeated miscarriages, General Pakenham, with fully five thousand good soldiers at his command, decided to wait an entire week for Major-General Lambert, who was then on his way with two fresh regiments. In the meanwhile Pakenham adopted a suggestion made first by Vice-Admiral Cochrane, to prepare for throwing a force across the river to turn Jackson's line from the opposite bank. The plan required that the Villeré canal should be extended through the levee to the river without the knowledge of the Americans. Perhaps Pakenham would have done better by dragging his boats across the intervening space; but he preferred to dig a canal, and the work, begun January 4, was done so successfully that until January 6, when it was completed, Jackson did not suspect the movement. On the same day Lambert's division arrived.

From this week of inaction the Americans gained little advantage. The lines were strengthened; but although the Kentucky reinforcements, more than two thousand in number, under General Thomas and John Adair, arrived January 4, they were ill provided with arms, and Jackson could furnish them neither with arms, clothing, nor equipment. The Louisiana militia were in the same condition. Jackson did his utmost to supply these wants; the people of New Orleans did more, and lent at last the few hundred muskets reserved against the danger of a slave insurrection, until in the end, if Adair was correct, a thousand of the Kentuckians were placed in the line of battle. Yet after all the reinforcements had been mustered, Jackson's main dependence was still on his artillery and his intrenchments. In the open field he could not meet the British force.

In his immediate front, Jackson had little to fear. Three thousand marksmen, behind intrenchments everywhere at least five feet high, defended by heavy guns and supported by the *Louisiana* on the river and a strong battery on the opposite shore, could defy twice or three times their number advancing across an open plain under fire of eight or ten heavy guns. The result of the artillery battle of January 1, as well as the reconnaissance of December 28, showed what the British general and his staff thought of their chances in a front attack. Twice they had refused to attempt it when Jackson's lines were unfinished; they were not likely to succeed when the lines were strengthened by another week of labor.

In his direct front, therefore, Jackson had reason to think that the British did not intend serious attack. Their next attempt could hardly fail to be a flanking movement. Jackson had been surprised, December 23, by such a movement, and feared nothing so much as to be surprised again. For this reason he still kept a large body of troops, three regiments of Louisiana militia, on the north of the city. "His greatest fear, and hence his strongest defence next to the one occupied by himself, was on the Chef Menteur road, where Governor Claiborne, at the head of the Louisiana militia, was posted." He kept close watch on the bayous which extended on his immediate flank, and constructed other lines in his rear to which he could retreat in case his left flank should be turned through the swamp. Apparently the idea did not occur to him that the British might more easily turn his right flank by throwing a force across the river; and when he learned January 7, that the British were engaged in making this movement, the time had already passed when he could prevent it.

No means had been provided for transporting troops directly from one bank of the river to the other. If obliged to protect the batteries established by Commodore Patterson on the west bank, Jackson must march troops from his lines back five miles to New Orleans, cross them by the ferry, and march them down the other shore. Such a movement required a whole day, and divided the army in a manner hazarding the safety of both wings.

Practically the west bank was undefended when Jackson, January 7, first heard that the British were about to occupy it. Commodore Patterson had mounted there, as has been told, a number of heavy guns in battery, but these guns were not in position to cover their own bank against attack from below. Major Latour was engaged with negroes in laying out lines of defence, but nothing was completed. In an advanced position, about a mile below the line of Jackson's works, a bastion had been raised close to the river, and near it a small redan, or salient, had been constructed. This work, which was untenable in case of attack in flank or rear, was occupied by four hundred and fifty Louisiana militia, commanded by General David Morgan. During the afternoon of January 7, after the British plan of attack was suspected, General Morgan caused three guns—one twelve-pounder and two six-pounders—to be mounted on his line. Late the same evening General Jackson ordered four hundred men of the Kentucky division to New Orleans, where they were to obtain muskets, then to cross the river, and march down the opposite shore to reinforce Morgan. The Kentuckians obeyed their orders, but they found only about seventy muskets at New Orleans; and not more than two hundred and fifty armed men, weary with marching and faint from want of food, reached Morgan's quarters at four o'clock on the morning of January 8. Adair, who should have known the number best, declared that only one hundred and seventy men were then in the ranks. They were sent a mile farther and stationed as an advanced line, with one hundred Louisiana militia.

Thus seven or eight hundred tired, ill-armed, and unprotected militia, divided in two bodies a mile apart, waited on the west bank to be attacked by a British column which was then in the act of crossing the river. Their defeat was almost certain. A thousand British troops could easily drive them away, capture all the batteries on the west bank, destroy the *Louisiana* as they had destroyed the *Carolina*, thus turning all Jackson's lines, and probably rendering necessary the evacuation of New Orleans. For this work Pakenham detached the Eighty-fifth regiment, about three hundred strong, the Fifth West India, two hundred seamen and two hundred marines—about twelve hundred men in all—under command of Colonel Thornton, who had led the light brigade at Bladensburg and across Lake Borgne to the Mississippi. The movement was ordered for the night of January 7, and was to be made in boats already collected in the Villeré canal.

With some hesitation Pakenham decided to make a simultaneous attack on Jackson. The arrangements for this assault were simple. The usual store of fascines and ladders was provided. Six of the eighteen-pound guns were once more mounted in battery about eight hundred yards from the American line, to cover the attack. The army, after detaching Thornton's corps, was organized in three divisions—one, under Major-General Gibbs, to attack Jackson's left; another, under Major-General Keane, to attack along the river-side; a third, the reserve, to be commanded by Major-General Lambert.

"The principal attack was to be made by Major-General Gibbs," said the British official report. The force assigned to Gibbs consisted of the Fourth, Twenty-first, and Forty-fourth regiments, with three companies of the Ninety-fifth—about two thousand two hundred rank-and-file. "The first brigade, consisting of the Fusileers and Forty-third, formed the reserve" under Major-General Keane, apparently also twelve hundred strong. Adding two hundred artillerists and five hundred black troops of the First West India regiment, employed as skirmishers along the edge of the swamp, the whole body of troops engaged on the east bank in the assault, according to the official report and returns of wounded, numbered about five thousand three hundred rank-and-file, consisting of the Fourth, Seventh (Fusileers), Twenty-first, Forty-third, Forty-fourth, Ninety-third, and Ninety-fifth regiments, of whom twenty-two hundred were to attack on the right, twelve hundred on the left, and twelve hundred were to remain in reserve.

Thus of the whole British force, some eight thousand rank-and-file, fifty-three hundred were to assault Jackson's line; twelve hundred were to cross the river and assault Morgan; eight hundred and fifty men were detailed for various duties; and the seamen, except two hundred with Colonel Thornton, must have been in the boats.

To meet this assault, Jackson held an overwhelming force, in which his mere numbers were the smallest element. According to a detailed account given by Jackson two years afterward, his left wing, near the swamp, was held by Coffee's brigade of eight hundred and four men; his centre, by Carroll's brigade of fourteen hundred and fourteen men; his right, near the river, by thirteen hundred and twenty-seven men, including all the regulars; while Adair's Kentucky brigade, numbering five hundred and twenty-five men, were in reserve. Adair claimed that the Kentuckians numbered fully one thousand. The dispute mattered little, for barely one third of the entire force, whatever it was, discharged a gun. Besides three thousand or thirty-five hundred men on the parapets and a thousand in reserve, Jackson had twelve pieces of artillery distributed along the line, covering every portion of the plain. The earth-wall behind which his men rested was in every part sufficiently high to require scaling, and the mud was so slippery as to afford little footing. Patterson's battery on the opposite shore increased in force till it contained three twenty-four-pounders and six twelve-pounders, covered the levee by which the British left must advance. The *Louisiana* took no part in the action, her men being engaged in working the guns on shore; but without the *Louisiana's* broadside, Jackson had more than twenty cannon in position. Such a force was sufficient to repel ten thousand men if the attack were made in open day.

Pakenham, aware of the probable consequences of attacking by daylight, arranged for moving before dawn; but his plan required a simultaneous advance on both banks of the river, and such a combination was liable to many accidents. According to the journal of Major Forrest, the British Assistant-Quartermaster-General, forty-seven boats were brought up the bayou on the evening of January 7:

"As soon as it was dark, the boats commenced to be crossed over into the river. A dam erected below the sternmost boat had raised the water about two feet. Still there was a very considerable fall from the river; and through which, for an extent of two hundred and fifty yards, the boats were dragged with incredible labor by the seamen. It required the whole night to effect this, and the day had dawned before the first detachment of Colonel Thornton's corps (about six hundred men) had embarked; and they just reached the opposite bank when the main attack commenced on the enemy's line."

At six o'clock in broad dawn the columns of Gibbs and Keane moved forward toward Jackson's works, which were lined with American troops waiting for the expected attack. Gibbs's column came first under fire, advancing near the swamp in close ranks of about sixty men in front. Three of the American batteries opened upon them. Coming within one hundred and fifty yards of the American line, the British column obliqued to the left to avoid the fire of the battery directly in face. As they came within musketry range the men faltered and halted, beginning a confused musketry fire. A few platoons advanced to the edge of the ditch, and then broke. Their officers tried in vain to rally them for another advance. Major-General Gibbs was mortally wounded, according to the official report, "within twenty yards of the glacis." Pakenham himself rode forward to rally Gibbs's column, and was instantly struck by a grape-shot and killed, nearly three hundred yards from the American line. "As I advanced with the reserve," said Lambert's report, "at about two hundred and fifty yards from the line, I had the mortification to observe the whole falling back upon me in the greatest confusion."

Keane's column on the left moved along the road and between the river and the levee. Pressing rapidly forward, greatly annoyed by Patterson's battery on the west bank, the head of this column reached the American line, and stormed an unfinished redoubt outside the main work at the edge of the river. The concentrated fire of the whole American right almost immediately drove the column back in disorder; the men who reached the redoubt were killed; Major-General Keane was severely wounded and carried off the field, while the casualties among officers of a lower grade were excessive. The Ninety-third regiment in Keane's brigade lost its lieutenant-colonel and two captains killed, and four more captains severely wounded; three hundred and forty-eight rank-and-file were wounded, ninety-nine were reported missing, and fifty-eight killed. These losses amounted to five hundred and five in seven hundred and seventy-five rank-and-file.

Lambert's report continued:—

"In this situation, finding that no impression had been made; that though many men had reached the ditch, they were either drowned or obliged to surrender, and that it was impossible to restore order in the regiments where they were—I placed the reserve in position until I could obtain such information as to determine me how to act to the best of my judgment, and whether or not I should resume the attack; and if so, I felt it could be done only by the reserve."

Just as the main attack ended, Colonel Thornton with his six hundred rank-and-file, having landed on the west bank, advanced against Morgan's line, routed it, turned the redoubt, and advanced on Patterson's heavy battery beyond. Patterson unable to use his guns had no choice but to spike his pieces and retreat. Thornton passed up the river a mile beyond Jackson's line, and needed only a field-piece and some hot shot to burn the *Louisiana* and march opposite New Orleans.

From the eastern shore Jackson watched the progress of Thornton with alarm. His official report of January 9 gave an idea of his emotions.

"Simultaneously with his advance on my lines," Jackson said, "the enemy had thrown over in his boats a considerable force to the other side of the river. These having landed were hardy enough to advance against the works of General Morgan; and what is strange and difficult to account for, at the very moment when their entire discomfiture was looked for with a confidence approaching to certainty, the Kentucky reinforcements ingloriously fled, drawing after them by their example the remainder of the forces, and thus yielding to the enemy that most formidable position. The batteries which had rendered me for many days the most important service, though bravely defended, were of course now abandoned, not however until the guns had been spiked. This unfortunate rout had totally changed the aspect of affairs. The enemy now occupied a position from which they might annoy us without hazard, and by means of which they might have been enabled to defeat in a great measure the effect of our success on this side the river."

John Adair, who was then in command of the Kentucky brigade, General Thomas being unwell, took great offence at Jackson's account of the battle on the west bank. "The detachment on the other side of the river," he reported to Governor Shelby, "were obliged to retire before a superior force. They have been calumniated by those who ought to have fought with them, but did not." The tone of Jackson's report, and his language afterward, showed a willingness to load the Kentucky troops on the west bank with the responsibility for a military oversight with which they had nothing to do; but the oversight was not the less serious, whoever was responsible for it. The Kentucky and Louisiana troops did not easily yield. The British returns of killed and wounded showed that Thornton's column suffered a considerable loss. Thornton himself was wounded; his regiment, the Eighty-fifth, numbering two hundred and ninety-eight rank-and-file, reported a loss of forty-three men killed, wounded, and missing, besides their colonel. Of one hundred sailors employed in the attack twenty were killed or wounded, besides Captain Money of the royal navy, "who, I am sorry to say, was severely wounded," said Thornton. The Americans made as good a resistance as could have been expected, and had they resisted longer they would merely have been captured when the next detachment of Thornton's column came up. The chief blame for the disaster did not rest on them.

Jackson was helpless to interpose. As he and his men, lining the river bank, watched the progress of Thornton's column on the opposite shore, Jackson could do nothing; but he ordered his men "that they should take off their hats, and give our troops on the right bank three cheers." Adair, who inclined to a severe judgment of Jackson's generalship, told the story more picturesquely:—

"I was standing by him when he gave his order, and with a smile, not of approbation, observed I was afraid they could not hear us. The distance from us to them, on a straight line, was upward of one mile and a half; there was a thick fog, and I confess I could not see the troops of either army. All I could discover was the blaze from the guns; and seeing that continue to progress up the river was the only knowledge we had that our men were retreating."

Jackson then ordered General Humbert, a French officer acting as a volunteer, to take four hundred men and cross the river at New Orleans to repulse the enemy, cost what it might; but had the enemy pressed his advantage, no force at Jackson's command could have stopped their advance, without causing the sacrifice of Jackson's lines. Fortunately, the only remaining British general, Lambert, was not disposed to make another effort. The eight regiments of regular troops which made the bulk of Pakenham's army had suffered severely in the assault. One of these regiments, the Eighty-fifth, was with Thornton on the west shore. Two, the Seventh and Forty-third, had been in the reserve, and except two companies had never approached the works within musket-shot, yet had lost fifty-two killed, and about one hundred wounded and missing, in an aggregate of less than eighteen hundred. The five remaining regiments— the Fourth, Twenty-first, Forty-fourth, Ninety-third, and Ninety-fifth—were nearly destroyed. They went into battle about three thousand strong; they lost seventeen hundred and fifty men killed, wounded, and missing. The total British loss was two thousand and thirty-six. The American loss was seventy-one. Even on the west bank the American loss was much less than that of the British.

The loss of three major-generals was almost as serious as the loss of one third of the regular Infantry. Lambert, the fourth major-general, weighed down by responsibility and defeat, had no wish but to escape. He recalled Thornton's corps the same evening from its position on the opposite bank, and the next day, January 9, began preparations for his difficult and hazardous retreat.

Pakenham's assault on Jackson's lines at New Orleans, January 8, repeated the assault made by Drummond, August 15, at Fort Erie. According to the British account of that battle, Drummond's engaged force numbered twenty-one hundred and forty men; the reserve, about one thousand. Drummond's direct attack, being made by night, was more successful than Pakenham's; his troops approached nearer and penetrated farther than those of Gibbs and Keane; but the consequences were the same. Of three thousand men, Drummond lost nine hundred and five. Of six thousand, engaged in the double action of Jan. 8, 1815, Pakenham lost two thousand and thirty-six. In each case the officers commanding the assaulting columns were killed or wounded, and the repulse was complete.

After the battle General Lambert's position was critical. His withdrawal of Thornton's corps from the west bank betrayed his intention of retiring, and his line of retreat was exposed to attack from the bayou which headed near Jackson's camp. Fortunately for him, Jackson was contented with checking his advance.

"Whether, after the severe loss he has sustained," wrote Jackson, five days after the battle, "he is preparing to return to his shipping, or to make still mightier efforts to attain his first object, I do not pretend to determine. It becomes me to act as though the latter were his intention."

If Jackson's inaction allowed Lambert to escape, it was likely to hazard a renewal of the attack from some other quarter; but the armies remained for ten days in their old positions without further hostilities, except from artillery fire, until on the night of January 18, after making careful preparations, the whole British force silently withdrew to fortified positions at the mouth of the bayou, disappearing as suddenly and mysteriously as it came, and leaving behind it only eight or, according to the American report, fourteen of the guns which had covered the river and held the *Louisiana* at a distance. At the mouth of the bayou the army remained until January 27, when it was re-embarked in the ships off Chandeleur's Island.

On the day of the battle of January 8, a British squadron appeared in the river below Fort St. Philip. Two bomb-vessels, under the protection of a sloop, a brig, and a schooner, bombarded the fort without effect until January 18, when they withdrew at the same time with the army above.

Notwithstanding the disastrous failure of the campaign before New Orleans, the British expedition, as it lay off Chandeleur Island February 1, still possessed nearly as much strength as when it appeared there December 11. Reinforced by a thousand fresh soldiers, Lambert determined to attack Mobile. "It was decided," reported Lambert, "that a force should be sent against Fort Bowyer, situated on the eastern point of the entrance of the bay, and from every information that could be obtained it was considered that a brigade would be sufficient for this object, with a respectable force of artillery." At daylight on the morning of February 8 a whole brigade and a heavy battering-train were disembarked in the rear of Fort Bowyer.

Jackson's determination to defend Mobile had already deprived him of the use of more than half the regular troops assigned to his military district, who remained inactive at Mobile during the months of December and January. They were commanded by General Winchester, whose record as a military officer was not reassuring. Although Fort Bowyer was known to be untenable against attack by land, Jackson not only retained Lieutenant-Colonel Lawrence there, but increased his force until he had three hundred and sixty men in his command—equal to the average strength of an entire regiment, or half the force of regulars which Jackson commanded at New Orleans. This garrison was only large enough to attract, not to repel, an enemy. The obvious criticism on such a course was afterward made by Armstrong:—

"After the arrival of the British armament the garrison of Fort Bowyer was not only continued but increased, though from its locality wholly unable to aid in any important purpose of the campaign. Nor was this the whole extent of the evil, for by the disposition made of this gallant corps it was not only subjected to present inaction, but ultimately . . . to the perils of a siege and the humiliation of a surrender."

Colonel Lawrence had no choice but to capitulate, which he did February 11. He had not even the opportunity to resist, for the British made regular approaches, and could not be prevented from capturing the place without

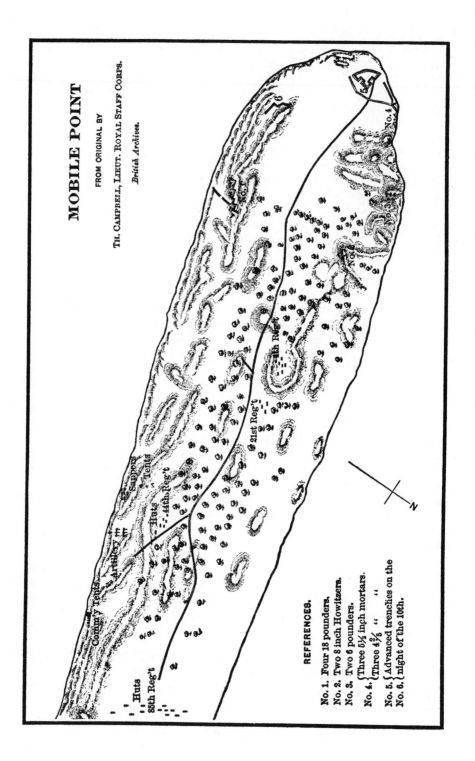

MOBILE POINT

FROM ORIGINAL BY

TH. CAMPBELL, LIEUT. ROYAL STAFF CORPS.

British Archives.

N

REFERENCES.

No. 1. Four 18 pounders.
No. 2. Two 8 inch Howitzers.
No. 3. Two 6 pounders.
No. 4. { Three 5½ inch mortars.
         Three 4⅖ "   "
No. 5. { Advanced trenches on the
No. 6. { night of the 10th.

Comm'y Tents
Artillery
Sappers
Huts
44th Reg't
Tents
21st Reg't
Huts
85th Reg't

the necessity of assault. Jackson reported to the Secretary of War that this event was one which he "little expected to happen but after the most gallant resistance; that it should have taken place without even a fire from the enemy's batteries is as astonishing as it is mortifying." In truth, the military arrangements, not Lawrence's defence, were responsible for the result; and Jackson had reason to fear that a greater disaster was at hand, for unless General Winchester should promptly evacuate Mobile, the disaster of the River Raisin was likely to be repeated on a larger scale.

CHAPTER XXVIII
THE MEETING AT GHENT

During the spring and summer of 1814 the task of diplomacy was less hopeful than that of arms. Brown and Izard with extreme difficulty defended the frontier; but Gallatin and Bayard could find no starting-point for negotiation. Allowed by Castlereagh's courtesy to visit England, they crossed the Channel in April, and established themselves in London. There Gallatin remained until June 21, waiting for the British government to act, and striving with tact, caution, and persistency to bring both governments on common ground; but the attempt was hopeless. England was beside herself with the intoxication of European success.

Although the English newspapers expressed a false idea of the general will, and were even at cross purposes with the Ministry in American matters, their tone was in some respects an indifferent barometer for measuring the elation or depression of the public temper, and exercised some influence, rather apparent than real, on the momentary attitudes of government. Had Castlereagh and his colleagues been really controlled by the press, no American peace could have been made. Whatever spirit of friendship for America might exist was necessarily silent, and only extravagant enmity found expression either in the press or in society.

Perhaps because ministers were believed to wish for peace with the United States, the London *Times,* which was not a ministerial journal, made itself conspicuous in demanding war. The *Times* had not previously shown a vindictive spirit, but it represented the Wellesley and Canning interest, which could discover no better course than that of being more English than England, and more patriotic than the Government. The *Times* was always ably written and well edited, but its language toward the United States showed too strong a connection with that of the Federalists, from whose public and private expressions the press of England formed its estimate of American character.

The *Times* indulged to excess in the pleasure of antipathy. Next to Napoleon, the chief victim of English hatred was Madison. For so mild a man Madison possessed a remarkable faculty of exciting invective. The English press surpassed the American Federalists in their allusions to him, and the *Times* was second to no English newspaper in the energy of its vituperation. "The lunatic ravings of the philosophic statesman of Washington" were in its political category of a piece with "his spaniel-like fawning on the Emperor of Russia. . . . The most abject of the tools of the deposed tyrant; . . . doubtless he expected to be named Prince of the Potomack or Grand Duke of Virginia." The *Sun* somewhat less abusively spoke of "that contemptible wretch Madison, and his gang"; but the *Times* habitually called him liar and impostor.

"Having disposed of all our enemies in Europe," the *Times* in the middle of April turned its attention to the United States. "Let us have no cant of moderation," was its starting-point. "There is no public feeling in the country stronger than that of indignation against the Americans; . . . conduct so base, so loathsome, so hateful. . . . As we urged the principle, No peace with Bonaparte! so we must maintain the doctrine of, No peace with James Madison!"

To this rule the *Times* steadily adhered with a degree of ill-temper not easily to be described, and with practical objects freely expressed. "Mr. Madison's dirty, swindling manoeuvres in respect to Louisiana and the Floridas remain to be punished," it declared April 27; and May 17 it pursued the idea: "He must fall a victim to the just vengeance of the Federalists. Let us persevere. Let us unmask the impostor. . . .Who cares about the impudence which they call a doctrine? . . . We shall demand indemnity. . . . We shall insist on security for Canada. . . . We shall inquire a little into the American title to Louisiana; and we shall not permit the base attack on Florida to go unpunished." May 18 it declared that Madison had put himself on record as a liar in the cause of his Corsican master. "He has lived an impostor, and he deserves to meet the fate of a traitor. That fate now stares him in the face." May 24 the *Times* resumed the topic: "They are struck to the heart with terror for their impending punishment; and oh may no false liberality, no mistaken lenity, no weak and cowardly policy, interpose to save them from the blow! Strike! chastise the savages, for such they are! . . . With Madison and his perjured set no treaty can be made, for no oath can bind them." When British commissioners were at last announced as ready to depart for Ghent to negotiate for peace with the United States, June 2, the *Times* gave them instructions: "Our demands may be couched in a single word—Submission!"

The *Morning Post*, a newspaper then carrying higher authority than the *Times*, used language if possible more abusive, and even discovered, Jan. 18, 1814, "a new trait in the character of the American government. Enjoying the reputation of being the most unprincipled and most contemptible on the face of the earth, they were already known to be impervious to any noble sentiment; but it is only of late that we find them insensible of the shame of defeat, destitute even of the brutish quality of being beaten into a sense of their unworthiness and their incapacity." Of Madison the *Morning Post* held the lowest opinion. He was "a despot in disguise; a miniature imitation" and miserable tool of Bonaparte, who wrote his Annual Message; a senseless betrayer of his country.

The *Times* and *Morning Post* were independent newspapers, and spoke only for themselves; but the *Courier* was supposed to draw inspiration from the Government, and commonly received the first knowledge of ministers' intentions. In temper the *Courier* seemed obliged to vie with its less favored rivals. The President's Annual Message of 1813 resembled in its opinion "all the productions of the vain and vulgar Cabinet;" it was "a compound of canting and hypocrisy, of exaggeration and falsehood, of coarseness without strength, of assertions without proof, of the meanest prejudices, and of the most malignant passions; of undisguised hatred of Great Britain, and of ill-concealed partiality and servility toward France." "We know of no man for whom we feel greater contempt than for Mr. Madison," said the *Courier* of May 24. These illustrations of what the *Courier* called "exaggeration and falsehood, of coarseness without strength, of assertions without proof, of the meanest prejudices, and of the most malignant passions" were probably in some degree a form as used by the *Courier*, which would at a hint from the Ministry adopt a different tone; but announcements of official acts and intentions were more serious, and claimed more careful attention.

Immediately after the capitulation of Paris, March 31, the Ministry turned its attention to the United States, and the *Courier* announced, April 15, that twenty thousand men were to go from the Garonne to America. Mr. Madison, the *Courier* added, had "made a pretty kettle of fish of it." Twenty thousand men were about two thirds of Wellington's English force, and their arrival in America would, as every Englishman believed, insure the success of the campaign. Not until these troops were embarked would the Ministry begin to negotiate; but in the middle of May the military measures were complete, and then the *Courier* began to prepare the public mind for terms of peace.

These terms were the same as those announced by the *Times*, except that the *Courier* did not object to treating with Madison. The United States were to be interdicted the fisheries; Spain was to be supported in recovering Louisiana; the right of impressment must be expressly conceded—anything short of this would be unwise and a disappointment. "There are points which must be conceded by America before we can put an end to the contest." Such language offered no apparent hope of peace; yet whatever hope existed lay in Castlereagh, who inspired it. Extravagant as the demands were, they fell short of the common expectation. The *Courier* admitted the propriety of negotiation; it insisted neither on Madison's retirement nor on a division of the Union, and it refrained from asserting the whole British demand, or making it an ultimatum.

The chief pressure on the Ministry came from Canada, and could not be ignored. The Canadian government returned to its old complaint that Canadian interests had been ignorantly and wantonly sacrificed by the treaty of 1783, and that the opportunity to correct the wrong should not be lost. The Canadian official *Gazette* insisted that the United States should be required to surrender the northern part of the state of New York, and that both banks of the St. Lawrence should be Canadian property. A line from Plattsburg to Sackett's Harbor would satisfy this necessity; but to secure Canadian interests, the British government should further insist on acquiring the east bank of the Niagara River, and on a guaranty of the Indian Territory from Sandusky to Kaskaskias, with the withdrawal of American military posts in the Northwest. A pamphlet was published in May to explain the subject for the use of the British negotiators, and the required territorial cessions were marked on a map. The control of the Lakes, the Ohio River as the Indian boundary, and the restitution of Louisiana were the chief sacrifices wished from the United States.

The cession of a part of Maine was rather assumed than claimed, and the fisheries were to be treated as wholly English. A memorial from Newfoundland, dated Nov. 8, 1813, pointed out the advantages which the war had already brought to British trade and fisheries by the exclusion of American competition, to the result of doubling the number of men employed on the Labrador shores; and the memorialists added—

"They cannot too often urge the important policy . . . of wholly excluding foreigners from sharing again in the advantages of a fishery from which a large proportion of our best national defence will be derived."

British confidence was at its highest point when the Emperor of Russia and the King of Prussia visited London, June 7, and received an enthusiastic welcome. Gallatin obtained an interview with the Czar, June 17, and hoped that Russian influence might moderate British demands; but the Czar could give him no encouragement. Gallatin wrote home an often-quoted despatch, dated June 13, warning the President that fifteen or twenty thousand men were on their way to America, and that the United States could expect no assistance from Europe.

"I have also the most perfect conviction," Gallatin continued, "that under the existing unpropitious circumstances of the world, America cannot by a continuance of the war compel Great Britain to yield any of the maritime points in dispute, and particularly to agree to any satisfactory arrangement on the subject of impressment; and that the most favorable terms of peace that can be expected are the *status ante bellum.*"

Even these terms, Gallatin added, depended on American success in withstanding the shock of the campaign. He did not say that at the time he wrote, the *status ante bellum* would be scouted by public opinion in England as favorable to the United States; but his estimate of the situation was more nearly exact than though he had consulted only the apparent passions of the British press.

"Lord Castlereagh," wrote Gallatin to Clay, "is, according to the best information I can collect, the best disposed man in the Cabinet." Yet Castlereagh did not venture at that stage to show a disposition for peace. He delayed the negotiation, perhaps wisely, six weeks after the American negotiators had assembled at Ghent; and his instructions to the British commissioners, dated July 28, reflected the demands of the press. They offered, not the *status ante bellum,* but the *uti possidetis,* as the starting-point of negotiation. "The state of possession must be considered as the territorial arrangement which would revive upon a peace, except so far as the same may be modified by any new treaty." The state of possession, in view of the orders that had then been given, or were to be given, for the invasion of the United States, was likely to cost the Americans half of Maine, between the Penobscot and the Passamaquoddy, Plattsburg, and the northern part of New York, Vermont, and New Hampshire; Fort Niagara, Mackinaw, and possibly New Orleans and Mobile. Besides this concession of the *uti possidetis,* or military occupation at the date of peace, the Americans were required at the outset to admit as a *sine qua non,* or condition precedent to any negotiation, that England's Indian allies, the tribes of the Northwestern Territory, should be included in the pacification, and that a definite boundary should be assigned to them under a mutual guaranty of both Powers. Eastport, or Moose Island, and the fishing privileges were to be regarded as British. With these instructions of July 28, the British commissioners, early in August, started for Ghent.

Between Castlereagh's ideas and those of Madison no relation existed. Gallatin and his colleagues at Ghent were provided with two sets of instructions. The first set had been written in 1813, for the expected negotiation at St. Petersburg. The second set was written in January, 1814, and was brought to Europe by Clay. Neither authorized the American commissioners to discuss such conditions as Castlereagh proposed. The President gave his negotiators authority to deal with questions of maritime law; but even there they were allowed to exercise no discretion on the chief issue in dispute. Monroe's latest letter, dated January 28, was emphatic. "On impressment, as to the right of the United States to be exempted from it, I have nothing to add," said the secretary; "the sentiments of the President have undergone no change on that important subject. This degrading practice must cease; our flag must protect the crew, or the United States cannot consider themselves an independent nation." The President would consent to exclude all British seamen, except those already naturalized, from American vessels, and to stipulate the surrender of British deserters; but the express abandonment of impressment was a *sine qua non* of treaty. "If this encroachment of Great Britain is not provided against," said Monroe, "the United States have appealed to arms in vain. If your efforts to accomplish it should fail, all further negotiations will cease, and you will return home without delay."

On territorial questions the two governments were equally wide apart. So far from authorizing a cession of territorial rights, Monroe instructed the American commissioners, both at St. Petersburg and at Ghent, "to bring to view the advantage to both countries which is promised by a transfer of the upper parts even the whole of Canada to the United States." The instructions of January 1 and January 28, 1814, reiterated the reasoning which should decide England voluntarily to cede Canada. "Experience has shown that Great Britain cannot participate in the dominion and navigation of the Lakes without incurring the danger of an early renewal of the war."

These instructions were subsequently omitted from the published documents, probably because the Ghent commissioners decided not to act upon them; but when the American negotiators met their British antagonists at Ghent, each party was under orders to exclude the other, if possible, from the Lakes, and the same divergence of opinion in regard to the results of two years' war extended over the whole field of negotiation. The British were ordered to begin by a *sine qua non* in regard to the Indians, which the Americans had no authority to consider. The Americans were ordered to impose a *sine qua non* in regard to impressments, which the British were forbidden to concede. The British were obliged to claim the basis of possession; the Americans were not even authorized to admit the status existing before the war. The Americans were required to negotiate about blockades, contraband and maritime rights of neutrals; the British could not admit such subjects into dispute. The British regarded their concessions of fishing-rights as terminated by the war; the Americans could not entertain the idea.

The diplomacy that should produce a treaty from such discordant material must show no ordinary excellence; yet even from that point of view the prospect was not encouraging. The British government made a peculiar choice of negotiators. The chief British commissioner, Lord Gambier, was unknown in diplomacy, or indeed in foreign affairs. A writer in the London *Morning Chronicle* of August 9 expressed the general surprise that Government could make no better selection for the chief of its commission than Lord Gambier, "who was a post-captain in 1794, and happened to fight the 'defence' decently in Lord Howe's action; who slumbered for some time as a Junior Lord of the Admiralty; who sung psalms, said prayers, and assisted in the burning of Copenhagen, for which he was made a lord."

Gambier showed no greater fitness for his difficult task than was to be expected from his training; and the second member of the commission, Henry Goulburn, could not supply Gambier's difficiencies. Goulburn was Under-Secretary of State to Lord Bathurst; he was a very young man, but a typical under-secretary, combining some of Francis James Jackson's temper with the fixed opinions of the elder Rose, and he had as little idea of diplomacy as was to be expected from an Under-Secretary of State for the colonies. The third and last member was William Adams, Doctor of Civil Law, whose professional knowledge was doubtless supposed to be valuable to the commission, but who was an unknown man, and remained one.

Experience had not convinced the British government that in dealing with the United States it required the best ability it could command. The mistake made by Lord Shelburne in 1783 was repeated by Lord Castlereagh in 1814. The miscalculation of relative ability which led the Foreign Office to assume that Gambier, Goulburn, and William Adams were competent to deal with Gallatin, J. Q. Adams, J. A. Bayard, Clay, and Russell was not reasonable. Probably the whole British public service, including Lords and Commons, could not at that day have produced four men competent to meet Gallatin, J. Q. Adams, Bayard, and Clay on the ground of American interests; and when Castlereagh opposed to them Gambier, Goulburn, and Dr. Adams, he sacrificed whatever advantage diplomacy offered; for in diplomacy as in generalship, the individual commanded success.

The only serious difficulty in the American commission was its excess of strength. By a natural reaction against the attempt to abolish diplomatic offices, the United States government sent into diplomacy its most vigorous men. Under favorable conditions, four minds and wills of so decided a character could not easily work together; but in the Ghent commission an additional difficulty was created by the unfortunate interference of the Senate. Originally Gallatin, as was due to his age, services, and ability, had been the head of the St. Petersburg commission; but the Senate refused to confirm the appointment. The President at last removed Gallatin from the Treasury, and renominated him as a member of the Ghent commission after the other members had been nominated and confirmed. The Senate then gave its approval—thus making Gallatin the last member of the commission instead of the first, and placing J. Q. Adams above them all.

Gallatin, was peculiarly fitted to moderate a discordant body like the negotiators, while Adams was by temperament little suited to the post of moderator, and by circumstances ill-qualified to appear as a proper representative of the commission in the eyes of its other members. Unless Gallatin were one of the loftiest characters and most loyal natures ever seen in American politics, Adams's chance of success in controlling the board was not within reasonable hope.

Gallatin was six years the senior, and represented the President, with the authority of close and continuous personal friendship. The board, including Adams himself, instinctively bowed to Gallatin's authority; but they were deferential to no one else, least of all to their nominal head. Bayard, whose age was the same as that of Adams, was still in name a Federalist; and although his party trusted him little more than it trusted Adams or William Pinkney, who had avowedly become Republicans, he was not the more disposed to follow Adams's leadership. Clay, though ten years their junior, was the most difficult of all to control; and Jonathan Russell, though a New Englander, preferred Clay's social charm, and perhaps also his political prospects, to the somewhat repellent temper and more than doubtful popularity of Adams.

Personal rivalry and jealousies counted for much in such a group; but these were not the only obstacles to Adams's influence. By a misfortune commonly reserved for men of the strongest wills, he represented no one but himself and a powerless minority. His State repudiated and, in a manner, ostracized him. Massachusetts gave him no support, even in defending her own rights; by every means in her power she deprived him of influence, and loaded him with the burden of her own unpopularity. Adams represented a community not only hostile to the war, but avowedly laboring to produce peace by means opposed to those employed at Ghent. If the Ghent commission should succeed in making a treaty, it could do so only by some sacrifice of Massachusetts which would ruin Adams at home. If the Ghent commission should fail, Adams must be equally ruined by any peace produced through the treasonable intrigues or overt rebellion of his State.

Such a head to a commission so constituted needed all the force of character which Adams had, and some qualities he did not possess, in order to retain enough influence to shape any project into a treaty that he could consent to sign; while Gallatin's singular tact and nobility of character were never more likely to fail than in the effort to make allowance for the difficulties of his chief's position. Had Castlereagh improved the opportunity by sending to Ghent one competent diplomatist, or even a well-informed and intelligent man of business, like Alexander Baring, he might probably have succeeded in isolating Adams, and in negotiating with the other four commissioners a treaty sacrificing Massachusetts.

The five American commissioners were ready to negotiate in June; but Castlereagh, for obvious reasons, wished delay, and deferred action until August, doubtless intending to prevent the signature of a treaty on the basis of *uti possidetis* until after September, when Sherbrooke and Prevost should have occupied the territory intended to be held. In May and June no one in England, unless it were Cobbett, entertained more than a passing doubt of British success on land and water; least of all did the three British commissioners expect to yield British demands. They came to impose terms, or to break negotiation. They were not sent to yield any point in dispute, or to seek a cessation of arms.

At one o'clock on the afternoon of August 8, the first conference took place in the Hotel des Pays Bas at Ghent. After the usual civilities and forms had passed, Goulburn took the lead, and presented the points which he and his colleagues were authorized to discuss—(1) Impressment and allegiance; (2) the Indians and their boundary, a *sine qua non;* (3) the Canadian boundary; (4) the privilege of landing and drying fish within British jurisdiction. Goulburn declared that it was not intended to contest the right of the United States to the fisheries, by which he probably meant the deep-sea fisheries; and he was understood to disavow the intention of acquiring territory by the revision of the Canada boundary; but he urged an immediate answer upon the question whether the Americans were instructed on the point made a *sine qua non* by the British government.

The Americans, seeing as yet only a small part of the British demands, were not so much surprised at Goulburn's points as unable to answer them. The next day they replied in conference that they had no authority to admit either Indian boundary or fisheries into question, being without instructions on these points; and in their turn presented subjects of discussion—blockades and indemnities; but professed themselves willing to discuss everything.

In the conversation following this reply, the British commissioners, with some apparent unwillingness, avowed the intention of erecting the Indian Territory into a barrier between the British possessions and the United States; and the American commissioners declined even to retire for consultation on the possibility of agreeing to such an article. The British commissioners then proposed to suspend conferences until they could receive further instructions, and their wish was followed. Both parties sent despatches to their governments.

Lord Castlereagh was prompt. As soon as was reasonably possible he sent more precise instructions. Dated August 14, these supplementary instructions gave to those of July 28 a distinct outline. They proposed the Indian boundary fixed by the Treaty of Greenville for the permanent barrier between British and American dominion, beyond which neither government should acquire land. They claimed also a "rectification" of the Canadian frontier, and the cession of Fort Niagara and Sackett's Harbor, besides a permanent prohibition on the United States from keeping either naval forces or land fortifications on the Lakes. Beyond these demands the British commissioners were not for the present to go, nor were they to ask for a direct cession of territory for Canada "with any view to an acquisition of territory as such, but for the purpose of securing her possessions and preventing future disputes;" yet a small cession of land in Maine was necessary for a road from Halifax to Quebec, and an arrangement of the Northwestern boundary was required to coincide with the free navigation of the Mississippi.

As soon as the new instructions reached Ghent the British commissioners summoned the Americans to another conference, August 19; and Goulburn, reading from Castlereagh's despatch, gave to the Americans a clear version of its contents. When he had finished, Gallatin asked what was to be done with the American citizens—perhaps one hundred thousand in number—already settled beyond the Greenville line, in Ohio, Indiana, Illinois, and Michigan? Goulburn and Dr. Adams replied that these people must shift for themselves. They added also that Moose Island and Eastport belonged to Great Britain as indisputably as the county of Northamptonshire, and were not a subject for discussion; but they would not then make a *sine qua non* of the proposition regarding the Lakes. The conference ended, leaving the Americans convinced that their answer to these demands would close the negotiation. Clay alone, whose knowledge of the Western game of brag stood him in good stead, insisted the British would recede.

The British commissioners the next day, August 20, sent an official note containing their demands, and the Americans before sending their reply forwarded the note to America, with despatches dated August 19 and 20, announcing that they intended to return "a unanimous and decided negative." They then undertook the task of drawing up their reply. Upon Adams as head of the commission fell the duty of drafting formal papers—a duty which, without common consent, no other member could assume. His draft met with little mercy, and the five gentlemen sat until eleven o'clock of August 24, "sifting, erasing, patching, and amending until we were all wearied, though none of us was yet satiated with amendment." At the moment when they gave final shape to the note which they believed would render peace impossible, the army of General Ross was setting fire to the Capitol at Washington, and President Madison was seeking safety in the Virginia woods.

Only to persons acquainted with the difficulties of its composition did the American note of August 24 show signs of its diverse origin. In dignified temper with reasoning creditable to its authors and decisive on its issues, it assured the British negotiators that any such arrangement as they required for the Indians was contrary to precedent in public law, was not founded on reciprocity, and was unnecessary for its professed object in regard to the Indians. The other demands were equally inadmissible:—

"They are founded neither on reciprocity, nor on any of the usual bases of negotiation, neither on that of *uti possidetis* nor of *status ante bellum*. They are above all dishonorable to the United States in demanding from them to abandon territory and a portion of their citizens; to admit a foreign interference in their domestic concerns, and to cease to exercise their natural rights on their own shores and in their own waters. A treaty concluded on such terms would be but an armistice."

The negotiators were ready to terminate the war, both parties restoring whatever territory might have been taken, and reserving their rights over their respective seamen; but such demands as were made by the British government could not be admitted even for reference.

The American reply was sent to the British commissioners August 25, "and will bring the negotiation," remarked J. Q. Adams, "very shortly to a close." The American commissioners prepared to quit Ghent and return to their several posts, while the British commissioners waited for instructions from London. Even Gallatin, who had clung to the hope that he could effect an arrangement, abandoned the idea, and believing that the British government had adopted a system of conquest, prepared for an immediate return to America. Goulburn also notified his Government that the negotiation was not likely to continue, and reported some confidential warnings from Bayard, that such conditions of peace would not only insure war, but would sacrifice the Federalist party. "It has not made the least impression upon me or upon my colleagues," reported Goulburn to Bathurst.

At that point the negotiation remained stationary for two months, kept alive by Liverpool, Castlereagh, and Bathurst, while they waited for the result of their American campaign. The despatch of August 20 crossed the Atlantic, and was communicated to Congress October 10, together with all other papers connected with the negotiation; but not until October 25 did the American commissioners write again to their Government.

CHAPTER XXIX

THE TREATY OF GHENT

The British note of August 19 and the American rejoinder of August 24, brought about a situation where Lord Castlereagh's influence could make itself felt. Castlereagh had signed the British instructions of July 28 and August 14, and himself brought the latter to Ghent, where he passed August 19, before going to Paris on his way to the Congress at Vienna. He was at Ghent when Goulburn and his colleagues held their conference and wrote their note of August 19; and he could not be supposed ignorant of their language or acts. Yet when he received at Paris letters from Goulburn, dated August 24 and 26, he expressed annoyance that the American commissioners should have been allowed to place England in the attitude of continuing the war for purposes of conquest, and still more that the British commissioners should be willing to accept that issue and break off negotiation upon it. In a letter to Lord Bathurst, who took charge of the negotiation in his absence, Castlereagh suggested ideas altogether different from those till then advanced in England.

"The substance of the question is," said Castlereagh, "Are we prepared to continue the war for territorial arrangements? And if not, is this the best time to make our peace, saving all our rights, and claiming the fisheries, which they do not appear to question? In which case the territorial questions might be reserved for ulterior discussion. Or is it desirable to take the chance of the campaign, and then to be governed by circumstances? . . . If we thought an immediate peace desirable, as they are ready to waive all the abstract questions, perhaps they might be prepared to sign a provisional article of Indian peace as distinct from limits, and relinquish their pretensions to the islands in Passamaquoddy Bay, and possibly to admit minor adjustments of frontier, including a right of communication from Quebec to Halifax across their territory. But while I state this, I feel the difficulty of so much letting down the question under present circumstances."

At the same time Castlereagh wrote to Goulburn, directing him to wait at Ghent for new instructions from London. Lord Liverpool shared his disapproval of the manner in which the British commissioners had managed the case, and replied to Castlereagh, September 2, that the Cabinet had already acted in the sense he wished:

"Our commissioners had certainly taken a very erroneous view of our policy. If the negotiation had been allowed to break off upon the two notes already presented, or upon such an answer as they were disposed to return, I am satisfied that the war would have become quite popular in America."

The idea that the war might become popular in America was founded chiefly on the impossibility of an Englishman's conceiving the contrary; but in truth the Ministry most feared that the war might become unpopular in England.

"It is very material to throw the rupture of the negotiation, if it is to take place, upon the Americans," wrote Liverpool, the same day, to the Duke of Wellington; "and not to allow them to say that we have brought forward points as ultimata which were only brought forward for discussion, and at the desire of the American commissioners themselves. The American note is a most impudent one, and, as to all its reasoning, capable of an irresistible answer."

New instructions were accordingly approved in Cabinet. Drawn by Bathurst, and dated September 1, they contained what Liverpool considered an "irresistible answer" to the American note of August 24; but their force of logic was weakened by the admission that the previous British demands though certainly stated as a *sine qua non*, were in reality not to be regarded as such. In private this retreat was covered by the pretext that it was intended only to keep the negotiation alive until better terms could be exacted.

"We cannot expect that the negotiation will proceed at present," continued Liverpool's letter to Castlereagh; "but I think it not unlikely, after our note has been delivered, that the American commissioners will propose to refer the subject to their Government. In that case the negotiation may be adjourned till the answer is received, and we shall know the result of the campaign before it can be resumed. If our commander does his duty, I am persuaded we shall have acquired by our arms every point on the Canadian frontier which we ought to insist on keeping."

Lord Gambier and his colleagues communicated their new instructions to the American negotiators in a long note dated September 4, and were answered by a still longer note dated September 9, which was also sent to London, and considered in Cabinet. Bathurst felt no anxiety about the negotiation in its actual stage. Goulburn wrote to him that "as long as we answer their notes, I believe that they will be ready to give us replies," and urged only that Sir George Prevost should hasten his reluctant movements in Canada. Bathurst wrote more instructions, dated September 16, directing his commissioners to abandon the demands for Indian territory and exclusive control of the Lakes, and to ask only that the Indians should be included in the peace. The British commissioners sent their note with these concessions to the Americans September 19; and then for the first time the Americans began to suspect the possibility of serious negotiation. For six weeks they had dealt only with the question whether they should negotiate at all.

The demand that the Indians should be included in the treaty was one that under favorable circumstances the Americans would have rejected; but none of them seriously thought of rejecting it as their affairs then stood. When the American commissioners discussed the subject among themselves, September 20, Adams proposed to break off the negotiation on that issue; but Gallatin good-naturedly overruled him, and Adams would not himself, on cool reflection, have ventured to take such responsibility. Indeed, he suggested an article for an Indian amnesty, practically accepting the British demand. He also yielded to Gallatin the ungrateful task of drafting the answers to the British notes; and thus Gallatin became in effect the head of the commission.

All Gallatin's abilities were needed to fill the place. In his entire public life he had never been required to manage so unruly a set of men. The British commissioners were trying, and especially Goulburn was aggressive in temper and domineering in tone; but with them Gallatin had little trouble. Adams and Clay were persons of a different type, as far removed from British heaviness as they were from the Virginian ease of temper which marked the Cabinet of Jefferson, or the incompetence which characterized that of Madison. Gallatin was obliged to exert all his faculties to control his colleagues; but whenever he succeeded, he enjoyed the satisfaction of feeling that he had colleagues worth controlling. They were bent on combat, if not with the British, at all events with each other; and Gallatin was partly amused and partly annoyed by the unnecessary energy of their attitude.

The first divergence occurred in framing the reply to the British note of September 19, which while yielding essentials made a series of complaints against the United States—and among the rest reproached them for their attempt to conquer Canada, and their actual seizure of Florida. Adams, who knew little about the secrets of Jefferson's and Madison's Administrations, insisted on resenting the British charges, and especially on justifying the United States government in its attacks upon Florida. Bayard protested that he could not support such a view, because he had himself publicly in Congress denounced the Government on the subject of Florida; and Gallatin was almost equally committed, for, as he frankly said, he had opposed in Cabinet for a whole year what had been done in Florida before he could succeed in stopping it. Clay said nothing, but he had strong reasons for wishing that the British negotiators should not be challenged to quote his notorious speeches on the conquest of Canada. Adams produced Monroe's instructions, and in the end compelled his colleagues to yield. His mistake in pressing such an issue was obvious to every one but himself, and would have been evident to him had he not been blinded by irritation at the British note. His colleagues retaliated by summarily rejecting as cant his argument that moral and religious duty required the Americans to take and settle the land of the Indians.

After much discussion their note was completed and sent, September 26, to the British commissioners, who forwarded it as usual to London, with a letter from Goulburn of the same date, written in the worst possible temper, and charging the American commissioners with making a variety of false and fraudulent statements. While the British Cabinet detained it longer than usual for consideration, the Americans at Ghent felt their position grow weaker day by day.

Nothing warranted a serious hope of peace. Goulburn and his colleagues showed no thought of yielding acceptable conditions. The London *Courier* of September 29 announced what might be taken for a semi-official expression of the Ministry:—

"Peace they (the Americans) may make, but it must be on condition that America has not a foot of land on the waters of the St. Lawrence, . . . no settlement on the Lakes, . . . no renewal of the treaties of 1783 and 1794; . . . and they must explicitly abandon their new-fangled principles of the law of nations."

Liverpool, writing to Castlereagh September 23, said that in his opinion the Cabinet had "now gone to the utmost justifiable point in concession, and if they (the Americans) are so unreasonable as to reject our proposals, we have nothing to do but to fight it out. The military accounts from America are on the whole satisfactory." The news of the cruel humiliation at Bladensburg and the burning of Washington arrived at Ghent October 1, and caused British and Americans alike to expect a long series of British triumphs, especially on Lake Champlain, where they knew the British force to be overwhelming.

Goulburn exerted himself to produce a rupture. His letter of September 26 to Bathurst treated the American offer of an Indian amnesty as a rejection of the British ultimatum. Again Lord Bathurst set him right by sending him, October 5, the draft of a reciprocal article replacing the Indians in their situation before the war; and the British commissioners in a note dated October 8, 1814, communicated this article once more as an ultimatum. Harrison's treaty of July 22 with the Wyandots, Delawares, Shawanees, and other tribes, binding them to take up arms against the British, had then arrived, and this news lessened the interest of both parties in the Indian question. None of the American negotiators were prepared to break off negotiations on that point at such a time, and Clay was so earnest to settle the matter that he took from Gallatin and Adams the task of writing the necessary acceptance of the British ultimatum. Gallatin and Clay decided to receive the British article as according entirely with the American offer of amnesty, and the note was so written.

With this cordial admission of the British ultimatum the Americans coupled an intimation that the time had come when an exchange of general projects for the proposed treaty should be made. More than two months of discussion had then resulted only in eliminating the Indians from the dispute, and in agreeing to maintain silence in regard to the Lakes. Another great difficulty which had been insuperable was voluntarily removed by President Madison and his Cabinet, who after long and obstinate resistance at last authorized the commissioners, by instructions dated June 27, to omit impressment from the treaty. Considering the frequent positive declarations of the United States government, besides the rejection of Monroe's treaty in 1807 and of Admiral Warren's and Sir George Prevost's armistice of 1812 for want of an explicit concession on that point, Monroe's letter of June 27 was only to be excused as an act of common-sense or of necessity. The President preferred to represent it as an act of common-sense, warranted by the peace in Europe, which promised to offer no further occasion for the claim or the denial of the British right. On the same principle the subject of blockades was withdrawn from discussion; and these concessions, balanced by the British withdrawal from the Indian ultimatum and the Lake armaments, relieved the American commissioners of all their insuperable difficulties.

The British commissioners were not so easily rescued from their untenable positions. The American note of October 13, sent as usual to London, was answered by Bathurst October 18 and 20, in instructions revealing the true British terms more completely than had yet been ventured. Bathurst at length came to the cardinal point of the negotiation. As the American commissioners had said in their note of August 24, the British government must choose between the two ordinary bases of treaties of peace—the state before the war or *status ante bellum*; and the state of possession, or *uti possidetis*. Until the middle of October, 1814, the *uti possidetis*, as a basis of negotiation, included whatever country might have been occupied by Sir George Prevost in his September campaign. Bathurst from the first intended to insist on the state of possession, but had not thought proper to avow it. His instructions of October 18 and 20 directed the British commissioners to come to the point, and to claim the basis of *uti possidetis* from the American negotiators:—

"On their admitting this to be the basis on which they are ready to negotiate, but not before they have admitted it, you will proceed to state the mutual accommodations which may be entered into in conformity with this basis. The British occupy Fort Michillimackinaw, Fort Niagara, and all the country east of the Penobscot. On the other hand the forces of the United States occupy Fort Erie and Fort Amherstburg [Malden]. On the government of the United States consenting to restore these two forts, Great Britain is ready to restore the forts of Castine and Machias, retaining Fort Niagara and Fort Michillimackinaw."

Thus the British demand, which had till then been intended to include half of Maine and the whole south bank of the St. Lawrence River from Plattsburg to Sackett's Harbor, suddenly fell to a demand for Moose Island, a right of way across the northern angle of Maine, Fort Niagara with five miles circuit, and the Island of Mackinaw. The reason for the new spirit of moderation was not far to seek. On the afternoon of October 17, while the British Cabinet was still deliberating on the basis of *uti possidetis*, news reached London that the British invasion of northern New York, from which so much had been expected, had totally failed, and that Prevost's large army had precipitately retreated into Canada. The London *Times* of October 19 was frank in its expressions of disappointment:—

"This is a lamentable event to the civilized world. . . . The subversion of that system of fraud and malignity which constitutes the whole policy of the Jeffersonian school . . . was an event to which we should have bent and yet must bend all our energies. The present American government must be displaced, or it will sooner or later plant its poisoned dagger in the heart of the parent State."

The failure of the attempt on Baltimore and Drummond's bloody repulse at Fort Erie became known at the same time, and coming together at a critical moment threw confusion into the Ministry and their agents in the press and the diplomatic service throughout Europe. The *Courier* of October 25 declared that "peace with America is neither practicable nor desirable till we have wiped away this late disaster;" but the *Morning Chronicle* of October 21-24 openly intimated that the game of war was at an end. October 31, the Paris correspondent of the London *Times* told of the cheers that rose from the crowds in the Palais Royal gardens at each recital of the Plattsburg defeat; and October 21 Goulburn wrote from Ghent to Bathurst—

"The news from America is very far from satisfactory. Even our brilliant success at Baltimore, as it did not terminate in the capture of the town, will be considered by the Americans as a victory and not as an escape. . . . If it were not for the want of fuel in Boston, I should be quite in despair."

In truth the blockade was the single advantage held by England; and even in that advantage the Americans had a share as long as their cruisers surrounded the British Islands. Liverpool wrote to Castlereagh, October 21, commenting severely on Prevost's failure, and finding consolation only in the thought that the Americans showed themselves even less patriotic than he had supposed them to be:—

"The capture and destruction of Washington has not united the Americans: quite the contrary. We have gained more credit with them by saving private property than we have lost by the destruction of their public works and buildings. Madison clings to office, and I am strongly inclined to think that the best thing for us is that he should remain there."

Castlereagh at Vienna found himself unable to make the full influence of England felt, so long as such mortifying disasters by land and sea proved her inability to deal with an enemy she persisted in calling contemptible.

On the American commissioners the news came, October 21, with the effect of a reprieve from execution. Gallatin was deeply moved; Adams could not believe the magnitude of the success; but as far as regarded their joint action, the overthrow of England's scheme produced no change. Their tone had always been high, and they saw no advantage to be gained by altering it. The British commissioners sent to them, October 21, the substance of the new instructions, offering the basis of *uti possidetis*, subject to modifications for mutual convenience. The Americans by common consent, October 23, declined to treat on that basis, or on any other than the mutual restoration of territory. They thought that the British government was still playing with them, when in truth Lord Bathurst had yielded the chief part of the original British demand, and had come to what the whole British empire regarded as essentials—the right of way to Quebec, and the exclusion of American fishermen from British shores and waters.

The American note of October 24, bluntly rejecting the basis of *uti possidetis*, created a feeling akin to consternation in the British Cabinet. At first, ministers assumed that the war must go on, and deliberated only on the point to be preferred for a rupture. "We still think it desirable to gain a little more time before the negotiation is brought to a close," wrote Liverpool to the Duke of Wellington, October 28; and on the same day he wrote to Castlereagh at Vienna to warn him that the American war "will probably now be of some duration," and treating of its embarrassments without disguise. The Czar's conduct at Vienna had annoyed and alarmed all the great Powers, and the American war gave him a decisive advantage over England; but even without the Russian complication, the prospect for ministers was not cheering.

"Looking to a continuance of the American war, our financial state is far from satisfactory," wrote Lord Liverpool; ". . . the American war will not cost us less than £10,000,000, in addition to our peace establishment and other expenses. We must expect, therefore, to hear it said that the property tax is continued for the purpose of securing a better frontier for Canada."

A week passed without bringing encouragement to the British Cabinet. On the contrary the Ministry learned that a vigorous prosecution of hostilities would cost much more than ten million pounds, and when Liverpool next wrote to Castlereagh, November 2, although he could still see "little prospect for our negotiations at Ghent ending in peace," he added that "the continuance of the

American war will entail upon us a prodigious expense, much more than we had any idea of." A Cabinet meeting was to be held the next day, November 3, to review the whole course of policy as to America.

Throughout the American difficulties, from first to last, the most striking quality shown by the British government was the want of intelligence which caused the war, and marked the conduct of both the war and the negotiations. If the foreign relations of every government were marked by the same character, politics could be no more than rivalry in the race to blunder; but in October, 1814, another quality almost equally striking became evident. The weakness of British councils was as remarkable as their want of intelligence. The government of England had exasperated the Americans to an animosity that could not forget or forgive, and every dictate of self-interest required that it should carry out its policy to the end. Even domestic politics in Parliament might have been more easily managed by drawing public criticism to America, while in no event could taxes be reduced to satisfy the public demand. Another year of war was the consistent and natural course for ministers to prefer.

So the Cabinet evidently thought; but instead of making a decision, the Cabinet council of November 3 resorted to the expedient of shifting responsibility upon the Duke of Wellington. The Duke was then Ambassador at Paris. His life had been threatened by angry officers of Napoleon, who could not forgive his victories at Vittoria and Toulouse. For his own security he might be sent to Canada, and if he went, he should go with full powers to close the war as he pleased.

The next day, November 4, Liverpool wrote to Wellington, explaining the wishes of the Cabinet, and inviting him to take the entire command in Canada, in order to bring the war to an honorable conclusion. Wellington replied November 9—and his words were the more interesting because, after inviting and receiving so decided an opinion from so high an authority, the Government could not easily reject it. Wellington began by reviewing the military situation, and closed by expressing his opinion on the diplomatic contest:—

"I have already told you and Lord Bathurst that I feel no objection to going to America, though I don't promise to myself much success there. I believe there are troops enough there for the defence of Canada forever, and even for the accomplishment of any reasonable offensive plan that could be formed from the Canadian frontier. I am quite sure that all the American armies of which I have ever read would not beat out of a field of battle the troops that went from Bordeaux last summer, if common precautions and care were taken of them. That which appears to me to be wanting in America is not a general, or a general officer and troops, but a naval superiority on the Lakes."

These views did not altogether accord with those of Americans, who could not see that the British generals made use of the Lakes even when controlling them, but who saw the troops of Wellington retire from one field of battle after another—at Plattsburg, Baltimore, and New Orleans—while taking more than common precautions. Wellington's military comments showed little interest in American affairs, and evidently he saw nothing to be gained by going to Canada. His diplomatic ideas betrayed the same bias:—

"In regard to your present negotiations, I confess that I think you have no right, from the state of the war, to demand any concession of territory from America. . . . You have not been able to carry it into the enemy's territory, notwithstanding your military success and now undoubted military superiority, and have not even cleared your own territory on the point of attack. You cannot on any principle of equality in negotiation claim a cession of territory excepting in exchange for other advantages which you have in your power. . . . Then if this reasoning be true, why stipulate for the *uti possidetis?* You can get no territory; indeed, the state of your military operations, however creditable, does not entitle you to demand any."

After such an opinion from the first military authority of England, the British Ministry had no choice but to abandon its claim for territory. Wellington's letter reached London about November 13, and was duly considered in the Cabinet. Liverpool wrote to Castlereagh, November 18, that the Ministry had made its decision; the claim for territory was to be abandoned. For this retreat he alleged various excuses—such as the unsatisfactory state of the negotiations at Vienna, and the alarming condition of France; the finances, the depression of rents, and the temper of Parliament. Such reasoning would have counted for nothing in the previous month of May, but six months wrought a change in public feeling. The war had lost public favor. Even the colonial and shipping interests and the navy were weary of it, while the army had little to expect from it but hard service and no increase of credit. Every Englishman who came in contact with Americans seemed to suffer. Broke, the only victor by sea, was a lifelong invalid; and Brock and Ross, the only victors on land, had paid for their success with their lives. Incessant disappointment made the war an unpleasant thought with Englishmen. The burning of Washington was an exploit of which they could not boast. The rate of marine insurance was a daily and intolerable annoyance. So rapidly did the war decline in favor, that in the first half of December it was declared to be decidedly unpopular by one of the most judicious English liberals, Francis Horner; although Horner held that the Americans, as the dispute then stood, were the aggressors. The tone of the press showed the same popular tendency, for while the *Times* grumbled loudly over the Canada campaign, the *Morning Chronicle* no longer concealed its hostility to the war, and ventured to sneer at it, talking of "the entire defeat and destruction of the last British fleet but one; for it has become necessary to particularize them now."

While the Cabinet still waited, the first instalment of Ghent correspondence to August 20, published in America October 10, returned to England November 18, and received no flattering attention. "We cannot compliment our negotiators," remarked the *Morning Chronicle;* and the *Times* was still less pleased. "The British government has been tricked into bringing forward demands which it had not the power to enforce. . . . Why treat at all with Mr. Madison?" In Parliament, November 19, the liberal opposition attacked the Government for setting up novel pretensions. Ministers needed no more urging, and Bathurst thenceforward could not be charged with waste of time.

During this interval of more than three weeks the negotiators at Ghent were left to follow their own devices. In order to provide the Americans with occupation, the British commissioners sent them a note dated October 31 calling for a counter-project, since the basis of *uti possidetis* was refused. This note, with all the others since August 20, was sent by the Americans to Washington on the same day, October 31; and then Gallatin and Adams began the task of drafting the formal project of a treaty. Immediately the internal discords of the commission broke into earnest dispute. A struggle began between the East and the West over the fisheries and the Mississippi.

The treaty of 1783 coupled the American right of fishing in British waters and curing fish on British shores with the British right of navigating the Mississippi River. For that arrangement the elder Adams was responsible. The fisheries were a Massachusetts interest. At Paris in 1783 John Adams, in season and out of season, with his colleagues and with the British negotiators, insisted, with the intensity of conviction, that the fishing rights which the New England people held while subjects of the British crown were theirs by no grant or treaty, but as a natural right, which could not be extinguished by war; and that where British subjects had a right to fish, whether on coasts or shores, in bays, inlets, creeks, or harbors, Americans had the same right, to be exercised wherever and whenever they pleased. John Adams's persistence secured the article of the definitive treaty, which, without expressly admitting a natural right, coupled the in-shore fisheries and the navigation of the Mississippi with the recognition of independence. In 1814 as in 1783 John Adams clung to his trophies, and his son would have waged indefinite war rather than break his father's heart by sacrificing what he had won; but at Ghent the son stood in isolation which the father in the worst times had never known. Massachusetts left him to struggle alone for a principle that needed not only argument but force to make it victorious. Governor Strong did not even write to him as he did to Pickering, that Massachusetts would give an equivalent in territory for the fisheries. As far as the State could influence the result, the fisheries were to be lost by default.

Had Adams encountered only British opposition he might have overborne it as his father had done; but since 1783 the West had become a political power, and Louisiana had been brought into the Union. If the fisheries were recognized as an indefeasible right by the treaty of 1783, the British liberty of navigating the Mississippi was another indefeasible right, which must revive with peace. The Western people naturally objected to such a proposition. Neither they nor the Canadians could be blamed for unwillingness to impose a mischievous servitude forever upon their shores, and Clay believed his popularity to depend on preventing an express recognition of the British right to navigate the Mississippi. Either Clay or Adams was sure to refuse signing any treaty which expressly sacrificed the local interests of either.

In this delicate situation only the authority and skill of Gallatin saved the treaty. At the outset of the discussion, October 30, Gallatin quietly took the lead from Adams's hands, and assumed the championship of the fisheries by proposing to renew both privileges, making the one an equivalent for the other. Clay resisted obstinately, while Gallatin gently and patiently overbore him. When Gallatin's proposal was put to the vote November 5, Clay and

Russell alone opposed it—and the support then given by Russell to Clay was never forgotten by Adams. Clay still refusing to sign the offer, Gallatin continued his pressure, until at last, November 10, Clay consented to insert, not in the project of treaty, but in the note which accompanied it, a paragraph declaring that the commissioners were not authorized to bring into discussion any of the rights hitherto enjoyed in the fisheries: "From their nature, and from the peculiar character of the treaty of 1783 by which they were recognized, no further stipulation has been deemed necessary by the Government of the United States to entitle them to the full enjoyment of all of them."

Clay signed the note, though unwillingly; and it was sent November 10, with the treaty project, to the British commissioners, who forwarded it to London, where it arrived at the time when the British Cabinet had at last decided on peace. Bathurst sent his reply in due course; and Goulburn's disgust was great to find that instead of breaking negotiation on the point of the fisheries as he wished, he was required once more to give way. "You know that I was never much inclined to give way to the Americans," he wrote, November 25. "I am still less inclined to do so after the statement of our demands with which the negotiation opened, and which has in every point of view proved most unfortunate."

The British reply, dated November 26, took no notice of the American reservation as to the fisheries, but inserted in the project the old right of navigating the Mississippi. Both Bathurst and Goulburn thought that their silence, after the American declaration, practically conceded the American right to the fisheries, though Gambier and Dr. Adams thought differently. In either case the British note of November 26, though satisfactory to Adams, was far from agreeable to Clay, who was obliged to endanger the peace in order to save the Mississippi. Adams strongly inclined to take the British project precisely as it was offered, but Gallatin overruled him, and Clay would certainly have refused to sign. In discussing the subject, November 28, Gallatin proposed to accept the article on the navigation of the Mississippi if the British would add a provision recognizing the fishing rights. Clay lost his temper, and intimated something more than willingness to let Massachusetts pay for the pleasure of peace; but during the whole day of November 29, Gallatin continued urging Clay and restraining Adams, until at last on the third day he brought the matter to the point he wished.

The result of this long struggle saved not indeed the fisheries, but the peace. Clay made no further protest, when, in conference with the British commissioners December 1, the Americans offered to renew both the disputed rights. Their proposal was sent to London, and was answered by Bathurst December 6, in a letter offering to set aside for future negotiation the terms under which the old fishing liberty and the navigation of the Mississippi should be continued for fair equivalents. The British commissioners communicated this suggestion in conference December 10, and threw new dissension among the Americans.

The British offer to reserve both disputed rights for future negotiation implied that both rights were forfeited, or subject to forfeit, by war—an admission which Adams could not make, but which the other commissioners could not reject. At that point Adams found himself alone. Even Gallatin admitted that the claim to the natural right of catching and curing fish on British shores was untenable, and could never be supported. Adams's difficulties were the greater because the question of peace and war was reduced to two points—the fisheries and Moose Island—both interesting to Massachusetts alone. Yet the Americans were unwilling to yield without another struggle, and decided still to resist the British claim as inconsistent with the admitted basis of the *status ante bellum*.

The struggle with the British commissioners then became warm. A long conference, December 12, brought no conclusion. The treaty of 1783 could neither be followed nor ignored, and perplexed the Englishmen as much as the Americans. During December 13, and December 14, Adams continued to press his colleagues to assert the natural right to the fisheries, and to insist on the permanent character of the treaty of 1783; but Gallatin would not consent to make that point an ultimatum. All the commissioners except Adams resigned themselves to the sacrifice of the fisheries; but Gallatin decided to make one more effort before abandoning the struggle, and with that object drew up a note rejecting the British stipulation because it implied the abandonment of a right, but offering either to be silent as to both the fisheries and the Mississippi, or to admit a general reference to further negotiation of all subjects in dispute, so expressed as to imply no abandonment of right.

The note was signed and sent December 14, and the Americans waited another week for the answer. Successful as they had been in driving their British antagonists from one position after another, they were not satisfied. Adams still feared that he might not be able to sign, and Clay was little better pleased. "He said we should make a damned bad treaty, and he did not know whether he would sign it or not." Whatever Adams thought of the treaty, his respect for at least two of his colleagues was expressed in terms of praise rarely used by him. Writing to his wife, September 27, Adams said: "Mr. Gallatin keeps and increases his influence over us all. It would have been an irreparable loss if our country had been deprived of the benefit of his talents in this negotiation." At the moment of final suspense he wrote again, December 16:

"Of the five members of the American mission, the Chevalier (Bayard) has the most perfect control of his temper, the most deliberate coolness; and it is the more meritorious because it is real self-command. His feelings are as quick and his spirits as high as those of any one among us, but he certainly has them under government. I can scarcely express to you how much both he and Mr. Gallatin have risen in my esteem since we have been here living together. Gallatin has not quite so constant a supremacy over his own emotions; yet he seldom yields to an ebullition of temper, and recovers from it immediately. He has a faculty, when discussion grows too warm, of turning off its edge by a joke, which I envy him more than all his other talents; and he has in his character one of the most extraordinary combinations of stubbornness and of flexibility that I ever met with in man. His greatest fault I think to be an ingenuity sometimes trenching upon ingenuousness."

Gallatin's opinion of Adams was not so enthusiastic as Adams's admiration for him. He thought Adams's chief fault to be that he lacked judgment "to a deplorable degree." Of Clay, whether in his merits or his faults, only one opinion was possible. Clay's character belonged to the simple Southern or Virginia type, somewhat affected, but not rendered more complex, by Western influence—and transparent beyond need of description or criticism.

The extraordinary patience and judgment of Gallatin, aided by the steady support of Bayard, carried all the American points without sacrificing either Adams or Clay, and with no quarrel of serious importance on any side. When Lord Bathurst received the American note of December 14, he replied December 19, yielding the last advantage he possessed: "The Prince Regent regrets to find that there does not appear any prospect of being able to arrive at such an arrangement with regard to the fisheries as would have the effect of coming to a full and satisfactory explanation on that subject"; but since this was the case, the disputed article might be altogether omitted.

Thus the treaty became simply a cessation of hostilities leaving every claim on either side open for future settlement. The formality of signature was completed December 24, and closed an era of American history. In substance, the treaty sacrificed much on both sides for peace. The Americans lost their claims for British spoliations, and were obliged to admit question of their right to Eastport and their fisheries in British waters; the British failed to establish their principles of impressment and blockade, and admitted question of their right to navigate the Mississippi and trade with the Indians. Perhaps at the moment the Americans were the chief losers; but they gained their greatest triumph in referring all their disputes to be settled by time, the final negotiator, whose decision they could safely trust.

CHAPTER XXX
THE CLOSE OF HOSTILITIES

England received the Treaty of Ghent with feelings of mixed anger and satisfaction. The *Morning Chronicle* seemed surprised at the extreme interest which the news excited. As early as November 24, when ministers made their decision to concede the American terms, the *Morning Chronicle* announced that "a most extraordinary sensation was produced yesterday" by news from Ghent, and by reports that ministers had abandoned their ground. When the treaty arrived, December 26, the same Whig newspaper, the next morning, while asserting that ministers had "humbled themselves in the dust and thereby brought discredit on the country," heartily approved what they had done; and added that "the city was in a complete state of hurricane during the whole of yesterday, but the storm did not attain its utmost height until toward the evening. . . . Purchases were made to the extent of many hundred thousand pounds." The importance of the United States to England was made more apparent by the act of peace than by the pressure of war. "At Birmingham," said the *Courier*, "an immense assemblage witnessed the arrival of the mail, and immediately took the horses out, and drew the mail to the post-office with the loudest acclamations,"—acclamations over a treaty universally regarded as discreditable.

The *Times* admitted the general joy, and denied only that it was universal. If the *Times* in any degree represented public opinion, the popular satisfaction at the peace was an extraordinary political symptom, for in its opinion the Government had accepted terms such as "might have been expected from an indulgent and liberal conqueror. . . . We have retired from the combat," it said, December 30, "with the stripes yet bleeding on our back—with the recent defeats at Plattsburg and on Lake Champlain unavenged." During several succeeding weeks the *Times* continued its extravagant complaints, which served only to give the Americans a new idea of the triumph they had won.

In truth, no one familiar with English opinion during the past ten years attempted to deny that the government of England must admit one or the other of two conclusions—either it had ruinously mismanaged its American policy before the war, or it had disgraced itself by the peace. The *Morning Chronicle*, while approving the treaty, declared that the Tories were on this point at odds with their own leaders: "Their attachment to the ministers, though strong, cannot reconcile them to this one step, though surely if they would look back with an impartial eye on the imbecility and error with which their idols conducted the war, they must acknowledge their prudence in putting an end to it. One of them very honestly said, two days ago, that if they had not put an end to the war, the war would have put an end to their Ministry." Whatever doubts existed about the temper of England before that time, no one doubted after the peace of Ghent that war with the United States was an unpopular measure with the British people.

Nevertheless the *Times* and the Tories continued their complaints until March 9, when two simultaneous pieces of news silenced criticism of the American treaty. The severe defeat at New Orleans became known at the moment when

Napoleon, having quitted Elba, began his triumphal return to Paris. These news, coming in the midst of Corn Riots, silenced further discussion of American relations, and left ministers free to redeem at Waterloo the failures they had experienced in America.

In the United States news of peace was slow to arrive. The British sloop-of-war *Favorite* bore the despatches, and was still at sea when the month of February began. The commissioners from Massachusetts and Connecticut, bearing the demands of the Hartford Convention, started for Washington. Every one was intent on the situation of New Orleans, where a disaster was feared. Congress seemed to have abandoned the attempt to provide means of defence, although it began another effort to create a bank on Dallas's plan. A large number of the most intelligent citizens believed that two announcements would soon be made—one, that New Orleans was lost; the other, that the negotiation at Ghent had ended in rupture. Under this double shock, the collapse of the national government seemed to its enemies inevitable.

In this moment of suspense, the first news arrived from New Orleans. To the extreme relief of the Government and the Republican majority in Congress, they learned, February 4, that the British invasion was defeated and New Orleans saved. The victory was welcomed by illuminations, votes of thanks, and rejoicings greater than had followed the more important success at Plattsburg, or the more brilliant battles at Niagara; for the success won at New Orleans relieved the Government from a load of anxiety, and postponed a crisis supposed to be immediately at hand. Half the influence of the Hartford Convention was destroyed by it; and the commissioners, who were starting for the capital, had reason to expect a reception less favorable by far than they would have met had the British been announced as masters of Louisiana. Yet the immediate effect of the news was not to lend new vigor to Congress, but rather to increase its inertness, and to encourage its dependence on militia, Treasury notes, and good fortune.

A week afterward, on the afternoon of Saturday, February 11, the British sloop-of-war *Favorite* sailed up New York harbor, and the city quickly heard rumors of peace. At eight o'clock that evening the American special messenger landed, bringing the official documents intrusted to his care; and when the news could no longer be doubted, the city burst into an uproar of joy. The messenger was slow in reaching Washington, where he arrived only on the evening of Tuesday, February 13, and delivered his despatches to the Secretary of State.

Had the treaty been less satisfactory than it was, the President would have hesitated long before advising its rejection, and the Senate could hardly have gained courage to reject it. In spite of rumors from London and significant speculations on the London Exchange, known in America in the middle of January, no one had seriously counted on a satisfactory peace, as was proved by the steady depression of government credit and of the prices of American staples. The reaction after the arrival of the news was natural, and so violent that few persons stopped to scrutinize the terms. Contrary to Clay's forebodings, the treaty, mere armistice though it seemed to be, was probably the most popular treaty ever negotiated by the United States. The President sent it to the

Senate February 15; and the next day, without suggestion of amendment, and apparently without a criticism, unless from Federalists, the Senate unanimously confirmed it, thirty-five senators uniting in approval.

Yet the treaty was not what the Government had expected in declaring the war, or such as it had a right to demand. The Republicans admitted it in private, and the Federalists proclaimed it in the press. Senator Gore wrote to Governor Strong: "The treaty must be deemed disgraceful to the Government who made the war and the peace, and will be so adjudged by all, after the first effusions of joy at relief have subsided." Opinions differed widely on the question where the disgrace belonged—whether to the Government who made the war, or to the people who refused to support it; but no one pretended that the terms of peace, as far as they were expressed in the treaty, were so good as those repeatedly offered by England more than two years before. Yet the treaty was universally welcomed, and not a thought of continued war found expression.

In New England the peace was received with extravagant delight. While the government messenger who carried the official news to Washington made no haste, a special messenger started from New York at ten o'clock Saturday night, immediately on the landing of the government messenger, and in thirty-two hours arrived in Boston. Probably the distance had rarely been travelled in less time, for the Boston *Centinel* announced the expense to be two hundred and twenty-five dollars; and such an outlay was seldom made for rapidity of travel or news. As the messenger passed from town to town he announced the tidings to the delighted people. Reaching the *Centinel* office, at Boston, early Monday morning, he delivered his bulletin, and a few minutes after it was published all the bells were set ringing; schools and shops were closed, and a general holiday taken; flags were hoisted, the British with the American; the militia paraded, and in the evening the city was illuminated. Yet the terms of peace were wholly unknown, and the people of Massachusetts had every reason to fear that their interests were sacrificed for the safety of the Union. Their rejoicing over the peace was as unreasoning as their hatred of the war.

Only along the Canadian frontier where the farmers had for three years made large profits by supplying both armies, the peace was received without rejoicing. South of New York, although less public delight was expressed, the relief was probably greater than in New England. Virginia had suffered most, and had felt the blockade with peculiar severity. A few weeks before the treaty was signed, Jefferson wrote:—

"By the total annihilation in value of the produce which was to give me sustenance and independence, I shall be like Tantalus—up to the shoulders in water, yet dying with thirst. We can make indeed enough to eat, drink, and clothe ourselves, but nothing for our salt, iron, groceries, and taxes which must be paid in money. For what can we raise for the market? Wheat?—we only give it to our horses, as we have been doing ever since harvest. Tobacco?—it is not worth the pipe it is smoked in."

While all Virginia planters were in this situation February 13, they awoke February 14 to find flour worth ten dollars a barrel, and groceries fallen fifty per cent. They were once more rich beyond their wants.

So violent and sudden a change in values had never been known in the United States. The New York market saw fortunes disappear and other fortunes created in the utterance of a single word. All imported articles dropped to low prices. Sugar which sold Saturday at twenty-six dollars a hundred-weight, sold Monday at twelve dollars and a half. Tea sank from two dollars and a quarter to one dollar a pound; tin fell from eighty to twenty-five dollars a box; cotton fabrics declined about fifty per cent. On the other hand flour, cotton, and the other chief staples of American produce rose in the same proportion. Nominally flour was worth seven and a half dollars on Saturday, though no large amounts could have been sold; On Monday the price was ten dollars, and all the wheat in the country was soon sold at that rate.

Owing to the derangement of currency, these prices expressed no precise specie value. The effect of the peace on the currency was for a moment to restore an apparent equilibrium. In New York the specie premium of twenty-two per cent was imagined for a time to have vanished. In truth, United States six-per-cents rose in New York from seventy-six to eighty-eight in paper; Treasury-notes from ninety-two to ninety-eight. In Philadelphia, on Saturday, six-per-cents sold at seventy-five; on Monday, at ninety-three. The paper depreciation remained about twenty per cent in New York, about twenty-four per cent in Philadelphia, and thirty per cent in Baltimore. The true value of six-per-cents was about sixty-eight; of Treasury notes about seventy-eight, after the announcement of peace.

As rapidly as possible the blockade was raised, and ships were hurried to sea with the harvests of three seasons for cargo; but some weeks still passed before all the operations of war were closed. The news of peace reached the British squadron below Mobile in time to prevent further advance on that place; but on the ocean a long time elapsed before fighting wholly ceased.

Some of the worst disasters as well as the greatest triumphs of the war occurred after the treaty of peace had been signed. The battle of New Orleans was followed by the loss of Fort Bowyer. At about the same time a British force occupied Cumberland Island on the southern edge of the Georgia coast, and January 13 attacked the fort at the entrance of the St. Mary's, and having captured it without loss, ascended the river the next day to the town of St. Mary's, which they seized, together with its merchandise and valuable ships in the river. Cockburn established his headquarters on Cumberland Island January 22, and threw the whole State of Georgia into agitation, while he waited for the arrival of a brigade with which an attack was to be made on Savannah.

The worst disaster of the naval war occurred January 15, when the frigate *President*—one of the three American forty-fours, under Stephen Decatur, the favorite ocean hero of the American service—suffered defeat and capture within fifty miles of Sandy Hook. No naval battle of the war was more disputed in its merits, although its occurrence in the darkest moments of national depression was almost immediately forgotten in the elation of the peace a few days later.

Secretary Jones retired from the Navy Department December 19, 1814, yielding the direction to B. W. Crowninshield of Massachusetts, but leaving a squadron ready for sea at New York under orders for distant service. The *Peacock* and *Hornet,* commanded by Warrington and Biddle, were to sail with a store-ship on a long cruise in Indian waters, where they were expected to ravage British shipping from the Cape of Good Hope to the China seas. With them Decatur was to go in the *President,* and at the beginning of the new year he waited only an opportunity to slip to sea past the blockading squadron. January 14 a strong westerly wind drove the British fleet out of sight. The *President* set sail, but in crossing the bar at night grounded, and continued for an hour or more to strike heavily, until the tide and strong wind forced her across. Decatur then ran along the Long Island coast some fifty miles, when he changed his course to the southeast, hoping that he had evaded the blockading squadrons. This course was precisely that which Captain Hayes, commanding the squadron, expected; and an hour before daylight the four British ships, standing to the northward and eastward, sighted the *President,* standing to the southward and eastward, not more than two miles on the weather-bow of the *Majestic*—the fifty-six-gun razee commanded by Captain Hayes.

The British ships promptly made chase. Captain Hayes's squadron, besides the *Majestic,* consisted of the *Endymion,* a fifty-gun frigate, with the *Pomone* and *Tenedos,* frigates like the *Guerrière, Macedonian,* and *Java,* armed with eighteen-pound guns. Only from the *Endymion* had Decatur much to fear, for the *Majestic* was slow and the other ships were weak; but the *Endymion* was a fast sailer, and especially adapted to meet the American frigates. The *Endymion,* according to British authority, was about one hundred and fifty-nine feet in length on the lower deck, and nearly forty-three feet in extreme breadth: the *President,* on the same authority, was about one hundred and seventy-three feet in length, and forty-four feet in breadth. The *Endymion* carried twenty-six long twenty-four-pounders on the maindeck; the *President* carried thirty. The *Endymion* mounted twenty-two thirty-two pound carronades on the spar deck; the *President* mounted twenty. The *Endymion* had also a long brass eighteen-pounder as a bow-chaser; the *President* a long twenty-four-pounder as a bow-chaser, and another as a stern-chaser. The *Endymion* was short-handed after her losses in action with the *Prince de Neufchatel,* and carried only three hundred and forty-six men; the *President* carried four hundred and fifty. The *Endymion* was the weaker ship, probably in the proportion of four to five; but for her immediate purpose she possessed a decisive advantage in superior speed, especially in light winds.

At two o'clock in the afternoon, the *Endymion* had gained so much on the *President* as to begin exchanging shots between the stern and bow-chasers. Soon after five o'clock, as the wind fell, the *Endymion* crept up on the *President's* starboard quarter, and "commenced close action." After bearing the enemy's fire for half an hour without reply, Decatur was obliged to alter his course and accept battle, or suffer himself to be crippled. The battle lasted two hours and a half, until eight o'clock when firing ceased; but at half-past nine, according to the *Pomone's* log, the *Endymion* fired two guns, which the *President* returned with one. According to Decatur's account the *Endymion* lay for half an hour under his stern, without firing, while the *President* was trying to escape. In truth the *Endymion* had no need to fire; she was busy bending new sails, while Decatur's ship, according to his official report, was crippled, and in want of wind could not escape.

In a letter written by Decatur to his wife immediately after the battle, he gave an account of what followed, as he understood it.

"The *Endymion,*" he began, . . . "was the leading ship of the enemy. She got close under my quarters and was cutting my rigging without my being able to bring a gun to bear upon her. To suffer this was making my capture certain, and that too without injury to the enemy. I therefore bore up for the *Endymion* and engaged her for two hours, when we silenced and beat her off. At this time the rest of the ships got within two miles of us. We made all the sail we could from them, but it was in vain. In three hours, the *Pomone* and *Tenedos* were alongside, and the *Majestic* and *Endymion* close to us. All that was now left for me to do was to receive the fire of the nearest ship and surrender."

The *Pomone's* account of the surrender completed the story:

"At eleven, being within gunshot of the *President* who was still steering to the eastward under a press of sail, with royal, top-gallant, topmast, and lower studding-sails set, finding how much we outsailed her our studding-sails were taken in, and immediately afterward we luffed to port and fired our starboard broadside. The enemy then also luffed to port, bringing his larboard broadside to bear, which was momentarily expected, as a few minutes previous to our closing her she hoisted a light abaft, which in night actions constitutes the ensign. Our second broadside was fired, and the *President* still luffing up as if intent to lay us on board, we hauled close to port, bracing the yards up, and setting the mainsail; the broadside was again to be fired into his bows, raking, when she hauled down the light, and we hailed demanding if she had surrendered. The reply was in the affirmative, and the firing immediately ceased. The *Tenedos,* who was not more than three miles off, soon afterward came up, and assisted the *Pomone* in securing the prize and removing the prisoners. At three quarters past twelve the *Endymion* came up, and the *Majestic* at three in the morning."

Between the account given by Decatur and that of the *Pomone's* log were some discrepancies. In the darkness many mistakes were inevitable; but if each party were taken as the best authority on its own side, the connected story seemed to show that Decatur, after beating off the *Endymion,* made every effort to escape, but was impressed by the conviction that if overtaken by the squadron, nothing was left but to receive the fire of the nearest ship, and surrender. The night was calm and the *President* made little headway. At eleven o'clock one of the pursuing squadron came up, and fired two broadsides. "Thus situated," reported Decatur, "with about one fifth of my crew killed and wounded, my ship crippled, and a more than fourfold force opposed to me, without a chance of escape left, I deemed it my duty to surrender."

The official Court of Inquiry on the loss of the *President* reported, a few months afterward, a warm approval of Decatur's conduct:

"We fear that we cannot express in a manner that will do justice to our feelings our admiration of the conduct of Commodore Decatur and his officers and crew. . . . As well during the chase as through his contest with the enemy

[he] evinced great judgment and skill, perfect coolness, the most determined resolution, and heroic courage."

The high praise thus bestowed was doubtless deserved, since the Court of Inquiry was composed of persons well qualified to judge; but Decatur's battle with the *Endymion* was far from repeating the success of his triumph over the *Macedonian*. Anxious to escape rather than to fight, Decatur in consequence failed either to escape or resist with effect. The action with the *Endymion* lasted three hours from the time when the British frigate gained the *President's* quarter. For the first half hour the *President* received the *Endymion's* broadsides without reply. During the last half hour the firing slackened and became intermittent. Yet for two hours the ships were engaged at close range, a part of the time within half musket-shot, in a calm sea, and in a parallel line of sailing. At all times of the battle, the ships were well within point-blank range, which for long twenty-four-pounders and thirty-two-pound carronades was about two hundred and fifty yards. Decatur had needed but an hour and a half to disable and capture the *Macedonian*, although a heavy swell disturbed his fire, and at no time were the ships within easy range for grape, which was about one hundred and fifty yards. The *Endymion* was a larger and better ship than the *Macedonian*, but the *President* was decidedly less efficient than the *United States*.

According to Captain Hope's report, the *Endymion* lost eleven men killed and fourteen wounded. The *President* reported twenty-five killed and sixty wounded. Of the two ships the *President* was probably the most severely injured. The masts of both were damaged, and two days afterward both were dismasted in a gale; but while the *President* lost all her masts by the board, the *Endymion* lost only her fore and main masts considerably above deck. On the whole, the injury inflicted by the *President* on the *Endymion* was less than in proportion to her relative strength, or to the length of time occupied in the action. Even on the supposition that the *President's* fire was directed chiefly against the *Endymion's* rigging, the injury done was not proportional to the time occupied in doing it. According to the *Pomone's* log, the *Endymion* was able to rejoin the squadron at quarter before one o'clock in the night. According to the *Endymion's* log, she repaired damages in an hour, and resumed the chase at nine o'clock.

The British ships were surprised that Decatur should have surrendered to the *Pomone* without firing a shot. Apparently the *Pomone's* broadside did little injury, and the *Tenedos* was not yet in range when the *Pomone* opened fire. The question of the proper time to surrender was to be judged by professional rules; and if resistance was hopeless, Decatur was doubtless justified in striking when he did; but his apparent readiness to do so hardly accorded with the popular conception of his character.

As usual the sloops were more fortunate than the frigate, and got to sea successfully, January 22, in a gale of wind which enabled them to run the blockade. Their appointed rendezvous was Tristan da Cunha. There the *Hornet* arrived on the morning of March 23, and before she had time to anchor sighted the British sloop-of-war *Penguin*—a new brig then cruising in search of the American privateer *Young Wasp*.

Captain Biddle of the *Hornet* instantly made chase, and Captain Dickinson of the *Penguin* bore up and stood for the enemy. According to British authority the vessels differed only by a "trifling disparity of force." In truth the American was somewhat superior in size, metal, and crew, although not so decisively as in most of the sloop battles. The *Hornet* carried eighteen thirty-two-pound carronades and two long twelve-pounders; the *Penguin* carried sixteen thirty-two-pound carronades, two long guns differently reported as twelve-pounders and six-pounders, and a twelve-pound carronade. The crews were apparently the same in number—about one hundred and thirty-two men. Captain Dickinson had equipped his vessel especially for the purpose of capturing heavy privateers, and was then looking for the *Young Wasp*—a vessel decidedly superior to the *Hornet*. Although he had reason to doubt his ability to capture the *Young Wasp*, he did not fear a combat with the *Hornet*, and showed his confidence by brushing up close alongside and firing a gun, while the *Hornet*, all aback, waited for him.

The result was very different from that of Decatur's two-hour battle with the *Endymion*. In little more than twenty minutes of close action the *Penguin's* foremast and bowsprit were gone, her captain killed, and thirty-eight men killed or wounded, or more than one fourth the crew. The brig was "a perfect wreck," according to the British official report, when the senior surviving officer hailed and surrendered. The *Hornet* was not struck in the hull, but was very much cut up in rigging and spars. She had two killed, and nine wounded. "It was evident," said Captain Biddle's report, "that our fire was greatly superior both in quickness and effect."

The *Penguin* was destroyed, and the *Hornet* and *Peacock* continued their cruise until April 27, when they chased for twenty-four hours a strange sail, which proved to be the British seventy-four *Cornwallis*. On discovering the character of the chase Biddle made off to windward, but found that the enemy "sailed remarkably fast and was very weatherly." At daylight of the 29th, the *Cornwallis* was within gunshot on the *Hornet's* lee-quarter. Her shot did not take effect, and Biddle, by lightening his ship, drew out of fire; but a few hours later the enemy again came up within three quarters of a mile, in a calm sea, and opened once more. Three shots struck the *Hornet*, but without crippling her. Biddle threw over everything that could be spared, except one long gun; and a fortunate change of wind enabled him a second time to creep out of fire. He escaped; but the loss of his guns, anchors, cables, and boats obliged him to make for San Salvador, where he heard the news of peace.

Captain Warrington in the *Peacock* continued his cruise to the Indian Ocean, and captured four Indiamen. In the Straits of Sunda, June 30, he encountered a small East India Company's cruiser, whose commander hailed and announced peace. Warrington replied, "directing him at the same time to haul his colors down if it were the case, in token of it—adding that if he did not, I should fire into him." The brig refused to strike its colors, and Warrington nearly destroyed her by a broadside. For this violence little excuse could be offered, for the *Nautilus* was not half the *Peacock's* strength, and could not have escaped. Warrington, like most officers of the American navy, remembered the *Chesapeake* too well.

The cruise of the *President, Peacock,* and *Hornet* ended in the loss of the *President,* the disabling of the *Hornet,* and the arrival of the *Peacock* alone at the point intended for their common cruising-ground. No other national vessels were at sea after peace was signed, except the *Constitution,* which late in December sailed from Boston under the command of Captain Charles Stewart—a Philadelphian of Irish descent, not thirty-nine years old, but since 1806 a captain in the United States service.

Cruising between Gibraltar and Madeira, at about one o'clock on the afternoon of February 20 Captain Stewart discovered two sail ahead, which he chased and overtook at six o'clock. Both were ship-rigged sloops-of-war. The larger of the two was the *Cyane.* Americans preferred to call her a frigate, but that designation, though vague at best, could hardly be applied to such a vessel. The *Cyane* was a frigate-built sloop-of-war, or corvette, like the *Little Belt,* carrying a regular complement of one hundred and eighty-five men. Her length on the lower deck was one hundred and eighteen feet, her breadth was thirty-two feet. She carried thirty-three guns, all carronades except two long-nines or twelves. Her companion, the *Levant,* was also a sloop-of-war of the larger sort, though smaller than the *Cyane.* She mounted twenty-one guns, all carronades except two long nine-pounders. Her regular crew was one hundred and thirty-five men and boys.

Either separately or together the British ships were decidedly unequal to the *Constitution,* which could, by remaining at long range, sink them both without receiving a shot in return. The *Constitution* carried thirty-two long twenty-four-pounders; while the two sloops could reply to these guns only by four long nine-pounders. The *Constitution* carried four hundred and fifty men; the two sloops at the time of the encounter carried three hundred and thirty-six seamen, marines, and officers. The *Constitution* was built of great strength; the two sloops had only the frames of their class. The utmost that the British captains could hope was that one of the two vessels might escape by the sacrifice of the other.

Instead of escaping, the senior officer, Captain George Douglass of the *Levant,* resolved to engage the frigate, "in the hopes, by disabling her, to prevent her intercepting two valuable convoys that sailed from Gibraltar about the same time as the *Levant* and *Cyane."* Captain Douglass knew his relative strength, for he had heard that the American frigate was on his course. Yet he seriously expected to disable her, and made a courageous attempt to do so.

The two ships, close together, tried first for the weather-gauge, but the *Constitution* outsailed them also on that point. They then bore up in hope of delaying the engagement till night, but the *Constitution* overhauled them too rapidly for the success of that plan. They then stood on the starboard tack, the *Cyane* astern, the *Levant* a half-cable length ahead, while the *Constitution* came up to windward and opened fire. Commodore Stewart's report described the result:

"At five minutes past six ranged up on the starboard side of the sternmost ship [the *Cyane*], about three hundred yards distant, and commenced the action by broadsides—both ships returning our fire with great spirit for about fifteen minutes. Then the fire of the enemy beginning to slacken, and the great column of smoke collected under our lee, induced us to cease our fire to ascertain their positions and conditions. In about three minutes the smoke clearing away, we found ourselves abreast of the headmost ship [the *Levant*], the sternmost ship luffing up for our starboard quarter."

Three hundred yards was a long range for carronades, especially in British sloops whose marksmanship was indifferent at best. According to the British court-martial on the officers of the *Cyane* and *Levant*, their carronades had little effect. If Stewart managed his ship as his duty required, the two sloops until that moment should have been allowed to make little effective return of the *Constitution's* broadside of sixteen twenty-four-pounders except by two nine-pounders. They were in the position of the *Essex* at Valparaiso. The *Cyane* naturally luffed up, in order to bring her carronades to bear, but she was already cut to pieces, and made the matter worse by closing.

"We poured a broadside into the headmost ship," continued the American account, "and then braced aback our main and mizzen topsails and backed astern under cover of the smoke abreast the sternmost ship, when the action was continued with spirit and considerable effect until thirty-five minutes past six, when the enemy's fire again slackened."

The *Levant*, after receiving two stern-raking fires, bore up at forty minutes past six and began to repair damages two miles to leeward. The *Cyane*, having become unmanageable, struck at ten minutes before seven. The most remarkable incident of the battle occurred after the *Cyane* struck, when the *Constitution* went after the *Levant* which was in sight to leeward. The little *Levant*, instead of running away, stood directly for the huge American frigate, more than three times her size, and ranging close alongside fired a broadside into her as the two ships passed on opposite tacks. Although the sloop received the *Constitution's* broadside in return, she was only captured at last after an hour's chase, at ten o'clock, much cut up in spars and rigging, but still sea-worthy, and with seven men killed and sixteen wounded, or only one casualty to six of her crew.

In truth, the injury inflicted by the *Constitution's* fire was not so great as might have been expected. The *Cyane* lost twelve killed and twenty-six wounded, if the American report was correct. Neither ship was dismasted or in a sinking condition. Both arrived safely, March 10, at Porto Praya. On the other hand, the *Constitution* was struck eleven times in the hull, and lost three men killed and twelve wounded, three of the latter mortally. She suffered more than in her battle with the *Guerrière*—a result creditable to the British ships, considering that in each case the *Constitution* could choose her own range.

Stewart took his prizes to the Cape de Verde Islands. At noon, March 11, while lying in port at Porto Praya, three British frigates appeared off the harbor, and Stewart instantly stood at sea, passing the enemy's squadron to windward within gunshot. The three frigates made chase, and at one o'clock, as the *Cyane* was dropping astern, Stewart signalled to her to tack ship, and either escape, if not pursued, or return to Porto Praya. The squadron paid no attention to the *Cyane*, but followed the *Constitution* and *Levant*. At three o'clock, the *Levant* falling behind, Stewart signalled her also to tack. Immediately the whole British squadron abandoned pursuit of the *Constitution* and followed the *Levant* to

Porto Praya, where they seized her under the guns of the Portuguese batteries. Meanwhile the *Constitution* and *Cyane* escaped, and reached the United States without further accident. The extraordinary blunders of the British squadron were never satisfactorily explained.

These combats and cruises, with the last ravages of the privateers, closed the war on the ocean as it had long ceased on land; and meanwhile the people of the United States had turned their energies to undertakings of a wholly different character.

CHAPTER XXXI
OBSERVATIONS ON THE AMERICAN CHARACTER

In the American character antipathy to war ranked first among political traits. The majority of Americans regarded war in a peculiar light, the consequence of comparative security. No European nation could have conducted a war, as the people of America conducted the War of 1812. The possibility of doing so without destruction explained the existence of the national trait, and assured its continuance. In politics, the divergence of America from Europe perpetuated itself in the popular instinct for peaceable methods. The Union took shape originally on the general lines that divided the civil from the military elements of the British constitution. The party of Jefferson and Gallatin was founded on dislike of every function of government necessary in a military system. Although Jefferson carried his pacific theories to an extreme, and brought about a military reaction, the reactionary movement was neither universal, violent, nor lasting; and society showed no sign of changing its convictions. With greater strength the country might acquire greater familiarity with warlike methods, but in the same degree was less likely to suffer any general change of habits. Nothing but prolonged intestine contests could convert the population of an entire continent into a race of warriors.

A people whose chief trait was antipathy to war, and to any system organized with military energy, could scarcely develop great results in national administration; yet the Americans prided themselves chiefly on their political capacity. Even the war did not undeceive them although the incapacity brought into evidence by the war was undisputed, and was most remarkable among the communities which believed themselves to be most gifted with political sagacity. Virginia and Massachusetts by turns admitted failure in dealing with issues so simple that the newest societies, like Tennessee and Ohio, understood them by instinct. That incapacity in national politics should appear as a leading trait in American character was unexpected by Americans, but might naturally result from their conditions. The better test of American character was not political but social, and was to be found not in the government but in the people.

The sixteen years of Jefferson's and Madison's rule furnished international tests of popular intelligence upon which Americans could depend. The ocean was the only open field for competition among nations. Americans enjoyed there no natural or artificial advantages over Englishmen, Frenchmen, or Spaniards; indeed, all these countries possessed navies, resources, and experience greater than were to be found in the United States. Yet the Americans developed, in the course of twenty years, a surprising degree of skill in naval affairs. The evidence of their success was to be found nowhere so complete as in the avowals of Englishmen who knew best the history of naval progress. The American invention of the fast-sailing schooner or clipper was the more remarkable because, of all American inventions, this alone sprang from direct competition with Europe. During ten centuries of struggle the nations of Europe had labored to obtain superiority over each other in ship-construction, yet Americans instantly made improvements which gave them superiority, and which Europeans were unable immediately to imitate even after seeing them. Not only were American vessels better in model, faster in sailing, easier and quicker in handling, and more economical in working than the European, but they were also better equipped. The English complained as a grievance that the Americans adopted new and unwarranted devices in naval warfare; that their vessels were heavier and better constructed, and their missiles of unusual shape and improper use. The Americans resorted to expedients that had not been tried before, and excited a mixture of irritation and respect in the English service, until Yankee smartness became a national misdemeanor.

The English admitted themselves to be slow to change their habits, but the French were both quick and scientific; yet Americans did on the ocean what the French, under stronger inducements, failed to do. The French privateer preyed upon British commerce for twenty years without seriously injuring it; but no sooner did the American privateer sail from French ports, than the rates of insurance doubled in London, and an outcry for protection arose among English shippers which the Admiralty could not calm. The British newspapers were filled with assertions that the American cruiser was the superior of any vessel of its class, and threatened to overthrow England's supremacy on the ocean.

Another test of relative intelligence was furnished by the battles at sea. Instantly after the loss of the *Guerrière* the English discovered and complained that American gunnery was superior to their own. They explained their inferiority by the length of time that had elapsed since their navy had found on the ocean an enemy to fight. Every vestige of hostile fleets had been swept away, until, after the battle of Trafalgar, British frigates ceased practice with their guns. Doubtless the British navy had become somewhat careless in the absence of a dangerous enemy, but Englishmen were themselves aware that some other cause must have affected their losses. Nothing showed that Nelson's line-of-battle ships, frigates, or sloops were as a rule better fought than the *Macedonian* and *Java*, the *Avon* and *Reindeer*. Sir Howard Douglas, the chief authority on the subject, attempted in vain to explain British reverses by the deterioration of British gunnery. His analysis showed only that American gunnery was extraordinarily good. Of all vessels, the sloop-of-war—on account of its smallness, its quick motion, and its more accurate armament of thirty-two-pound carronades—offered the best test of relative gunnery, and Sir Howard Douglas in commenting upon the destruction of the *Peacock* and *Avon* could only say—

"In these two actions it is clear that the fire of the British vessels was thrown too high, and that the ordnance of their opponents were expressly and carefully aimed at and took effect chiefly in the hull."

The battle of the *Hornet* and *Penguin* as well as those of the *Reindeer* and *Avon*, showed that the excellence of American gunnery continued till the close of the war. Whether at point-blank range or at long-distance practice, the Americans used guns as they had never been used at sea before.

None of the reports of former British victories showed that the British fire had been more destructive at any previous time than in 1812, and no report of any commander since the British navy existed showed so much damage inflicted on an opponent in so short a time as was proved to have been inflicted on themselves by the reports of British commanders in the American war. The strongest proof of American superiority was given by the best British officers, like Broke, who strained every nerve to maintain an equality with American gunnery. So instantaneous and energetic was the effort that, according to the British historian of the war, "a British forty-six-gun frigate of 1813 was half as effective again as a British forty-six-gun frigate of 1812"; and, as he justly said, "the slaughtered crews and the shattered hulks" of the captured British ships proved that no want of their old fighting qualities accounted for their repeated and almost habitual mortifications.

Unwilling as the English were to admit the superior skill of Americans on the ocean, they did not hesitate to admit it, in certain respects, on land. The American rifle in American hands was affirmed to have no equal in the world. This admission could scarcely be withheld after the lists of killed and wounded which followed almost every battle; but the admission served to check a wider inquiry. In truth, the rifle played but a small part in the war. Winchester's men at the river Raisin may have owed their over-confidence, as the British Forty-first owed its losses, to that weapon, and at New Orleans five or six hundred of Coffee's men, who were out of range, were armed with the rifle, but the surprising losses of the British were commonly due to artillery and musketry fire. At New Orleans the artillery was chiefly engaged. The artillery battle of January 1, according to British accounts, amply proved the superiority of American gunnery on that occasion, which was probably the fairest test during the war. The battle of January 8 was also chiefly an artillery battle; the main British column never arrived within fair musket range; Pakenham was killed by a grape-shot, and the main column of his troops halted more than one hundred yards from the parapet.

The best test of British and American military qualities, both for men and weapons, was Scott's battle of Chippawa. Nothing intervened to throw a doubt over the fairness of the trial. Two parallel lines of regular soldiers, practically equal in numbers, armed with similar weapons, moved in close order toward each other, across a wide open plain, without cover or advantage of position, stopping at intervals to load and fire, until one line broke and retired At the same time, two three-gun batteries, the British being the heavier, maintained a steady fire from positions opposite each other. According to the reports, the two infantry lines in the centre never came nearer than eighty yards. Major-General Riall reported that then, owing to severe losses, his troops broke and could not be rallied. Comparison of the official reports showed that the British lost in killed and wounded four hundred and sixty-nine men; the Americans, two hundred and ninety-six. Some doubts always affect the returns of wounded, because the severity of the wound cannot be known; but dead men tell their own tale. Riall reported one hundred and forty-eight killed; Scott reported sixty-one. The severity of the losses showed that the battle was sharply contested, and proved the personal bravery of both armies. Marksmanship decided the result, and the returns proved that the American fire was superior to that of the British in the proportion of more than fifty per cent if estimated by the entire loss, and of two hundred and forty-two to one hundred if estimated by the deaths alone.

The conclusion seemed incredible, but it was supported by the results of the naval battles. The Americans showed superiority amounting in some cases to twice the efficiency of their enemies in the use of weapons. The best French critic of the naval war, Jurien de la Gravière said: "An enormous superiority in the rapidity and precision of their fire can alone explain the difference in the losses sustained by the combatants." So far from denying this conclusion the British press constantly alleged it, and the British officers complained of it. The discovery caused great surprise, and in both British services much attention was at once directed to improvement in artillery and musketry. Nothing could exceed the frankness with which Englishmen avowed their inferiority. According to Sir Francis Head, "gunnery was in naval warfare in the extraordinary state of ignorance we have just described, when our lean children, the American people, taught us, rod in hand, our first lesson in the art." The English textbook on Naval Gunnery, written by Major-General Sir Howard Douglas immediately after the peace, devoted more attention to the short American war than to all the battles of Napoleon, and began by admitting that Great Britain had "entered with too great confidence on war with a marine much more expert than that of any of our European enemies." The admission appeared "objectionable" even to the author; but he did not add, what was equally true, that it applied as well to the land as to the sea service.

No one questioned the bravery of the British forces, or the ease with which they often routed larger bodies of militia but the losses they inflicted were rarely as great as those they suffered. Even at Bladensburg, where they met little resistance, their loss was several times greater than that of the Americans. At Plattsburg, where the intelligence and quickness of Macdonough and his men alone won the victory, his ships were in effect stationary batteries, and enjoyed the same superiority in gunnery. "The *Saratoga*," said his official report, "had fifty-five round-shot in her hull; the *Confiance*, one hundred and five. The enemy's shot passed principally just over our heads, as there were not twenty whole hammocks in the nettings at the close of the action."

The greater skill of the Americans was not due to special training, for the British service was better trained in gunnery, as in everything else, than the motley armies and fleets that fought at New Orleans and on the Lakes. Critics constantly said that every American had learned from his childhood the use of the rifle, but he certainly had not learned to use cannon in shooting birds or hunting deer, and he knew less than the Englishman about the handling of artillery and muskets. The same intelligence that selected the rifle and the long pivot-gun for favorite weapons was shown in handling the carronades, and every other instrument however clumsy.

Another significant result of the war was the sudden development of scientific engineering in the United States. This branch of the military service owed its efficiency and almost its existence to the military school at West Point, established in 1802. The school was at first much neglected by government. The number of graduates before the year 1812 was very small; but at the outbreak of the war the corps of engineers was already efficient. Its chief was Colonel Joseph Gardner Swift, of Massachusetts, the first graduate of the academy: Colonel Swift planned the defences of New York harbor. The lieutenant-colonel in 1812 was Walker Keith Armistead, of Virginia—the third graduate, who planned the defences of Norfolk. Major William McRee, of North Carolina, became chief engineer to General Brown, and constructed the fortifications at Fort Erie, which cost the British General Gordon Drummond the loss of half his army, besides the mortification of defeat. Captain Eleazer Derby Wood, of New York, constructed Fort Meigs, which enabled Harrison to defeat the attack of Proctor in May, 1813. Captain Joseph Gilbert Totten, of New York, was chief engineer to General Izard at Plattsburg, where he directed the fortifications that stopped the advance of Prevost's great army. None of the works constructed by a graduate of West Point was captured by the enemy; and had an engineer been employed at Washington by Armstrong and Winder, the city would have been easily saved.

Perhaps without exaggeration the West Point Academy might be said to have decided, next to the navy, the result of the war. The works at New Orleans were simple in character, and as far as they were due to engineering skill were directed by Major Latour, a Frenchman; but the war was already ended when the battle of New Orleans was fought. During the critical campaign of 1814, the West Point engineers doubled the capacity of the little American army for resistance, and introduced a new and scientific character into American life.

INDEX

OTHER COOPER SQUARE PRESS TITLES OF INTEREST

HANNIBAL
G. P. Baker
366 pp., 3 b/w illus., 5 maps
0-8154-1005-0
$16.95

WOLFE AT QUEBEC
The Man Who Won the
French and Indian War
Christopher Hibbert
208 pp., 1 b/w illus., 4 maps
0-8154-1016-6
$15.95

CANARIS
Hitler's Master Spy
Heinz Höhne
736 pp., 21 b/w photos, 1 map, 2 diagrams
0-8154-1007-7
$19.95

MENGELE
The Complete Story
Gerald L. Posner and John Ware
New introduction by Michael Berenbaum
408 pp., 41 b/w photos
0-8154-1006-9
$17.95

Available at bookstores; or call 1-800-462-6420

Cooper Square Press

150 Fifth Avenue
Suite 911
New York, NY 10011